BATMAN
DARK
VICTORY

VP-Executive Editor **Dan DiDio**

Editor-original series **Mark Chiarello**

Editor-collected edition **Nick J. Napolitano**

Senior Art Director **Robbin Brosterman**

President & Publisher **Paul Levitz**

VP-Design & Retail Product Development **Georg Brewer**

Senior VP-Creative Director **Richard Bruning**

Senior VP-Finance & Operations **Patrick Caldon**

VP-Finance **Chris Caramalis**

VP-Managing Editor **Terri Cunningham**

VP-Manufacturing **Alison Gill**

VP-Book Trade Sales **Rich Johnson**

VP-General Manager, WildStorm **Hank Kanalz**

Senior VP & General Counsel **Lillian Laserson**

Editorial Director-WildStorm **Jim Lee**

VP-Advertising & Custom Publishing **David McKillips**

VP-Business Development **John Nee**

Senior VP-Creative Affairs **Gregory Noveck**

Senior VP-Brand Management **Cheryl Rubin**

VP-Sales & Marketing **Bob Wayne**

B A T M A N :   D A R K   V I C T O R Y

DC Comics, 1700 Broadway, New York, NY 10019
A Warner Bros. Entertainment Company
Printed in Canada. Third Printing.

ISBN: 1 56389 868 3

Cover illustration by Tim Sale.

BATMAN
DARK VICTORY

JEPH LOEB
WRITER

TIM SALE
ARTIST

GREGORY WRIGHT
COLORIST

RICHARD STARKINGS
LETTERER

ARCHIE GOODWIN
INSPIRATION

**BATMAN CREATED
BY BOB KANE**

I N T R O D U C T I O N

The first time I met my Girl, I drew her a picture of Batman on a tablecloth. I was showing off, of course, and having at that point three Batman Halloween Specials under my belt, felt pretty confident that whatever else I may be lacking, I could still draw a pretty girl an impressive picture of Batman.

Except that apparently I couldn't. She told me later it was a pretty lame drawing, but somehow she forgave that, saw something in me anyway, and we fell in love.

She had a boy who was seven years old at the time, and a few months later for his birthday I drew another picture of Batman, somewhat better (or at least bigger) than the first, and this time I cast her boy as Robin. An impish contrast to Batman, he leapt through the air with roller blades on his feet and a street hockey stick in his fist.

That was my first and last picture of the Boy Wonder until Jeph called one day with a story he wanted to tell:

"But I *hate* Robin, he doesn't make any *sense*, he's so colorful, Batman's a loner, he can't escape the tragedy that shaped his life, blah, blah blah," I said.

"That's the point. You wait and see." Jeph said.

What he saw, and this is the talent that is Loeb, was a way to filter a Reality through Comic Book Melodrama and find the poignancy, the sentiment. Batman is a loner. What sense did it make for him to have a companion? Or for us to give him one? Jeph's answer lay in the contrast: His depiction of Dick as an extroverted, talky little kid, and the conflicts in personalities that arose from that (helped immeasurably by the now eleven-year-old in my life), made sense to me.

It will come as no surprise to anyone who has ever looked at my work that I love visual contrasts—heavy blacks and thin lines, big panels on the same page with tiny, dense backgrounds and big empty spaces. It heightens the comedy or drama in each scene, and when I realized that the figures of Batman and Robin gave me the opportunity to play with that — big, hulking super-hero and little kid — Jeph had won me over.

So thank you, Jeph, Trevor and Jane. And thank you, Bruce and Dick, for the adult and child in all of us.

T I M S A L E J U N E , 2 0 0 1

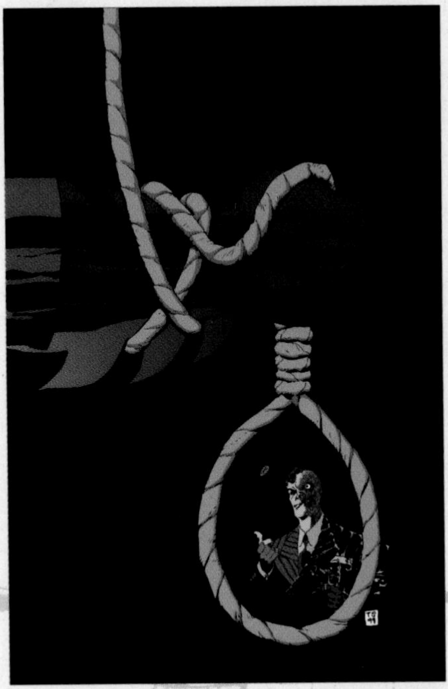

PROLOGUE

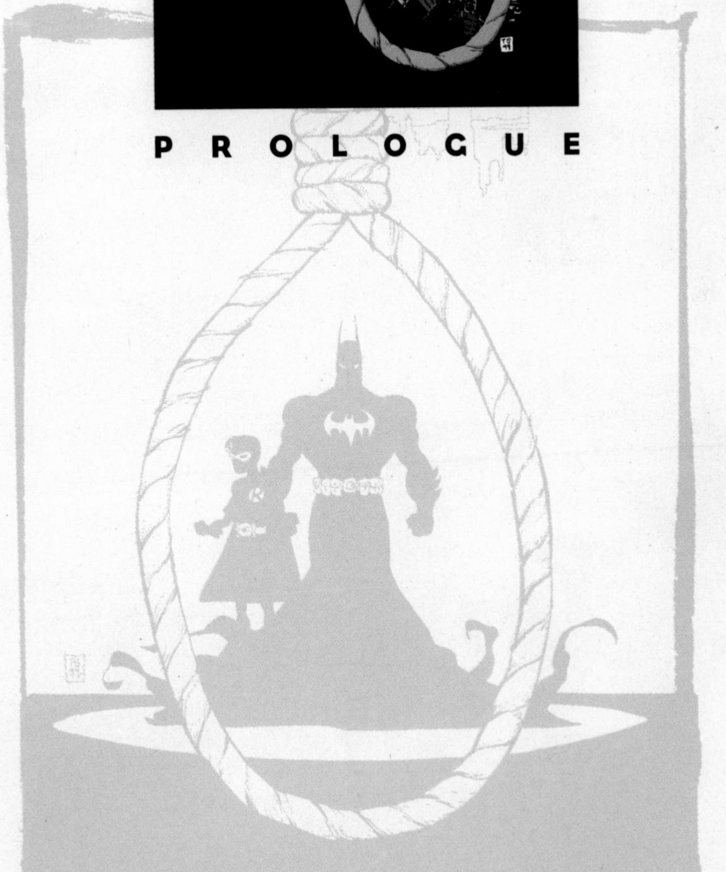

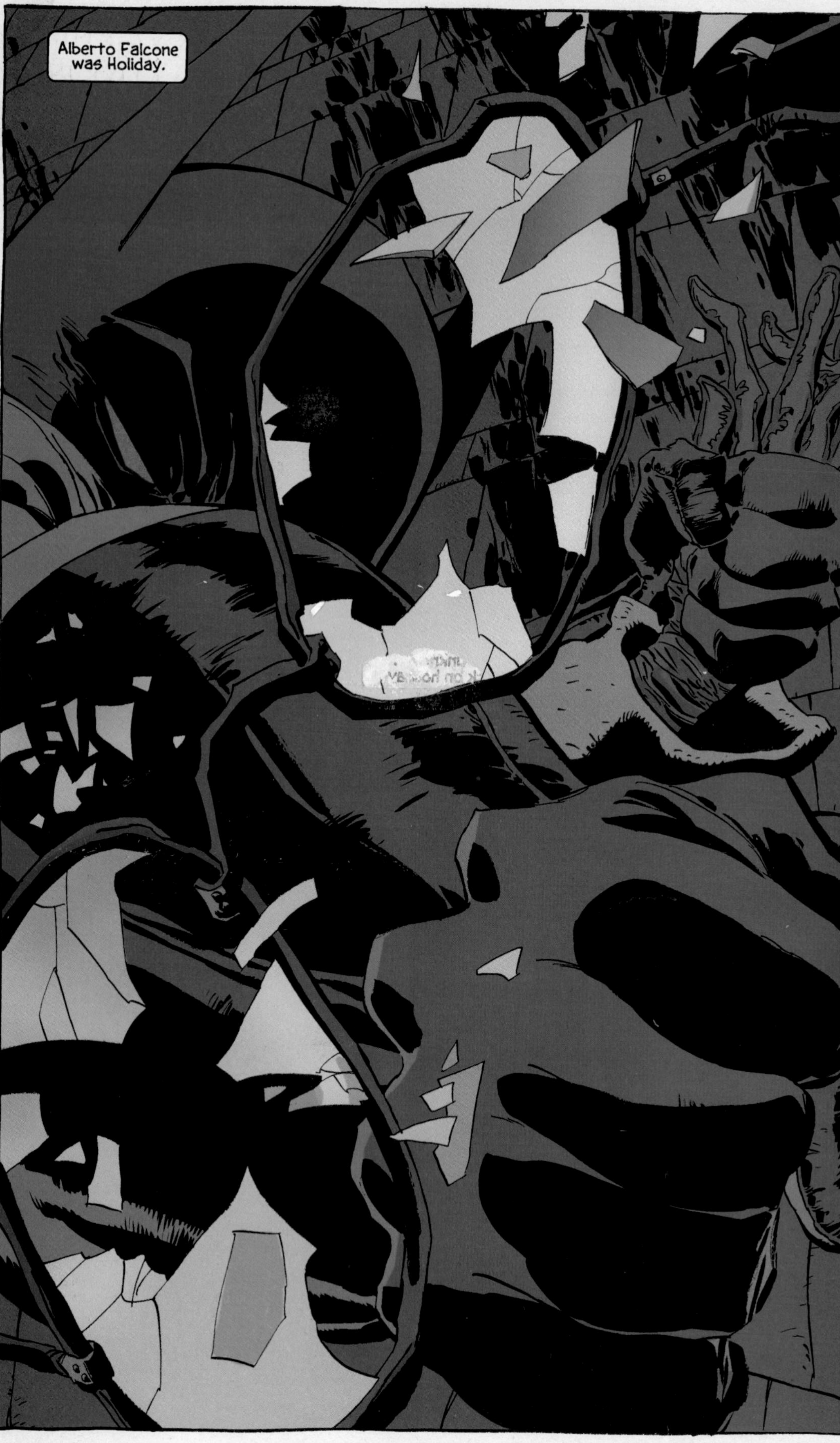
Alberto Falcone
was Holiday.

The son of Carmine "The Roman" Falcone, Gotham City's "Untouchable" Crime Lord...

...this serial killer held Gotham City in his grasp for nearly a year.

His identity was unknown. Only that he struck on holidays.

I suspected Harvey Dent. Gotham City's then District Attorney.

He was my friend.

I was wrong.

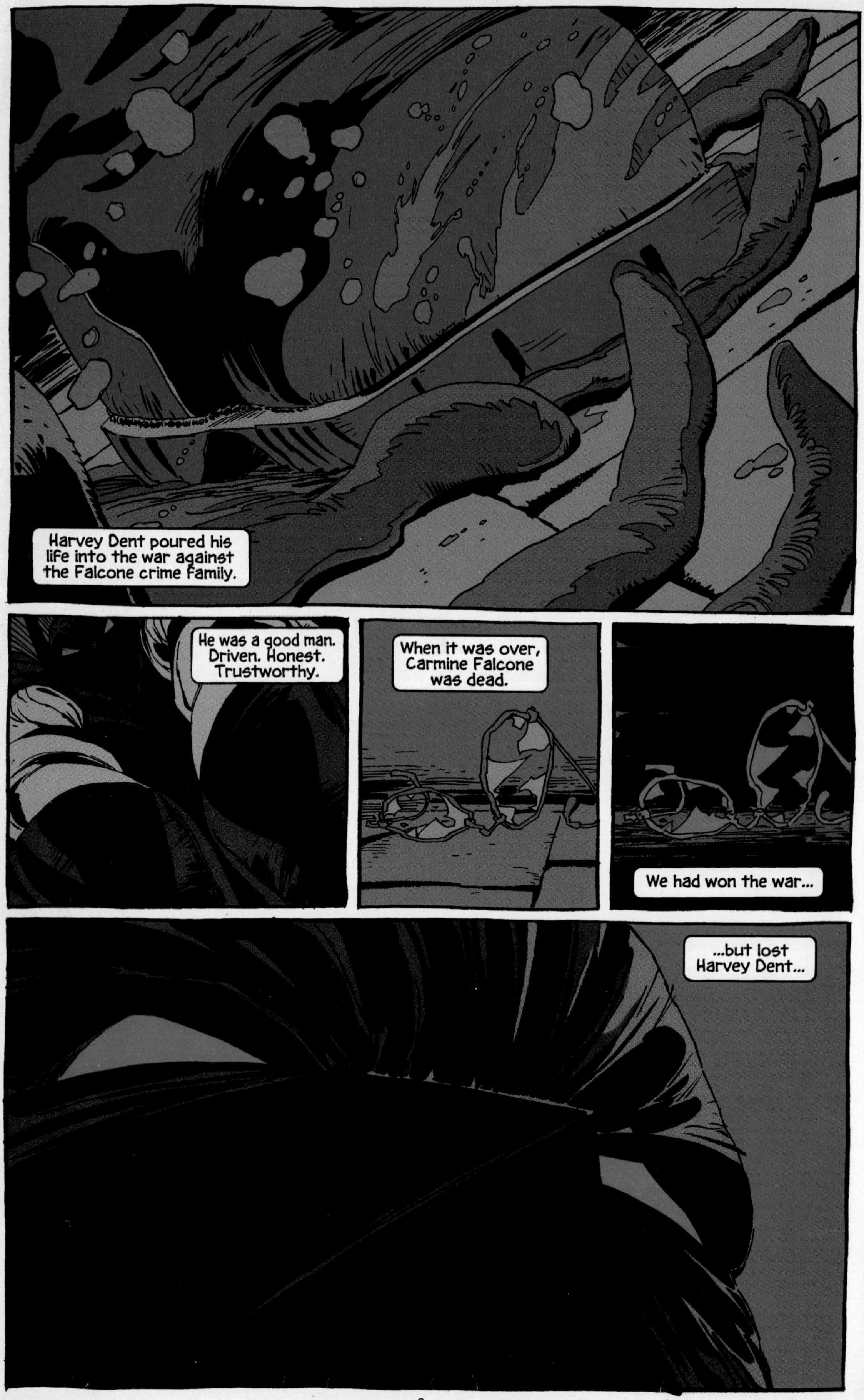
Harvey Dent poured his life into the war against the Falcone crime family.
He was a good man. Driven. Honest. Trustworthy.
When it was over, Carmine Falcone was dead.
We had won the war...
...but lost Harvey Dent...

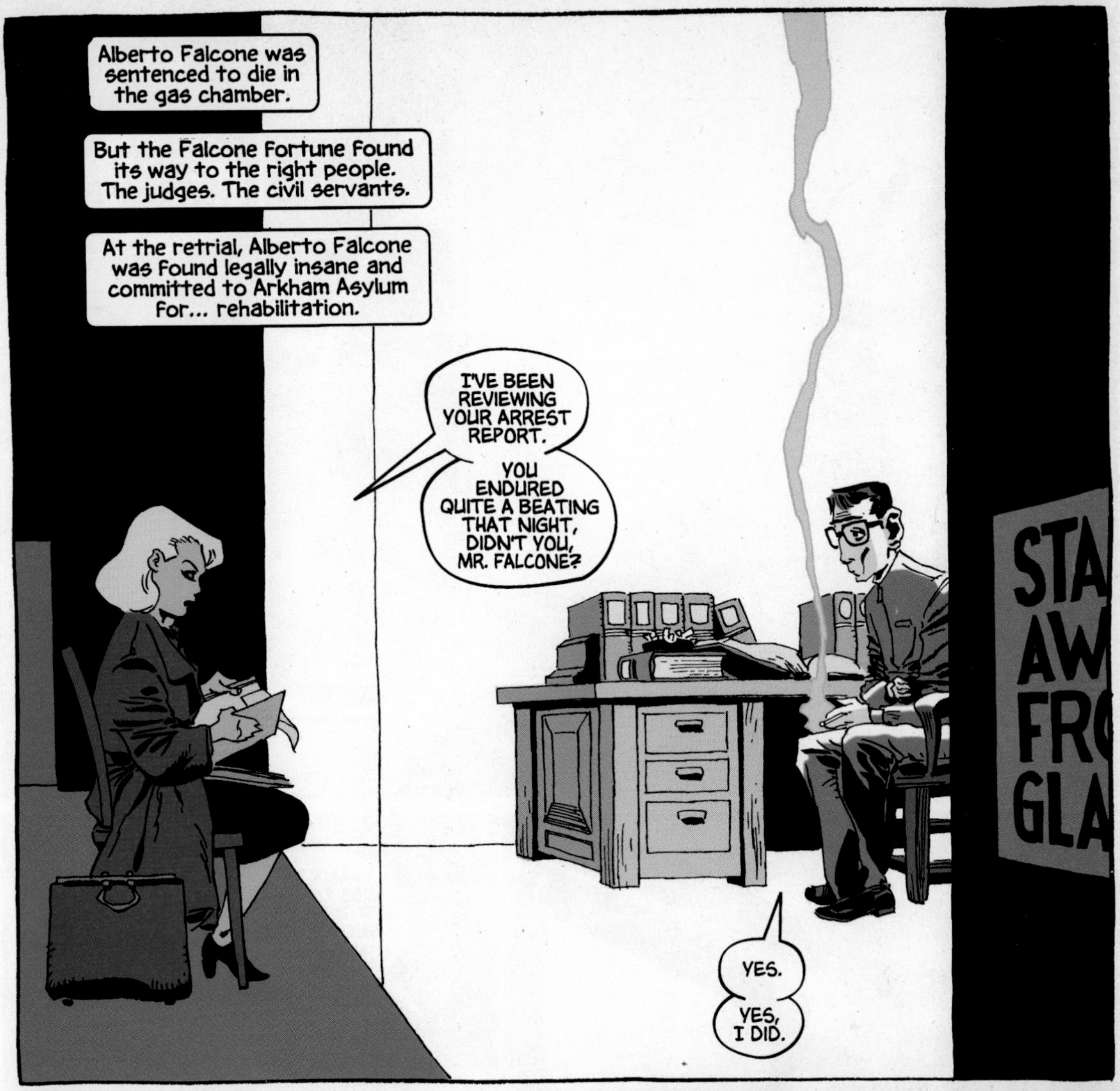
Alberto Falcone was sentenced to die in the gas chamber.
But the Falcone fortune found its way to the right people. The judges. The civil servants.
At the retrial, Alberto Falcone was found legally insane and committed to Arkham Asylum for... rehabilitation.
I'VE BEEN REVIEWING YOUR ARREST REPORT.
YOU ENDURED QUITE A BEATING THAT NIGHT, DIDN'T YOU, MR. FALCONE?
YES.
YES, I DID.

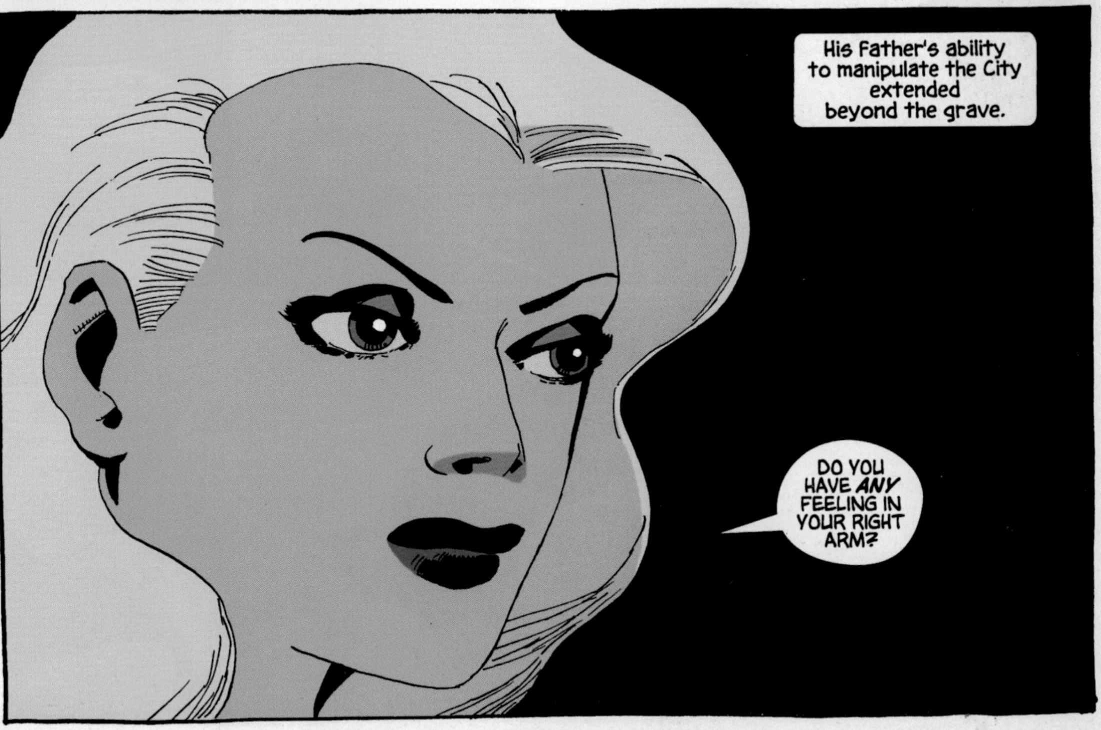
His father's ability to manipulate the City extended beyond the grave.
DO YOU HAVE *ANY* FEELING IN YOUR RIGHT ARM?

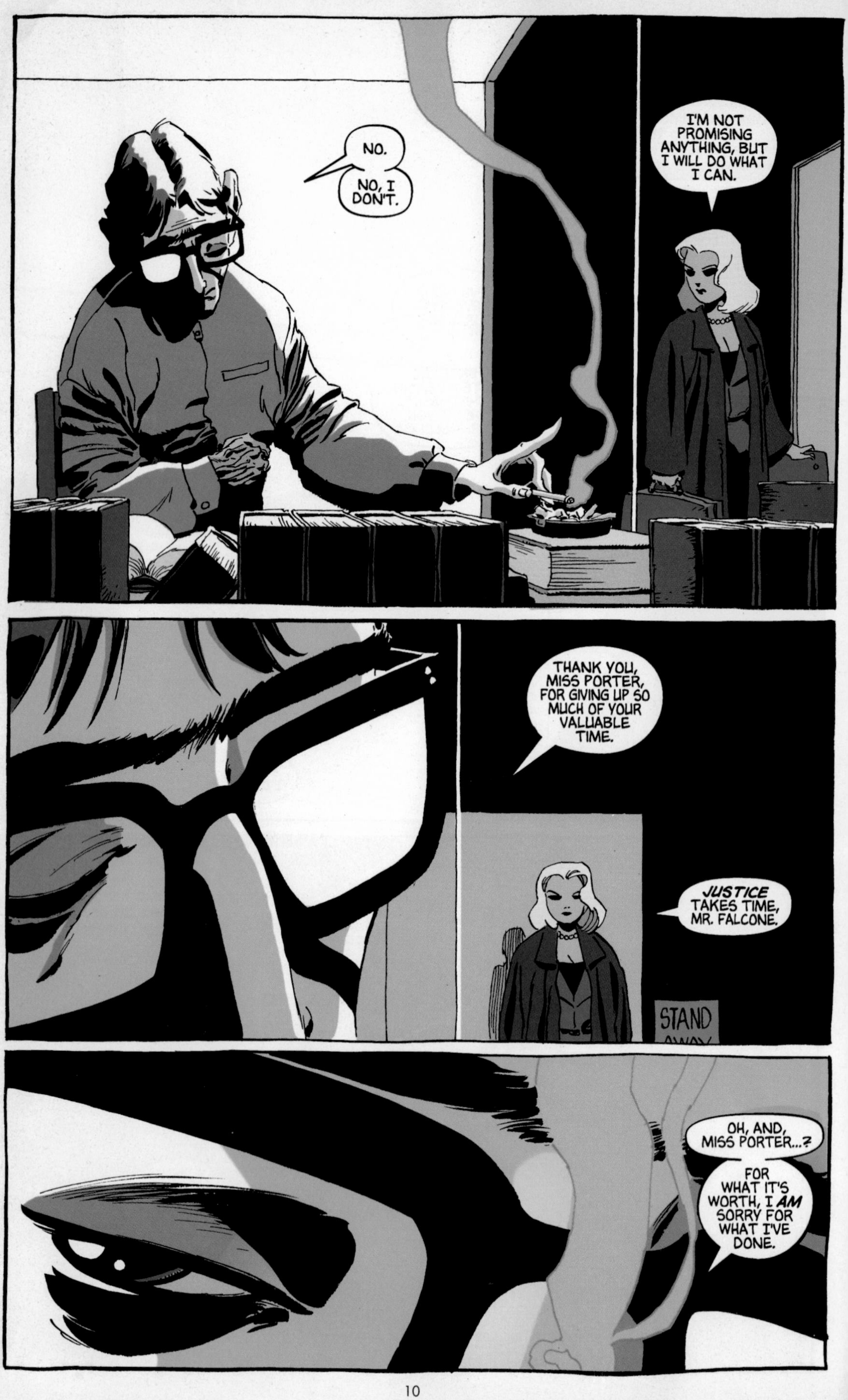
NO.
NO, I DON'T.
I'M NOT PROMISING ANYTHING, BUT I WILL DO WHAT I CAN.
THANK YOU, MISS PORTER, FOR GIVING UP SO MUCH OF YOUR VALUABLE TIME.
JUSTICE TAKES TIME, MR. FALCONE.
STAND
OH, AND, MISS PORTER...?
FOR WHAT IT'S WORTH, I AM SORRY FOR WHAT I'VE DONE.

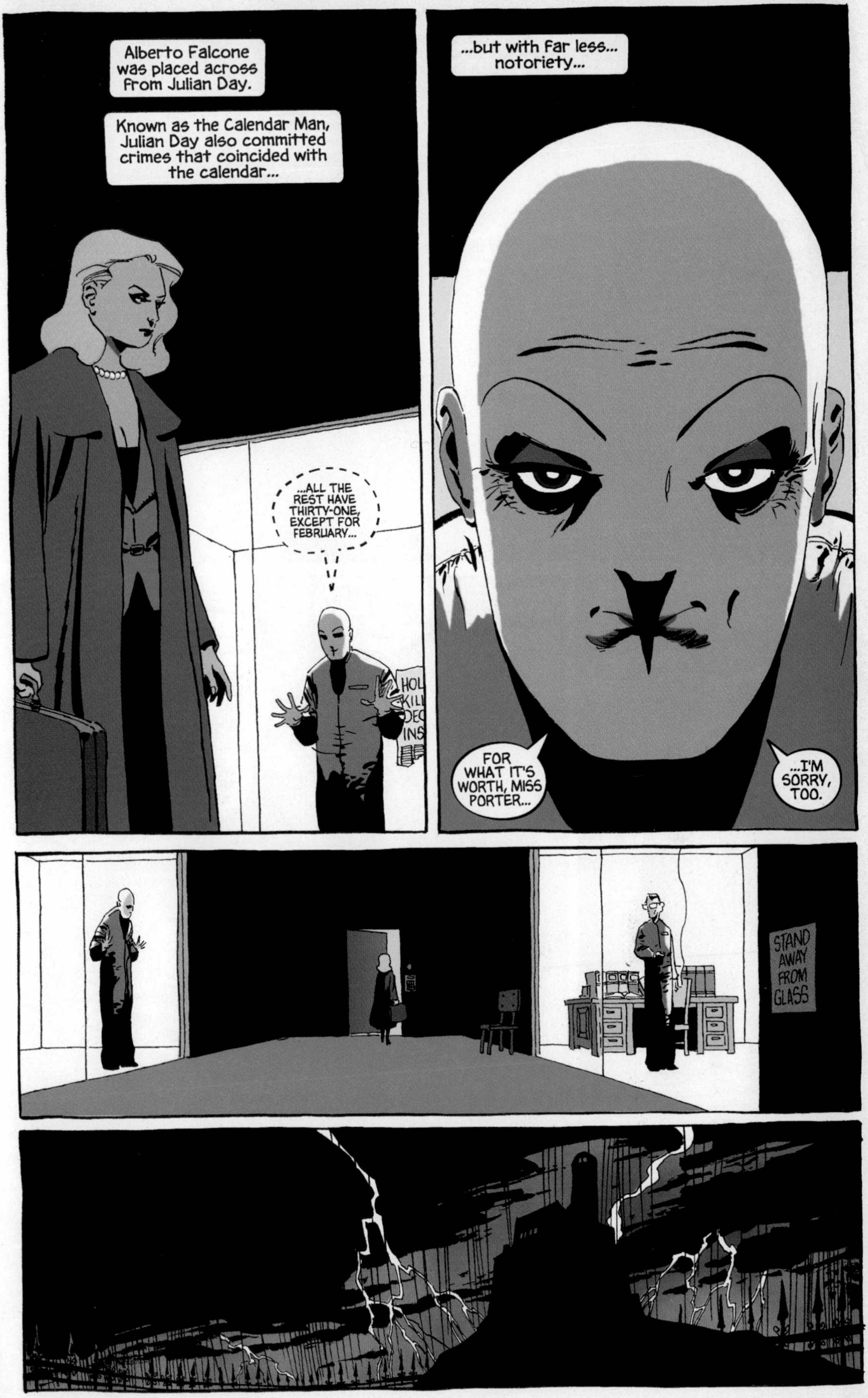
Alberto Falcone was placed across from Julian Day.
Known as the Calendar Man, Julian Day also committed crimes that coincided with the calendar...
...ALL THE REST HAVE THIRTY-ONE, EXCEPT FOR FEBRUARY...
...but with far less... notoriety...
FOR WHAT IT'S WORTH, MISS PORTER...
...I'M SORRY, TOO.
STAND AWAY FROM GLASS

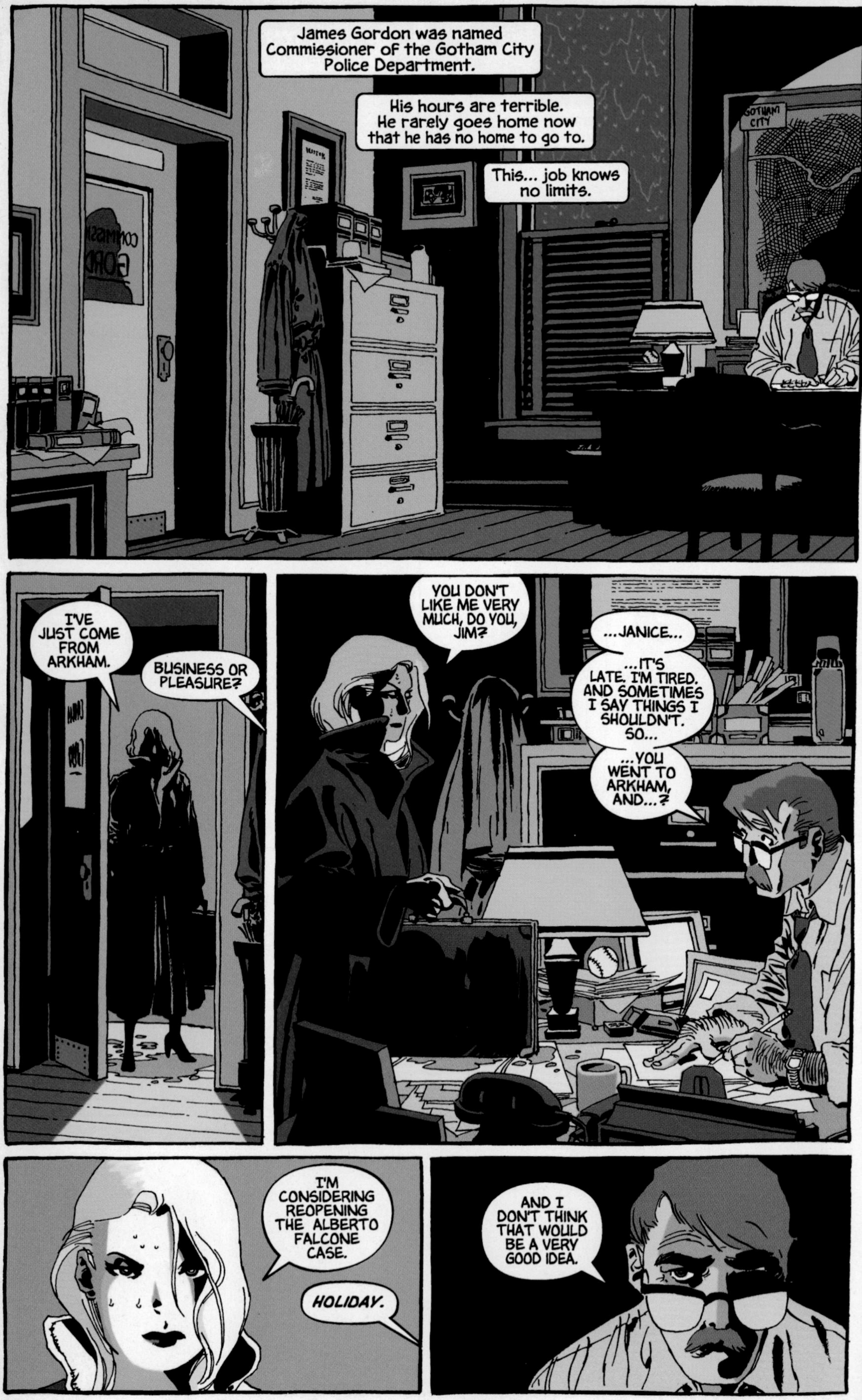
James Gordon was named Commissioner of the Gotham City Police Department.
His hours are terrible. He rarely goes home now that he has no home to go to.
This... job knows no limits.
GOTHAM CITY
I'VE JUST COME FROM ARKHAM.
BUSINESS OR PLEASURE?
YOU DON'T LIKE ME VERY MUCH, DO YOU, JIM?
...JANICE...
...IT'S LATE. I'M TIRED. AND SOMETIMES I SAY THINGS I SHOULDN'T. SO...
...YOU WENT TO ARKHAM, AND...?
I'M CONSIDERING REOPENING THE ALBERTO FALCONE CASE.
HOLIDAY.
AND I DON'T THINK THAT WOULD BE A VERY GOOD IDEA.

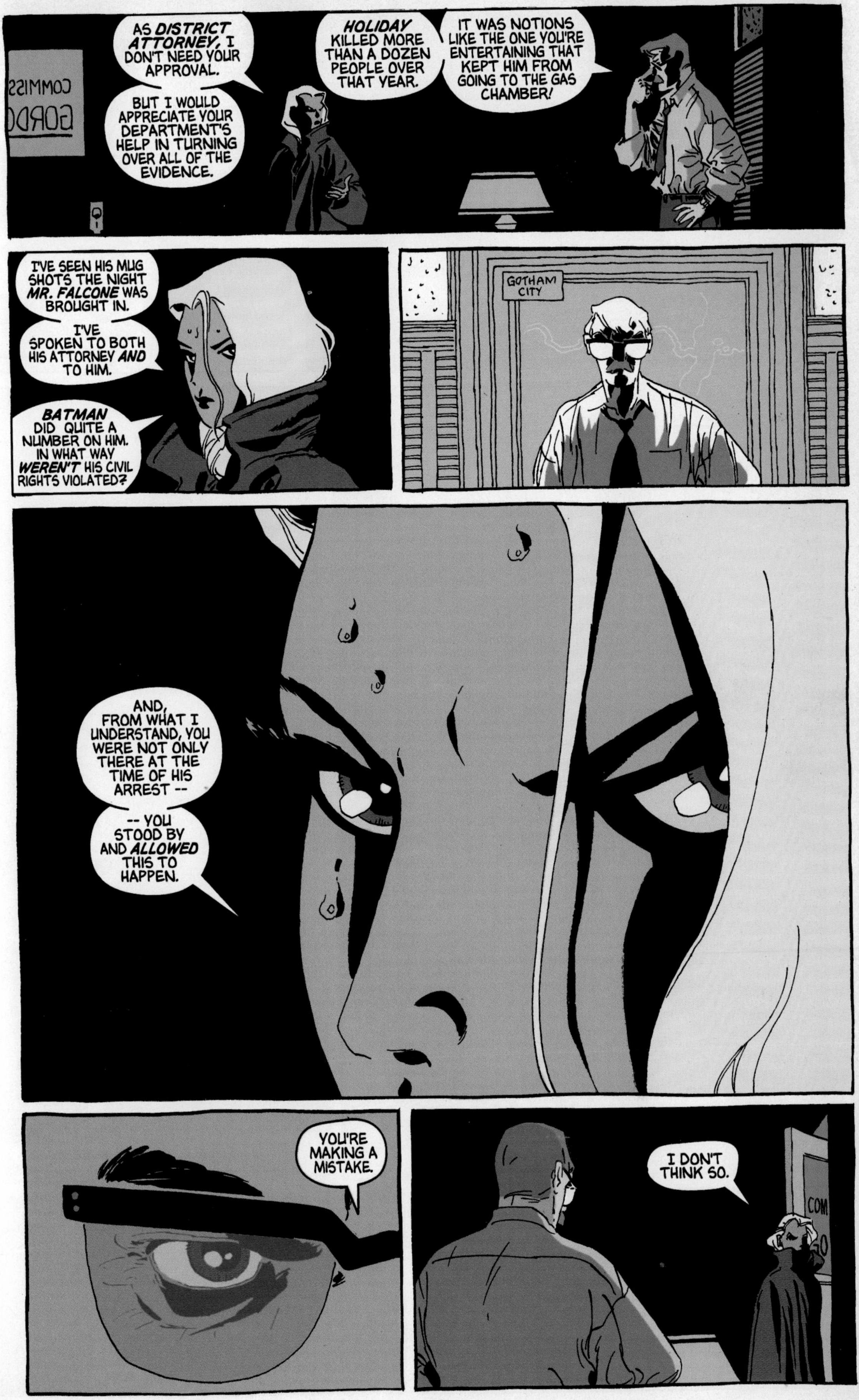
COMMISS
GORDO
AS DISTRICT ATTORNEY, I DON'T NEED YOUR APPROVAL.
BUT I WOULD APPRECIATE YOUR DEPARTMENT'S HELP IN TURNING OVER ALL OF THE EVIDENCE.
HOLIDAY KILLED MORE THAN A DOZEN PEOPLE OVER THAT YEAR.
IT WAS NOTIONS LIKE THE ONE YOU'RE ENTERTAINING THAT KEPT HIM FROM GOING TO THE GAS CHAMBER!
I'VE SEEN HIS MUG SHOTS THE NIGHT MR. FALCONE WAS BROUGHT IN.
I'VE SPOKEN TO BOTH HIS ATTORNEY AND TO HIM.
BATMAN DID QUITE A NUMBER ON HIM. IN WHAT WAY WEREN'T HIS CIVIL RIGHTS VIOLATED?
GOTHAM CITY
AND, FROM WHAT I UNDERSTAND, YOU WERE NOT ONLY THERE AT THE TIME OF HIS ARREST --
-- YOU STOOD BY AND ALLOWED THIS TO HAPPEN.
YOU'RE MAKING A MISTAKE.
I DON'T THINK SO.

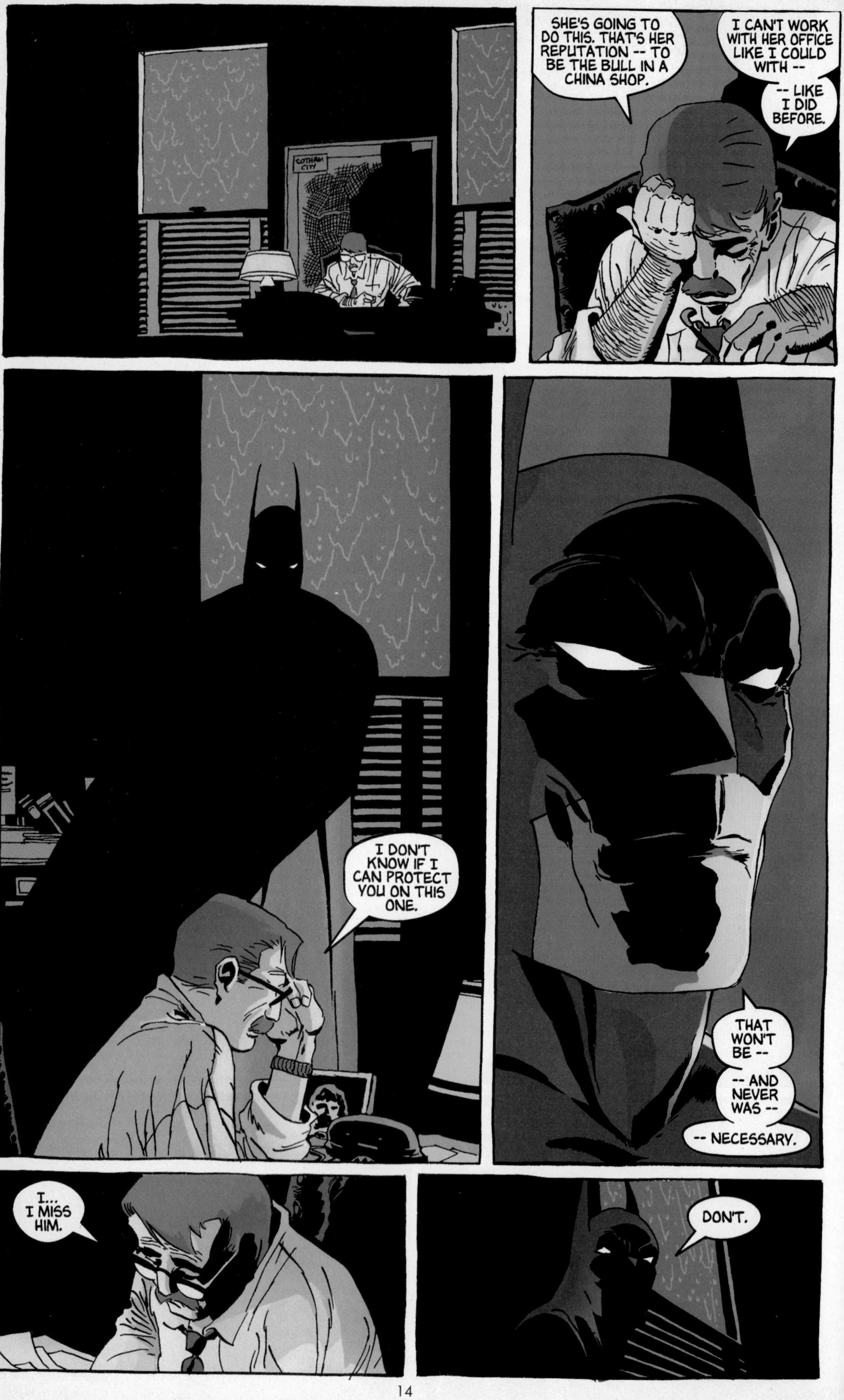
SHE'S GOING TO DO THIS. THAT'S HER REPUTATION -- TO BE THE BULL IN A CHINA SHOP.
I CAN'T WORK WITH HER OFFICE LIKE I COULD WITH --
-- LIKE I DID BEFORE.
I DON'T KNOW IF I CAN PROTECT YOU ON THIS ONE.
THAT WON'T BE --
-- AND NEVER WAS --
-- NECESSARY.
I... I MISS HIM.
DON'T.

HOW CAN YOU BE SO COLD-HEARTED?

HE WAS MY FRIEND. I GOT DRUNK WITH HIM. WE PLAYED CARDS UNTIL FOUR IN THE MORNING.

NO MATTER WHAT HE'S BECOME, HARVEY WAS YOUR FRIEND, TOO...

It was on a night like this that I ran to my father. The thunder and lightning rumbled through the house.

Instead of comforting me, he held me at arm's length.

BATMAN...?

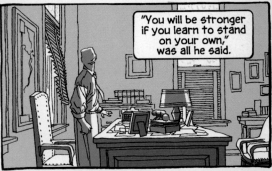

"You will be stronger if you learn to stand on your own," was all he said.

GOTHAM CITY

DAMN...

This storm that rages in Gotham City tonight...

...is only the beginning...

LOEB SALE 1999

I

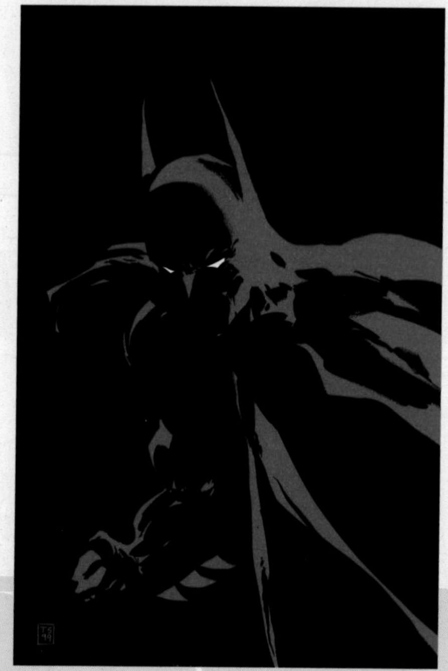

W A R

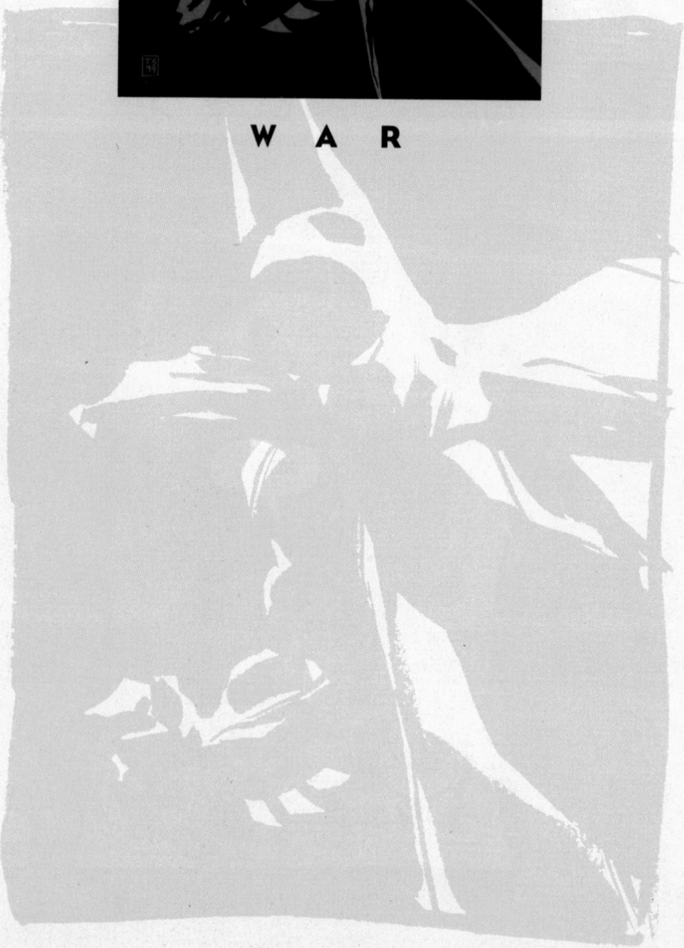

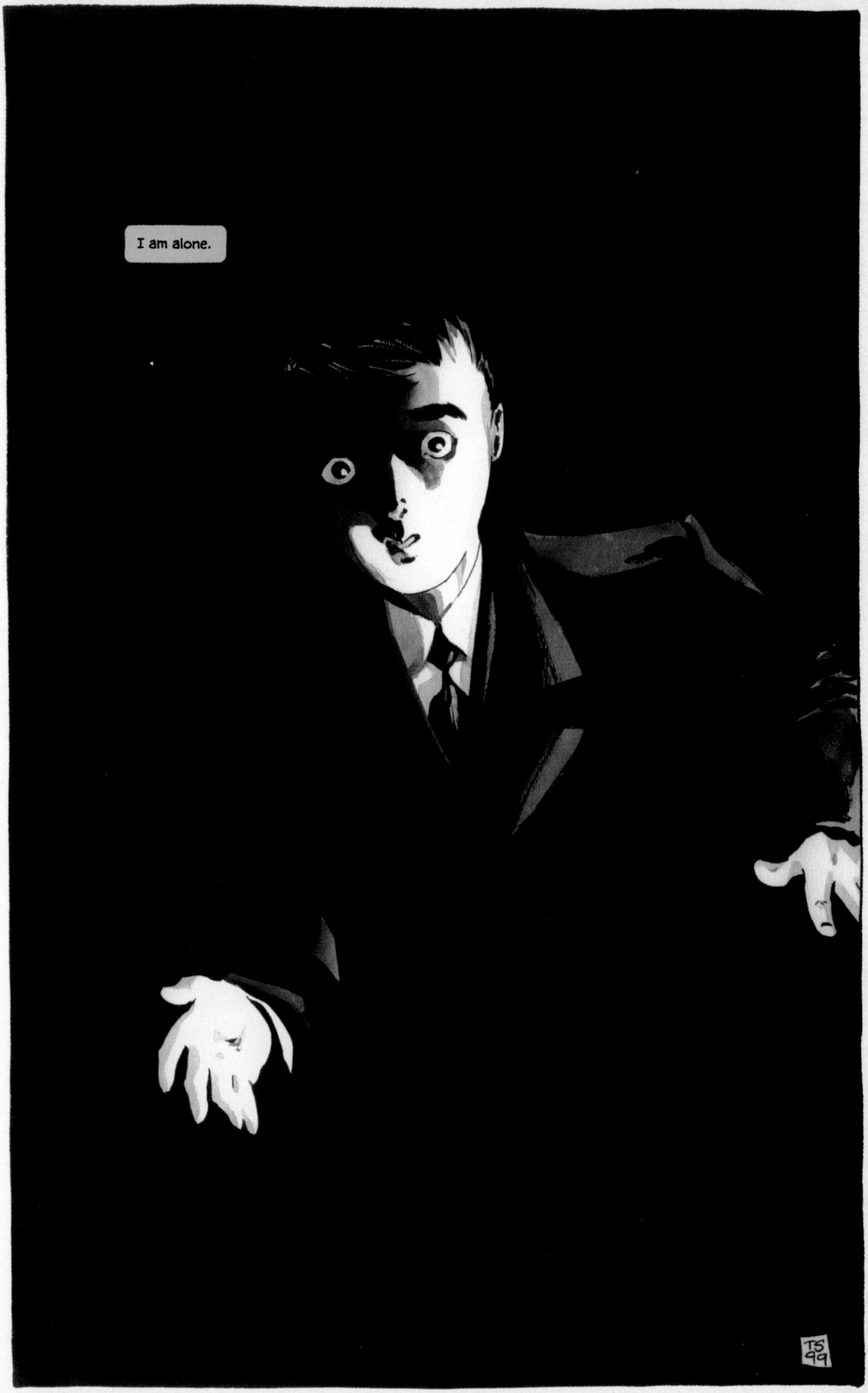
I am alone.
TS 99

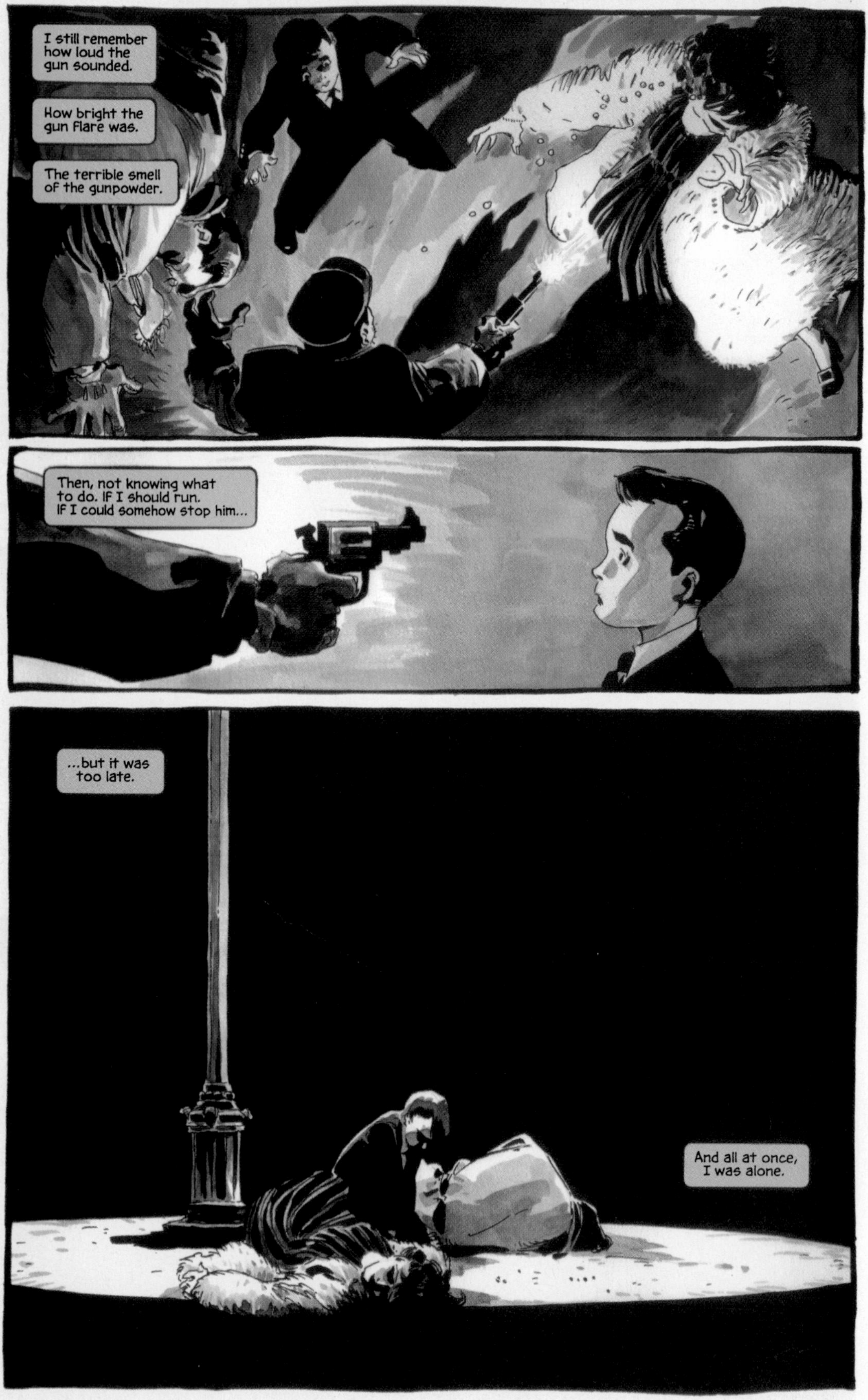
I still remember how loud the gun sounded.
How bright the gun flare was.
The terrible smell of the gunpowder.
Then, not knowing what to do. If I should run. If I could somehow stop him...
...but it was too late.
And all at once, I was alone.

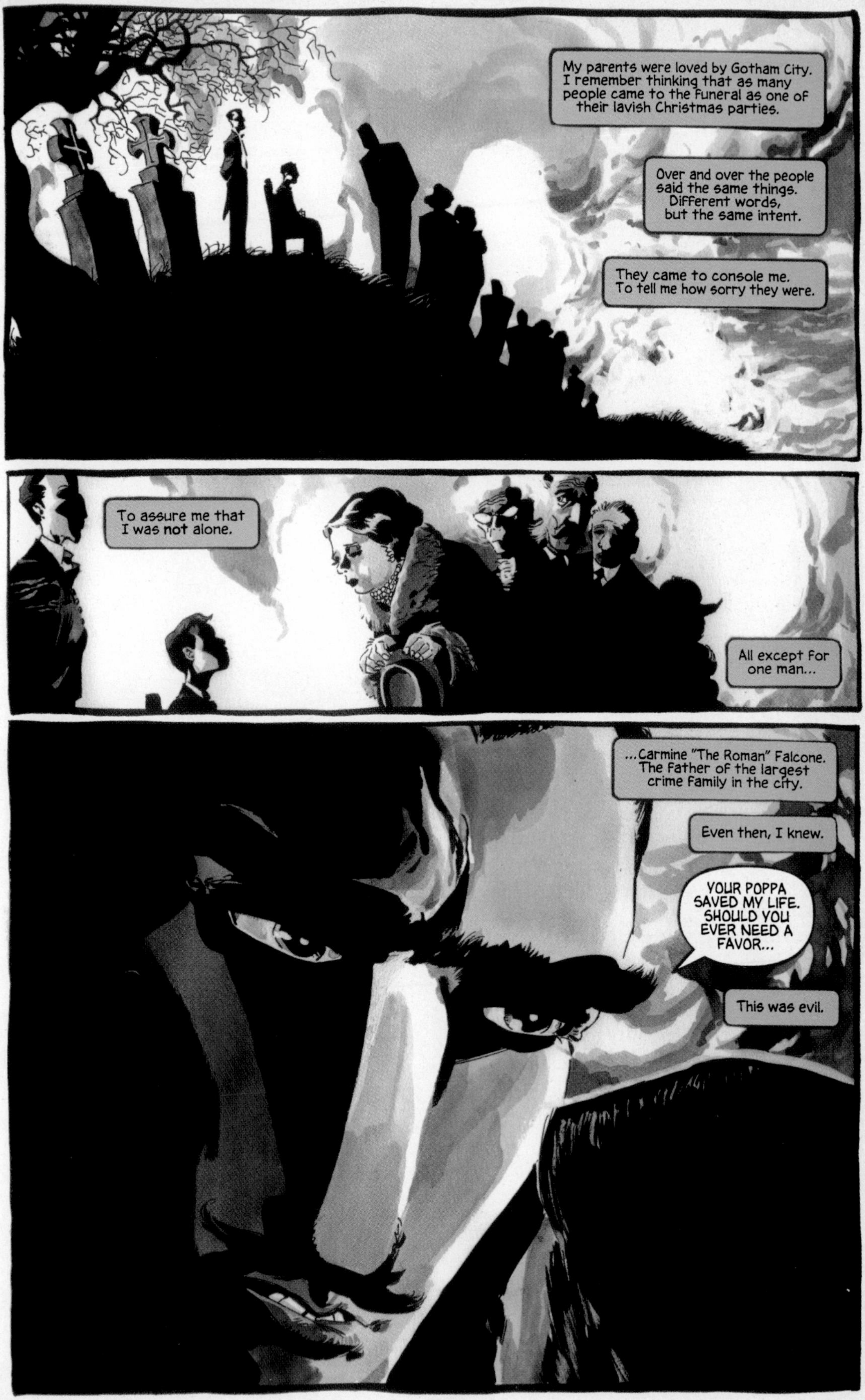
My parents were loved by Gotham City. I remember thinking that as many people came to the funeral as one of their lavish Christmas parties.
Over and over the people said the same things. Different words, but the same intent.
They came to console me. To tell me how sorry they were.
To assure me that I was **not** alone.
All except for one man...
...Carmine "The Roman" Falcone. The father of the largest crime family in the city.
Even then, I knew.
YOUR POPPA SAVED MY LIFE. SHOULD YOU EVER NEED A FAVOR...
This was evil.

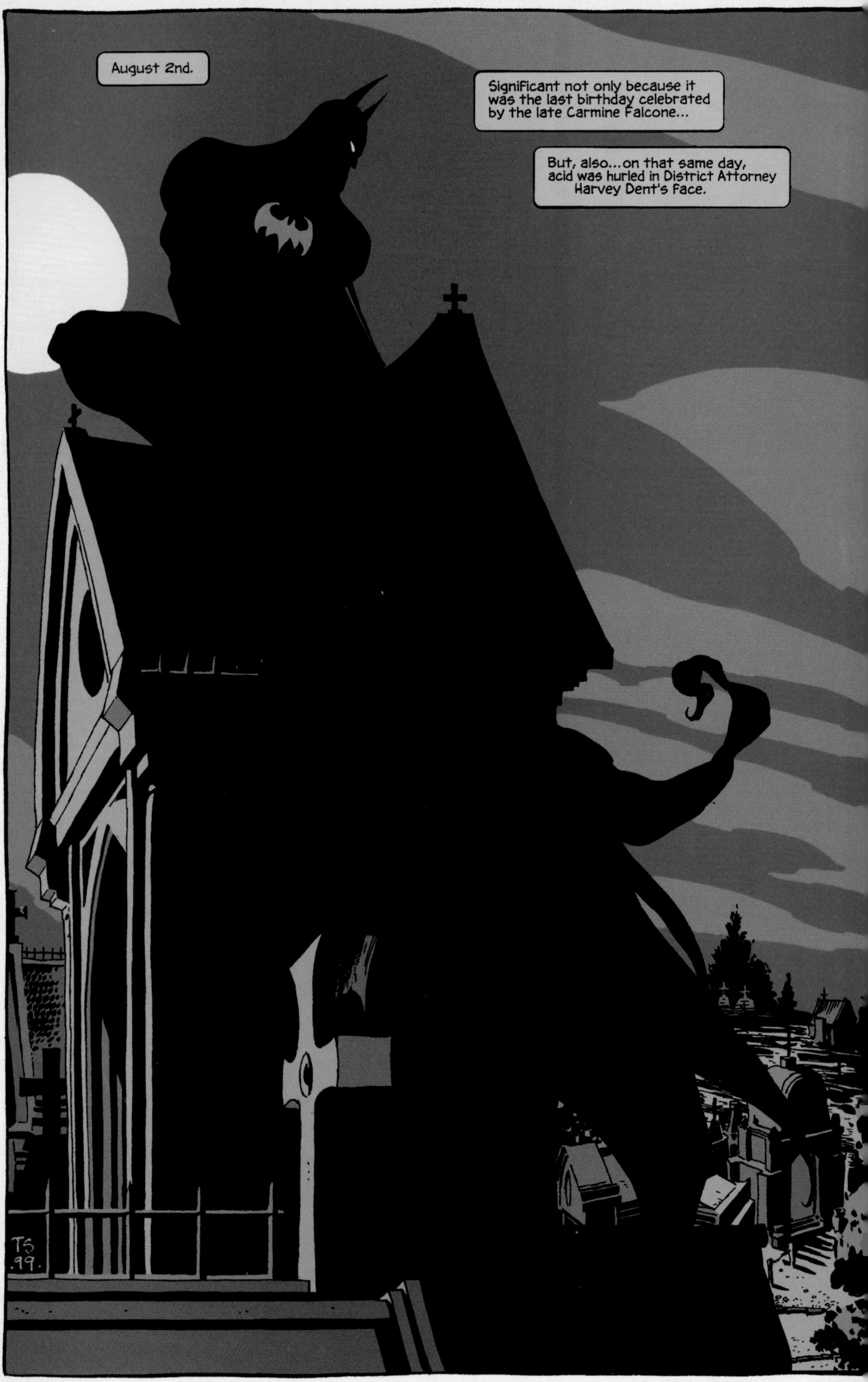
August 2nd.
Significant not only because it was the last birthday celebrated by the late Carmine Falcone...
But, also...on that same day, acid was hurled in District Attorney Harvey Dent's Face.
TS .99.

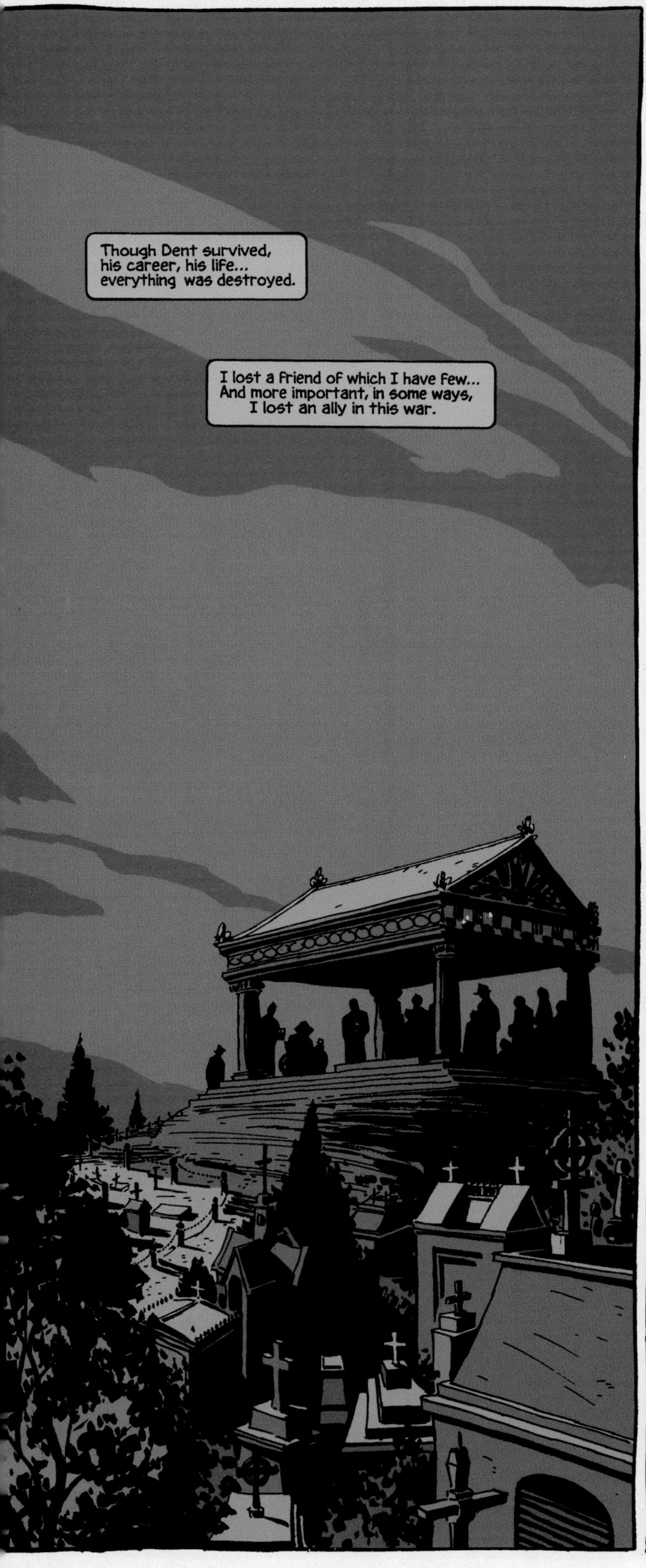
Though Dent survived, his career, his life... everything was destroyed.
I lost a friend of which I have few... And more important, in some ways, I lost an ally in this war.

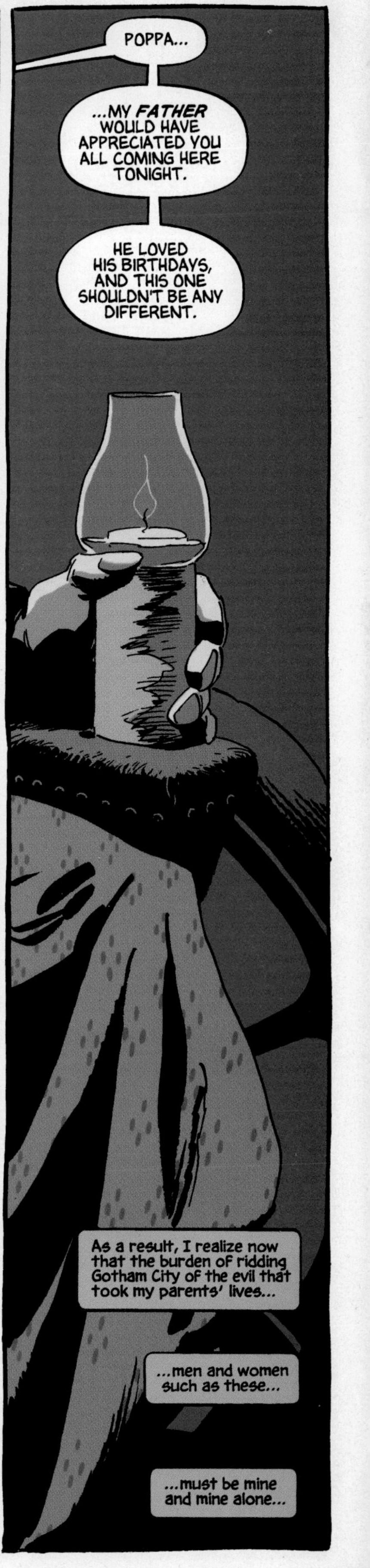
POPPA...
...MY FATHER WOULD HAVE APPRECIATED YOU ALL COMING HERE TONIGHT.
HE LOVED HIS BIRTHDAYS, AND THIS ONE SHOULDN'T BE ANY DIFFERENT.
As a result, I realize now that the burden of ridding Gotham City of the evil that took my parents' lives...
...men and women such as these...
...must be mine and mine alone...

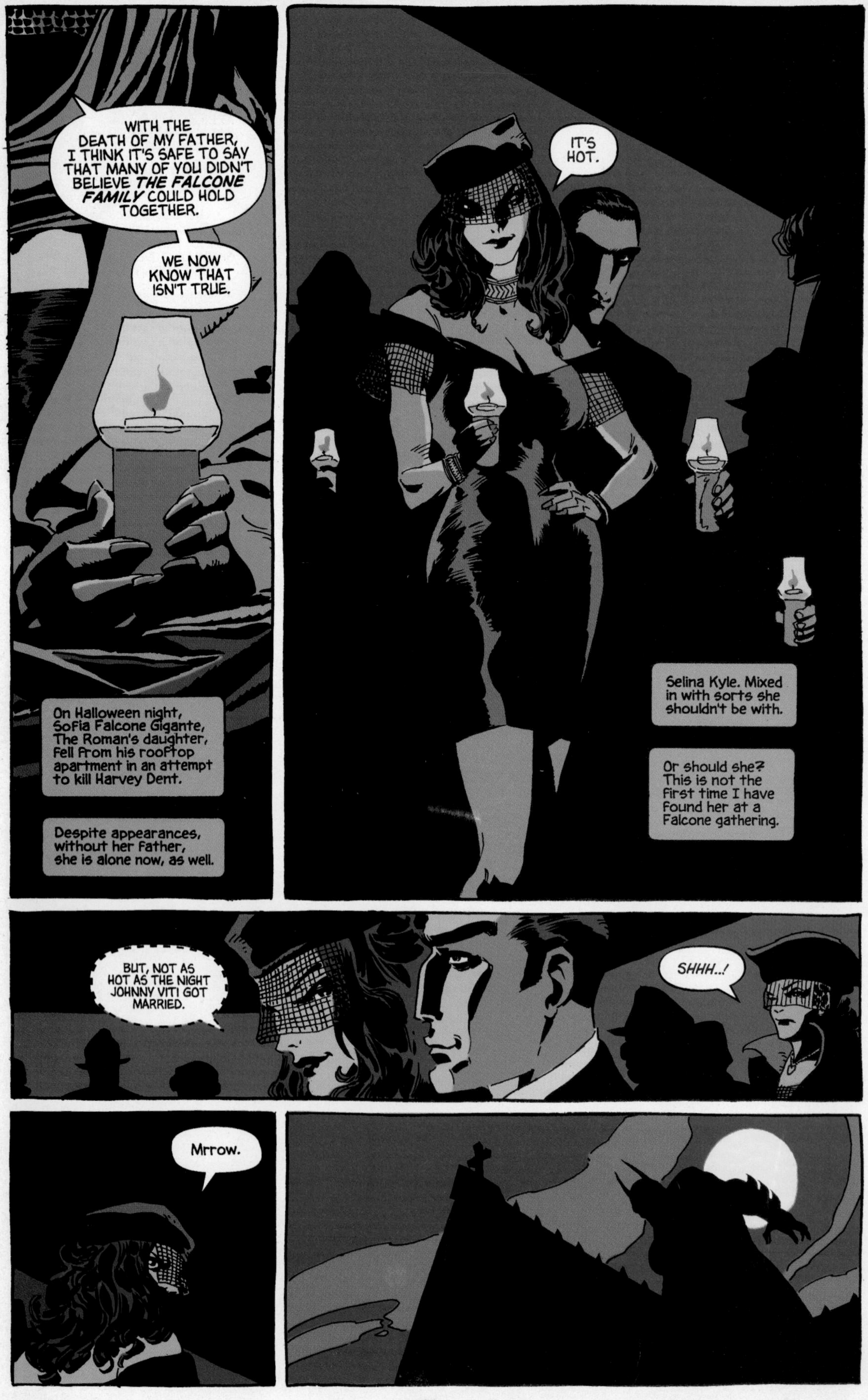
WITH THE DEATH OF MY FATHER, I THINK IT'S SAFE TO SAY THAT MANY OF YOU DIDN'T BELIEVE THE FALCONE FAMILY COULD HOLD TOGETHER.
WE NOW KNOW THAT ISN'T TRUE.
On Halloween night, Sofia Falcone Gigante, The Roman's daughter, fell from his rooftop apartment in an attempt to kill Harvey Dent.
Despite appearances, without her father, she is alone now, as well.
IT'S HOT.
Selina Kyle. Mixed in with sorts she shouldn't be with.
Or should she? This is not the first time I have found her at a Falcone gathering.
BUT, NOT AS HOT AS THE NIGHT JOHNNY VITI GOT MARRIED.
SHHH..!
Mrrow.

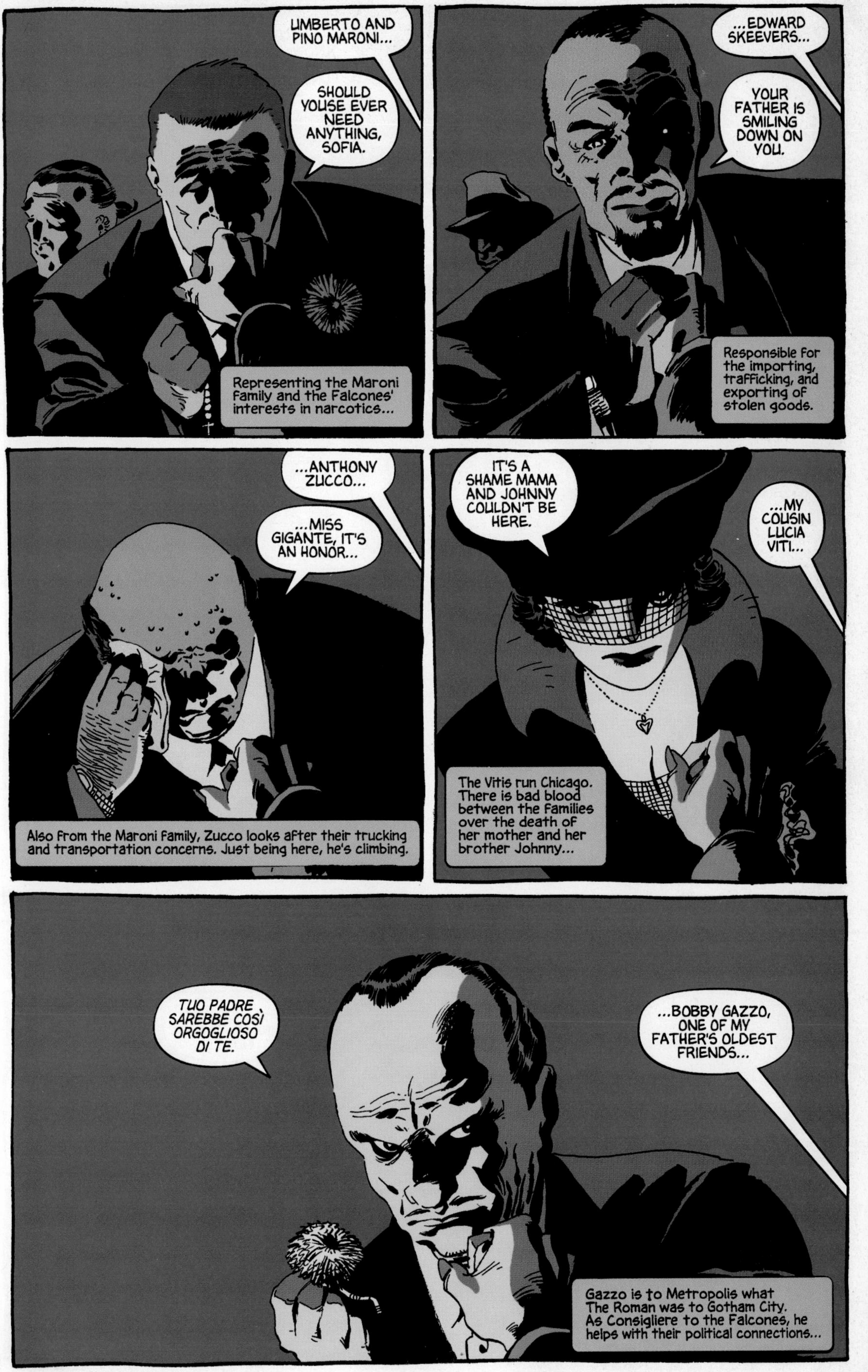
UMBERTO AND PINO MARONI...
SHOULD YOUSE EVER NEED ANYTHING, SOFIA.
Representing the Maroni family and the Falcones' interests in narcotics...
...EDWARD SKEEVERS...
YOUR FATHER IS SMILING DOWN ON YOU.
Responsible for the importing, trafficking, and exporting of stolen goods.
...ANTHONY ZUCCO...
...MISS GIGANTE, IT'S AN HONOR...
Also from the Maroni family, Zucco looks after their trucking and transportation concerns. Just being here, he's climbing.
IT'S A SHAME MAMA AND JOHNNY COULDN'T BE HERE.
...MY COUSIN LUCIA VITI...
The Vitis run Chicago. There is bad blood between the families over the death of her mother and her brother Johnny...
...BOBBY GAZZO, ONE OF MY FATHER'S OLDEST FRIENDS...
TUO PADRE SAREBBE COSÌ ORGOGLIOSO DI TE.
Gazzo is to Metropolis what The Roman was to Gotham City. As Consigliere to the Falcones, he helps with their political connections...

AS MANY OF YOU KNOW, I COULD NOT ATTEND MY FATHER'S FUNERAL DUE TO MY... CONDITION.

MY BROTHER, *MARIO*, WAS OUT OF THE COUNTRY AND MY *OTHER* BROTHER, *ALBERTO*...IS STILL NOT WELL...

SLEEP WELL, POPPA. DREAM THE DREAMS OF KINGS...

ALL OF YOU ARE MI FAMILIA NOW...

TOGETHER, WE WILL MAKE HISTORY IN GOTHAM CITY BY RESTORING THE BALANCE OF POWER *AWAY* FROM THE SO-CALLED *FREAKS* WHO HAVE USURPED SO MUCH OF OUR TERRITORIES.

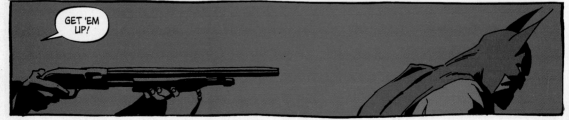

GET 'EM UP!

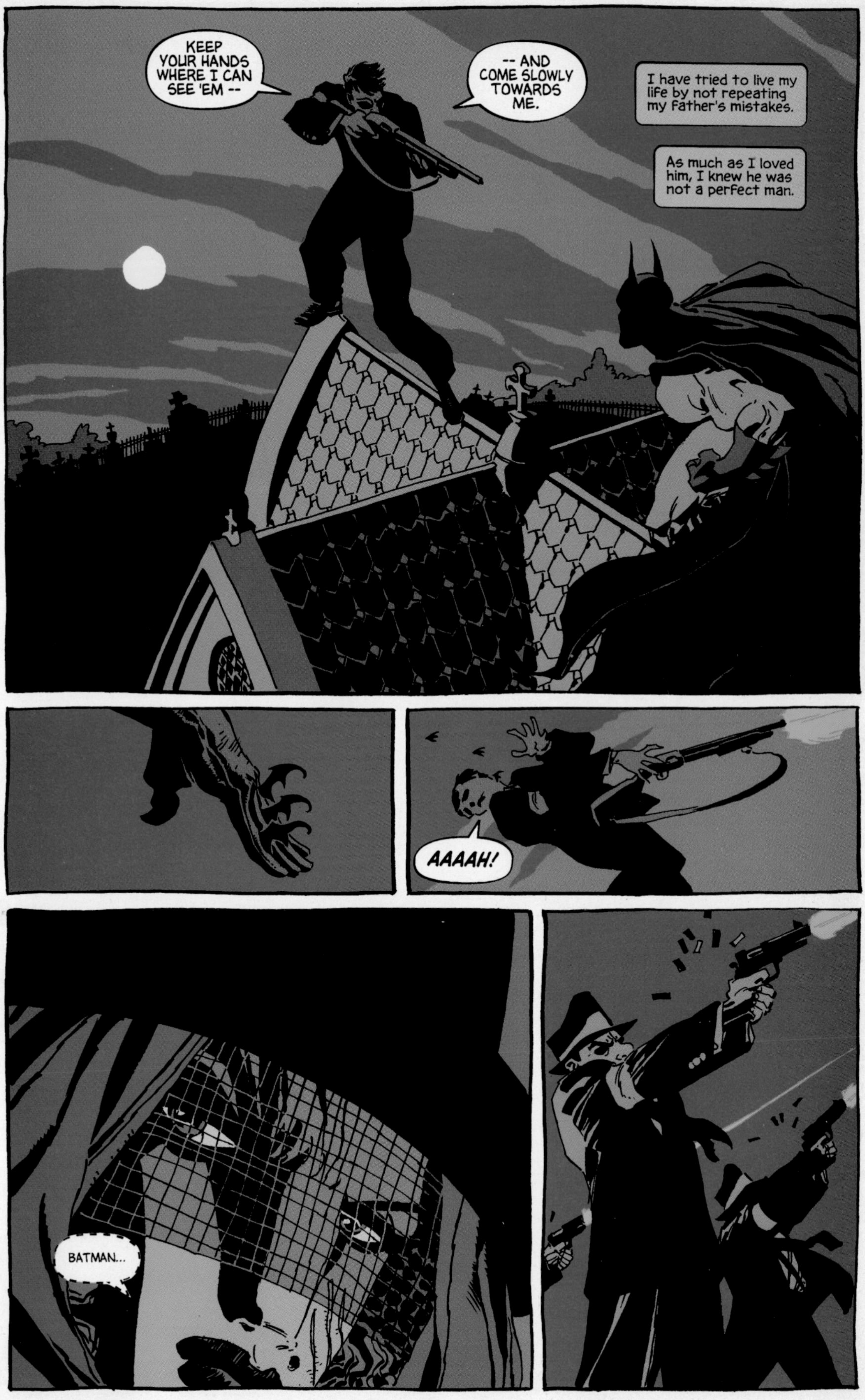
KEEP YOUR HANDS WHERE I CAN SEE 'EM --
-- AND COME SLOWLY TOWARDS ME.
I have tried to live my life by not repeating my father's mistakes.
As much as I loved him, I knew he was not a perfect man.
AAAAH!
BATMAN...

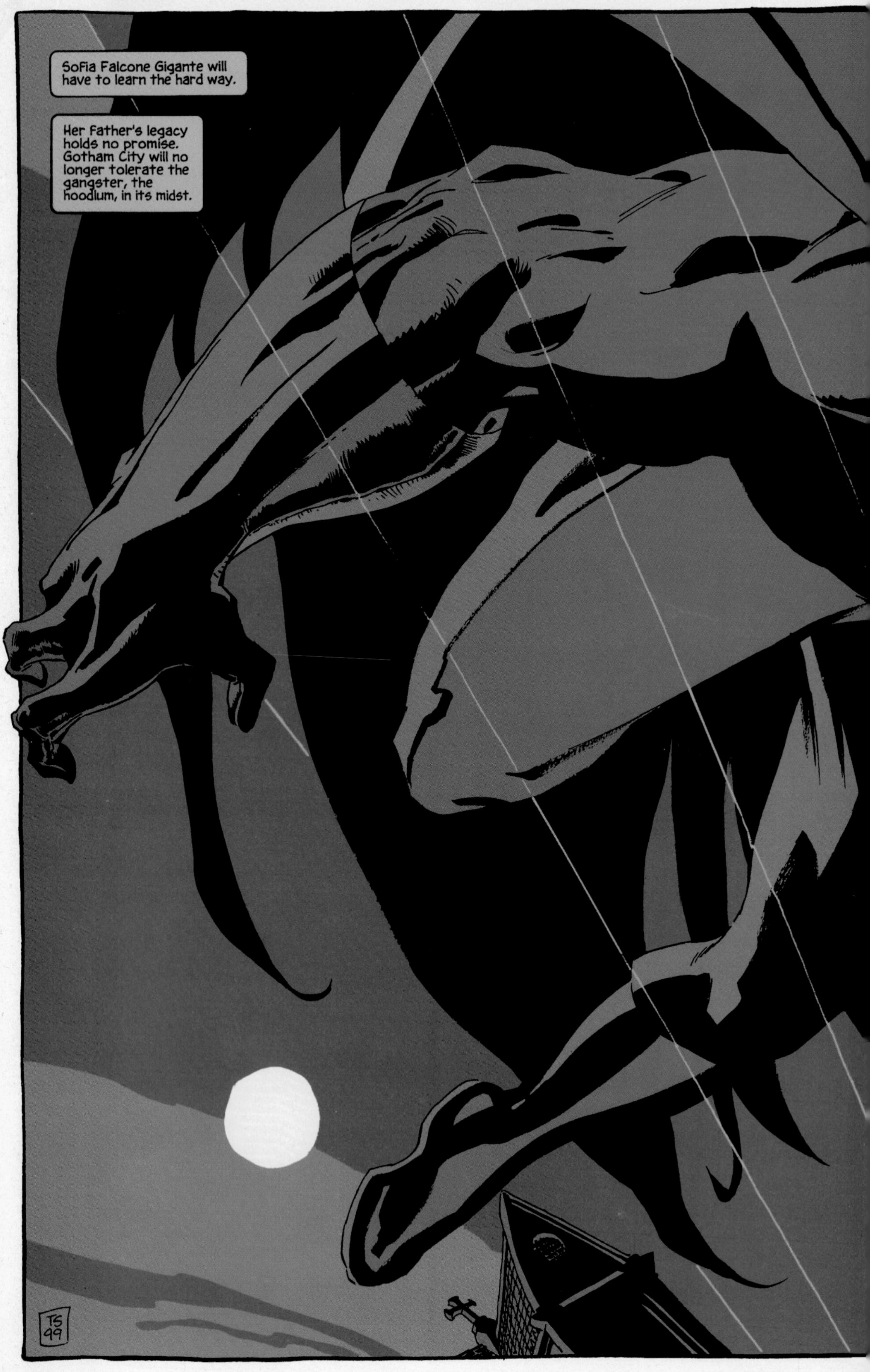
Sofia Falcone Gigante will have to learn the hard way.
Her father's legacy holds no promise. Gotham City will no longer tolerate the gangster, the hoodlum, in its midst.
TS 99

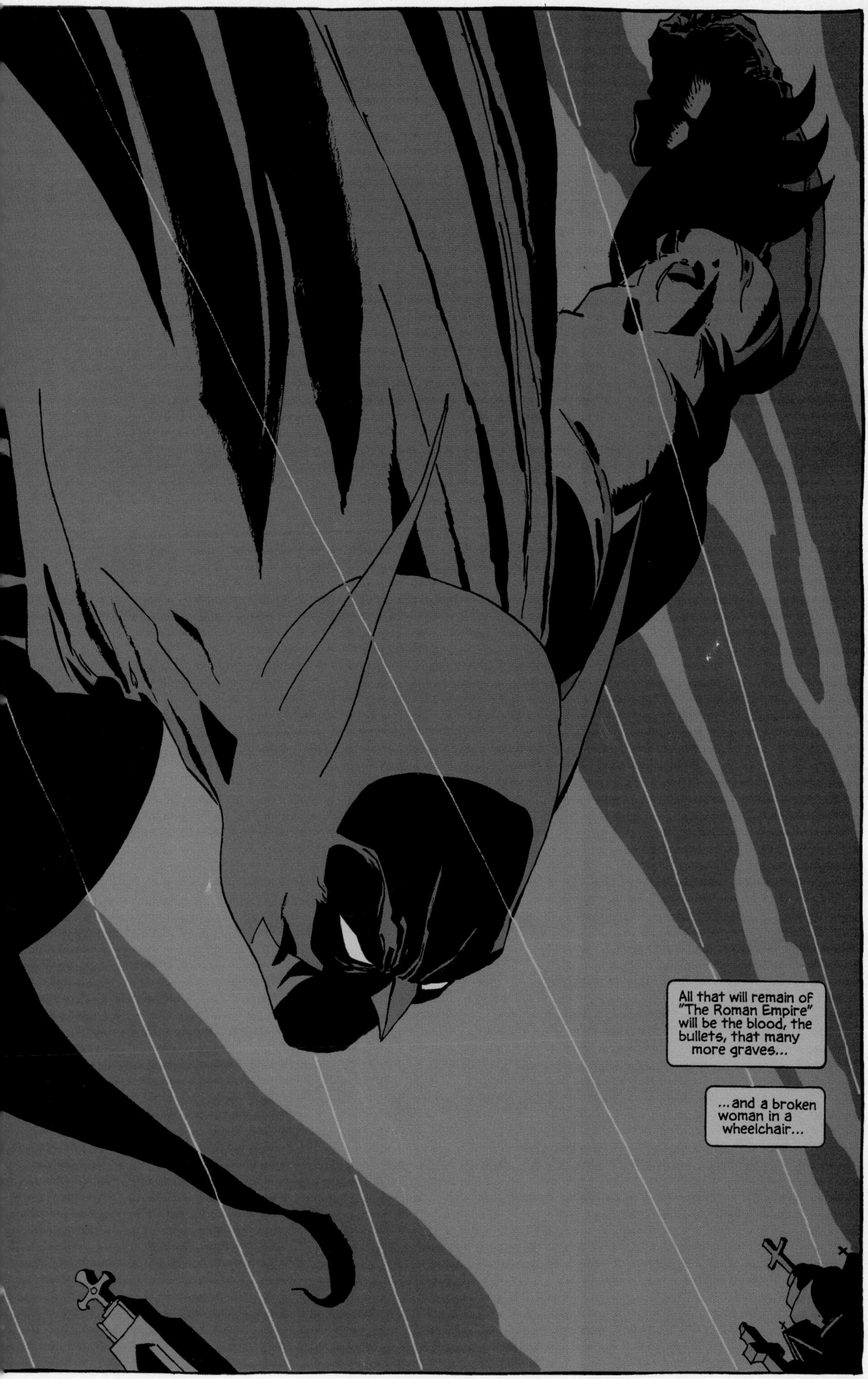
All that will remain of "The Roman Empire" will be the blood, the bullets, that many more graves...
...and a broken woman in a wheelchair...

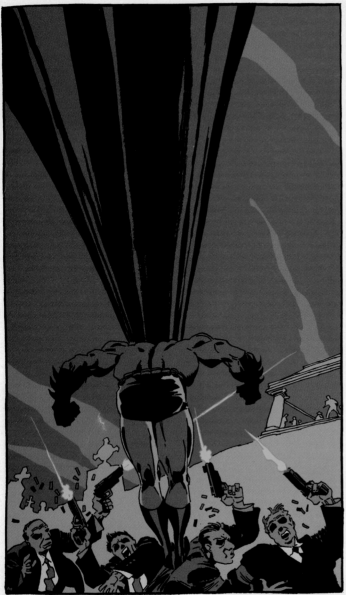

LET'S GET BACK TO THE CAR. WE DO *NOT* WANT TO BE PART OF THIS.

WE SHOULD GO, TOO --

-- SELINA...?

URK

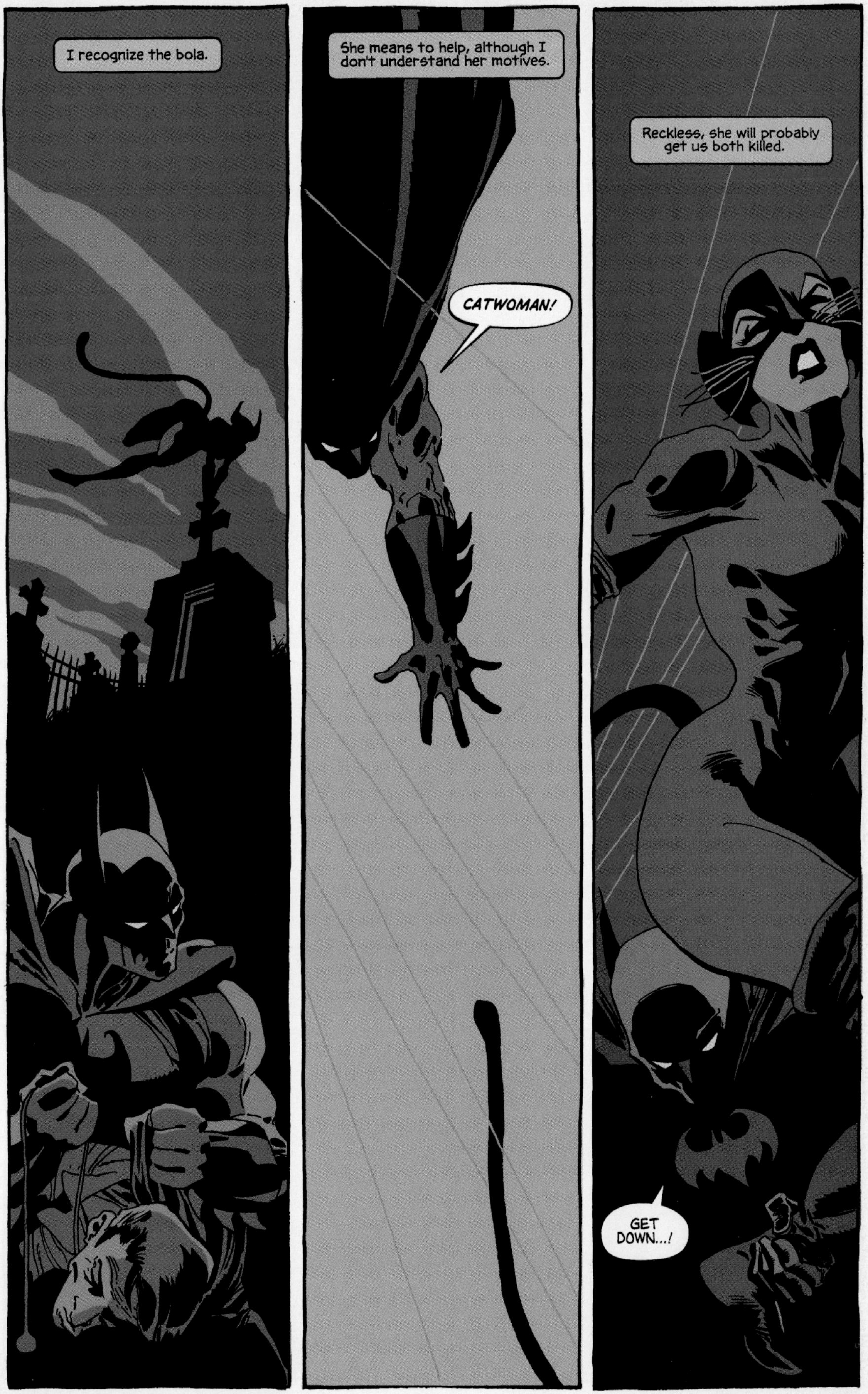
I recognize the bola.
She means to help, although I don't understand her motives.
CATWOMAN!
Reckless, she will probably get us both killed.
GET DOWN...!

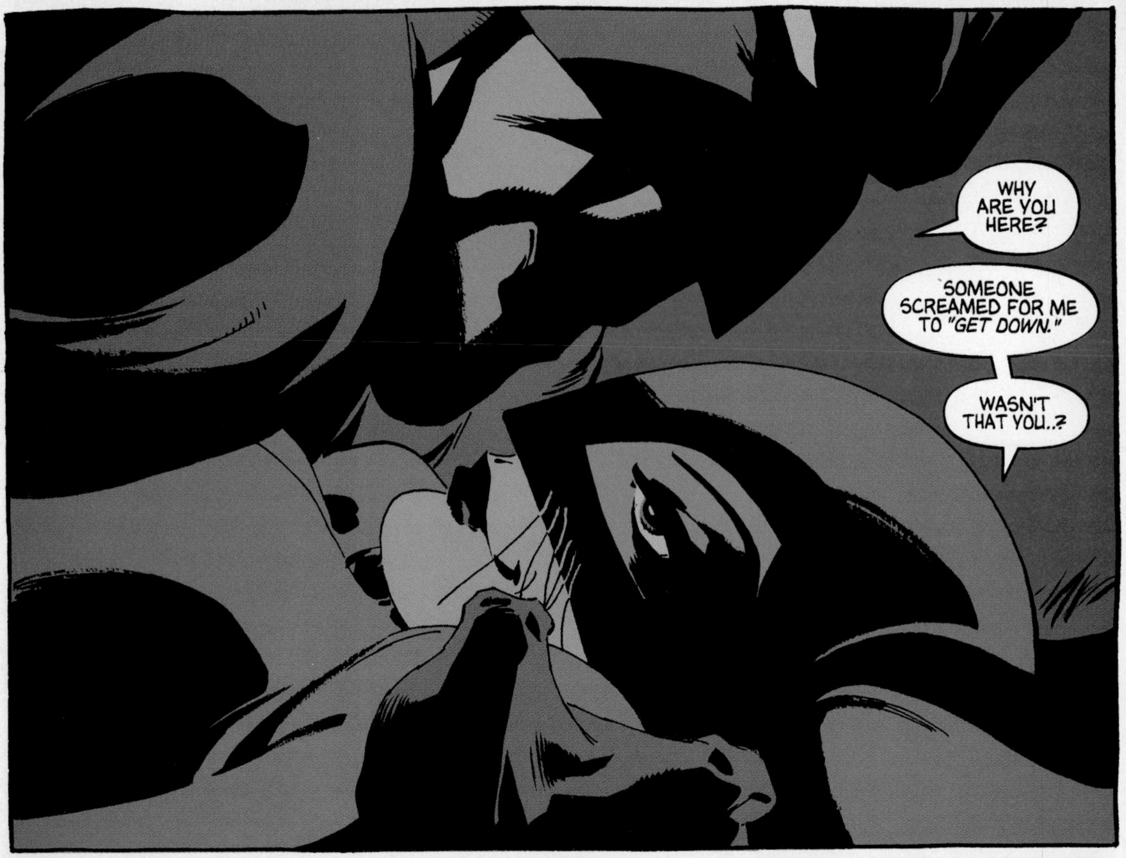
WHY ARE YOU HERE?
SOMEONE SCREAMED FOR ME TO "GET DOWN."
WASN'T THAT YOU..?

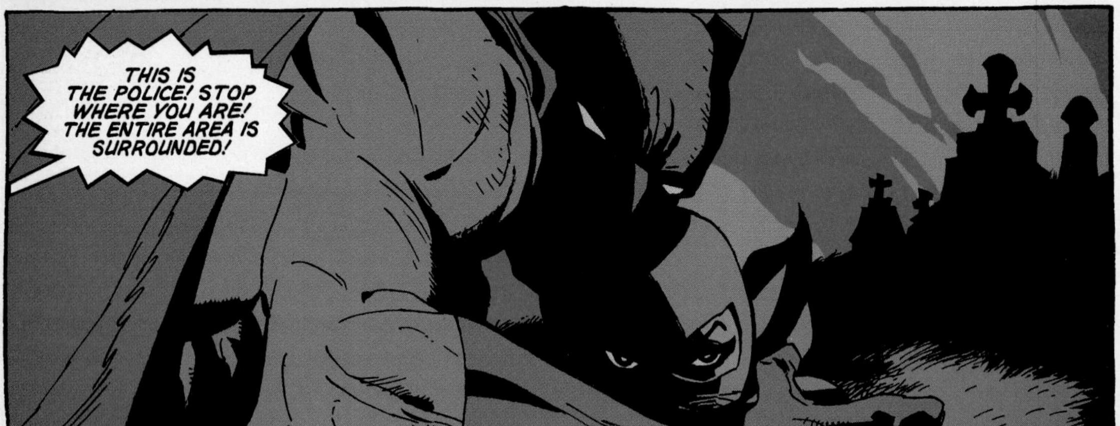
THIS IS THE POLICE! STOP WHERE YOU ARE! THE ENTIRE AREA IS SURROUNDED!

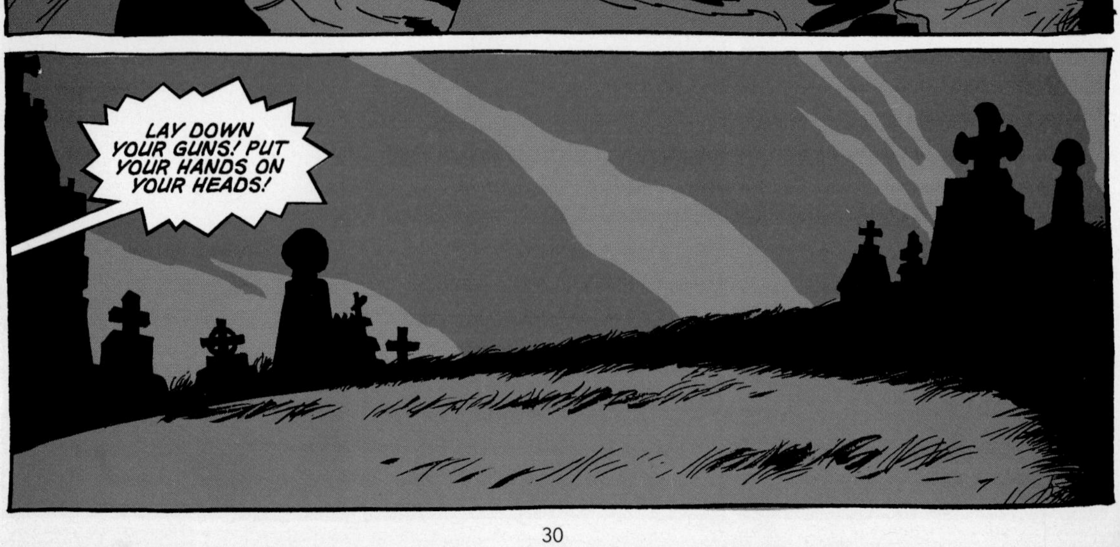
LAY DOWN YOUR GUNS! PUT YOUR HANDS ON YOUR HEADS!

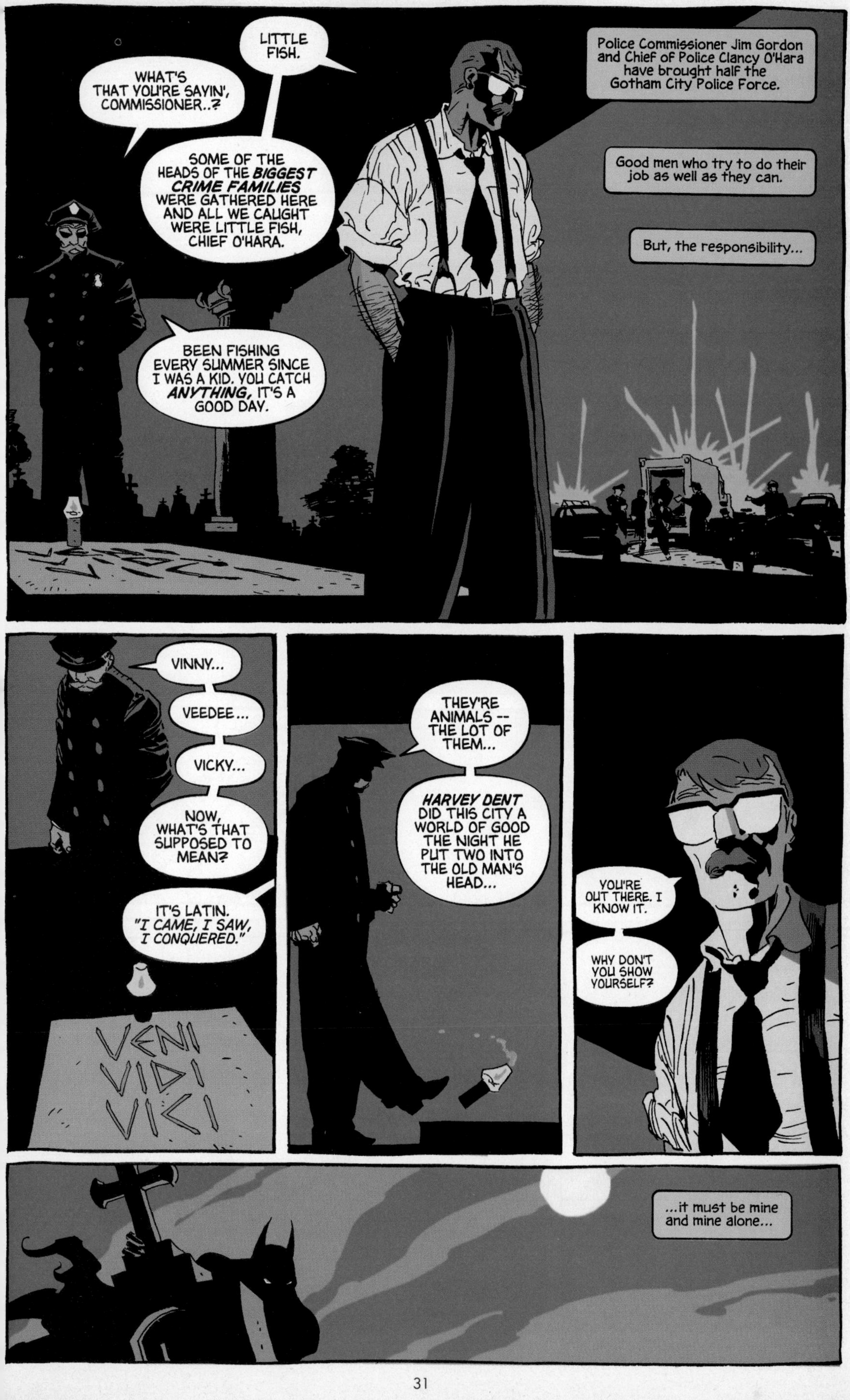
WHAT'S THAT YOU'RE SAYIN', COMMISSIONER..?
LITTLE FISH.
SOME OF THE HEADS OF THE *BIGGEST CRIME FAMILIES* WERE GATHERED HERE AND ALL WE CAUGHT WERE LITTLE FISH, CHIEF O'HARA.
BEEN FISHING EVERY SUMMER SINCE I WAS A KID. YOU CATCH *ANYTHING,* IT'S A GOOD DAY.
Police Commissioner Jim Gordon and Chief of Police Clancy O'Hara have brought half the Gotham City Police Force.
Good men who try to do their job as well as they can.
But, the responsibility...
VINNY...
VEEDEE...
VICKY...
NOW, WHAT'S THAT SUPPOSED TO MEAN?
IT'S LATIN. *"I CAME, I SAW, I CONQUERED."*
VENI VIDI VICI
THEY'RE ANIMALS -- THE LOT OF THEM...
HARVEY DENT DID THIS CITY A WORLD OF GOOD THE NIGHT HE PUT TWO INTO THE OLD MAN'S HEAD...
YOU'RE OUT THERE. I KNOW IT.
WHY DON'T YOU SHOW YOURSELF?
...it must be mine and mine alone...

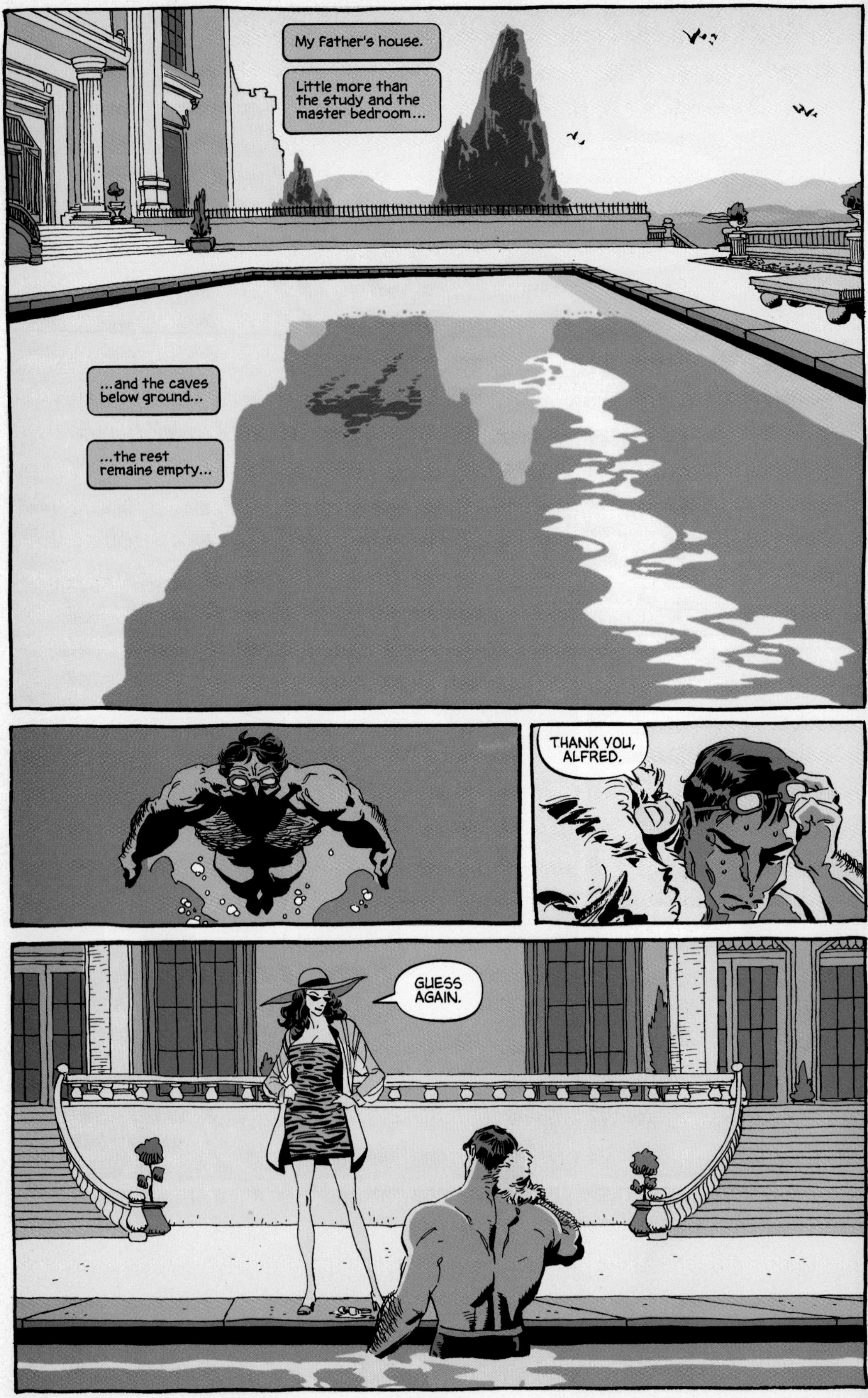
My father's house.
Little more than the study and the master bedroom...
...and the caves below ground...
...the rest remains empty...
THANK YOU, ALFRED.
GUESS AGAIN.

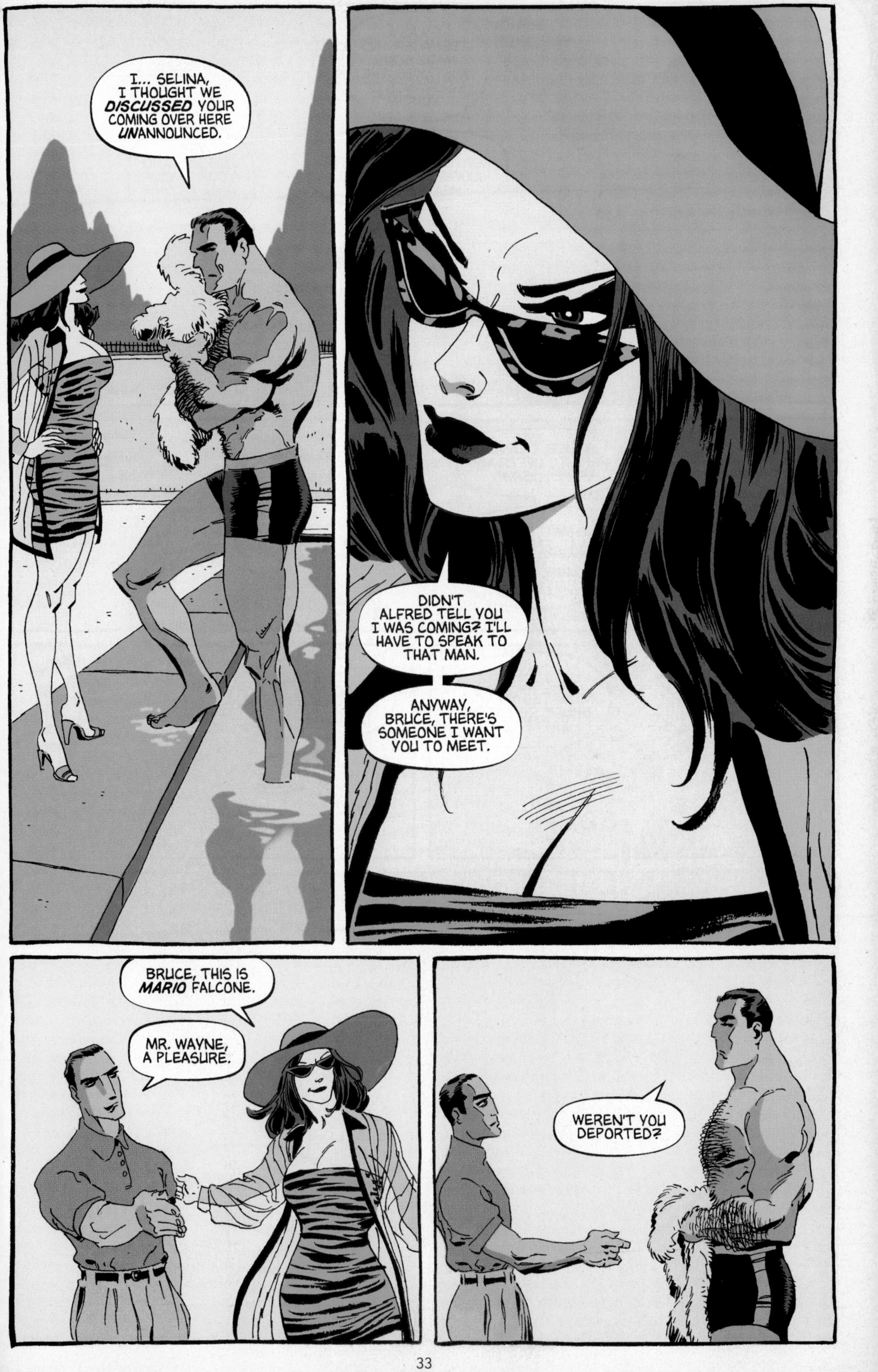
I... SELINA, I THOUGHT WE DISCUSSED YOUR COMING OVER HERE UNANNOUNCED.
DIDN'T ALFRED TELL YOU I WAS COMING? I'LL HAVE TO SPEAK TO THAT MAN.
ANYWAY, BRUCE, THERE'S SOMEONE I WANT YOU TO MEET.
BRUCE, THIS IS MARIO FALCONE.
MR. WAYNE, A PLEASURE.
WEREN'T YOU DEPORTED?

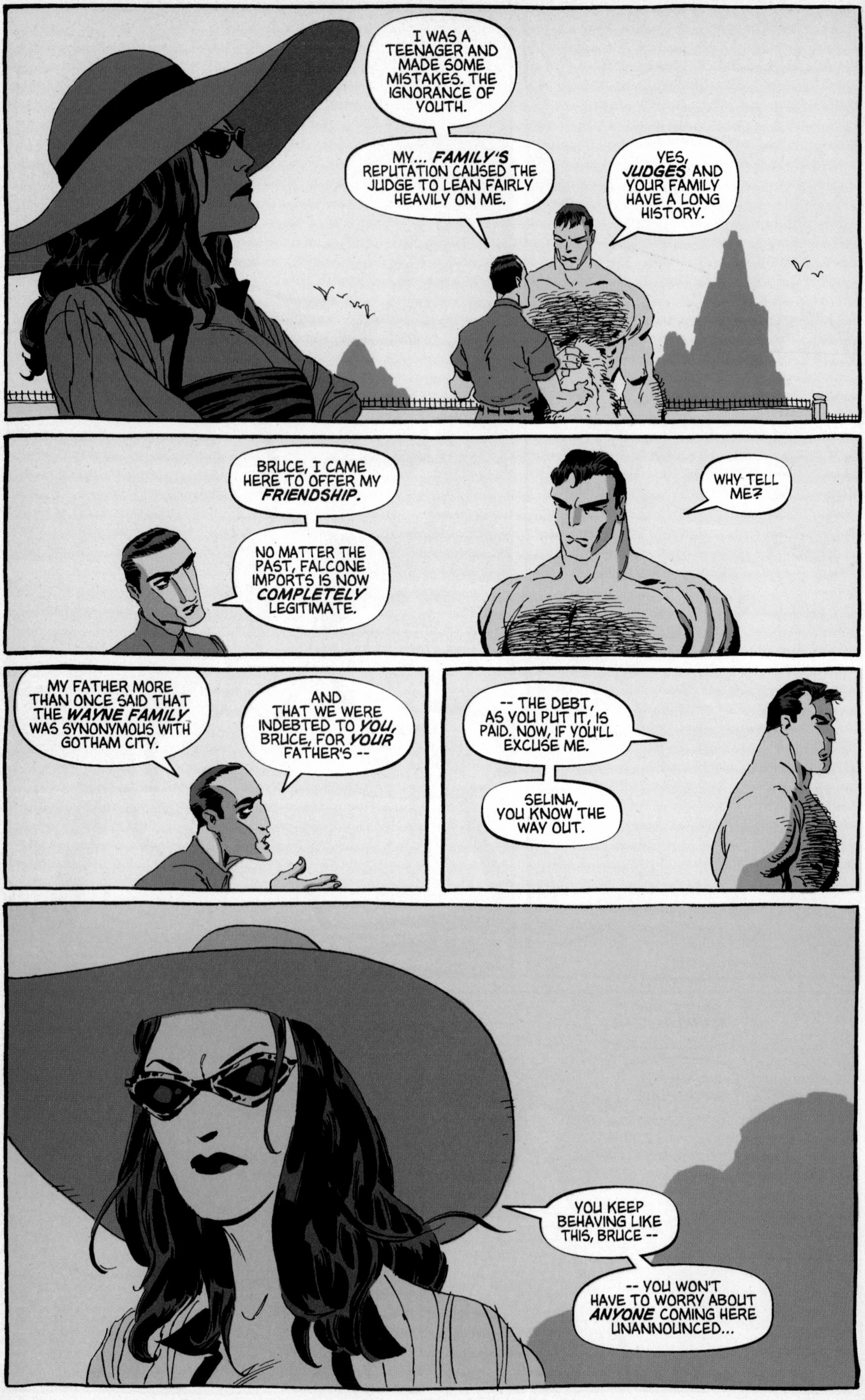
I WAS A TEENAGER AND MADE SOME MISTAKES. THE IGNORANCE OF YOUTH.
MY... FAMILY'S REPUTATION CAUSED THE JUDGE TO LEAN FAIRLY HEAVILY ON ME.
YES, JUDGES AND YOUR FAMILY HAVE A LONG HISTORY.
BRUCE, I CAME HERE TO OFFER MY FRIENDSHIP.
NO MATTER THE PAST, FALCONE IMPORTS IS NOW COMPLETELY LEGITIMATE.
WHY TELL ME?
MY FATHER MORE THAN ONCE SAID THAT THE WAYNE FAMILY WAS SYNONYMOUS WITH GOTHAM CITY.
AND THAT WE WERE INDEBTED TO YOU, BRUCE, FOR YOUR FATHER'S --
-- THE DEBT, AS YOU PUT IT, IS PAID. NOW, IF YOU'LL EXCUSE ME.
SELINA, YOU KNOW THE WAY OUT.
YOU KEEP BEHAVING LIKE THIS, BRUCE --
-- YOU WON'T HAVE TO WORRY ABOUT ANYONE COMING HERE UNANNOUNCED...

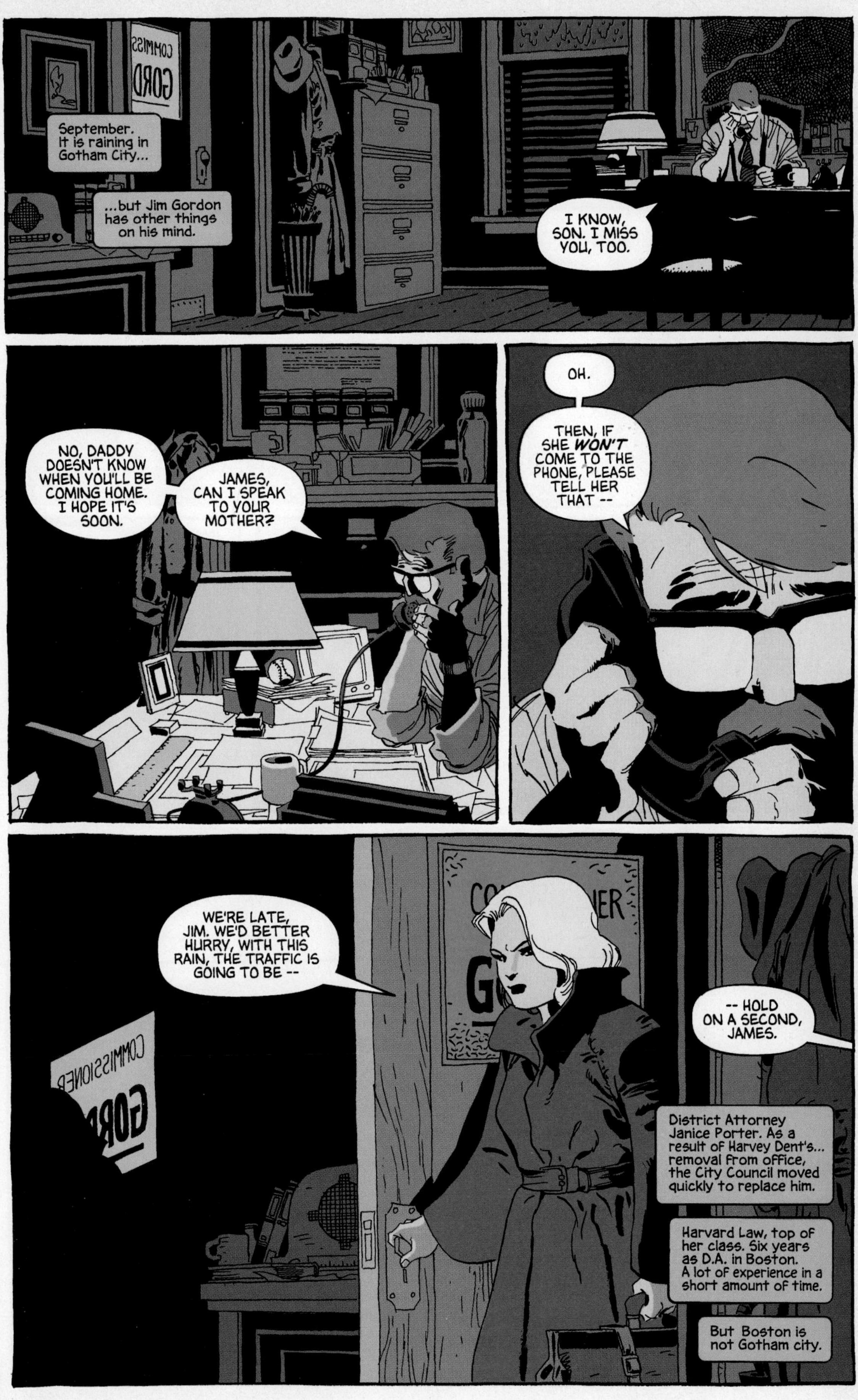
September.
It is raining in Gotham City...
...but Jim Gordon has other things on his mind.
I KNOW, SON. I MISS YOU, TOO.
NO, DADDY DOESN'T KNOW WHEN YOU'LL BE COMING HOME. I HOPE IT'S SOON.
JAMES, CAN I SPEAK TO YOUR MOTHER?
OH.
THEN, IF SHE WON'T COME TO THE PHONE, PLEASE TELL HER THAT --
WE'RE LATE, JIM. WE'D BETTER HURRY, WITH THIS RAIN, THE TRAFFIC IS GOING TO BE --
-- HOLD ON A SECOND, JAMES.
District Attorney Janice Porter. As a result of Harvey Dent's... removal from office, the City Council moved quickly to replace him.
Harvard Law, top of her class. Six years as D.A. in Boston. A lot of experience in a short amount of time.
But Boston is not Gotham city.

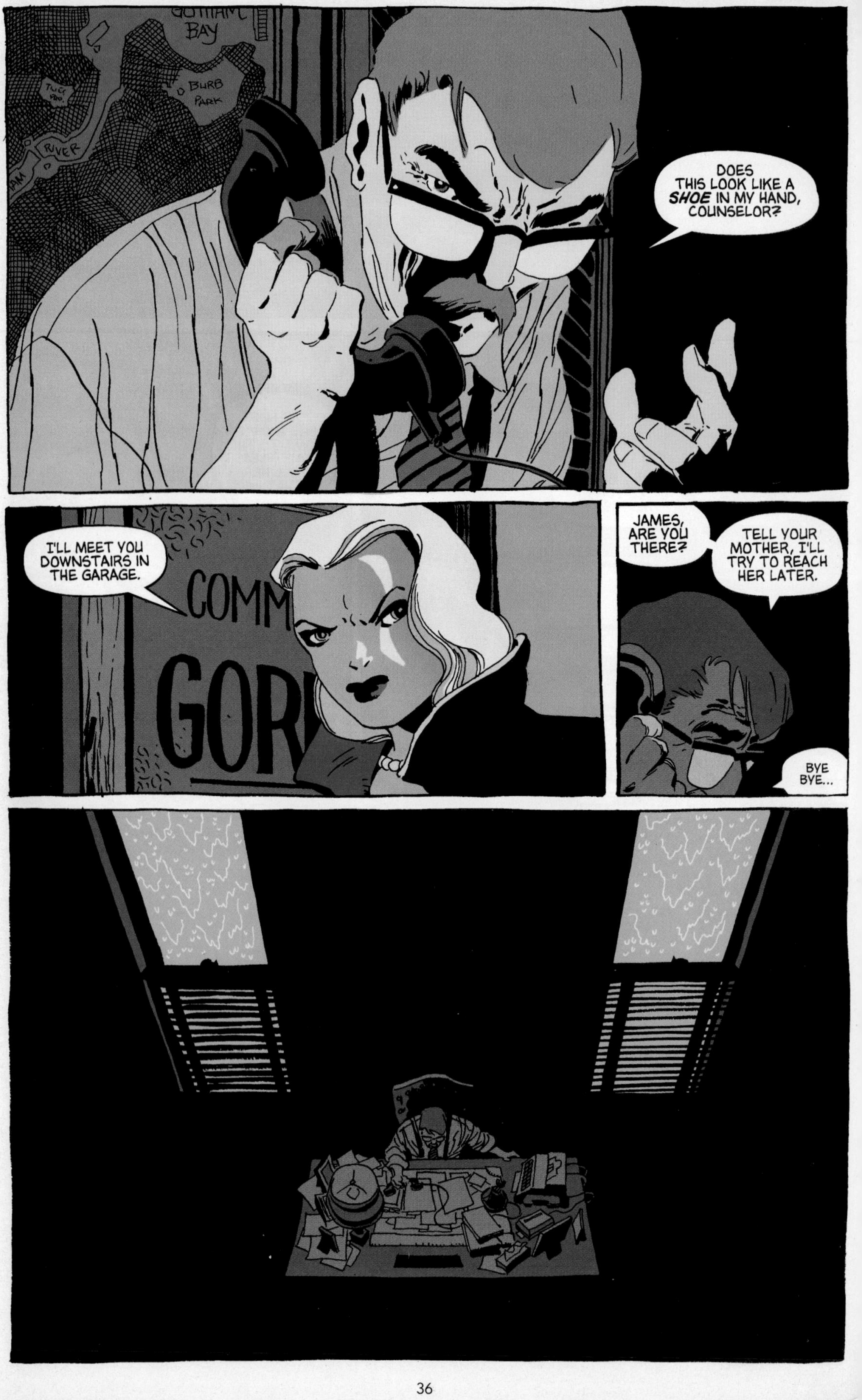
BAY
BURB PARK
RIVER
DOES THIS LOOK LIKE A SHOE IN MY HAND, COUNSELOR?
I'LL MEET YOU DOWNSTAIRS IN THE GARAGE.
JAMES, ARE YOU THERE?
TELL YOUR MOTHER, I'LL TRY TO REACH HER LATER.
BYE BYE...

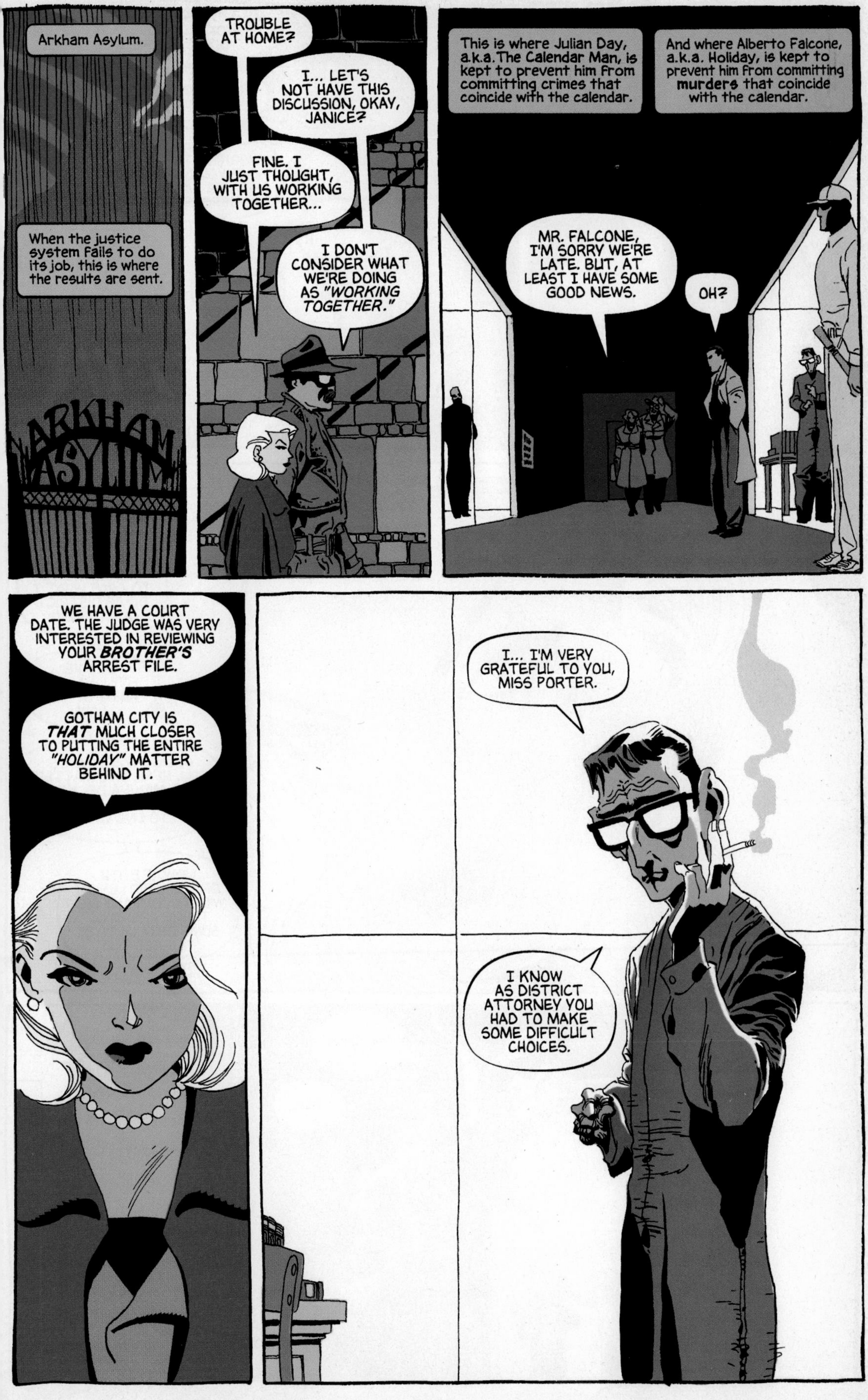
Arkham Asylum.
When the justice system fails to do its job, this is where the results are sent.
ARKHAM ASYLUM
TROUBLE AT HOME?
I... LET'S NOT HAVE THIS DISCUSSION, OKAY, JANICE?
FINE. I JUST THOUGHT, WITH US WORKING TOGETHER...
I DON'T CONSIDER WHAT WE'RE DOING AS "WORKING TOGETHER."
This is where Julian Day, a.k.a. The Calendar Man, is kept to prevent him from committing crimes that coincide with the calendar.
And where Alberto Falcone, a.k.a. Holiday, is kept to prevent him from committing **murders** that coincide with the calendar.
MR. FALCONE, I'M SORRY WE'RE LATE. BUT, AT LEAST I HAVE SOME GOOD NEWS.
OH?
WE HAVE A COURT DATE. THE JUDGE WAS VERY INTERESTED IN REVIEWING YOUR ***BROTHER'S*** ARREST FILE.
GOTHAM CITY IS ***THAT*** MUCH CLOSER TO PUTTING THE ENTIRE *"HOLIDAY"* MATTER BEHIND IT.
I... I'M VERY GRATEFUL TO YOU, MISS PORTER.
I KNOW AS DISTRICT ATTORNEY YOU HAD TO MAKE SOME DIFFICULT CHOICES.

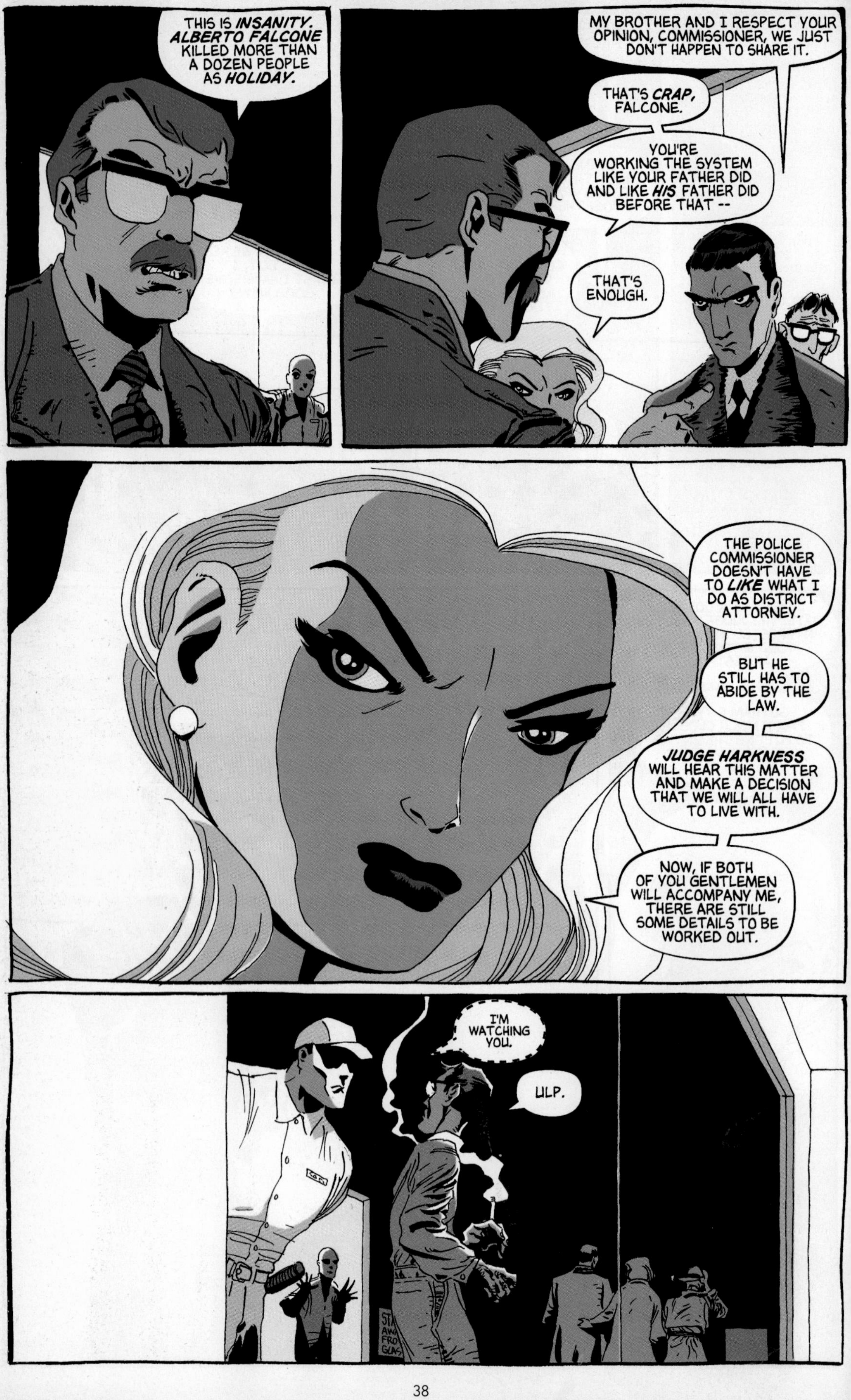

THIS IS INSANITY. ALBERTO FALCONE KILLED MORE THAN A DOZEN PEOPLE AS HOLIDAY.
MY BROTHER AND I RESPECT YOUR OPINION, COMMISSIONER, WE JUST DON'T HAPPEN TO SHARE IT.
THAT'S CRAP, FALCONE.
YOU'RE WORKING THE SYSTEM LIKE YOUR FATHER DID AND LIKE HIS FATHER DID BEFORE THAT --
THAT'S ENOUGH.
THE POLICE COMMISSIONER DOESN'T HAVE TO LIKE WHAT I DO AS DISTRICT ATTORNEY.
BUT HE STILL HAS TO ABIDE BY THE LAW.
JUDGE HARKNESS WILL HEAR THIS MATTER AND MAKE A DECISION THAT WE WILL ALL HAVE TO LIVE WITH.
NOW, IF BOTH OF YOU GENTLEMEN WILL ACCOMPANY ME, THERE ARE STILL SOME DETAILS TO BE WORKED OUT.
I'M WATCHING YOU.
ULP.

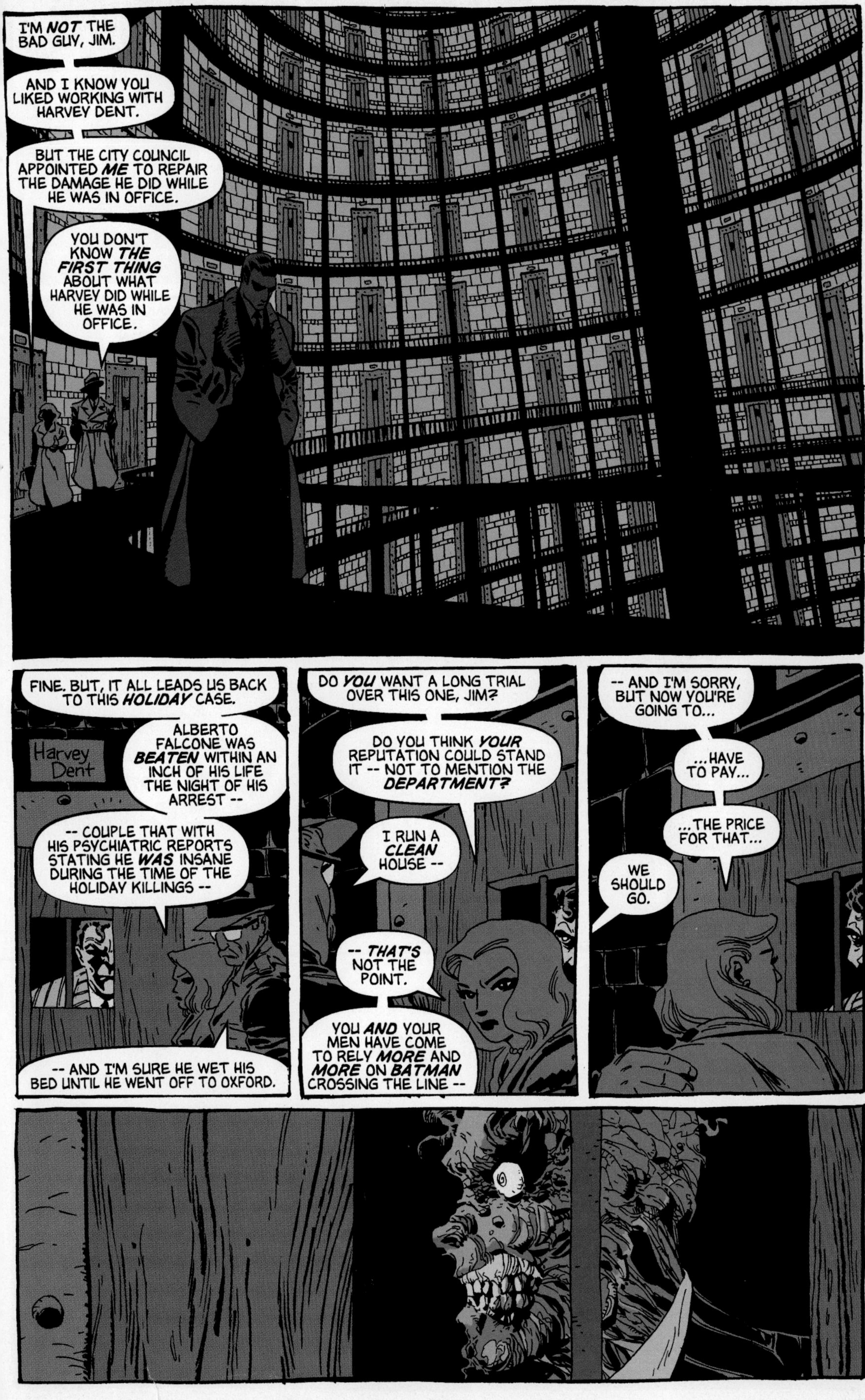
I'M NOT THE BAD GUY, JIM.
AND I KNOW YOU LIKED WORKING WITH HARVEY DENT.
BUT THE CITY COUNCIL APPOINTED ME TO REPAIR THE DAMAGE HE DID WHILE HE WAS IN OFFICE.
YOU DON'T KNOW THE FIRST THING ABOUT WHAT HARVEY DID WHILE HE WAS IN OFFICE.
FINE. BUT, IT ALL LEADS US BACK TO THIS HOLIDAY CASE.
Harvey Dent
ALBERTO FALCONE WAS BEATEN WITHIN AN INCH OF HIS LIFE THE NIGHT OF HIS ARREST --
-- COUPLE THAT WITH HIS PSYCHIATRIC REPORTS STATING HE WAS INSANE DURING THE TIME OF THE HOLIDAY KILLINGS --
-- AND I'M SURE HE WET HIS BED UNTIL HE WENT OFF TO OXFORD.
DO YOU WANT A LONG TRIAL OVER THIS ONE, JIM?
DO YOU THINK YOUR REPUTATION COULD STAND IT -- NOT TO MENTION THE DEPARTMENT?
I RUN A CLEAN HOUSE --
-- THAT'S NOT THE POINT.
YOU AND YOUR MEN HAVE COME TO RELY MORE AND MORE ON BATMAN CROSSING THE LINE --
-- AND I'M SORRY, BUT NOW YOU'RE GOING TO...
...HAVE TO PAY...
...THE PRICE FOR THAT...
WE SHOULD GO.

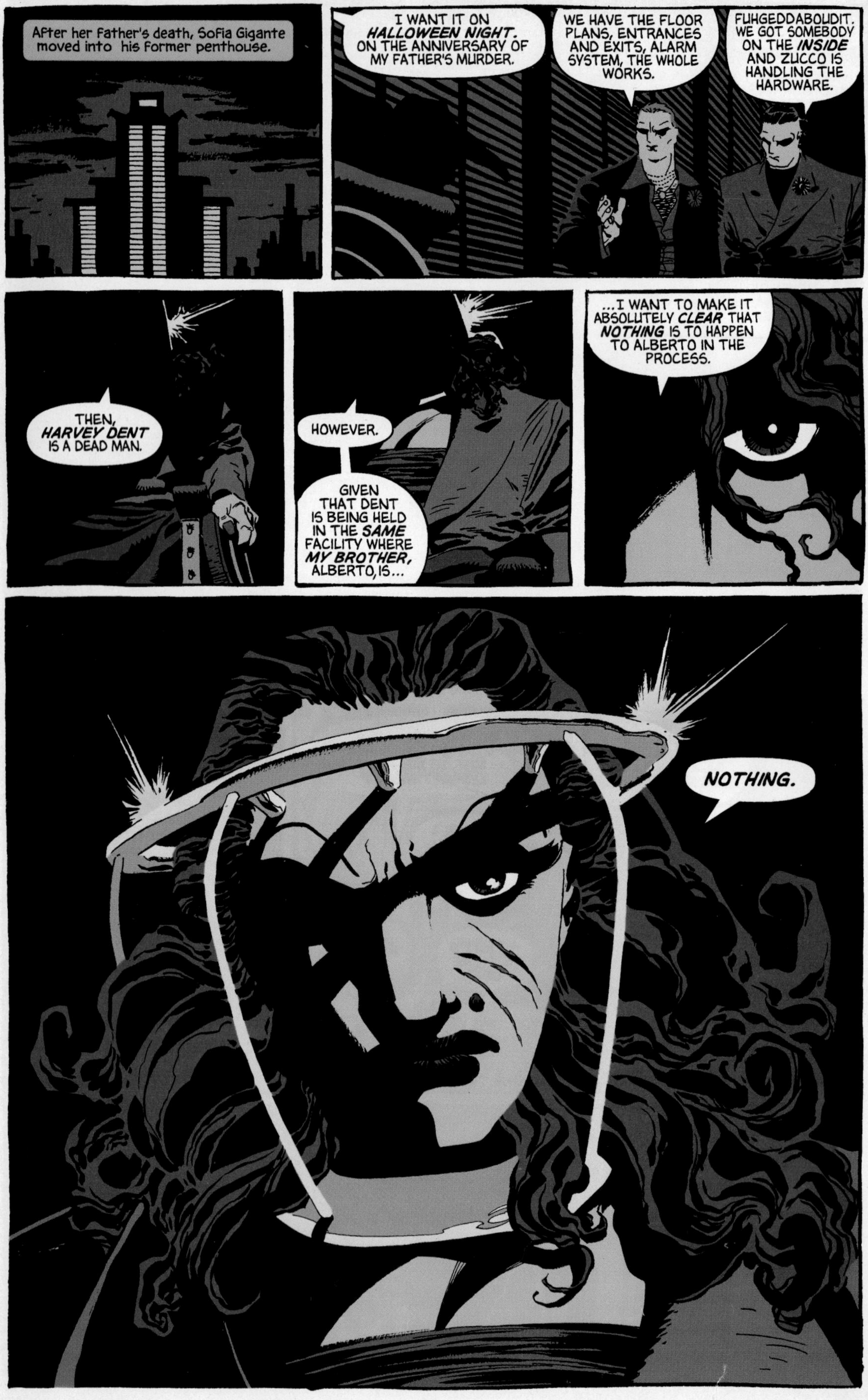
After her father's death, Sofia Gigante moved into his former penthouse.
I WANT IT ON HALLOWEEN NIGHT. ON THE ANNIVERSARY OF MY FATHER'S MURDER.
WE HAVE THE FLOOR PLANS, ENTRANCES AND EXITS, ALARM SYSTEM, THE WHOLE WORKS.
FUHGEDDABOUDIT. WE GOT SOMEBODY ON THE INSIDE AND ZUCCO IS HANDLING THE HARDWARE.
THEN, HARVEY DENT IS A DEAD MAN.
HOWEVER.
GIVEN THAT DENT IS BEING HELD IN THE SAME FACILITY WHERE MY BROTHER, ALBERTO, IS...
...I WANT TO MAKE IT ABSOLUTELY CLEAR THAT NOTHING IS TO HAPPEN TO ALBERTO IN THE PROCESS.
NOTHING.

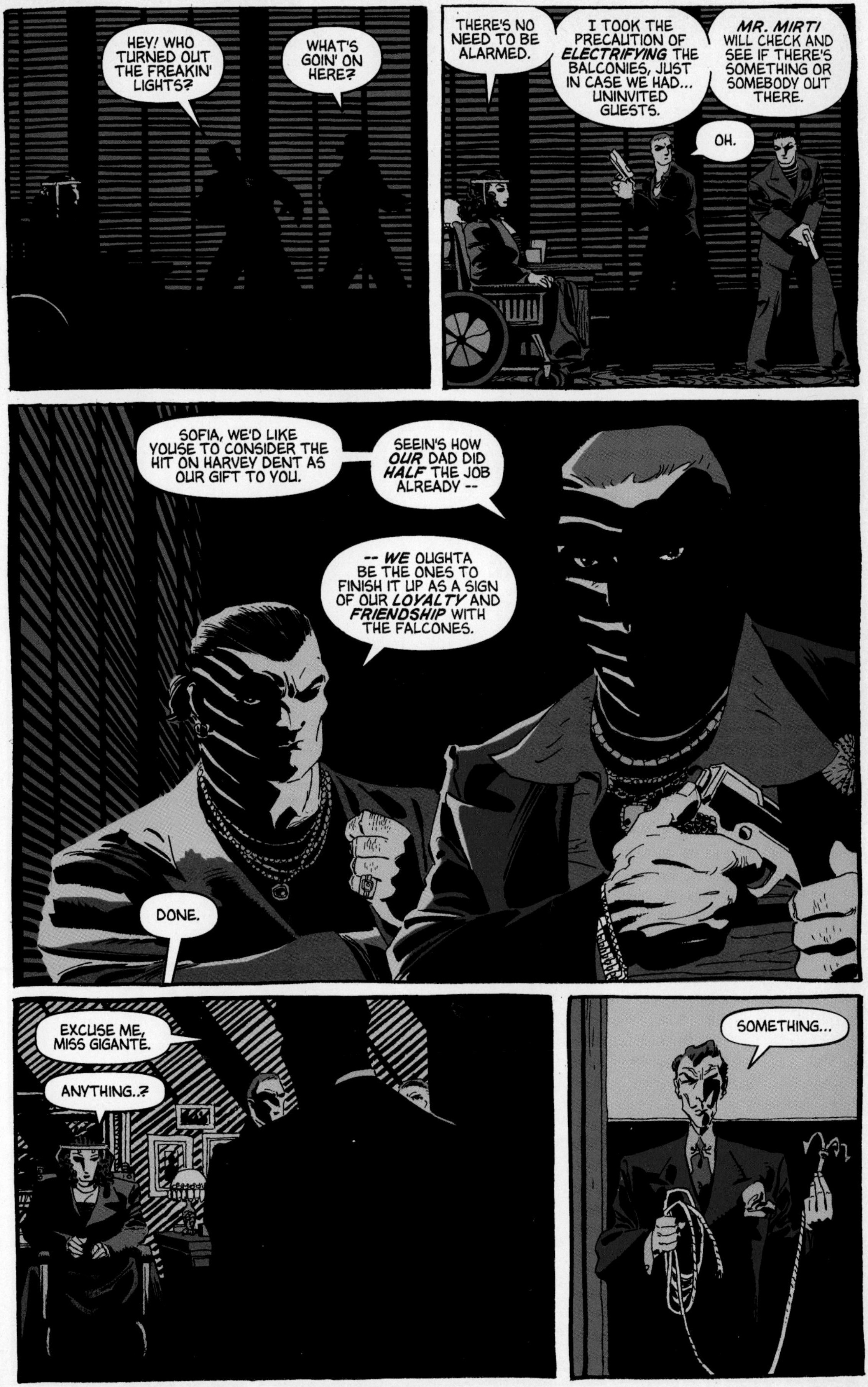
HEY! WHO TURNED OUT THE FREAKIN' LIGHTS?
WHAT'S GOIN' ON HERE?
THERE'S NO NEED TO BE ALARMED.
I TOOK THE PRECAUTION OF ELECTRIFYING THE BALCONIES, JUST IN CASE WE HAD... UNINVITED GUESTS.
MR. MIRTI WILL CHECK AND SEE IF THERE'S SOMETHING OR SOMEBODY OUT THERE.
OH.
SOFIA, WE'D LIKE YOUSE TO CONSIDER THE HIT ON HARVEY DENT AS OUR GIFT TO YOU.
SEEIN'S HOW OUR DAD DID HALF THE JOB ALREADY --
-- WE OUGHTA BE THE ONES TO FINISH IT UP AS A SIGN OF OUR LOYALTY AND FRIENDSHIP WITH THE FALCONES.
DONE.
EXCUSE ME, MISS GIGANTE.
ANYTHING..?
SOMETHING...

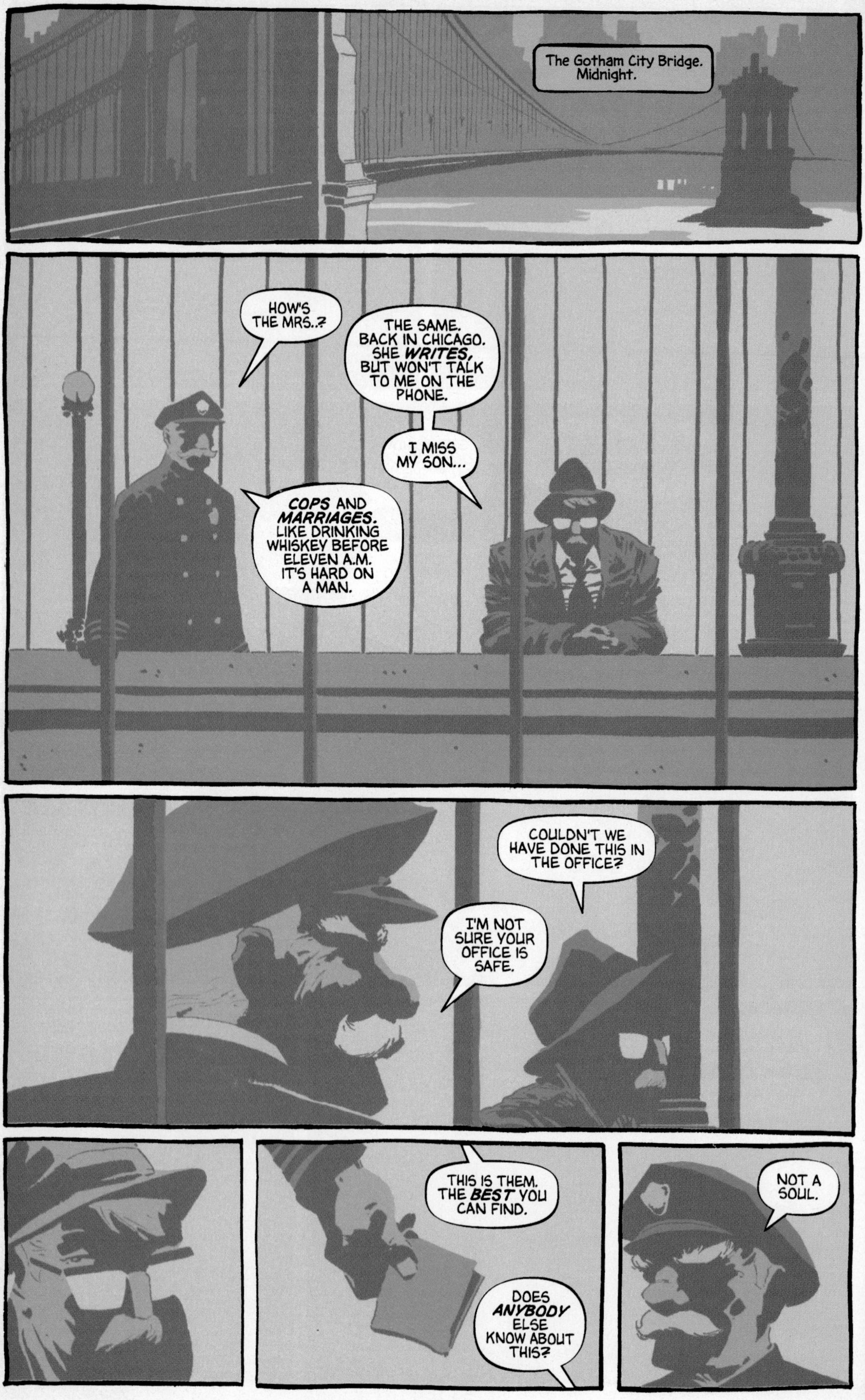
The Gotham City Bridge. Midnight.
HOW'S THE MRS..?
THE SAME. BACK IN CHICAGO. SHE *WRITES,* BUT WON'T TALK TO ME ON THE PHONE.
I MISS MY SON...
COPS AND *MARRIAGES.* LIKE DRINKING WHISKEY BEFORE ELEVEN A.M. IT'S HARD ON A MAN.
COULDN'T WE HAVE DONE THIS IN THE OFFICE?
I'M NOT SURE YOUR OFFICE IS SAFE.
THIS IS THEM. THE *BEST* YOU CAN FIND.
DOES *ANYBODY* ELSE KNOW ABOUT THIS?
NOT A SOUL.

THIS WAS MY FIRST BEAT. I *STILL* WALK HOME THIS WAY EVERY NIGHT, JUST TO REMEMBER WHERE I CAME FROM.

IT *WAS* DIFFERENT THEN, WASN'T IT, CLANCY?

IT WAS ROUGH, BUT WE HELD ON TO IT. A *COP* MEANT SOMETHING BACK THEN.

UP UNTIL THE WAYNE MURDERS.

THOMAS AND MARTHA WAYNE..?

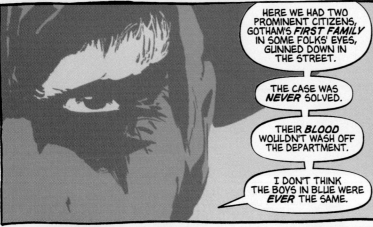

HERE WE HAD TWO PROMINENT CITIZENS, GOTHAM'S *FIRST FAMILY* IN SOME FOLKS' EYES, GUNNED DOWN IN THE STREET.

THE CASE WAS *NEVER* SOLVED.

THEIR *BLOOD* WOULDN'T WASH OFF THE DEPARTMENT.

I DON'T THINK THE BOYS IN BLUE WERE *EVER* THE SAME.

WHAT ABOUT NOW?

DO YOU THINK WE CAN MAKE BEING A *COP* MEAN SOMETHING AGAIN?

YOU REALLY WANT TO KNOW WHAT *I* THINK?

YOU SHOULD GO TALK TO THE BAT.

YOU NEED TO TELL HIM WHAT'S GOING ON...

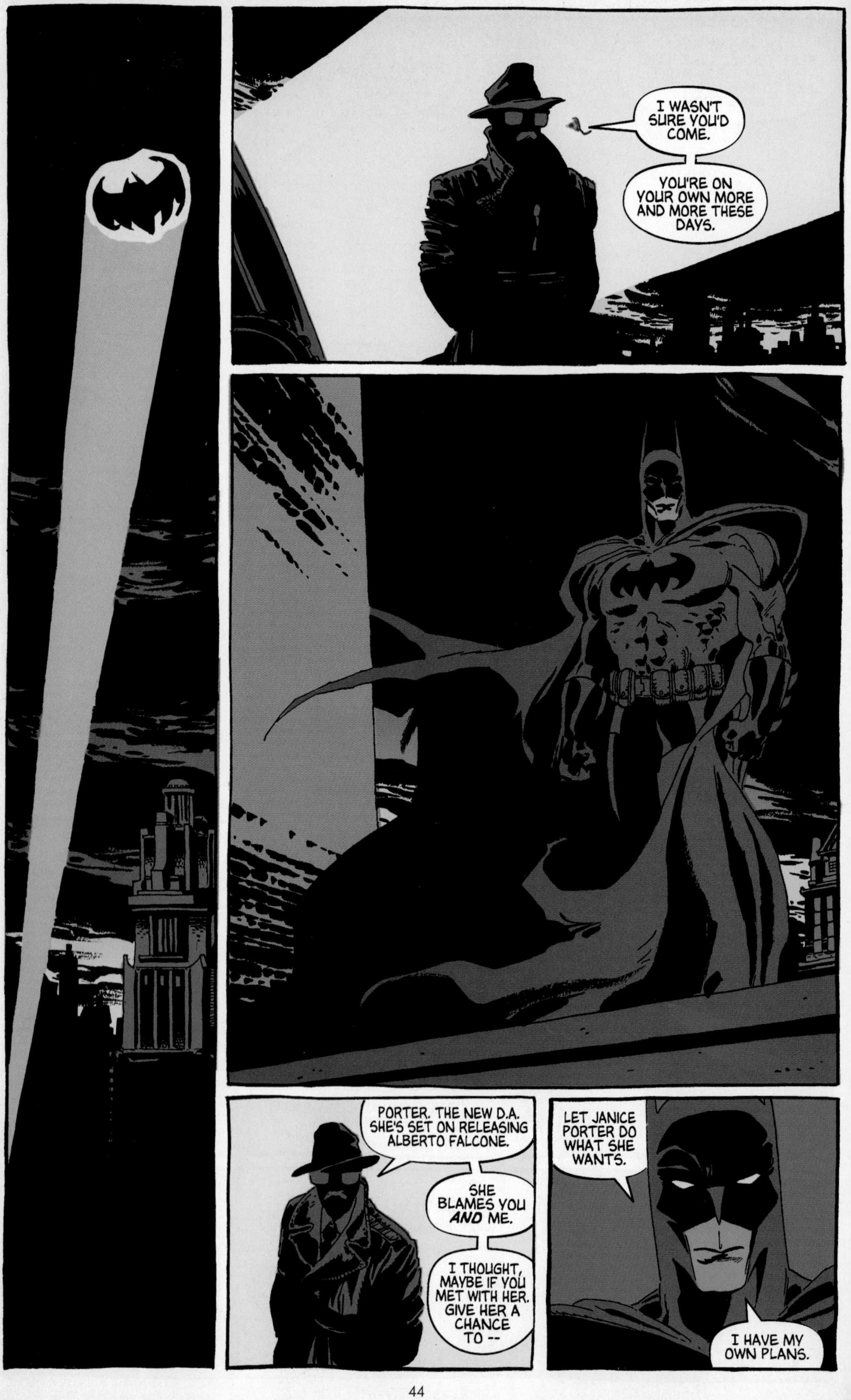
I WASN'T SURE YOU'D COME.
YOU'RE ON YOUR OWN MORE AND MORE THESE DAYS.
PORTER. THE NEW D.A. SHE'S SET ON RELEASING ALBERTO FALCONE.
SHE BLAMES YOU *AND* ME.
I THOUGHT, MAYBE IF YOU MET WITH HER. GIVE HER A CHANCE TO --
LET JANICE PORTER DO WHAT SHE WANTS.
I HAVE MY OWN PLANS.

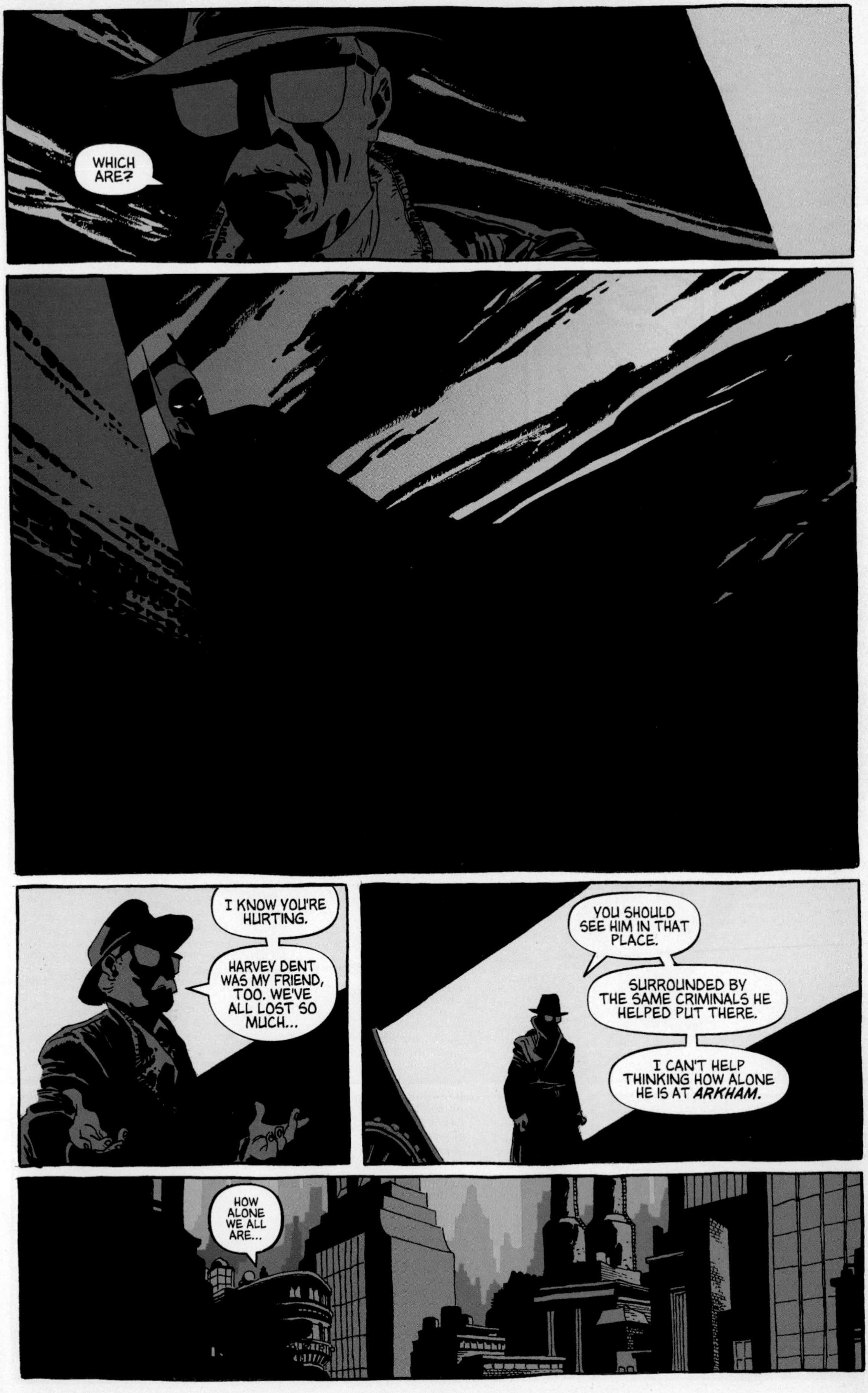
WHICH ARE?
I KNOW YOU'RE HURTING.
HARVEY DENT WAS MY FRIEND, TOO. WE'VE ALL LOST SO MUCH...
YOU SHOULD SEE HIM IN THAT PLACE.
SURROUNDED BY THE SAME CRIMINALS HE HELPED PUT THERE.
I CAN'T HELP THINKING HOW ALONE HE IS AT ARKHAM.
HOW ALONE WE ALL ARE...

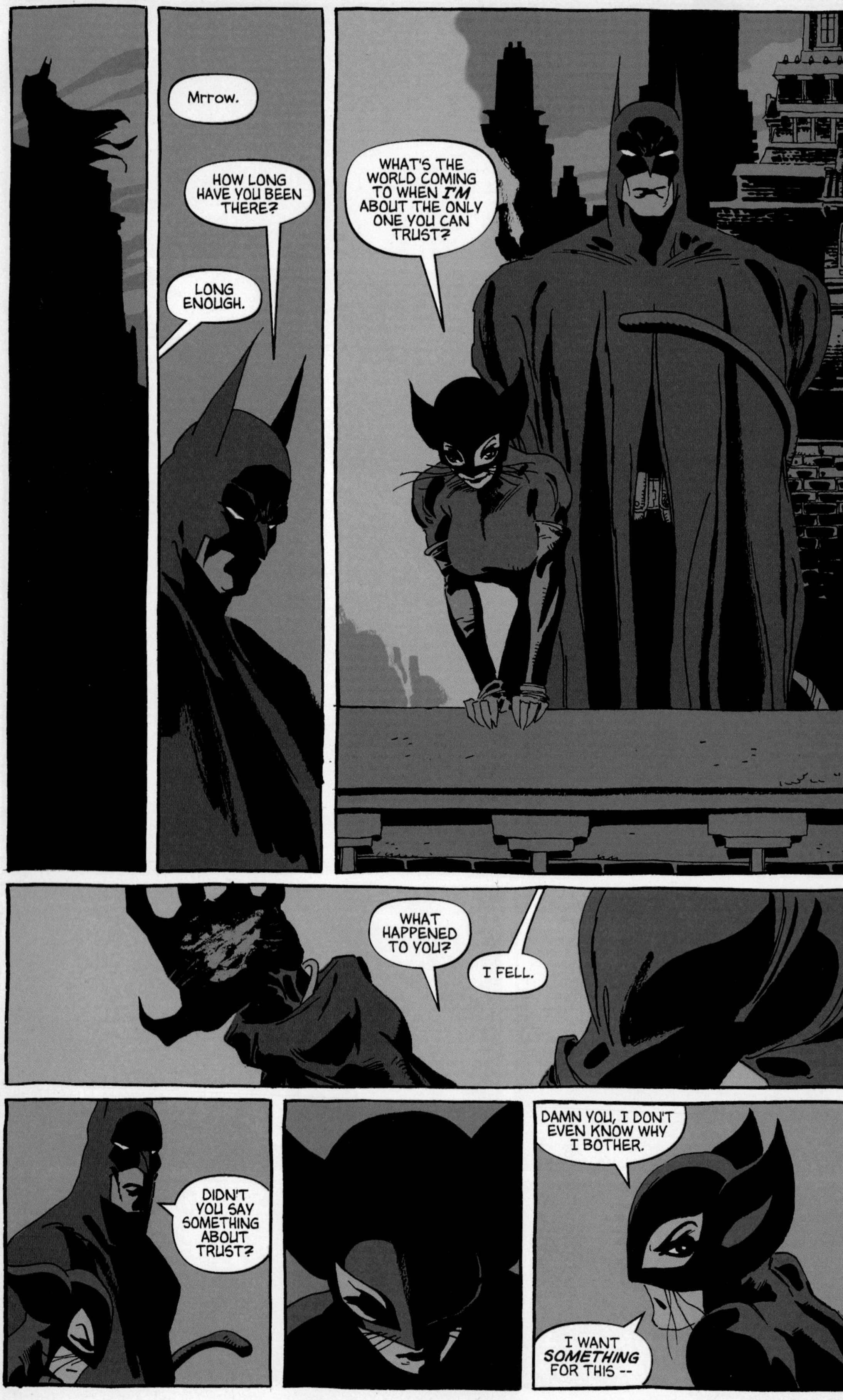
Mrrow.
HOW LONG HAVE YOU BEEN THERE?
LONG ENOUGH.
WHAT'S THE WORLD COMING TO WHEN *I'M* ABOUT THE ONLY ONE YOU CAN TRUST?
WHAT HAPPENED TO YOU?
I FELL.
DIDN'T YOU SAY SOMETHING ABOUT TRUST?
DAMN YOU, I DON'T EVEN KNOW WHY I BOTHER.
I WANT *SOMETHING* FOR THIS --

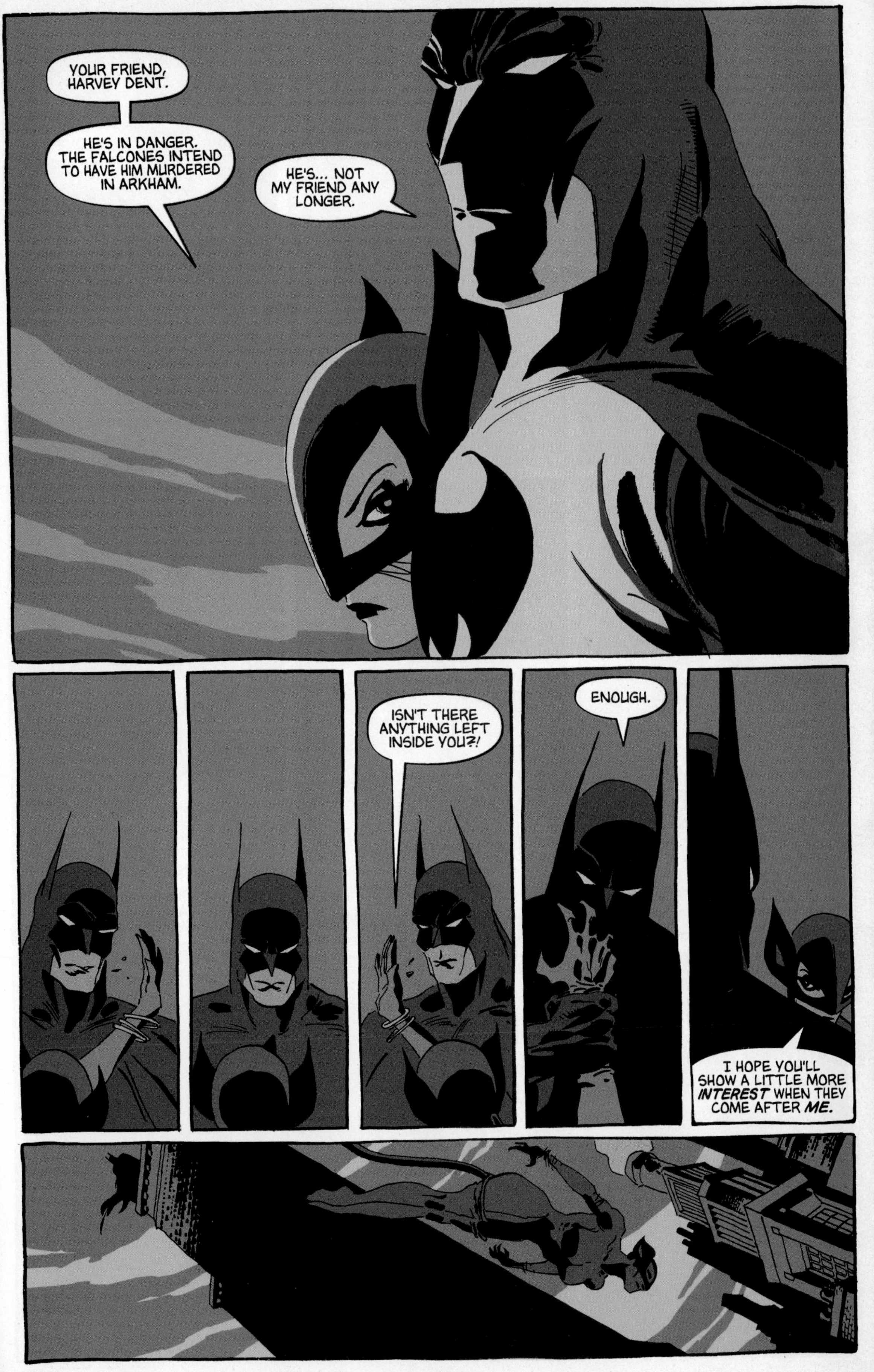
YOUR FRIEND, HARVEY DENT.
HE'S IN DANGER. THE FALCONES INTEND TO HAVE HIM MURDERED IN ARKHAM.
HE'S... NOT MY FRIEND ANY LONGER.
ISN'T THERE ANYTHING LEFT INSIDE YOU?!
ENOUGH.
I HOPE YOU'LL SHOW A LITTLE MORE *INTEREST* WHEN THEY COME AFTER *ME.*

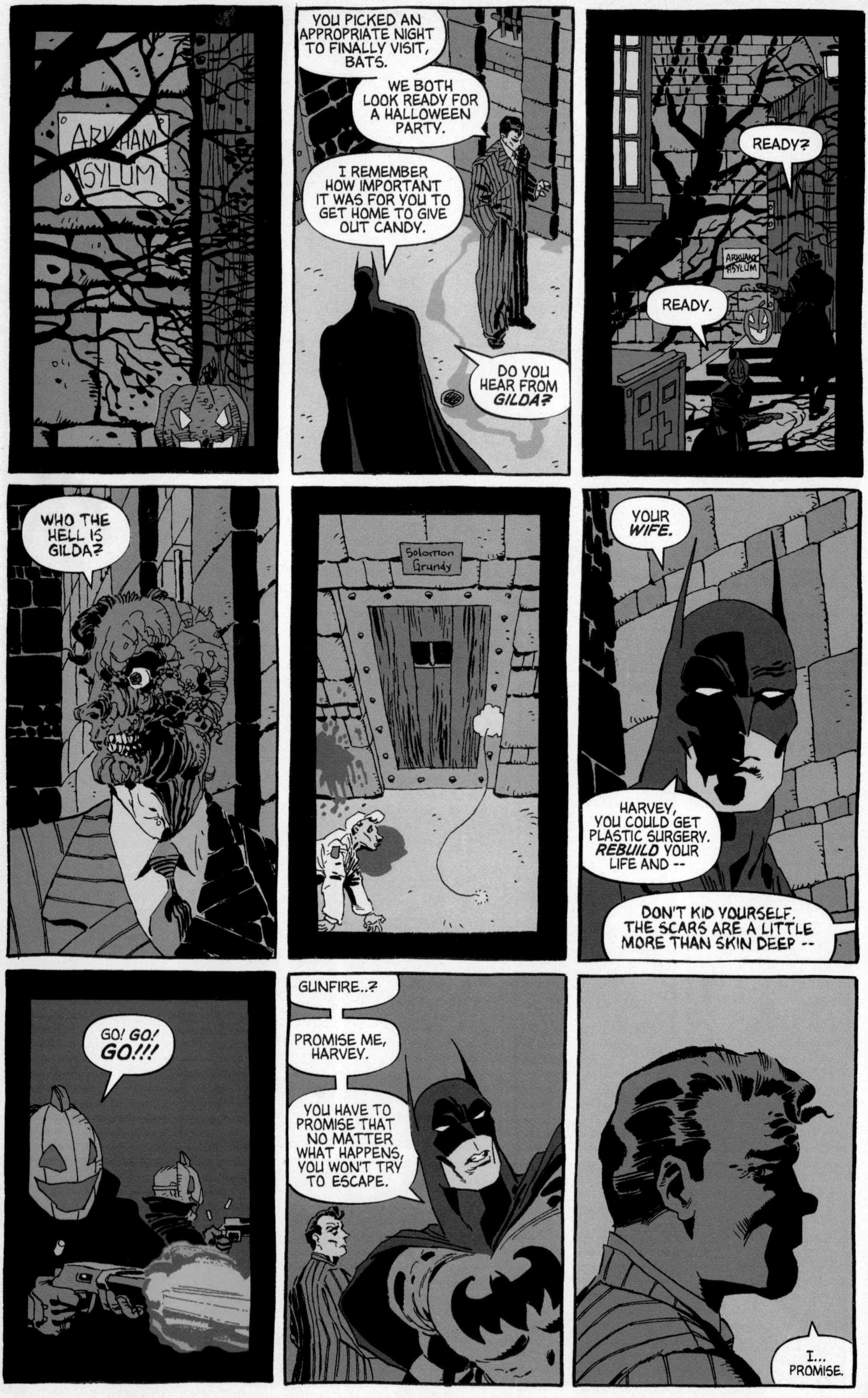
ARKHAM ASYLUM
YOU PICKED AN APPROPRIATE NIGHT TO FINALLY VISIT, BATS.
WE BOTH LOOK READY FOR A HALLOWEEN PARTY.
I REMEMBER HOW IMPORTANT IT WAS FOR YOU TO GET HOME TO GIVE OUT CANDY.
DO YOU HEAR FROM GILDA?
ARKHAM ASYLUM
READY?
READY.
WHO THE HELL IS GILDA?
Solomon Grundy
YOUR WIFE.
HARVEY, YOU COULD GET PLASTIC SURGERY. REBUILD YOUR LIFE AND --
DON'T KID YOURSELF. THE SCARS ARE A LITTLE MORE THAN SKIN DEEP --
GO! GO! GO!!!
GUNFIRE..?
PROMISE ME, HARVEY.
YOU HAVE TO PROMISE THAT NO MATTER WHAT HAPPENS, YOU WON'T TRY TO ESCAPE.
I... PROMISE.

BOLT THAT DOOR! NO ONE GETS IN OR OUT!

YOU DON'T HAVE TO BOLT THE --

-- YOU'RE AN IDIOT, HARVEY.

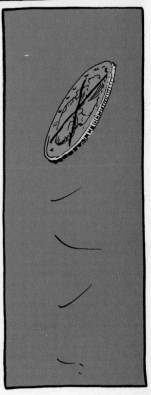

I have... miscalculated. From Catwoman's warning, I assumed that there would be an assassination attempt on Harvey.

And on Harvey alone.

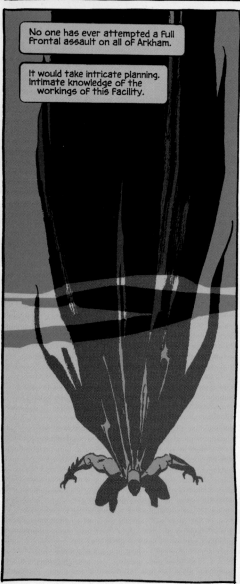

No one has ever attempted a full frontal assault on all of Arkham.

It would take intricate planning. Intimate knowledge of the workings of this facility.

YOU ARE *NOT* LEAVING, HATTER.

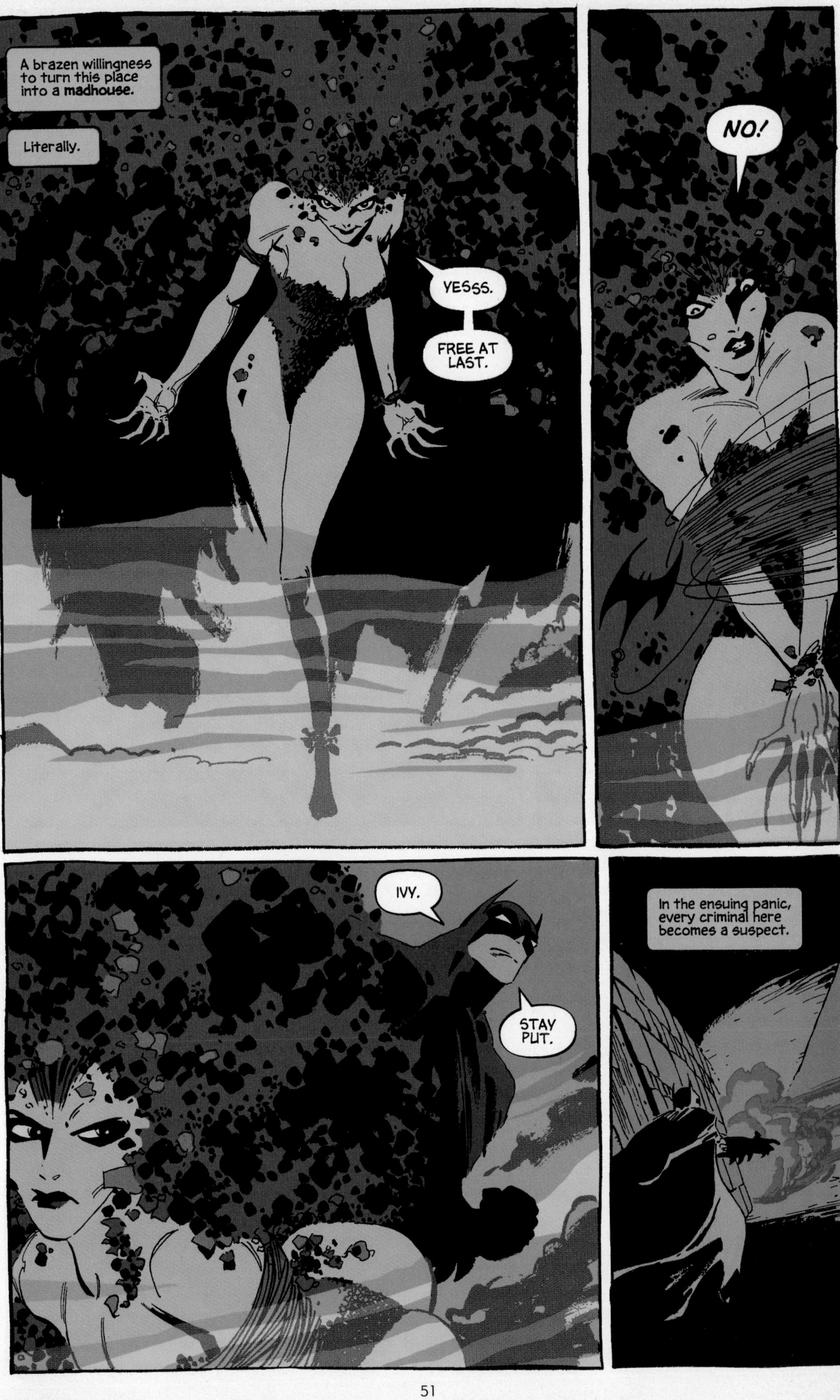
A brazen willingness to turn this place into a madhouse.
Literally.
YESSS.
FREE AT LAST.
NO!
IVY.
STAY PUT.
In the ensuing panic, every criminal here becomes a suspect.

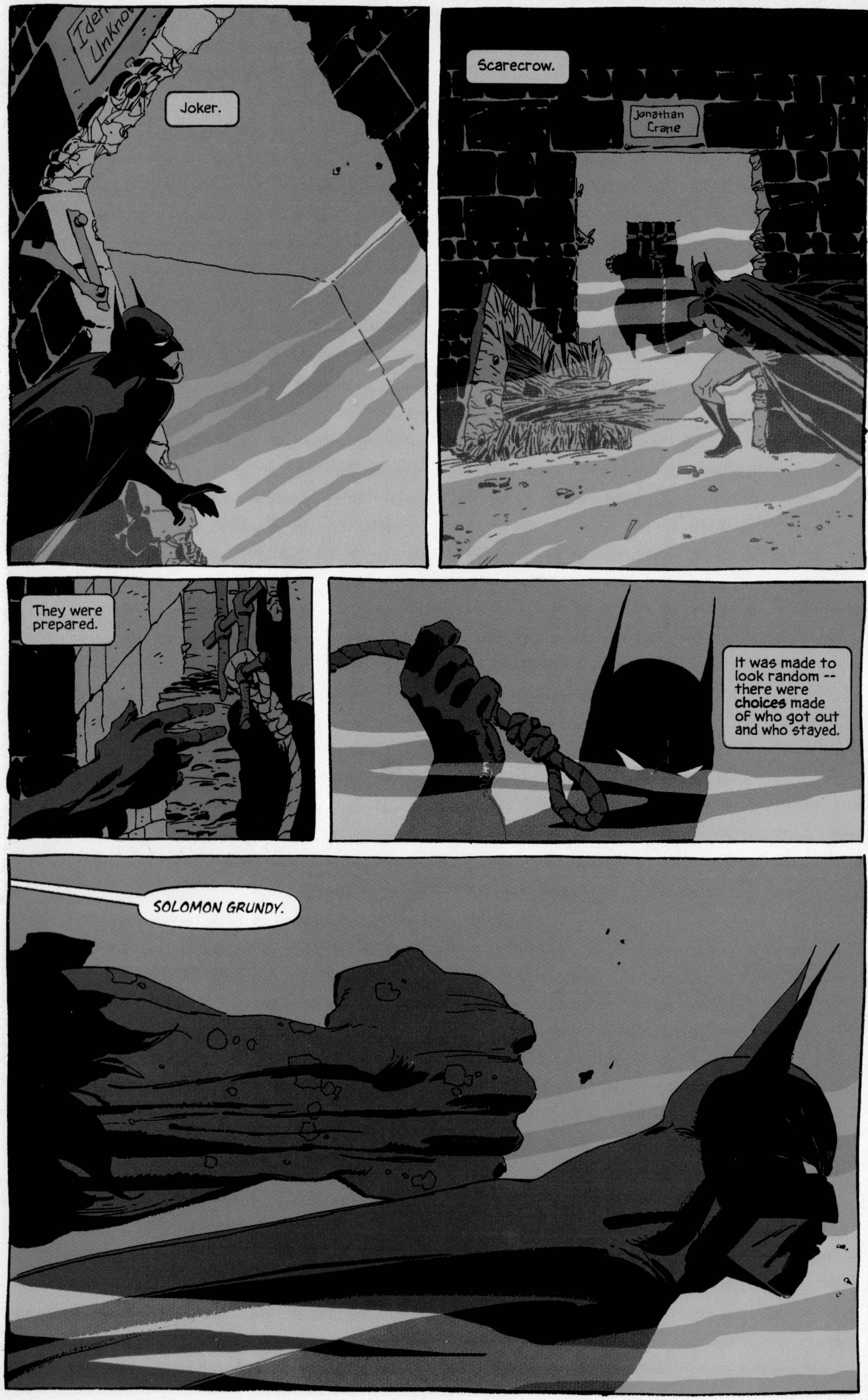
Joker.
Scarecrow.
Jonathan Crane
They were prepared.
It was made to look random -- there were **choices** made of who got out and who stayed.
SOLOMON GRUNDY.

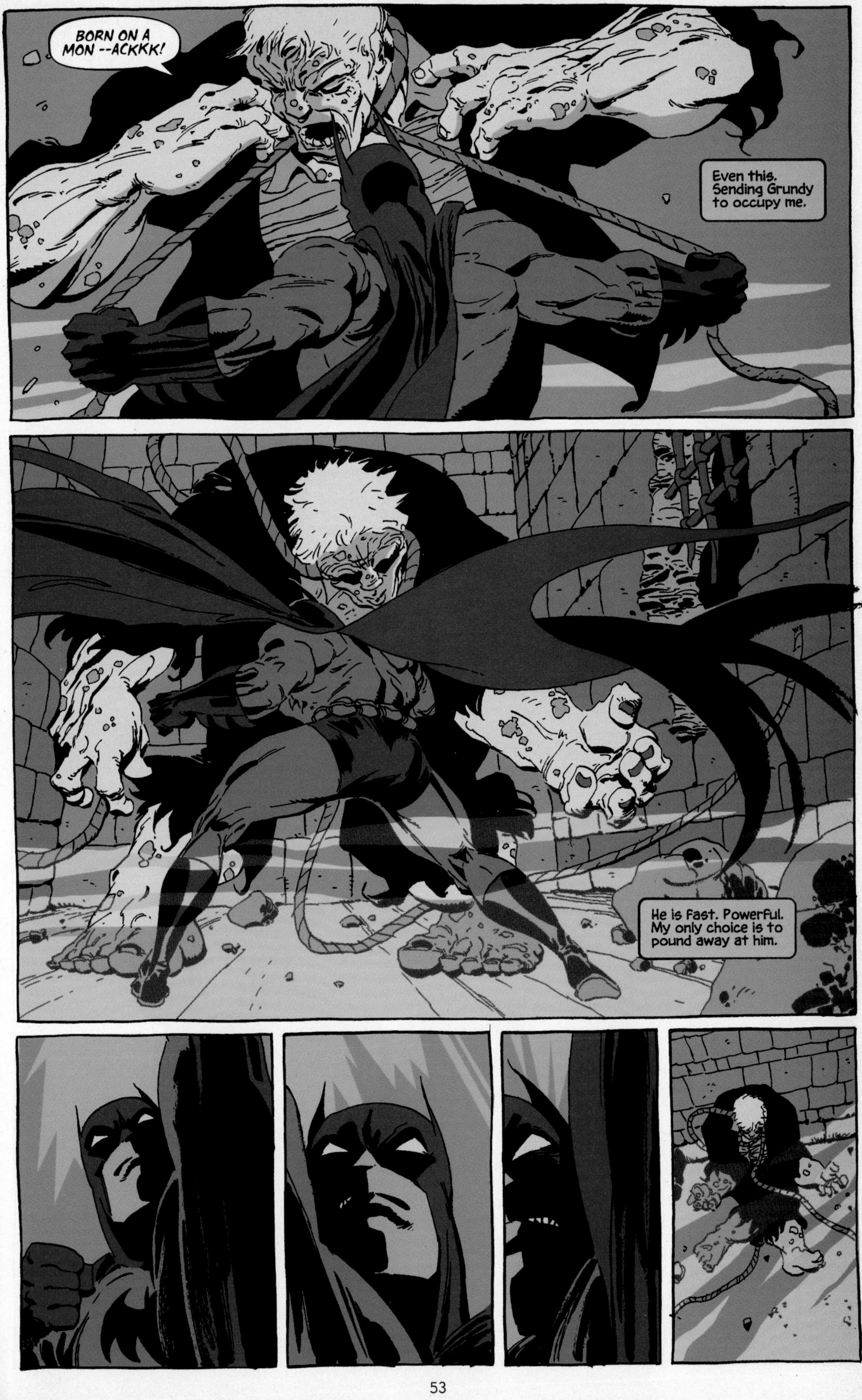
BORN ON A MON --ACKKK!
Even this. Sending Grundy to occupy me.
He is fast. Powerful. My only choice is to pound away at him.

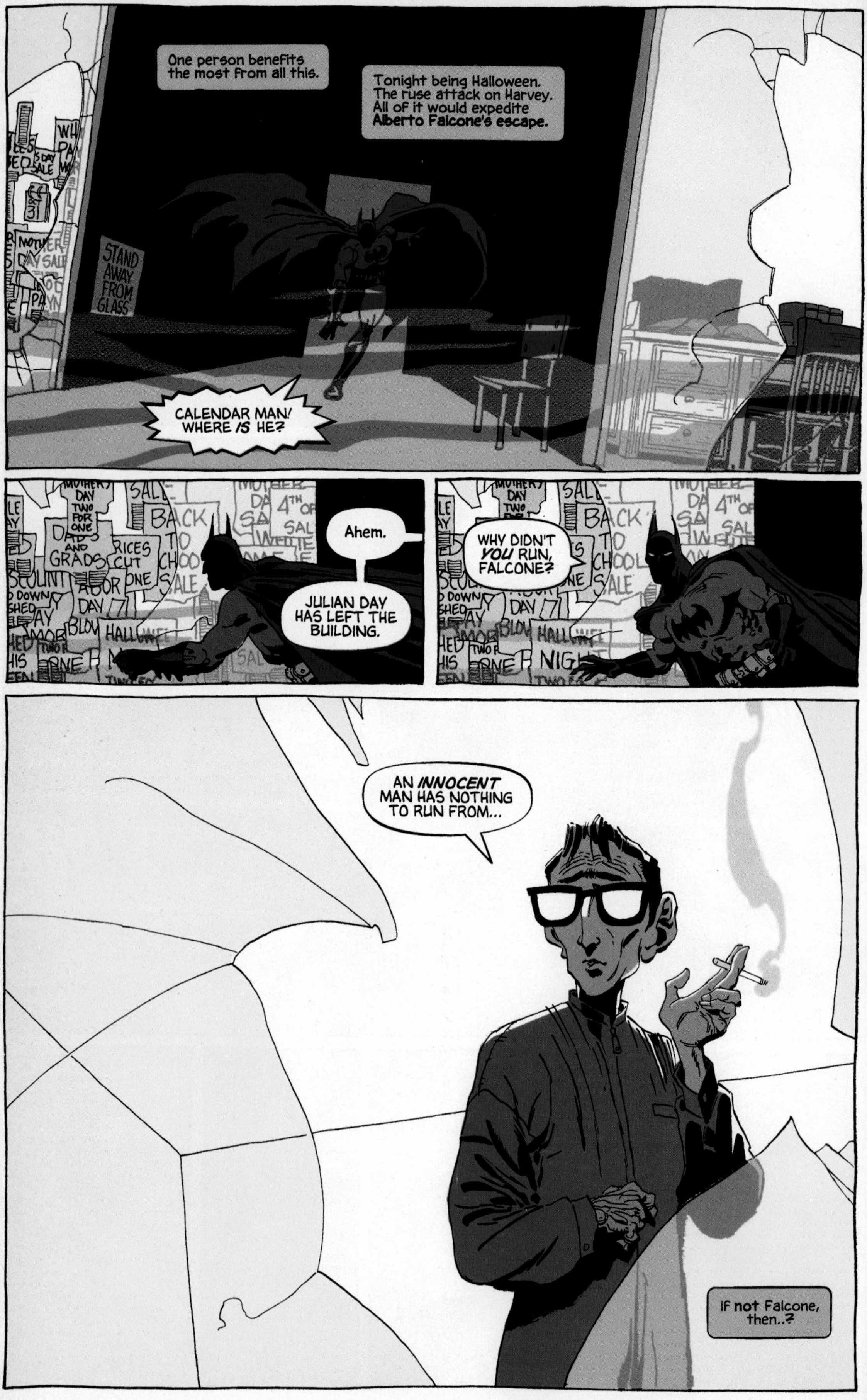
One person benefits the most from all this.
Tonight being Halloween. The ruse attack on Harvey. All of it would expedite **Alberto Falcone's escape.**
STAND AWAY FROM GLASS
CALENDAR MAN! WHERE *IS* HE?
Ahem.
JULIAN DAY HAS LEFT THE BUILDING.
WHY DIDN'T *YOU* RUN, FALCONE?
AN *INNOCENT* MAN HAS NOTHING TO RUN FROM...
If **not** Falcone, then..?

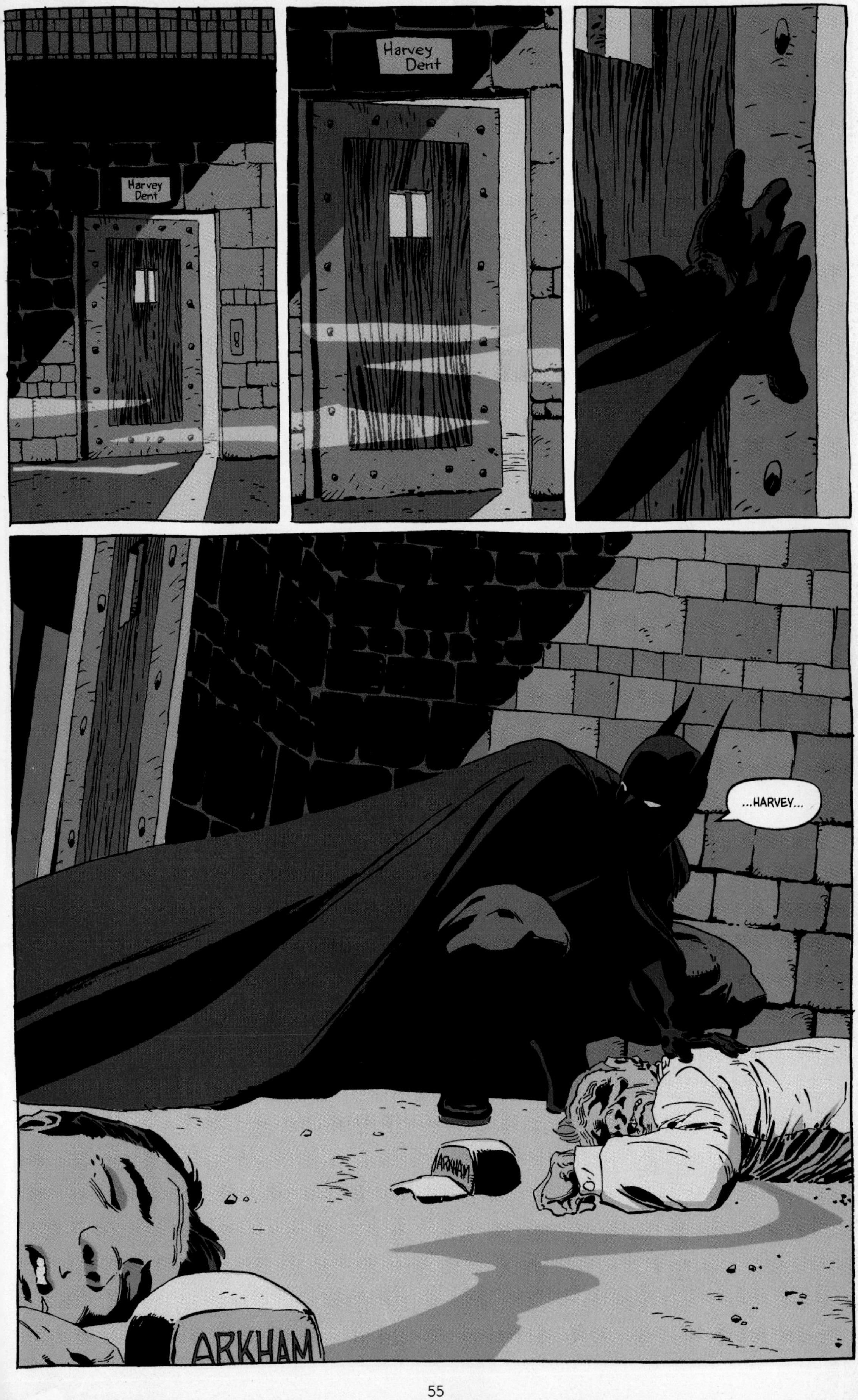
Harvey Dent
Harvey Dent
...HARVEY...
ARKHAM
ARKHAM

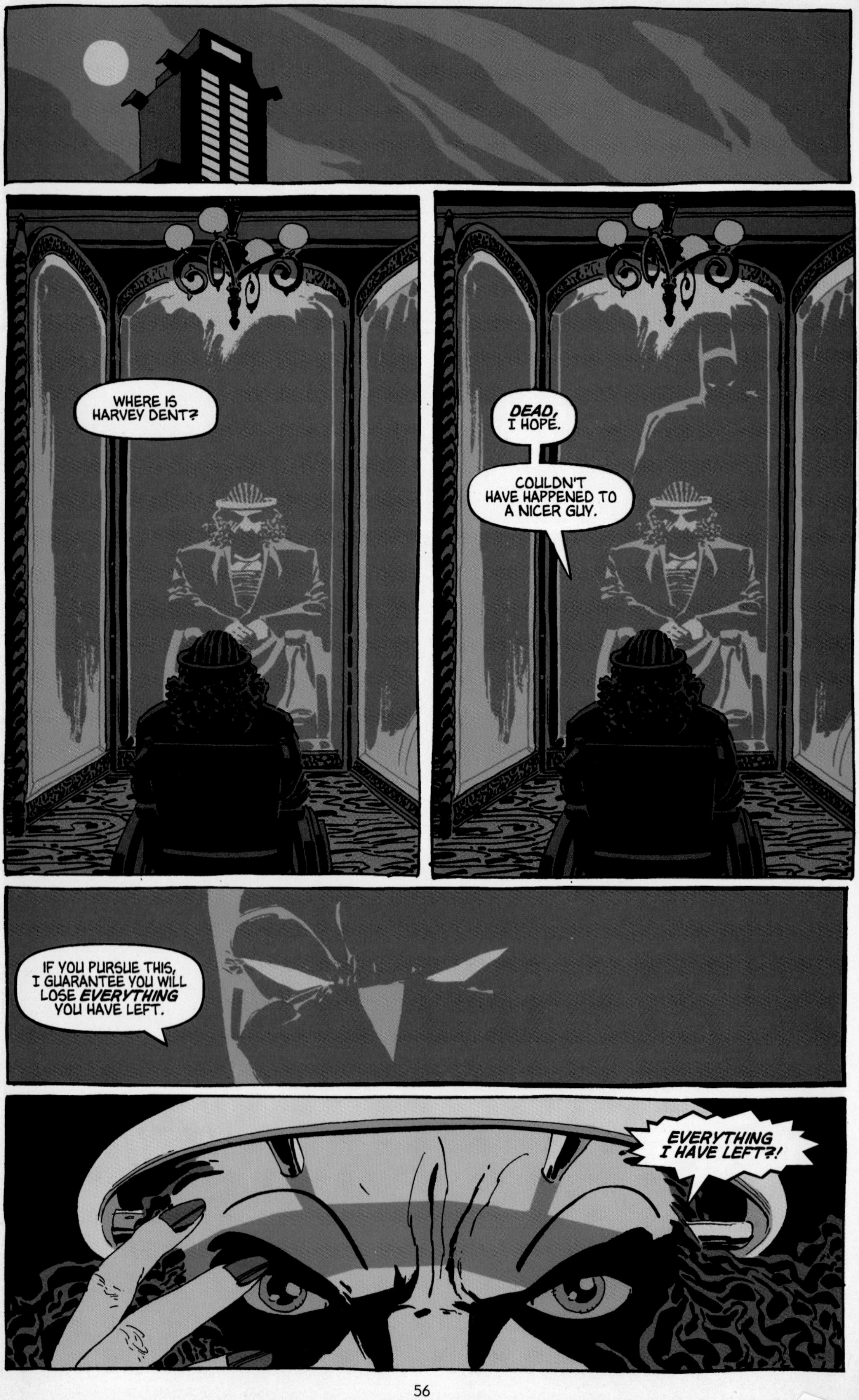
WHERE IS HARVEY DENT?
DEAD, I HOPE.
COULDN'T HAVE HAPPENED TO A NICER GUY.
IF YOU PURSUE THIS, I GUARANTEE YOU WILL LOSE EVERYTHING YOU HAVE LEFT.
EVERYTHING I HAVE LEFT?!

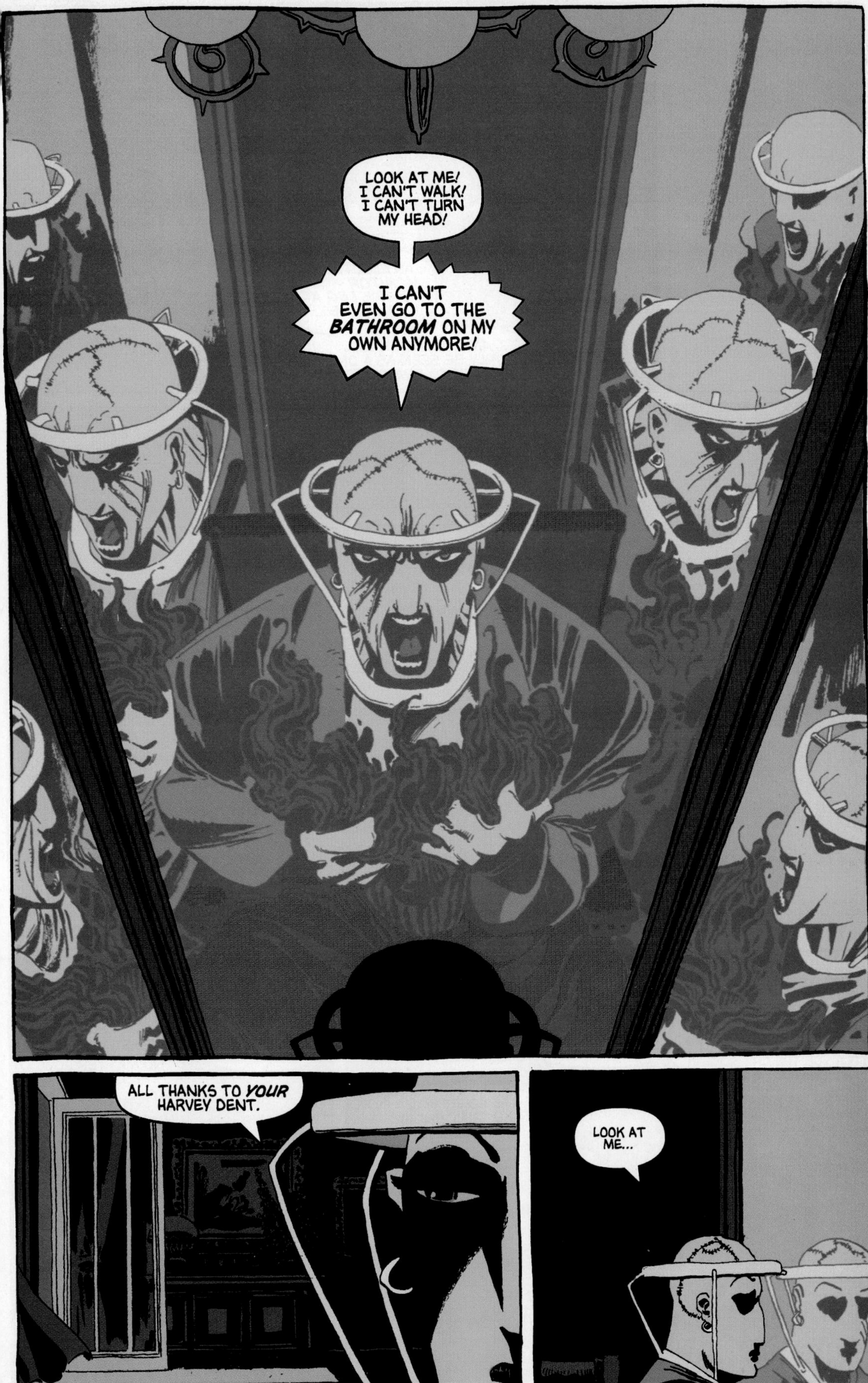
LOOK AT ME! I CAN'T WALK! I CAN'T TURN MY HEAD!
I CAN'T EVEN GO TO THE BATHROOM ON MY OWN ANYMORE!
ALL THANKS TO YOUR HARVEY DENT.
LOOK AT ME...

November. Gotham City Court House. Docket Nine. Judge Harkness presiding.

YOU UNDERSTAND, MR. MARIO FALCONE, THAT BY RELEASING *YOUR BROTHER* INTO *YOUR* CUSTODY --

YOU MUST TAKE *FULL* RESPONSIBILITY FOR HIM.

YES, YOUR HONOR.

I INTEND TO KEEP HIM ON A VERY SHORT LEASH.

AN *ELECTRONIC MONITOR* WILL BE ON HIS *LEG* AT ALL TIMES.

ANY VIOLATION WILL NOT ONLY BE SEEN AS A ONE-WAY TICKET BACK TO *PRISON* FOR HIM --

-- I WILL ALSO MAKE IT MY *PERSONAL* BUSINESS TO SEE THAT IMMIGRATION TAKES ANOTHER LOOK AT THE DEPORTATION OF *YOU*, SIR.

YOU'LL REGRET THIS FOR THE REST OF YOUR LIFE!

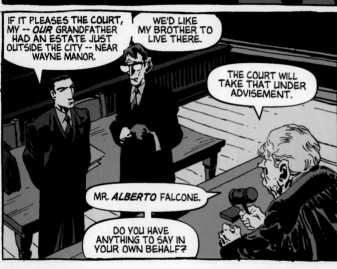

IF IT PLEASES *THE COURT*, MY -- *OUR* GRANDFATHER HAD AN ESTATE JUST OUTSIDE THE CITY -- NEAR WAYNE MANOR.

WE'D LIKE MY BROTHER TO LIVE THERE.

THE COURT WILL TAKE THAT UNDER ADVISEMENT.

MR. *ALBERTO* FALCONE.

DO YOU HAVE ANYTHING TO SAY IN YOUR OWN BEHALF?

ONLY THAT I *AM* SORRY, YOUR HONOR.

AND I'M GRATEFUL FOR BEING GIVEN A SECOND CHANCE, NO MATTER HOW RESTRICTED.

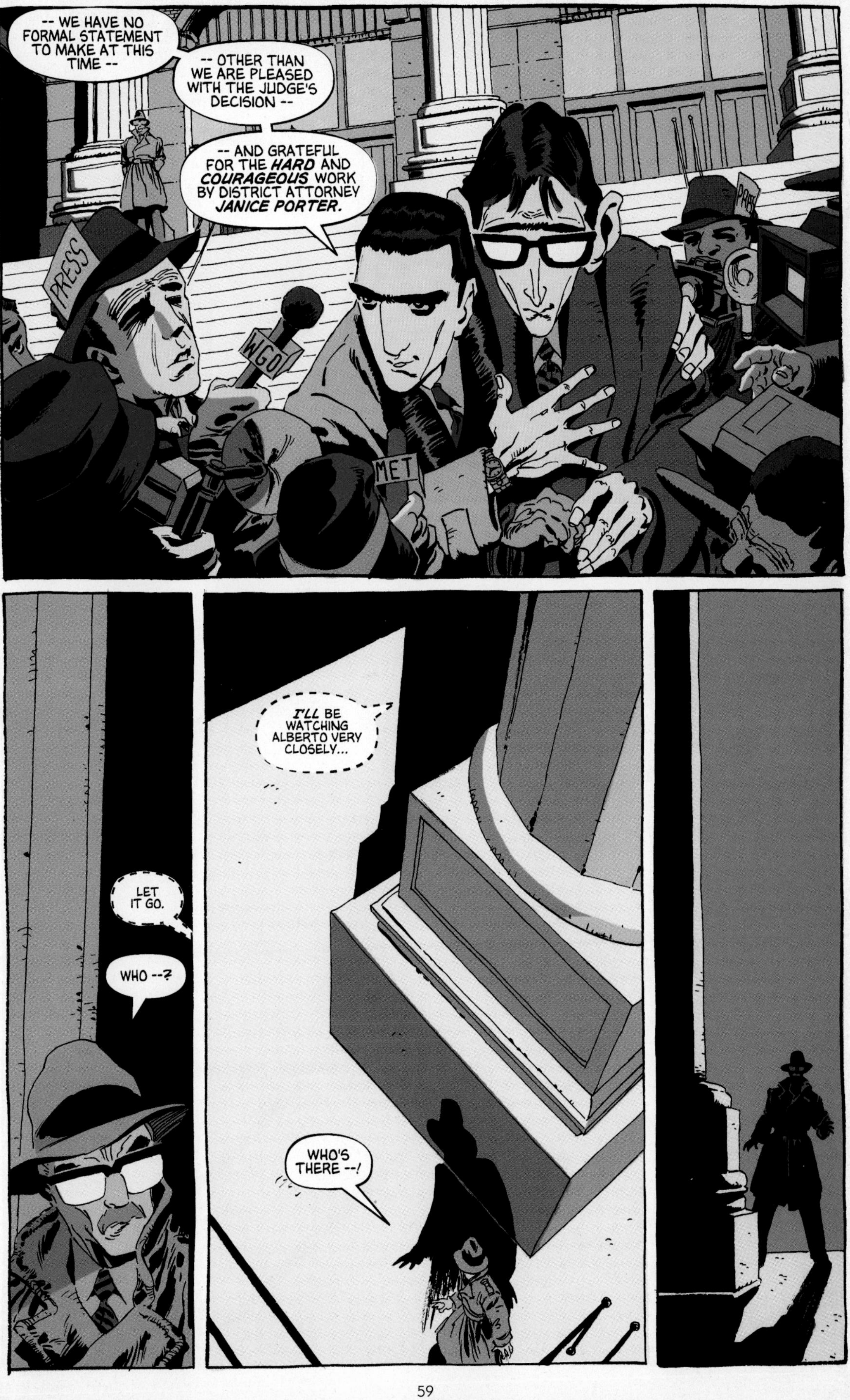
-- WE HAVE NO FORMAL STATEMENT TO MAKE AT THIS TIME --
-- OTHER THAN WE ARE PLEASED WITH THE JUDGE'S DECISION --
-- AND GRATEFUL FOR THE HARD AND COURAGEOUS WORK BY DISTRICT ATTORNEY JANICE PORTER.
PRESS
WGO
MET
LET IT GO.
WHO --?
I'LL BE WATCHING ALBERTO VERY CLOSELY...
WHO'S THERE --!

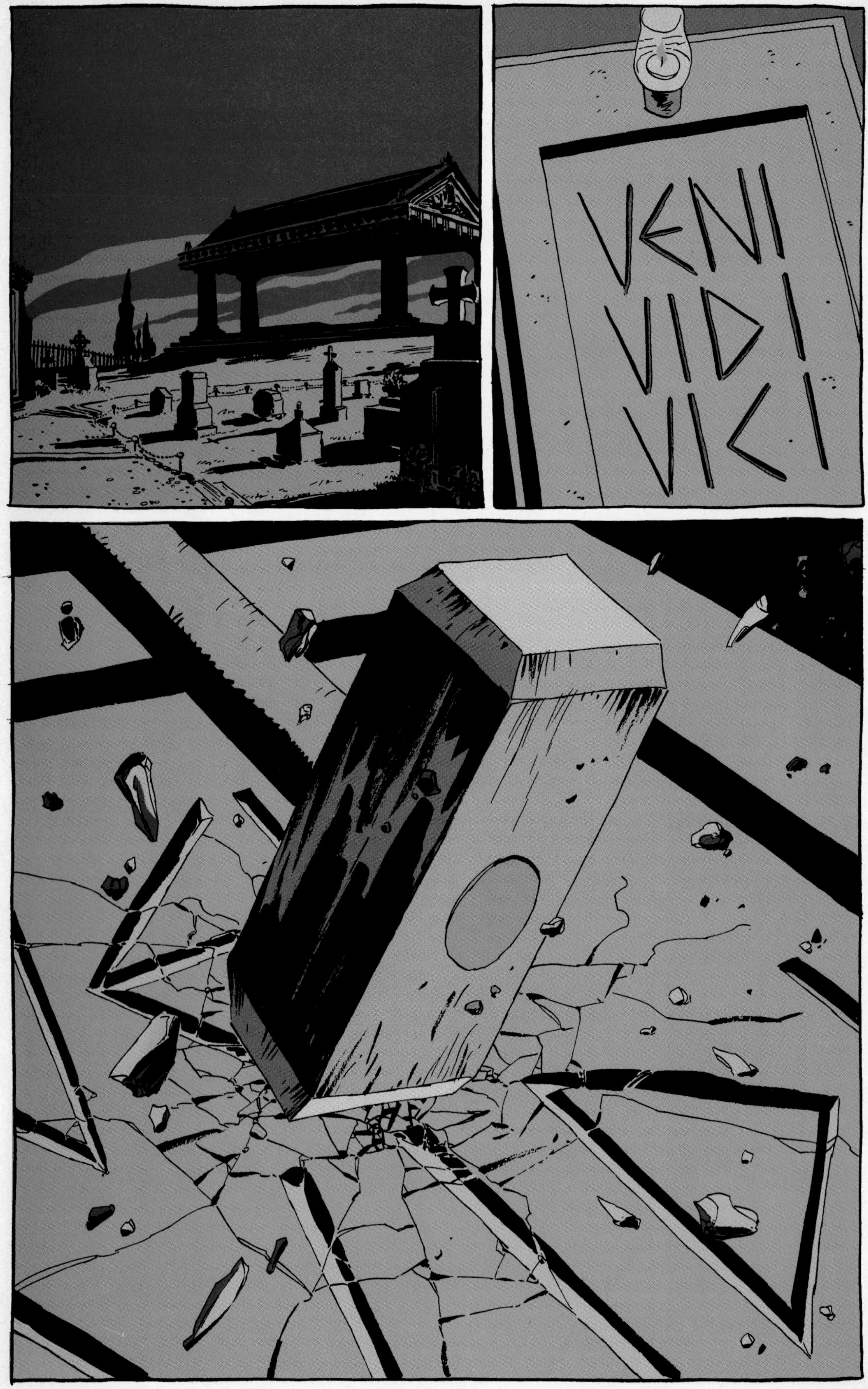
VENI
VIDI
VICI

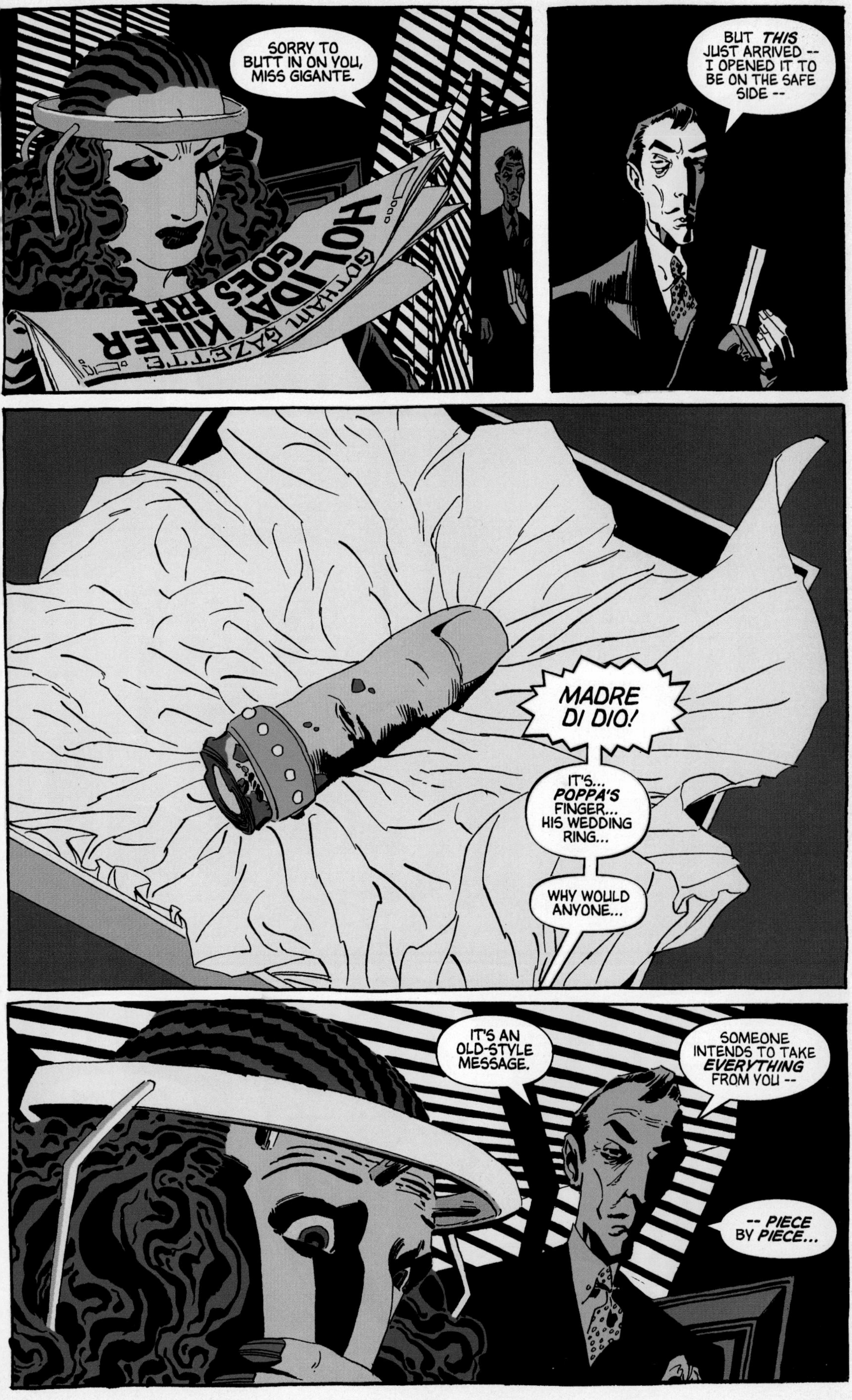
SORRY TO BUTT IN ON YOU, MISS GIGANTE.
GOTHAM GAZETTE
HOLIDAY KILLER GOES FREE
BUT *THIS* JUST ARRIVED -- I OPENED IT TO BE ON THE SAFE SIDE --
MADRE DI DIO!
IT'S... *POPPA'S* FINGER... HIS WEDDING RING...
WHY WOULD ANYONE...
IT'S AN OLD-STYLE MESSAGE.
SOMEONE INTENDS TO TAKE *EVERYTHING* FROM YOU --
-- *PIECE* BY *PIECE...*

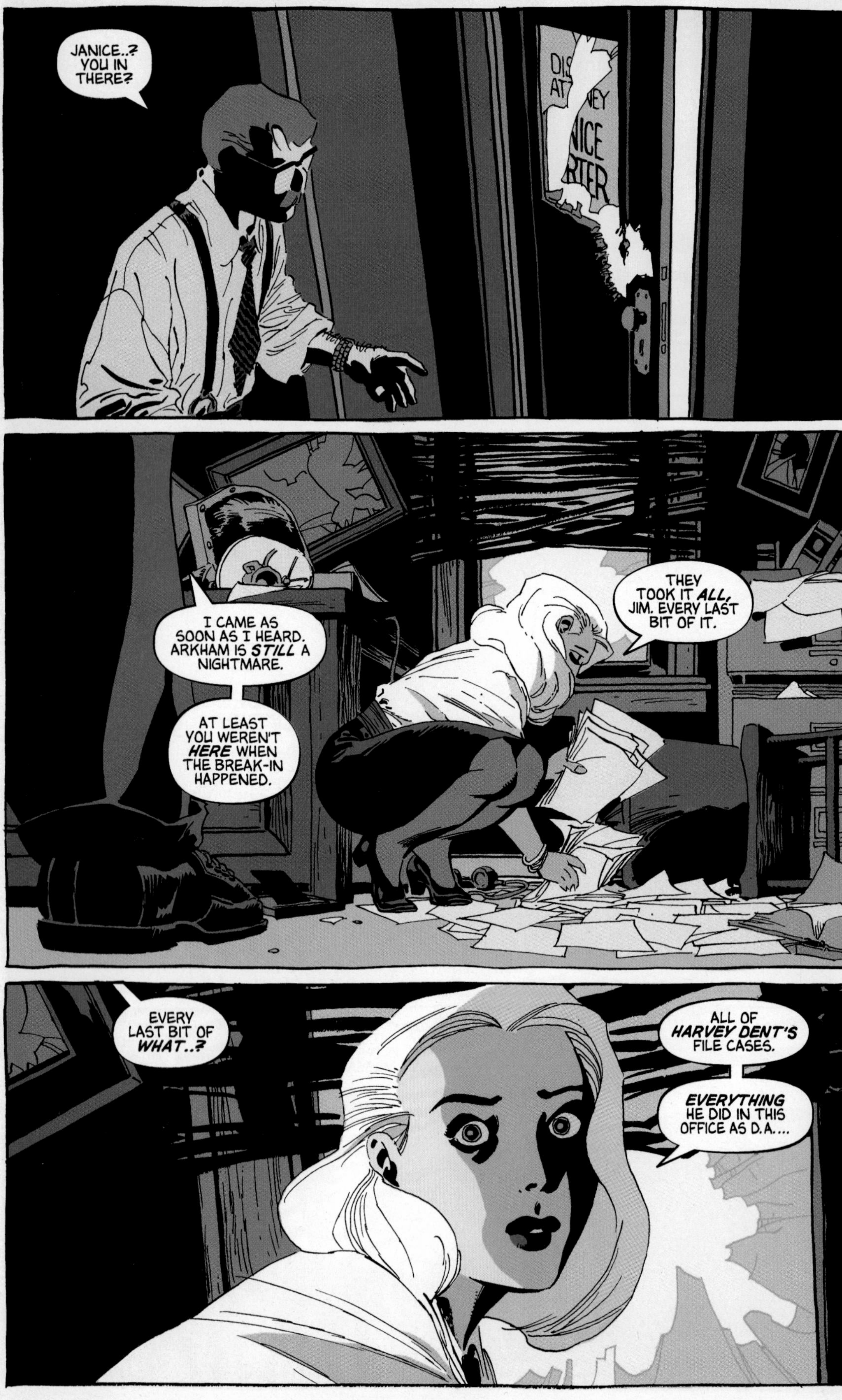
JANICE..? YOU IN THERE?
I CAME AS SOON AS I HEARD. ARKHAM IS STILL A NIGHTMARE.
AT LEAST YOU WEREN'T HERE WHEN THE BREAK-IN HAPPENED.
THEY TOOK IT ALL, JIM. EVERY LAST BIT OF IT.
EVERY LAST BIT OF WHAT..?
ALL OF HARVEY DENT'S FILE CASES.
EVERYTHING HE DID IN THIS OFFICE AS D.A....

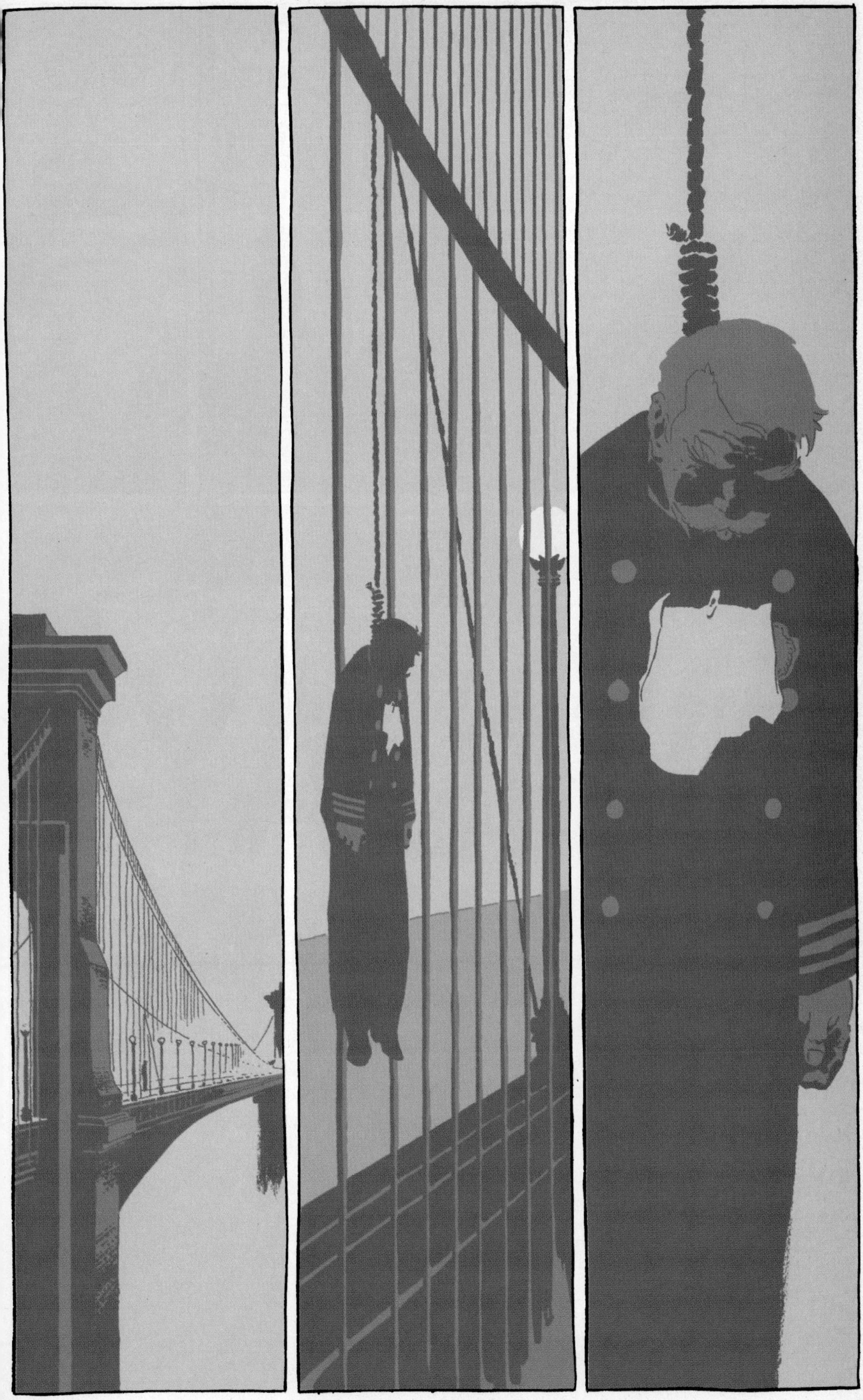

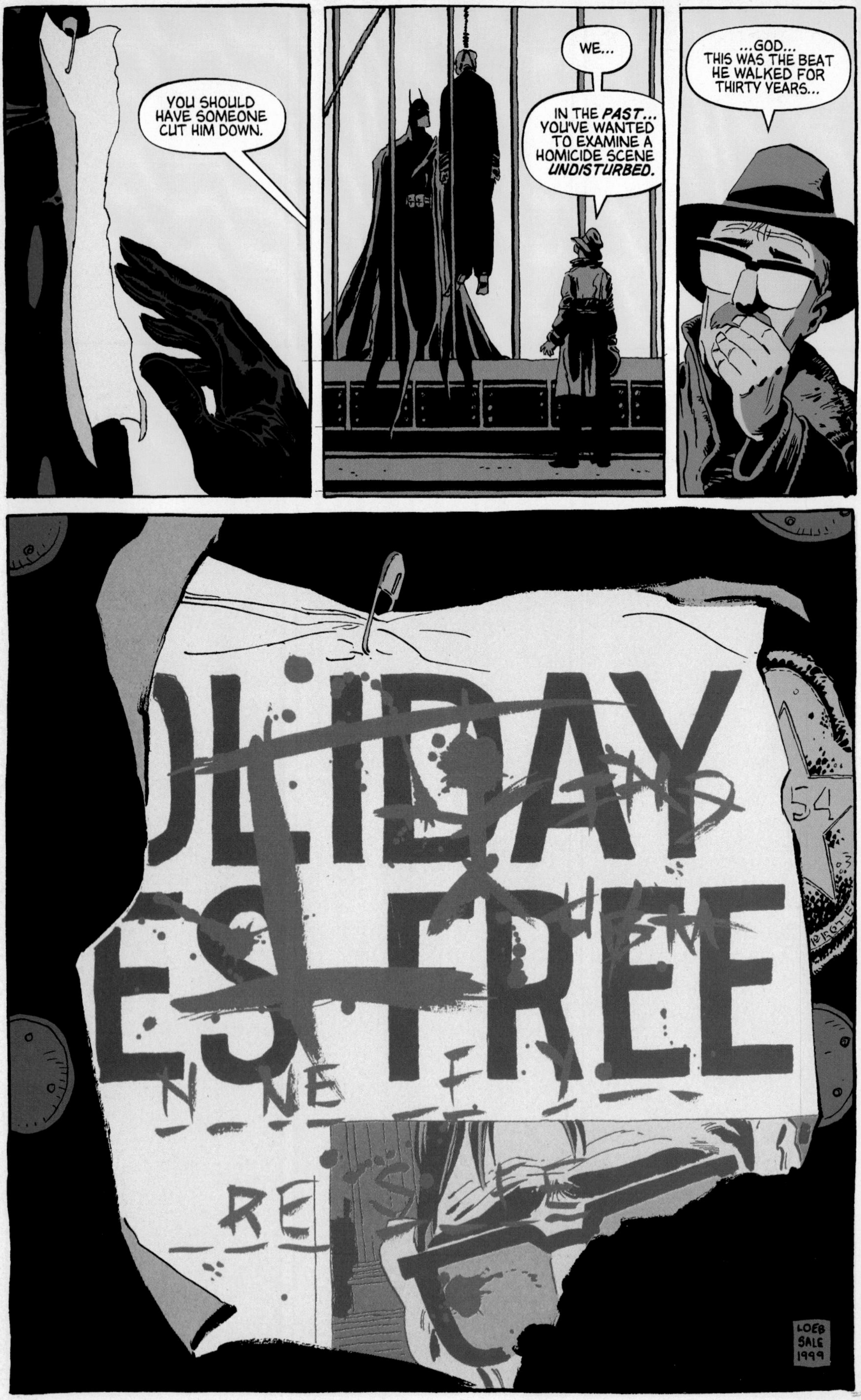
YOU SHOULD HAVE SOMEONE CUT HIM DOWN.
WE...
IN THE PAST... YOU'VE WANTED TO EXAMINE A HOMICIDE SCENE UNDISTURBED.
...GOD... THIS WAS THE BEAT HE WALKED FOR THIRTY YEARS...
LOEB SALE 1999

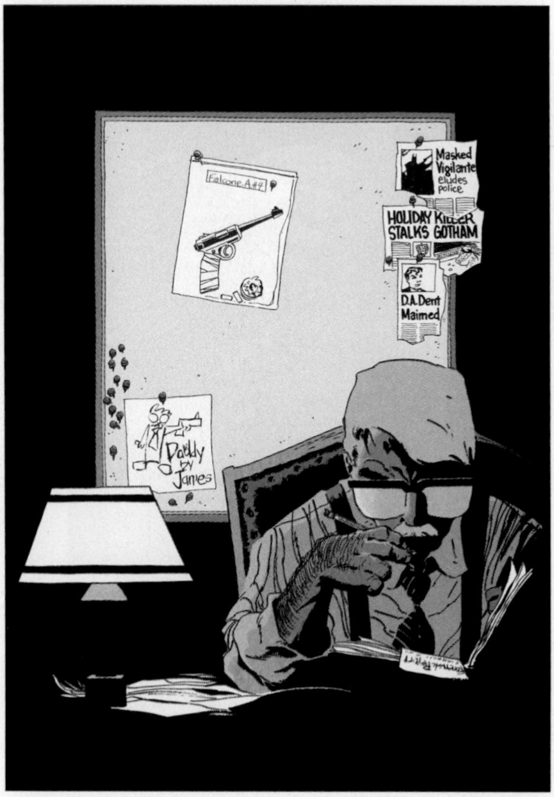
Falcone A#4
Masked Vigilante eludes police
HOLIDAY KILLER STALKS GOTHAM
D.A. Dent Maimed
Daddy by James

2

S E C R E T S

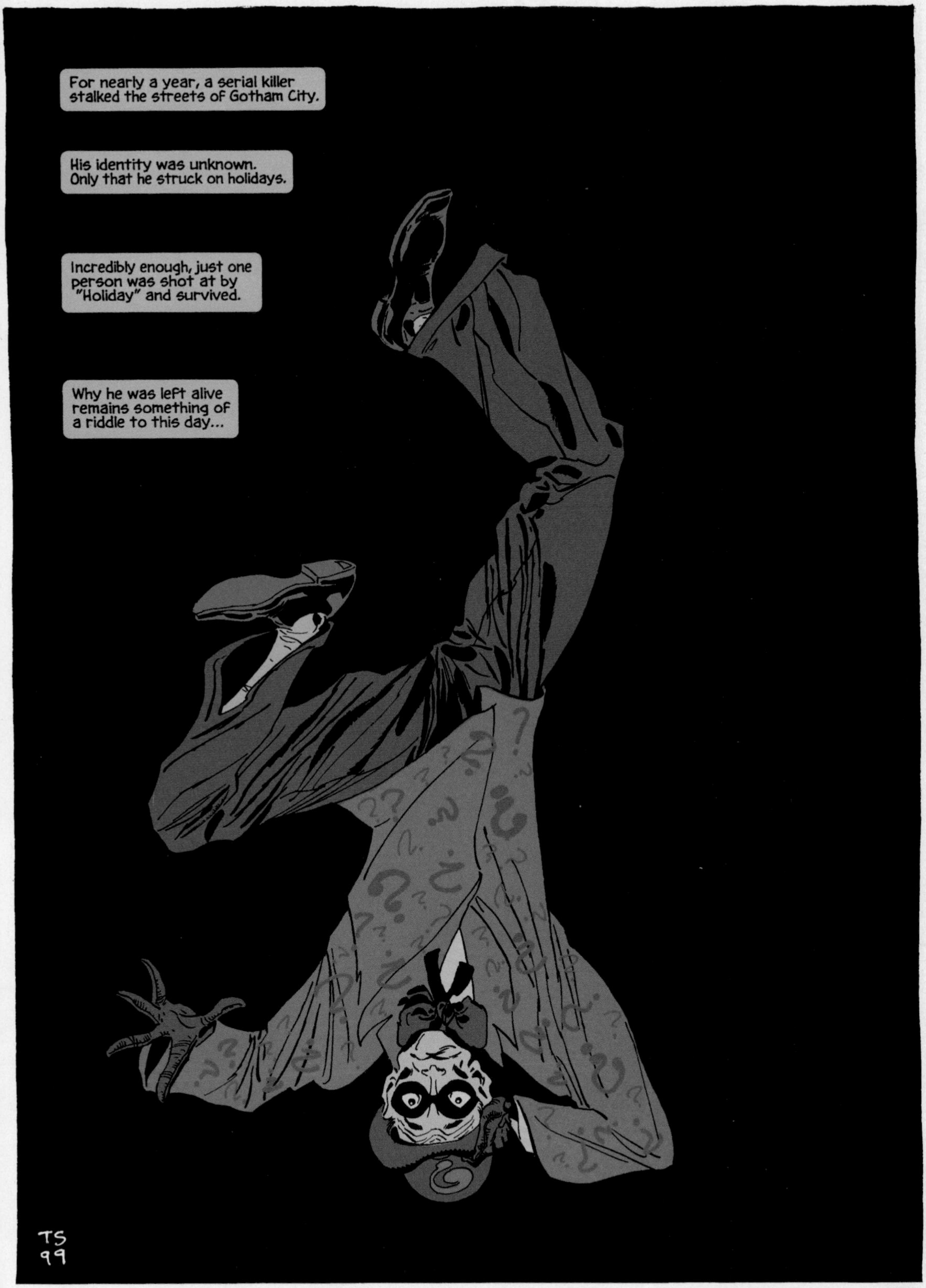
For nearly a year, a serial killer stalked the streets of Gotham City.
His identity was unknown. Only that he struck on holidays.
Incredibly enough, just one person was shot at by "Holiday" and survived.
Why he was left alive remains something of a riddle to this day...
TS 99

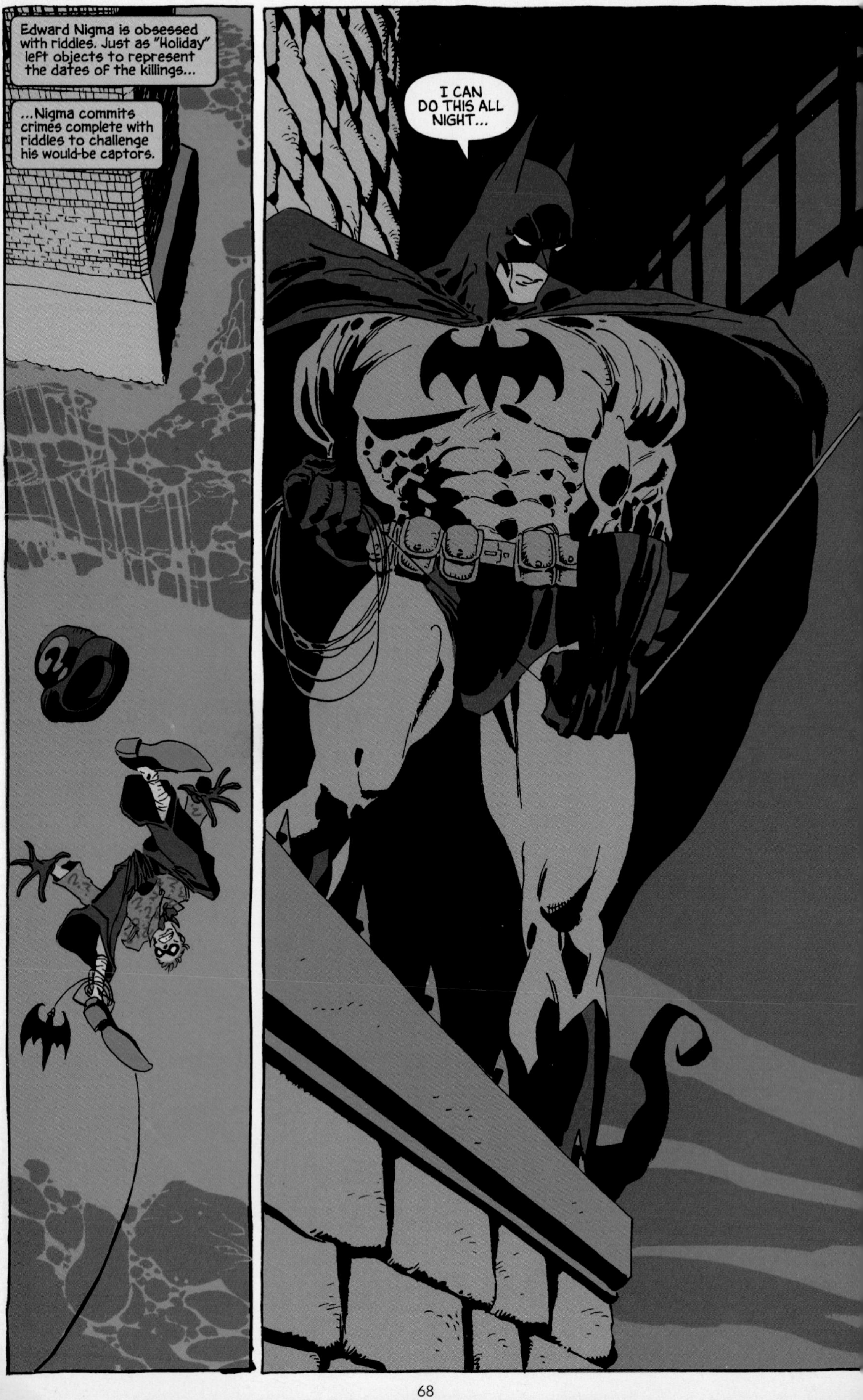
Edward Nigma is obsessed with riddles. Just as "Holiday" left objects to represent the dates of the killings...
...Nigma commits crimes complete with riddles to challenge his would-be captors.
I CAN DO THIS ALL NIGHT...

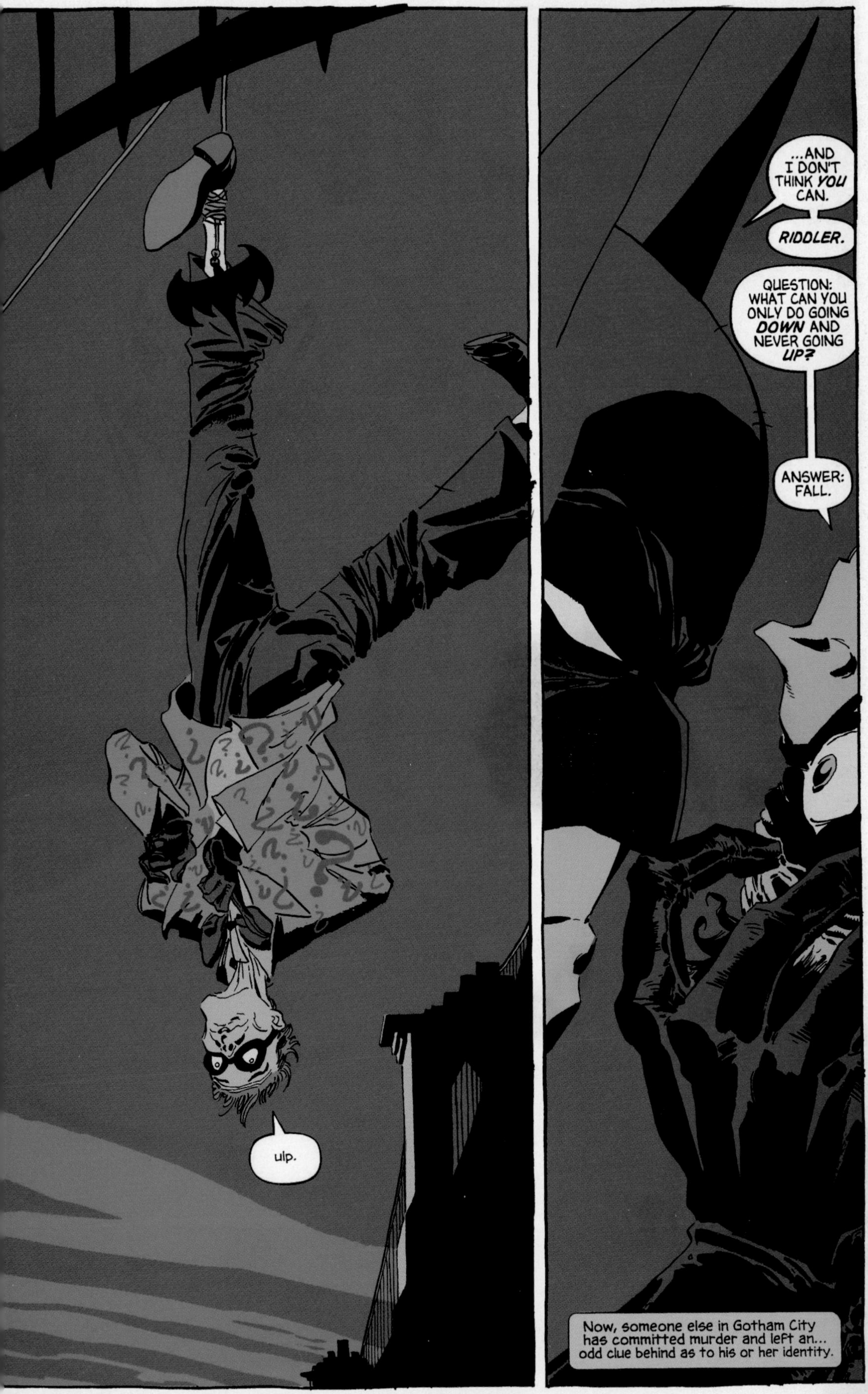
ulp.
...AND I DON'T THINK YOU CAN.
RIDDLER.
QUESTION: WHAT CAN YOU ONLY DO GOING DOWN AND NEVER GOING UP?
ANSWER: FALL.
Now, someone else in Gotham City has committed murder and left an... odd clue behind as to his or her identity.

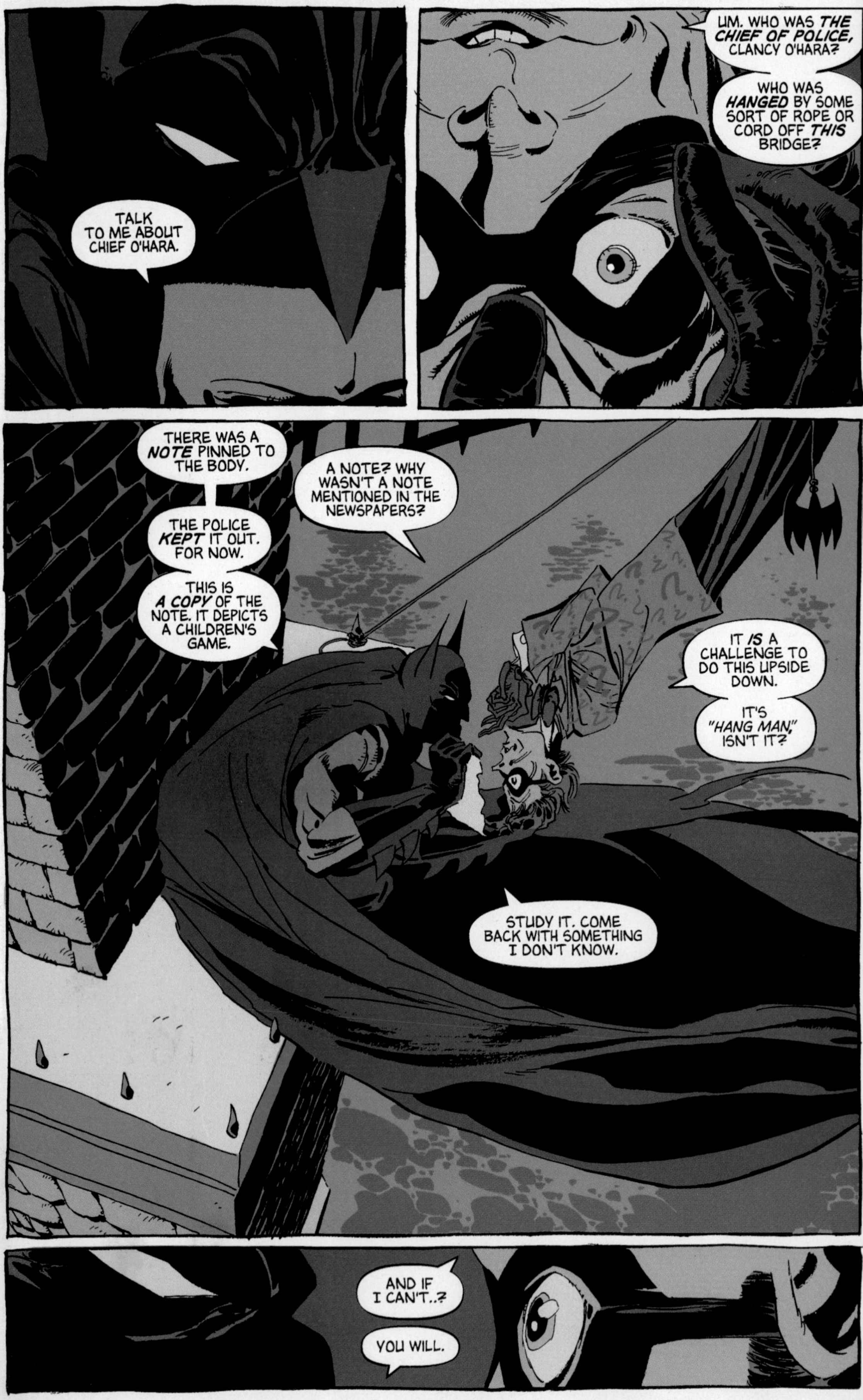

TALK TO ME ABOUT CHIEF O'HARA.
UM. WHO WAS THE CHIEF OF POLICE, CLANCY O'HARA?
WHO WAS HANGED BY SOME SORT OF ROPE OR CORD OFF THIS BRIDGE?
THERE WAS A NOTE PINNED TO THE BODY.
A NOTE? WHY WASN'T A NOTE MENTIONED IN THE NEWSPAPERS?
THE POLICE KEPT IT OUT. FOR NOW.
THIS IS A COPY OF THE NOTE. IT DEPICTS A CHILDREN'S GAME.
IT IS A CHALLENGE TO DO THIS UPSIDE DOWN.
IT'S "HANG MAN," ISN'T IT?
STUDY IT. COME BACK WITH SOMETHING I DON'T KNOW.
AND IF I CAN'T..?
YOU WILL.

I ALWAYS LIKED THE VIEW FROM THAT CHAIR.

O'Hara's death weighs the heaviest on Jim Gordon.

As the newly appointed Police Commissioner, he'll be flooded with pressure from both inside the Department and out...

GIL. I WISH YOU HAD LET ME KNOW YOU WERE COMING DOWNTOWN. I COULD HAVE --

-- YOU COULD HAVE *WHAT*, JIMMY?

MADE SURE YOU WERE *OUT* FOR LUNCH?

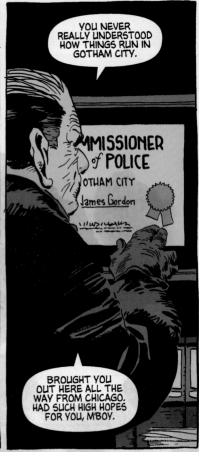

YOU NEVER REALLY UNDERSTOOD HOW THINGS RUN IN GOTHAM CITY.

MMISSIONER of POLICE

OTHAM CITY

James Gordon

BROUGHT YOU OUT HERE ALL THE WAY FROM CHICAGO. HAD SUCH HIGH HOPES FOR YOU, M'BOY.

Gotham City

I DIDN'T *TAKE* YOUR JOB, GIL.

YOU LOST IT IN A CESSPOOL OF *CORRUPTION* AND *GRAFT*.

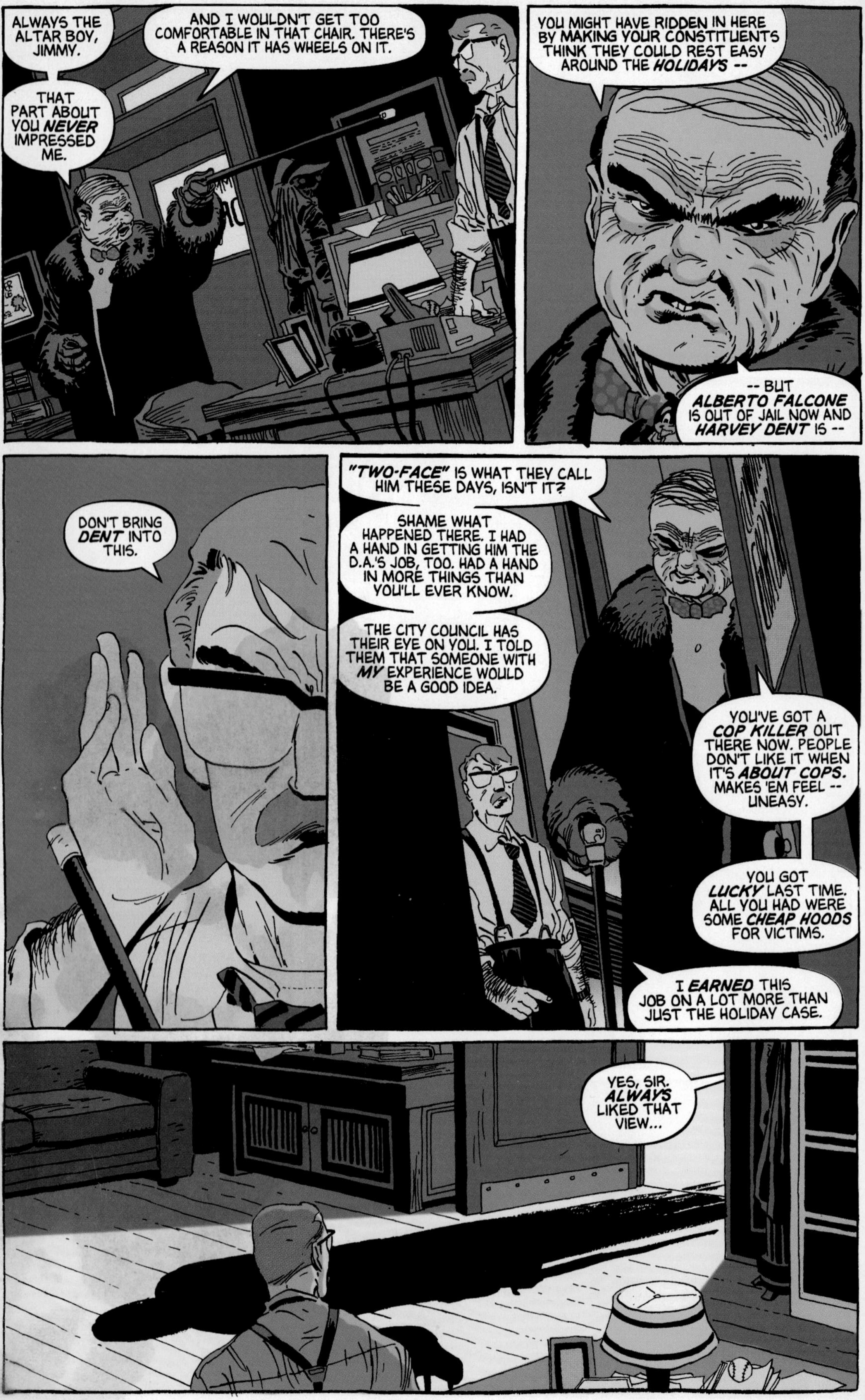
ALWAYS THE ALTAR BOY, JIMMY.
AND I WOULDN'T GET TOO COMFORTABLE IN THAT CHAIR. THERE'S A REASON IT HAS WHEELS ON IT.
THAT PART ABOUT YOU NEVER IMPRESSED ME.
YOU MIGHT HAVE RIDDEN IN HERE BY MAKING YOUR CONSTITUENTS THINK THEY COULD REST EASY AROUND THE HOLIDAYS --
-- BUT ALBERTO FALCONE IS OUT OF JAIL NOW AND HARVEY DENT IS --
DON'T BRING DENT INTO THIS.
"TWO-FACE" IS WHAT THEY CALL HIM THESE DAYS, ISN'T IT?
SHAME WHAT HAPPENED THERE. I HAD A HAND IN GETTING HIM THE D.A.'S JOB, TOO. HAD A HAND IN MORE THINGS THAN YOU'LL EVER KNOW.
THE CITY COUNCIL HAS THEIR EYE ON YOU. I TOLD THEM THAT SOMEONE WITH MY EXPERIENCE WOULD BE A GOOD IDEA.
YOU'VE GOT A COP KILLER OUT THERE NOW. PEOPLE DON'T LIKE IT WHEN IT'S ABOUT COPS. MAKES 'EM FEEL -- UNEASY.
YOU GOT LUCKY LAST TIME. ALL YOU HAD WERE SOME CHEAP HOODS FOR VICTIMS.
I EARNED THIS JOB ON A LOT MORE THAN JUST THE HOLIDAY CASE.
YES, SIR. ALWAYS LIKED THAT VIEW...

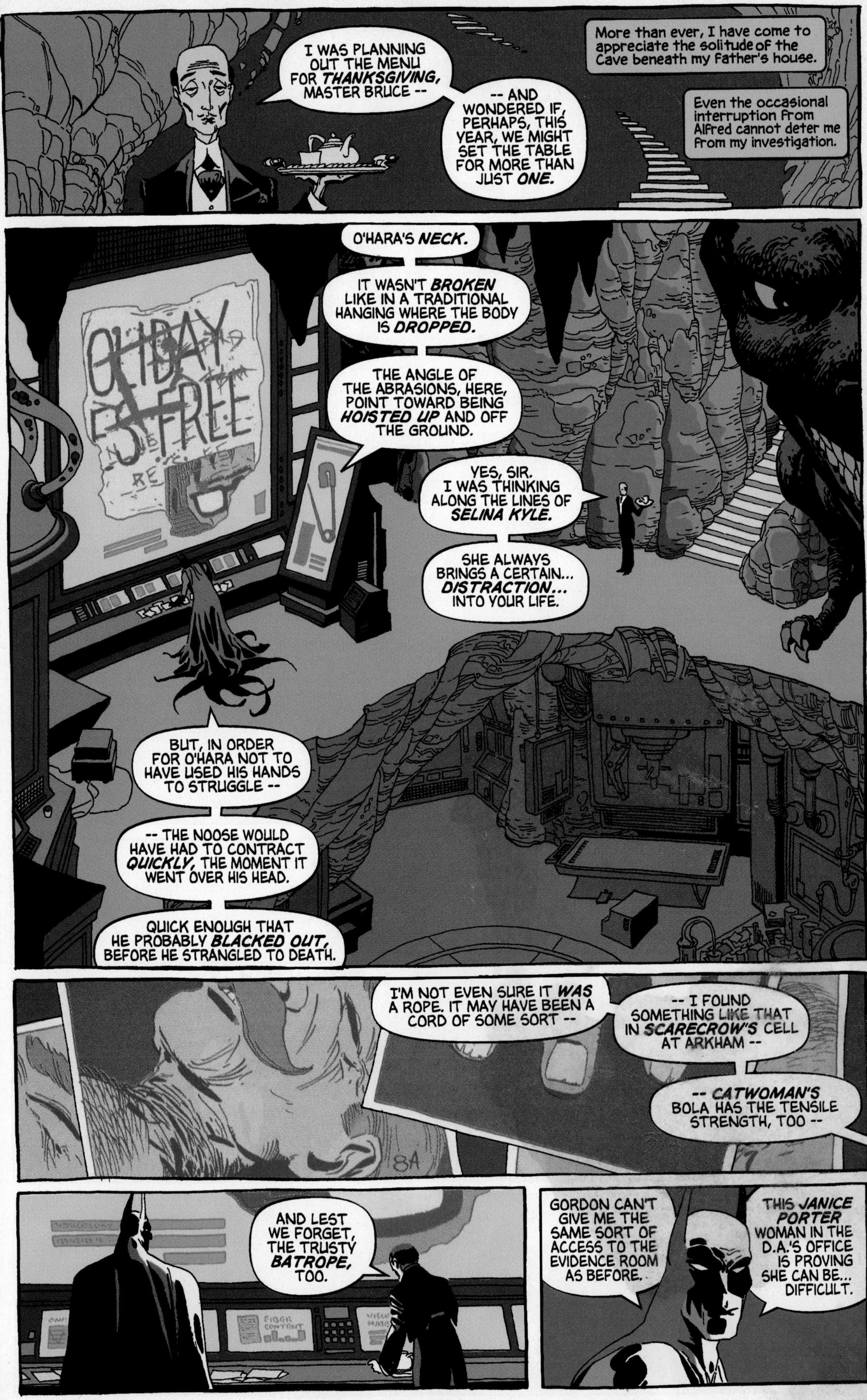
More than ever, I have come to appreciate the solitude of the Cave beneath my father's house.
Even the occasional interruption from Alfred cannot deter me from my investigation.
I WAS PLANNING OUT THE MENU FOR THANKSGIVING, MASTER BRUCE --
-- AND WONDERED IF, PERHAPS, THIS YEAR, WE MIGHT SET THE TABLE FOR MORE THAN JUST ONE.
O'HARA'S NECK.
IT WASN'T BROKEN LIKE IN A TRADITIONAL HANGING WHERE THE BODY IS DROPPED.
THE ANGLE OF THE ABRASIONS, HERE, POINT TOWARD BEING HOISTED UP AND OFF THE GROUND.
YES, SIR. I WAS THINKING ALONG THE LINES OF SELINA KYLE.
SHE ALWAYS BRINGS A CERTAIN... DISTRACTION... INTO YOUR LIFE.
BUT, IN ORDER FOR O'HARA NOT TO HAVE USED HIS HANDS TO STRUGGLE --
-- THE NOOSE WOULD HAVE HAD TO CONTRACT QUICKLY, THE MOMENT IT WENT OVER HIS HEAD.
QUICK ENOUGH THAT HE PROBABLY BLACKED OUT, BEFORE HE STRANGLED TO DEATH.
I'M NOT EVEN SURE IT WAS A ROPE. IT MAY HAVE BEEN A CORD OF SOME SORT --
-- I FOUND SOMETHING LIKE THAT IN SCARECROW'S CELL AT ARKHAM --
-- CATWOMAN'S BOLA HAS THE TENSILE STRENGTH, TOO --
AND LEST WE FORGET, THE TRUSTY BATROPE, TOO.
GORDON CAN'T GIVE ME THE SAME SORT OF ACCESS TO THE EVIDENCE ROOM AS BEFORE.
THIS JANICE PORTER WOMAN IN THE D.A.'S OFFICE IS PROVING SHE CAN BE... DIFFICULT.

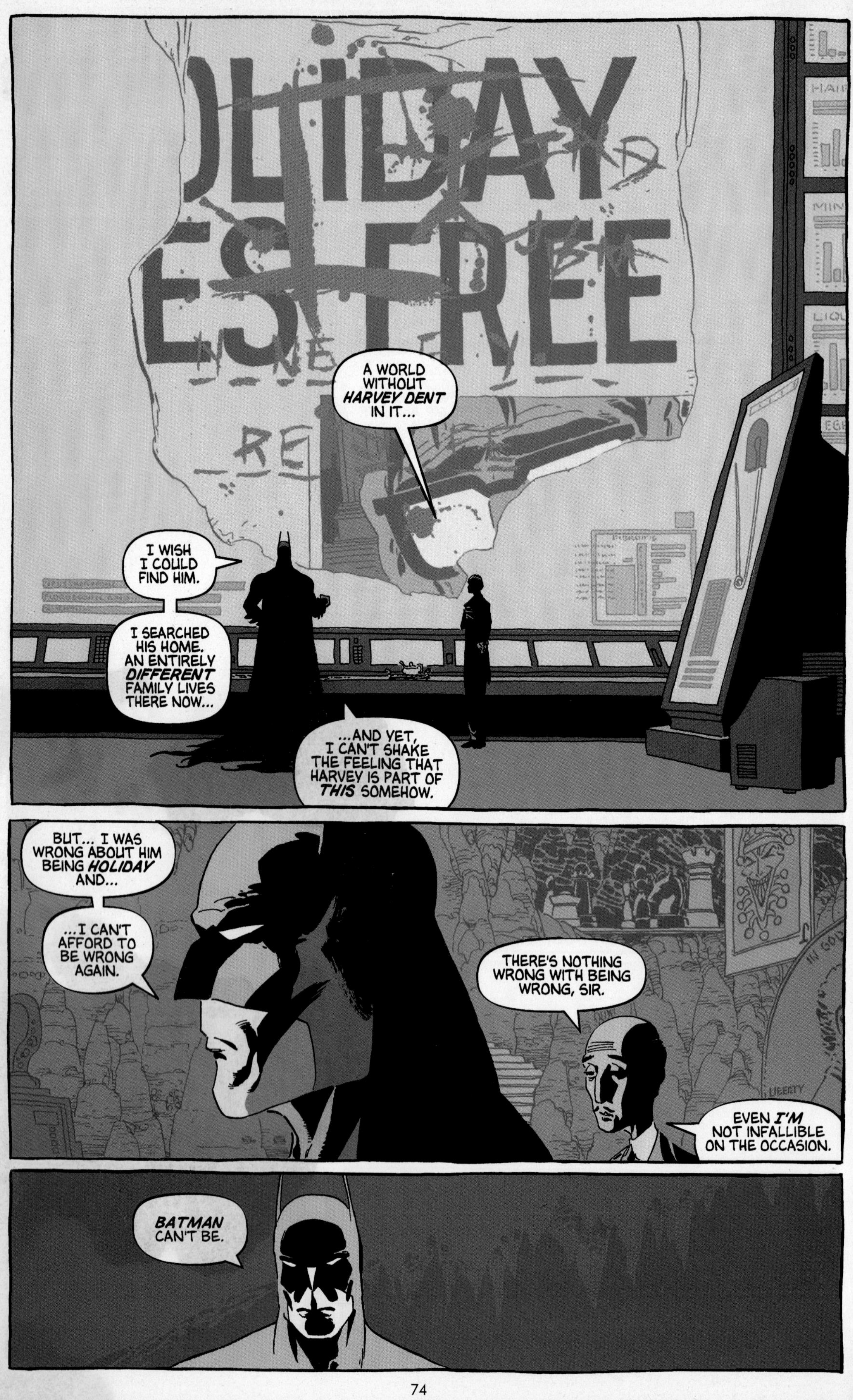
A WORLD WITHOUT HARVEY DENT IN IT...
I WISH I COULD FIND HIM.
I SEARCHED HIS HOME. AN ENTIRELY DIFFERENT FAMILY LIVES THERE NOW...
...AND YET, I CAN'T SHAKE THE FEELING THAT HARVEY IS PART OF THIS SOMEHOW.
BUT... I WAS WRONG ABOUT HIM BEING HOLIDAY AND...
...I CAN'T AFFORD TO BE WRONG AGAIN.
THERE'S NOTHING WRONG WITH BEING WRONG, SIR.
EVEN I'M NOT INFALLIBLE ON THE OCCASION.
BATMAN CAN'T BE.

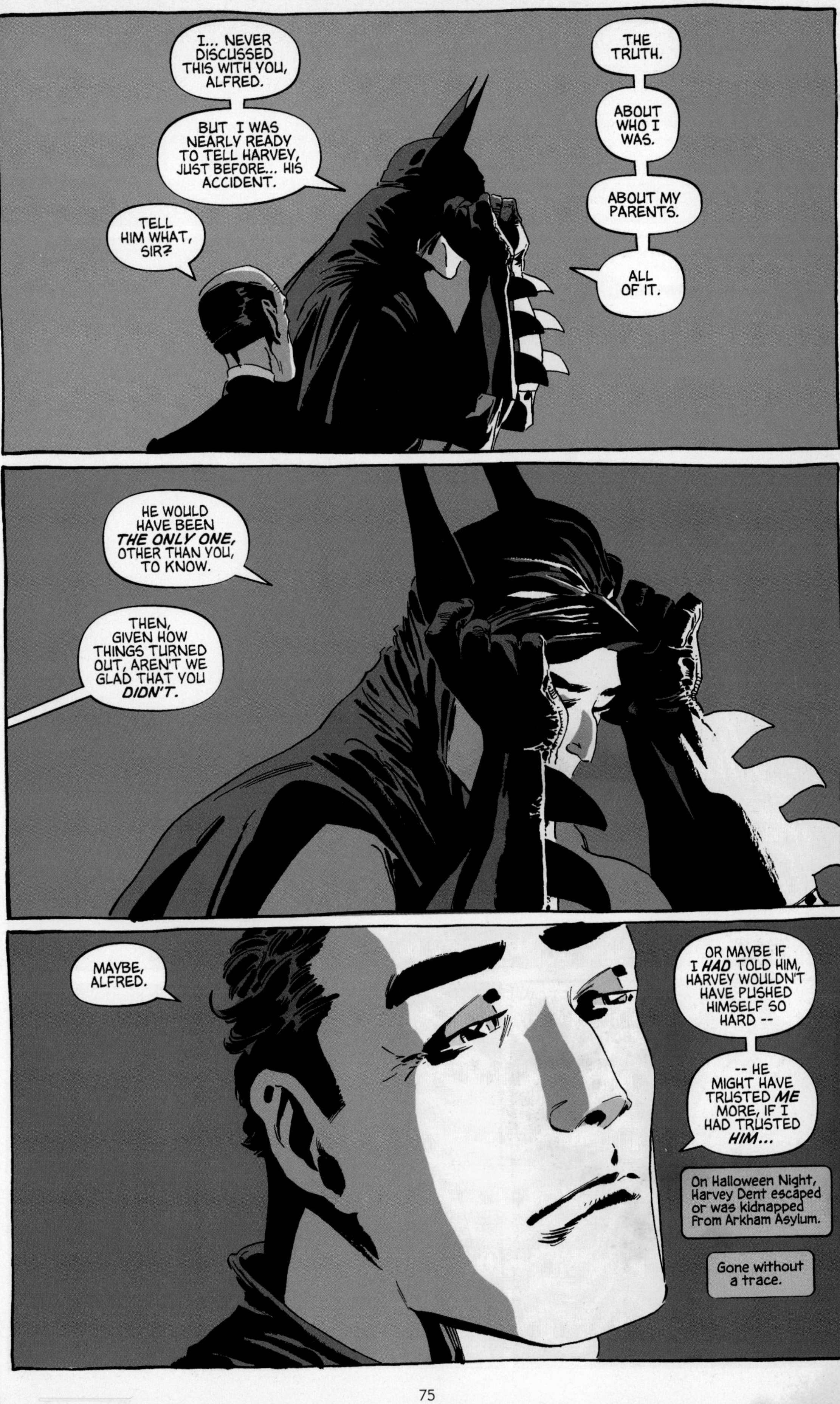
I... NEVER DISCUSSED THIS WITH YOU, ALFRED.
BUT I WAS NEARLY READY TO TELL HARVEY, JUST BEFORE... HIS ACCIDENT.
TELL HIM WHAT, SIR?
THE TRUTH.
ABOUT WHO I WAS.
ABOUT MY PARENTS.
ALL OF IT.
HE WOULD HAVE BEEN THE ONLY ONE, OTHER THAN YOU, TO KNOW.
THEN, GIVEN HOW THINGS TURNED OUT, AREN'T WE GLAD THAT YOU DIDN'T.
MAYBE, ALFRED.
OR MAYBE IF I HAD TOLD HIM, HARVEY WOULDN'T HAVE PUSHED HIMSELF SO HARD --
-- HE MIGHT HAVE TRUSTED ME MORE, IF I HAD TRUSTED HIM...
On Halloween Night, Harvey Dent escaped or was kidnapped from Arkham Asylum.
Gone without a trace.

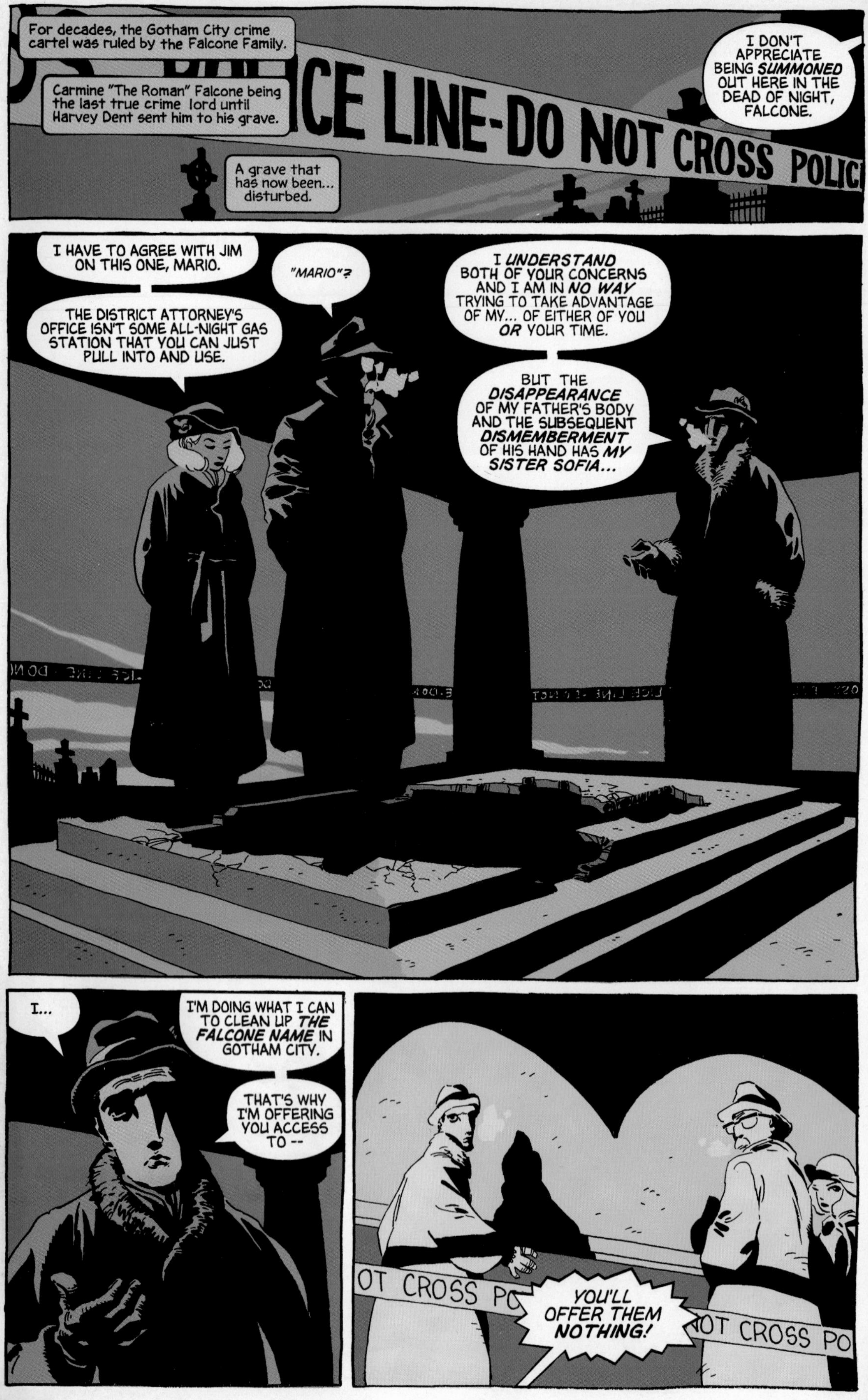
For decades, the Gotham City crime cartel was ruled by the Falcone Family.
Carmine "The Roman" Falcone being the last true crime lord until Harvey Dent sent him to his grave.
A grave that has now been... disturbed.
I DON'T APPRECIATE BEING SUMMONED OUT HERE IN THE DEAD OF NIGHT, FALCONE.
ICE LINE-DO NOT CROSS POLIC
I HAVE TO AGREE WITH JIM ON THIS ONE, MARIO.
THE DISTRICT ATTORNEY'S OFFICE ISN'T SOME ALL-NIGHT GAS STATION THAT YOU CAN JUST PULL INTO AND USE.
"MARIO"?
I UNDERSTAND BOTH OF YOUR CONCERNS AND I AM IN NO WAY TRYING TO TAKE ADVANTAGE OF MY... OF EITHER OF YOU OR YOUR TIME.
BUT THE DISAPPEARANCE OF MY FATHER'S BODY AND THE SUBSEQUENT DISMEMBERMENT OF HIS HAND HAS MY SISTER SOFIA...
I...
I'M DOING WHAT I CAN TO CLEAN UP THE FALCONE NAME IN GOTHAM CITY.
THAT'S WHY I'M OFFERING YOU ACCESS TO --
OT CROSS PO
YOU'LL OFFER THEM NOTHING!
NOT CROSS PO

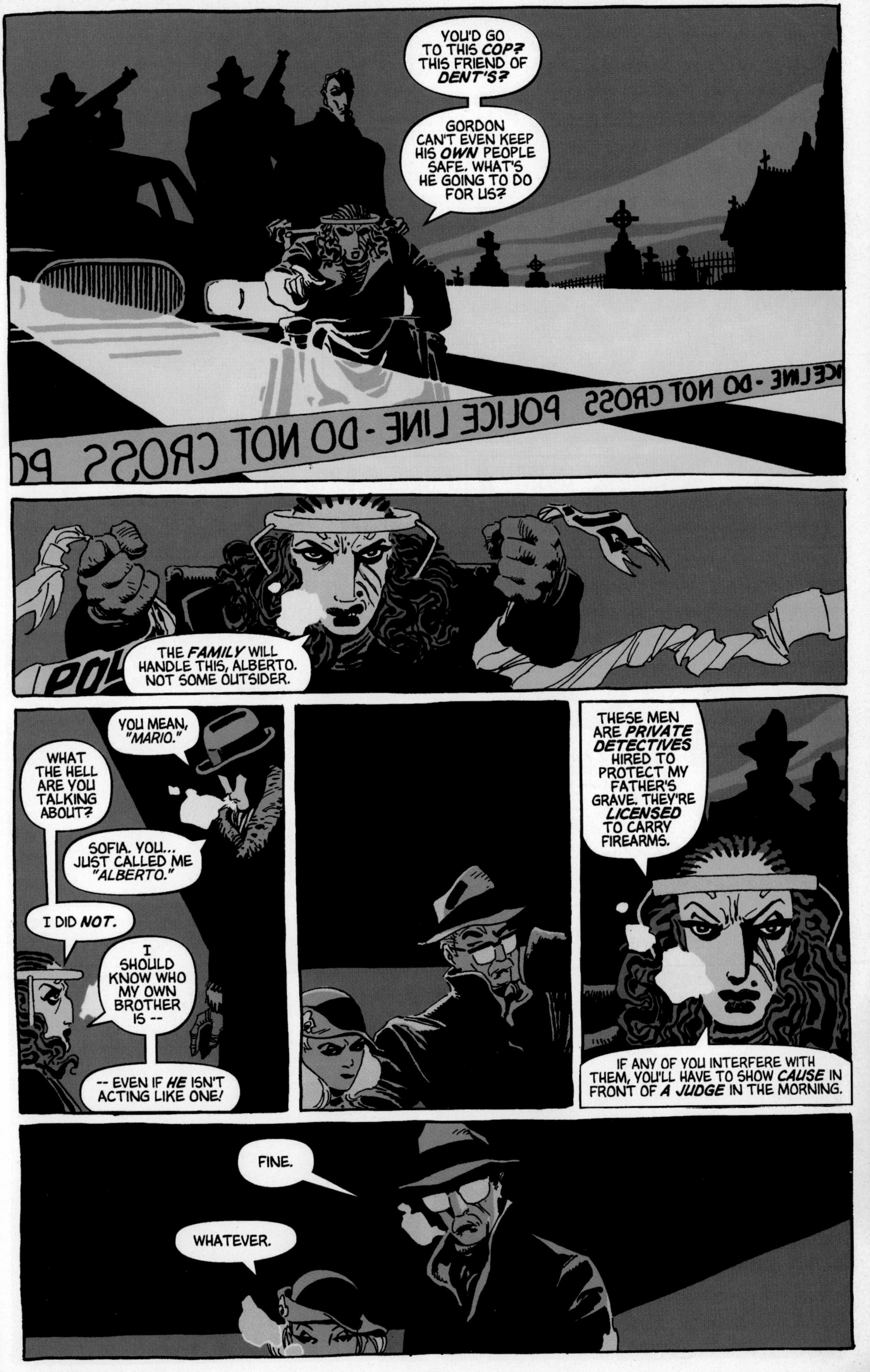
YOU'D GO TO THIS COP? THIS FRIEND OF DENT'S?
GORDON CAN'T EVEN KEEP HIS OWN PEOPLE SAFE. WHAT'S HE GOING TO DO FOR US?
POLICE LINE - DO NOT CROSS
THE FAMILY WILL HANDLE THIS, ALBERTO. NOT SOME OUTSIDER.
WHAT THE HELL ARE YOU TALKING ABOUT?
YOU MEAN, "MARIO."
SOFIA. YOU... JUST CALLED ME "ALBERTO."
I DID NOT.
I SHOULD KNOW WHO MY OWN BROTHER IS --
-- EVEN IF HE ISN'T ACTING LIKE ONE!
THESE MEN ARE PRIVATE DETECTIVES HIRED TO PROTECT MY FATHER'S GRAVE. THEY'RE LICENSED TO CARRY FIREARMS.
IF ANY OF YOU INTERFERE WITH THEM, YOU'LL HAVE TO SHOW CAUSE IN FRONT OF A JUDGE IN THE MORNING.
FINE.
WHATEVER.

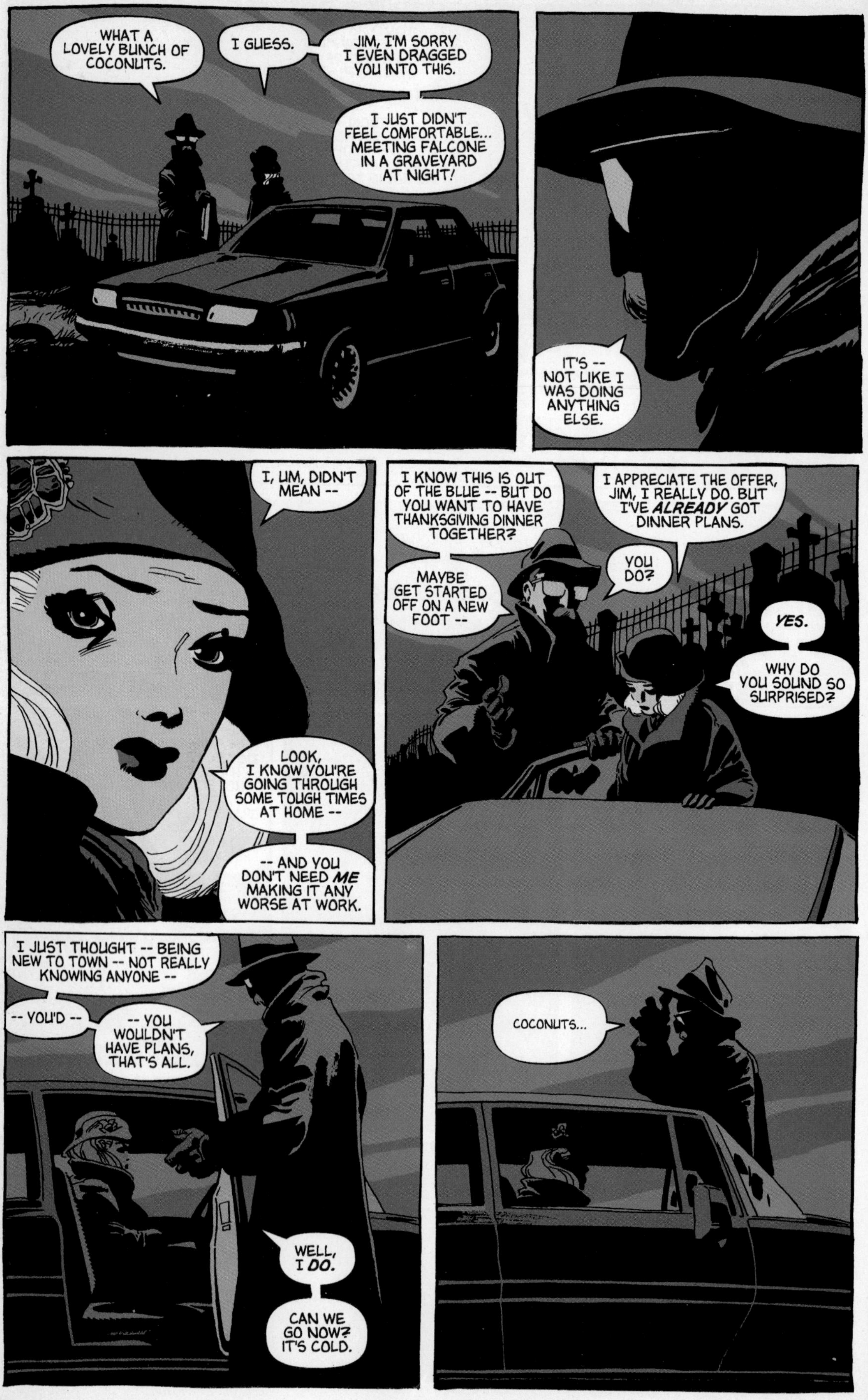
WHAT A LOVELY BUNCH OF COCONUTS.
I GUESS.
JIM, I'M SORRY I EVEN DRAGGED YOU INTO THIS.
I JUST DIDN'T FEEL COMFORTABLE... MEETING FALCONE IN A GRAVEYARD AT NIGHT!
IT'S -- NOT LIKE I WAS DOING ANYTHING ELSE.
I, UM, DIDN'T MEAN --
LOOK, I KNOW YOU'RE GOING THROUGH SOME TOUGH TIMES AT HOME --
-- AND YOU DON'T NEED ME MAKING IT ANY WORSE AT WORK.
I KNOW THIS IS OUT OF THE BLUE -- BUT DO YOU WANT TO HAVE THANKSGIVING DINNER TOGETHER?
MAYBE GET STARTED OFF ON A NEW FOOT --
I APPRECIATE THE OFFER, JIM, I REALLY DO. BUT I'VE ALREADY GOT DINNER PLANS.
YOU DO?
YES.
WHY DO YOU SOUND SO SURPRISED?
I JUST THOUGHT -- BEING NEW TO TOWN -- NOT REALLY KNOWING ANYONE --
-- YOU'D --
-- YOU WOULDN'T HAVE PLANS, THAT'S ALL.
WELL, I DO.
CAN WE GO NOW? IT'S COLD.
COCONUTS...

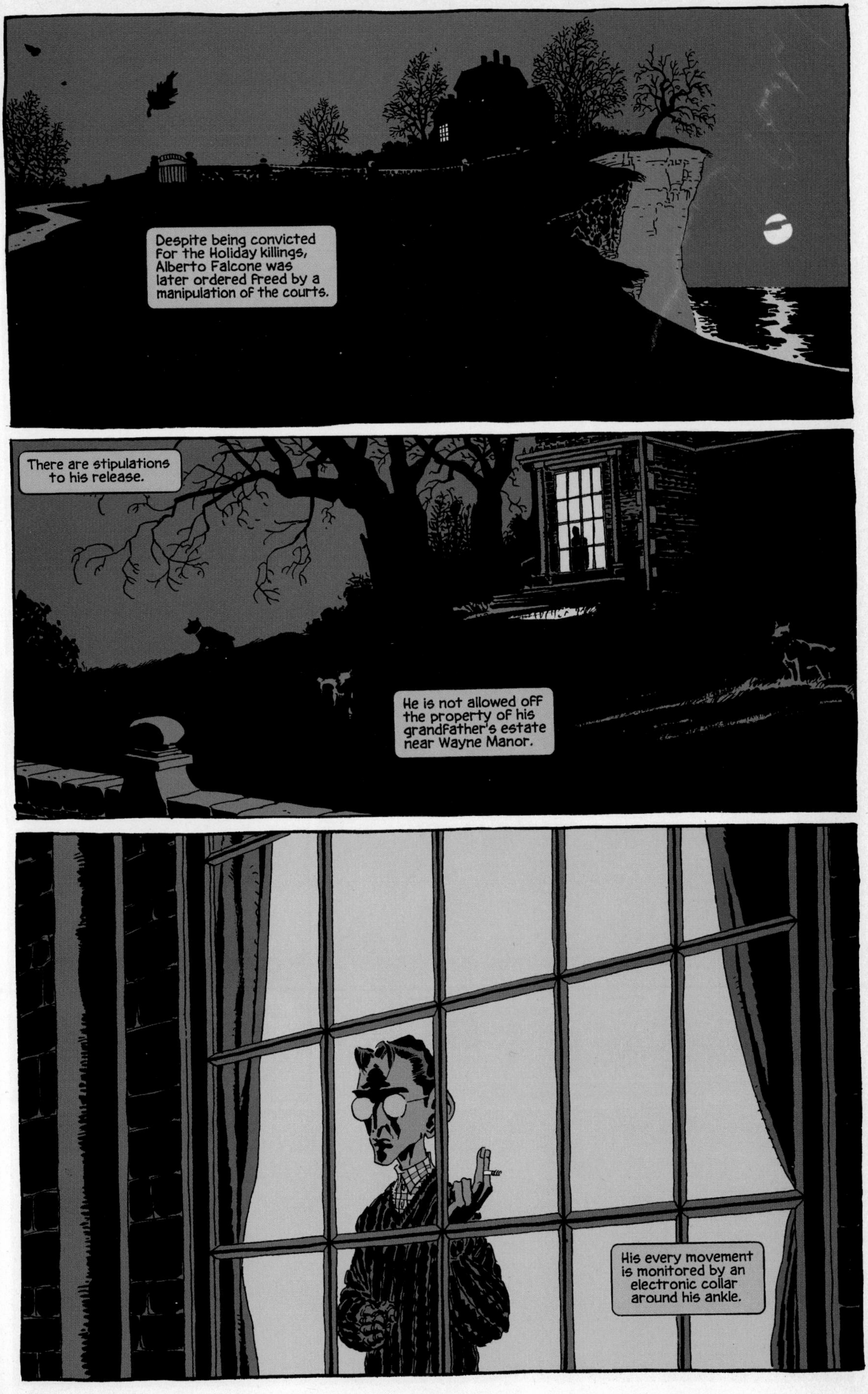
Despite being convicted for the Holiday killings, Alberto Falcone was later ordered freed by a manipulation of the courts.
There are stipulations to his release.
He is not allowed off the property of his grandfather's estate near Wayne Manor.
His every movement is monitored by an electronic collar around his ankle.

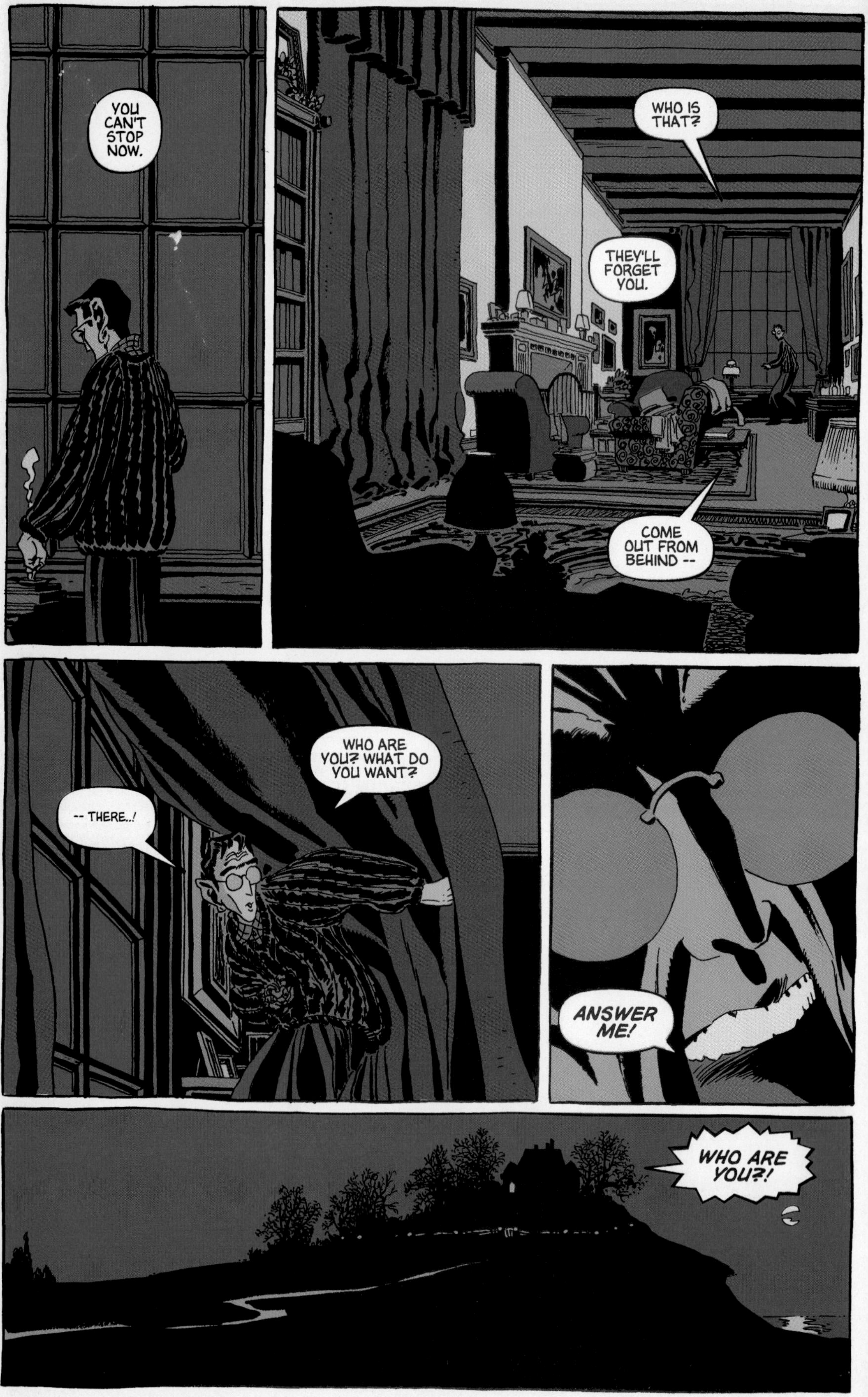
YOU CAN'T STOP NOW.
WHO IS THAT?
THEY'LL FORGET YOU.
COME OUT FROM BEHIND --
-- THERE..!
WHO ARE YOU? WHAT DO YOU WANT?
ANSWER ME!
WHO ARE YOU?!

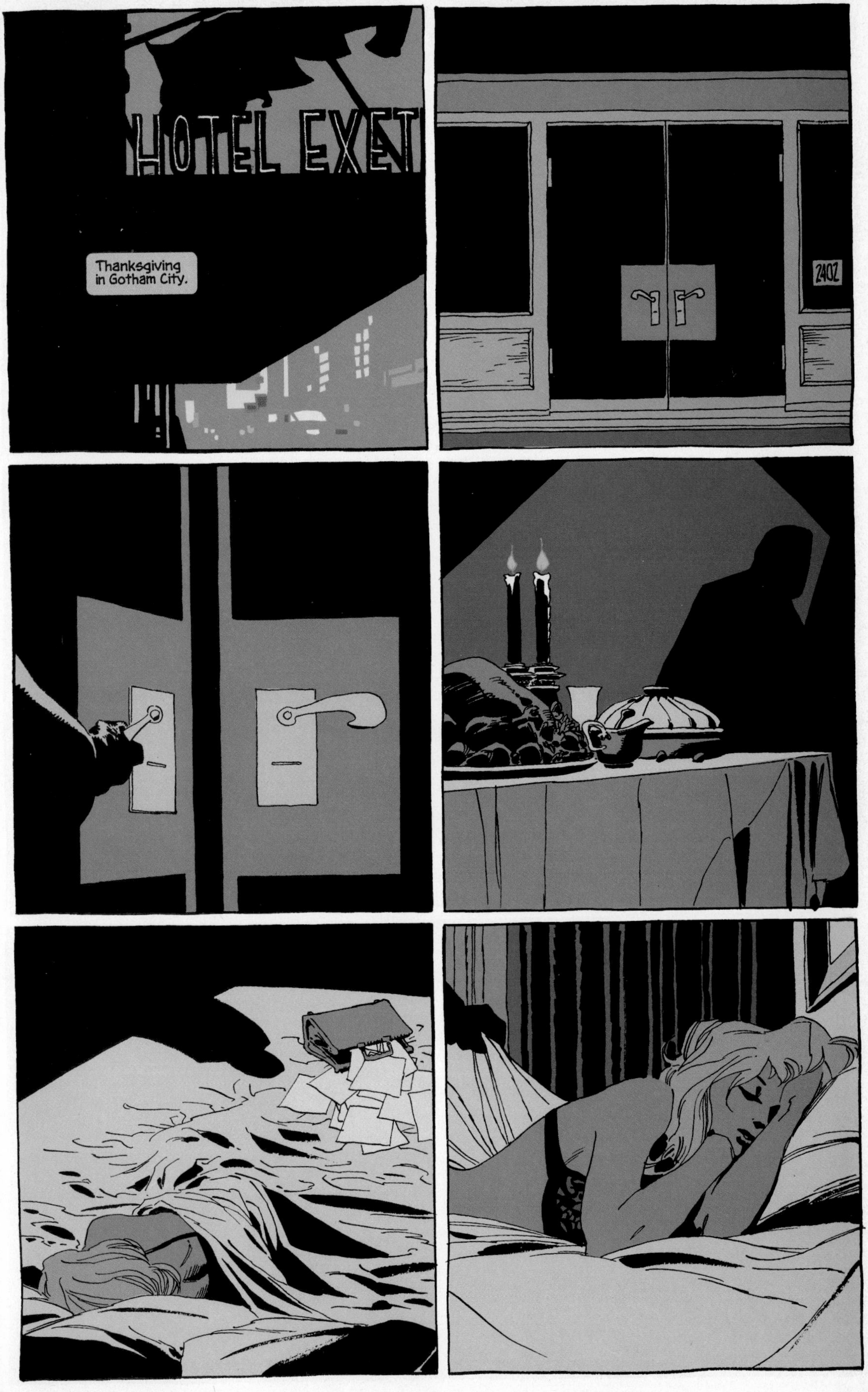
HOTEL EXET
Thanksgiving in Gotham City.
2402

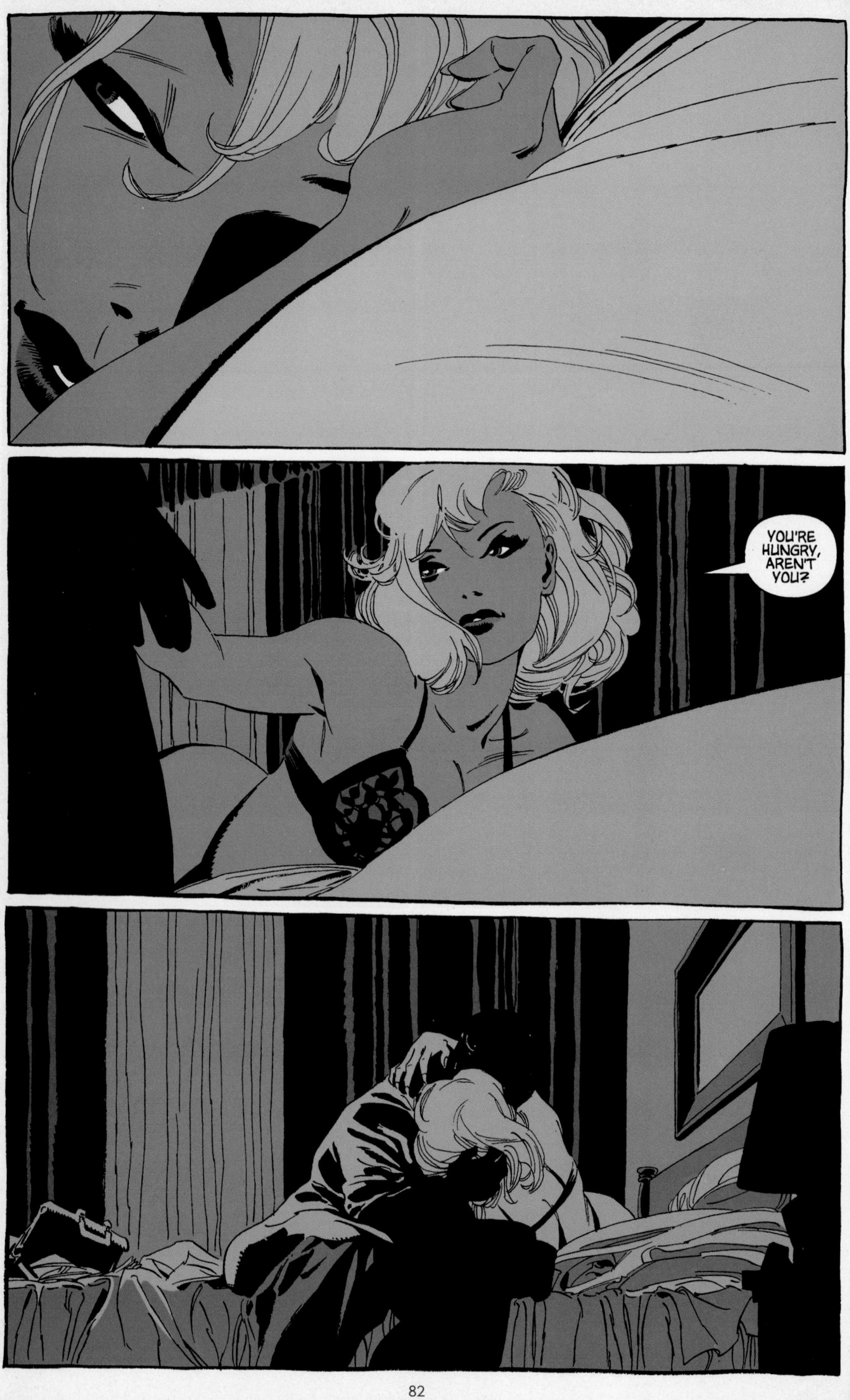
YOU'RE HUNGRY, AREN'T YOU?

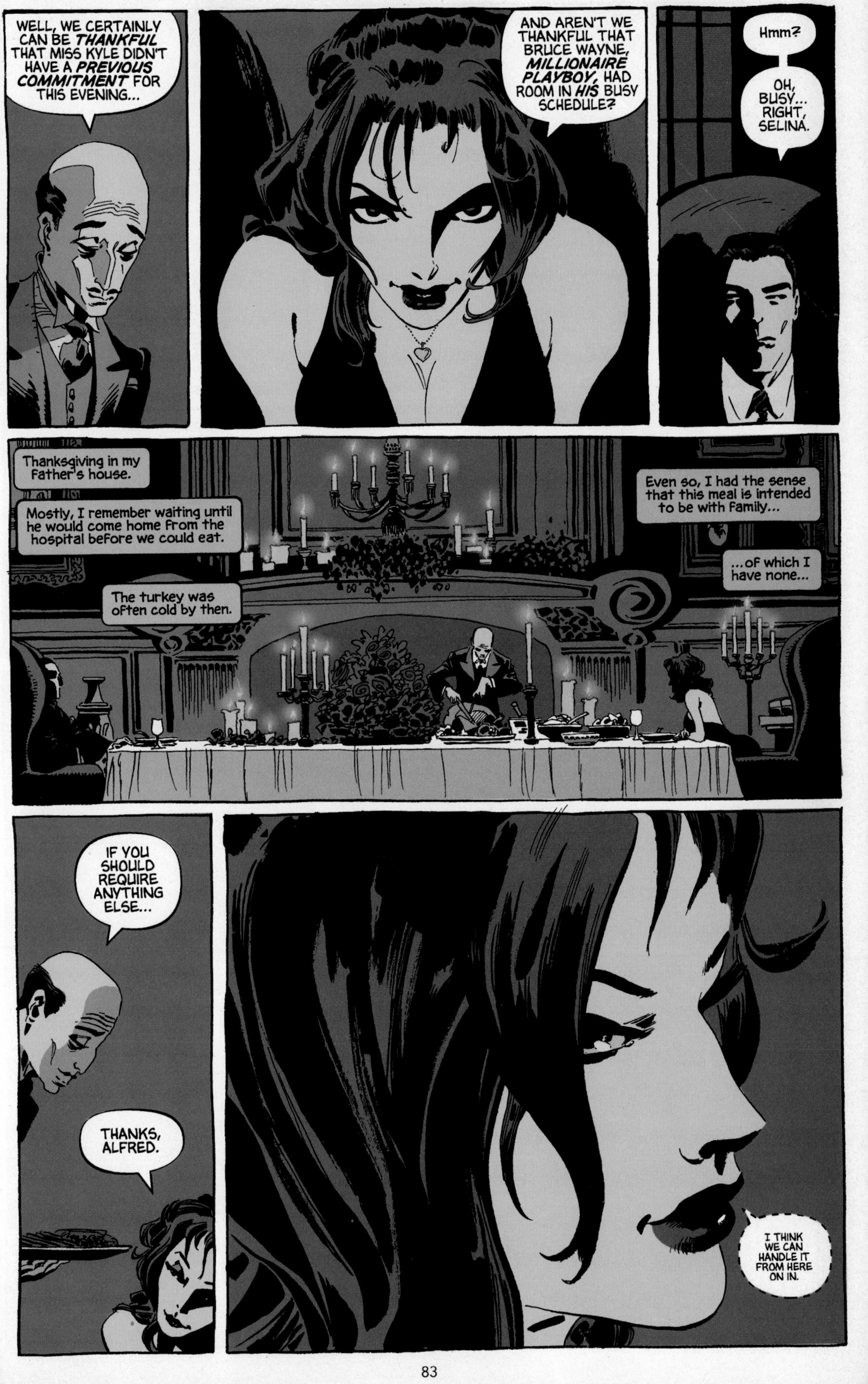
WELL, WE CERTAINLY CAN BE *THANKFUL* THAT MISS KYLE DIDN'T HAVE A *PREVIOUS COMMITMENT* FOR THIS EVENING...
AND AREN'T WE THANKFUL THAT BRUCE WAYNE, *MILLIONAIRE PLAYBOY,* HAD ROOM IN *HIS* BUSY SCHEDULE?
Hmm?
OH, BUSY... RIGHT, SELINA.
Thanksgiving in my Father's house.
Mostly, I remember waiting until he would come home from the hospital before we could eat.
The turkey was often cold by then.
Even so, I had the sense that this meal is intended to be with Family...
...of which I have none...
IF YOU SHOULD REQUIRE ANYTHING ELSE...
THANKS, ALFRED.
I THINK WE CAN HANDLE IT FROM HERE ON IN.

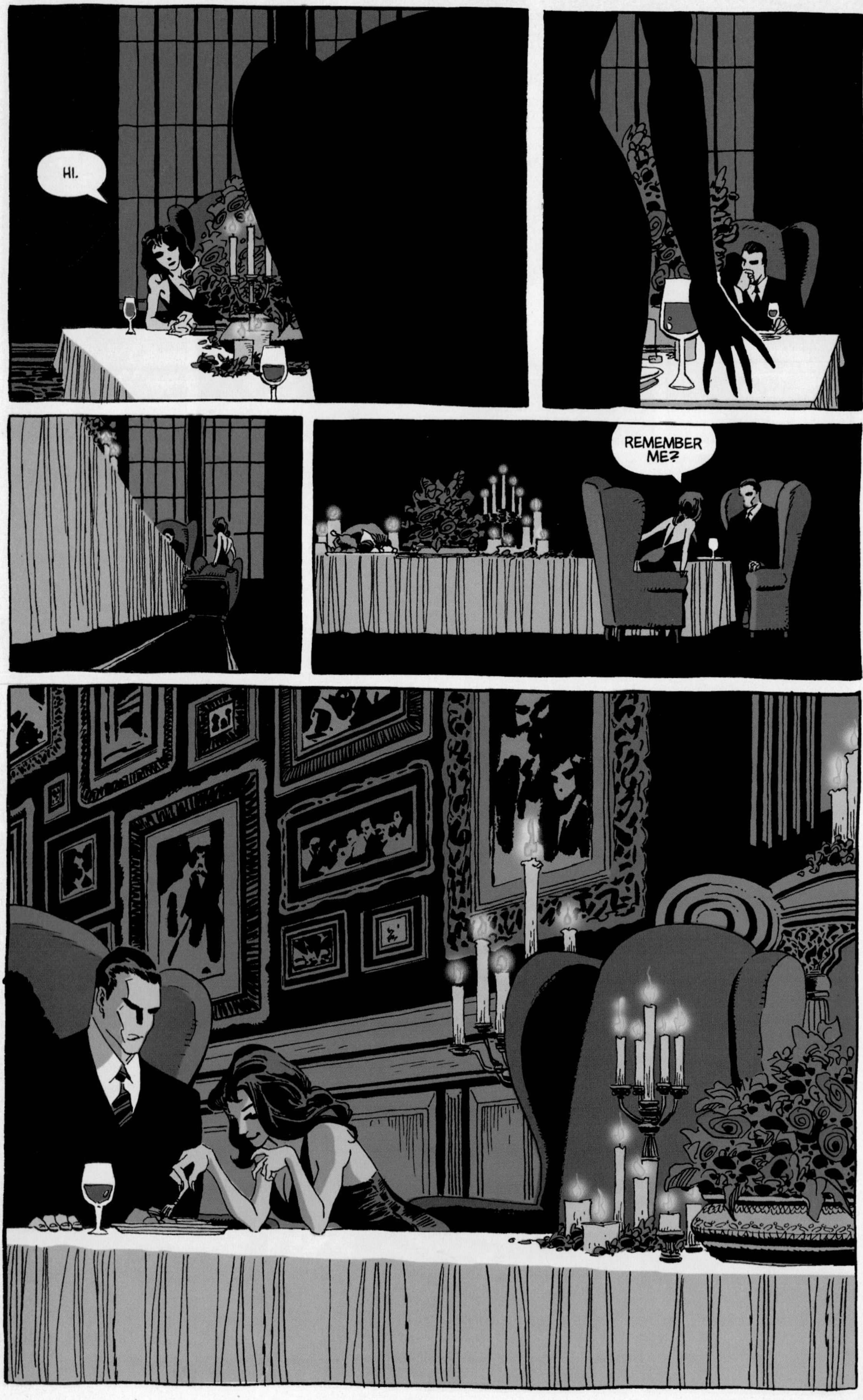
HI.
REMEMBER ME?

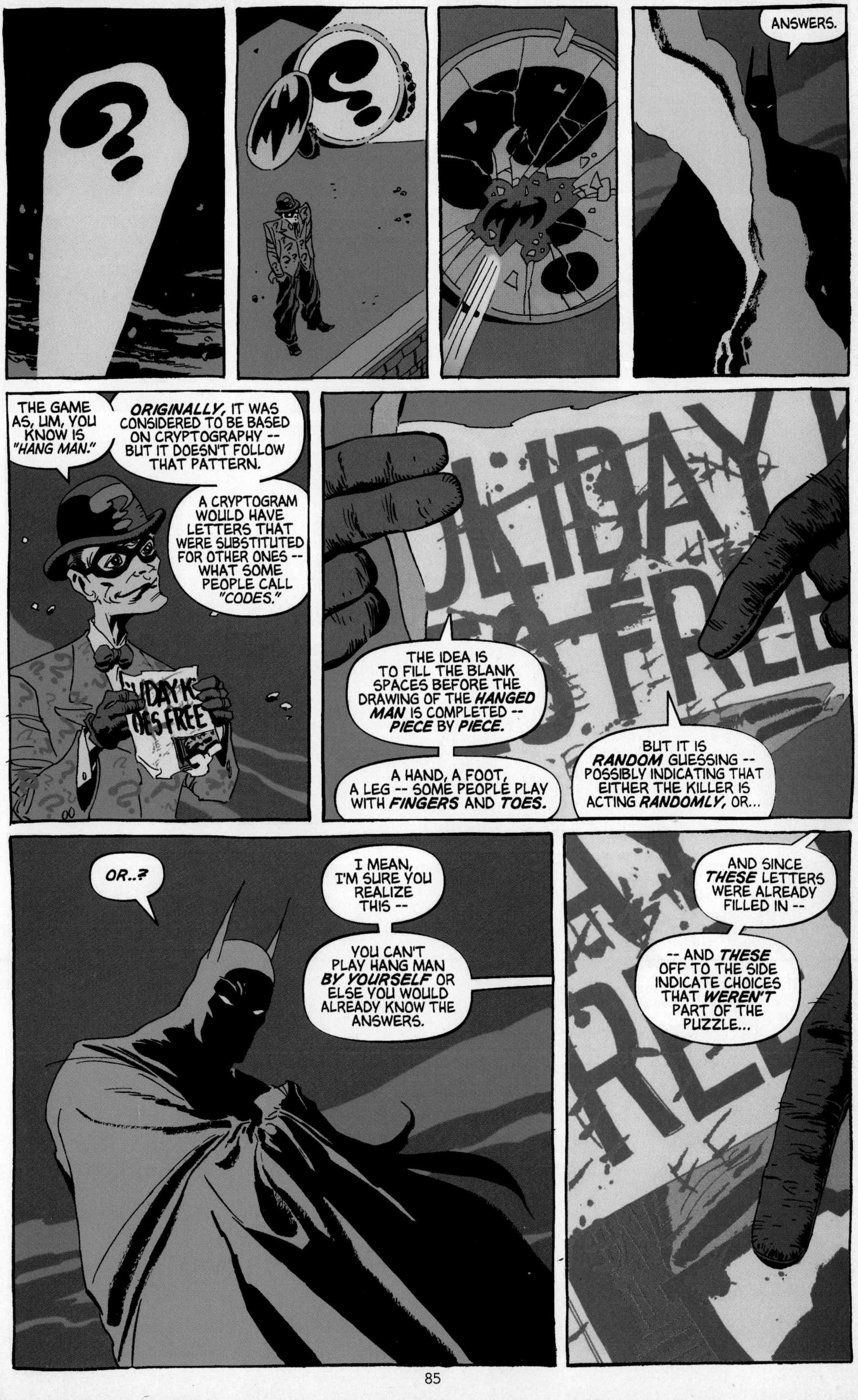
ANSWERS.
THE GAME AS, UM, YOU KNOW IS "HANG MAN."
ORIGINALLY, IT WAS CONSIDERED TO BE BASED ON CRYPTOGRAPHY -- BUT IT DOESN'T FOLLOW THAT PATTERN.
A CRYPTOGRAM WOULD HAVE LETTERS THAT WERE SUBSTITUTED FOR OTHER ONES -- WHAT SOME PEOPLE CALL "CODES."
THE IDEA IS TO FILL THE BLANK SPACES BEFORE THE DRAWING OF THE HANGED MAN IS COMPLETED -- PIECE BY PIECE.
A HAND, A FOOT, A LEG -- SOME PEOPLE PLAY WITH FINGERS AND TOES.
BUT IT IS RANDOM GUESSING -- POSSIBLY INDICATING THAT EITHER THE KILLER IS ACTING RANDOMLY, OR...
OR..?
I MEAN, I'M SURE YOU REALIZE THIS --
YOU CAN'T PLAY HANG MAN BY YOURSELF OR ELSE YOU WOULD ALREADY KNOW THE ANSWERS.
AND SINCE THESE LETTERS WERE ALREADY FILLED IN --
-- AND THESE OFF TO THE SIDE INDICATE CHOICES THAT WEREN'T PART OF THE PUZZLE...

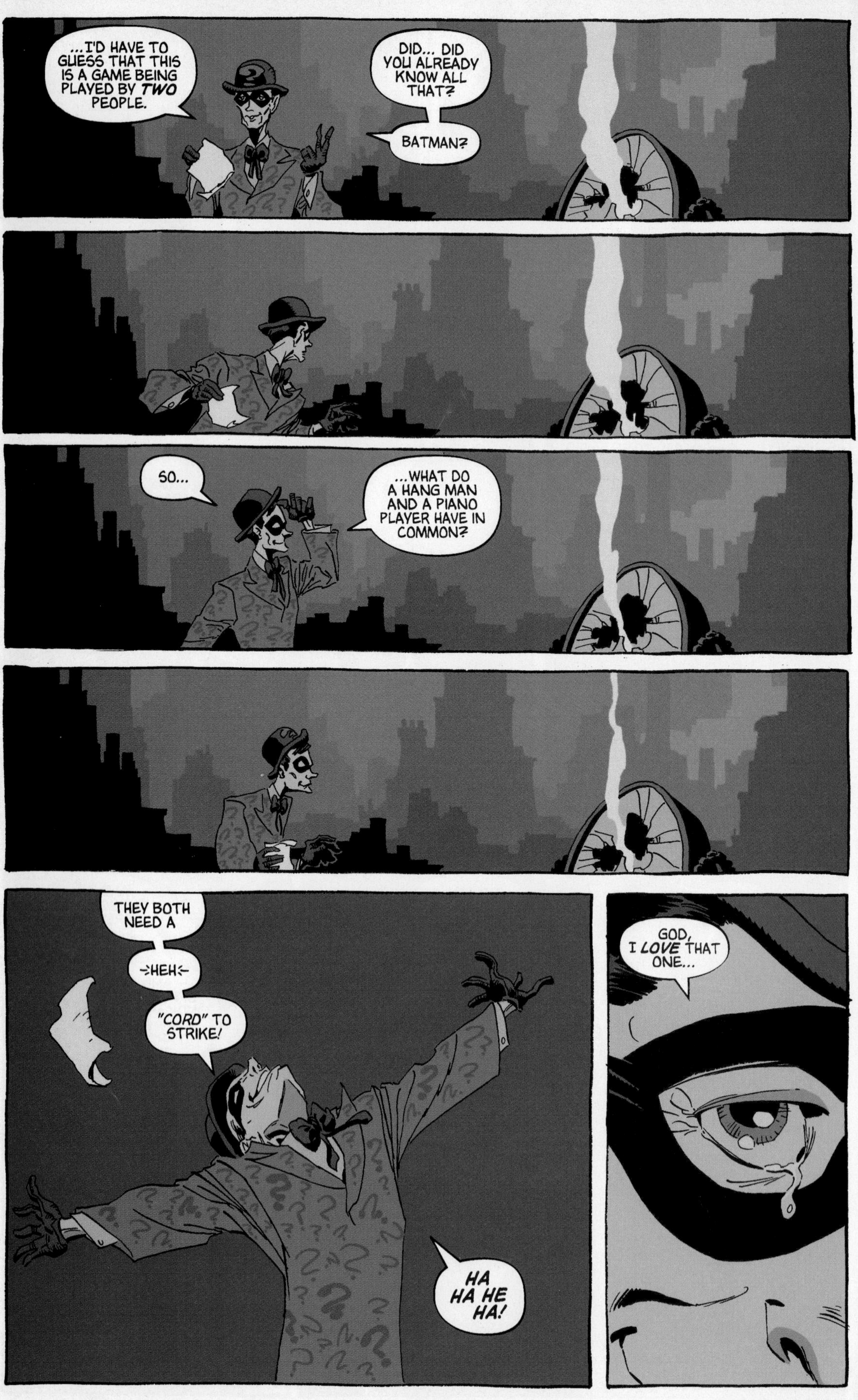
...I'D HAVE TO GUESS THAT THIS IS A GAME BEING PLAYED BY *TWO* PEOPLE.
DID... DID YOU ALREADY KNOW ALL THAT?
BATMAN?
SO...
...WHAT DO A HANG MAN AND A PIANO PLAYER HAVE IN COMMON?
THEY BOTH NEED A
-HEH-
"CORD" TO STRIKE!
HA HA HE HA!
GOD, I *LOVE* THAT ONE...

Former Commissioner Gillian B. Loeb was everything that was wrong with the Gotham City Police Department.

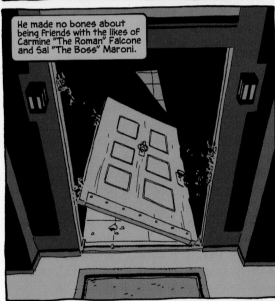

He made no bones about being friends with the likes of Carmine "The Roman" Falcone and Sal "The Boss" Maroni.

So corrupt, many thought he actually flaunted it because no one would dare to take him down.

We did, though. Myself, then-Lieutenant James Gordon...

COMMISSIO
POLIC
GOTHAM C
Gillian B. Loeb

...and a young, courageous District Attorney named Harvey Dent...

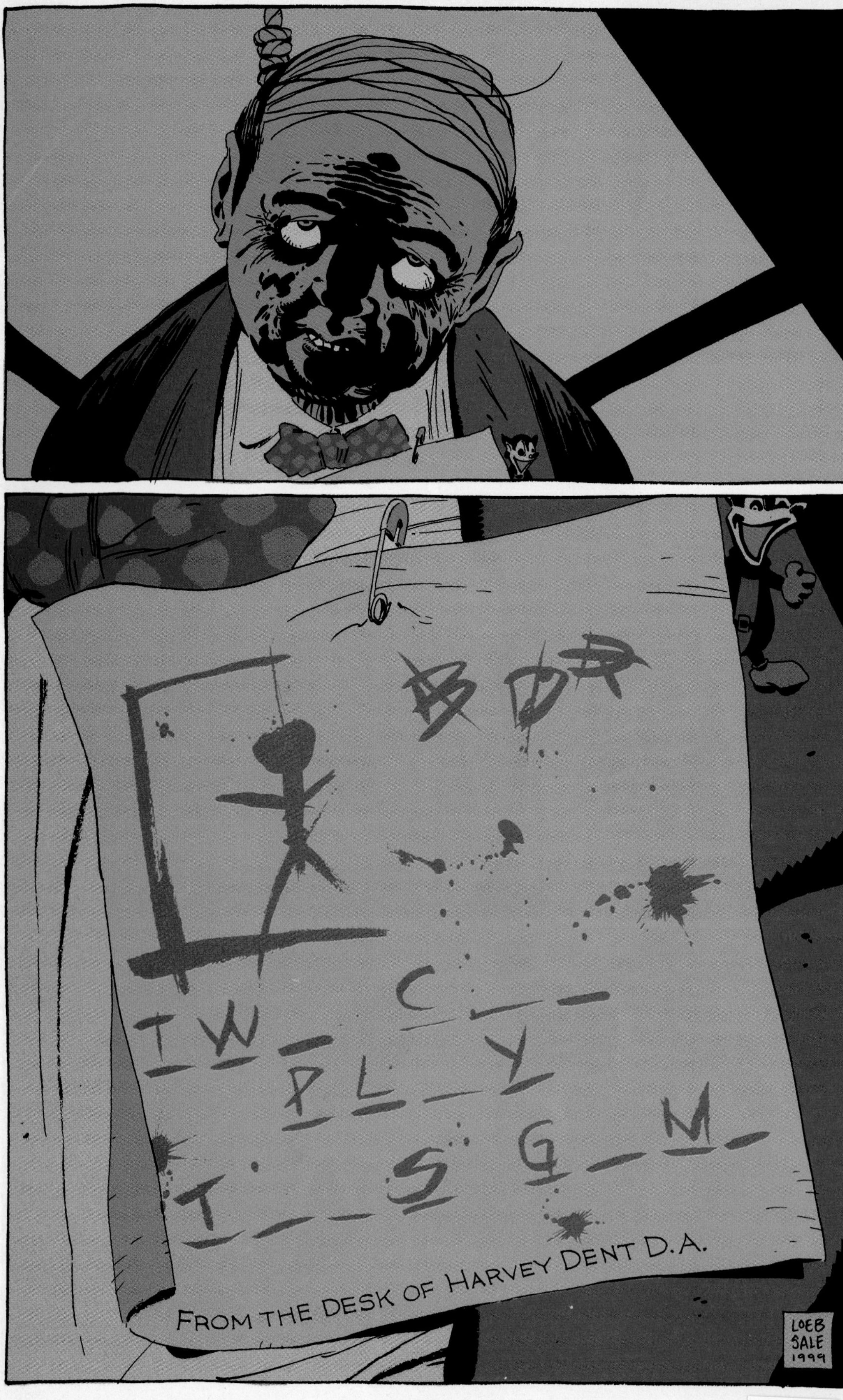
FROM THE DESK OF HARVEY DENT D.A.
LOEB SALE 1999

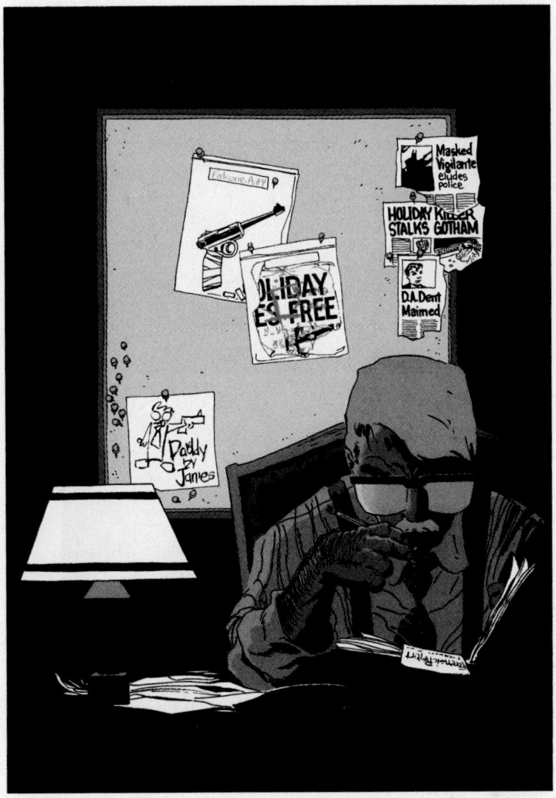

Falcone, A. #4
Masked Vigilante eludes police
HOLIDAY KILLER STALKS GOTHAM
OLIDAY
ES FREE
D.A. Dent Maimed
Daddy by James

3

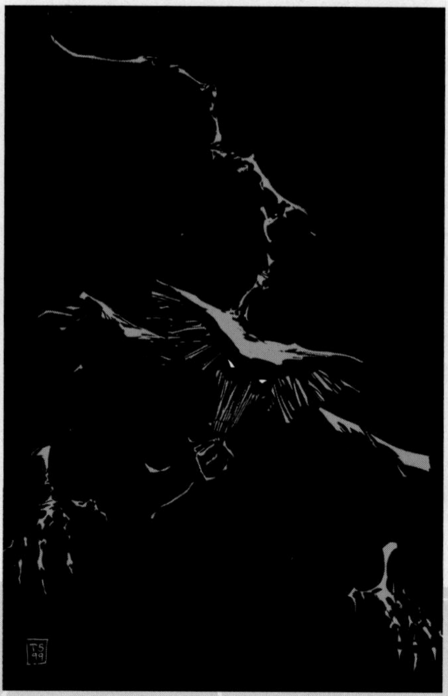

T O Y S

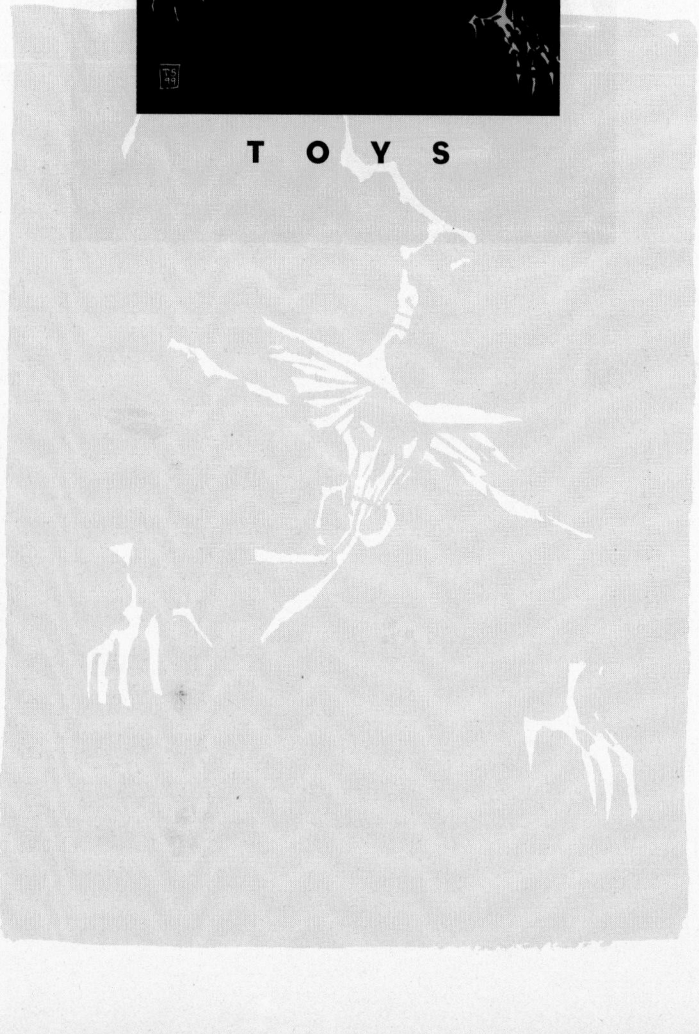

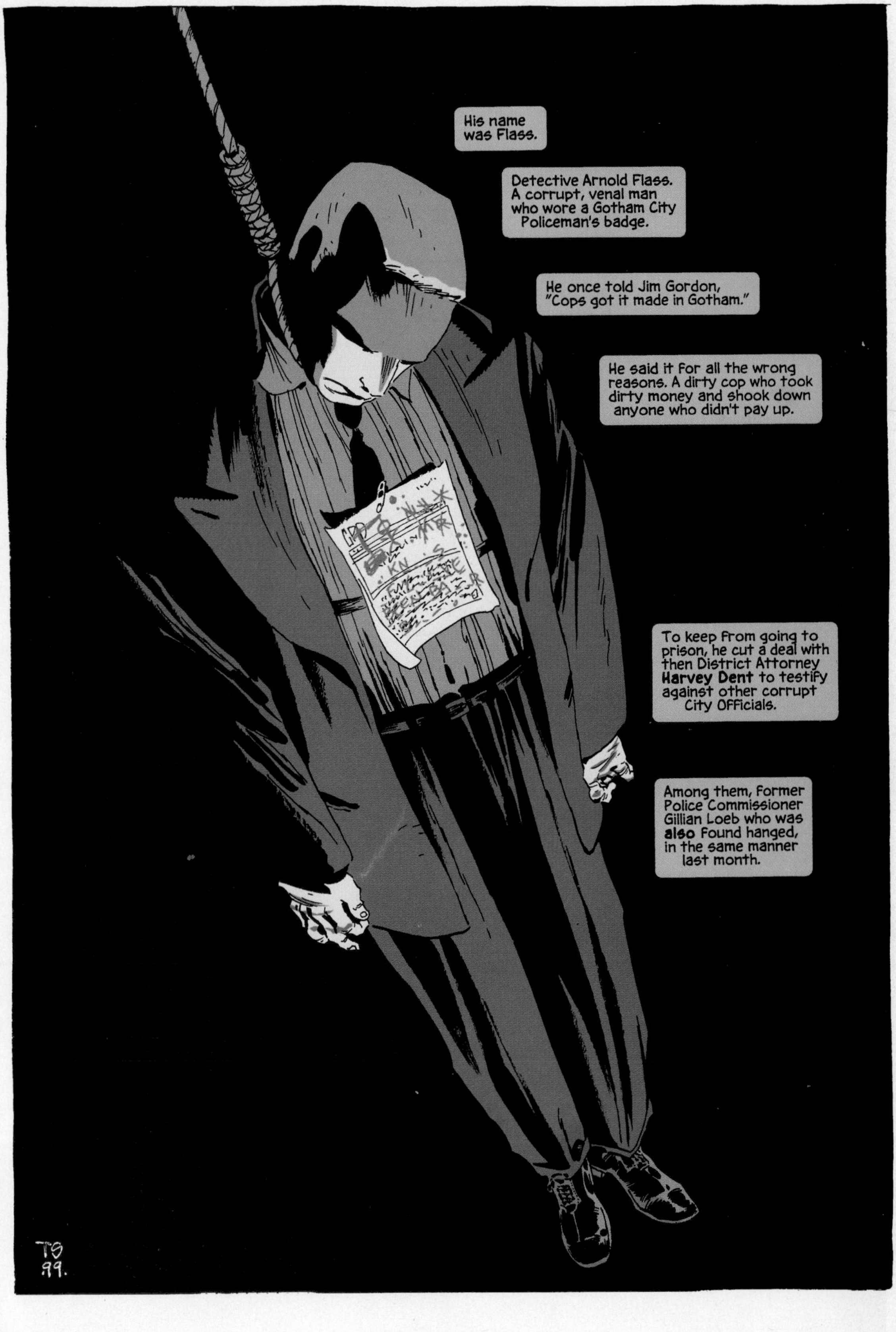
His name was Flass.
Detective Arnold Flass. A corrupt, venal man who wore a Gotham City Policeman's badge.
He once told Jim Gordon, "Cops got it made in Gotham."
He said it for all the wrong reasons. A dirty cop who took dirty money and shook down anyone who didn't pay up.
To keep from going to prison, he cut a deal with then District Attorney **Harvey Dent** to testify against other corrupt City Officials.
Among them, Former Police Commissioner Gillian Loeb who was **also** found hanged, in the same manner last month.
TS 99.

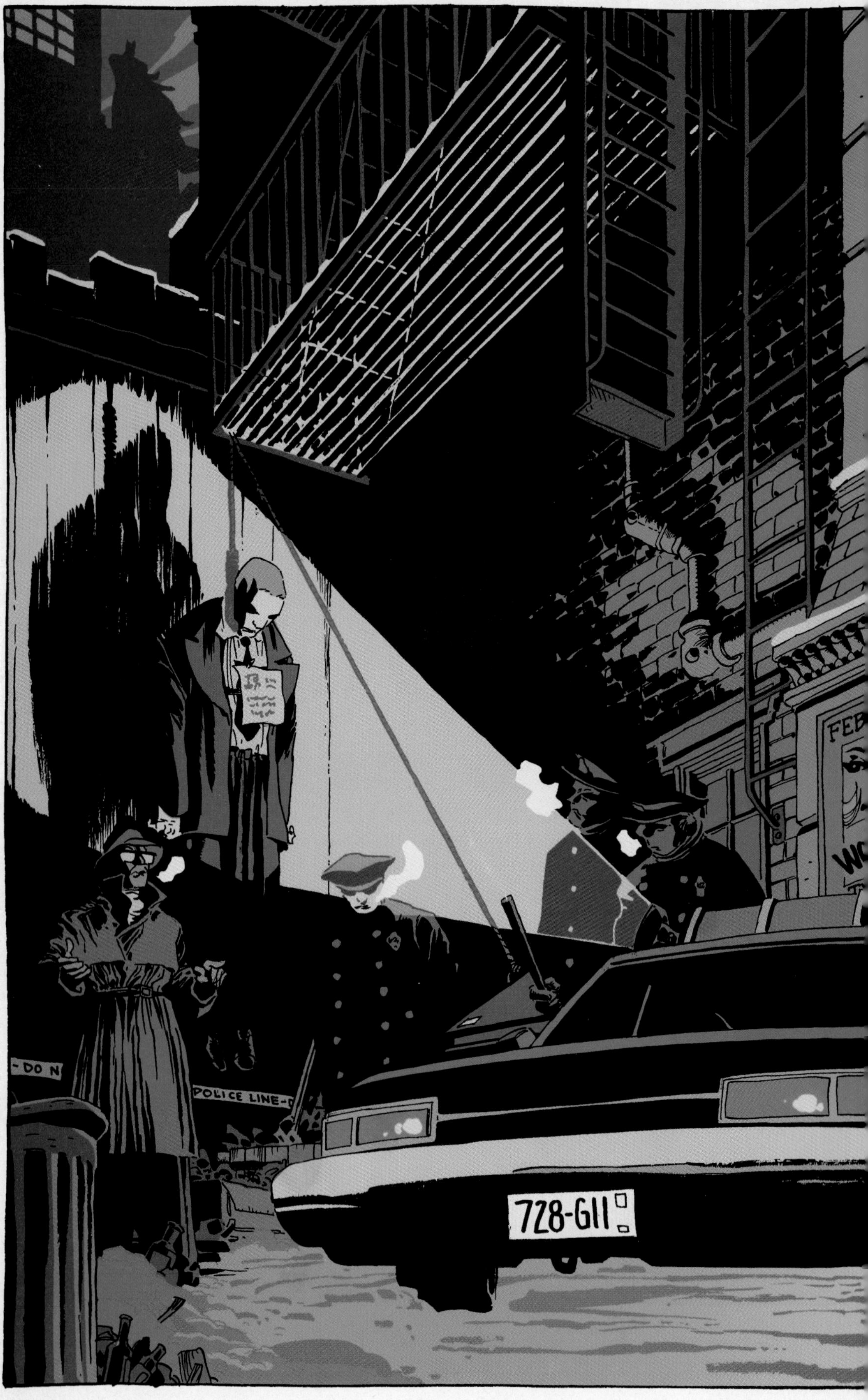

- DO N
POLICE LINE-D
728-GII
FEB
WO

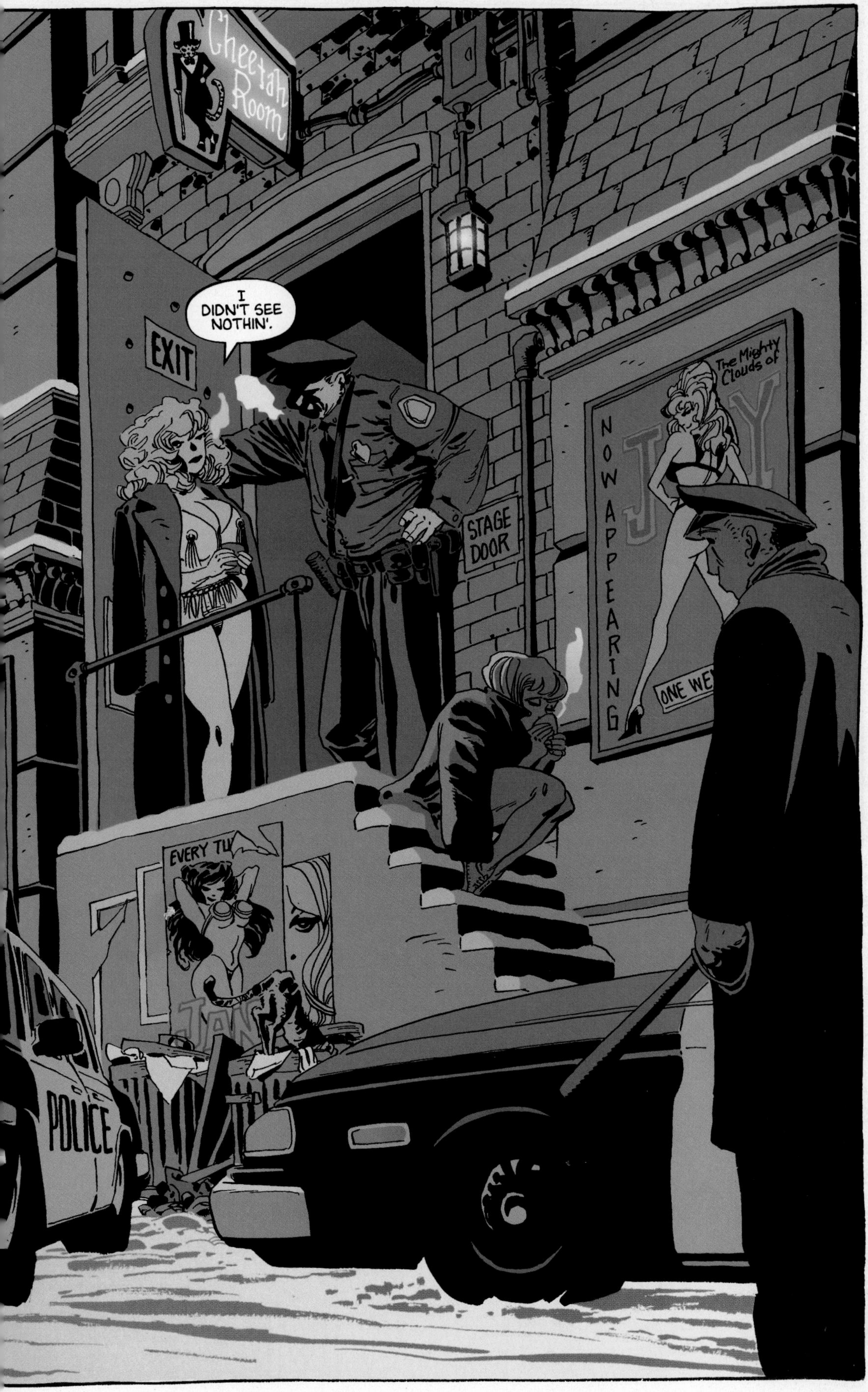
Cheetah Room
I DIDN'T SEE NOTHIN'.
EXIT
STAGE DOOR
The Mighty Clouds of
JOY
NOW APPEARING
ONE WE
EVERY TU
POLICE

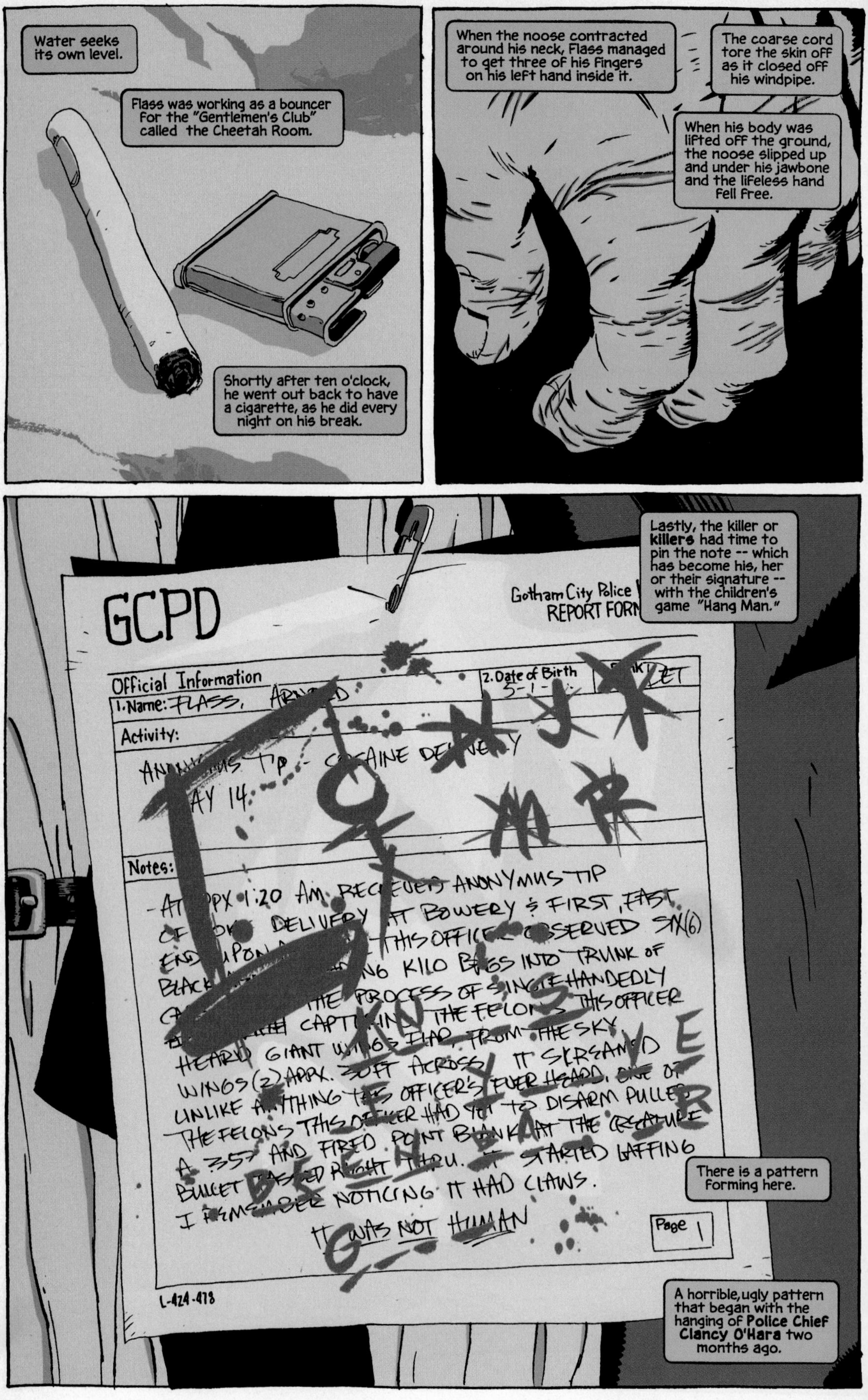

Water seeks its own level.
Flass was working as a bouncer for the "Gentlemen's Club" called the Cheetah Room.
Shortly after ten o'clock, he went out back to have a cigarette, as he did every night on his break.
When the noose contracted around his neck, Flass managed to get three of his fingers on his left hand inside it.
The coarse cord tore the skin off as it closed off his windpipe.
When his body was lifted off the ground, the noose slipped up and under his jawbone and the lifeless hand fell free.
Lastly, the killer or killers had time to pin the note -- which has become his, her or their signature -- with the children's game "Hang Man."
GCPD
Gotham City Police
REPORT FORM
Official Information
1. Name: FLASS,
2. Date of Birth
Activity:
Notes:
IT WAS NOT HUMAN
Page 1
L-424-478
There is a pattern forming here.
A horrible, ugly pattern that began with the hanging of Police Chief Clancy O'Hara two months ago.

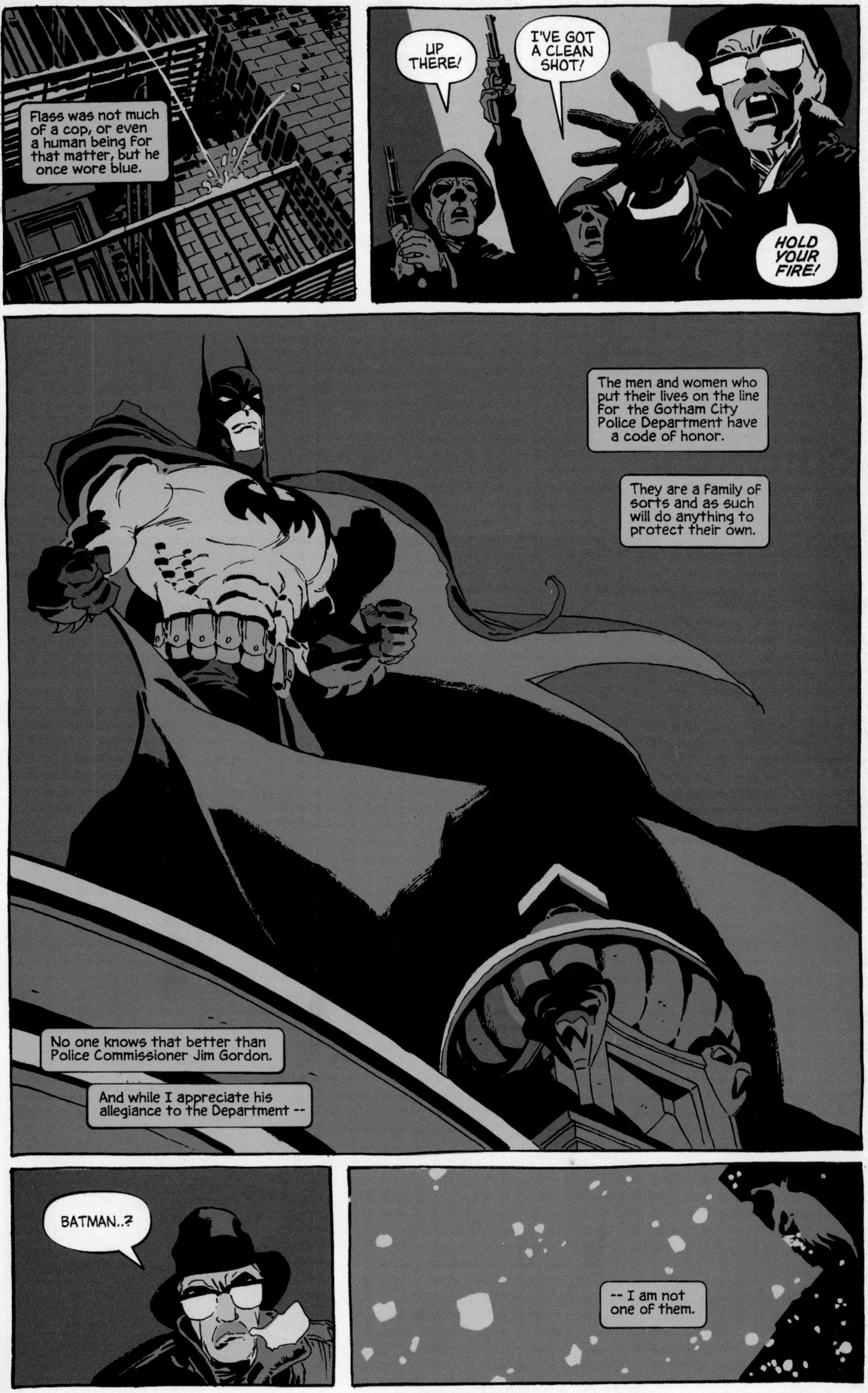
Flass was not much of a cop, or even a human being for that matter, but he once wore blue.
UP THERE!
I'VE GOT A CLEAN SHOT!
HOLD YOUR FIRE!
The men and women who put their lives on the line for the Gotham City Police Department have a code of honor.
They are a family of sorts and as such will do anything to protect their own.
No one knows that better than Police Commissioner Jim Gordon.
And while I appreciate his allegiance to the Department --
BATMAN..?
-- I am not one of them.

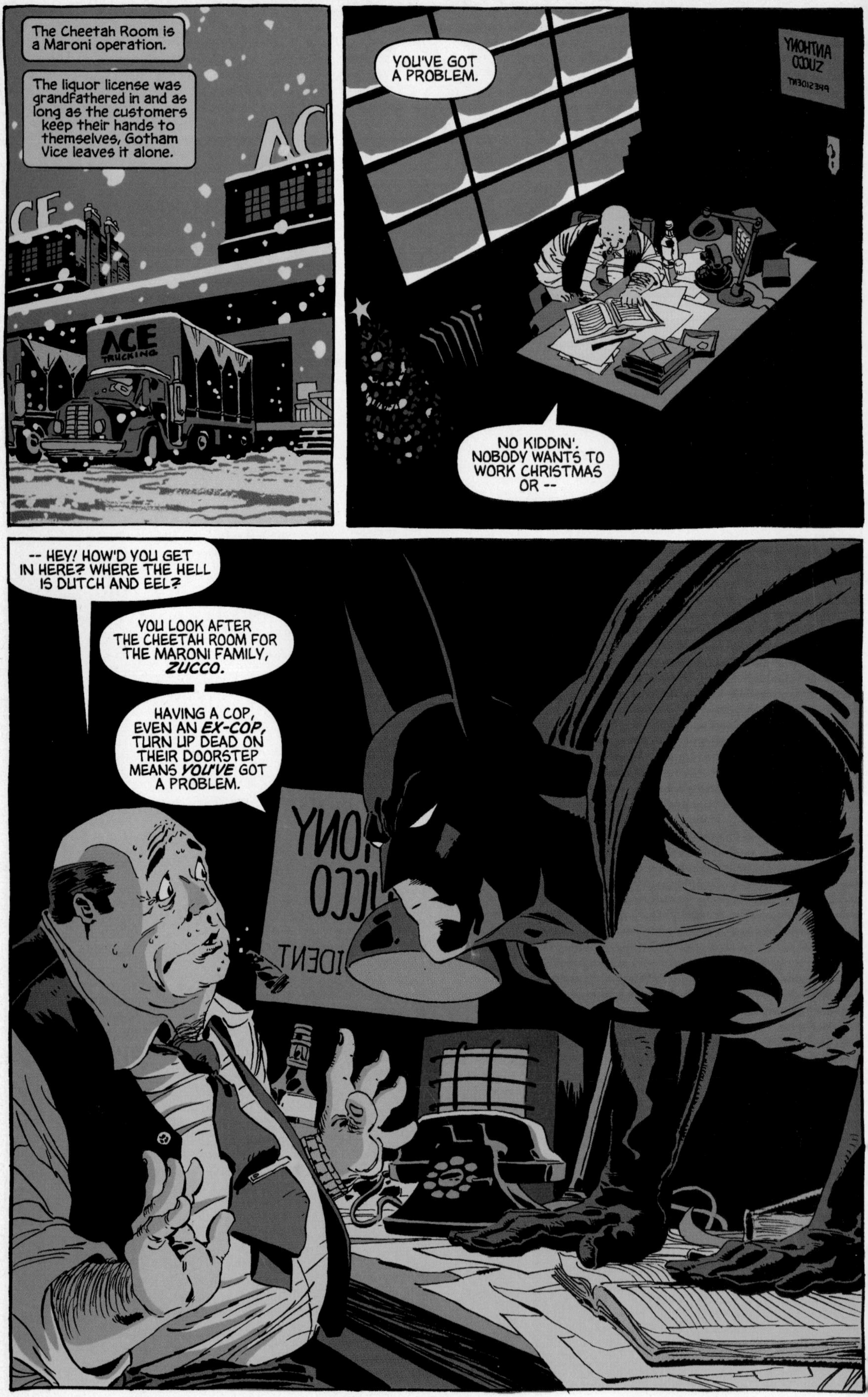

The Cheetah Room is a Maroni operation.
The liquor license was grandfathered in and as long as the customers keep their hands to themselves, Gotham Vice leaves it alone.
ACE TRUCKING
YOU'VE GOT A PROBLEM.
NO KIDDIN'. NOBODY WANTS TO WORK CHRISTMAS OR --
-- HEY! HOW'D YOU GET IN HERE? WHERE THE HELL IS DUTCH AND EEL?
YOU LOOK AFTER THE CHEETAH ROOM FOR THE MARONI FAMILY, ZUCCO.
HAVING A COP, EVEN AN EX-COP, TURN UP DEAD ON THEIR DOORSTEP MEANS YOU'VE GOT A PROBLEM.

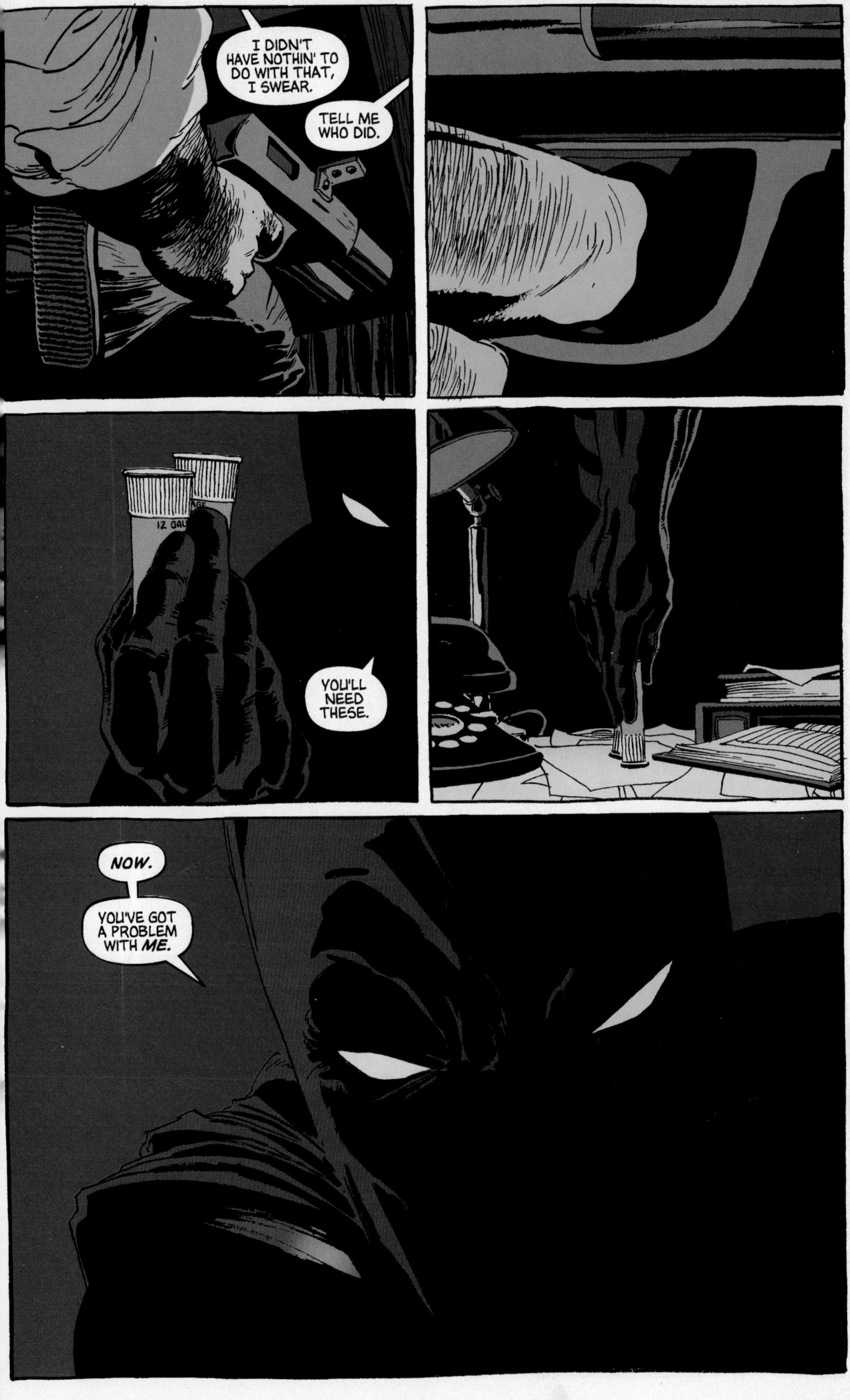
I DIDN'T HAVE NOTHIN' TO DO WITH THAT, I SWEAR.
TELL ME WHO DID.
12 GAUGE
YOU'LL NEED THESE.
NOW.
YOU'VE GOT A PROBLEM WITH *ME*.

YOU DIDN'T COME BY AND COLLECT THE RECEIPTS TONIGHT.

WHY?

I... I WAS SUPPOSED TO MEET A GUY IN THE ALLEY OUT BACK AT AROUND TEN. ABOUT SOME TRANSPORTATION STUFF.

I GET THERE A LITTLE LATE AND THERE'S COPS ALL OVER THE PLACE. SO, I COME BACK HERE. I SWEAR.

M-MY HEAD'S GONNA SPLIT OPEN!

A NAME, ZUCCO.

A NAME.

HE -- HE'S ONE OF YOU GUYS!

ONE OF *WHAT* "GUYS"?

A FREAK! LIKE YOU WITH A MASK AND ALL THAT!

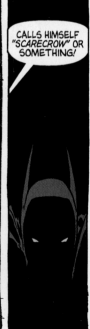

CALLS HIMSELF "SCARECROW" OR SOMETHING!

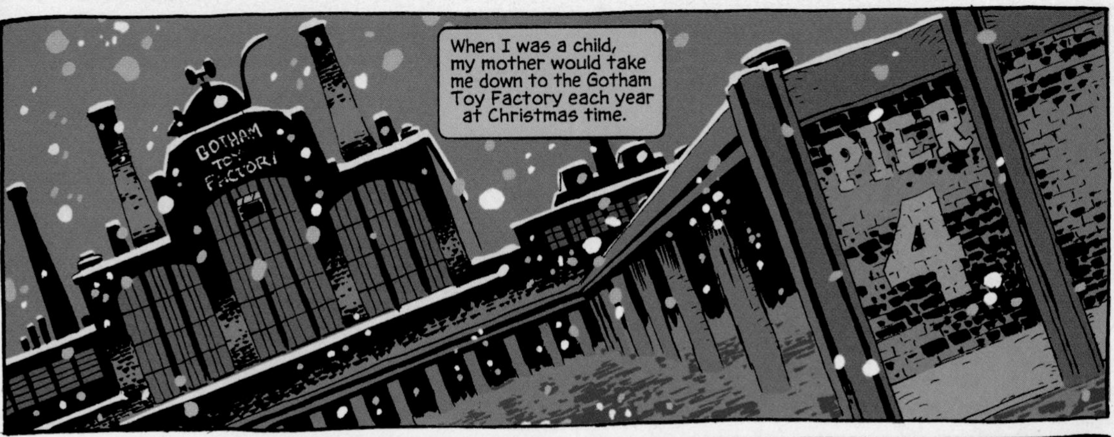
When I was a child, my mother would take me down to the Gotham Toy Factory each year at Christmas time.
GOTHAM TOY FACTORY
PIER 4

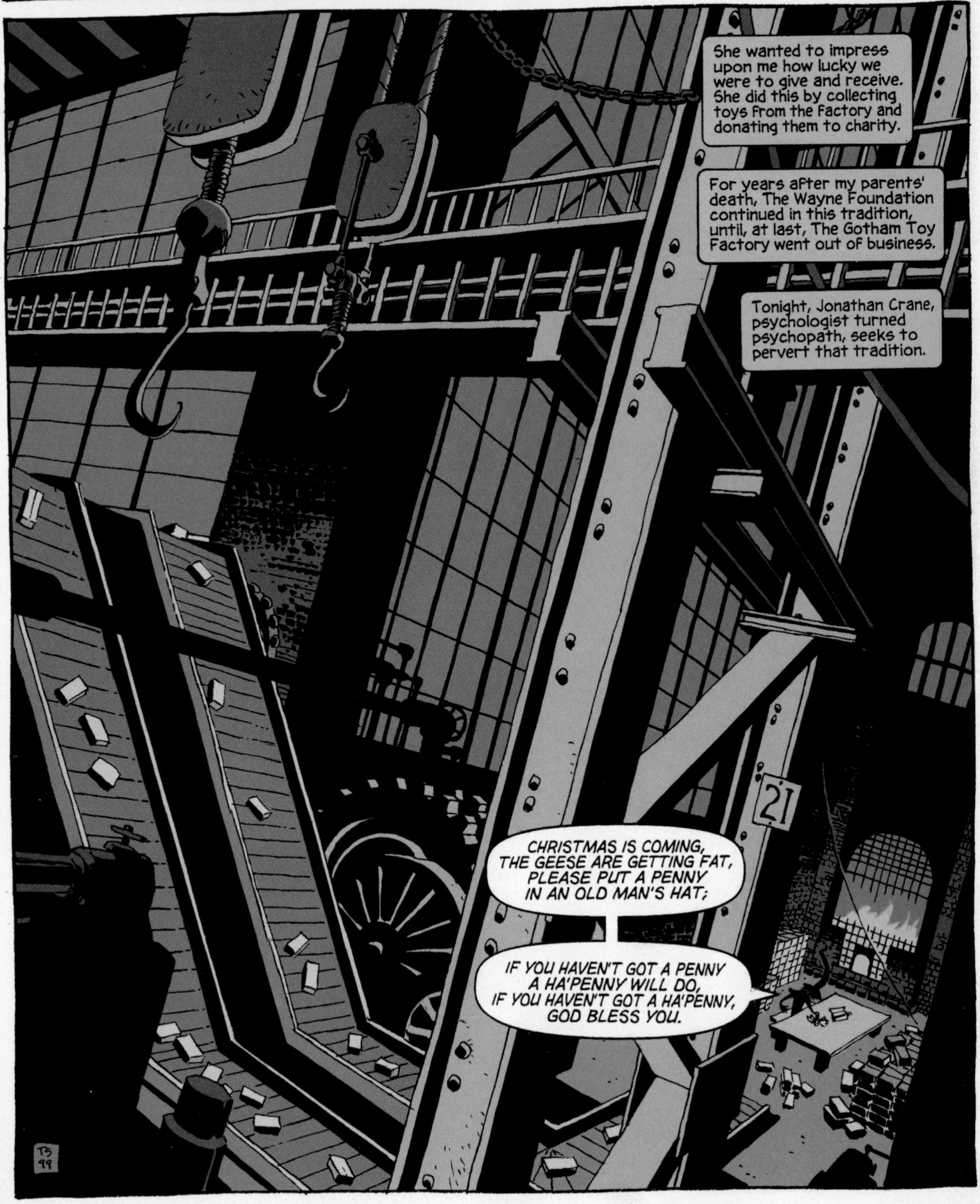
She wanted to impress upon me how lucky we were to give and receive. She did this by collecting toys from the Factory and donating them to charity.
For years after my parents' death, The Wayne Foundation continued in this tradition, until, at last, The Gotham Toy Factory went out of business.
Tonight, Jonathan Crane, psychologist turned psychopath, seeks to pervert that tradition.
21
CHRISTMAS IS COMING, THE GEESE ARE GETTING FAT, PLEASE PUT A PENNY IN AN OLD MAN'S HAT;
IF YOU HAVEN'T GOT A PENNY A HA'PENNY WILL DO, IF YOU HAVEN'T GOT A HA'PENNY, GOD BLESS YOU.
TS 99

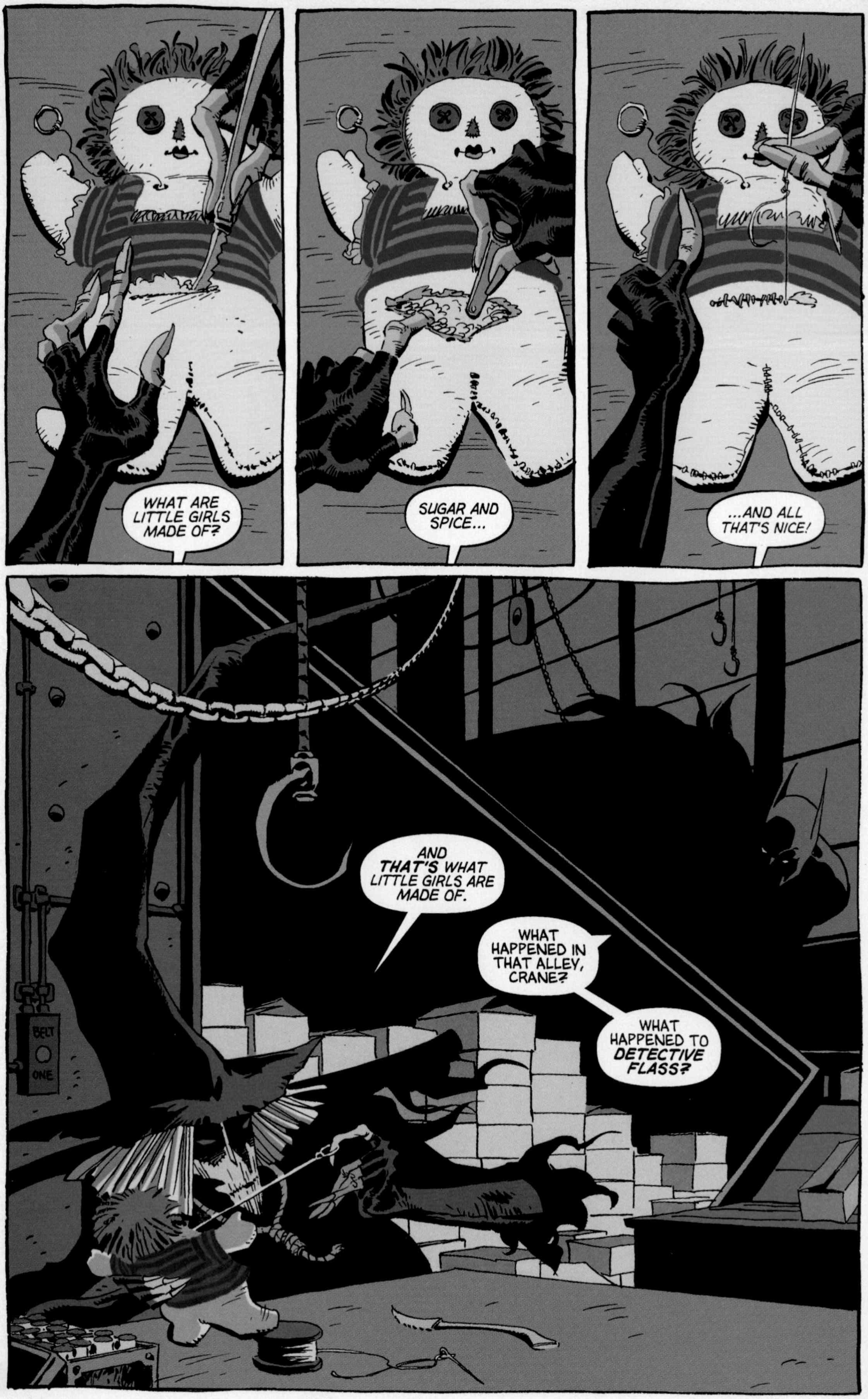
WHAT ARE LITTLE GIRLS MADE OF?
SUGAR AND SPICE...
...AND ALL THAT'S NICE!
AND THAT'S WHAT LITTLE GIRLS ARE MADE OF.
WHAT HAPPENED IN THAT ALLEY, CRANE?
WHAT HAPPENED TO DETECTIVE FLASS?
BELT ONE

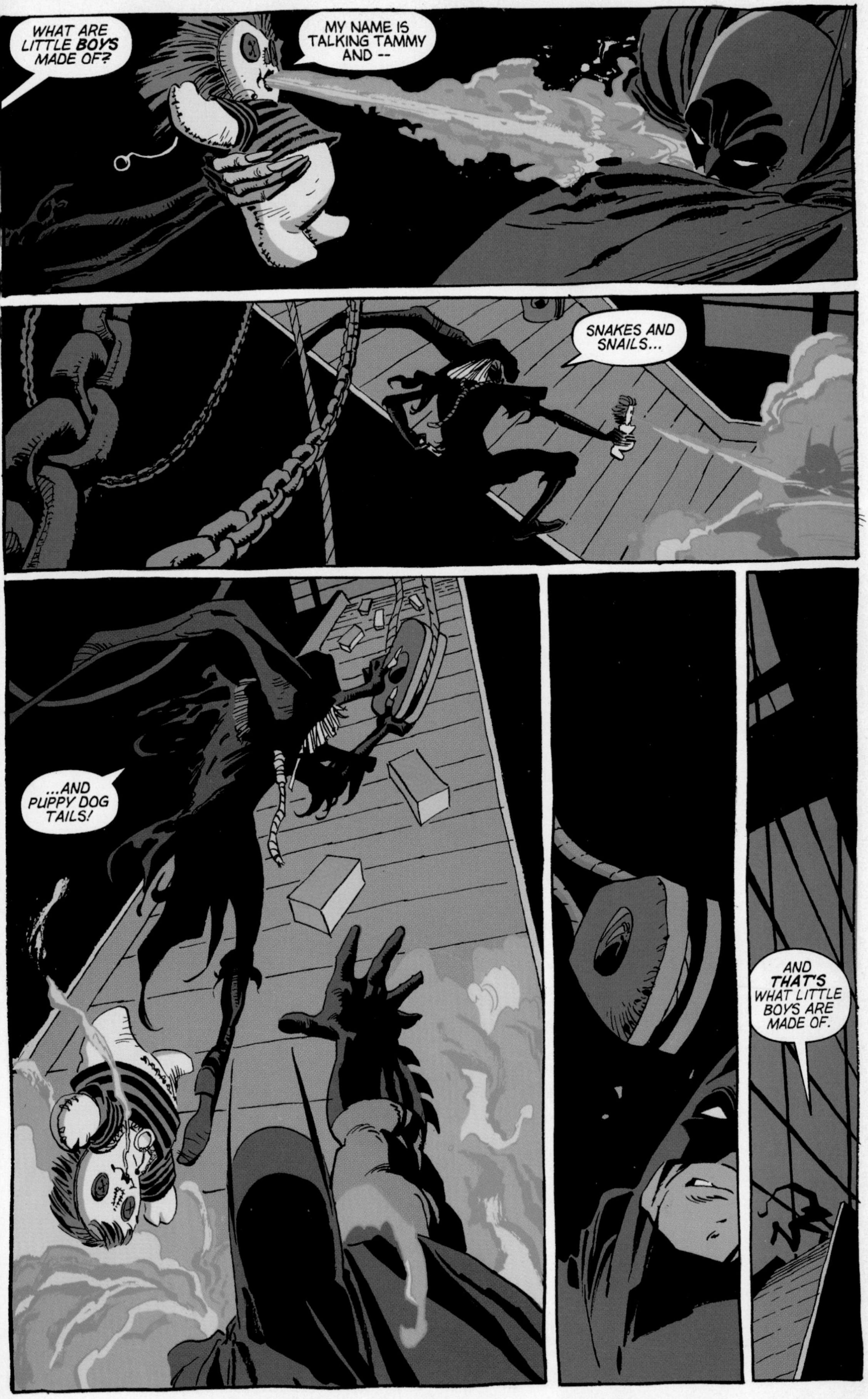
WHAT ARE LITTLE BOYS MADE OF?
MY NAME IS TALKING TAMMY AND --
SNAKES AND SNAILS...
...AND PUPPY DOG TAILS!
AND THAT'S WHAT LITTLE BOYS ARE MADE OF.

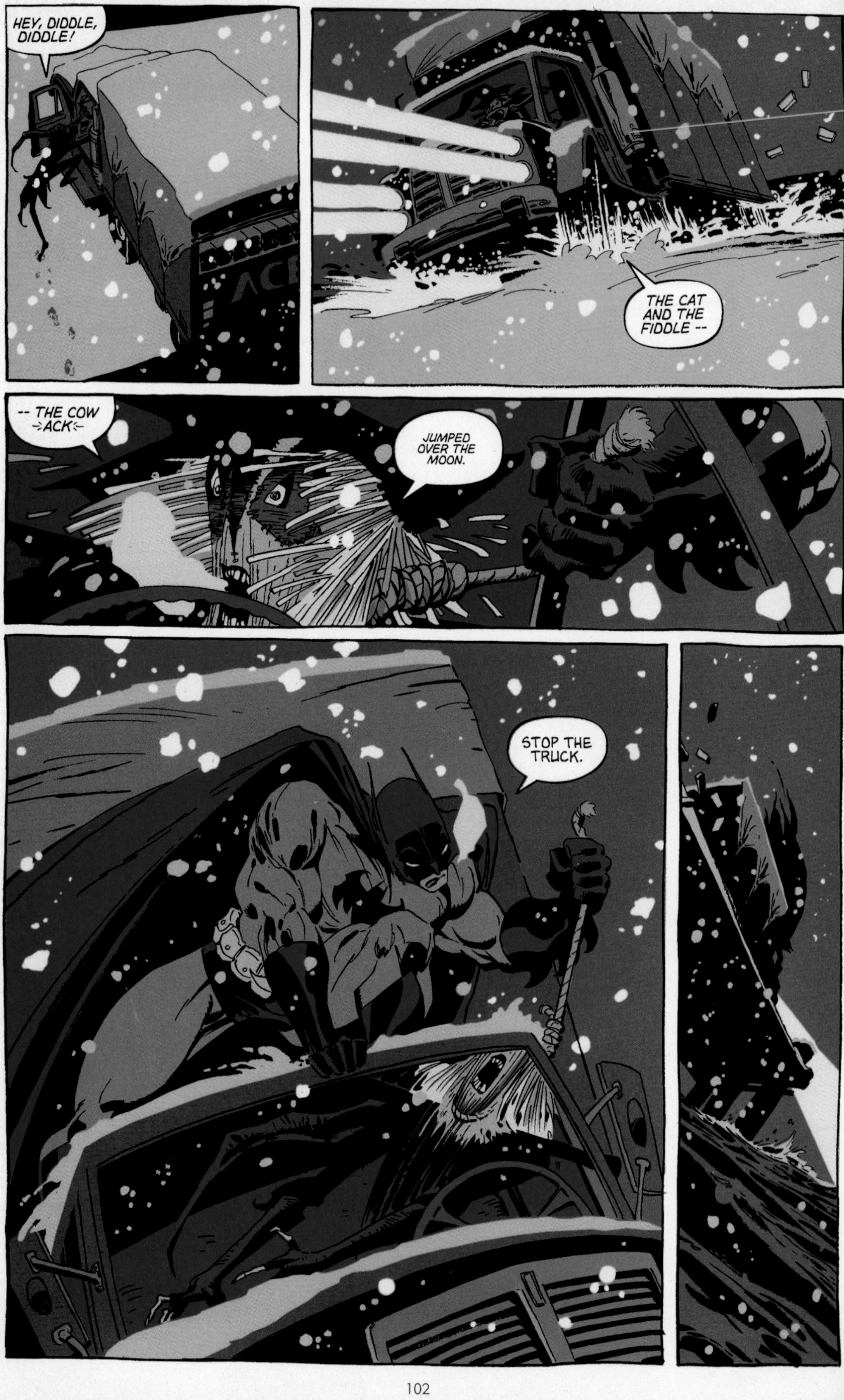
HEY, DIDDLE, DIDDLE!
ACE
THE CAT AND THE FIDDLE --
-- THE COW ->ACK<-
JUMPED OVER THE MOON.
STOP THE TRUCK.

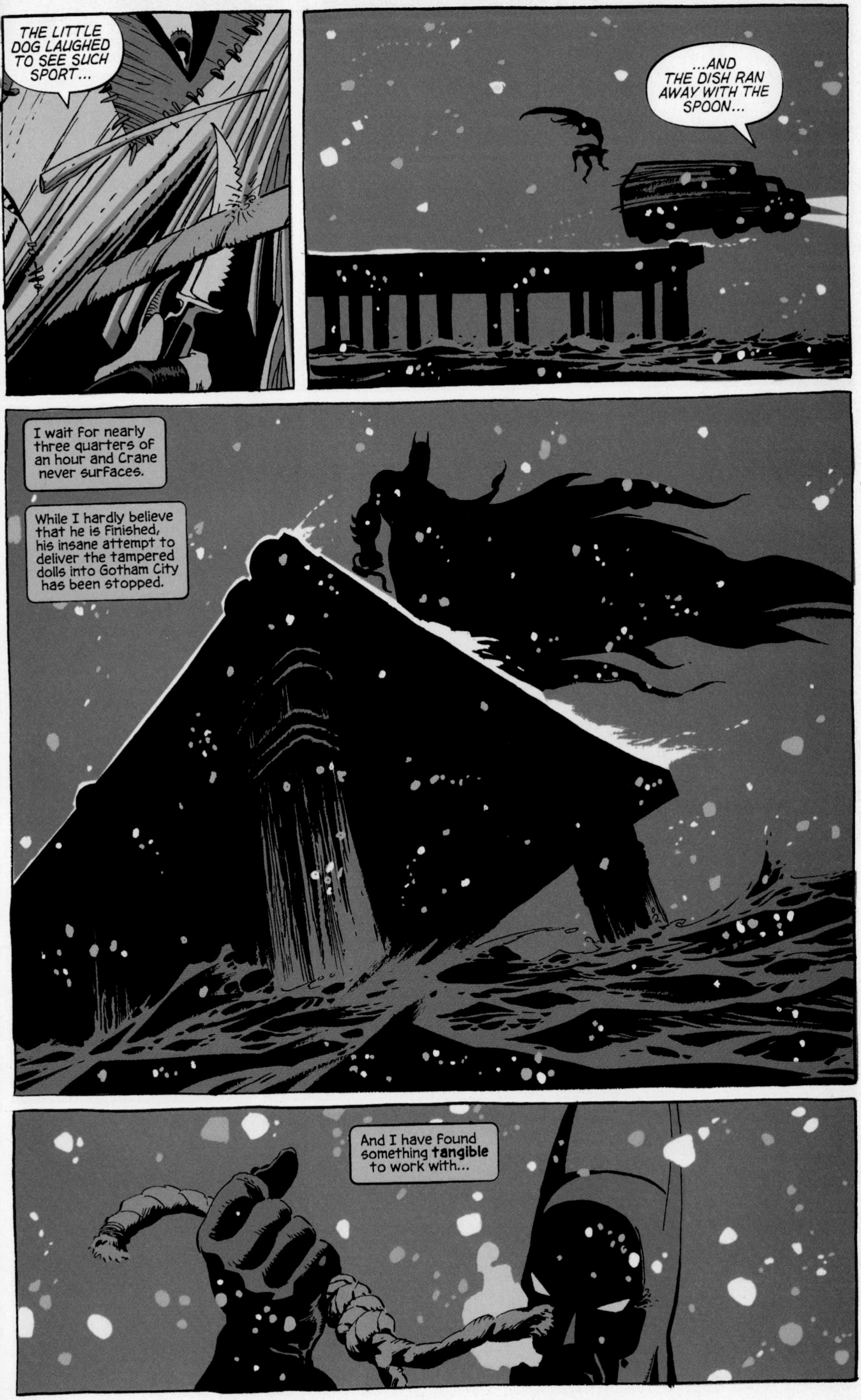
THE LITTLE DOG LAUGHED TO SEE SUCH SPORT...
...AND THE DISH RAN AWAY WITH THE SPOON...
I wait for nearly three quarters of an hour and Crane never surfaces.
While I hardly believe that he is finished, his insane attempt to deliver the tampered dolls into Gotham City has been stopped.
And I have found something **tangible** to work with...

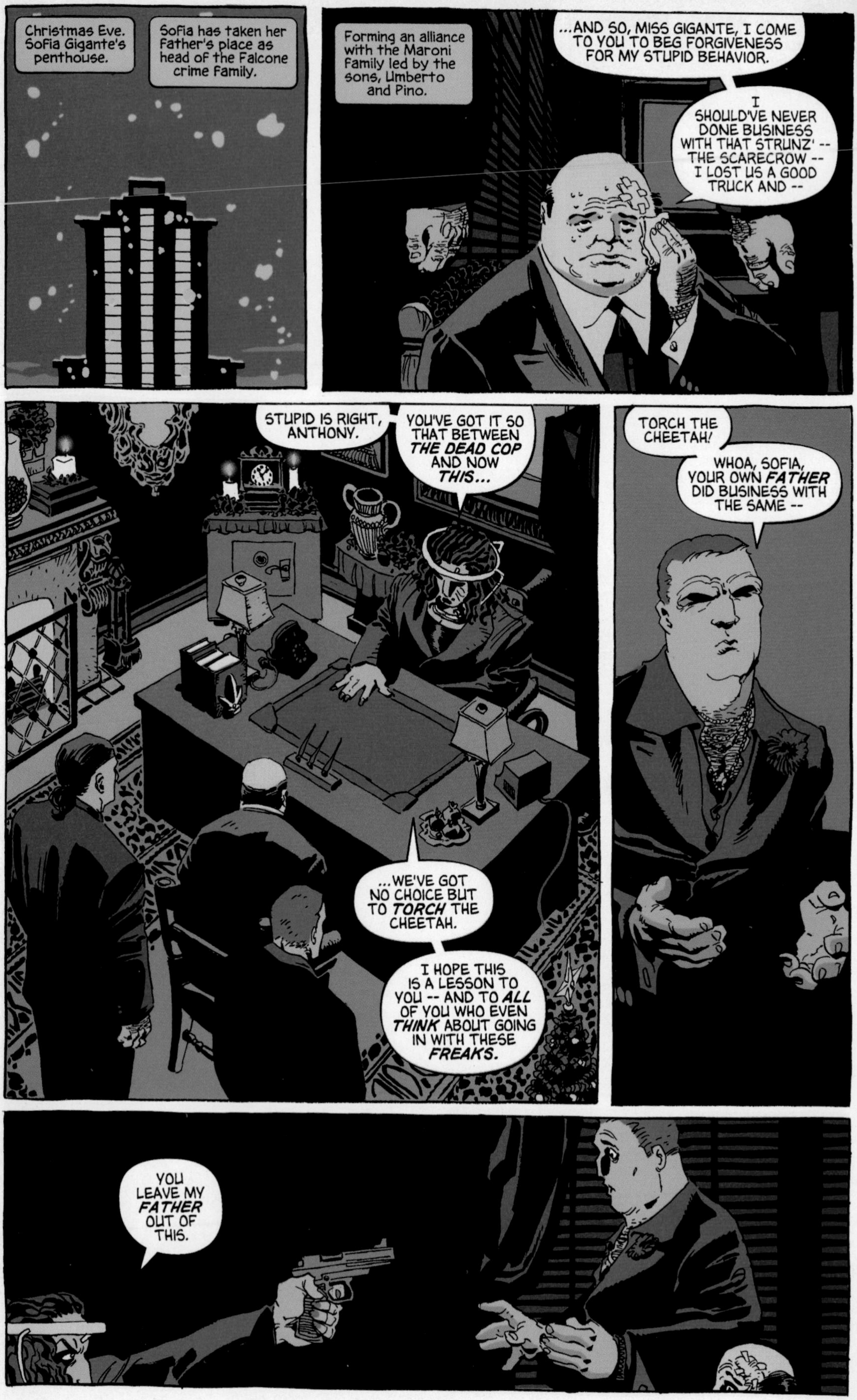
Christmas Eve. Sofia Gigante's penthouse.
Sofia has taken her father's place as head of the Falcone crime family.
Forming an alliance with the Maroni family led by the sons, Umberto and Pino.
...AND SO, MISS GIGANTE, I COME TO YOU TO BEG FORGIVENESS FOR MY STUPID BEHAVIOR.
I SHOULD'VE NEVER DONE BUSINESS WITH THAT STRUNZ' -- THE SCARECROW -- I LOST US A GOOD TRUCK AND --
STUPID IS RIGHT, ANTHONY.
YOU'VE GOT IT SO THAT BETWEEN THE DEAD COP AND NOW THIS...
...WE'VE GOT NO CHOICE BUT TO TORCH THE CHEETAH.
I HOPE THIS IS A LESSON TO YOU -- AND TO ALL OF YOU WHO EVEN THINK ABOUT GOING IN WITH THESE FREAKS.
TORCH THE CHEETAH!
WHOA, SOFIA, YOUR OWN FATHER DID BUSINESS WITH THE SAME --
YOU LEAVE MY FATHER OUT OF THIS.

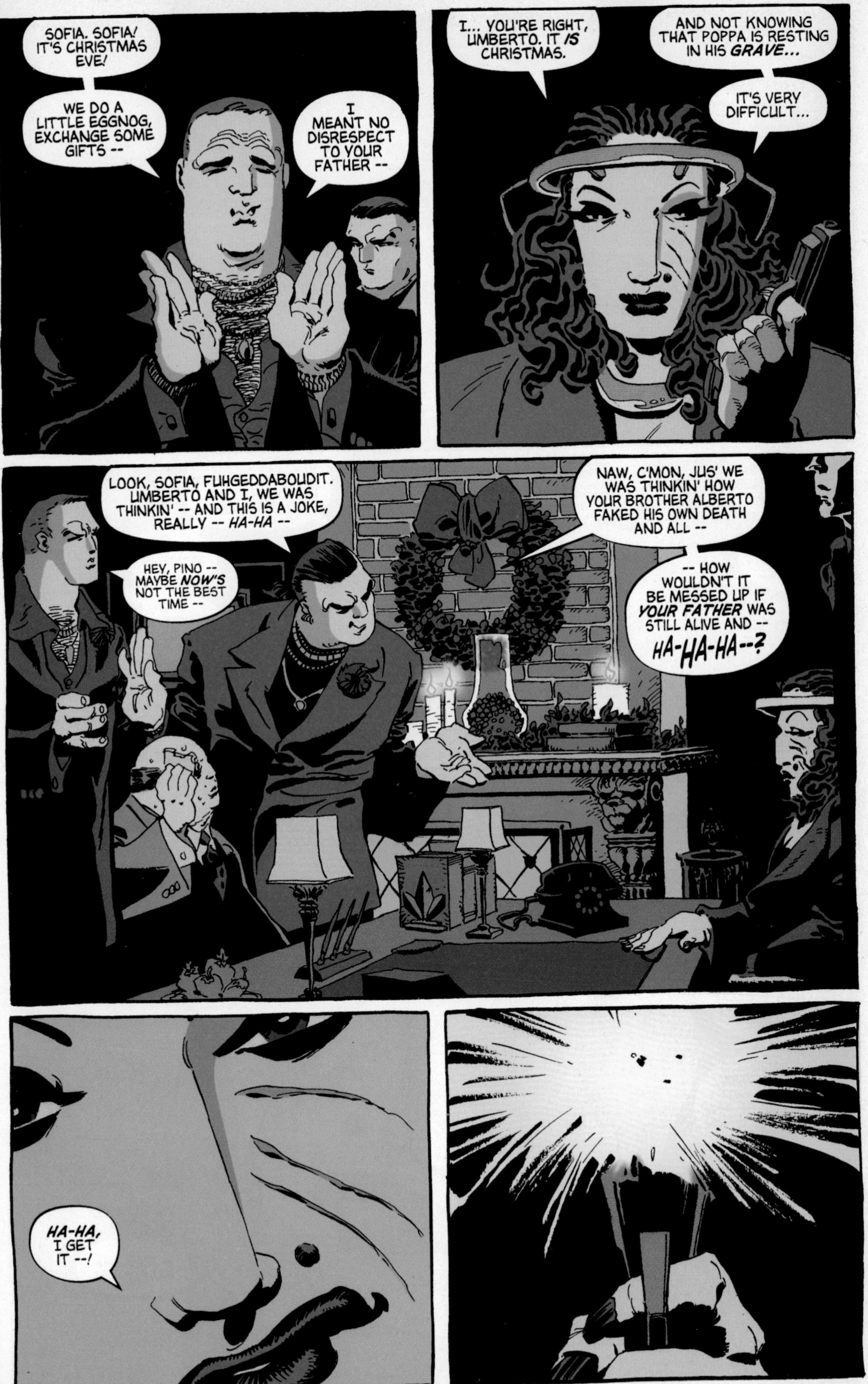
SOFIA. SOFIA! IT'S CHRISTMAS EVE!
WE DO A LITTLE EGGNOG, EXCHANGE SOME GIFTS --
I MEANT NO DISRESPECT TO YOUR FATHER --
I... YOU'RE RIGHT, UMBERTO. IT *IS* CHRISTMAS.
AND NOT KNOWING THAT POPPA IS RESTING IN HIS *GRAVE...*
IT'S VERY DIFFICULT...
LOOK, SOFIA, FUHGEDDABOUDIT. UMBERTO AND I, WE WAS THINKIN' -- AND THIS IS A JOKE, REALLY -- *HA-HA* --
HEY, PINO -- MAYBE *NOW'S* NOT THE BEST TIME --
NAW, C'MON, JUS' WE WAS THINKIN' HOW YOUR BROTHER ALBERTO FAKED HIS OWN DEATH AND ALL --
-- HOW WOULDN'T IT BE MESSED UP IF *YOUR FATHER* WAS STILL ALIVE AND --
HA-HA-HA--?
HA-HA, I GET IT --!

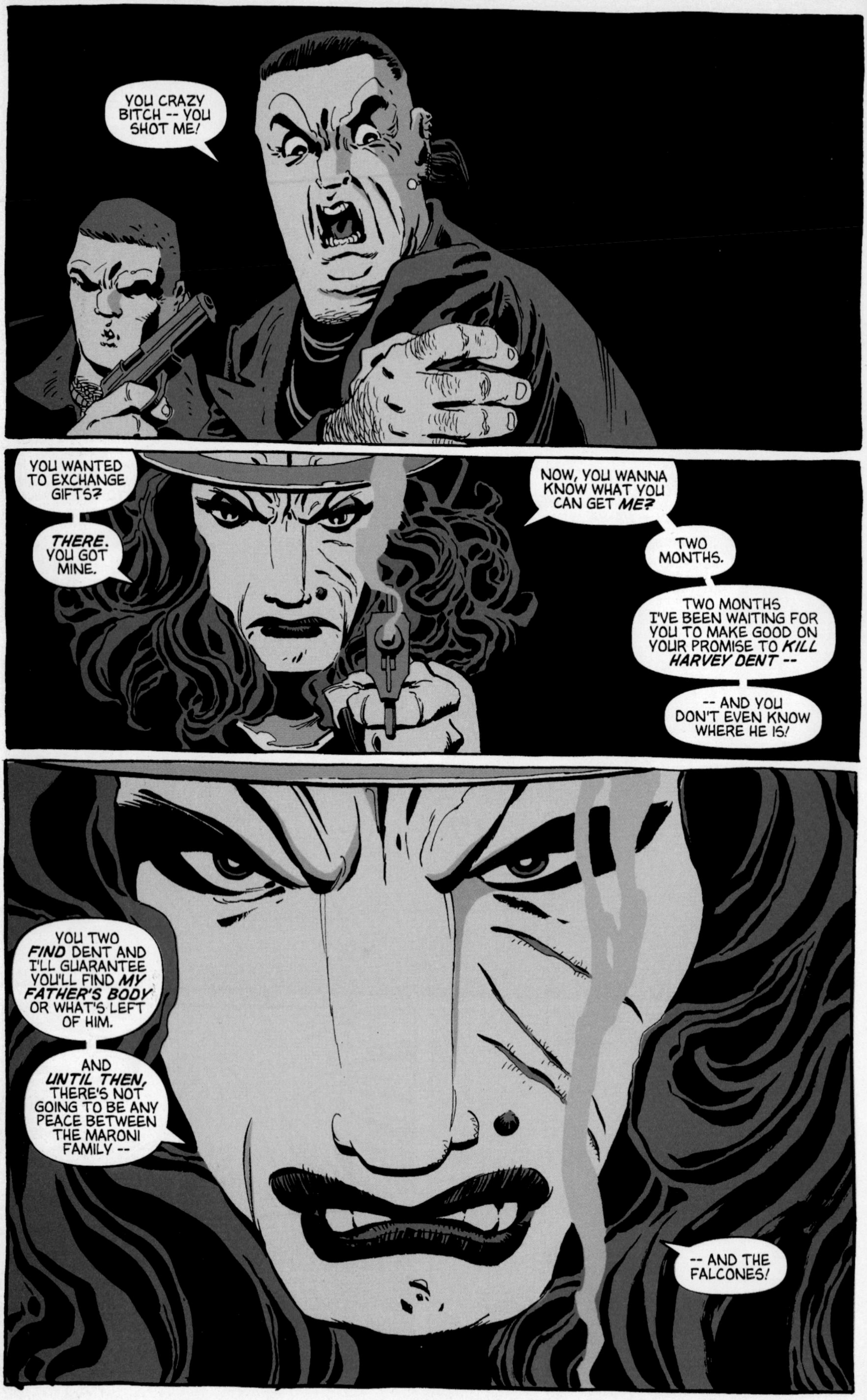
YOU CRAZY BITCH -- YOU SHOT ME!
YOU WANTED TO EXCHANGE GIFTS?
THERE. YOU GOT MINE.
NOW, YOU WANNA KNOW WHAT YOU CAN GET *ME?*
TWO MONTHS.
TWO MONTHS I'VE BEEN WAITING FOR YOU TO MAKE GOOD ON YOUR PROMISE TO *KILL HARVEY DENT --*
-- AND YOU DON'T EVEN KNOW WHERE HE IS!
YOU TWO *FIND* DENT AND I'LL GUARANTEE YOU'LL FIND *MY FATHER'S BODY* OR WHAT'S LEFT OF HIM.
AND *UNTIL THEN,* THERE'S NOT GOING TO BE ANY PEACE BETWEEN THE MARONI FAMILY --
-- AND THE FALCONES!

Wayne Manor.

Hmmph.

AM I *JUST* WASTING MY TIME, ALFRED?

MISS..?

THIS IS ONE GIRL WHO ISN'T USED TO BEING *STOOD UP* ON CHRISTMAS EVE.

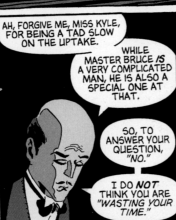

AH, FORGIVE ME, MISS KYLE, FOR BEING A TAD SLOW ON THE UPTAKE.

WHILE MASTER BRUCE *IS* A VERY COMPLICATED MAN, HE IS ALSO A SPECIAL ONE AT THAT.

SO, TO ANSWER YOUR QUESTION, "NO."

I DO *NOT* THINK YOU ARE "WASTING YOUR TIME."

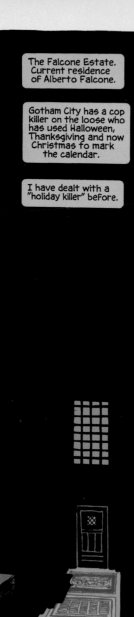

The Falcone Estate. Current residence of Alberto Falcone.

Gotham City has a cop killer on the loose who has used Halloween, Thanksgiving and now Christmas to mark the calendar.

I have dealt with a "holiday killer" before.

I'M LOOKING FOR A *MURDERER.*

HIS KILLINGS FOLLOW A PATTERN.

JUST LIKE YOURS DID.

"HOLIDAY."

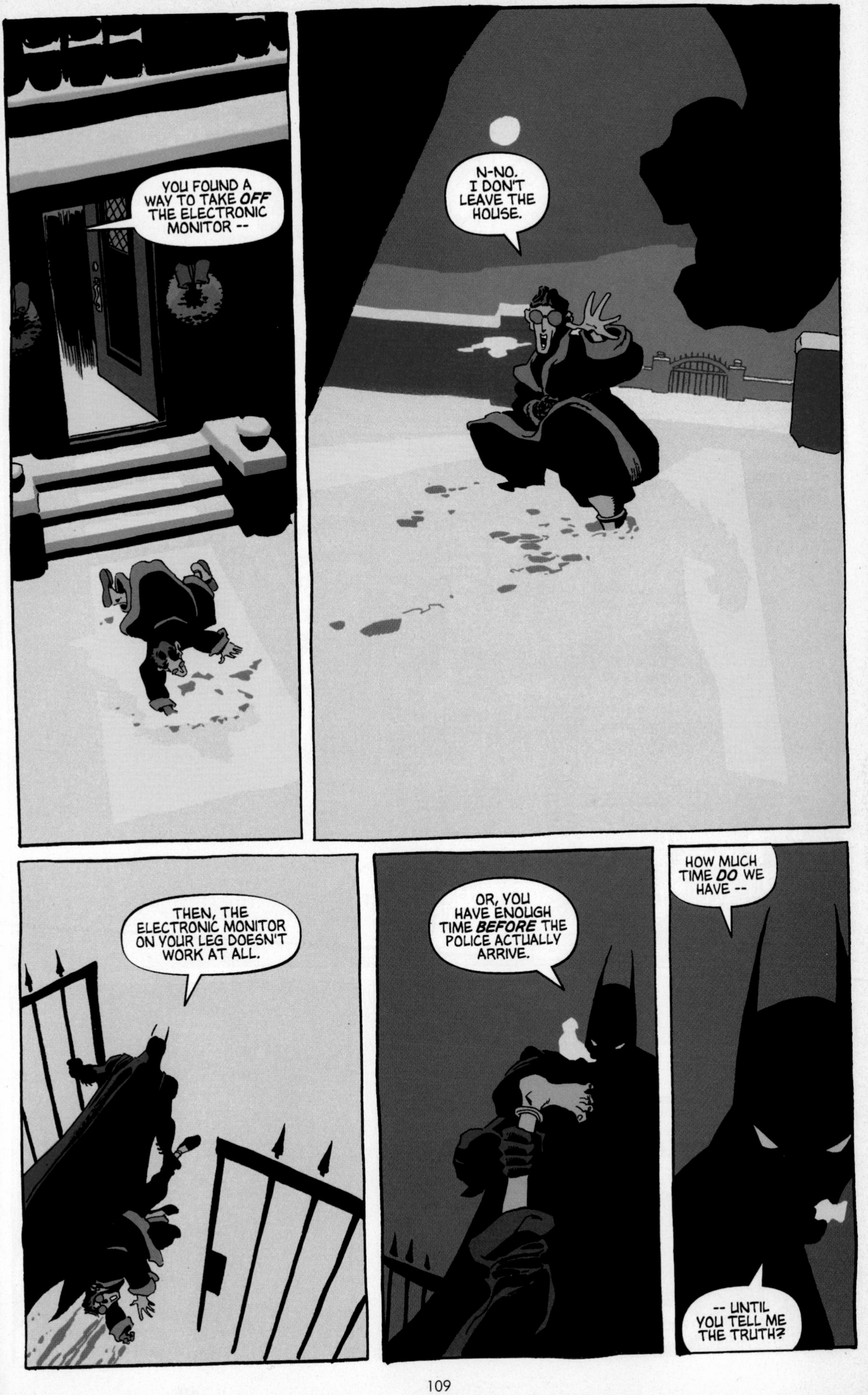
YOU FOUND A WAY TO TAKE OFF THE ELECTRONIC MONITOR --
N-NO. I DON'T LEAVE THE HOUSE.
THEN, THE ELECTRONIC MONITOR ON YOUR LEG DOESN'T WORK AT ALL.
OR, YOU HAVE ENOUGH TIME BEFORE THE POLICE ACTUALLY ARRIVE.
HOW MUCH TIME DO WE HAVE --
-- UNTIL YOU TELL ME THE TRUTH?

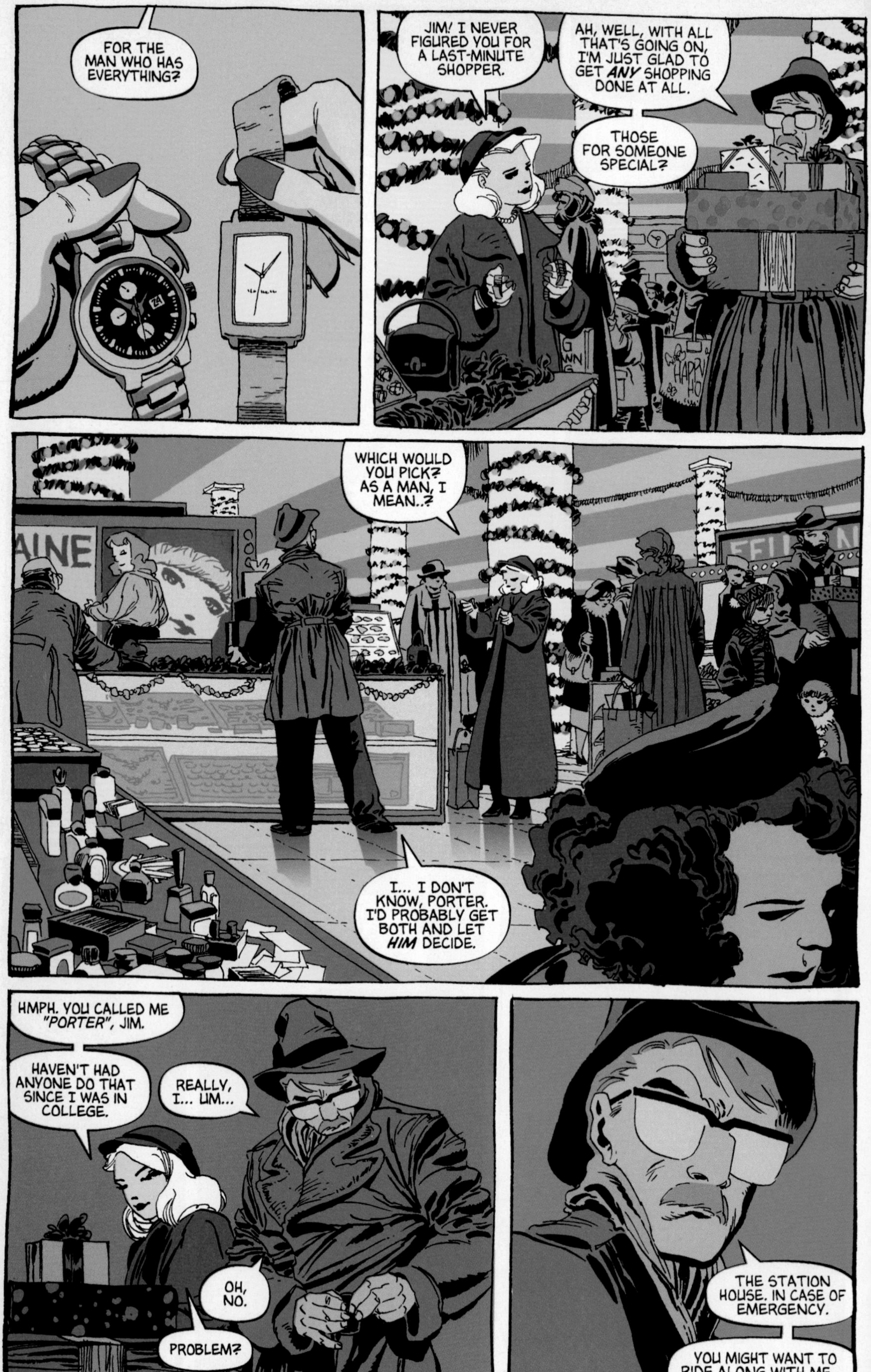
FOR THE MAN WHO HAS EVERYTHING?
JIM! I NEVER FIGURED YOU FOR A LAST-MINUTE SHOPPER.
AH, WELL, WITH ALL THAT'S GOING ON, I'M JUST GLAD TO GET ANY SHOPPING DONE AT ALL.
THOSE FOR SOMEONE SPECIAL?
WHICH WOULD YOU PICK? AS A MAN, I MEAN..?
I... I DON'T KNOW, PORTER. I'D PROBABLY GET BOTH AND LET HIM DECIDE.
HMPH. YOU CALLED ME "PORTER", JIM.
HAVEN'T HAD ANYONE DO THAT SINCE I WAS IN COLLEGE.
REALLY, I... UM...
OH, NO.
PROBLEM?
THE STATION HOUSE. IN CASE OF EMERGENCY.
YOU MIGHT WANT TO RIDE ALONG WITH ME...

THE WHOLE... INCIDENT IS VERY DISTURBING.

WE'D LIKE TO SEE YOUR BROTHER, MR. FALCONE.

I'D RATHER YOU DIDN'T.

I JUST GOT HIM TO BED AND GIVEN HIM SOMETHING TO HELP HIM SLEEP.

AND... HE'S CLAIMING *BATMAN* CAME HERE AND ATTACKED HIM?

I'M AFRAID SO. SOMETHING TO DO WITH THE... *"HANG MAN"* KILLINGS...

YOU'RE TAKING THIS PRETTY LIGHTLY.

I'M NOT SURE *WHAT* TO BELIEVE.

AS MY BROTHER'S GUARDIAN, I'M CONCERNED, OF COURSE --

-- BUT, HE TOLD ME --

HOW SHOULD I SAY THIS --?

TRY *HONESTLY.* THAT'S ALWAYS A GOOD START.

JIM...

YES, WELL, MY BROTHER TOLD ME HE'S BEEN *HEARING VOICES* IN THE HOUSE.

VOICES..?

HE CLAIMS THE HOUSE IS... *HAUNTED* BY MY LATE FATHER.

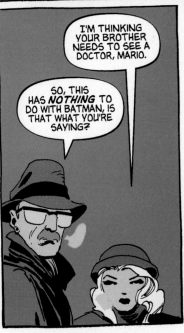

I'M THINKING YOUR BROTHER NEEDS TO SEE A DOCTOR, MARIO.

SO, THIS HAS *NOTHING* TO DO WITH BATMAN, IS THAT WHAT YOU'RE SAYING?

I'M SAYING I FIND THE ENTIRE INCIDENT DISTURBING AND IT BEARS INVESTIGATION.

BUT... WHAT I *DO* KNOW IS, IF BATMAN WAS INVOLVED IN *ANY* WAY --

-- I CAN'T BE HELD RESPONSIBLE FOR HOW *MY SISTER SOFIA* WILL REACT...

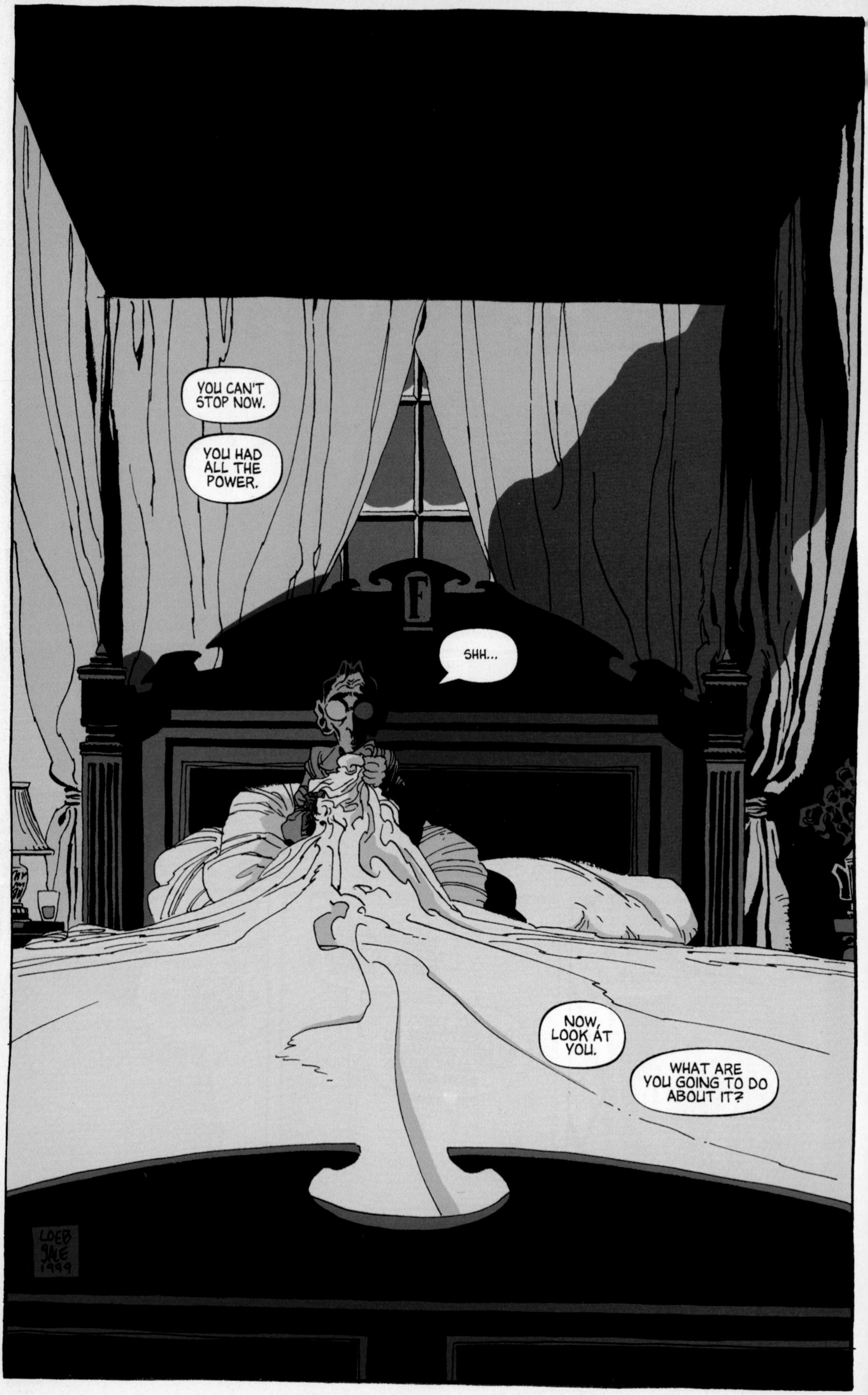
YOU CAN'T STOP NOW.
YOU HAD ALL THE POWER.
SHH...
NOW, LOOK AT YOU.
WHAT ARE YOU GOING TO DO ABOUT IT?
LOEB SALE 1999

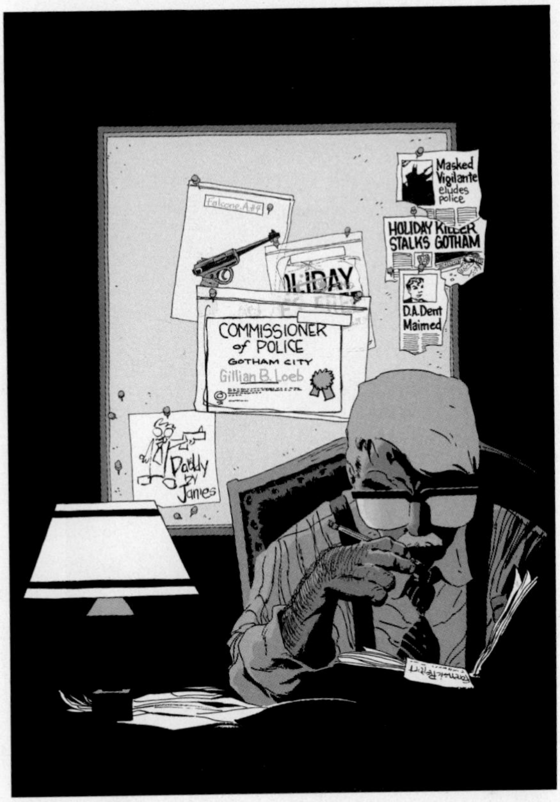
Masked Vigilante eludes police
HOLIDAY KILLER STALKS GOTHAM
D.A. Dent Maimed
COMMISSIONER of POLICE
GOTHAM CITY
Gillian B. Loeb
Daddy by James

4

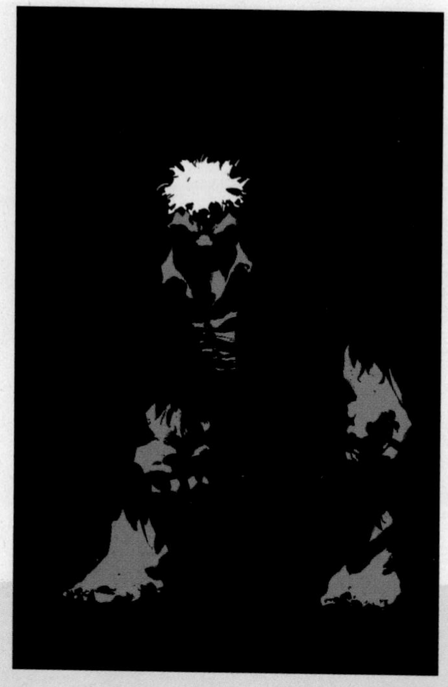

L O S T

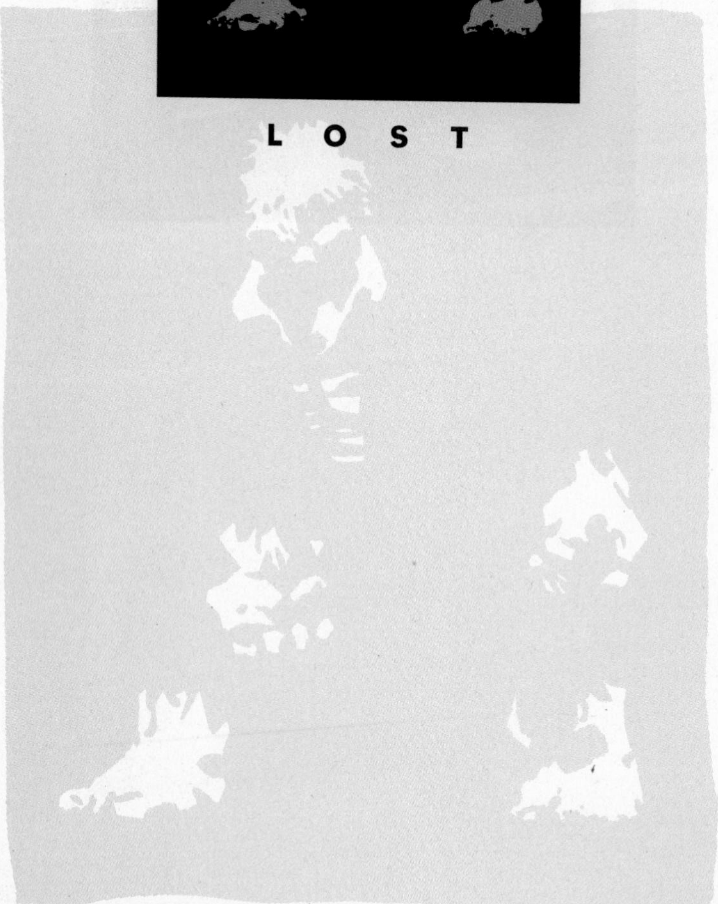

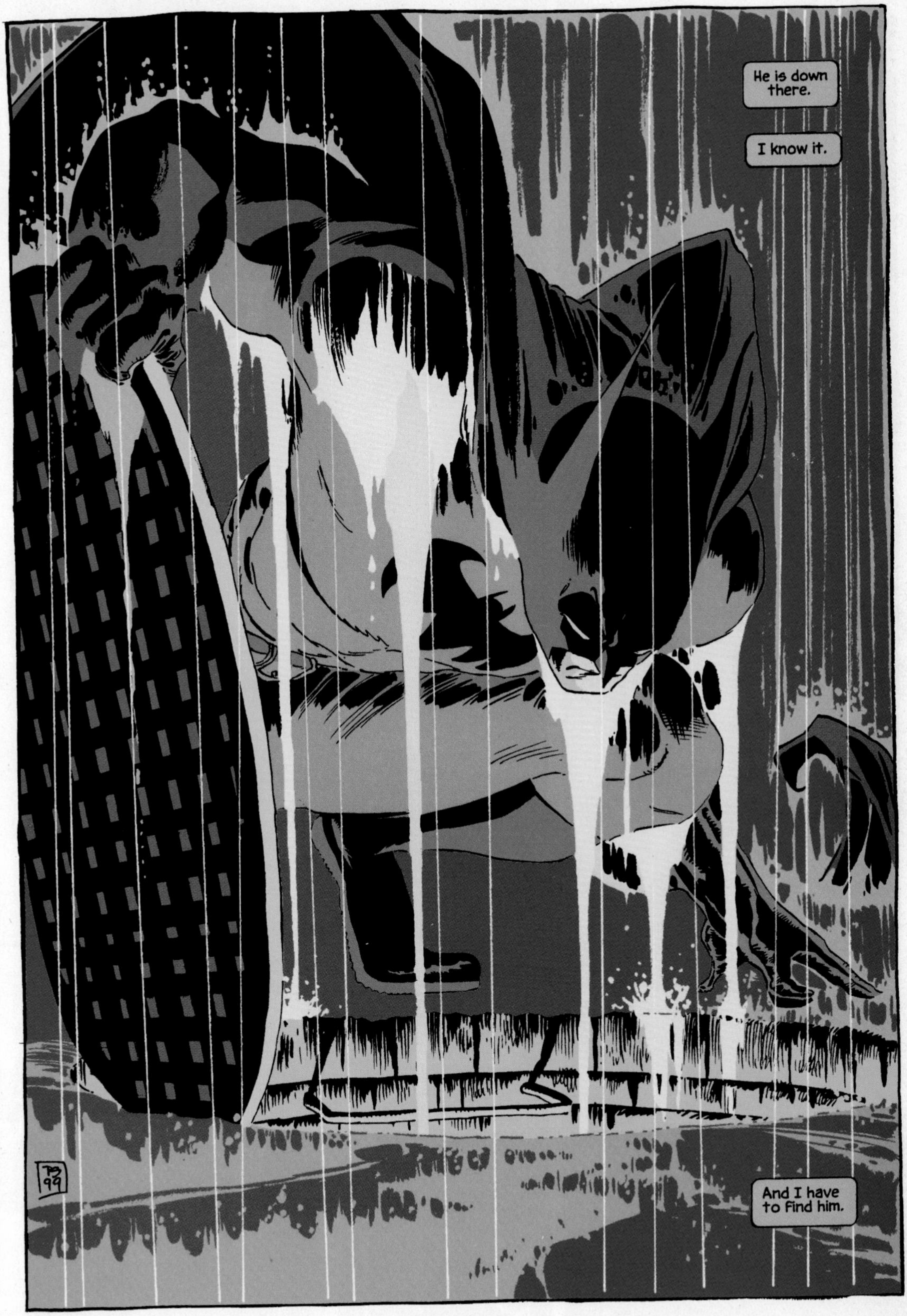
He is down there.
I know it.
And I have to find him.

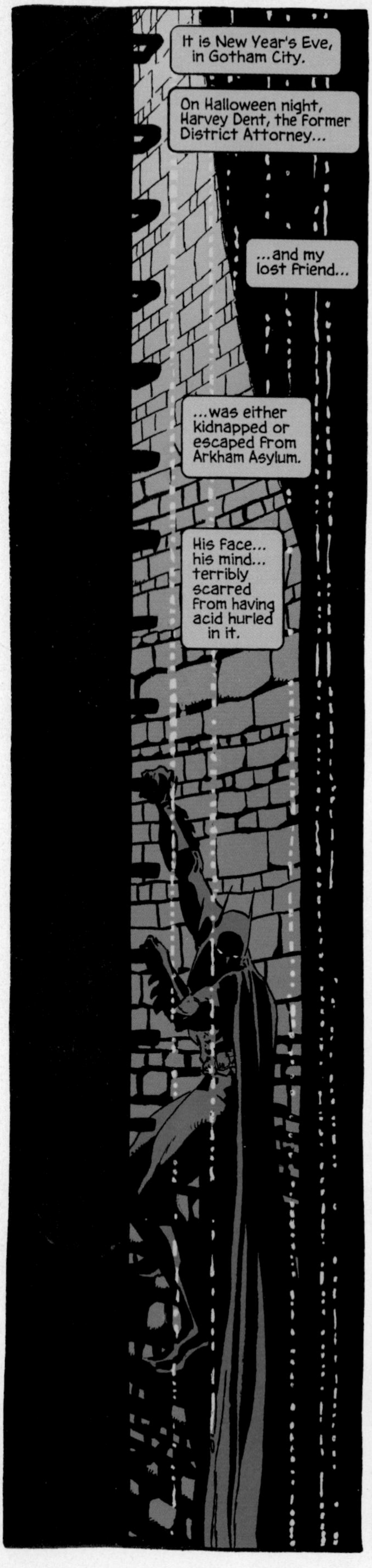
It is New Year's Eve, in Gotham City.
On Halloween night, Harvey Dent, the Former District Attorney...
...and my lost friend...
...was either kidnapped or escaped from Arkham Asylum.
His face... his mind... terribly scarred from having acid hurled in it.

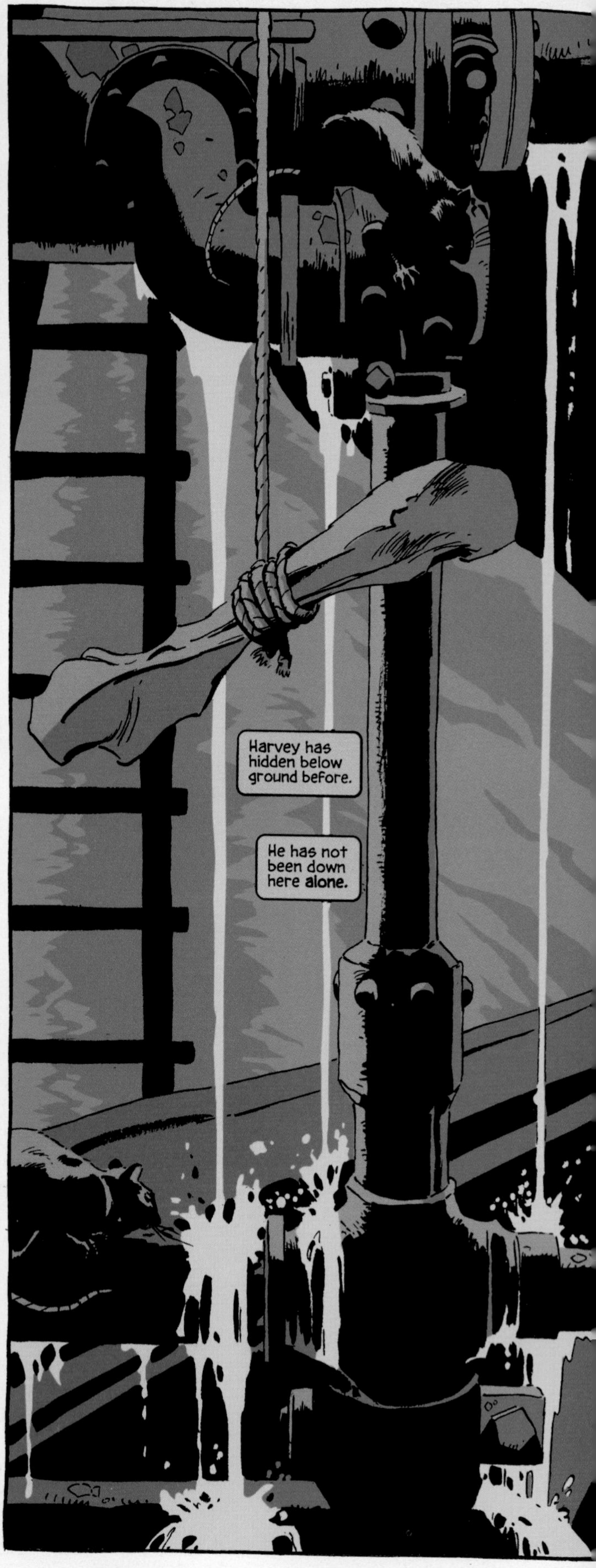
Harvey has hidden below ground before.
He has not been down here alone.

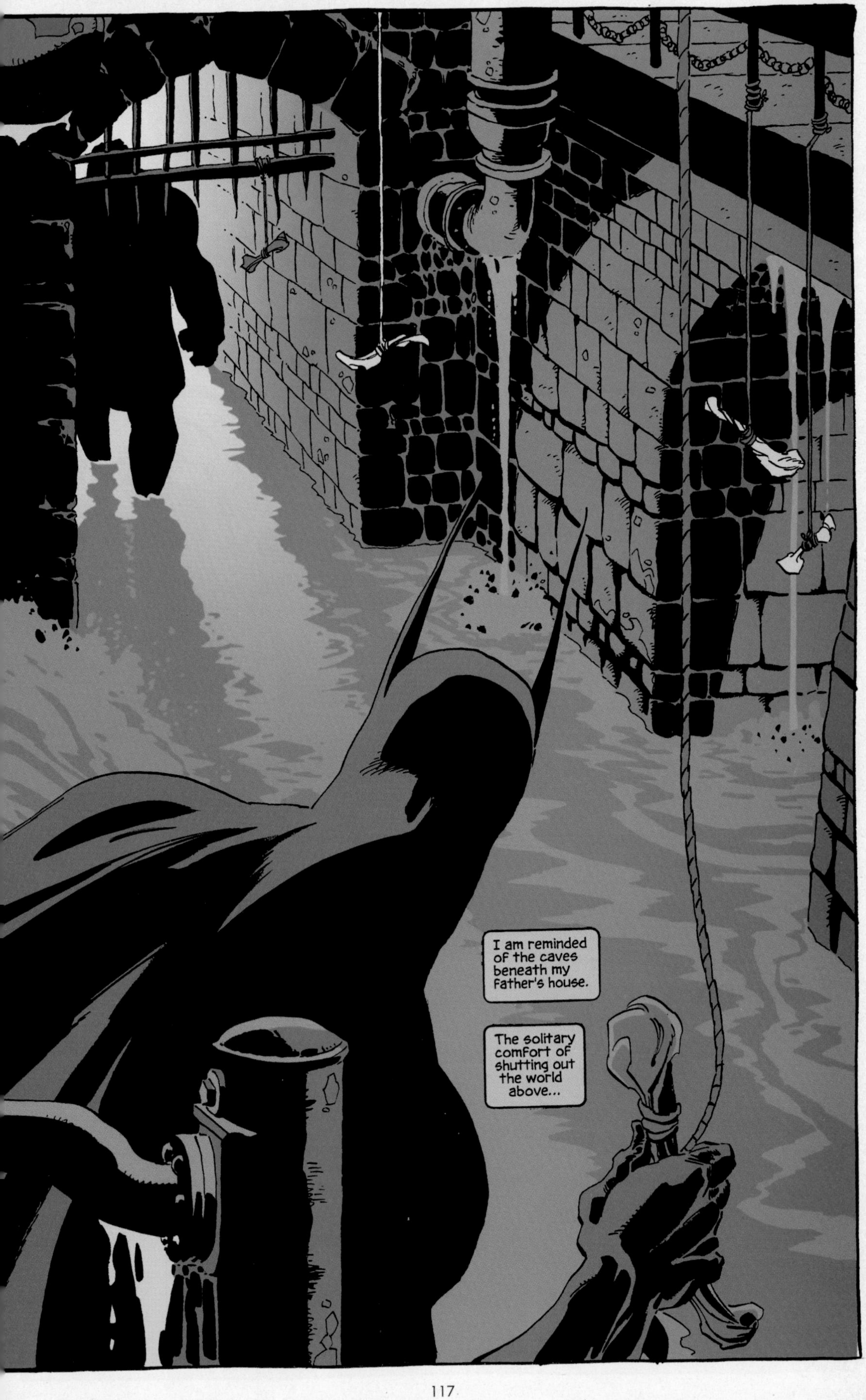
I am reminded of the caves beneath my father's house.
The solitary comfort of shutting out the world above...

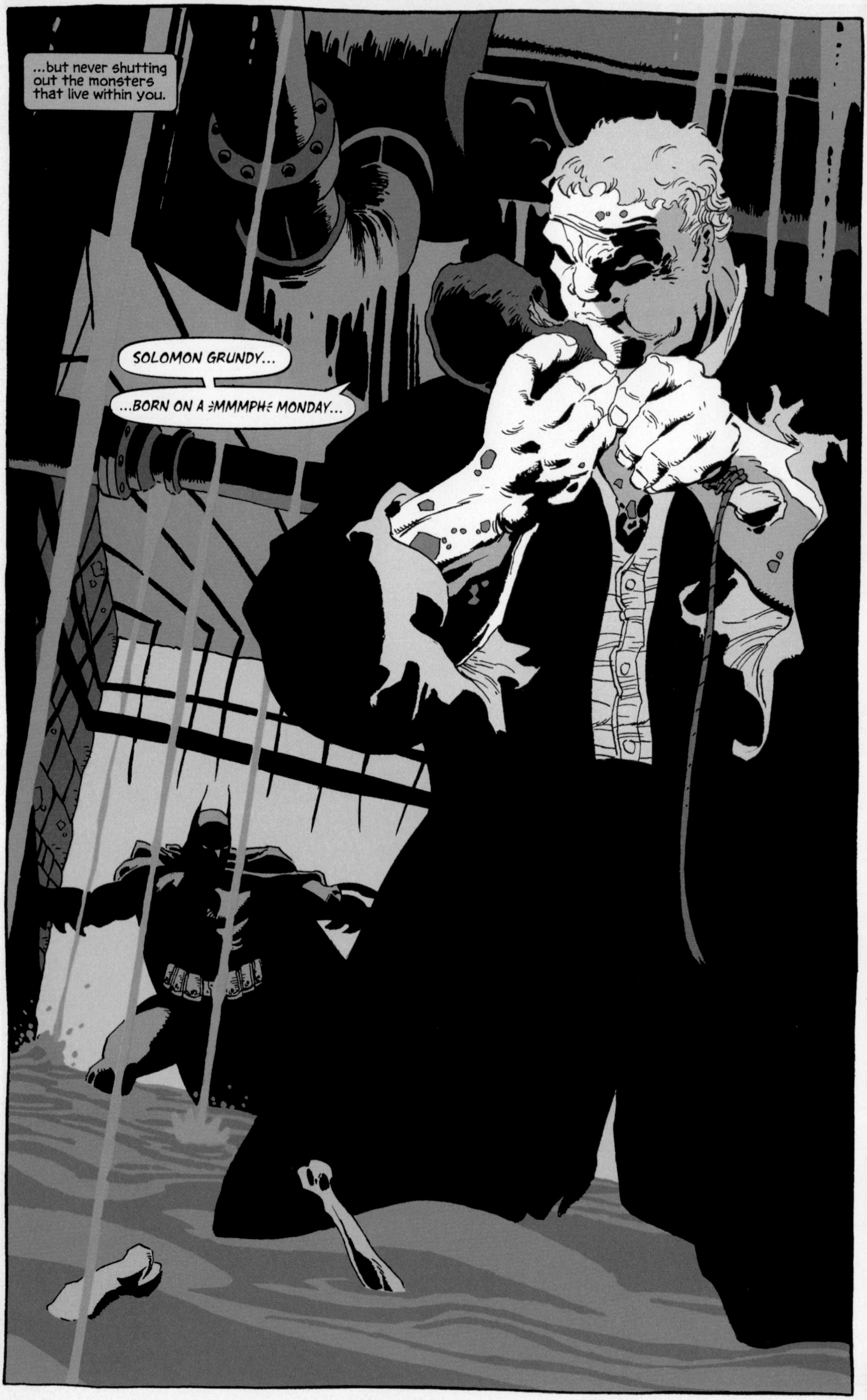
...but never shutting out the monsters that live within you.
SOLOMON GRUNDY...
...BORN ON A ≡MMMPH≡ MONDAY...

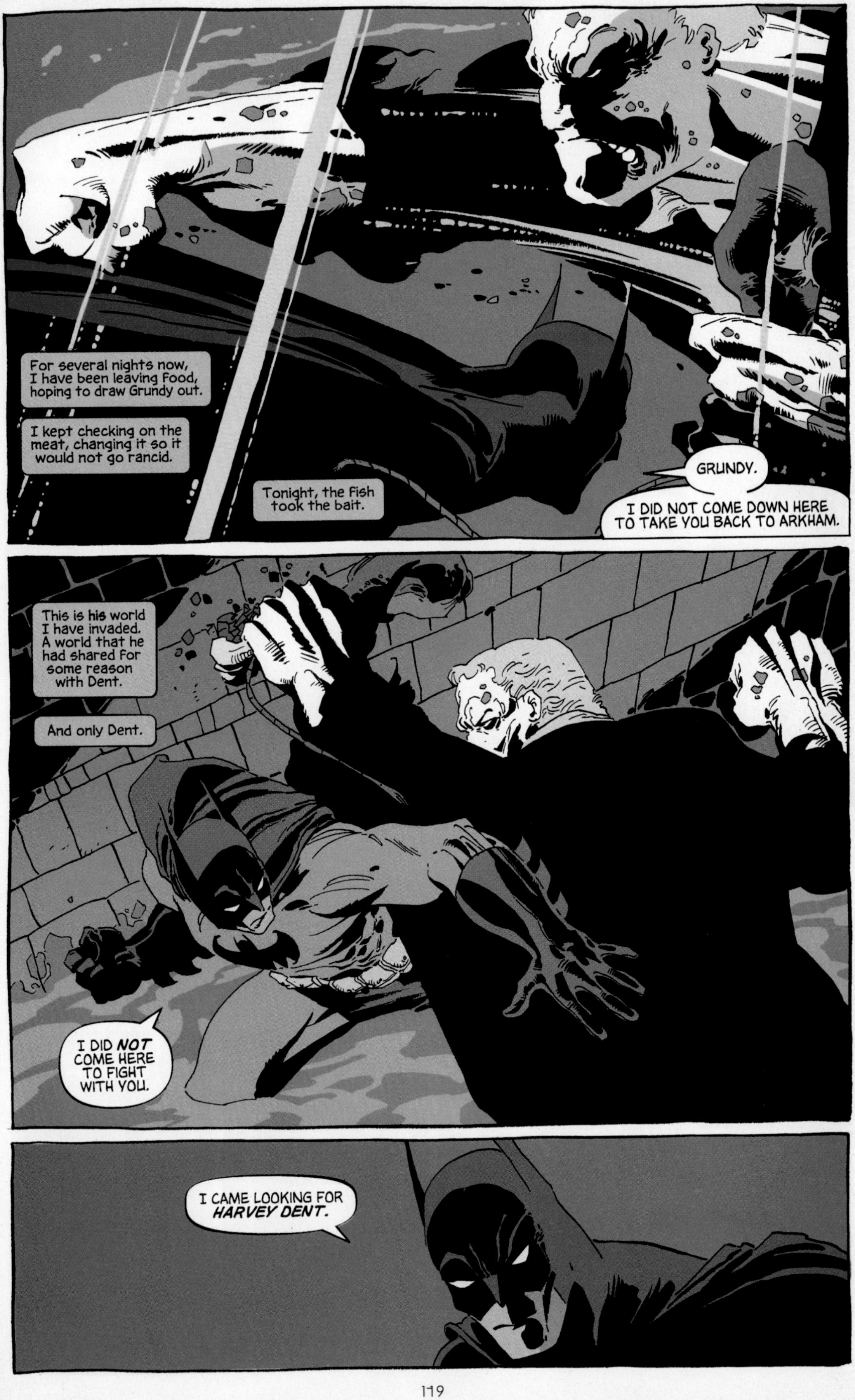
For several nights now, I have been leaving food, hoping to draw Grundy out.
I kept checking on the meat, changing it so it would not go rancid.
Tonight, the Fish took the bait.
GRUNDY.
I DID NOT COME DOWN HERE TO TAKE YOU BACK TO ARKHAM.
This is his world I have invaded. A world that he had shared for some reason with Dent.
And only Dent.
I DID *NOT* COME HERE TO FIGHT WITH YOU.
I CAME LOOKING FOR *HARVEY DENT*.

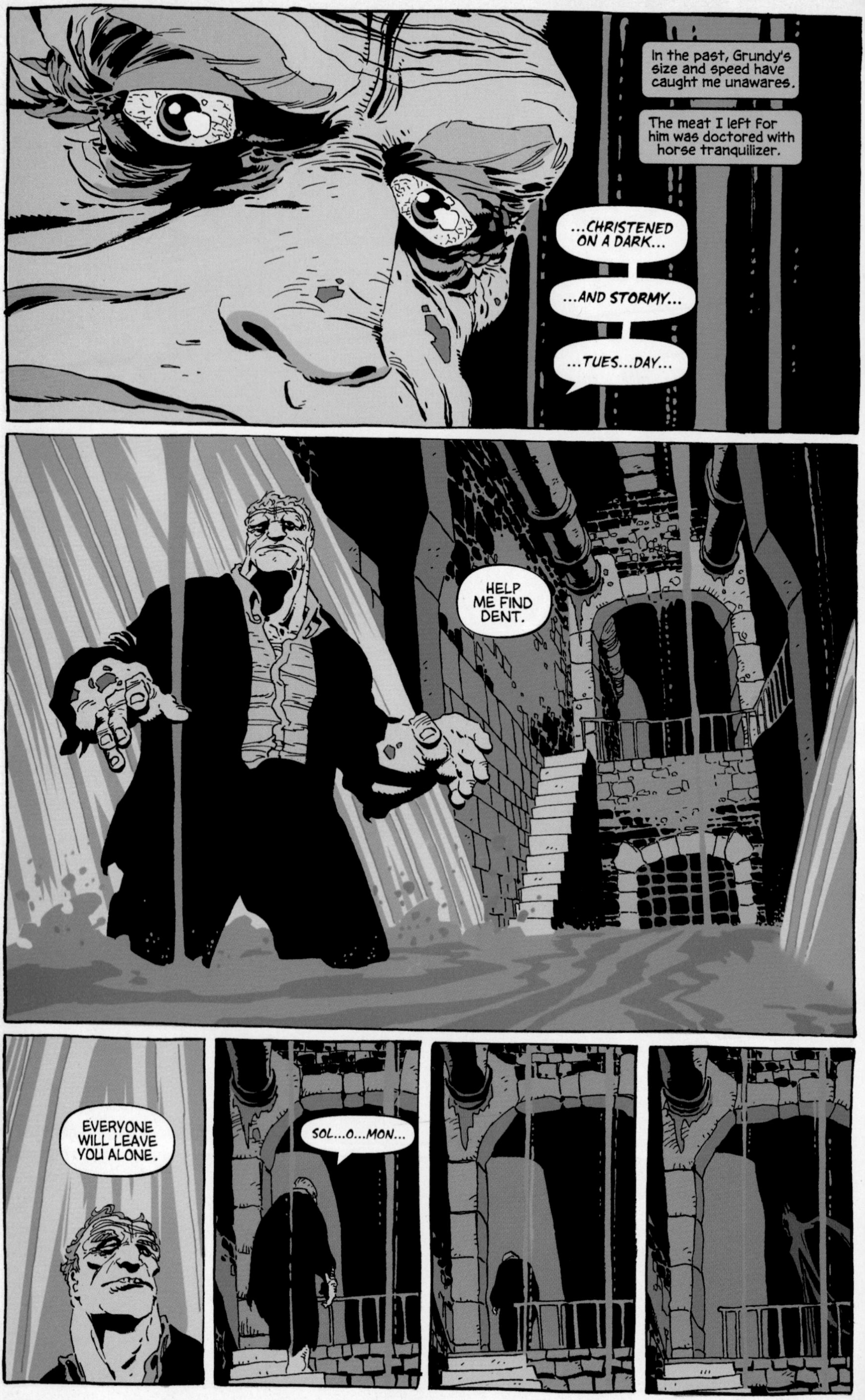
In the past, Grundy's size and speed have caught me unawares.
The meat I left for him was doctored with horse tranquilizer.
...CHRISTENED ON A DARK...
...AND STORMY...
...TUES...DAY...
HELP ME FIND DENT.
EVERYONE WILL LEAVE YOU ALONE.
SOL...O...MON...

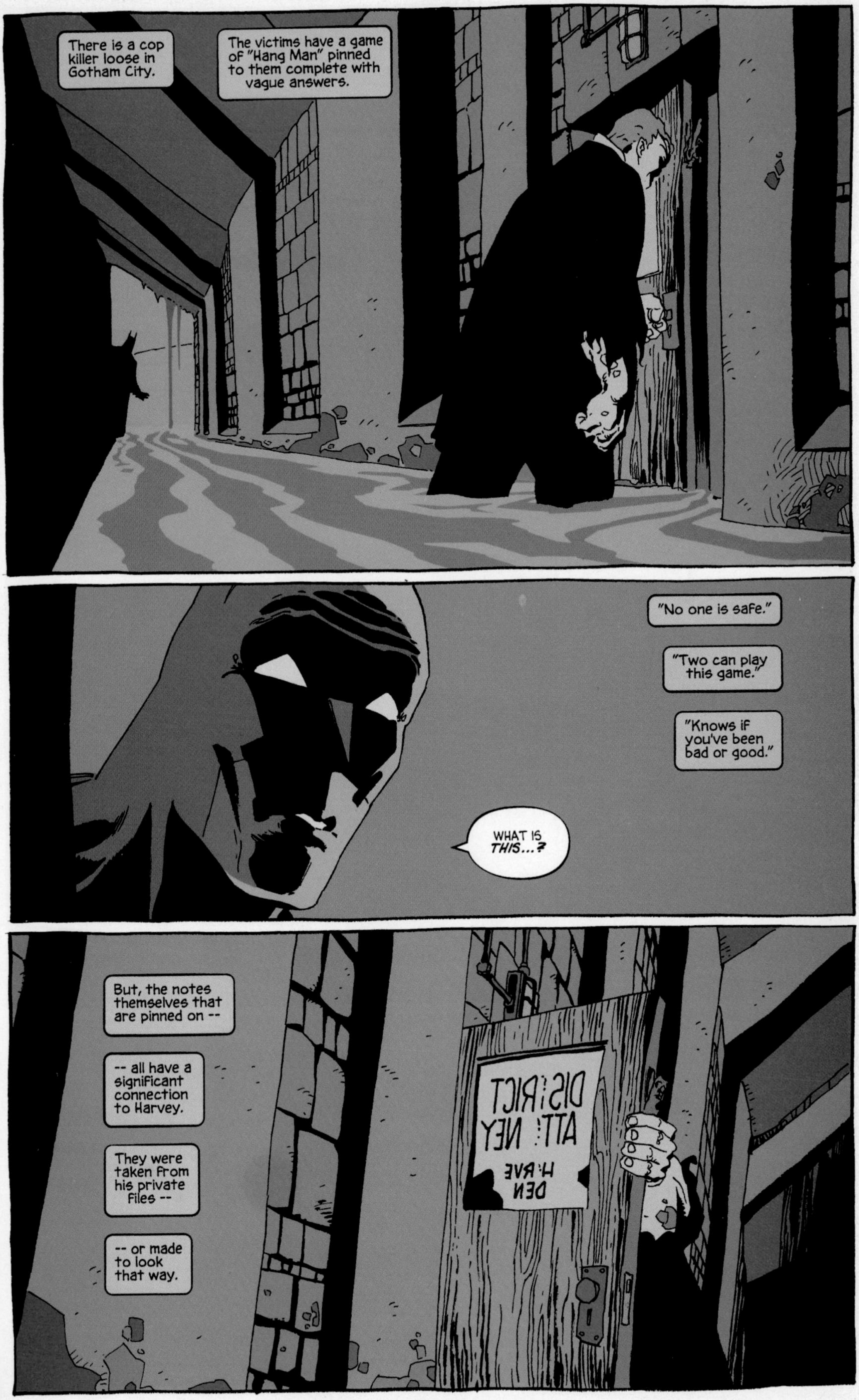
There is a cop killer loose in Gotham City.
The victims have a game of "Hang Man" pinned to them complete with vague answers.
"No one is safe."
"Two can play this game."
"Knows if you've been bad or good."
WHAT IS THIS...?
But, the notes themselves that are pinned on --
-- all have a significant connection to Harvey.
They were taken from his private files --
-- or made to look that way.

GOTHAM CITY
POLICE DEPT

DENIED
CTD 52
...endiary device...
...terrorist known as THE BAT...

$\$\%\%\%\%$

JUSTICE

A
Harry Dent
DISTRICT ATTORNEY

OH,
GOD...
NO...

DID...DID
YOU KNOW
HIM?

HIS NAME
WAS *BRANDEN*.
HE HEADED UP THE
SPECIAL WEAPONS
UNIT IN GOTHAM
FOR YEARS.

HE WAS A *ZEALOT*,
NEVER KNEW THE MEANING
OF EXCESSIVE FORCE.

WHEN
COMMISSIONER LOEB
GOT BROOMED,
HE WENT TOO.

BUT,
HE DIDN'T
DESERVE THIS...

SS-POLICE LI

JIM...!

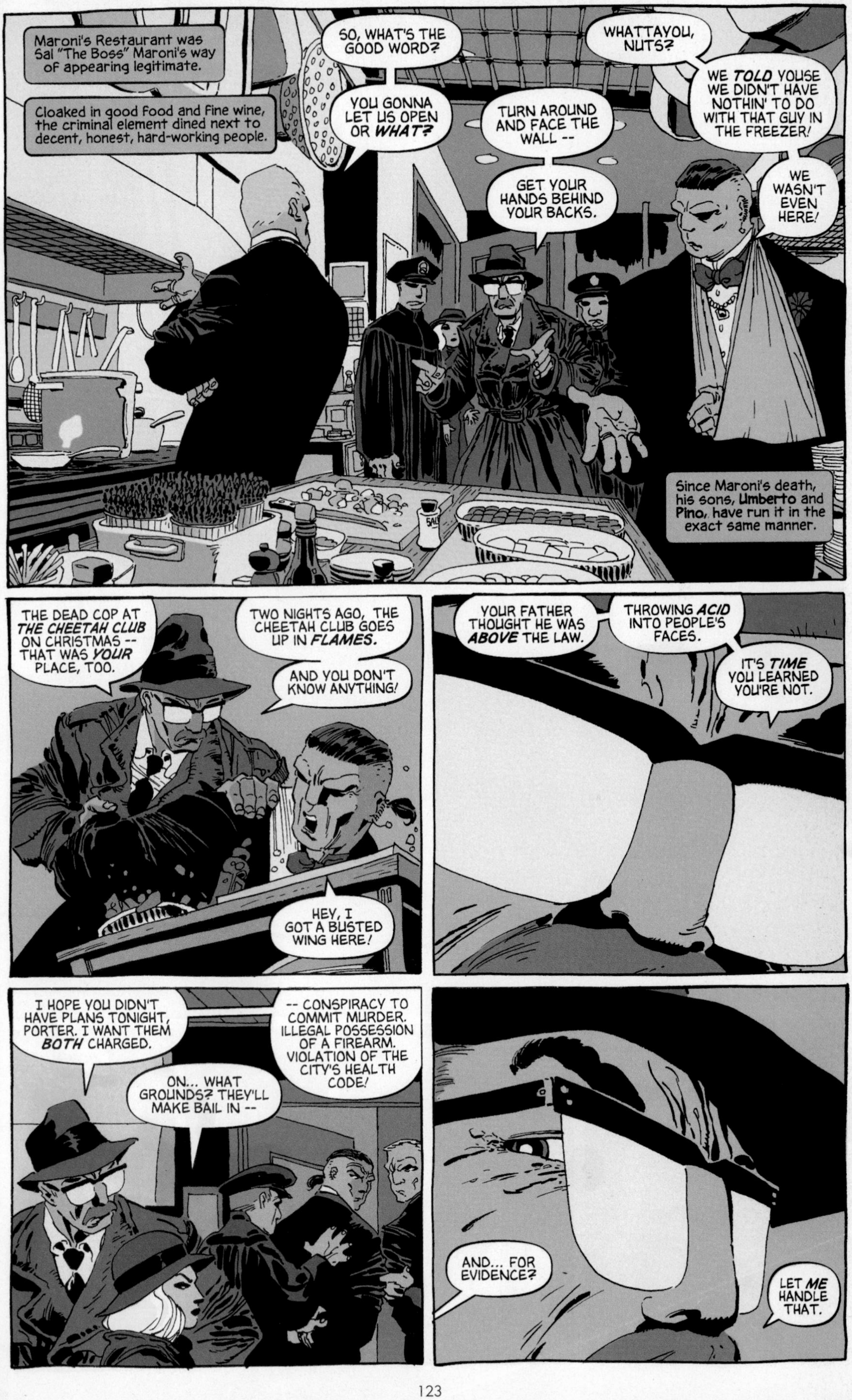

Maroni's Restaurant was Sal "The Boss" Maroni's way of appearing legitimate.
Cloaked in good food and fine wine, the criminal element dined next to decent, honest, hard-working people.
SO, WHAT'S THE GOOD WORD?
YOU GONNA LET US OPEN OR WHAT?
TURN AROUND AND FACE THE WALL --
GET YOUR HANDS BEHIND YOUR BACKS.
WHATTAYOU, NUTS?
WE TOLD YOUSE WE DIDN'T HAVE NOTHIN' TO DO WITH THAT GUY IN THE FREEZER!
WE WASN'T EVEN HERE!
Since Maroni's death, his sons, Umberto and Pino, have run it in the exact same manner.
THE DEAD COP AT THE CHEETAH CLUB ON CHRISTMAS -- THAT WAS YOUR PLACE, TOO.
TWO NIGHTS AGO, THE CHEETAH CLUB GOES UP IN FLAMES.
AND YOU DON'T KNOW ANYTHING!
HEY, I GOT A BUSTED WING HERE!
YOUR FATHER THOUGHT HE WAS ABOVE THE LAW.
THROWING ACID INTO PEOPLE'S FACES.
IT'S TIME YOU LEARNED YOU'RE NOT.
I HOPE YOU DIDN'T HAVE PLANS TONIGHT, PORTER. I WANT THEM BOTH CHARGED.
ON... WHAT GROUNDS? THEY'LL MAKE BAIL IN --
-- CONSPIRACY TO COMMIT MURDER. ILLEGAL POSSESSION OF A FIREARM. VIOLATION OF THE CITY'S HEALTH CODE!
AND... FOR EVIDENCE?
LET ME HANDLE THAT.

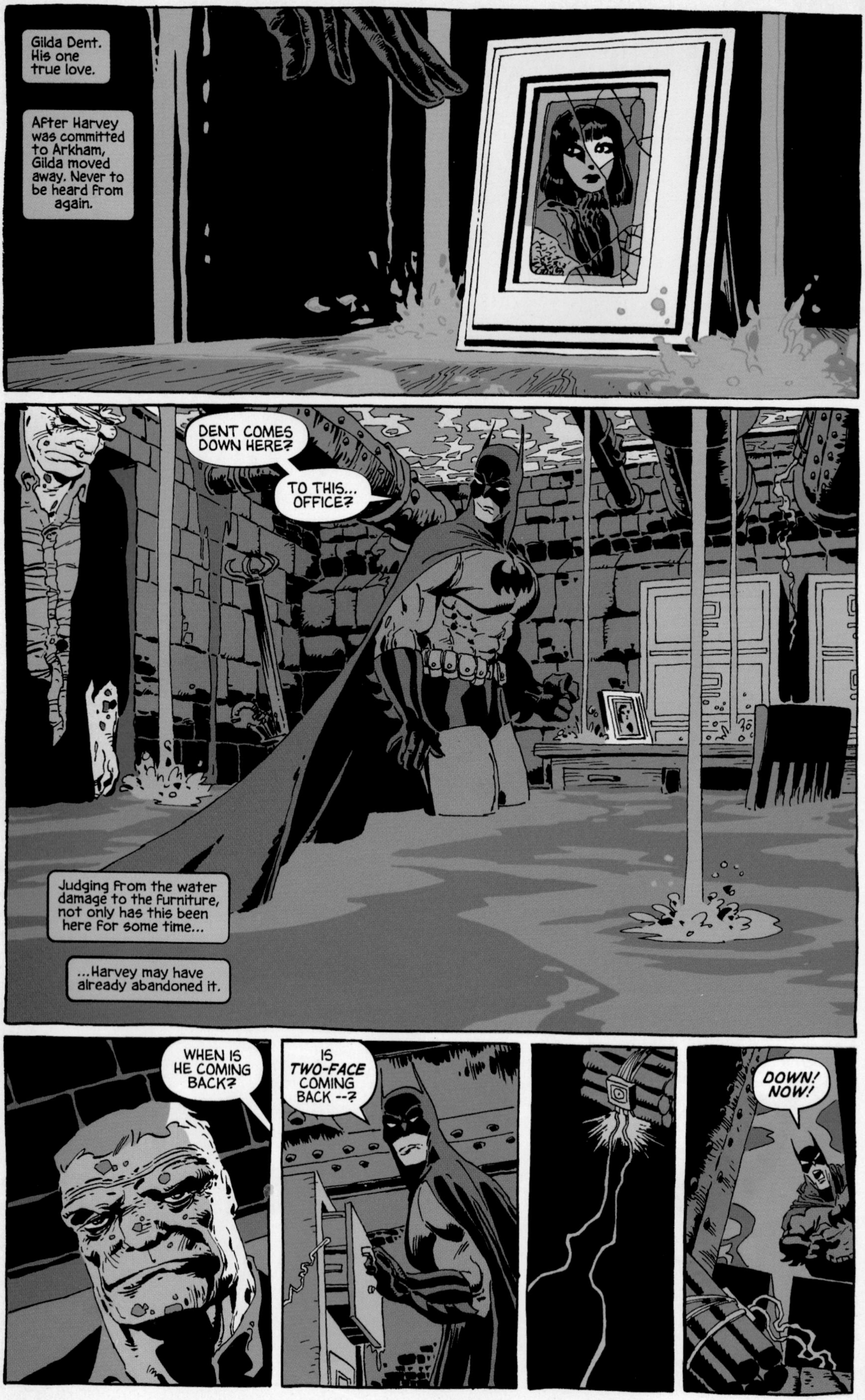

Gilda Dent. His one true love.
After Harvey was committed to Arkham, Gilda moved away. Never to be heard from again.
DENT COMES DOWN HERE?
TO THIS... OFFICE?
Judging from the water damage to the furniture, not only has this been here for some time...
...Harvey may have already abandoned it.
WHEN IS HE COMING BACK?
IS TWO-FACE COMING BACK --?
DOWN! NOW!

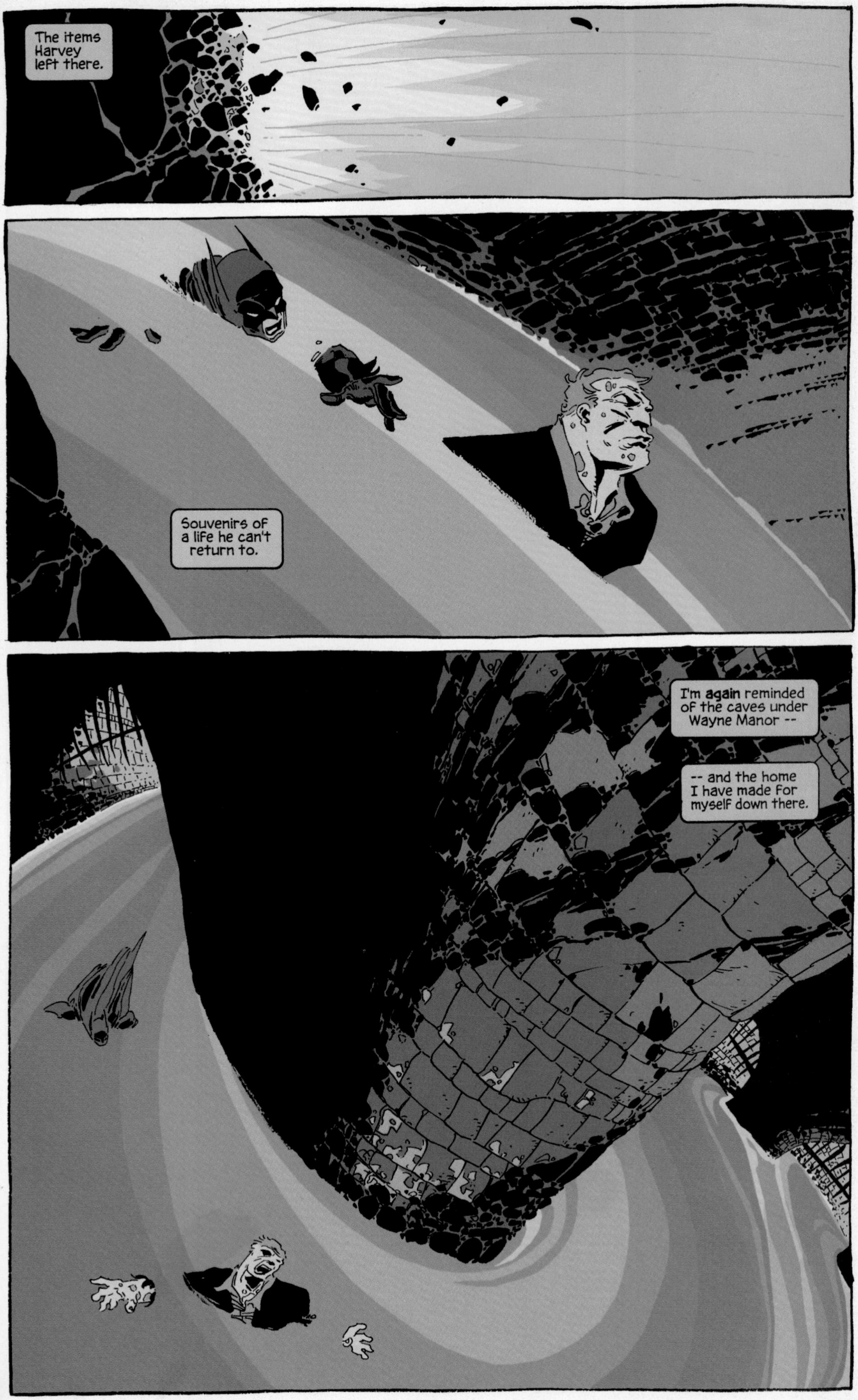
The items Harvey left there.
Souvenirs of a life he can't return to.
I'm **again** reminded of the caves under Wayne Manor --
-- and the home I have made for myself down there.

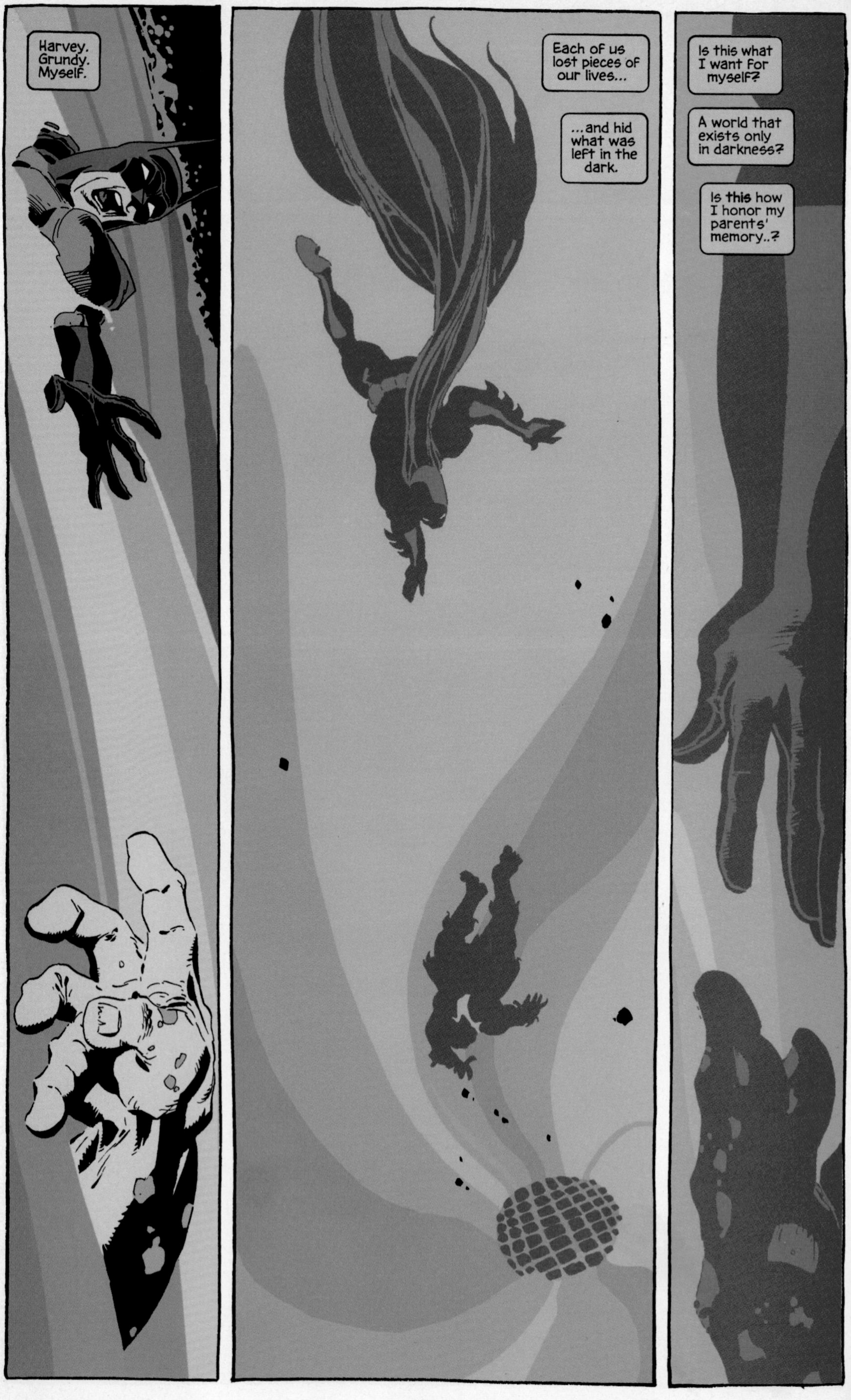
Harvey. Grundy. Myself.
Each of us lost pieces of our lives...
...and hid what was left in the dark.
Is this what I want for myself?
A world that exists only in darkness?
Is this how I honor my parents' memory..?

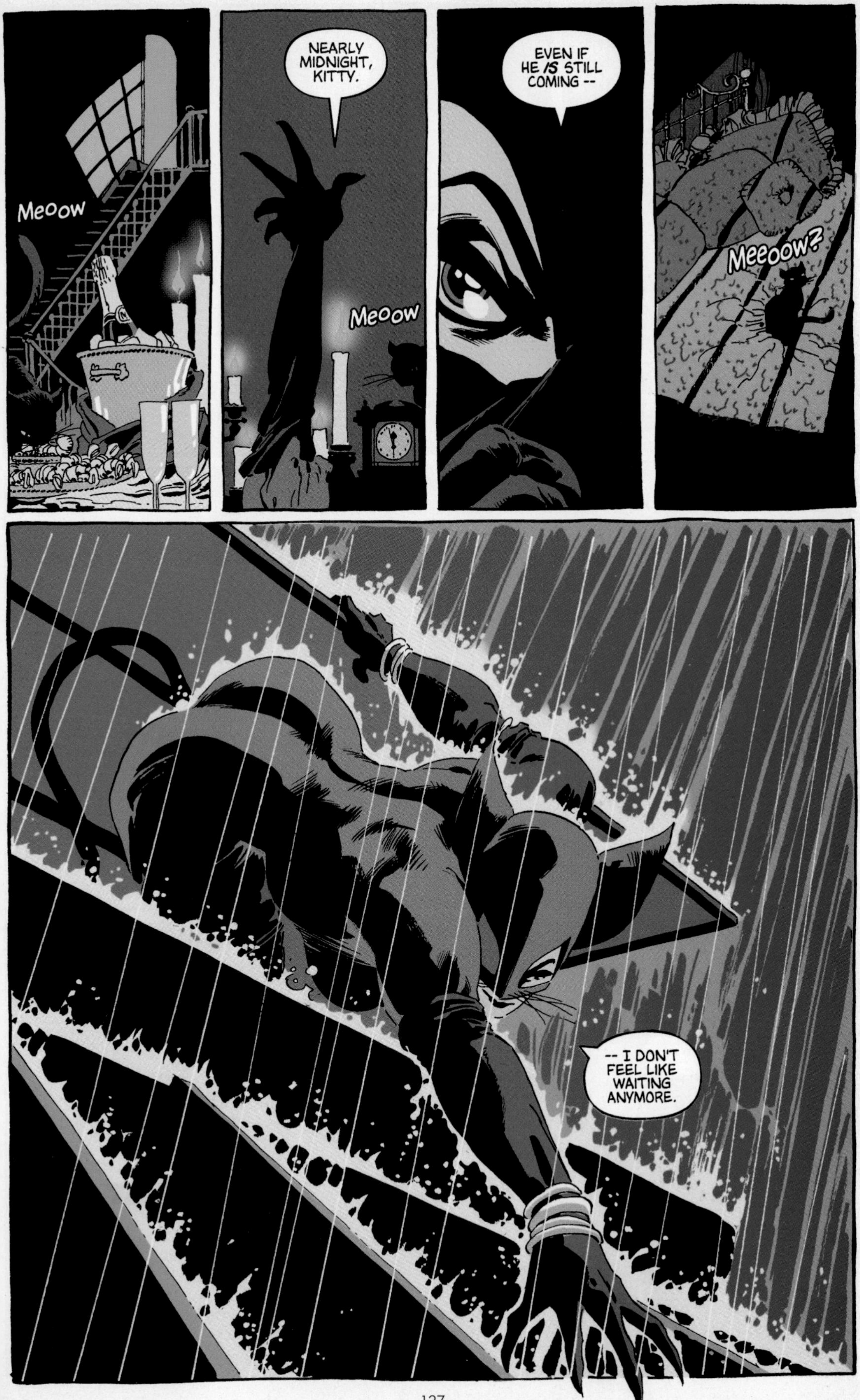
Meoow
NEARLY MIDNIGHT, KITTY.
Meoow
EVEN IF HE IS STILL COMING --
Meeoow?
-- I DON'T FEEL LIKE WAITING ANYMORE.

Sofia Gigante's penthouse. She is now head of the Falcone crime family.

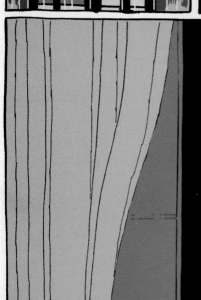

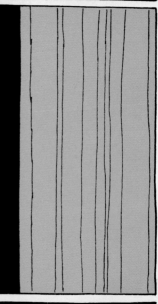

Mrrow...

TWO SHOTS.

NINE LIVES.

I'D QUIT WHILE YOU'RE AHEAD.

WHAT DO YOU WANT?

I WANT TO TALK TO YOU ABOUT... YOUR FATHER.

WHAT'S HE TO YOU?

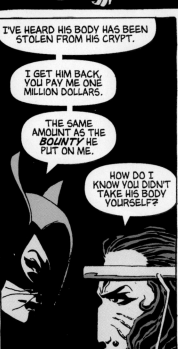

I'VE HEARD HIS BODY HAS BEEN STOLEN FROM HIS CRYPT.

I GET HIM BACK, YOU PAY ME ONE MILLION DOLLARS.

THE SAME AMOUNT AS THE BOUNTY HE PUT ON ME.

HOW DO I KNOW YOU DIDN'T TAKE HIS BODY YOURSELF?

YOU DON'T.

BUT EITHER WAY, YOU GET HIM BACK AND I GET THE MILLION DOLLARS.

WHY WOULD YOU WANT THE JOB?

MAYBE IT'S THE MONEY.

MAYBE I'M JUST CURIOUS AS TO WHO TOOK HIM AND WHY.

MAYBE IT'S NONE OF YOUR DAMN BUSINESS.

YOU REALLY CAN'T GET OUT OF THAT CHAIR, CAN YOU, SOFIA?

GO TO HELL.

I HAVEN'T HEARD YOU SAY "NO" TO MY OFFER.

SO, I'LL TAKE THAT AS A "YES."

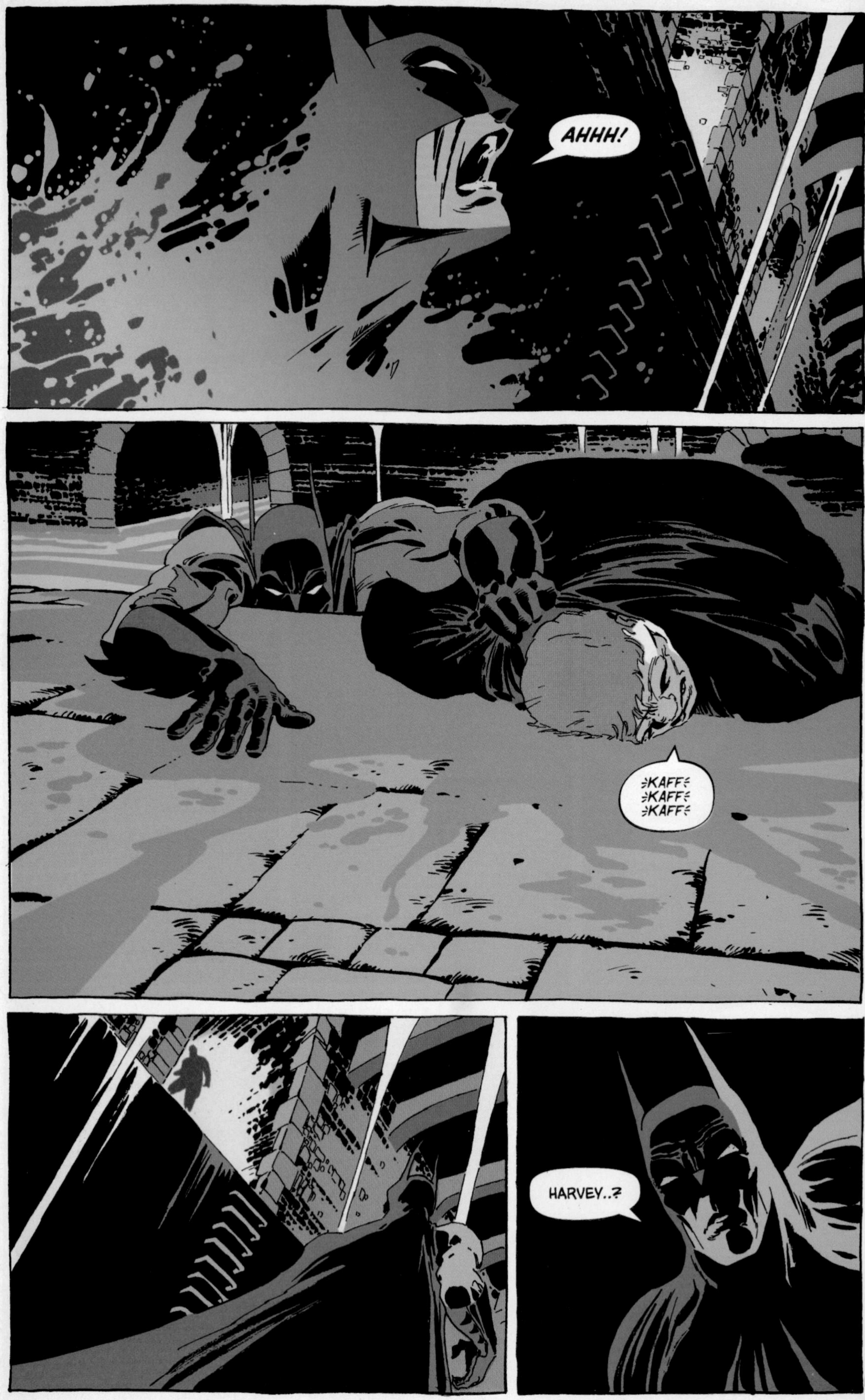
AHHH!
KAFF KAFF KAFF
HARVEY..?

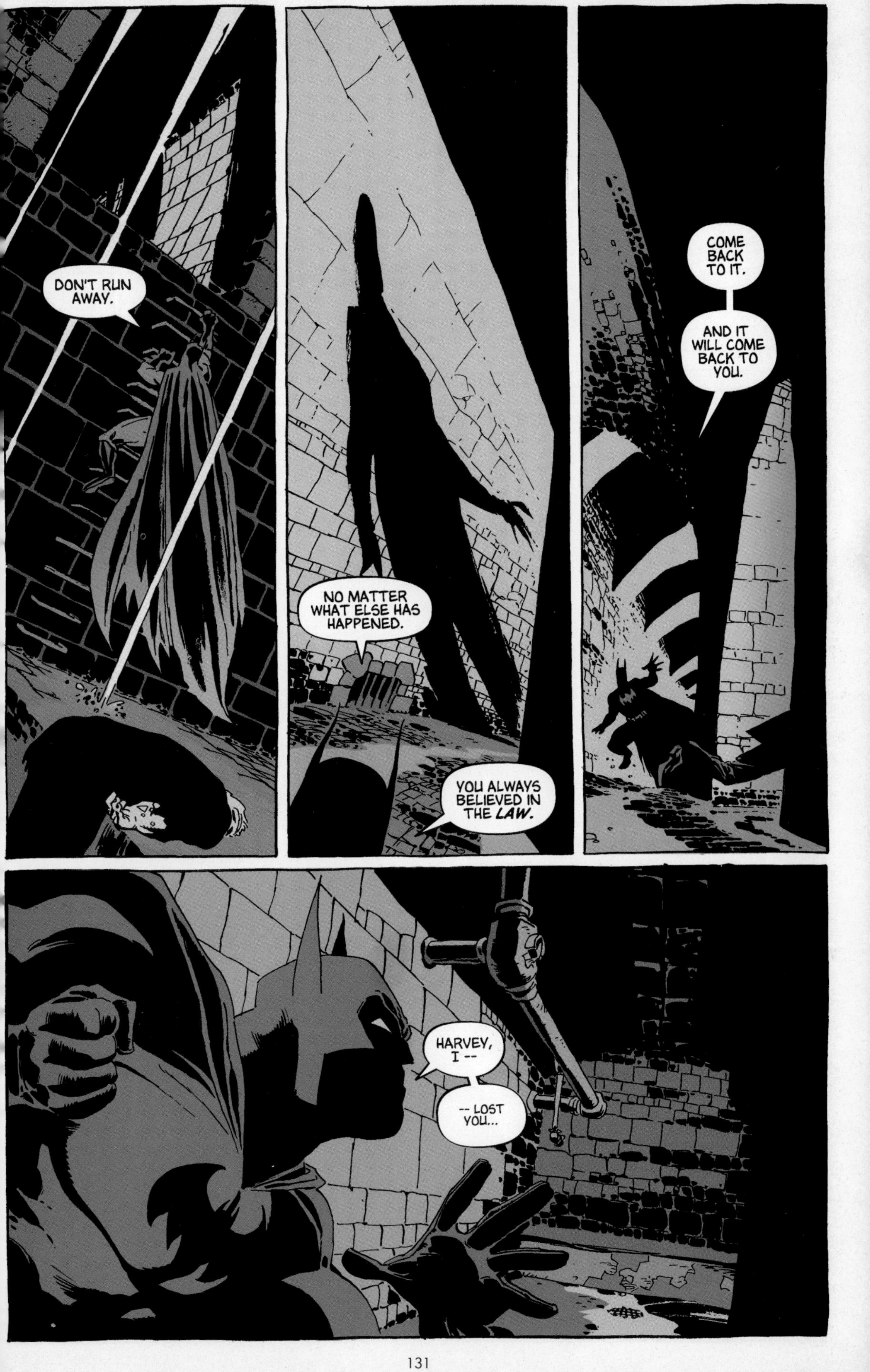
DON'T RUN AWAY.
NO MATTER WHAT ELSE HAS HAPPENED.
YOU ALWAYS BELIEVED IN THE *LAW.*
COME BACK TO IT.
AND IT WILL COME BACK TO YOU.
HARVEY, I --
-- LOST YOU...

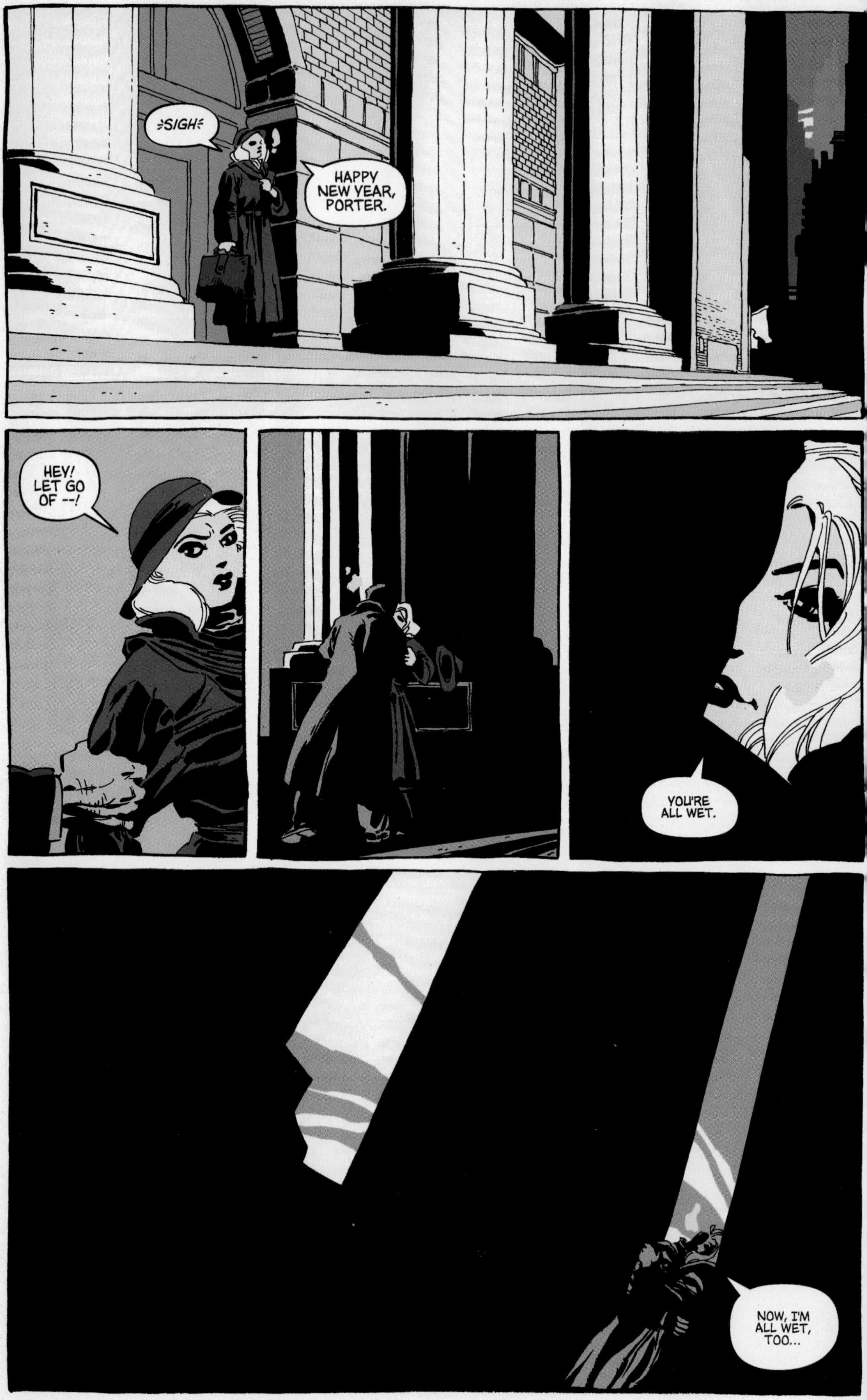

SIGH
HAPPY NEW YEAR, PORTER.
HEY! LET GO OF --!
YOU'RE ALL WET.
NOW, I'M ALL WET, TOO...

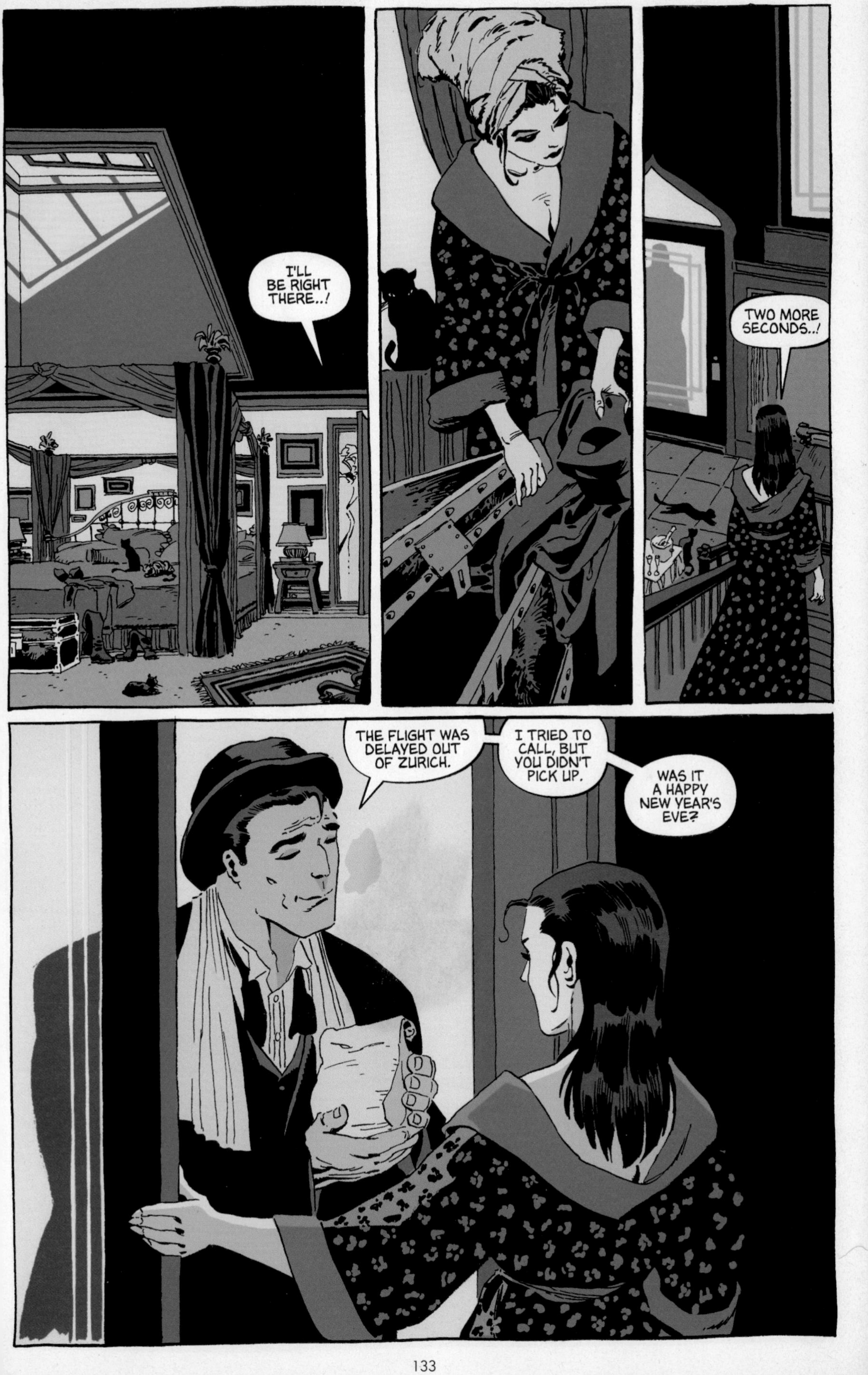
I'LL BE RIGHT THERE..!
TWO MORE SECONDS..!
THE FLIGHT WAS DELAYED OUT OF ZURICH.
I TRIED TO CALL, BUT YOU DIDN'T PICK UP.
WAS IT A HAPPY NEW YEAR'S EVE?

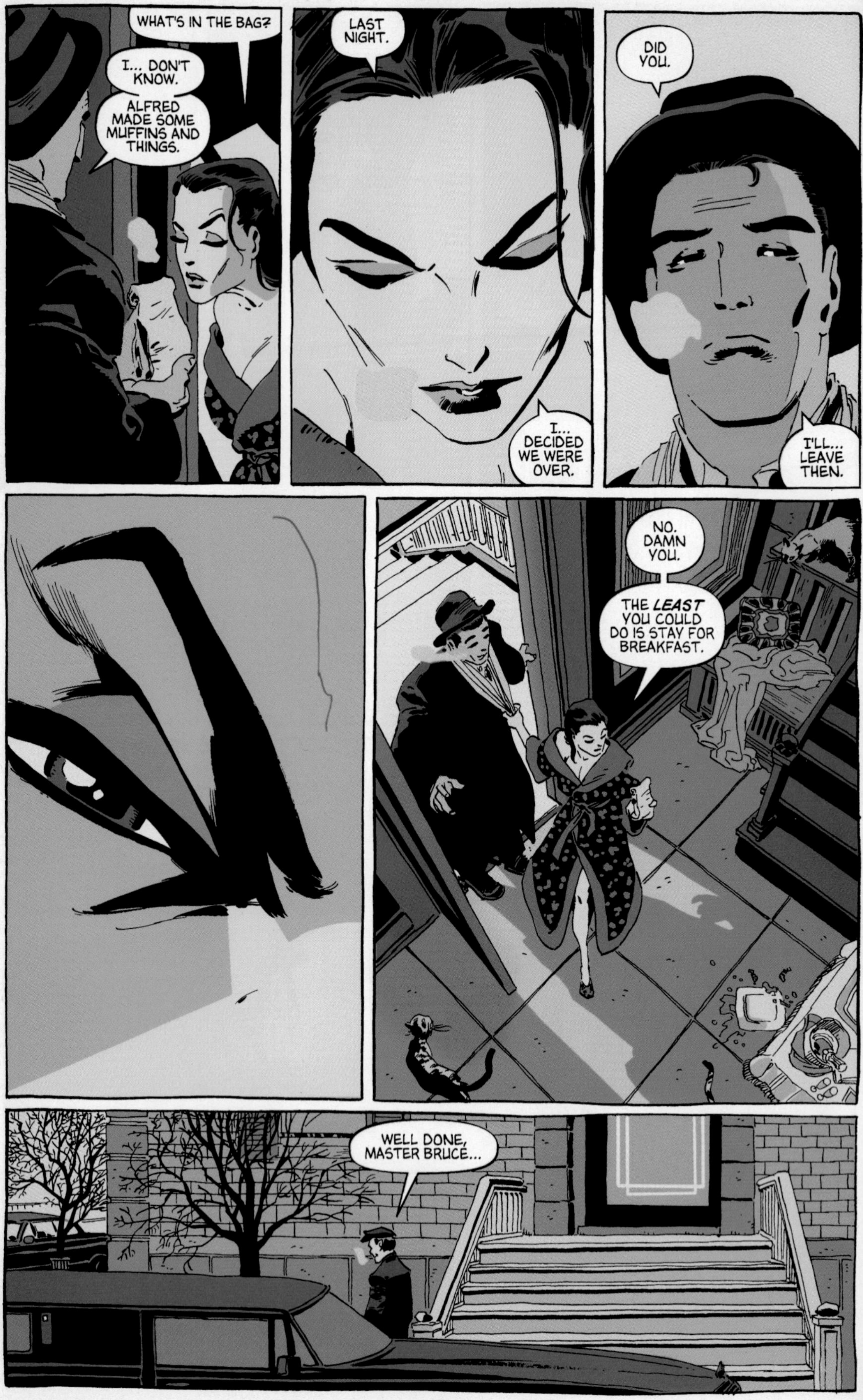
WHAT'S IN THE BAG?
I... DON'T KNOW.
ALFRED MADE SOME MUFFINS AND THINGS.
LAST NIGHT.
I... DECIDED WE WERE OVER.
DID YOU.
I'LL... LEAVE THEN.
NO. DAMN YOU.
THE LEAST YOU COULD DO IS STAY FOR BREAKFAST.
WELL DONE, MASTER BRUCE...

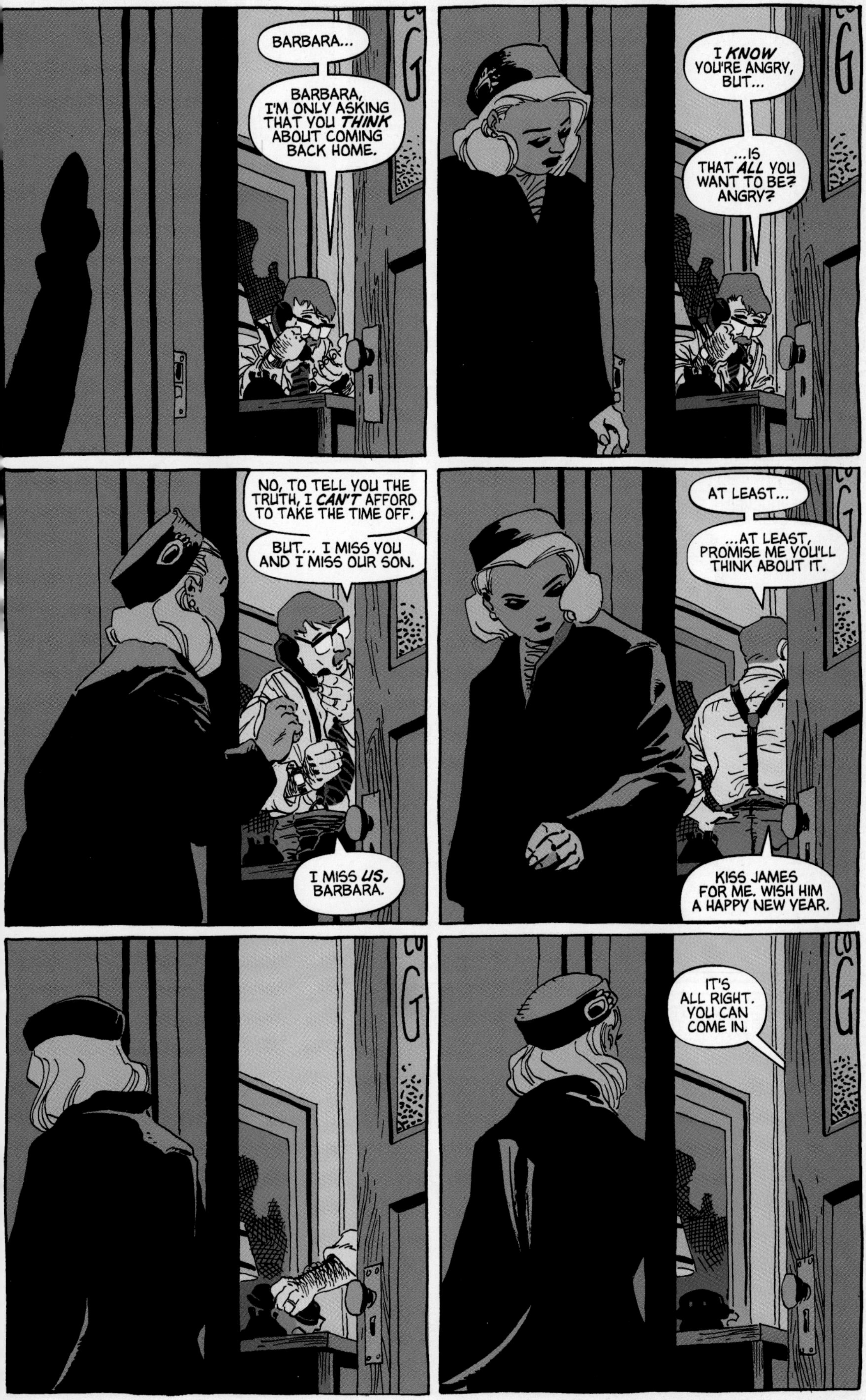
BARBARA...
BARBARA, I'M ONLY ASKING THAT YOU *THINK* ABOUT COMING BACK HOME.
I *KNOW* YOU'RE ANGRY, BUT...
...IS THAT *ALL* YOU WANT TO BE? ANGRY?
NO, TO TELL YOU THE TRUTH, I *CAN'T* AFFORD TO TAKE THE TIME OFF.
BUT... I MISS YOU AND I MISS OUR SON.
I MISS *US,* BARBARA.
AT LEAST...
...AT LEAST, PROMISE ME YOU'LL THINK ABOUT IT.
KISS JAMES FOR ME. WISH HIM A HAPPY NEW YEAR.
IT'S ALL RIGHT. YOU CAN COME IN.

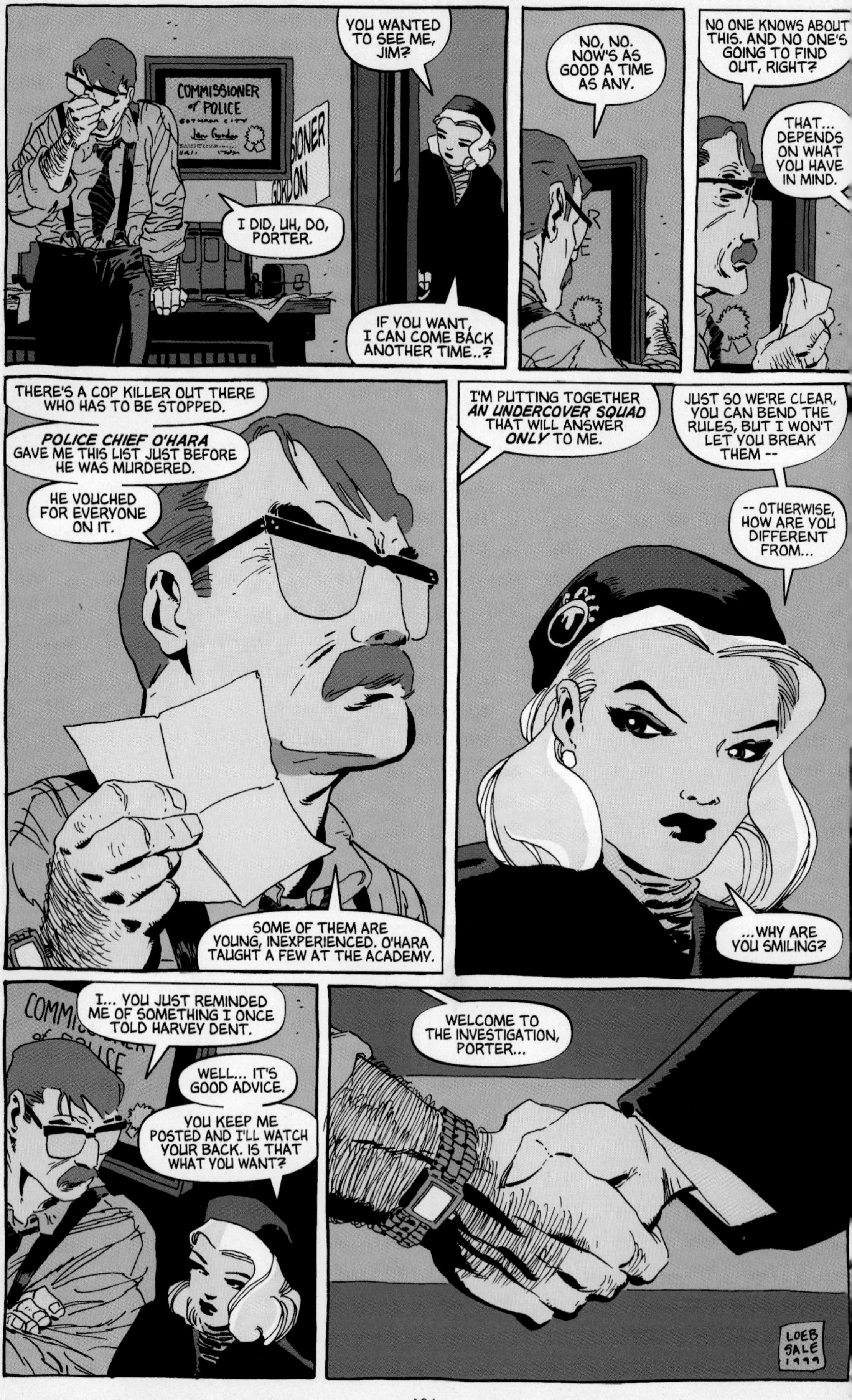
COMMISSIONER of POLICE GOTHAM CITY
YOU WANTED TO SEE ME, JIM?
I DID, UH, DO, PORTER.
IF YOU WANT, I CAN COME BACK ANOTHER TIME..?
NO, NO. NOW'S AS GOOD A TIME AS ANY.
NO ONE KNOWS ABOUT THIS. AND NO ONE'S GOING TO FIND OUT, RIGHT?
THAT... DEPENDS ON WHAT YOU HAVE IN MIND.
THERE'S A COP KILLER OUT THERE WHO HAS TO BE STOPPED.
POLICE CHIEF O'HARA GAVE ME THIS LIST JUST BEFORE HE WAS MURDERED.
HE VOUCHED FOR EVERYONE ON IT.
SOME OF THEM ARE YOUNG, INEXPERIENCED. O'HARA TAUGHT A FEW AT THE ACADEMY.
I'M PUTTING TOGETHER *AN UNDERCOVER SQUAD* THAT WILL ANSWER *ONLY* TO ME.
JUST SO WE'RE CLEAR, YOU CAN BEND THE RULES, BUT I WON'T LET YOU BREAK THEM --
-- OTHERWISE, HOW ARE YOU DIFFERENT FROM...
...WHY ARE YOU SMILING?
I... YOU JUST REMINDED ME OF SOMETHING I ONCE TOLD HARVEY DENT.
WELL... IT'S GOOD ADVICE.
YOU KEEP ME POSTED AND I'LL WATCH YOUR BACK. IS THAT WHAT YOU WANT?
WELCOME TO THE INVESTIGATION, PORTER...
LOEB SALE 1999

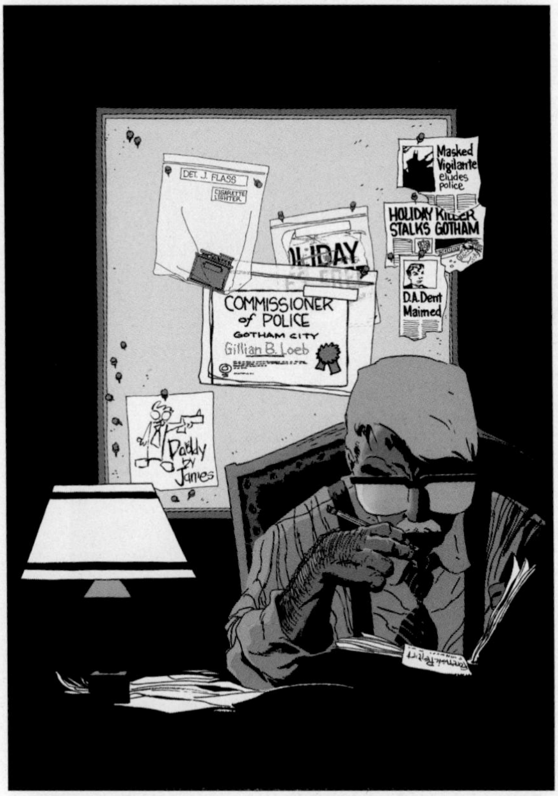
DET. J. FLASS
CIGARETTE LIGHTER
Masked Vigilante eludes police
HOLIDAY KILLER STALKS GOTHAM
D.A. Dent Maimed
COMMISSIONER of POLICE
GOTHAM CITY
Gillian B. Loeb
Daddy by James

5

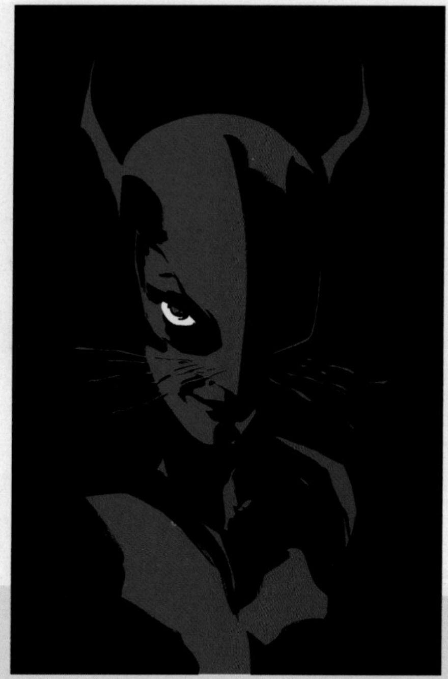

LOVE

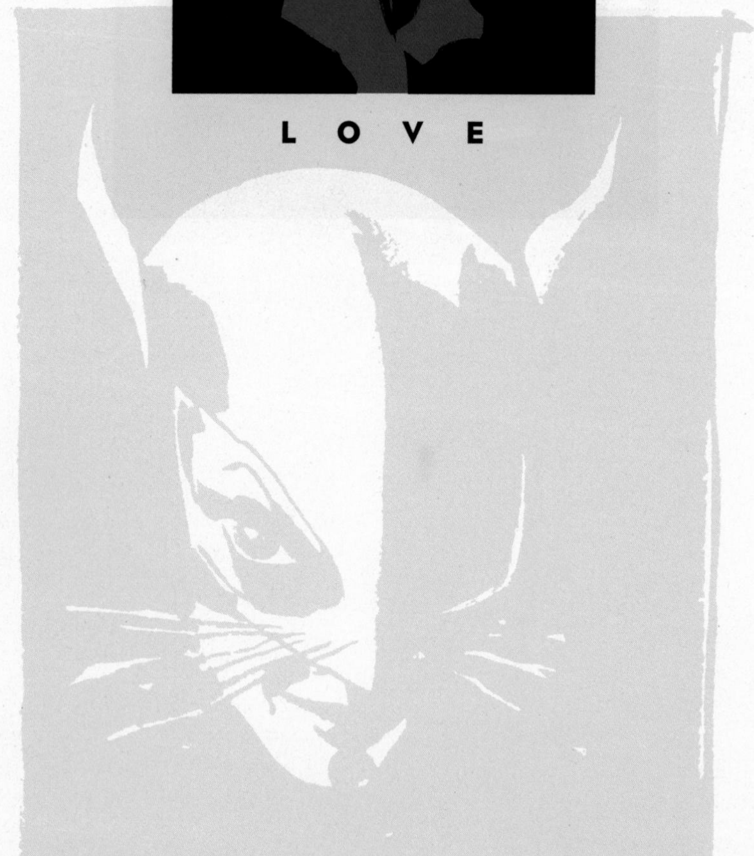

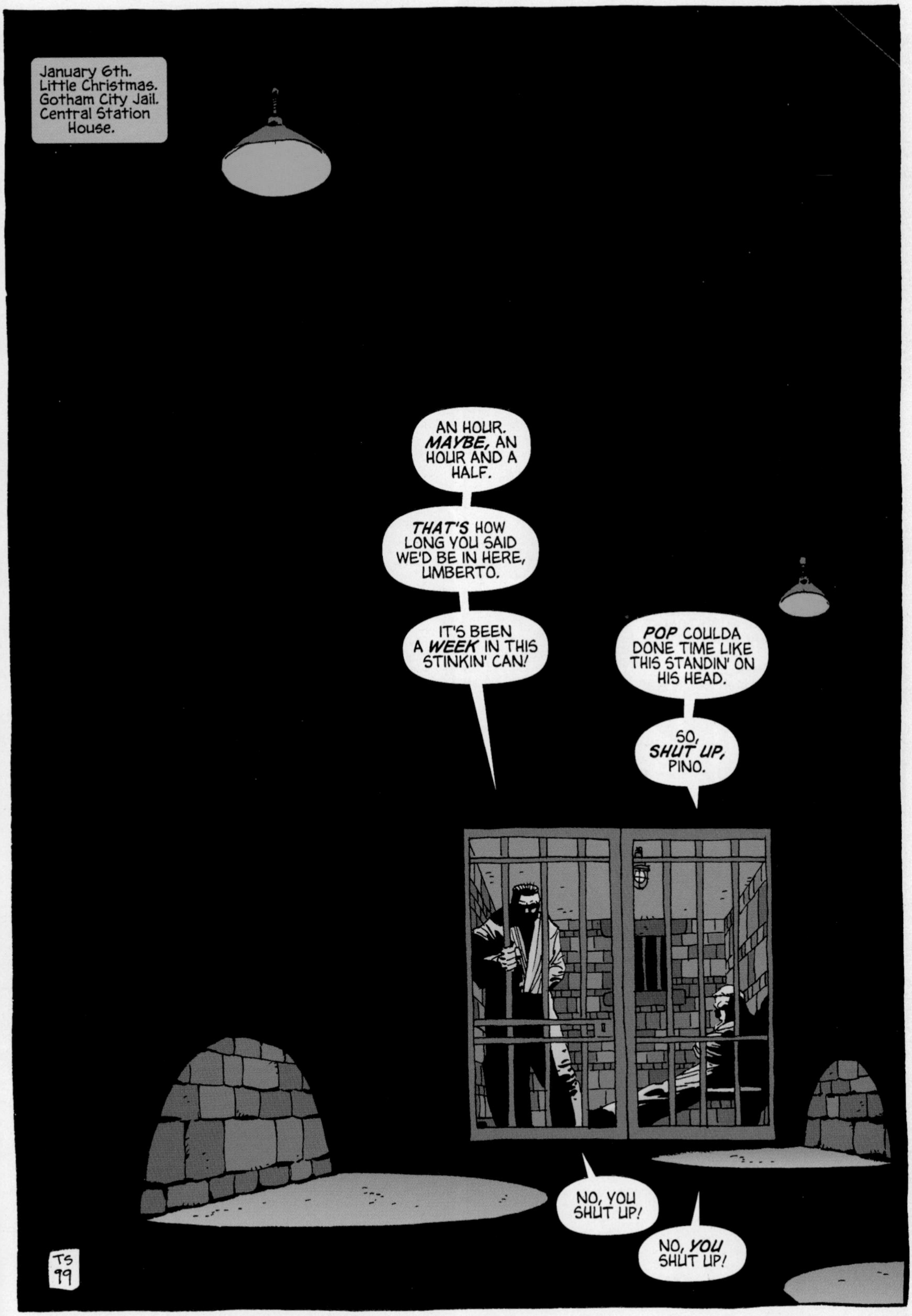

January 6th.
Little Christmas.
Gotham City Jail.
Central Station House.
AN HOUR. *MAYBE,* AN HOUR AND A HALF.
THAT'S HOW LONG YOU SAID WE'D BE IN HERE, UMBERTO.
IT'S BEEN A *WEEK* IN THIS STINKIN' CAN!
POP COULDA DONE TIME LIKE THIS STANDIN' ON HIS HEAD.
SO, *SHUT UP,* PINO.
NO, YOU SHUT UP!
NO, *YOU* SHUT UP!
TS 99

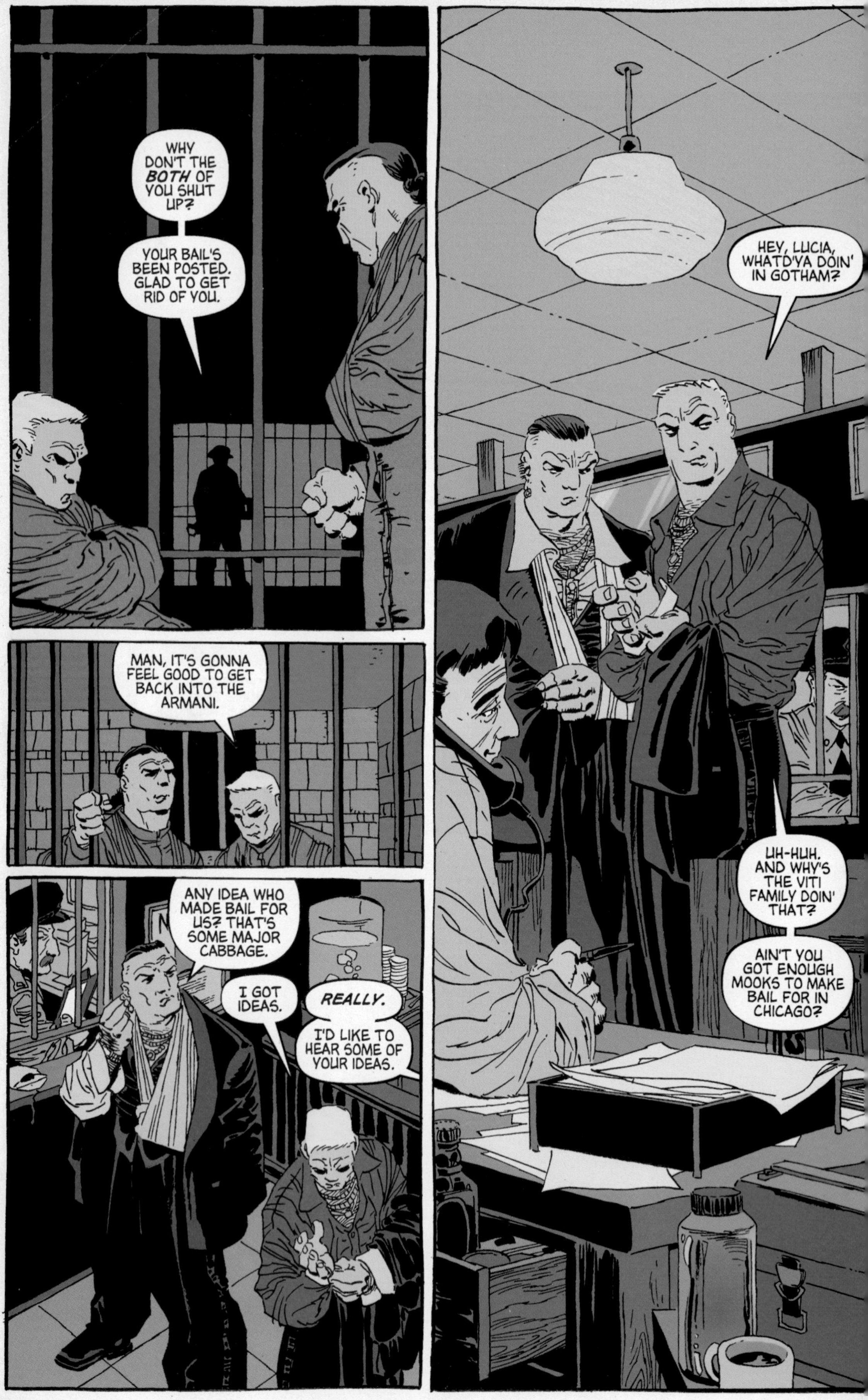
WHY DON'T THE *BOTH* OF YOU SHUT UP?
YOUR BAIL'S BEEN POSTED. GLAD TO GET RID OF YOU.
MAN, IT'S GONNA FEEL GOOD TO GET BACK INTO THE ARMANI.
ANY IDEA WHO MADE BAIL FOR US? THAT'S SOME MAJOR CABBAGE.
I GOT IDEAS.
REALLY.
I'D LIKE TO HEAR SOME OF YOUR IDEAS.
HEY, LUCIA, WHATD'YA DOIN' IN GOTHAM?
UH-HUH. AND WHY'S THE VITI FAMILY DOIN' THAT?
AIN'T YOU GOT ENOUGH MOOKS TO MAKE BAIL FOR IN CHICAGO?

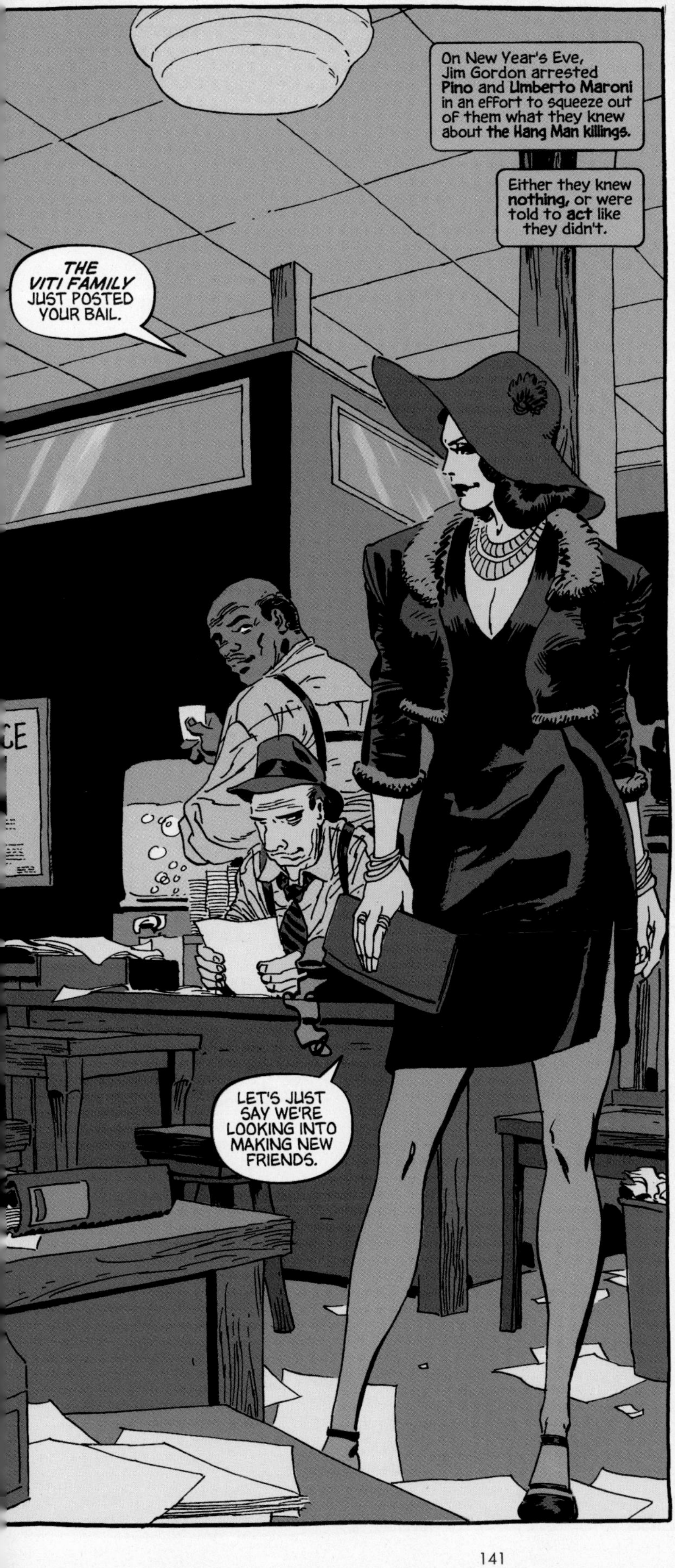
On New Year's Eve, Jim Gordon arrested Pino and Umberto Maroni in an effort to squeeze out of them what they knew about the Hang Man killings.
Either they knew nothing, or were told to act like they didn't.
THE VITI FAMILY JUST POSTED YOUR BAIL.
LET'S JUST SAY WE'RE LOOKING INTO MAKING NEW FRIENDS.
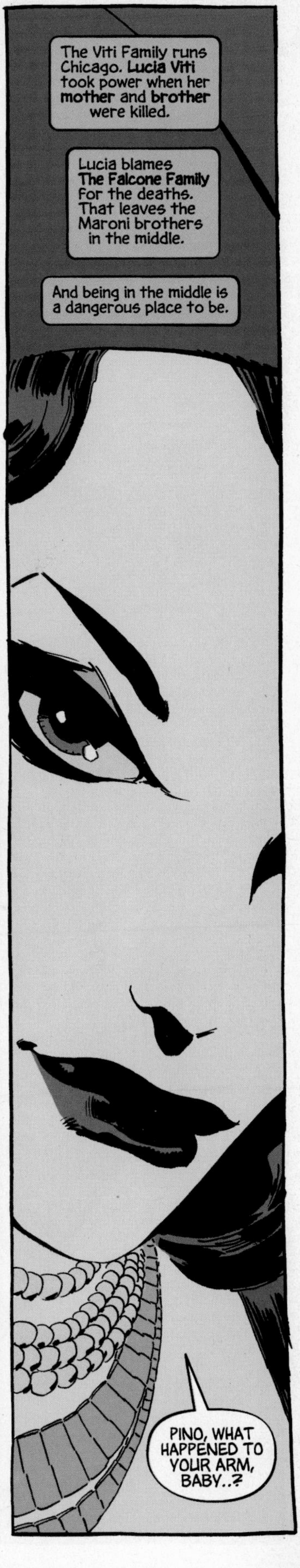
The Viti Family runs Chicago. Lucia Viti took power when her mother and brother were killed.
Lucia blames The Falcone Family for the deaths. That leaves the Maroni brothers in the middle.
And being in the middle is a dangerous place to be.
PINO, WHAT HAPPENED TO YOUR ARM, BABY..?

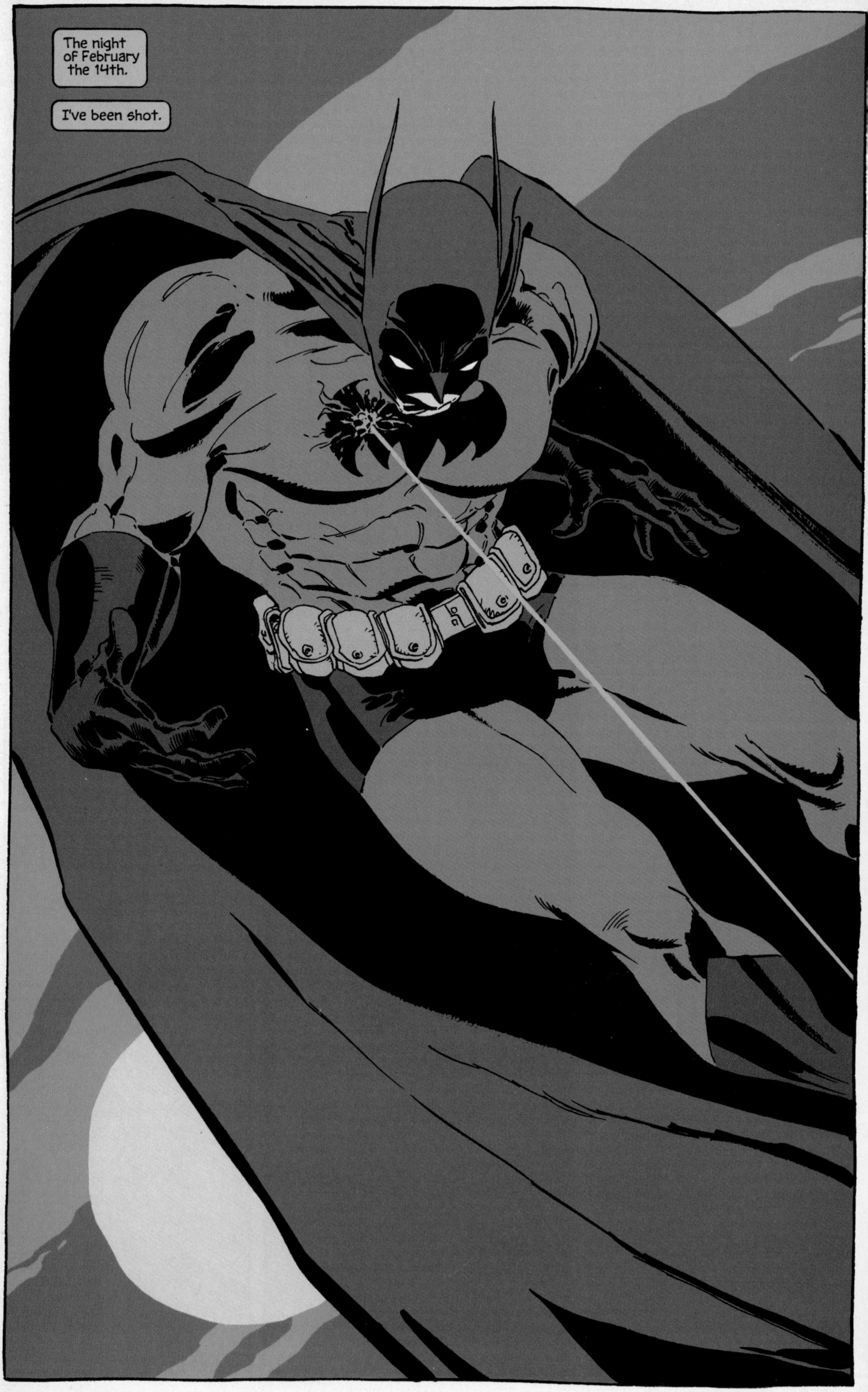
The night of February the 14th.
I've been shot.

There is a killer loose in Gotham City.

Four men have been hanged. All on holidays. One per month.

Other than the manner of the killings, they had **one** thing in common.

They were all **cops**.

Cops who worked Gotham when I -- when **both** Jim Gordon and I started here.

The victims all had different ranks. Police Chief O'Hara. Commissioner Loeb. Detective Flass. Lieutenant Branden.

When **Branden** was killed on New Year's, I started looking into who else was under his command.

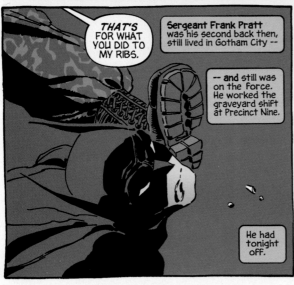

THAT'S FOR WHAT YOU DID TO MY RIBS.

Sergeant Frank Pratt was his second back then, still lived in Gotham City --

-- and still was on the force. He worked the graveyard shift at Precinct Nine.

He had tonight off.

≥URK≥

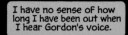

I have no sense of how long I have been out when I hear Gordon's voice.

BATMAN. BATMAN, CAN YOU HEAR ME?

Alfred always insists I wear the kevlar vest underneath the costume -- despite how it hampers my movement.

Even so, the impact of the bullet feels like I cracked a rib.

Hard to breathe.

WHERE -- WHERE IS PRATT?

Gordon has some new faces with him. They don't like me, which is fine. I'm not here to be liked.

WHERE IS HE?

HE'S DEAD.

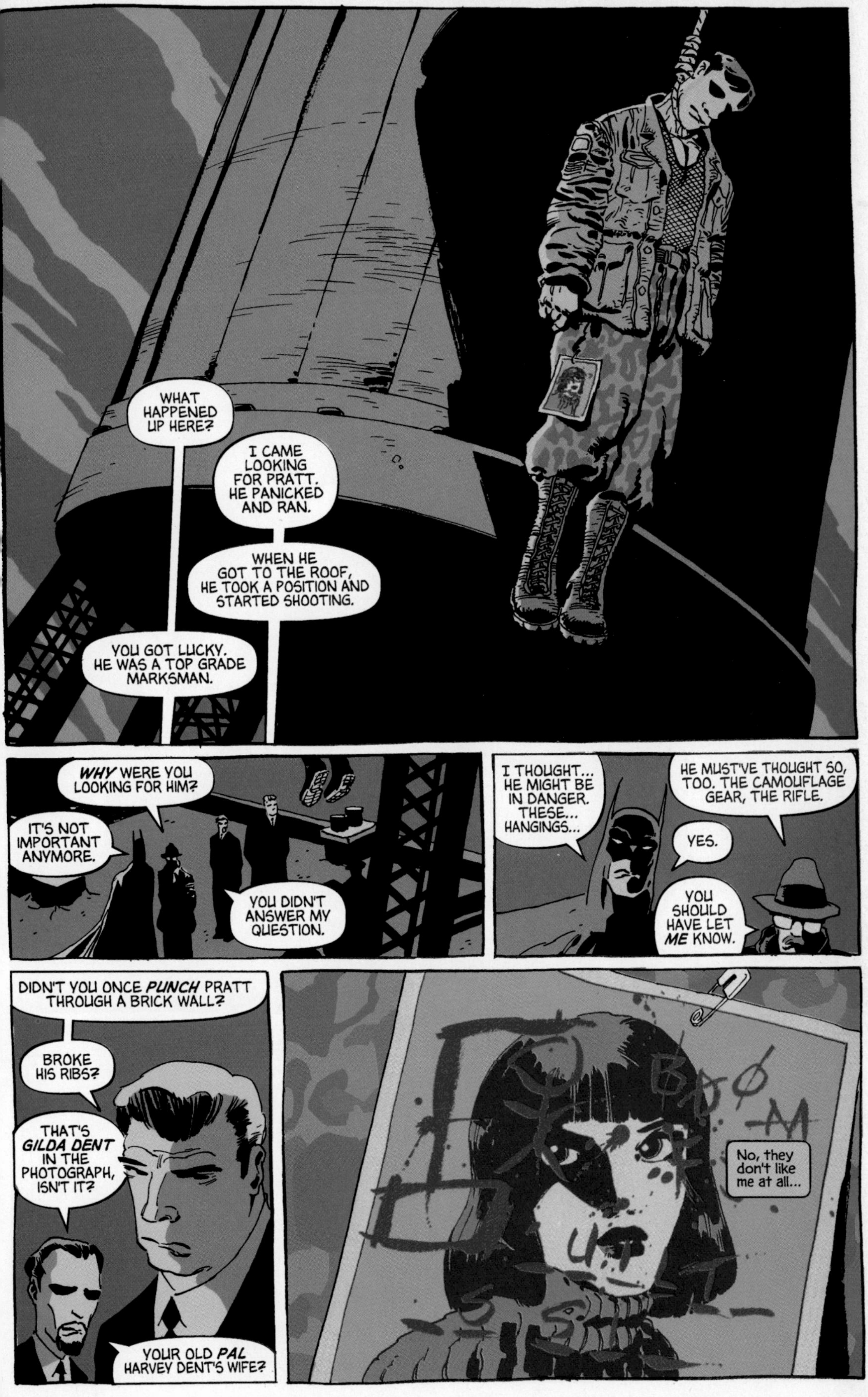
WHAT HAPPENED UP HERE?
I CAME LOOKING FOR PRATT. HE PANICKED AND RAN.
WHEN HE GOT TO THE ROOF, HE TOOK A POSITION AND STARTED SHOOTING.
YOU GOT LUCKY. HE WAS A TOP GRADE MARKSMAN.
WHY WERE YOU LOOKING FOR HIM?
IT'S NOT IMPORTANT ANYMORE.
YOU DIDN'T ANSWER MY QUESTION.
I THOUGHT... HE MIGHT BE IN DANGER. THESE... HANGINGS...
HE MUST'VE THOUGHT SO, TOO. THE CAMOUFLAGE GEAR, THE RIFLE.
YES.
YOU SHOULD HAVE LET ME KNOW.
DIDN'T YOU ONCE PUNCH PRATT THROUGH A BRICK WALL?
BROKE HIS RIBS?
THAT'S GILDA DENT IN THE PHOTOGRAPH, ISN'T IT?
YOUR OLD PAL HARVEY DENT'S WIFE?
No, they don't like me at all...

For weeks now, I've been hearing that **Catwoman** is on the prowl.

Leaving a trail that is too easy **not** to Follow.

WHO'S NEXT?

MEN

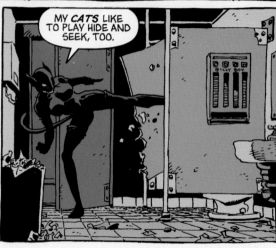

MY **CATS** LIKE TO PLAY HIDE AND SEEK, TOO.

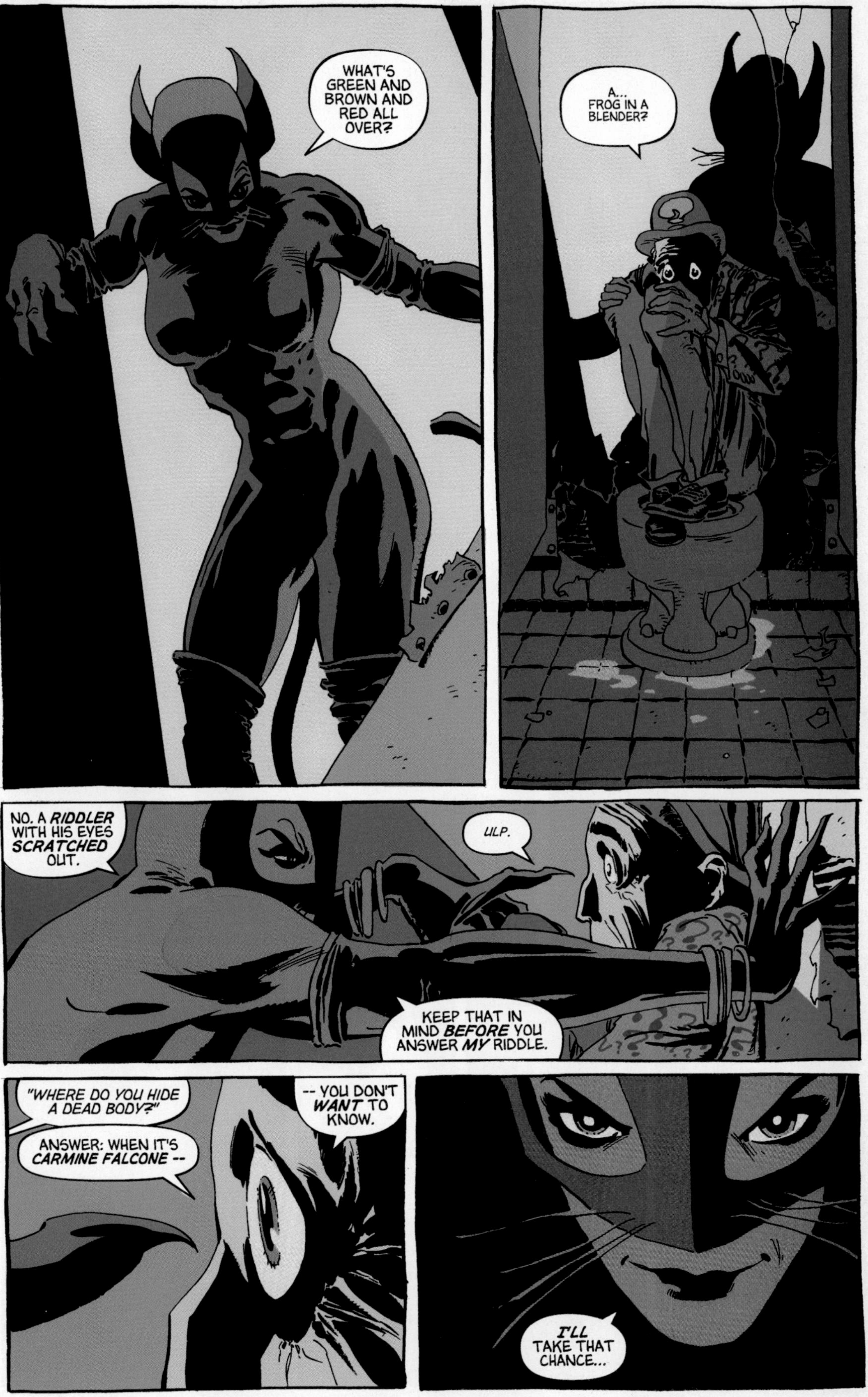
WHAT'S GREEN AND BROWN AND RED ALL OVER?
A... FROG IN A BLENDER?
NO. A RIDDLER WITH HIS EYES SCRATCHED OUT.
ULP.
KEEP THAT IN MIND BEFORE YOU ANSWER MY RIDDLE.
"WHERE DO YOU HIDE A DEAD BODY?"
ANSWER: WHEN IT'S CARMINE FALCONE --
-- YOU DON'T WANT TO KNOW.
I'LL TAKE THAT CHANCE...

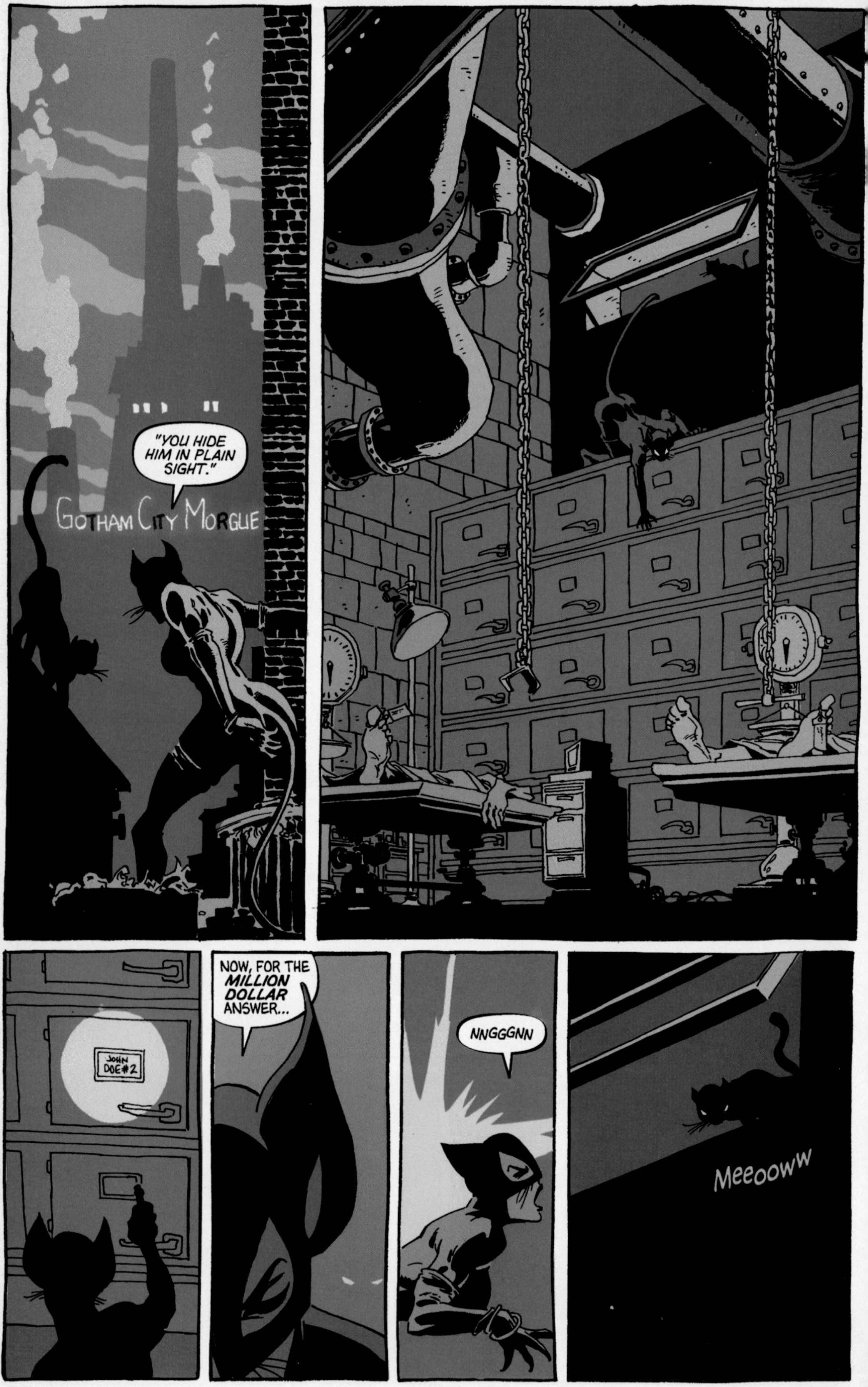
"YOU HIDE HIM IN PLAIN SIGHT."
GOTHAM CITY MORGUE
JOHN DOE #2
NOW, FOR THE MILLION DOLLAR ANSWER...
NNGGGNN
Meeooww

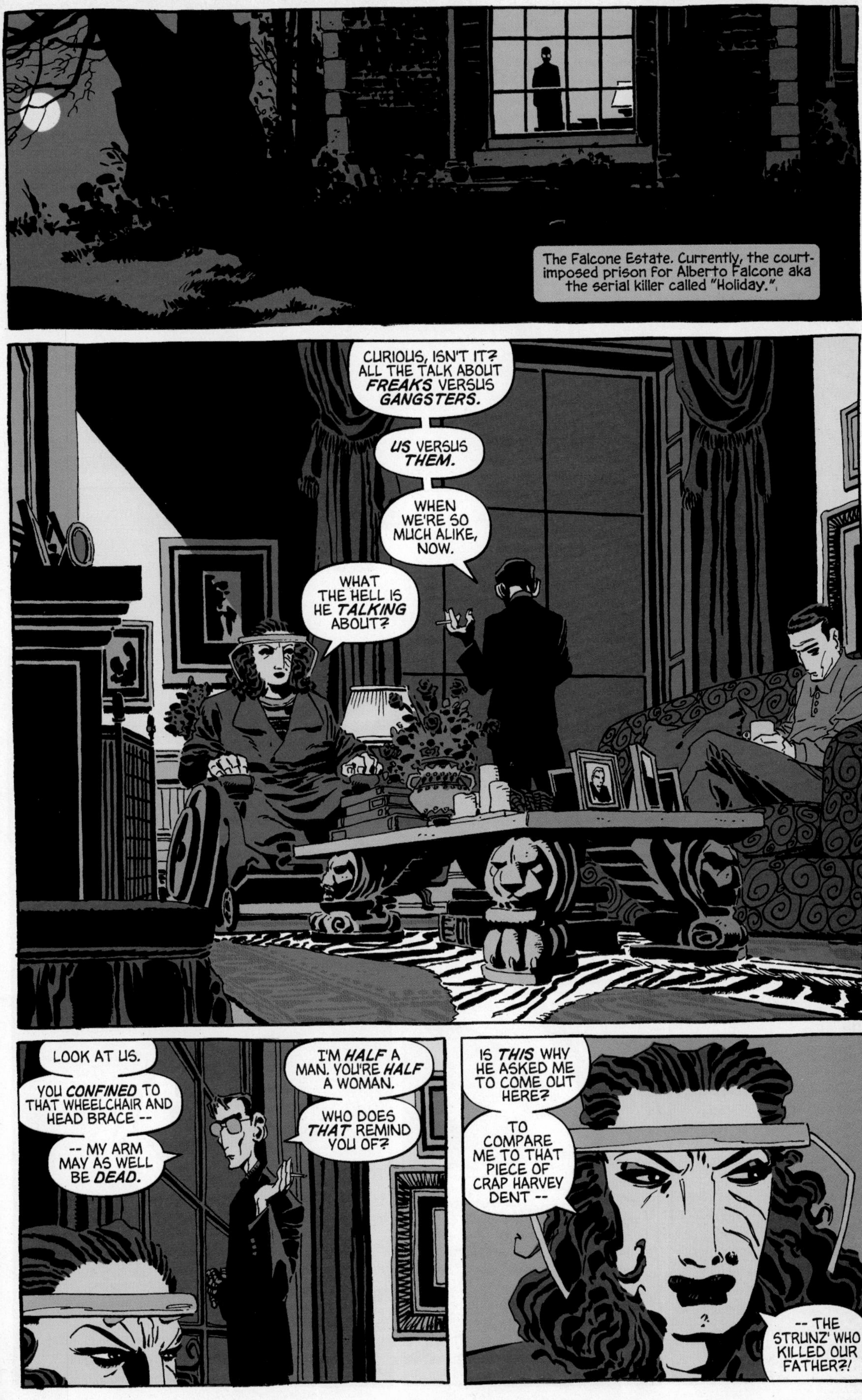
The Falcone Estate. Currently, the court-imposed prison for Alberto Falcone aka the serial killer called "Holiday."
CURIOUS, ISN'T IT? ALL THE TALK ABOUT FREAKS VERSUS GANGSTERS.
US VERSUS THEM.
WHEN WE'RE SO MUCH ALIKE, NOW.
WHAT THE HELL IS HE TALKING ABOUT?
LOOK AT US.
YOU CONFINED TO THAT WHEELCHAIR AND HEAD BRACE --
-- MY ARM MAY AS WELL BE DEAD.
I'M HALF A MAN. YOU'RE HALF A WOMAN.
WHO DOES THAT REMIND YOU OF?
IS THIS WHY HE ASKED ME TO COME OUT HERE?
TO COMPARE ME TO THAT PIECE OF CRAP HARVEY DENT --
-- THE STRUNZ' WHO KILLED OUR FATHER?!

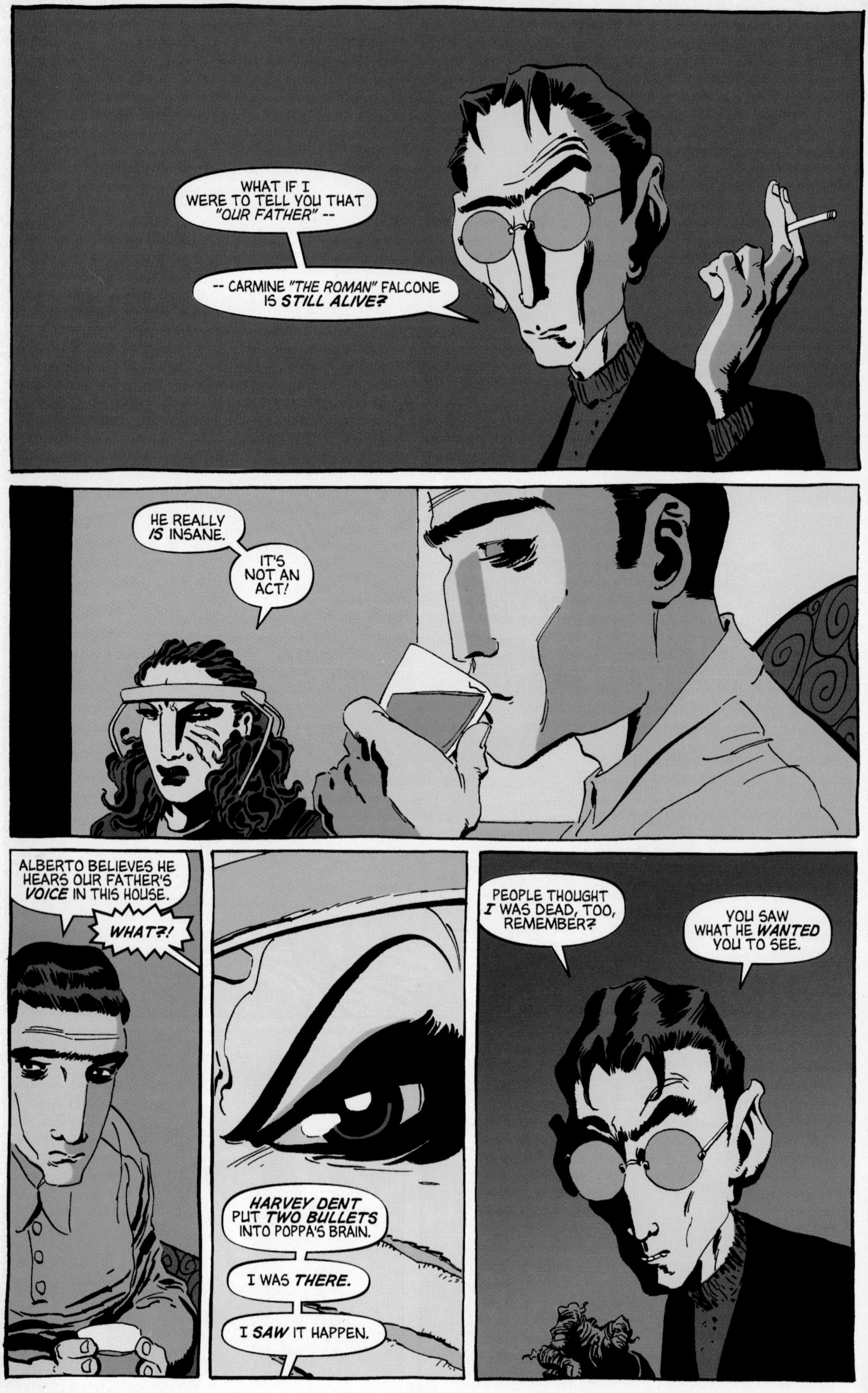
WHAT IF I WERE TO TELL YOU THAT "OUR FATHER" --
-- CARMINE "THE ROMAN" FALCONE IS STILL ALIVE?
HE REALLY IS INSANE.
IT'S NOT AN ACT!
ALBERTO BELIEVES HE HEARS OUR FATHER'S VOICE IN THIS HOUSE.
WHAT?!
HARVEY DENT PUT TWO BULLETS INTO POPPA'S BRAIN.
I WAS THERE.
I SAW IT HAPPEN.
PEOPLE THOUGHT I WAS DEAD, TOO, REMEMBER?
YOU SAW WHAT HE WANTED YOU TO SEE.

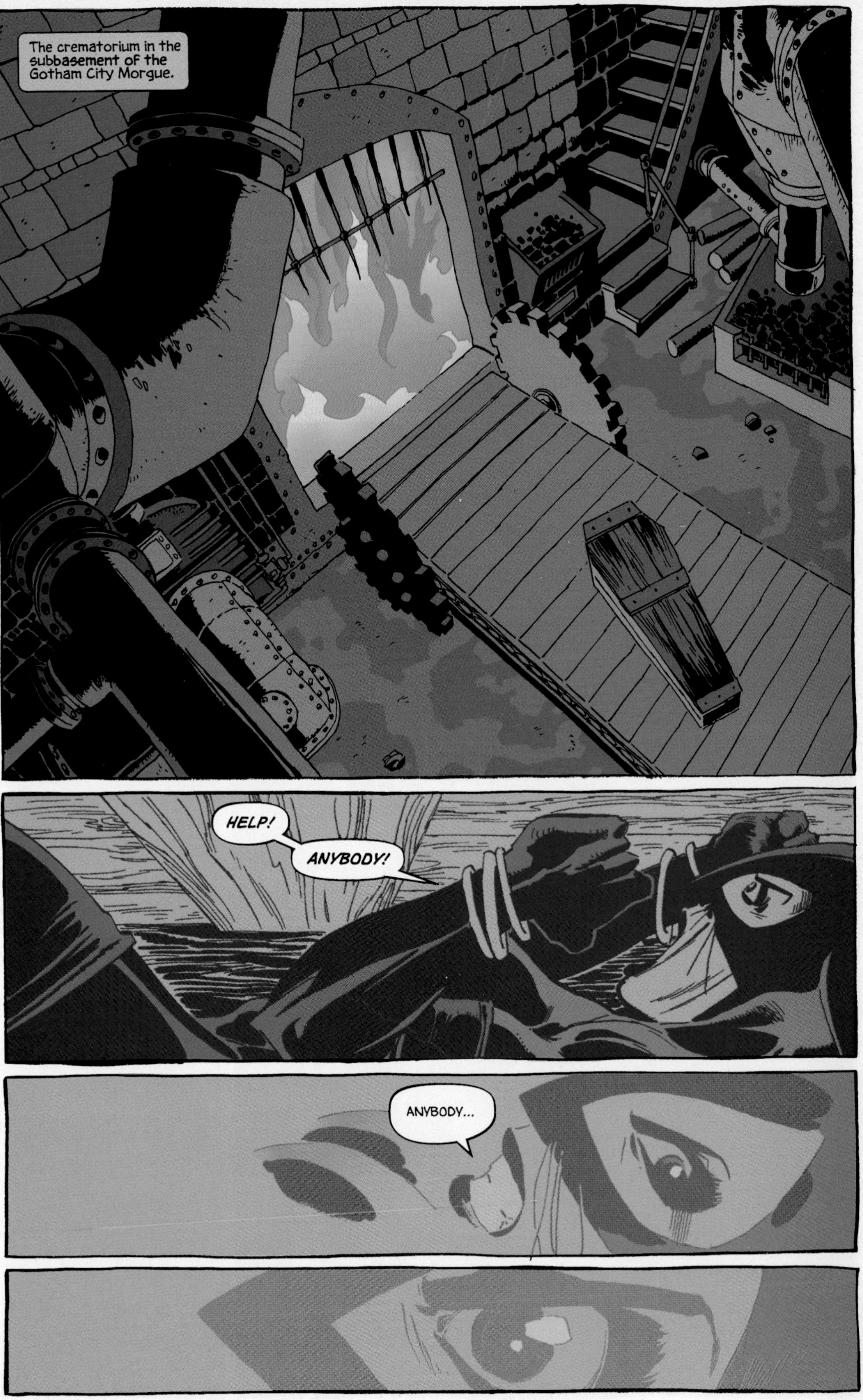
The crematorium in the subbasement of the Gotham City Morgue.
HELP!
ANYBODY!
ANYBODY...

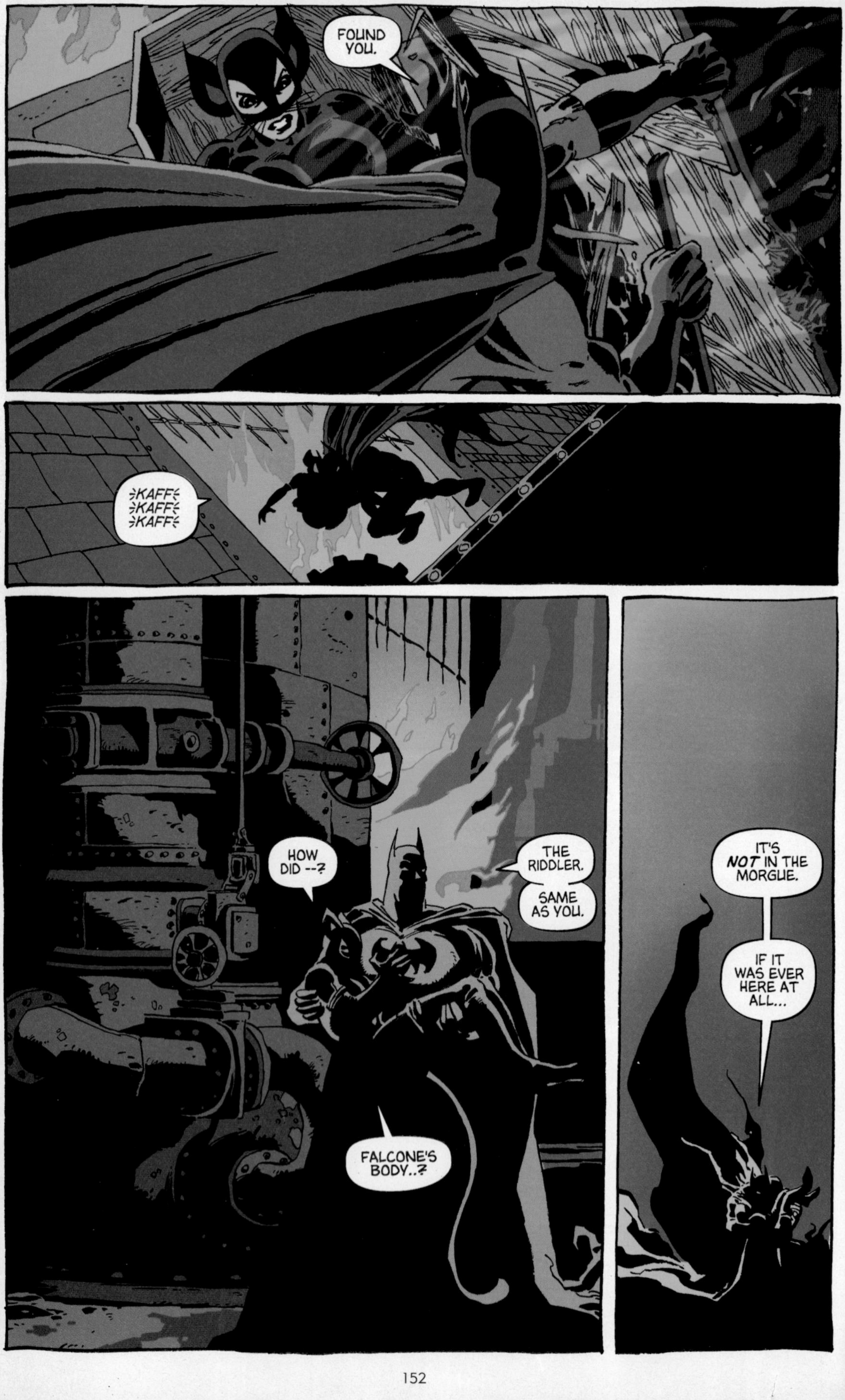
FOUND YOU.
KAFF KAFF KAFF
HOW DID --?
THE RIDDLER.
SAME AS YOU.
FALCONE'S BODY..?
IT'S NOT IN THE MORGUE.
IF IT WAS EVER HERE AT ALL...

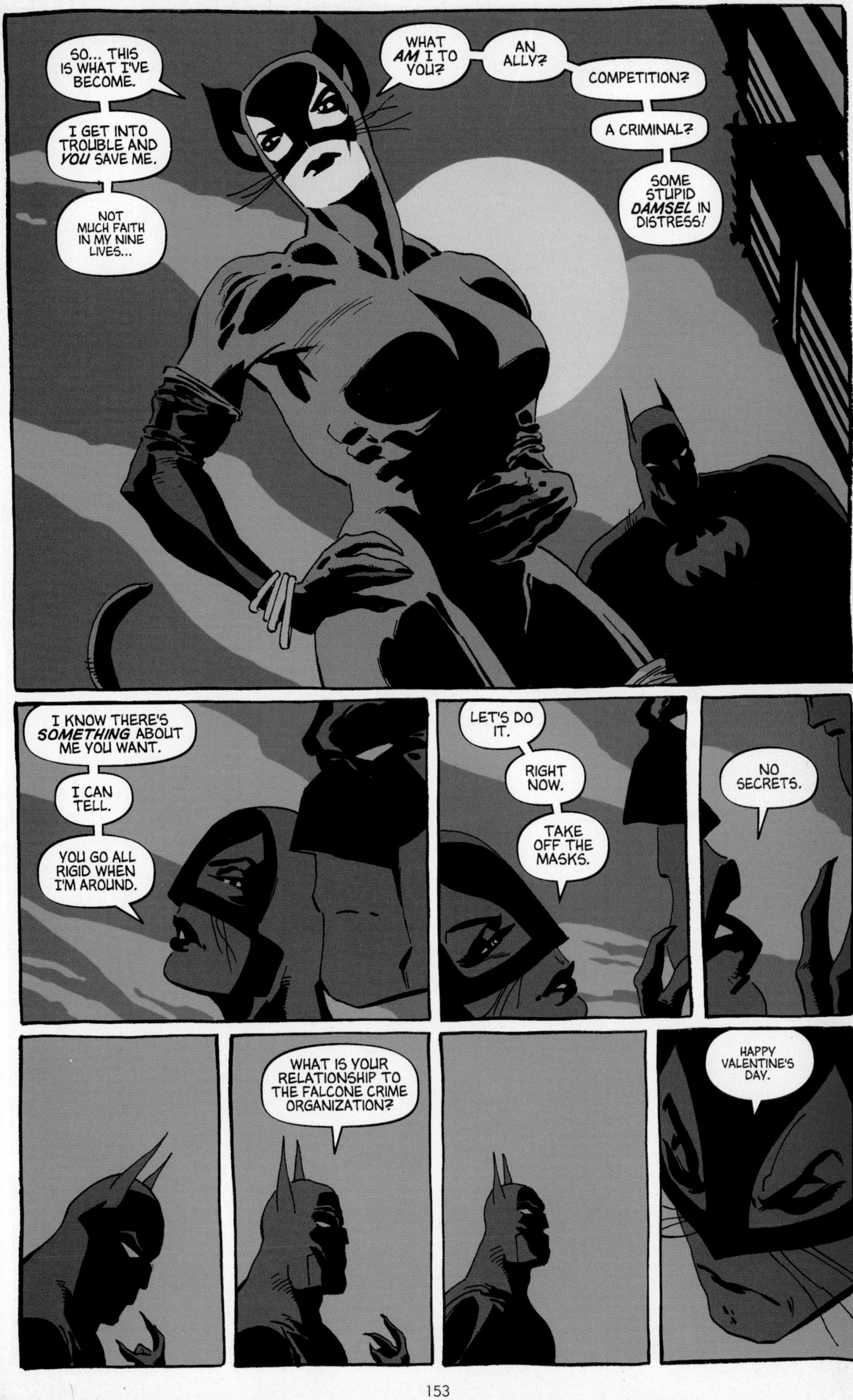

SO... THIS IS WHAT I'VE BECOME.
I GET INTO TROUBLE AND YOU SAVE ME.
NOT MUCH FAITH IN MY NINE LIVES...
WHAT AM I TO YOU?
AN ALLY?
COMPETITION?
A CRIMINAL?
SOME STUPID DAMSEL IN DISTRESS!
I KNOW THERE'S SOMETHING ABOUT ME YOU WANT.
I CAN TELL.
YOU GO ALL RIGID WHEN I'M AROUND.
LET'S DO IT.
RIGHT NOW.
TAKE OFF THE MASKS.
NO SECRETS.
WHAT IS YOUR RELATIONSHIP TO THE FALCONE CRIME ORGANIZATION?
HAPPY VALENTINE'S DAY.

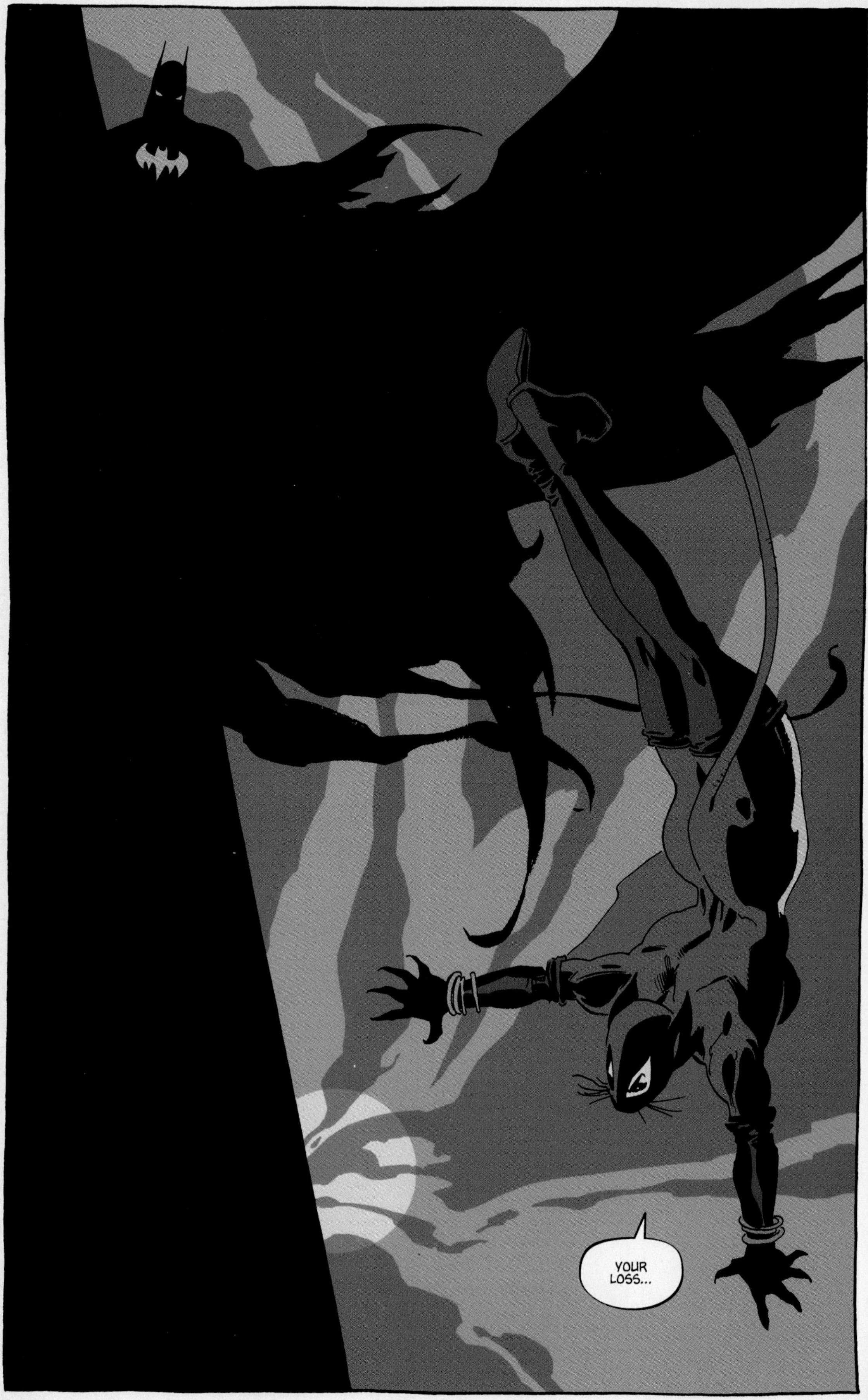
YOUR LOSS...

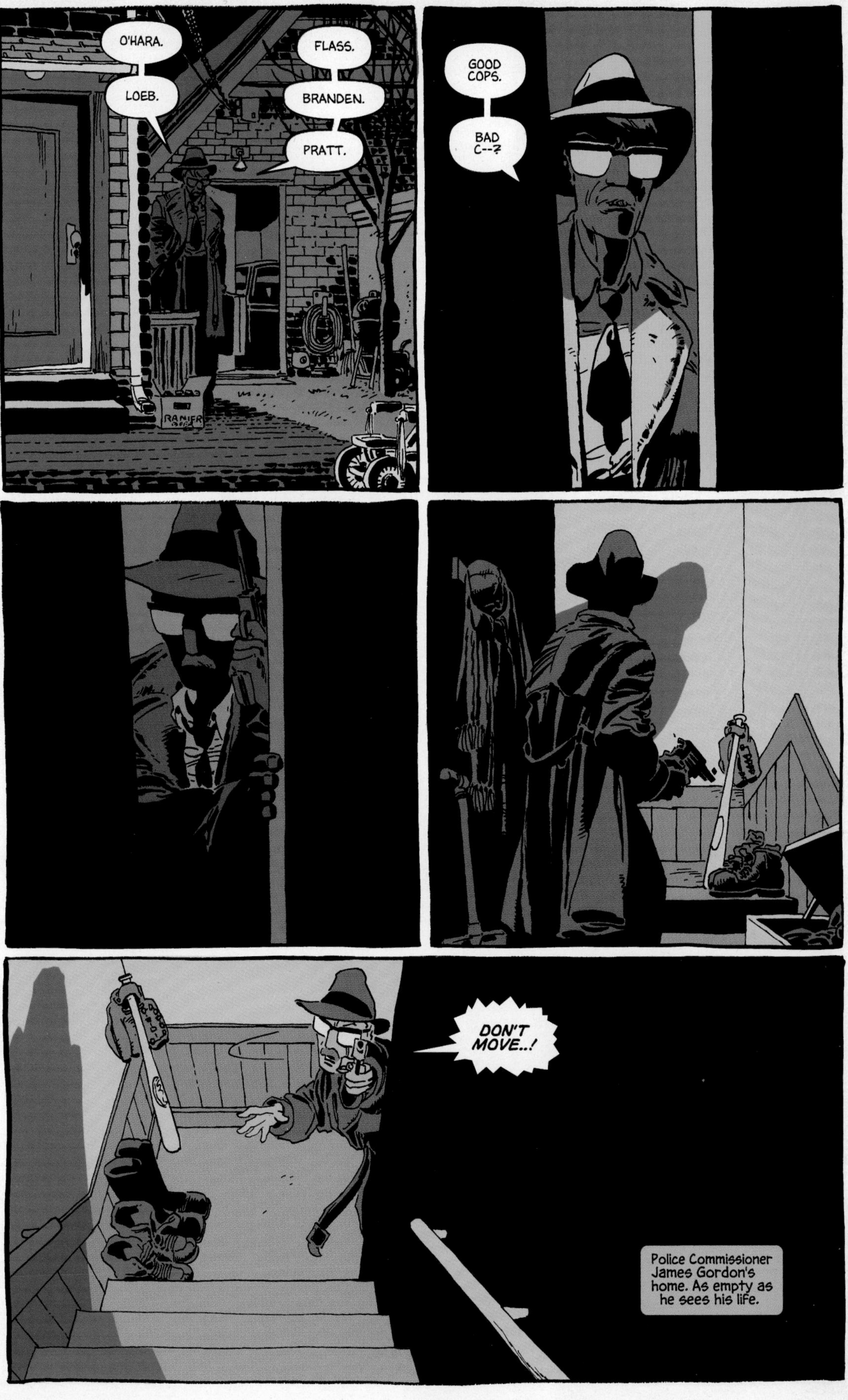
O'HARA.
LOEB.
FLASS.
BRANDEN.
PRATT.
RANIER
GOOD COPS.
BAD C--?
DON'T MOVE..!
Police Commissioner James Gordon's home. As empty as he sees his life.

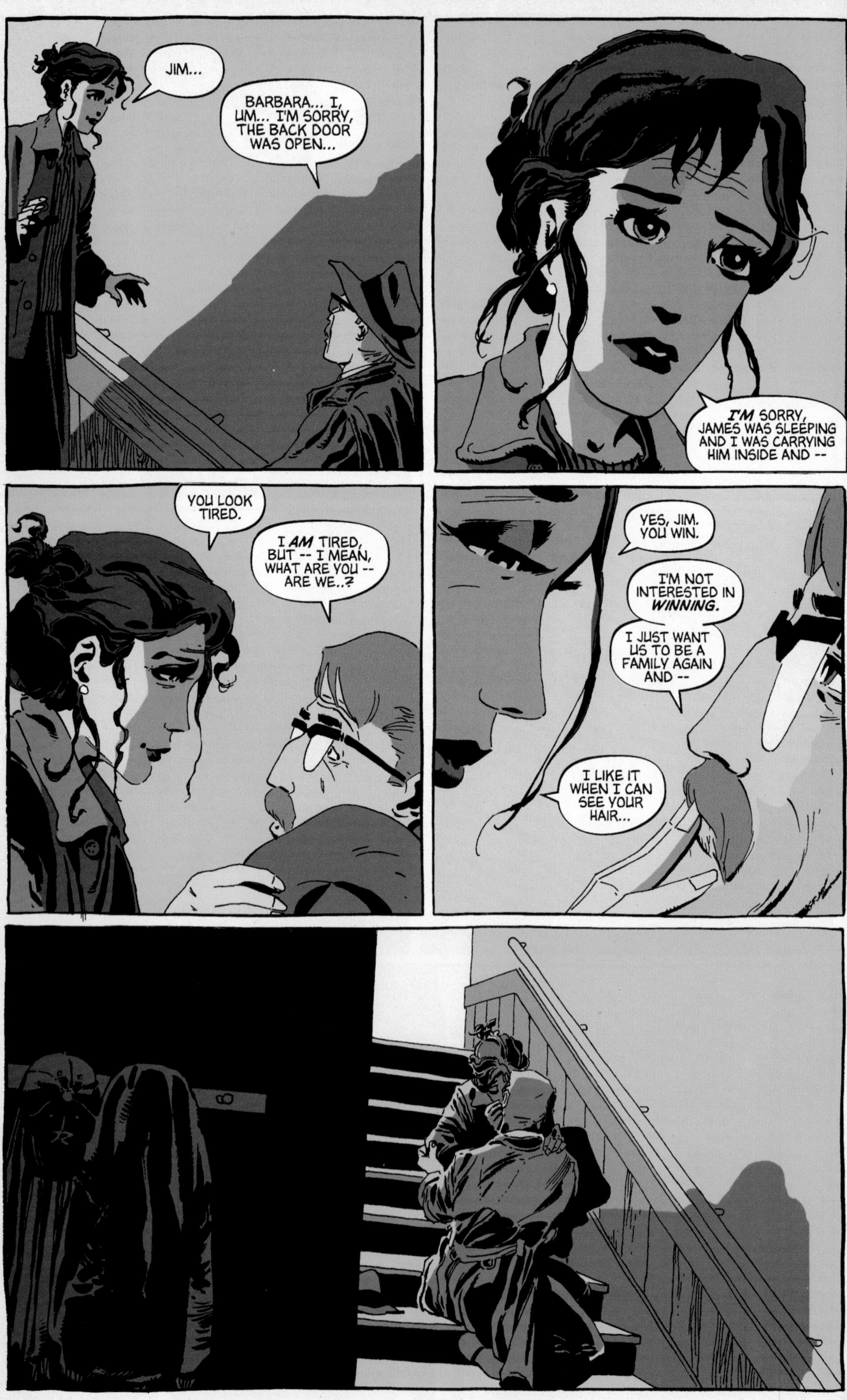
JIM...
BARBARA... I, UM... I'M SORRY, THE BACK DOOR WAS OPEN...
I'M SORRY, JAMES WAS SLEEPING AND I WAS CARRYING HIM INSIDE AND --
YOU LOOK TIRED.
I AM TIRED, BUT -- I MEAN, WHAT ARE YOU -- ARE WE..?
YES, JIM. YOU WIN.
I'M NOT INTERESTED IN WINNING.
I JUST WANT US TO BE A FAMILY AGAIN AND --
I LIKE IT WHEN I CAN SEE YOUR HAIR...

The morning of February the 15th. Selina Kyle's brownstone.

The moving truck out front is one of Anthony Zucco's. **The Maronis** own the company. Coincidence?

WHAT'S GOING ON HERE?

WHAT'S IT LOOK LIKE? THE LADY'S *MOVIN'*.

WHAT? WHERE?

TALK TO THE BOSS INSIDE.

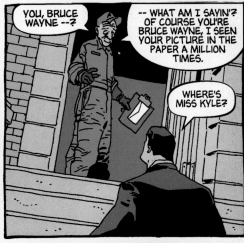

YOU, BRUCE WAYNE --?

-- WHAT AM I SAYIN'? OF COURSE YOU'RE BRUCE WAYNE, I SEEN YOUR PICTURE IN THE PAPER A MILLION TIMES.

WHERE'S MISS KYLE?

SHE SAID TO GIVE THIS TO YOU IF YOU SHOWED UP, OTHERWISE TAPE IT TO THE DOOR.

IS THERE A FORWARDING ADDRESS?

NAW. ALL THIS IS GOIN' INTA STORAGE.

SAY, WOULDYA MIND LOCKIN' UP?

THAT'S THE LAST PIECE GOIN' ON THE TRUCK AND WE GOT A SCHEDULE TO KEEP.

AND, I MEAN, IF I CAN'T TRUST A GUY LIKE YOU...

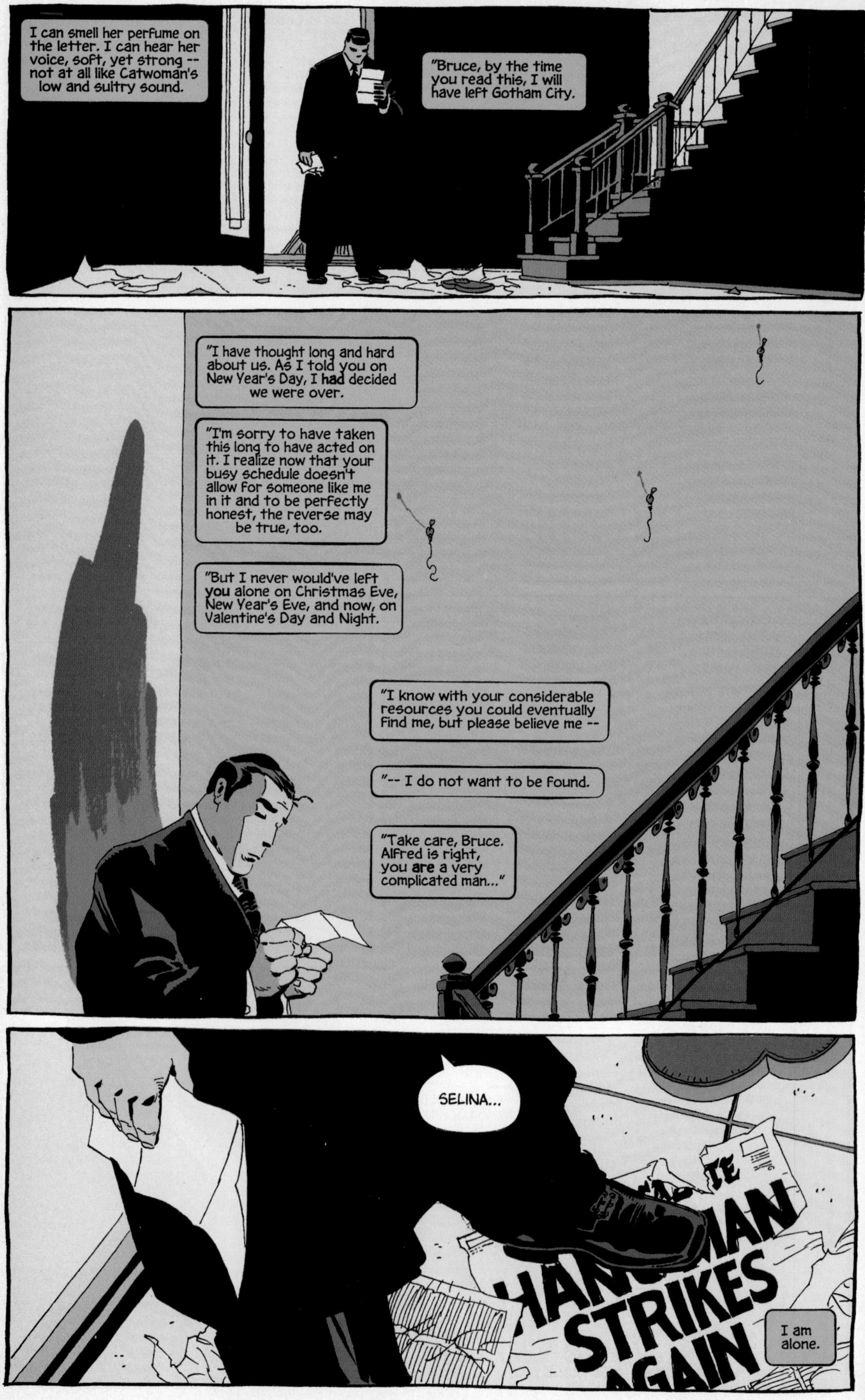

I can smell her perfume on the letter. I can hear her voice, soft, yet strong -- not at all like Catwoman's low and sultry sound.
"Bruce, by the time you read this, I will have left Gotham City.
"I have thought long and hard about us. As I told you on New Year's Day, I **had** decided we were over.
"I'm sorry to have taken this long to have acted on it. I realize now that your busy schedule doesn't allow for someone like me in it and to be perfectly honest, the reverse may be true, too.
"But I never would've left **you** alone on Christmas Eve, New Year's Eve, and now, on Valentine's Day and Night.
"I know with your considerable resources you could eventually find me, but please believe me --
"-- I do not want to be found.
"Take care, Bruce. Alfred is right, you **are** a very complicated man..."
SELINA...
STRIKES AGAIN
I am alone.

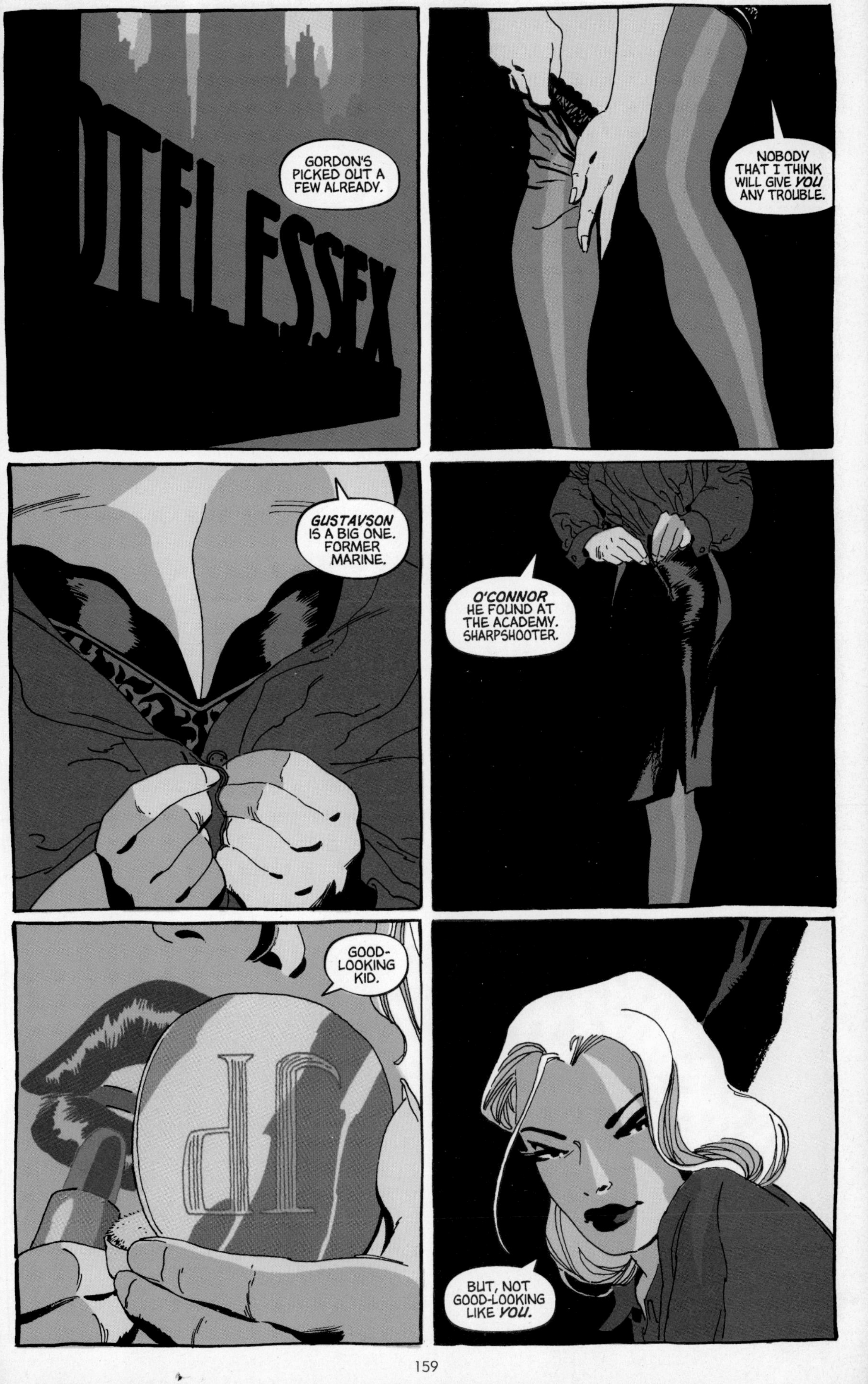
GORDON'S PICKED OUT A FEW ALREADY.
NOBODY THAT I THINK WILL GIVE *YOU* ANY TROUBLE.
GUSTAVSON IS A BIG ONE. FORMER MARINE.
O'CONNOR HE FOUND AT THE ACADEMY. SHARPSHOOTER.
GOOD-LOOKING KID.
BUT, NOT GOOD-LOOKING LIKE *YOU*.

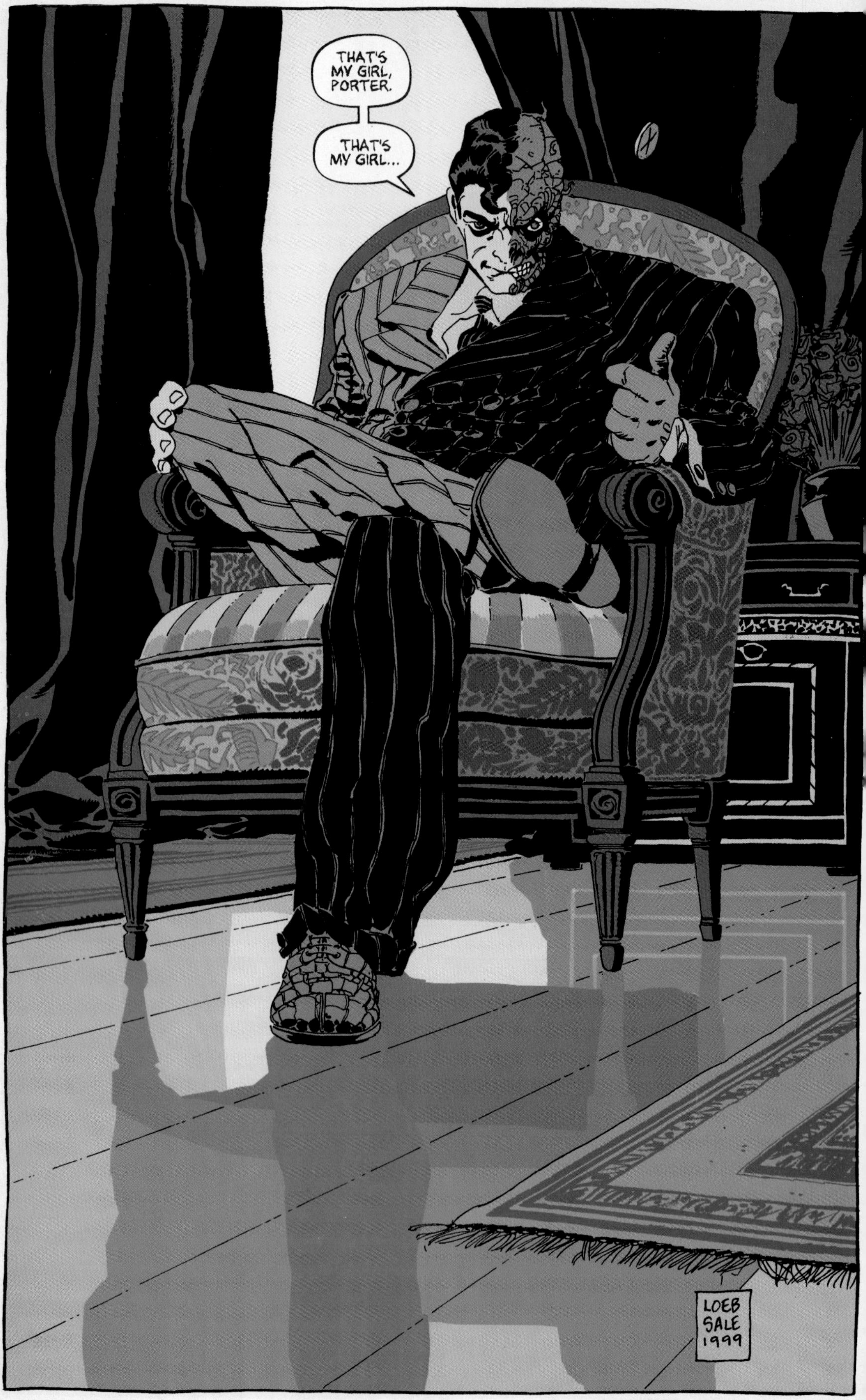
THAT'S MY GIRL, PORTER.
THAT'S MY GIRL...
LOEB SALE 1999

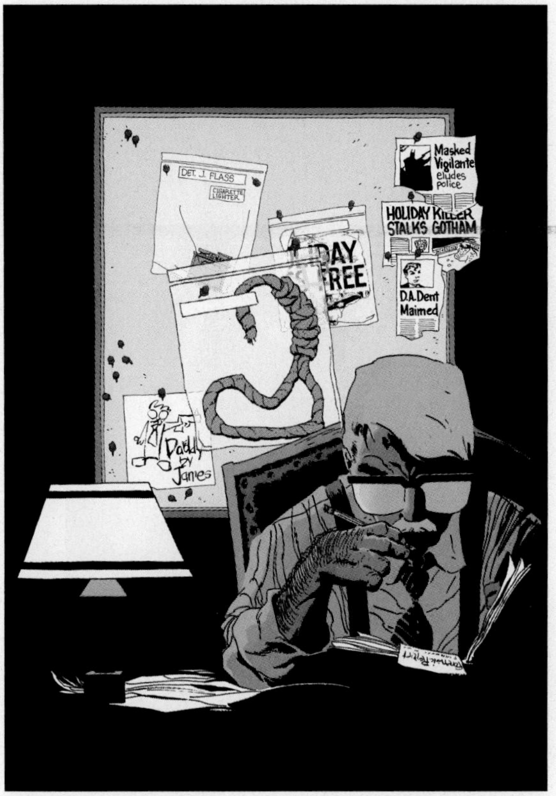
DET. J. FLASS
CIGARETTE LIGHTER
Masked Vigilante eludes police
HOLIDAY KILLER STALKS GOTHAM
D.A. Dent Maimed
Daddy by James

HATE

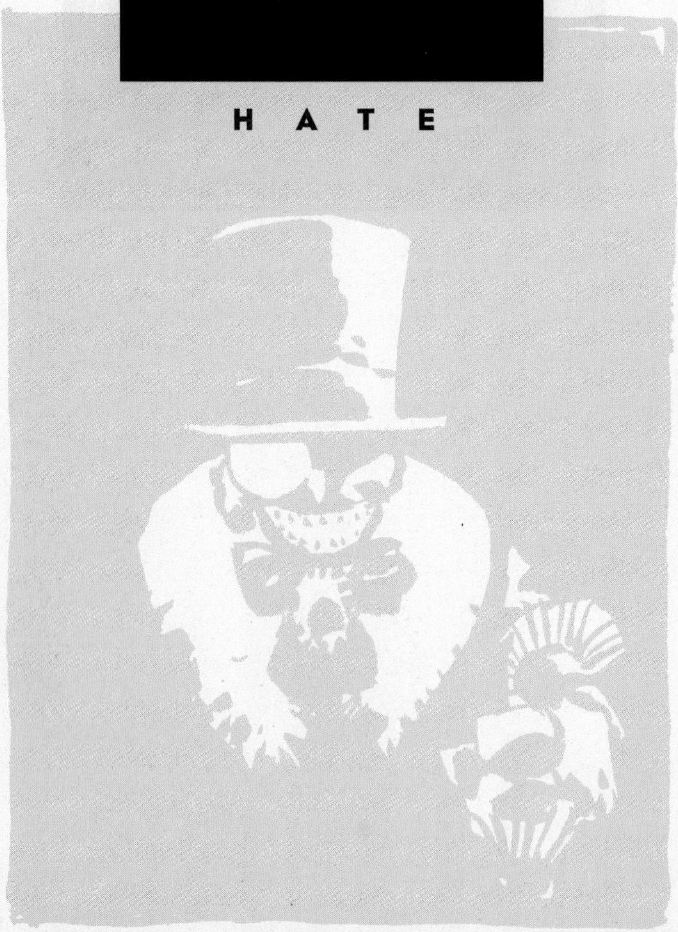

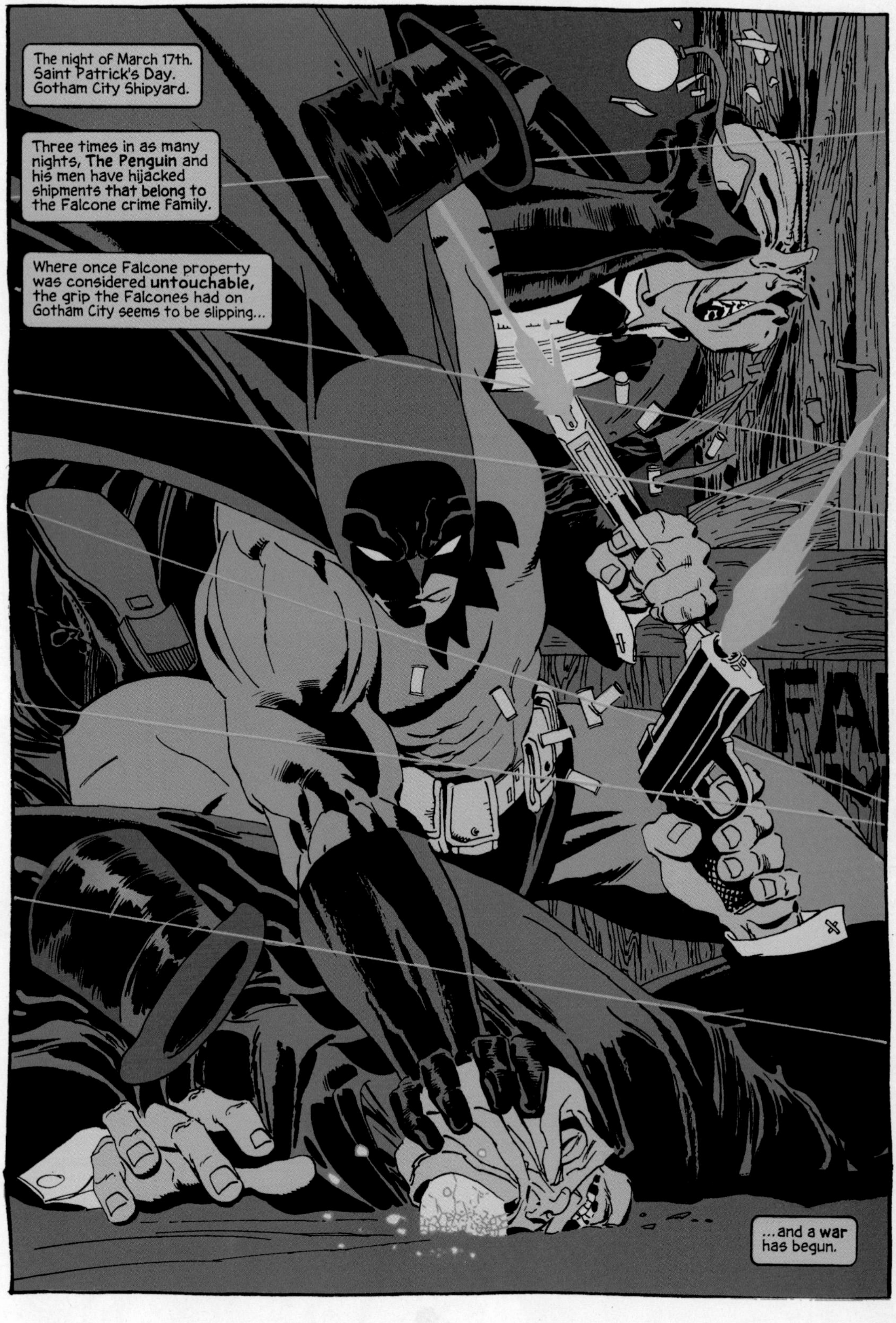
The night of March 17th. Saint Patrick's Day. Gotham City Shipyard.
Three times in as many nights, **The Penguin** and his men have hijacked shipments that belong to the Falcone crime Family.
Where once Falcone property was considered **untouchable**, the grip the Falcones had on Gotham City seems to be slipping...
...and a **war** has begun.

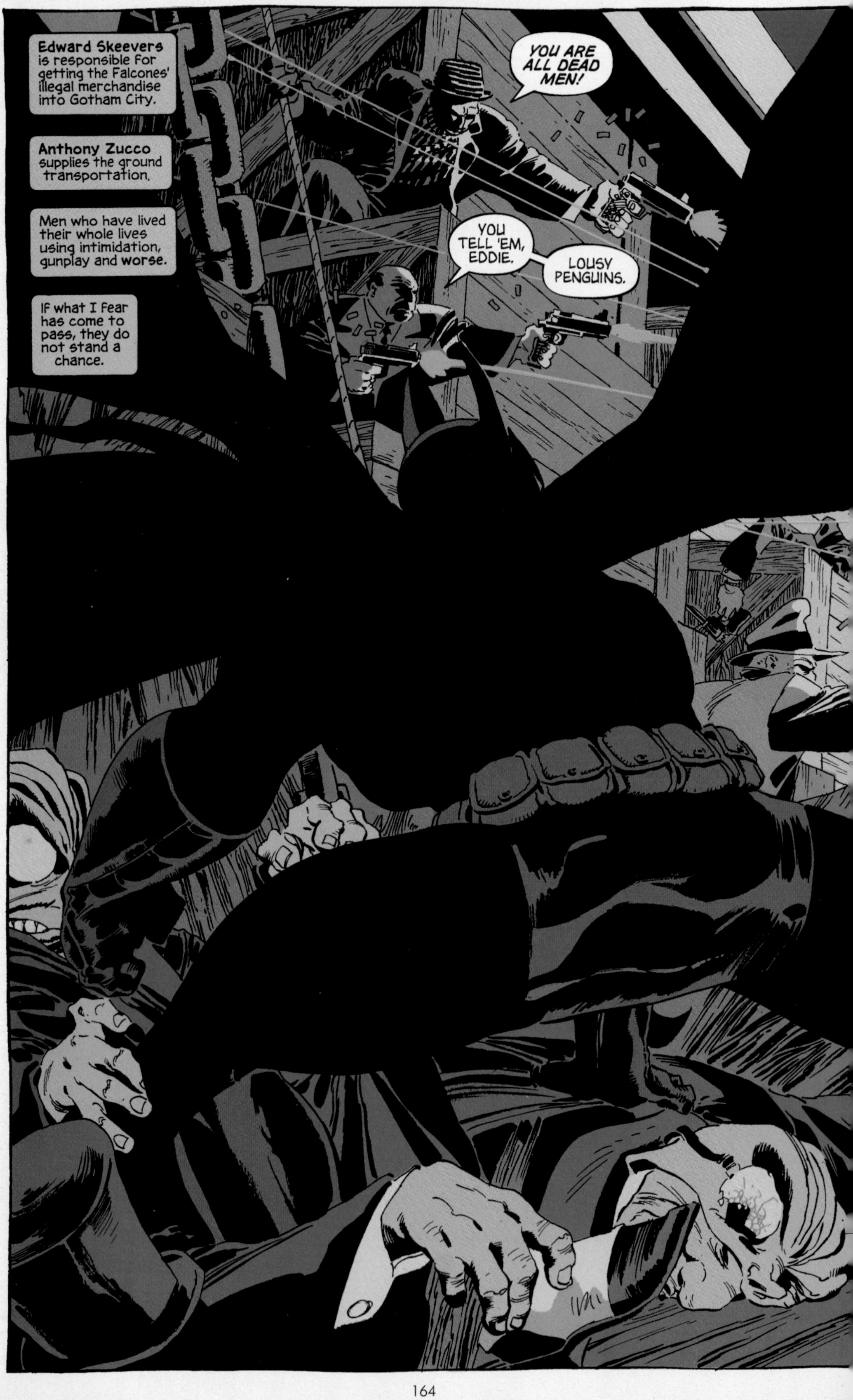

Edward Skeevers is responsible for getting the Falcones' illegal merchandise into Gotham City.
Anthony Zucco supplies the ground transportation.
Men who have lived their whole lives using intimidation, gunplay and worse.
If what I fear has come to pass, they do not stand a chance.
YOU ARE ALL DEAD MEN!
YOU TELL 'EM, EDDIE.
LOUSY PENGUINS.

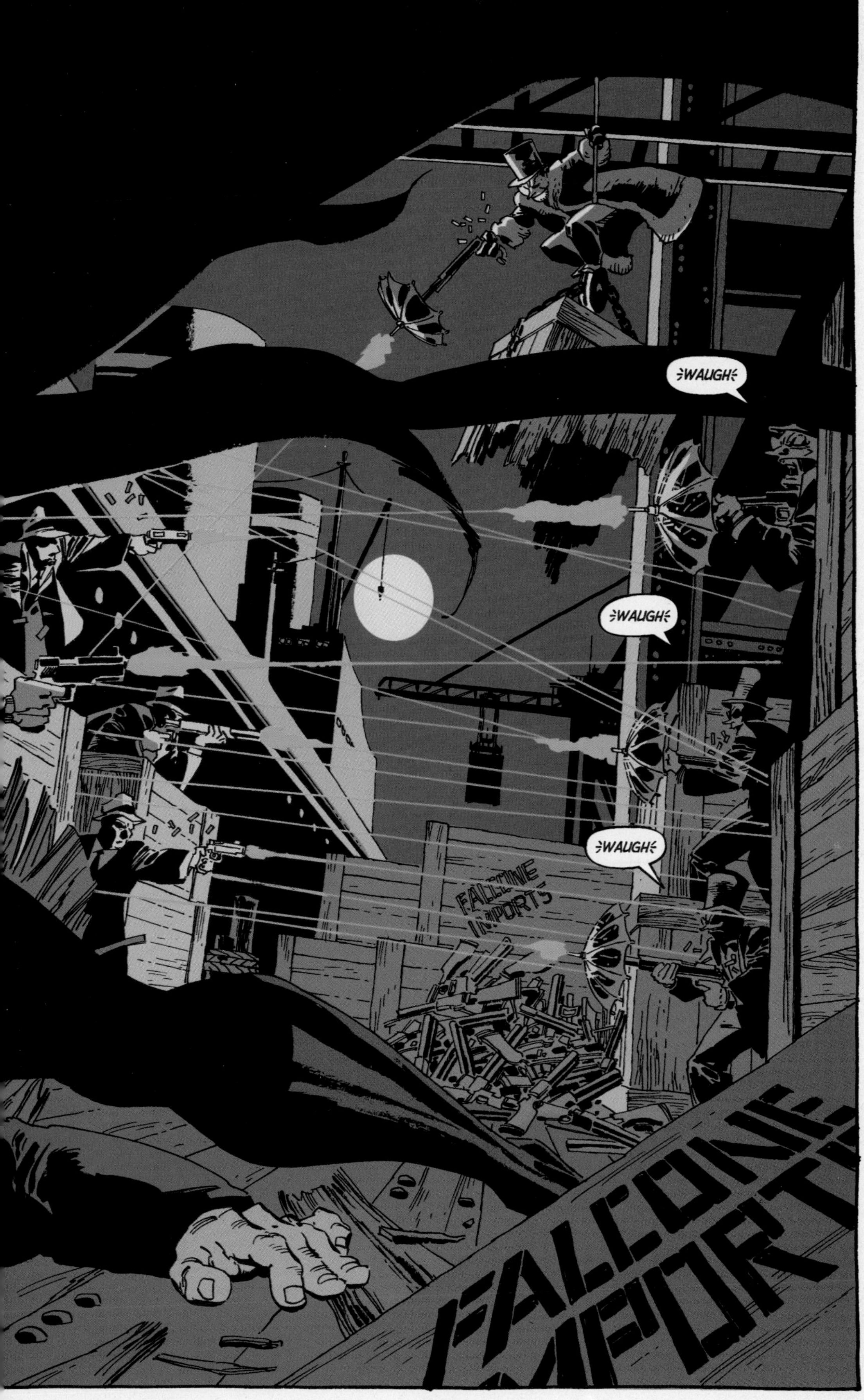
WAUGH
WAUGH
WAUGH
FALCONE IMPORTS
FALCONE IMPORTS

AW, CRAP, THAT'S THE *BATMAN!*

WHOSE SIDE DO YOU FIGURE *HE'S* ON, ZUCCO?

HOW THE HELL SHOULD I KNOW?

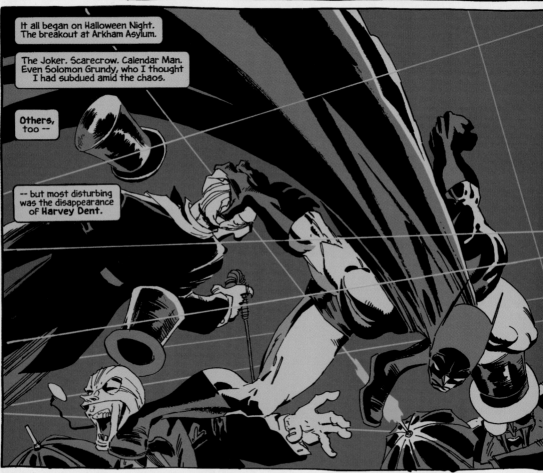

It all began on Halloween Night. The breakout at Arkham Asylum.

The Joker. Scarecrow. Calendar Man. Even Solomon Grundy, who I thought I had subdued amid the chaos.

Others, too --

-- but most disturbing was the disappearance of **Harvey Dent.**

‡UGHNN‡

EDDIE!

The Former District Attorney. My ally. My... friend.

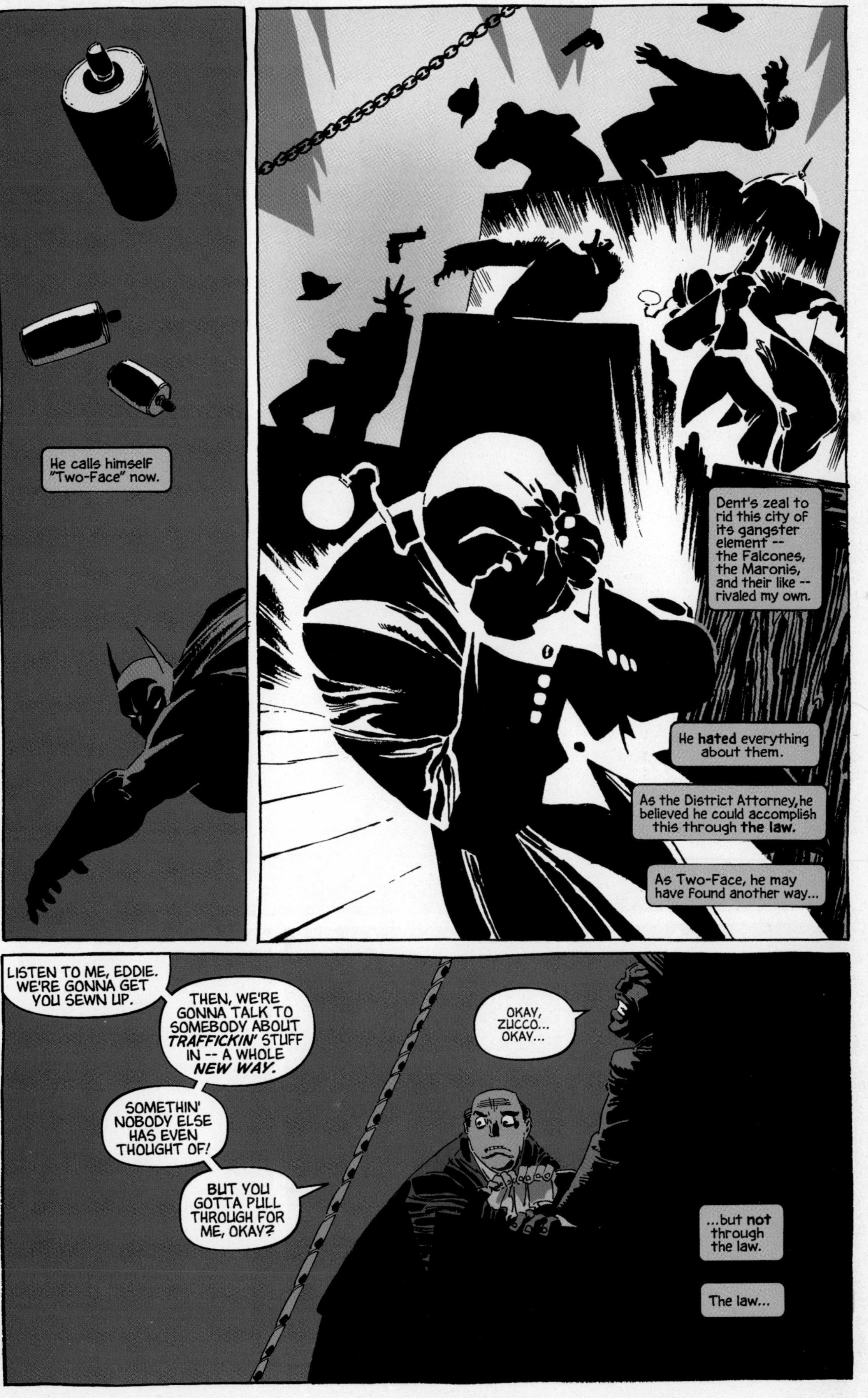
He calls himself "Two-Face" now.
Dent's zeal to rid this city of its gangster element -- the Falcones, the Maronis, and their like -- rivaled my own.
He hated everything about them.
As the District Attorney, he believed he could accomplish this through the law.
As Two-Face, he may have found another way...
LISTEN TO ME, EDDIE. WE'RE GONNA GET YOU SEWN UP.
THEN, WE'RE GONNA TALK TO SOMEBODY ABOUT TRAFFICKIN' STUFF IN -- A WHOLE NEW WAY.
SOMETHIN' NOBODY ELSE HAS EVEN THOUGHT OF!
BUT YOU GOTTA PULL THROUGH FOR ME, OKAY?
OKAY, ZUCCO... OKAY...
...but not through the law.
The law...

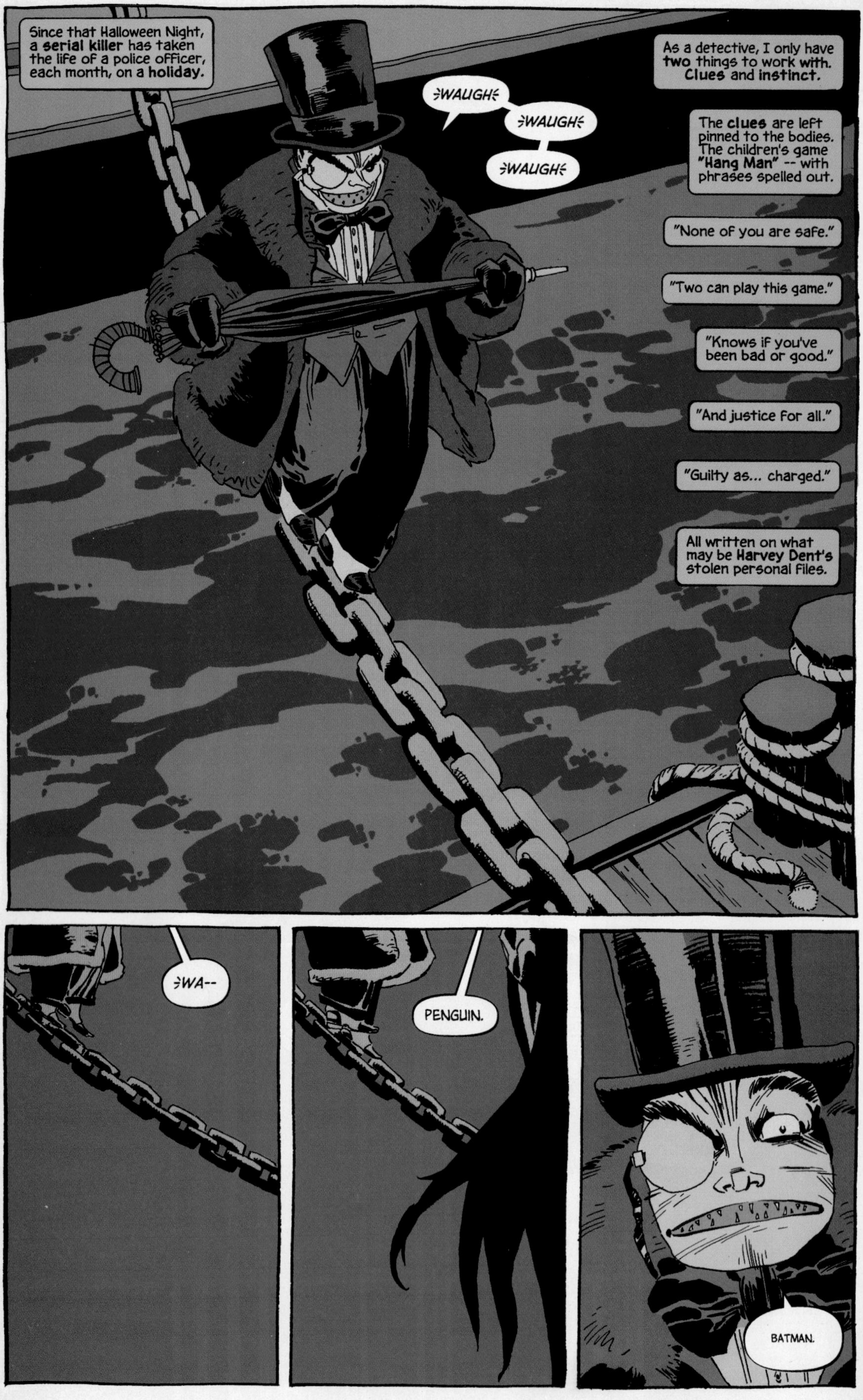
Since that Halloween Night, a serial killer has taken the life of a police officer, each month, on a holiday.
WAUGH
WAUGH
WAUGH
As a detective, I only have two things to work with. Clues and instinct.
The clues are left pinned to the bodies. The children's game "Hang Man" -- with phrases spelled out.
"None of you are safe."
"Two can play this game."
"Knows if you've been bad or good."
"And justice for all."
"Guilty as... charged."
All written on what may be Harvey Dent's stolen personal files.
WA--
PENGUIN.
BATMAN.

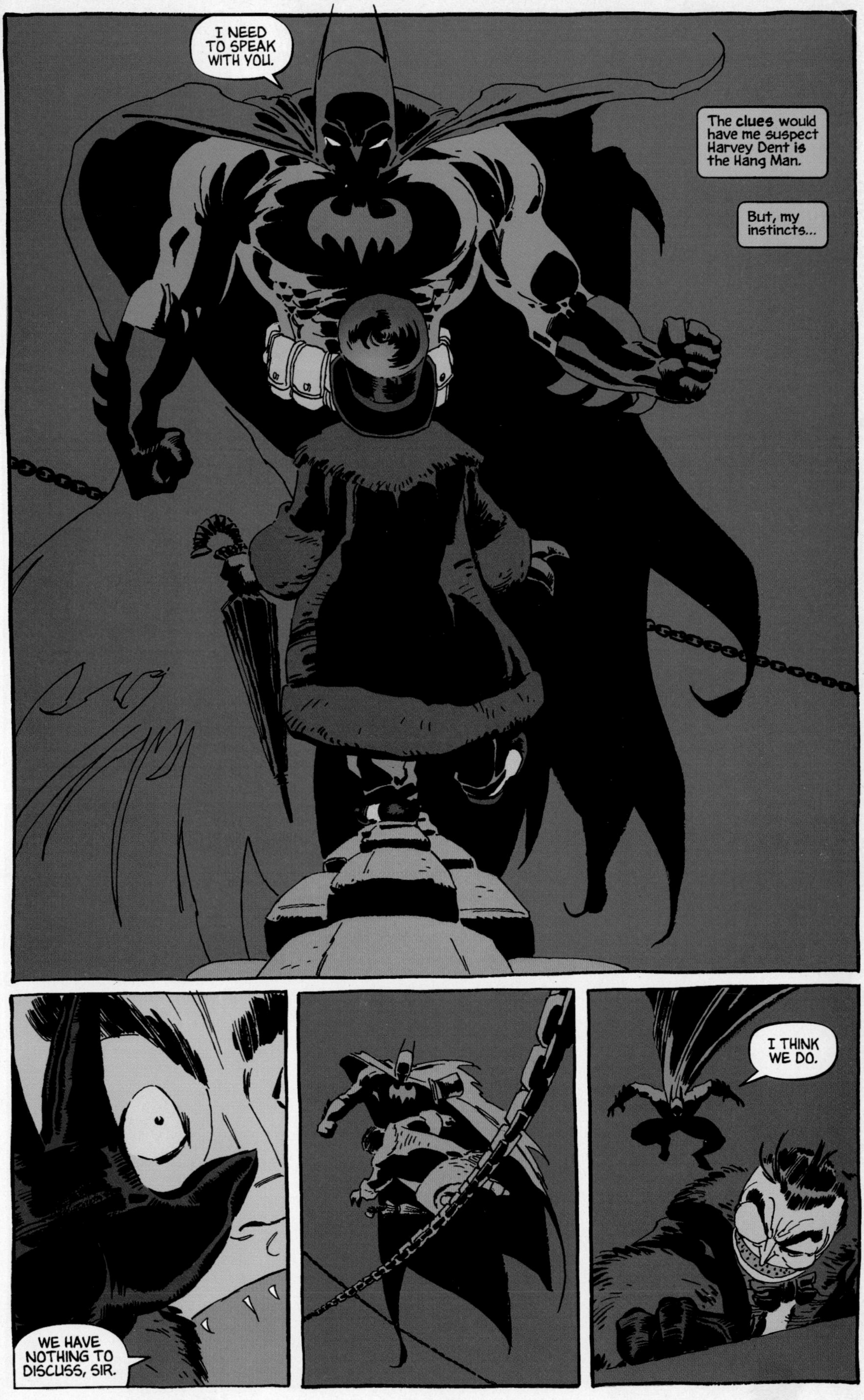
I NEED TO SPEAK WITH YOU.
The clues would have me suspect Harvey Dent is the Hang Man.
But, my instincts...
WE HAVE NOTHING TO DISCUSS, SIR.
I THINK WE DO.

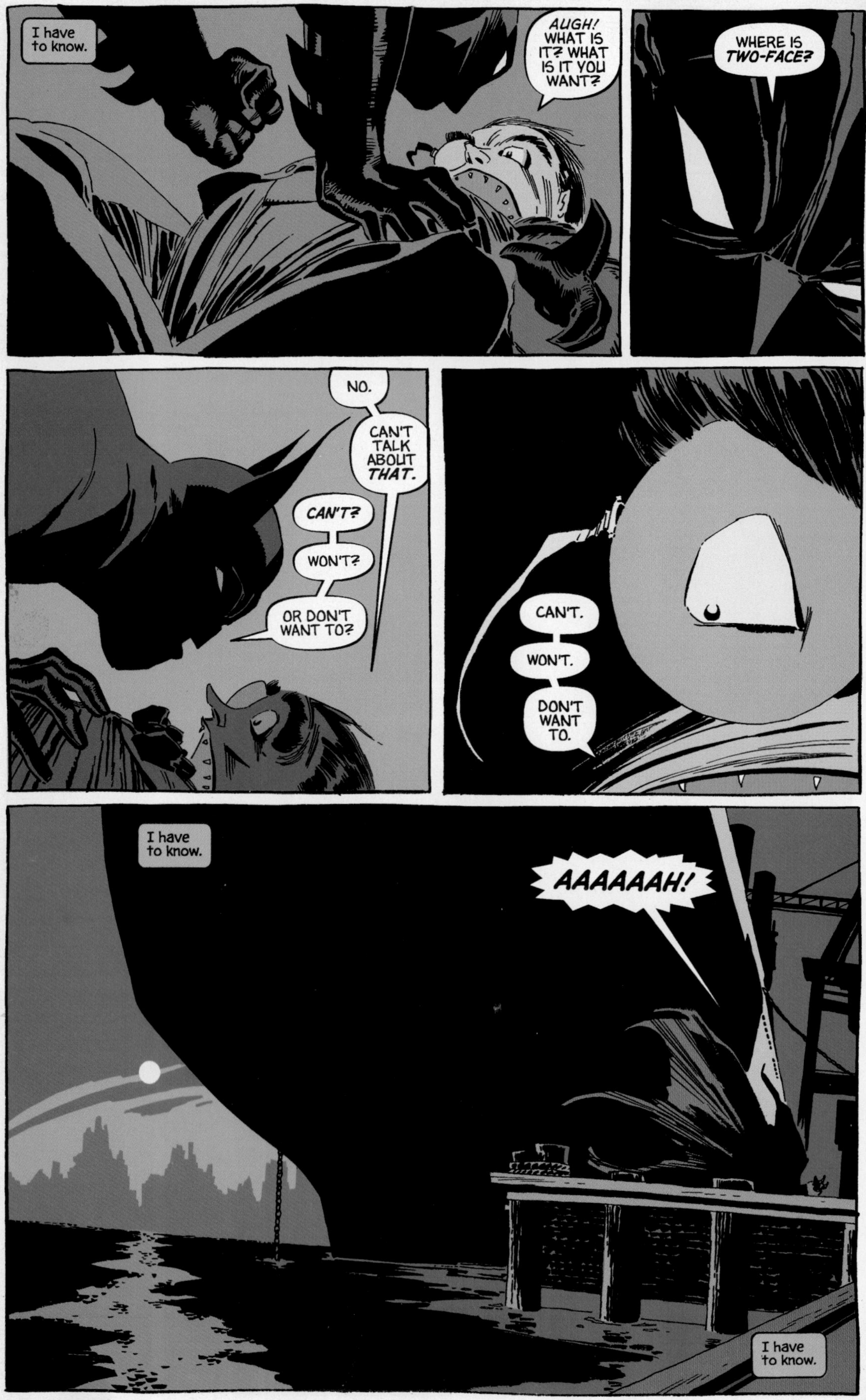
I have to know.
AUGH! WHAT IS IT? WHAT IS IT YOU WANT?
WHERE IS TWO-FACE?
NO.
CAN'T TALK ABOUT THAT.
CAN'T?
WON'T?
OR DON'T WANT TO?
CAN'T.
WON'T.
DON'T WANT TO.
I have to know.
AAAAAAH!
I have to know.

The rooftop of the G.C.P.D. Central Station.

SO, WE ALL AGREE.

IF WE NEED TO MEET, IT'S *ONLY* TO BE UP HERE -- *NEVER* IN MY OFFICE.

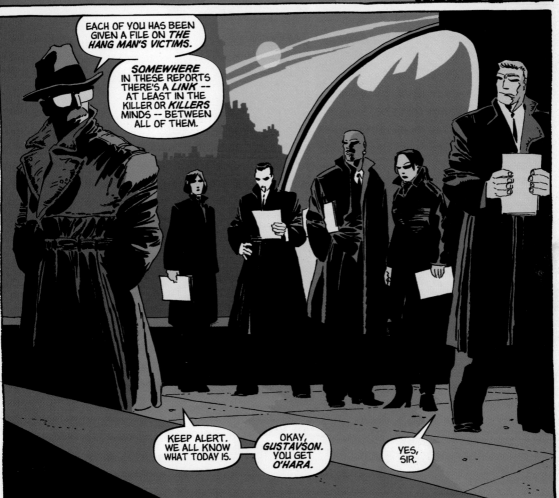

EACH OF YOU HAS BEEN GIVEN A FILE ON *THE HANG MAN'S VICTIMS.*

SOMEWHERE IN THESE REPORTS THERE'S A *LINK* -- AT LEAST IN THE KILLER OR *KILLERS* MINDS -- BETWEEN ALL OF THEM.

KEEP ALERT. WE ALL KNOW WHAT TODAY IS.

OKAY, *GUSTAVSON.* YOU GET *O'HARA.*

YES, SIR.

LOPEZ. YOU GET *LOEB.*

Ugh. CAN'T I HAVE ANYONE ELSE?

NO.

KING. YOU GET *FLASS.* DO YOU HAVE A PROBLEM WITH THAT?

SHOULD I?

O'CONNOR. I WANT YOU TO HAVE *BRANDEN.*

COMMISH. I THOUGHT I SAW SOMETHIN' MOVE --

WE'RE *ALL* A LITTLE JUMPY, O'CONNOR.

I GUESS THAT LEAVES ME *PRATT,* SIR.

THAT'S RIGHT, *WILCOX,* IT DOES.

AND HEAVEN HELP US, LET THESE BE THE LAST OF THEM.

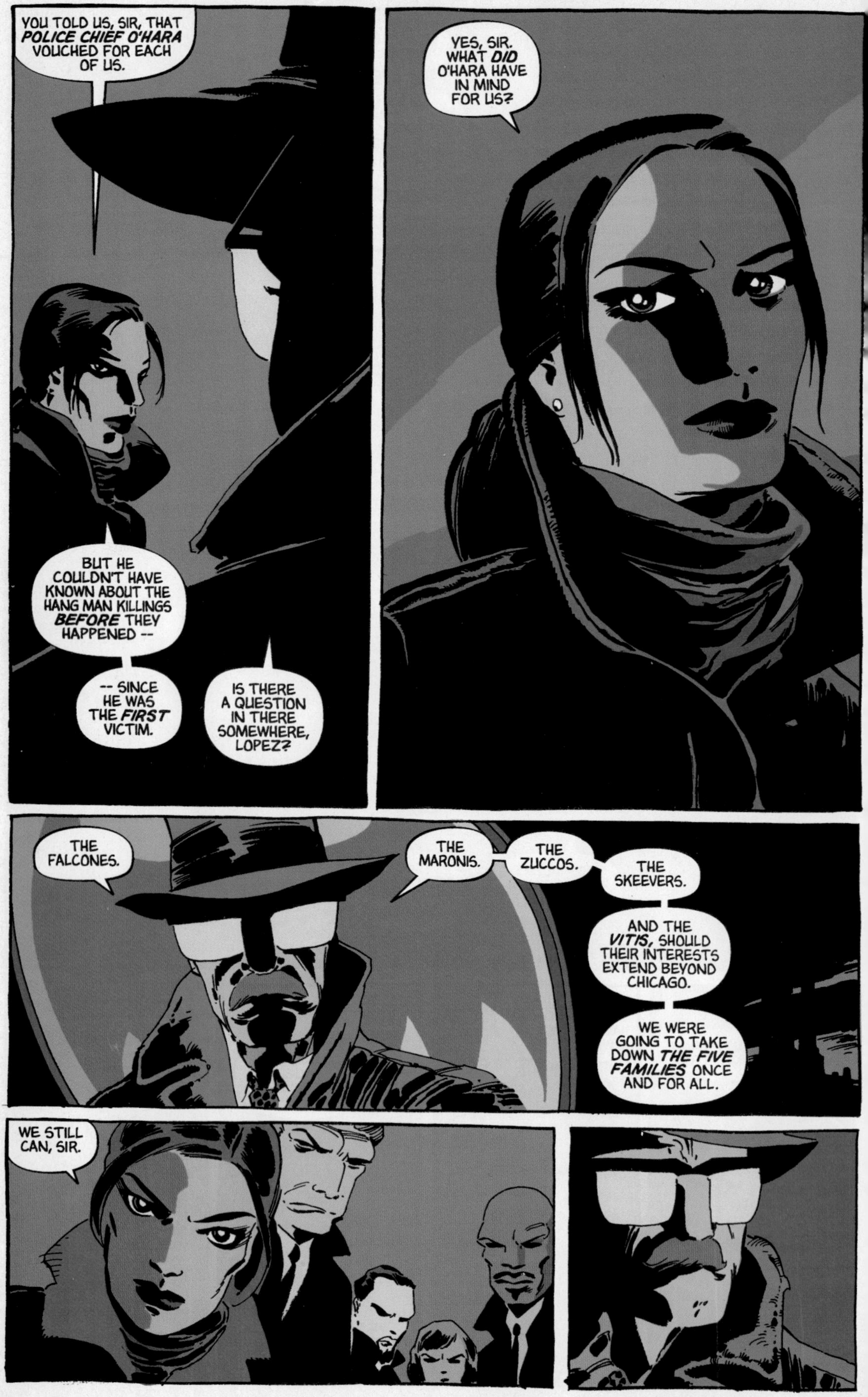

YOU TOLD US, SIR, THAT POLICE CHIEF O'HARA VOUCHED FOR EACH OF US.
BUT HE COULDN'T HAVE KNOWN ABOUT THE HANG MAN KILLINGS BEFORE THEY HAPPENED --
-- SINCE HE WAS THE FIRST VICTIM.
IS THERE A QUESTION IN THERE SOMEWHERE, LOPEZ?
YES, SIR. WHAT DID O'HARA HAVE IN MIND FOR US?
THE FALCONES.
THE MARONIS.
THE ZUCCOS.
THE SKEEVERS.
AND THE VITIS, SHOULD THEIR INTERESTS EXTEND BEYOND CHICAGO.
WE WERE GOING TO TAKE DOWN THE FIVE FAMILIES ONCE AND FOR ALL.
WE STILL CAN, SIR.

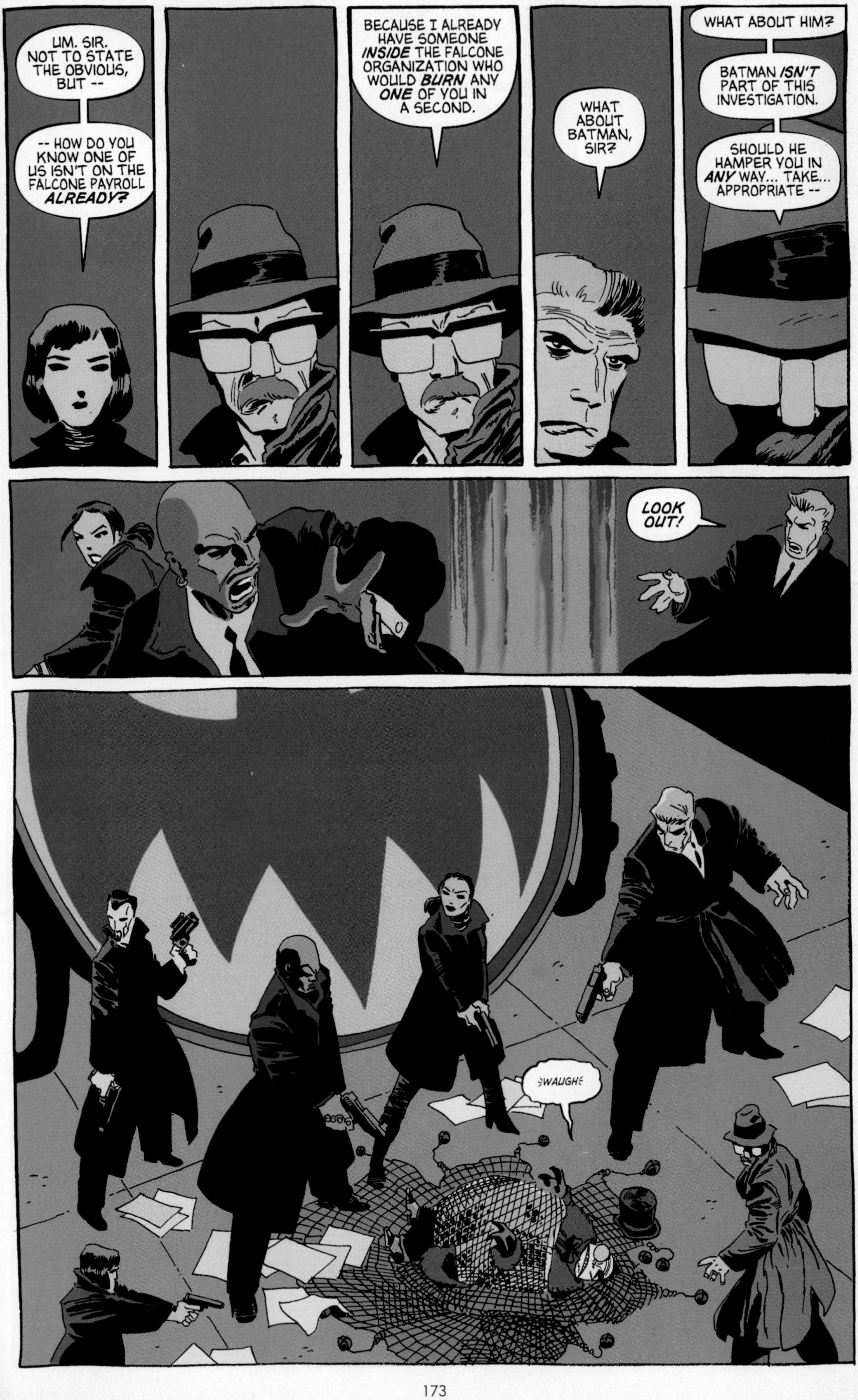
UM. SIR. NOT TO STATE THE OBVIOUS, BUT --
-- HOW DO YOU KNOW ONE OF US ISN'T ON THE FALCONE PAYROLL ALREADY?
BECAUSE I ALREADY HAVE SOMEONE INSIDE THE FALCONE ORGANIZATION WHO WOULD BURN ANY ONE OF YOU IN A SECOND.
WHAT ABOUT BATMAN, SIR?
WHAT ABOUT HIM?
BATMAN ISN'T PART OF THIS INVESTIGATION.
SHOULD HE HAMPER YOU IN ANY WAY... TAKE... APPROPRIATE --
LOOK OUT!
≯WAUGH≮

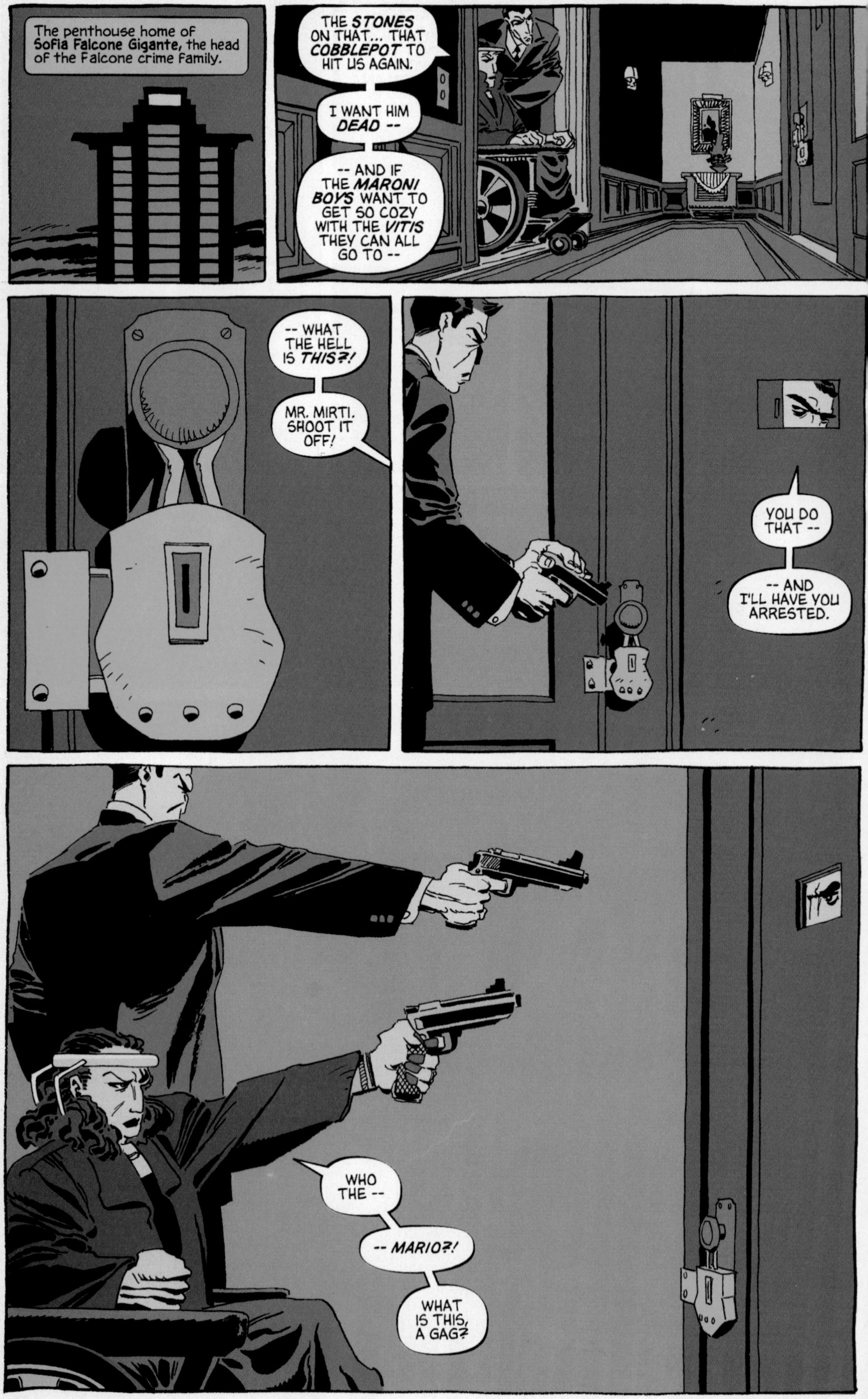
The penthouse home of Sofia Falcone Gigante, the head of the Falcone crime family.
THE STONES ON THAT... THAT COBBLEPOT TO HIT US AGAIN.
I WANT HIM DEAD --
-- AND IF THE MARONI BOYS WANT TO GET SO COZY WITH THE VITIS THEY CAN ALL GO TO --
-- WHAT THE HELL IS THIS?!
MR. MIRTI. SHOOT IT OFF!
YOU DO THAT --
-- AND I'LL HAVE YOU ARRESTED.
WHO THE --
-- MARIO?!
WHAT IS THIS, A GAG?

I TOLD YOU, *SISTER*, THE "FALCONE" NAME COULD NO LONGER BE USED FOR *ILLEGITIMATE* ACTIVITIES --

-- LIKE *THIS* EVENING'S FIASCO AT THE SHIPYARD.

AS THE *MAJORITY* SHAREHOLDER IN *FALCONE IMPORTS*, I HAVE SEIZED YOUR ASSETS, INCLUDING *THIS* PENTHOUSE --

-- AND YOU, BY COURT ORDER, ARE NO LONGER ALLOWED TO USE THE FALCONE *NAME*.

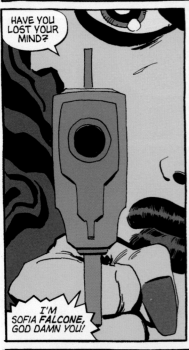

HAVE YOU LOST YOUR MIND?

I'M SOFIA *FALCONE*, GOD DAMN YOU!

NOT ANY LONGER, YOU AREN'T.

YOU CAN CALL YOURSELF SOFIA *GIGANTE* -- YOU CAN CALL YOURSELF SOFIA *SMITH*, FOR ALL I CARE.

GOTHAM CITY IS CHANGING.

AND YOU'VE BEEN LEFT BEHIND.

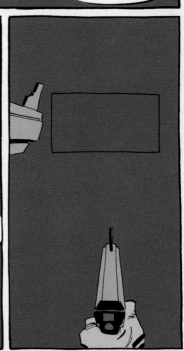

GOD DAMN YOU.

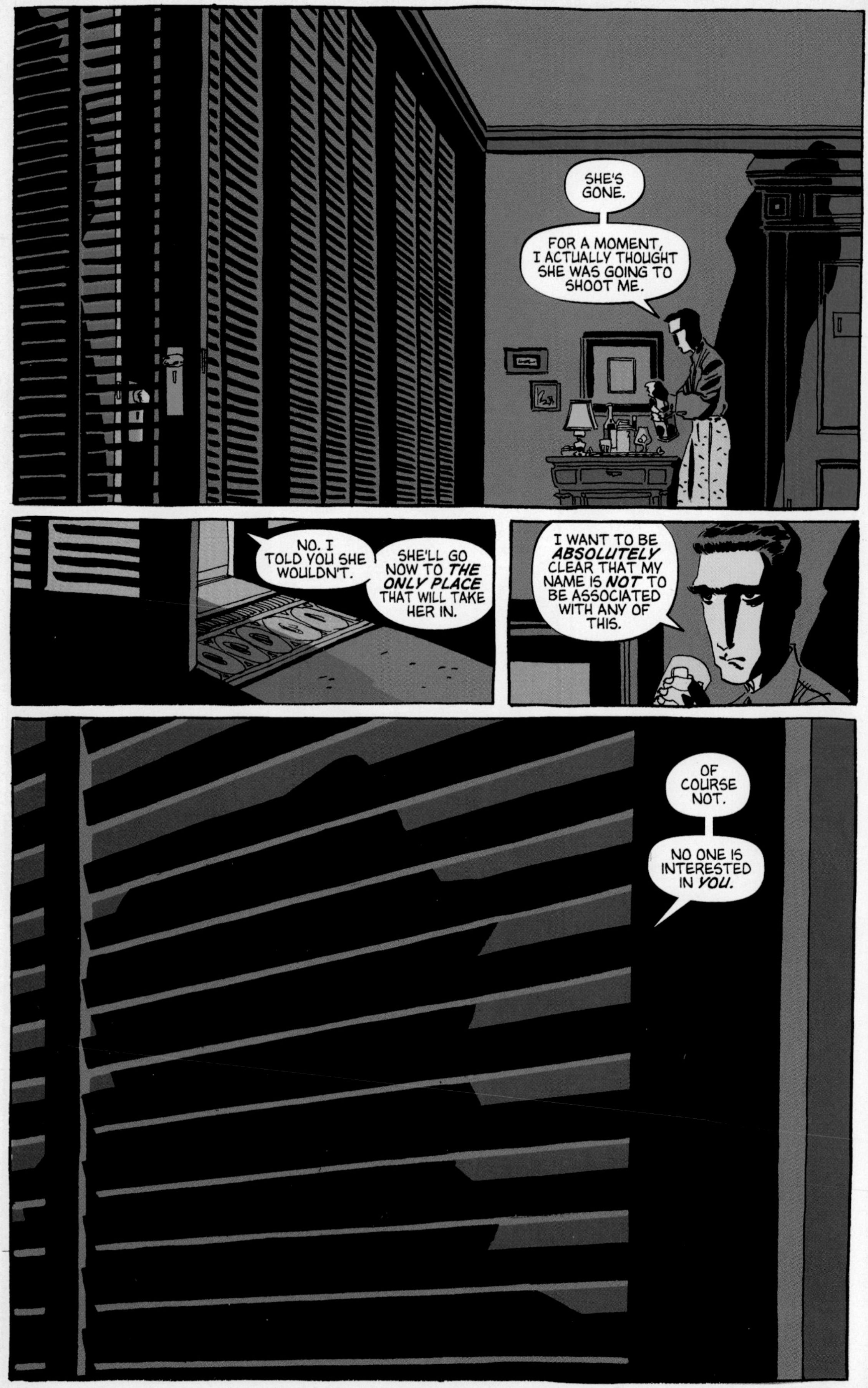
SHE'S GONE.
FOR A MOMENT, I ACTUALLY THOUGHT SHE WAS GOING TO SHOOT ME.
NO. I TOLD YOU SHE WOULDN'T.
SHE'LL GO NOW TO *THE ONLY PLACE* THAT WILL TAKE HER IN.
I WANT TO BE *ABSOLUTELY* CLEAR THAT MY NAME IS *NOT* TO BE ASSOCIATED WITH ANY OF THIS.
OF COURSE NOT.
NO ONE IS INTERESTED IN *YOU.*

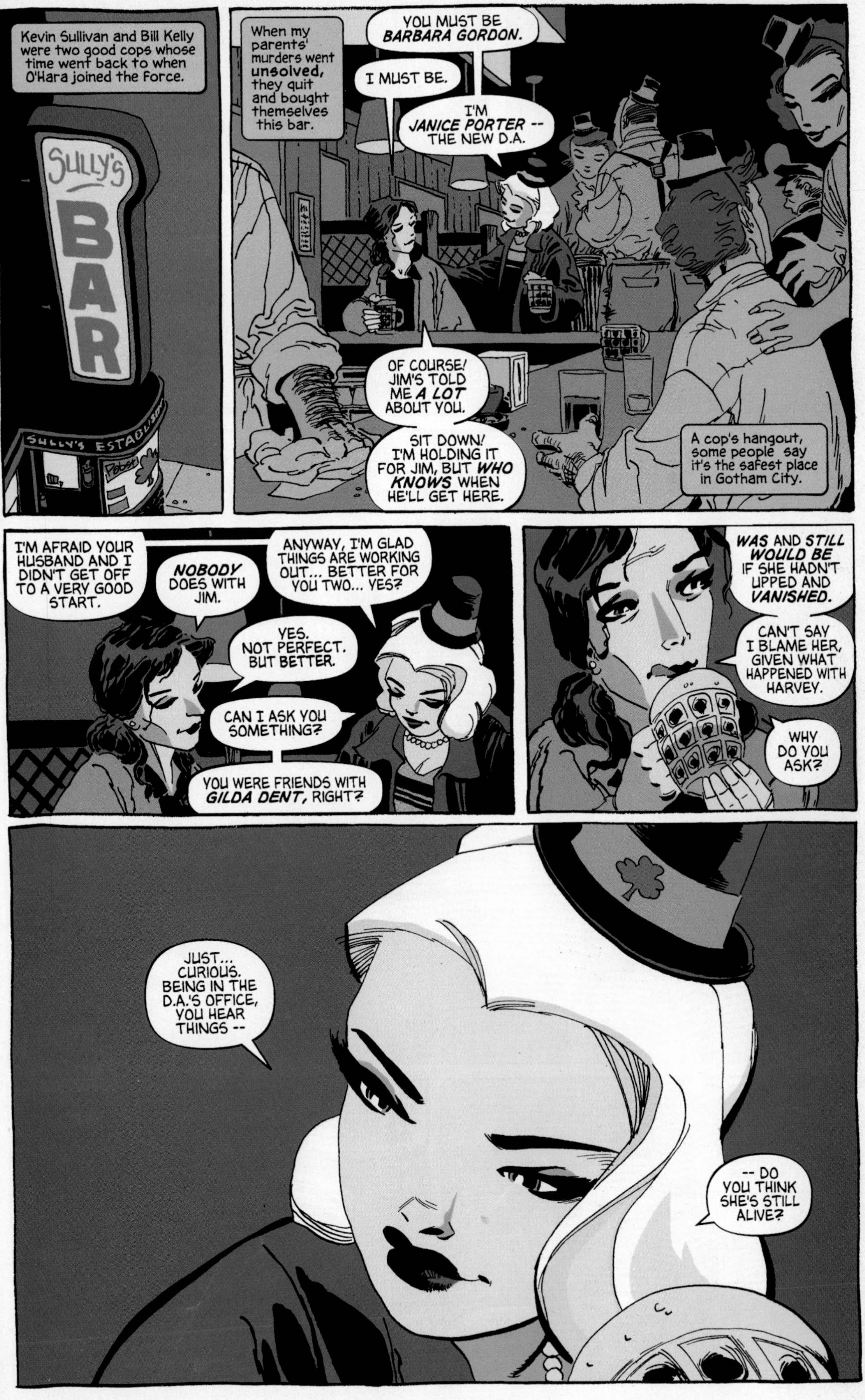
Kevin Sullivan and Bill Kelly were two good cops whose time went back to when O'Hara joined the Force.
SULLY'S BAR
When my parents' murders went unsolved, they quit and bought themselves this bar.
YOU MUST BE BARBARA GORDON.
I MUST BE.
I'M JANICE PORTER -- THE NEW D.A.
OF COURSE! JIM'S TOLD ME A LOT ABOUT YOU.
SIT DOWN! I'M HOLDING IT FOR JIM, BUT WHO KNOWS WHEN HE'LL GET HERE.
A cop's hangout, some people say it's the safest place in Gotham City.
I'M AFRAID YOUR HUSBAND AND I DIDN'T GET OFF TO A VERY GOOD START.
NOBODY DOES WITH JIM.
ANYWAY, I'M GLAD THINGS ARE WORKING OUT... BETTER FOR YOU TWO... YES?
YES. NOT PERFECT. BUT BETTER.
CAN I ASK YOU SOMETHING?
YOU WERE FRIENDS WITH GILDA DENT, RIGHT?
WAS AND STILL WOULD BE IF SHE HADN'T UPPED AND VANISHED.
CAN'T SAY I BLAME HER, GIVEN WHAT HAPPENED WITH HARVEY.
WHY DO YOU ASK?
JUST... CURIOUS. BEING IN THE D.A.'S OFFICE, YOU HEAR THINGS --
-- DO YOU THINK SHE'S STILL ALIVE?

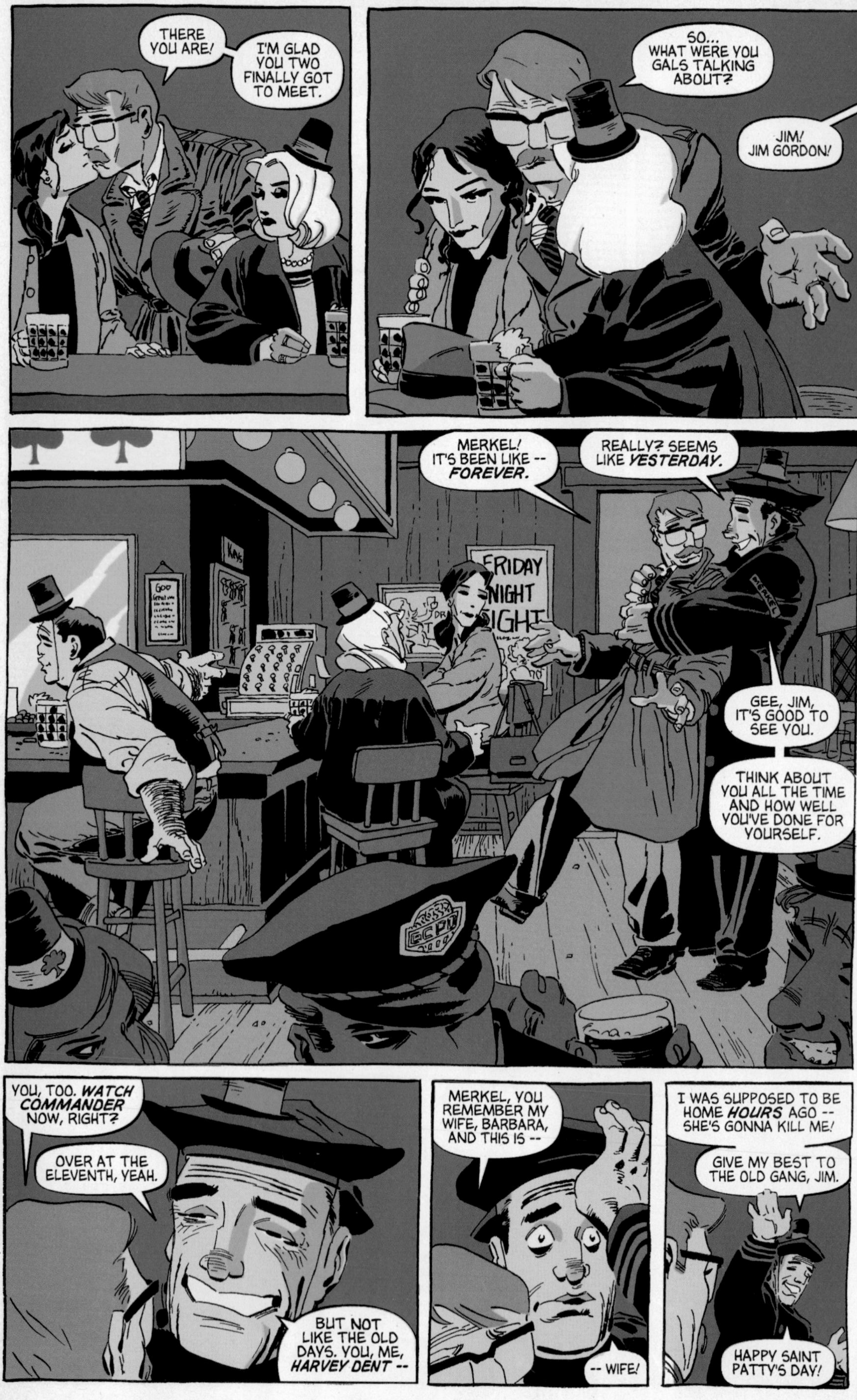
THERE YOU ARE!
I'M GLAD YOU TWO FINALLY GOT TO MEET.
SO... WHAT WERE YOU GALS TALKING ABOUT?
JIM! JIM GORDON!
MERKEL! IT'S BEEN LIKE -- FOREVER.
REALLY? SEEMS LIKE YESTERDAY.
FRIDAY NIGHT FIGHT
GEE, JIM, IT'S GOOD TO SEE YOU.
THINK ABOUT YOU ALL THE TIME AND HOW WELL YOU'VE DONE FOR YOURSELF.
YOU, TOO. WATCH COMMANDER NOW, RIGHT?
OVER AT THE ELEVENTH, YEAH.
BUT NOT LIKE THE OLD DAYS. YOU, ME, HARVEY DENT --
MERKEL, YOU REMEMBER MY WIFE, BARBARA, AND THIS IS --
-- WIFE!
I WAS SUPPOSED TO BE HOME HOURS AGO -- SHE'S GONNA KILL ME!
GIVE MY BEST TO THE OLD GANG, JIM.
HAPPY SAINT PATTY'S DAY!

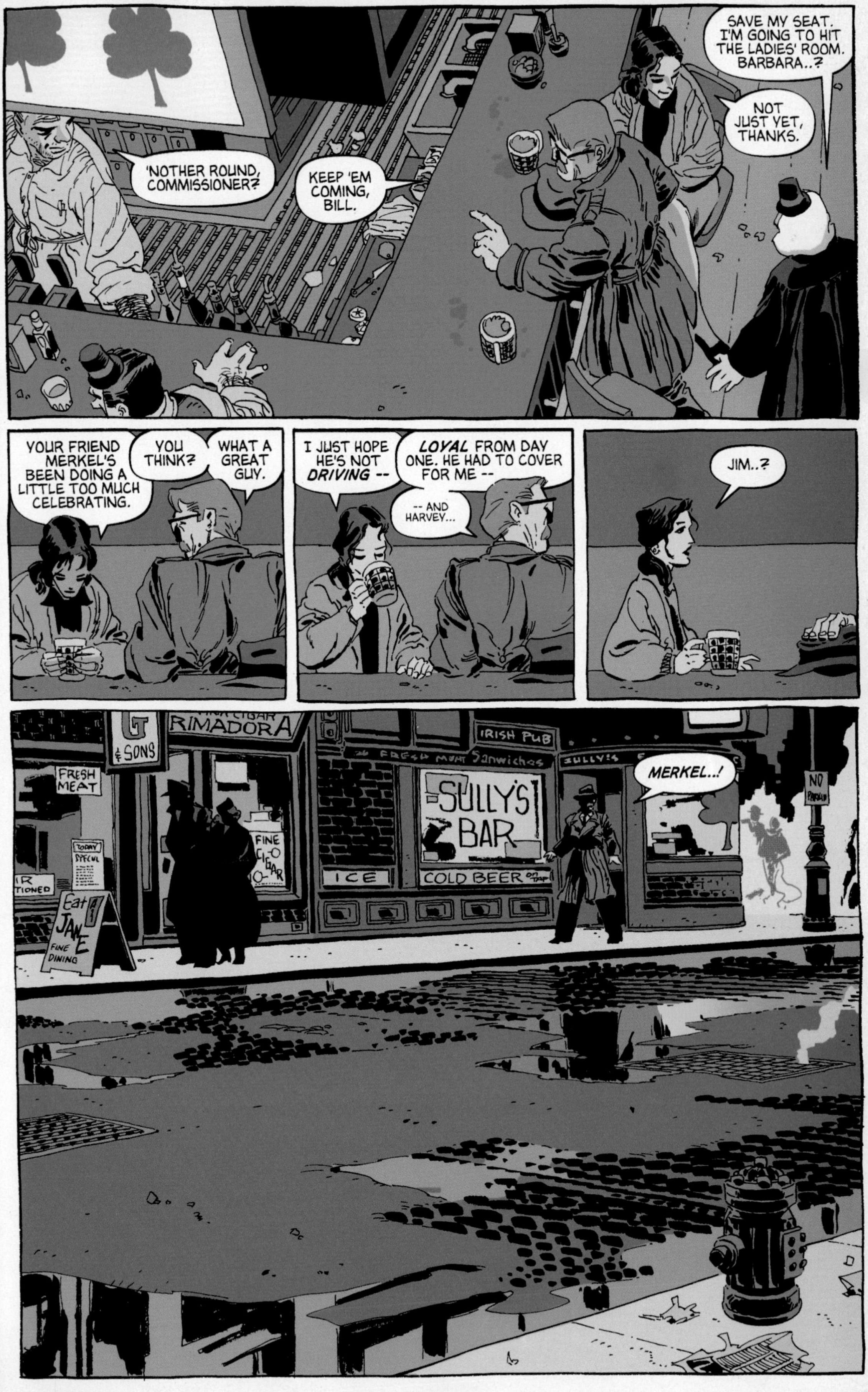

'NOTHER ROUND, COMMISSIONER?
KEEP 'EM COMING, BILL.
SAVE MY SEAT. I'M GOING TO HIT THE LADIES' ROOM. BARBARA..?
NOT JUST YET, THANKS.
YOUR FRIEND MERKEL'S BEEN DOING A LITTLE TOO MUCH CELEBRATING.
YOU THINK?
WHAT A GREAT GUY.
I JUST HOPE HE'S NOT DRIVING --
LOYAL FROM DAY ONE. HE HAD TO COVER FOR ME --
-- AND HARVEY...
JIM..?
RIMADORA
FRESH MEAT
& SONS
IRISH PUB
SULLY'S BAR
ICE
COLD BEER ON TAP
FINE CIGAR
Eat JANE FINE DINING
NO PARKING
MERKEL..!

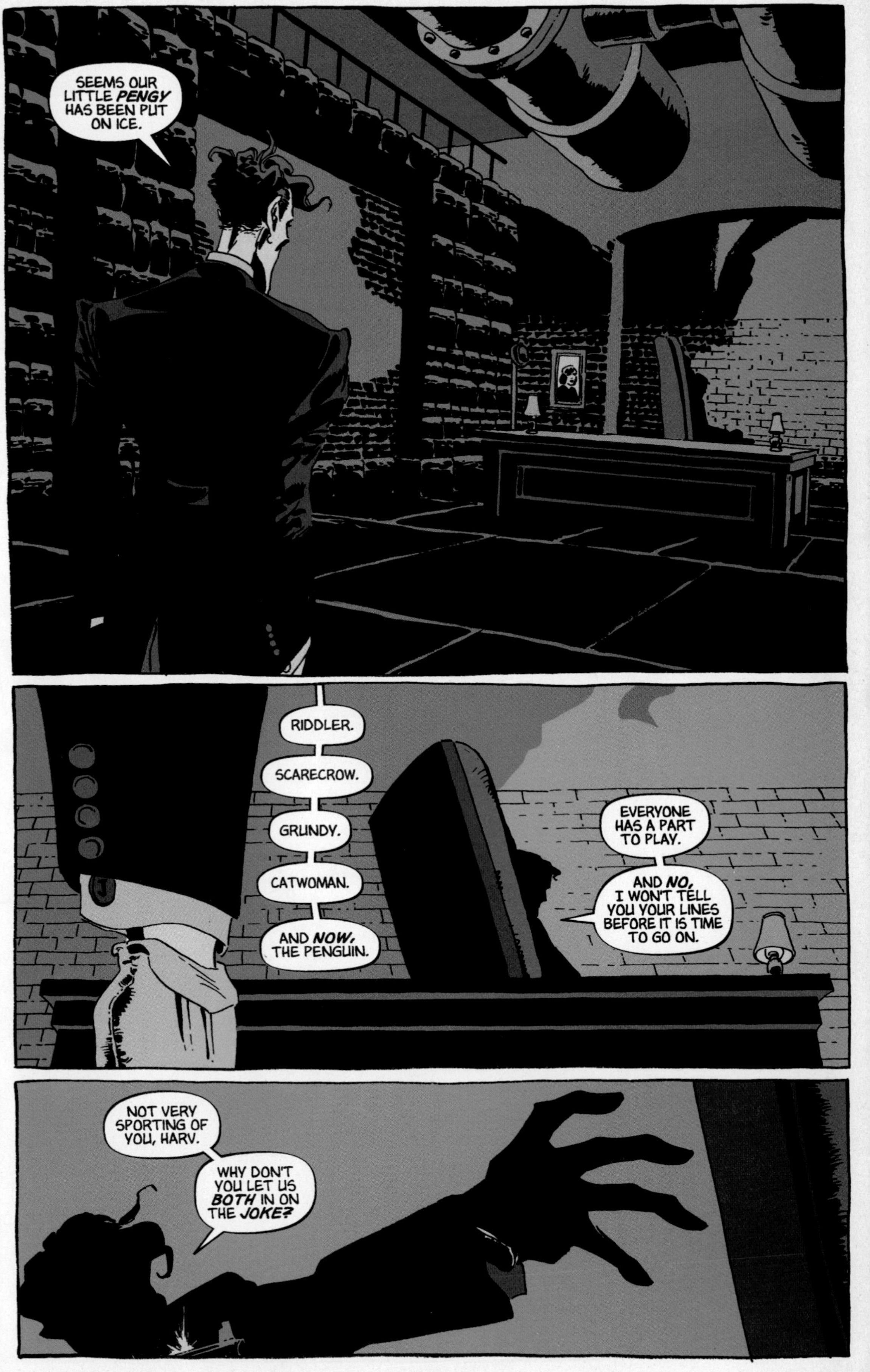
SEEMS OUR LITTLE PENGY HAS BEEN PUT ON ICE.
RIDDLER.
SCARECROW.
GRUNDY.
CATWOMAN.
AND NOW, THE PENGUIN.
EVERYONE HAS A PART TO PLAY.
AND NO, I WON'T TELL YOU YOUR LINES BEFORE IT IS TIME TO GO ON.
NOT VERY SPORTING OF YOU, HARV.
WHY DON'T YOU LET US BOTH IN ON THE JOKE?

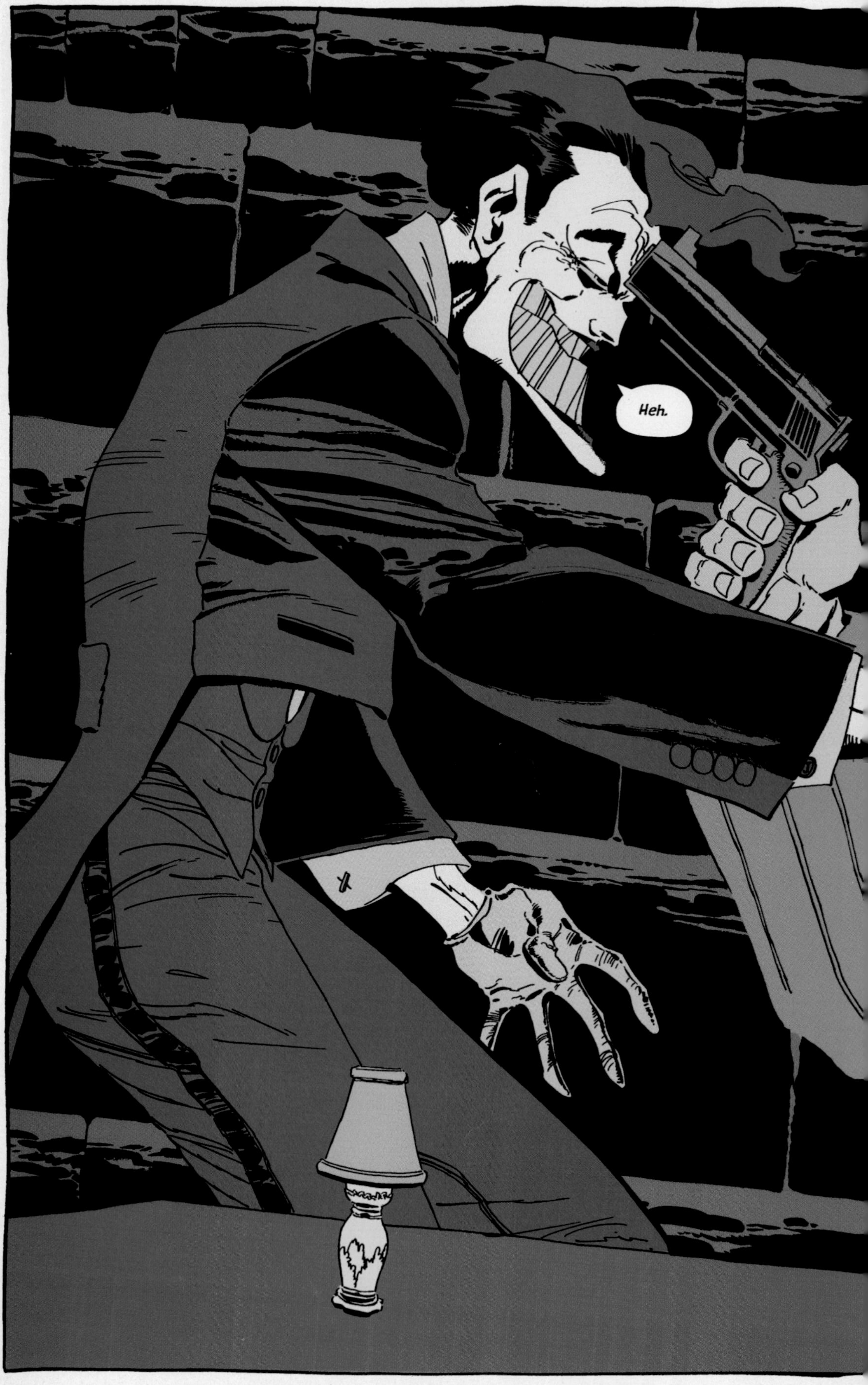
Heh.

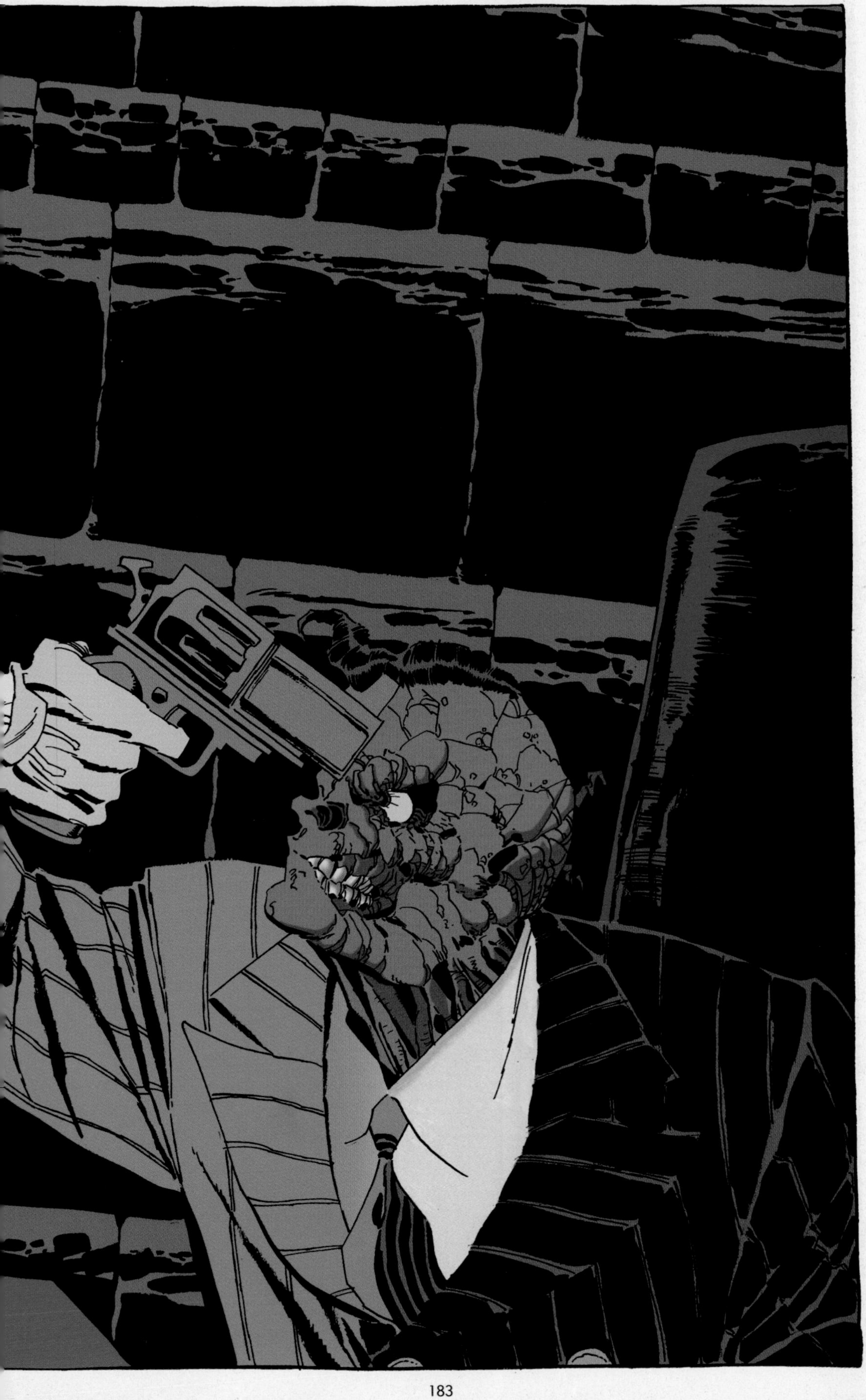

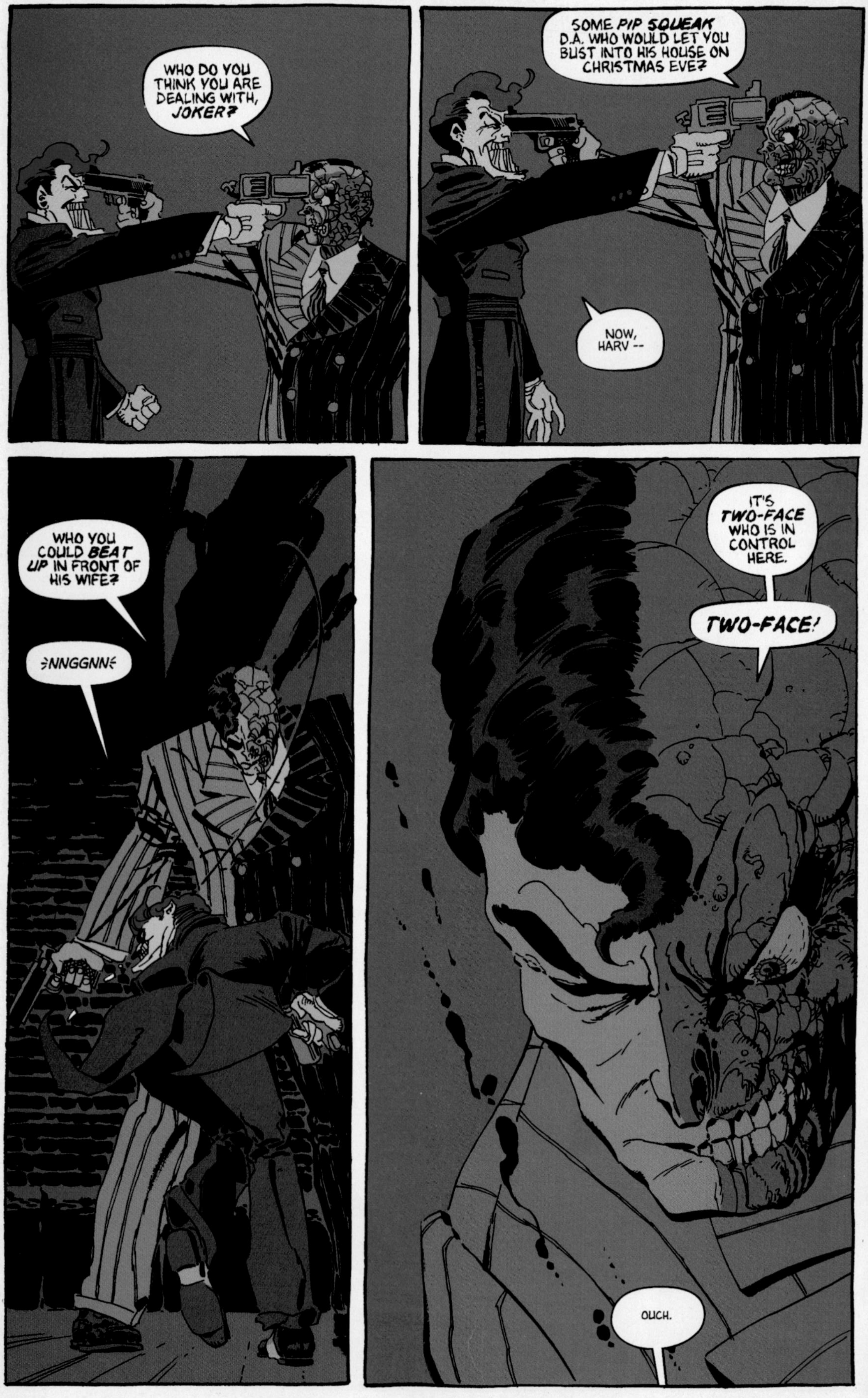
WHO DO YOU THINK YOU ARE DEALING WITH, JOKER?
SOME PIP SQUEAK D.A. WHO WOULD LET YOU BUST INTO HIS HOUSE ON CHRISTMAS EVE?
NOW, HARV --
WHO YOU COULD BEAT UP IN FRONT OF HIS WIFE?
NNGGNN
IT'S TWO-FACE WHO IS IN CONTROL HERE.
TWO-FACE!
OUCH.

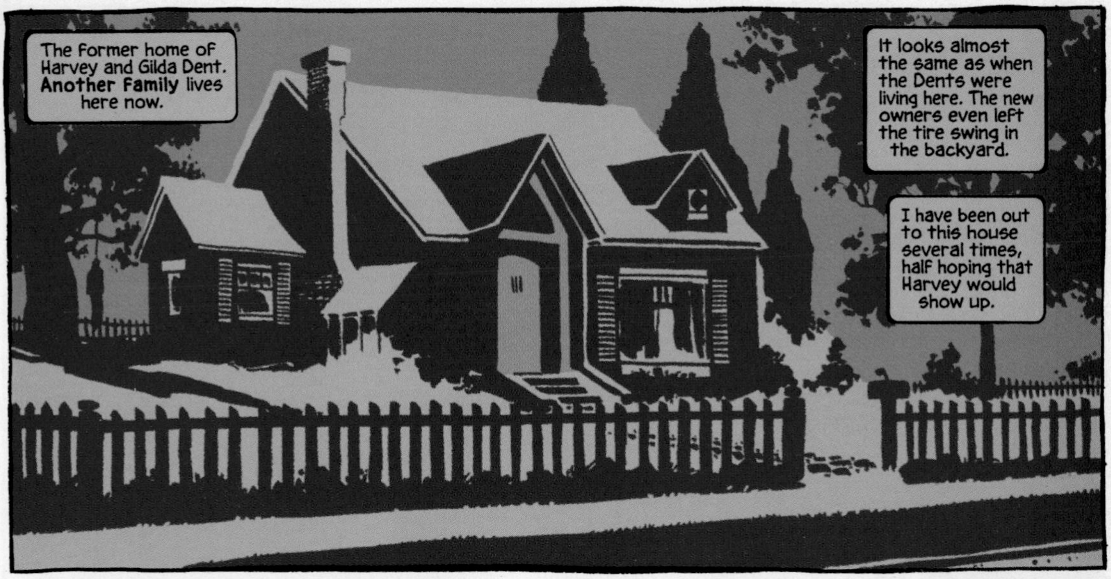
The former home of Harvey and Gilda Dent. **Another Family** lives here now.
It looks almost the same as when the Dents were living here. The new owners even left the tire swing in the backyard.
I have been out to this house several times, half hoping that Harvey would show up.

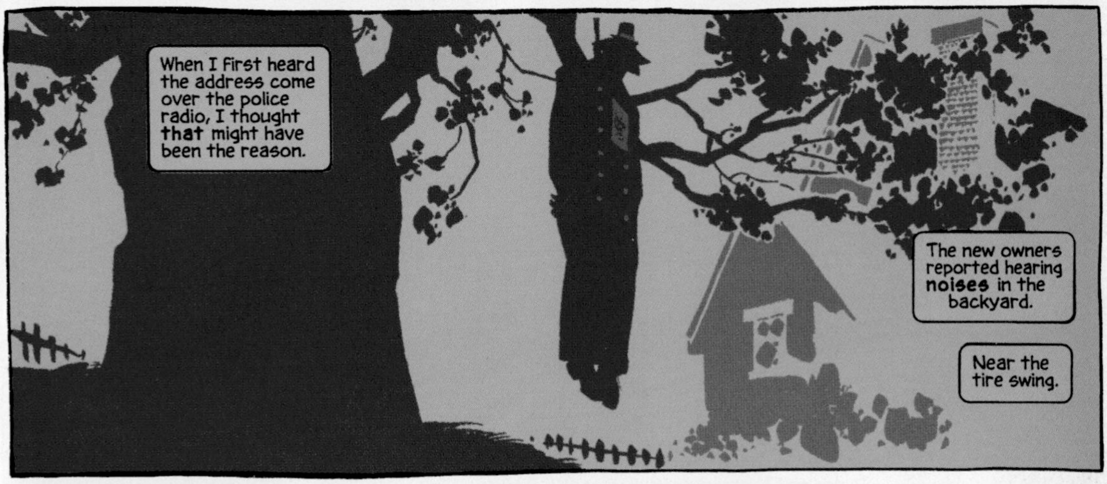
When I first heard the address come over the police radio, I thought **that** might have been the reason.
The new owners reported hearing **noises** in the backyard.
Near the tire swing.

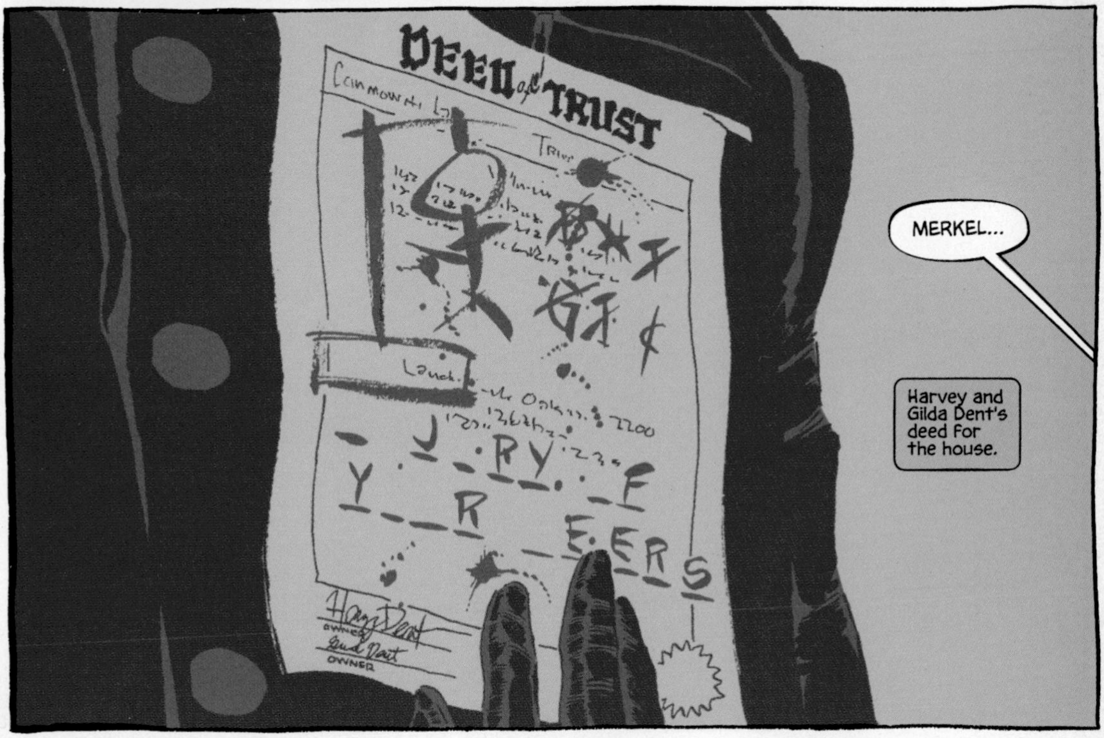
DEED of TRUST
MERKEL...
Harvey and Gilda Dent's deed for the house.

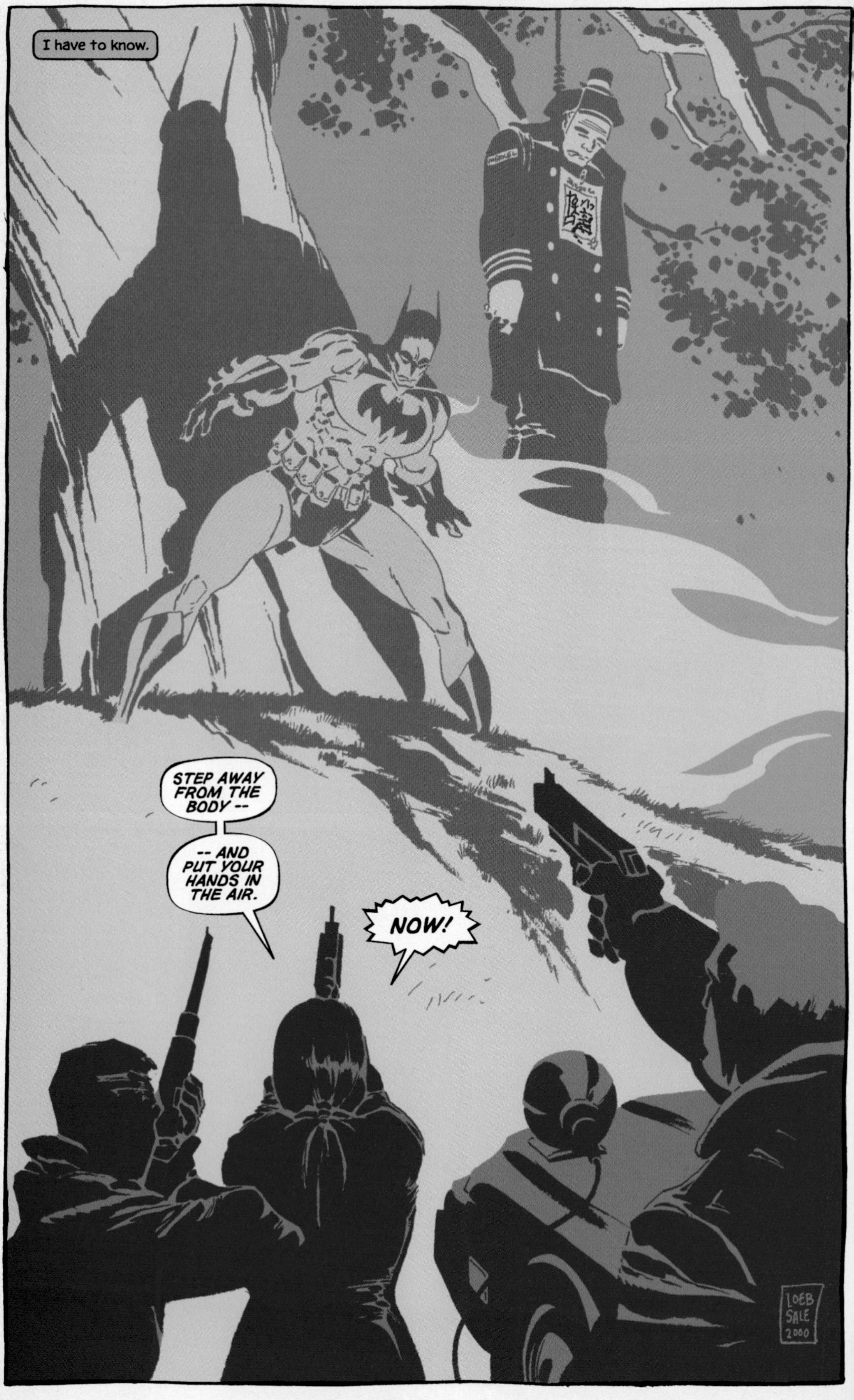
I have to know.
STEP AWAY FROM THE BODY --
-- AND PUT YOUR HANDS IN THE AIR.
NOW!
LOEB SALE 2000

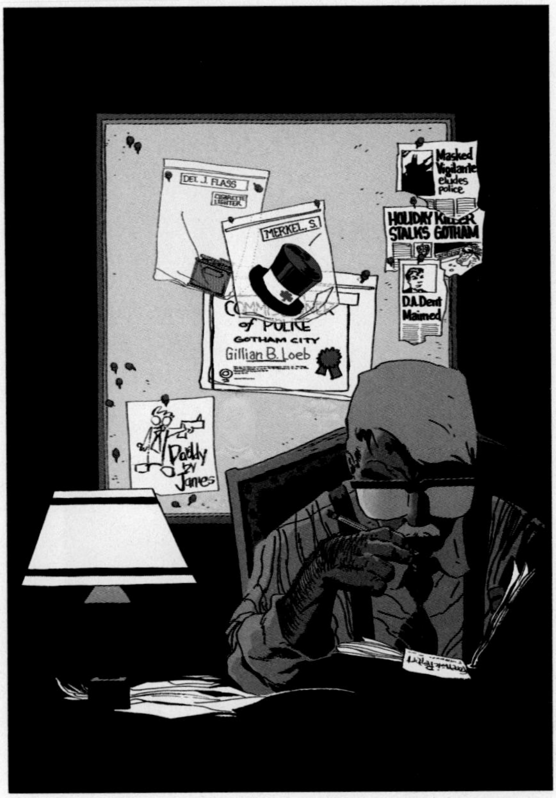
DET. J. FLASS
CIGARETTE LIGHTER
MERKEL, S.
of POLICE
GOTHAM CITY
Gillian B. Loeb
Masked Vigilante eludes police
HOLIDAY
STALKS GOTHAM
D.A. Dent Maimed
Daddy by James

7

F O O L S

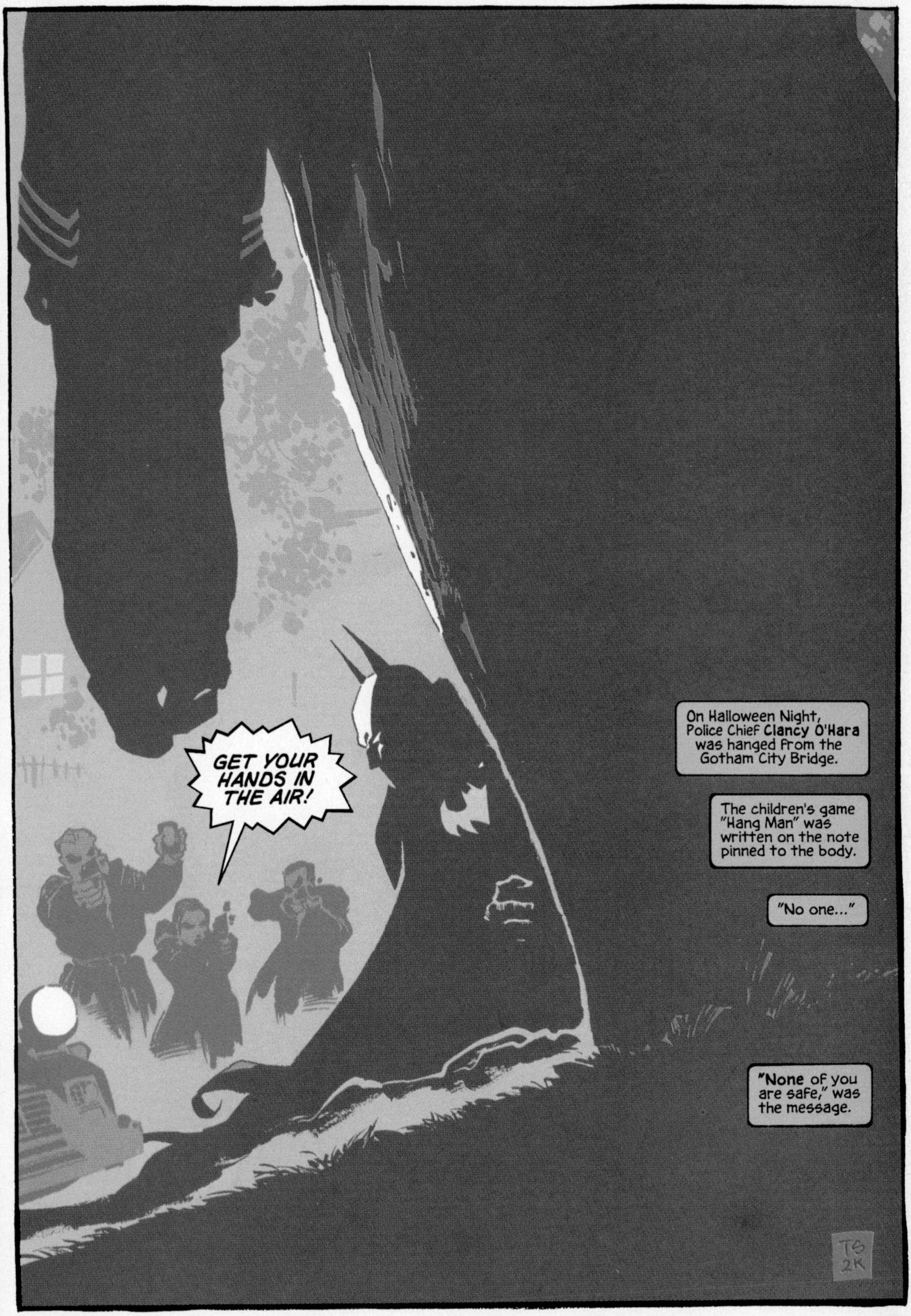
GET YOUR HANDS IN THE AIR!
On Halloween Night, Police Chief Clancy O'Hara was hanged from the Gotham City Bridge.
The children's game "Hang Man" was written on the note pinned to the body.
"No one..."
"None of you are safe," was the message.
TS 2K

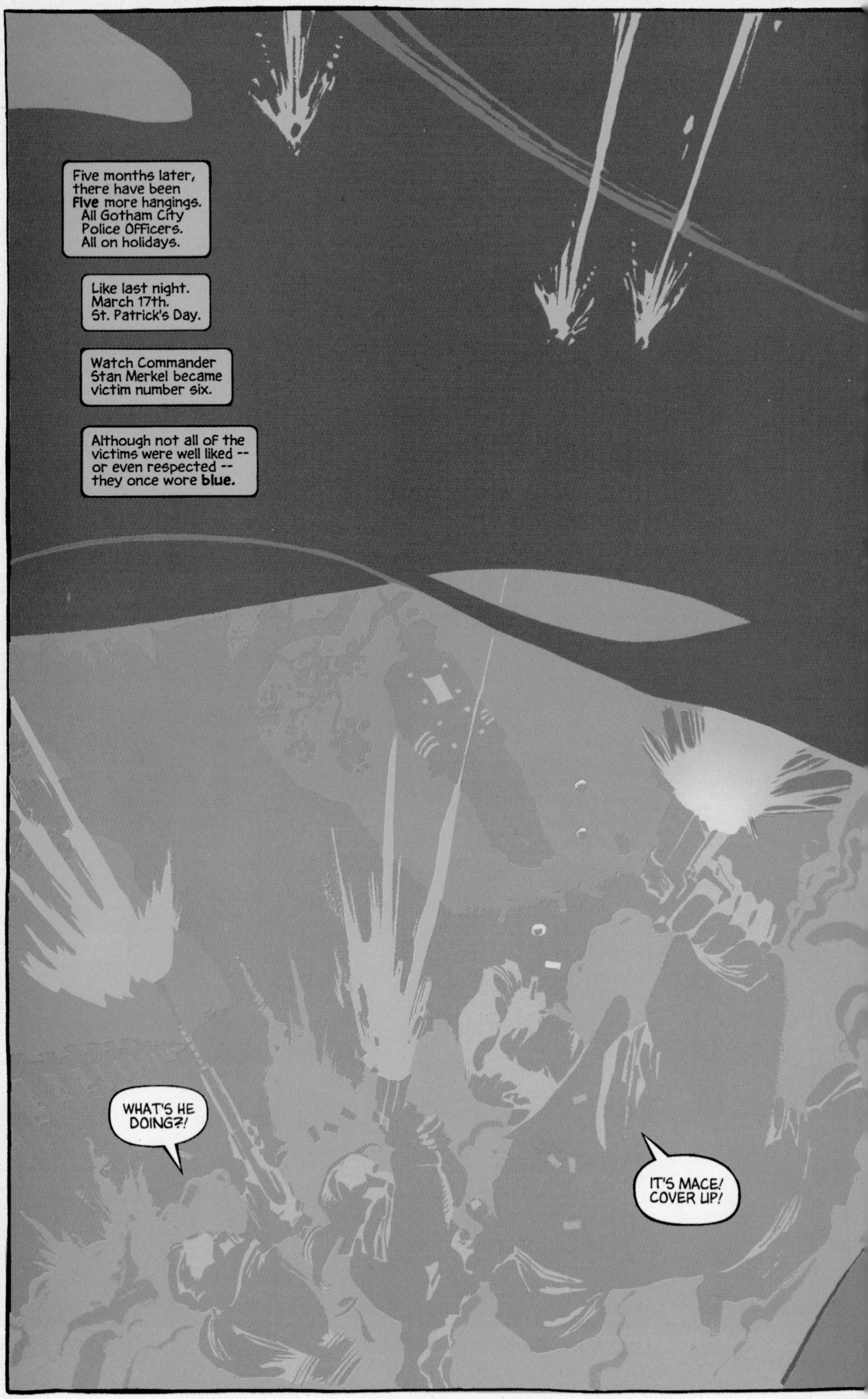

Five months later, there have been **five** more hangings. All Gotham City Police Officers. All on holidays.
Like last night. March 17th. St. Patrick's Day.
Watch Commander Stan Merkel became victim number six.
Although not all of the victims were well liked -- or even respected -- they once wore **blue.**
WHAT'S HE DOING?!
IT'S MACE! COVER UP!

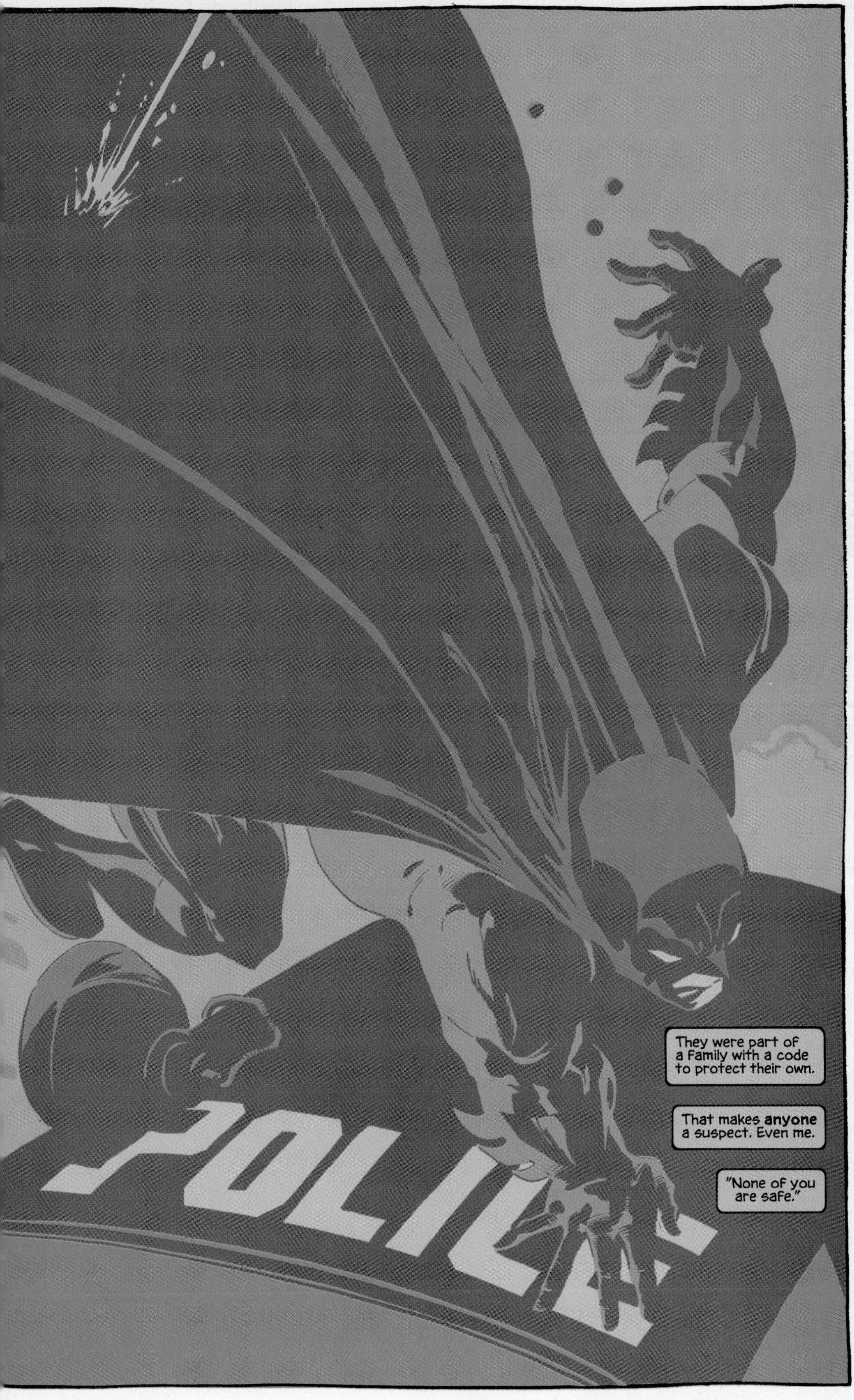
They were part of a family with a code to protect their own.
That makes **anyone** a suspect. Even me.
"None of you are safe."
POLICE

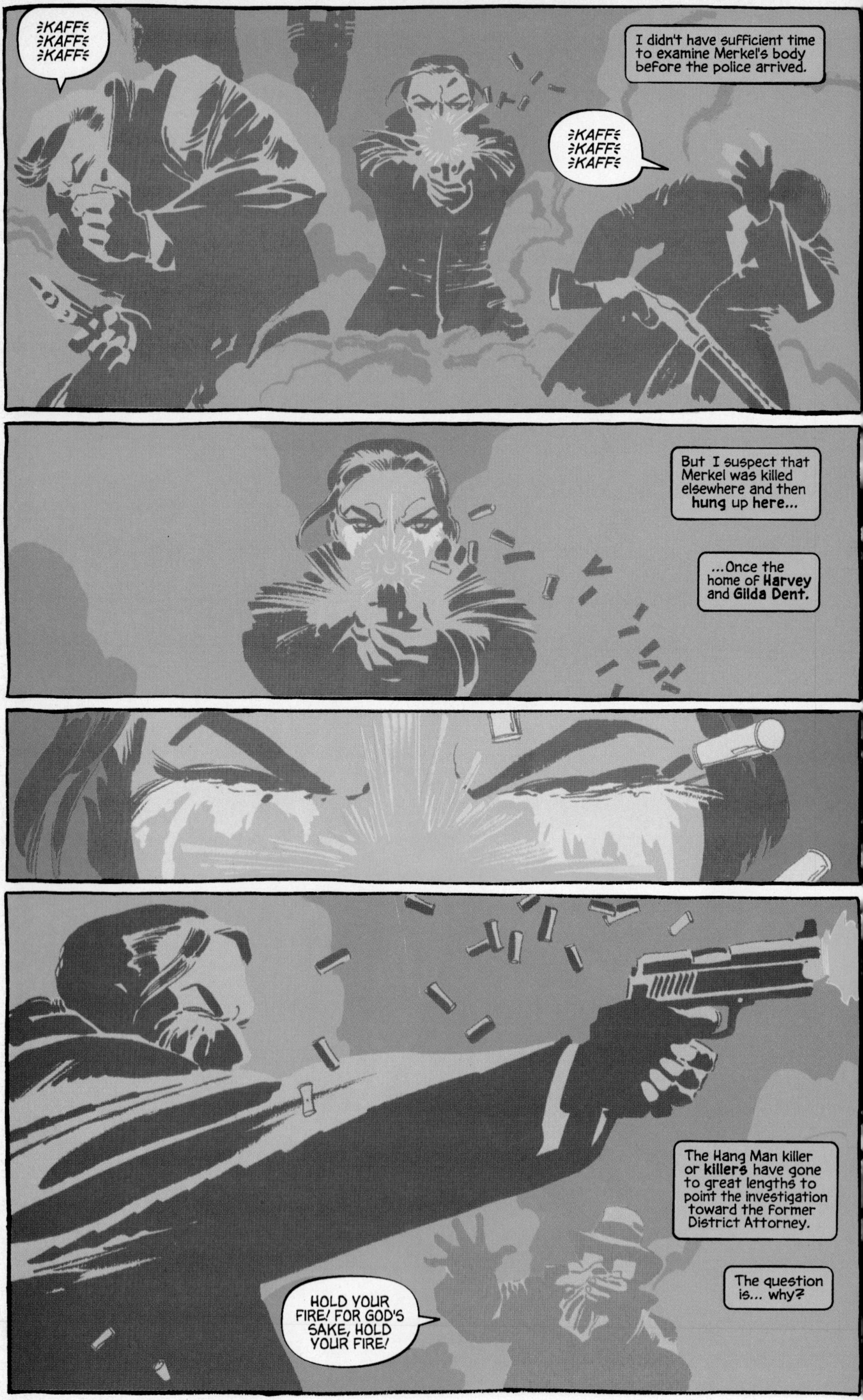

ƎKAFFƐ ƎKAFFƐ ƎKAFFƐ
I didn't have sufficient time to examine Merkel's body before the police arrived.
ƎKAFFƐ ƎKAFFƐ ƎKAFFƐ
But I suspect that Merkel was killed elsewhere and then hung up here...
...Once the home of Harvey and Gilda Dent.
The Hang Man killer or killers have gone to great lengths to point the investigation toward the former District Attorney.
The question is... why?
HOLD YOUR FIRE! FOR GOD'S SAKE, HOLD YOUR FIRE!

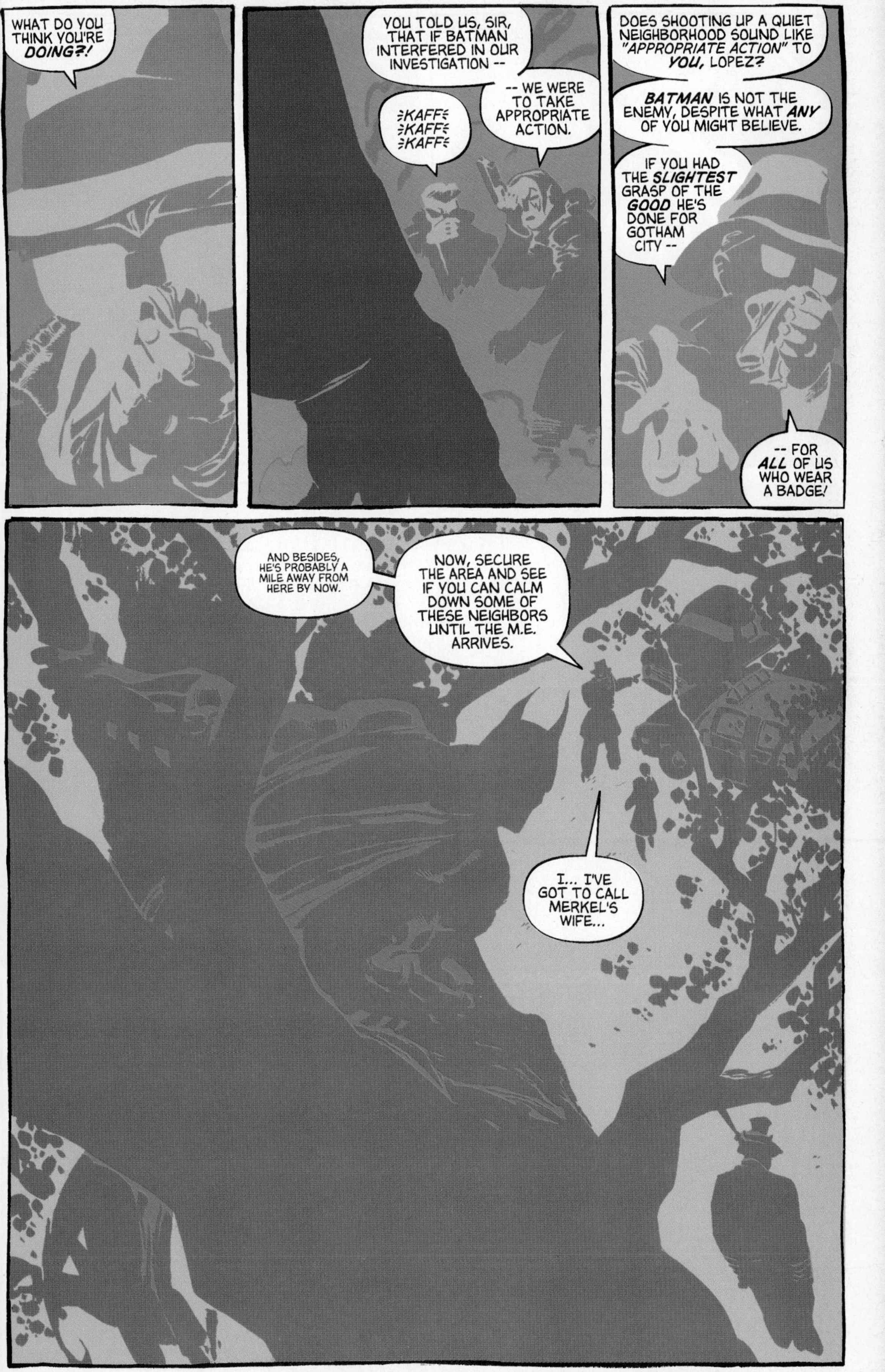
WHAT DO YOU THINK YOU'RE DOING?!
YOU TOLD US, SIR, THAT IF BATMAN INTERFERED IN OUR INVESTIGATION --
-- WE WERE TO TAKE APPROPRIATE ACTION.
KAFF KAFF KAFF
DOES SHOOTING UP A QUIET NEIGHBORHOOD SOUND LIKE "APPROPRIATE ACTION" TO YOU, LOPEZ?
BATMAN IS NOT THE ENEMY, DESPITE WHAT ANY OF YOU MIGHT BELIEVE.
IF YOU HAD THE SLIGHTEST GRASP OF THE GOOD HE'S DONE FOR GOTHAM CITY --
-- FOR ALL OF US WHO WEAR A BADGE!
NOW, SECURE THE AREA AND SEE IF YOU CAN CALM DOWN SOME OF THESE NEIGHBORS UNTIL THE M.E. ARRIVES.
AND BESIDES, HE'S PROBABLY A MILE AWAY FROM HERE BY NOW.
I... I'VE GOT TO CALL MERKEL'S WIFE...

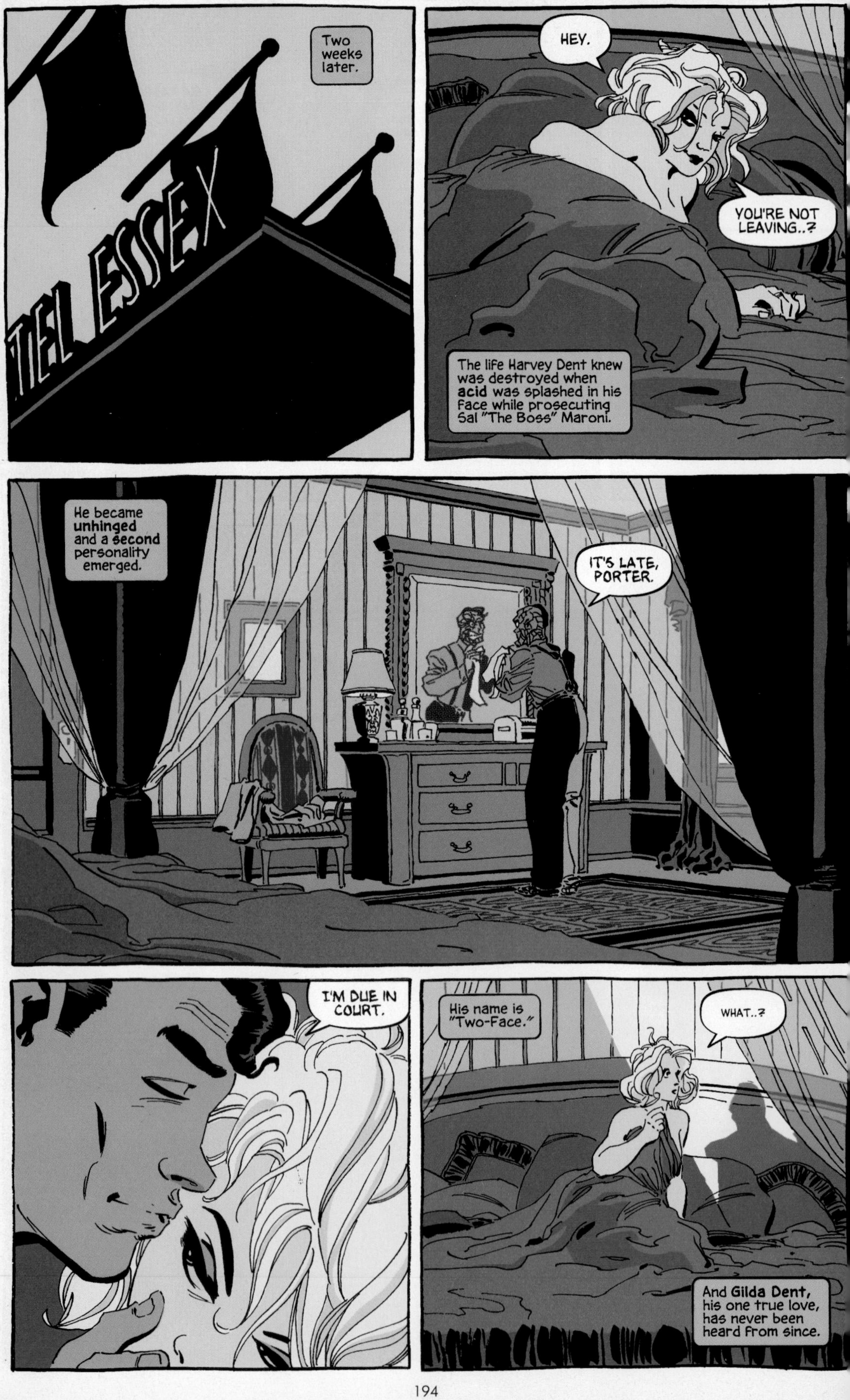
Two weeks later.
TEL ESSEX
HEY.
YOU'RE NOT LEAVING..?
The life Harvey Dent knew was destroyed when **acid** was splashed in his face while prosecuting Sal "The Boss" Maroni.
He became **unhinged** and a **second** personality emerged.
IT'S LATE, PORTER.
I'M DUE IN COURT.
His name is "Two-Face."
WHAT..?
And **Gilda Dent,** his one true love, has never been heard from since.

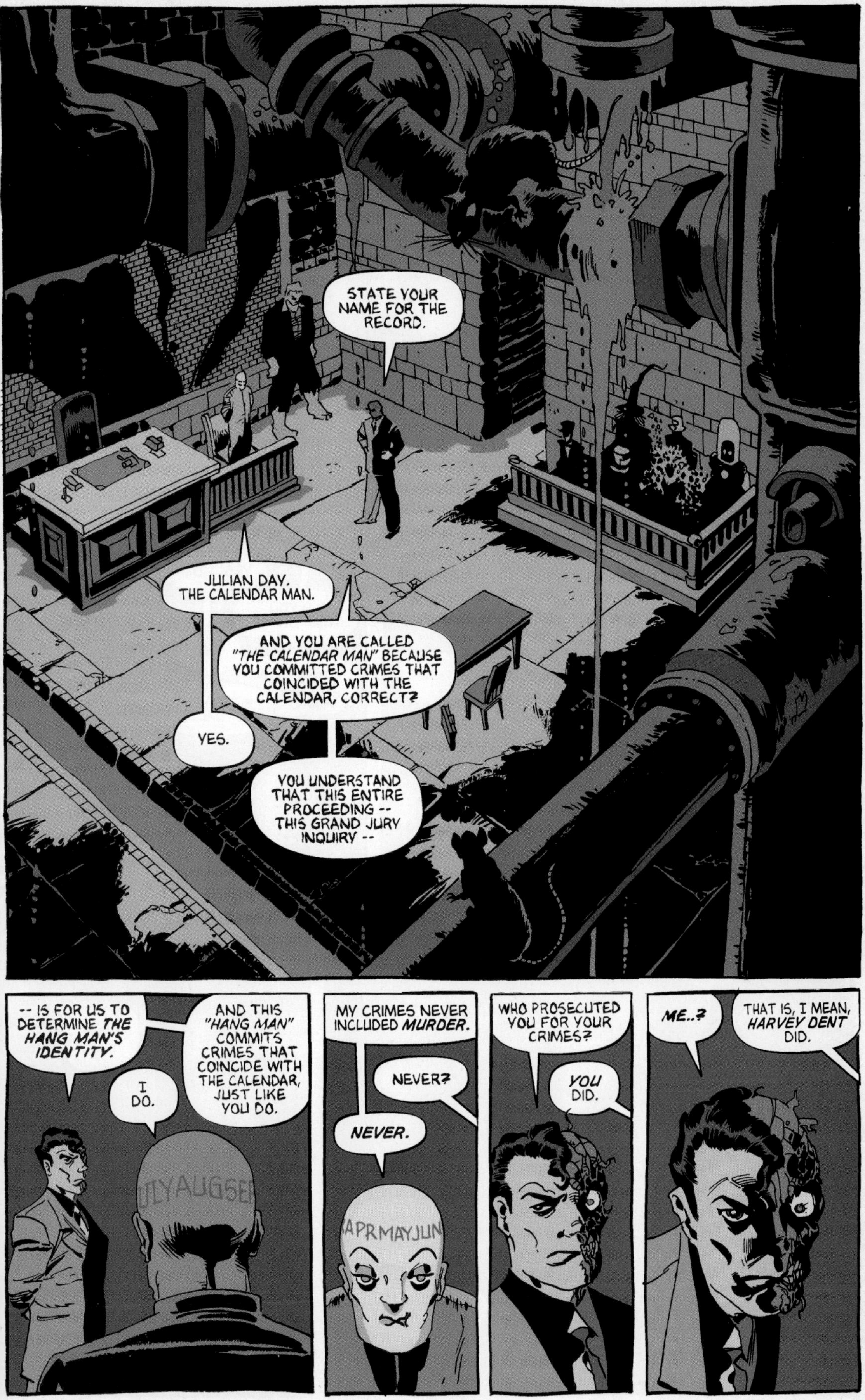
STATE YOUR NAME FOR THE RECORD.
JULIAN DAY. THE CALENDAR MAN.
AND YOU ARE CALLED "THE CALENDAR MAN" BECAUSE YOU COMMITTED CRIMES THAT COINCIDED WITH THE CALENDAR, CORRECT?
YES.
YOU UNDERSTAND THAT THIS ENTIRE PROCEEDING -- THIS GRAND JURY INQUIRY --
-- IS FOR US TO DETERMINE THE HANG MAN'S IDENTITY.
I DO.
AND THIS "HANG MAN" COMMITS CRIMES THAT COINCIDE WITH THE CALENDAR, JUST LIKE YOU DO.
ULYAUGSEP
MY CRIMES NEVER INCLUDED MURDER.
NEVER?
NEVER.
APRMAYJUN
WHO PROSECUTED YOU FOR YOUR CRIMES?
YOU DID.
ME..?
THAT IS, I MEAN, HARVEY DENT DID.

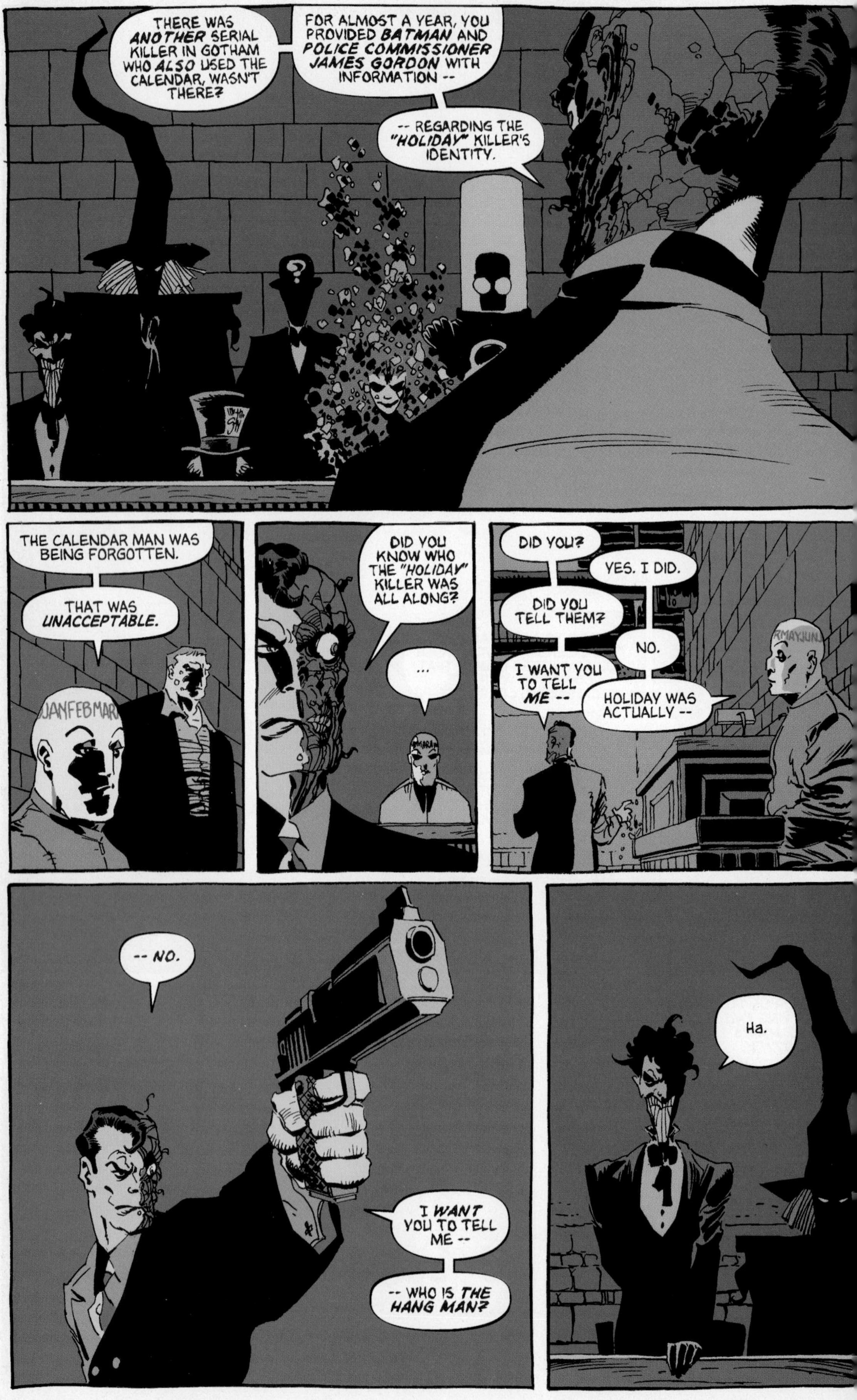
THERE WAS ANOTHER SERIAL KILLER IN GOTHAM WHO ALSO USED THE CALENDAR, WASN'T THERE?
FOR ALMOST A YEAR, YOU PROVIDED BATMAN AND POLICE COMMISSIONER JAMES GORDON WITH INFORMATION --
-- REGARDING THE "HOLIDAY" KILLER'S IDENTITY.
THE CALENDAR MAN WAS BEING FORGOTTEN.
THAT WAS UNACCEPTABLE.
JANFEBMAR
DID YOU KNOW WHO THE "HOLIDAY" KILLER WAS ALL ALONG?
...
DID YOU?
YES. I DID.
DID YOU TELL THEM?
NO.
I WANT YOU TO TELL ME --
HOLIDAY WAS ACTUALLY --
-- NO.
I WANT YOU TO TELL ME --
-- WHO IS THE HANG MAN?
Ha.

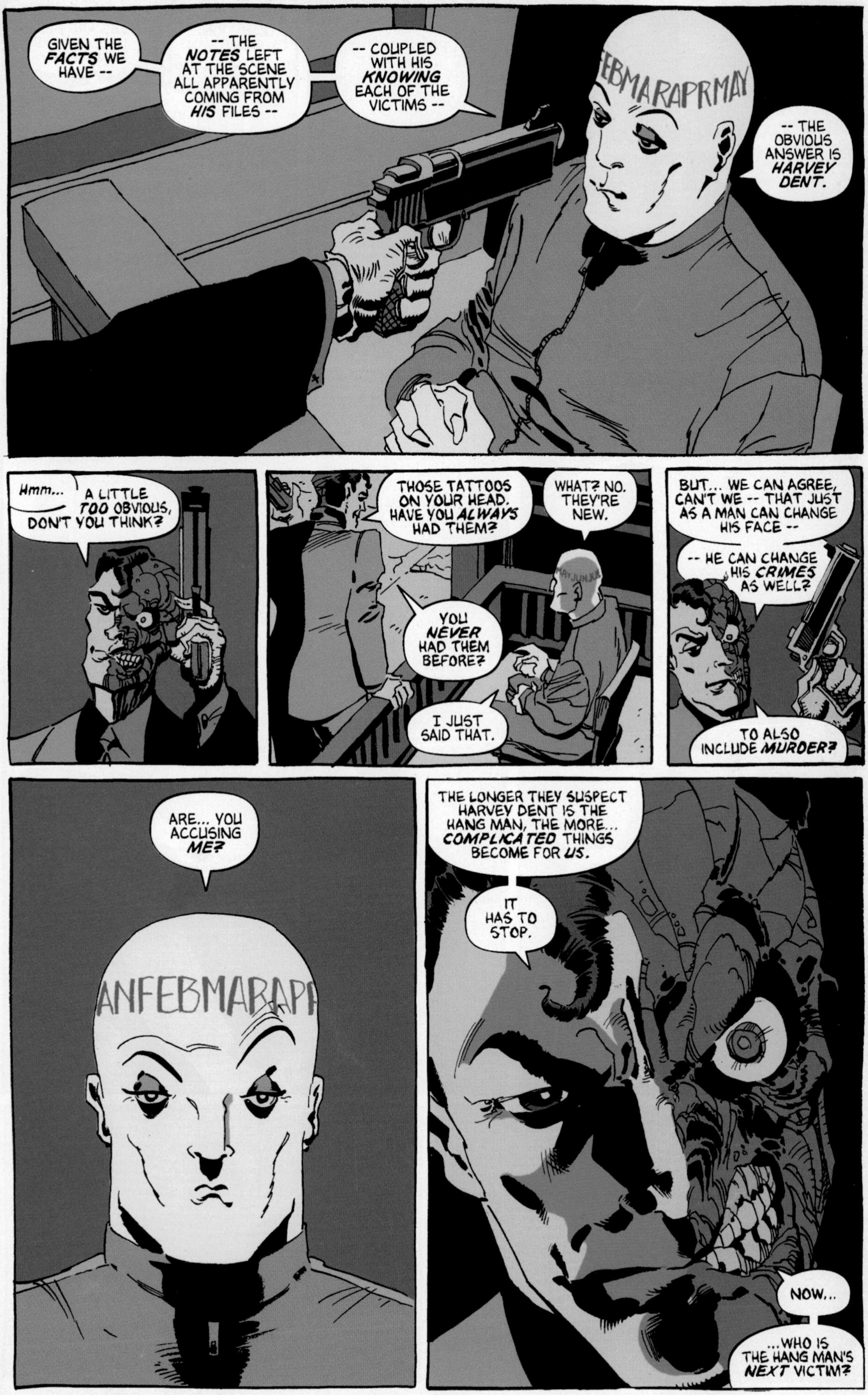
GIVEN THE FACTS WE HAVE --
-- THE NOTES LEFT AT THE SCENE ALL APPARENTLY COMING FROM HIS FILES --
-- COUPLED WITH HIS KNOWING EACH OF THE VICTIMS --
FEBMARAPRMAY
-- THE OBVIOUS ANSWER IS HARVEY DENT.
Hmm...
A LITTLE TOO OBVIOUS, DON'T YOU THINK?
THOSE TATTOOS ON YOUR HEAD. HAVE YOU ALWAYS HAD THEM?
WHAT? NO. THEY'RE NEW.
YOU NEVER HAD THEM BEFORE?
I JUST SAID THAT.
BUT... WE CAN AGREE, CAN'T WE -- THAT JUST AS A MAN CAN CHANGE HIS FACE --
-- HE CAN CHANGE HIS CRIMES AS WELL?
TO ALSO INCLUDE MURDER?
ARE... YOU ACCUSING ME?
ANFEBMARAPR
THE LONGER THEY SUSPECT HARVEY DENT IS THE HANG MAN, THE MORE... COMPLICATED THINGS BECOME FOR US.
IT HAS TO STOP.
NOW...
...WHO IS THE HANG MAN'S NEXT VICTIM?

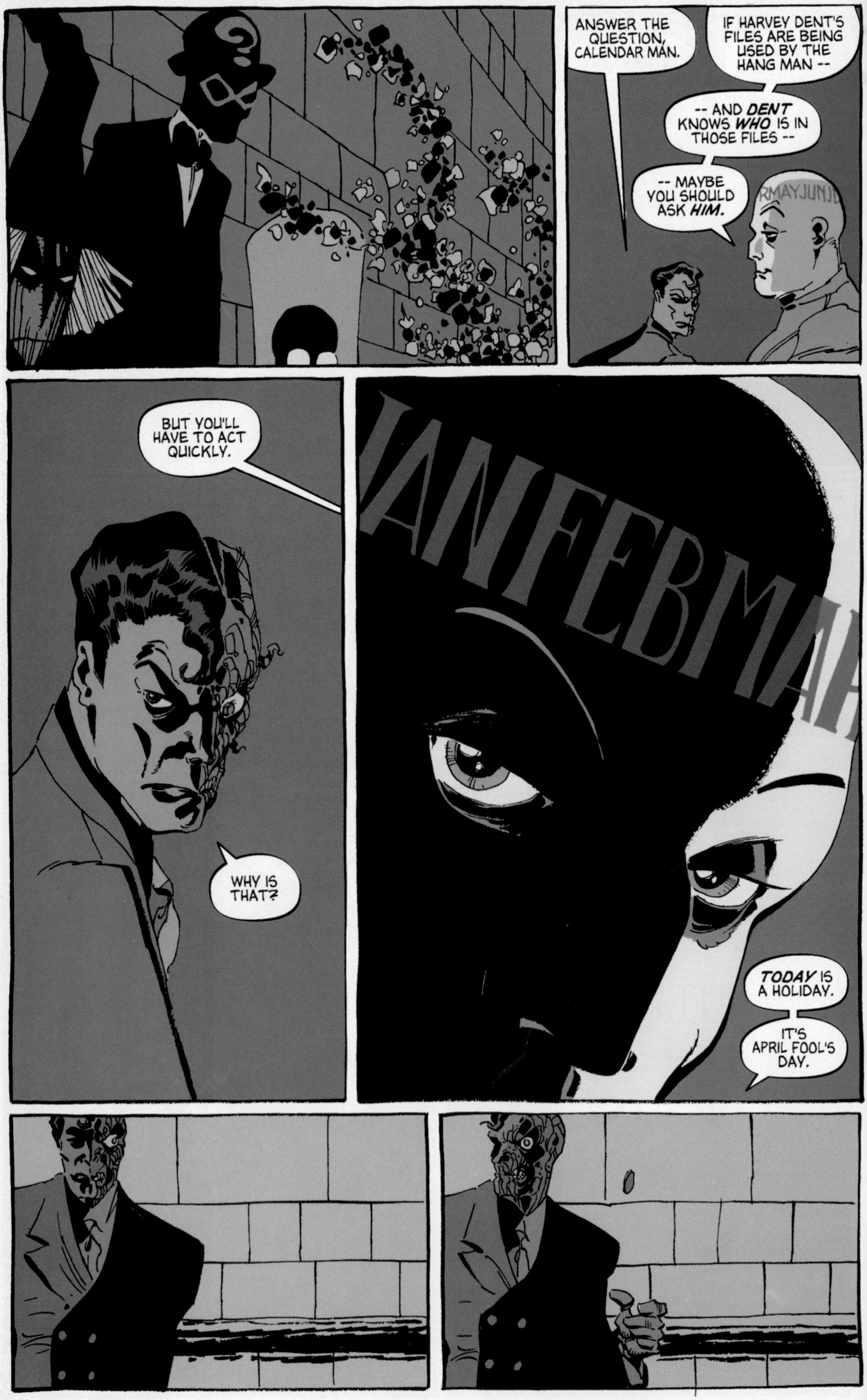
ANSWER THE QUESTION, CALENDAR MAN.
IF HARVEY DENT'S FILES ARE BEING USED BY THE HANG MAN --
-- AND DENT KNOWS WHO IS IN THOSE FILES --
-- MAYBE YOU SHOULD ASK HIM.
RMAYJUNJU
BUT YOU'LL HAVE TO ACT QUICKLY.
JANFEBMAR
WHY IS THAT?
TODAY IS A HOLIDAY.
IT'S APRIL FOOL'S DAY.

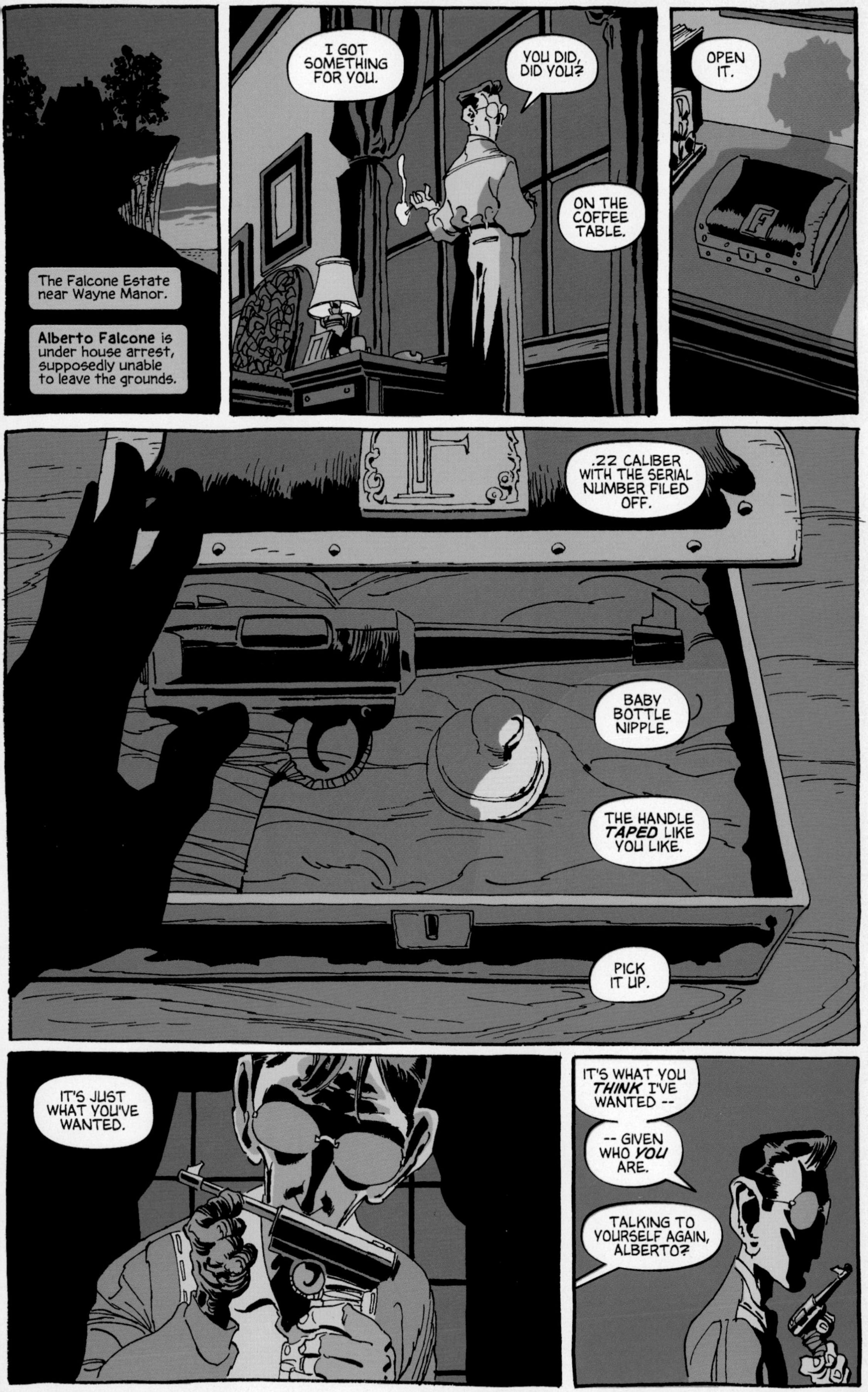
The Falcone Estate near Wayne Manor.
Alberto Falcone is under house arrest, supposedly unable to leave the grounds.
I GOT SOMETHING FOR YOU.
YOU DID, DID YOU?
ON THE COFFEE TABLE.
OPEN IT.
.22 CALIBER WITH THE SERIAL NUMBER FILED OFF.
BABY BOTTLE NIPPLE.
THE HANDLE TAPED LIKE YOU LIKE.
PICK IT UP.
IT'S JUST WHAT YOU'VE WANTED.
IT'S WHAT YOU THINK I'VE WANTED --
-- GIVEN WHO YOU ARE.
TALKING TO YOURSELF AGAIN, ALBERTO?

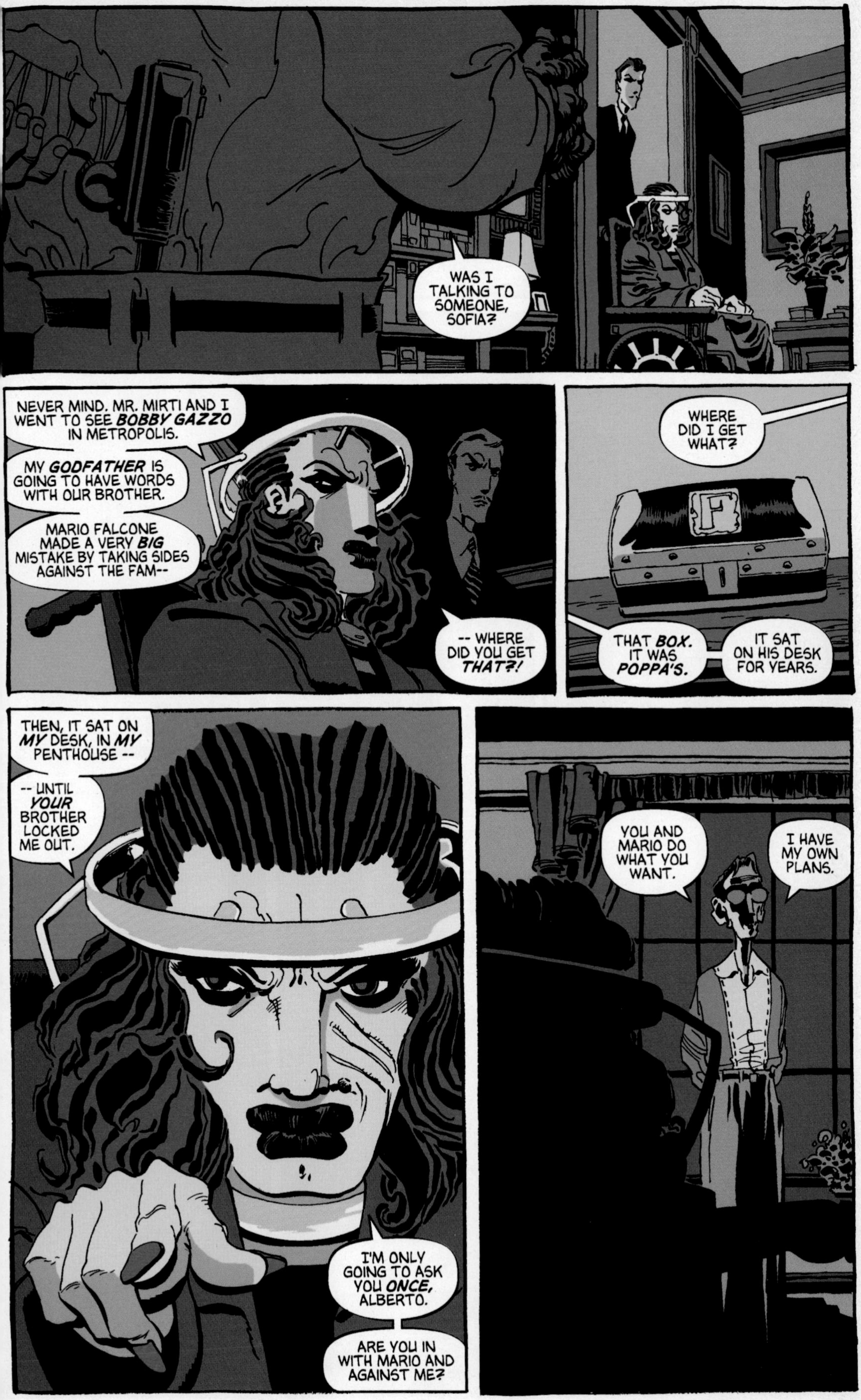
WAS I TALKING TO SOMEONE, SOFIA?
NEVER MIND. MR. MIRTI AND I WENT TO SEE BOBBY GAZZO IN METROPOLIS.
MY GODFATHER IS GOING TO HAVE WORDS WITH OUR BROTHER.
MARIO FALCONE MADE A VERY BIG MISTAKE BY TAKING SIDES AGAINST THE FAM--
-- WHERE DID YOU GET THAT?!
WHERE DID I GET WHAT?
THAT BOX. IT WAS POPPA'S.
IT SAT ON HIS DESK FOR YEARS.
THEN, IT SAT ON MY DESK, IN MY PENTHOUSE --
-- UNTIL YOUR BROTHER LOCKED ME OUT.
I'M ONLY GOING TO ASK YOU ONCE, ALBERTO.
ARE YOU IN WITH MARIO AND AGAINST ME?
YOU AND MARIO DO WHAT YOU WANT.
I HAVE MY OWN PLANS.

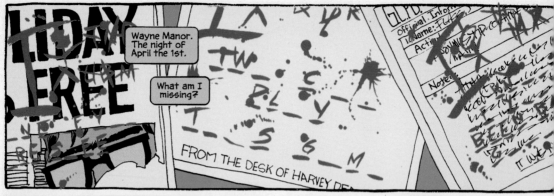

Wayne Manor. The night of April the 1st.

What am I missing?

FROM THE DESK OF HARVEY DEN

The notes themselves. The **way** the Hang Man game is being played.

There are **mistakes.** Discarded letters which are part of the puzzles.

Insufficient discarded letters to actually build the Hanged Man.

It's almost as if...

...there is **no way** to win the game.

Do the discarded letters mean anything?

"B" for Batman?

"J" for Joker?

"D" for... Dent.

"D" for Dent.

I can't ignore that the notes were all written on things relating to Harvey.

A torn newspaper headline of "HOLIDAY GOES FREE."

His stationery. Police reports from his cases. The deed to his house.

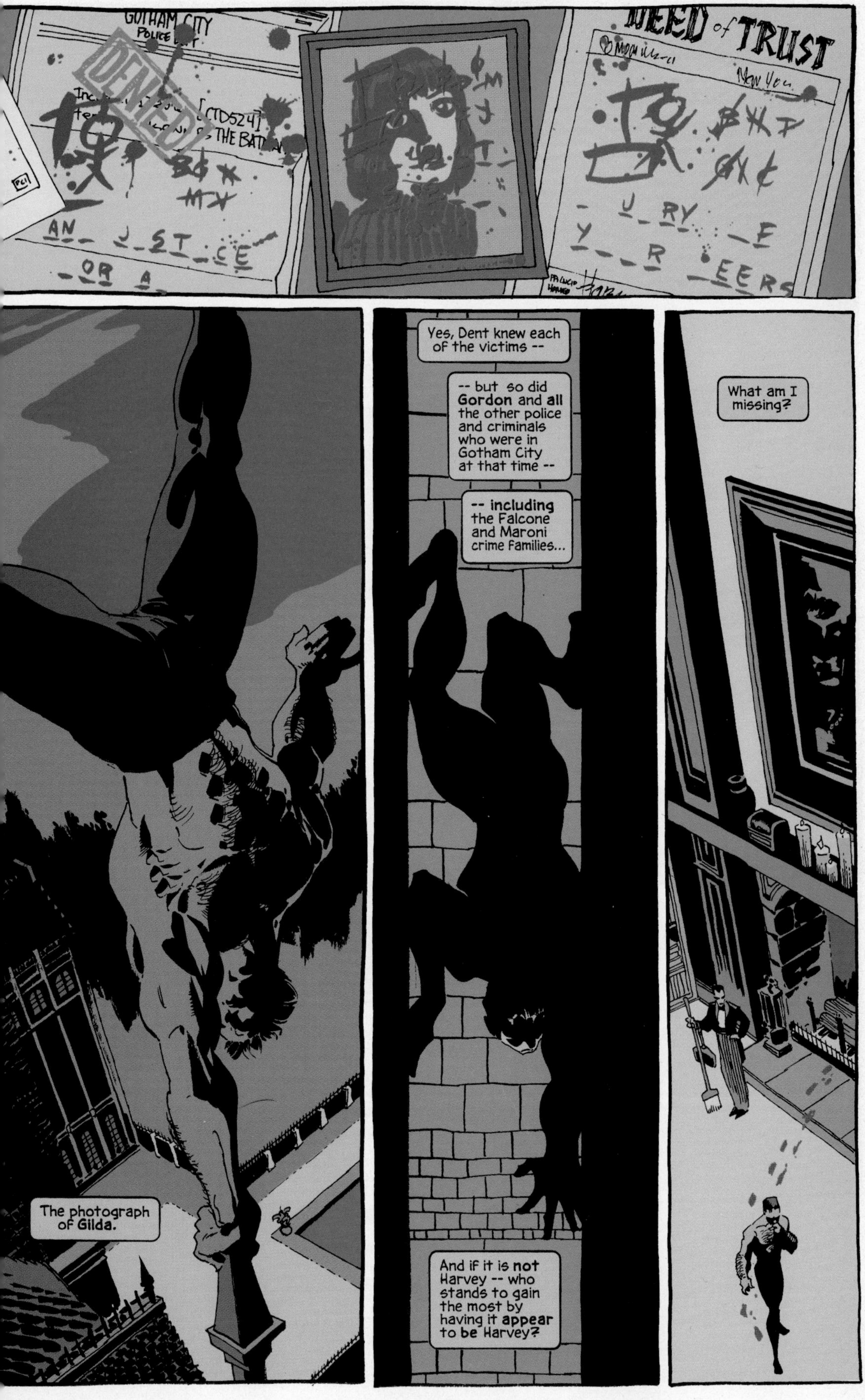
GOTHAM CITY
POLICE DEPT
DENIED
THE BATMAN
AN_ J_ST_CE
_OR A
DEED of TRUST
New York
_ J_RY
Y__R _E
_EERS
The photograph of Gilda.
Yes, Dent knew each of the victims --
-- but so did Gordon and all the other police and criminals who were in Gotham City at that time --
-- including the Falcone and Maroni crime families...
And if it is not Harvey -- who stands to gain the most by having it appear to be Harvey?
What am I missing?

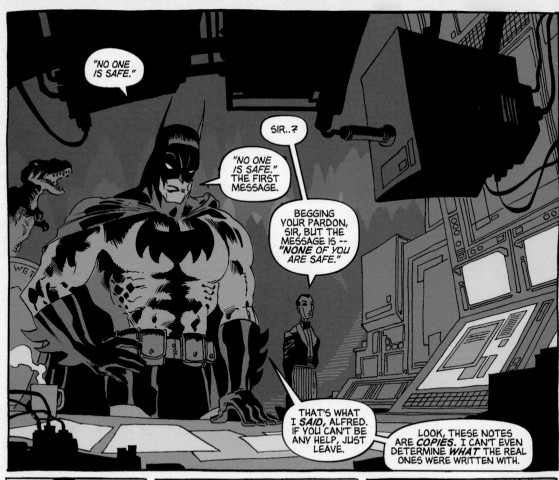

"NO ONE IS SAFE."

SIR..?

"NO ONE IS SAFE." THE FIRST MESSAGE.

BEGGING YOUR PARDON, SIR, BUT THE MESSAGE IS -- *"NONE OF YOU ARE SAFE."*

THAT'S WHAT I *SAID*, ALFRED. IF YOU CAN'T BE ANY HELP, JUST LEAVE.

LOOK, THESE NOTES ARE *COPIES.* I CAN'T EVEN DETERMINE *WHAT* THE REAL ONES WERE WRITTEN WITH.

PAINT? CRAYON? *BLOOD?*

AND IF IT *IS* BLOOD -- WHOSE BLOOD?

THIS NEW D.A. -- *PORTER.* SHE'S GOT THEM ALL *CONVINCED* THAT I'LL CONTAMINATE THE EVIDENCE. SOIL THE INVESTIGATION.

ME.

MAYBE I SHOULD BE INVESTIGATING *HER...*

MASTER BRUCE.

PERHAPS I COULD BE OF SOME SERVICE IF YOU WOULD TELL ME THE *ORDER* IN WHICH THE KILLINGS TOOK PLACE.

WHAT..?

THE ORDER. STARTING WITH THE FIRST.

O'HARA. LOEB. PRATT. UM... BRANDEN. MERKEL.

PRATT CAME *AFTER* BRANDEN.

AND YOU DID NOT MENTION *FLASS.* HE WAS THIRD.

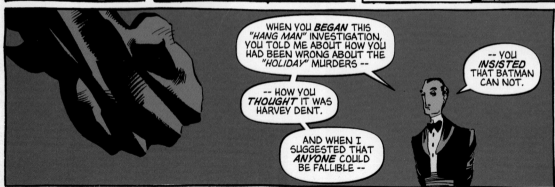

WHEN YOU *BEGAN* THIS "HANG MAN" INVESTIGATION, YOU TOLD ME ABOUT HOW YOU HAD BEEN WRONG ABOUT THE "HOLIDAY" MURDERS --

-- HOW YOU *THOUGHT* IT WAS HARVEY DENT.

AND WHEN I SUGGESTED THAT *ANYONE* COULD BE FALLIBLE --

-- YOU *INSISTED* THAT BATMAN CAN NOT.

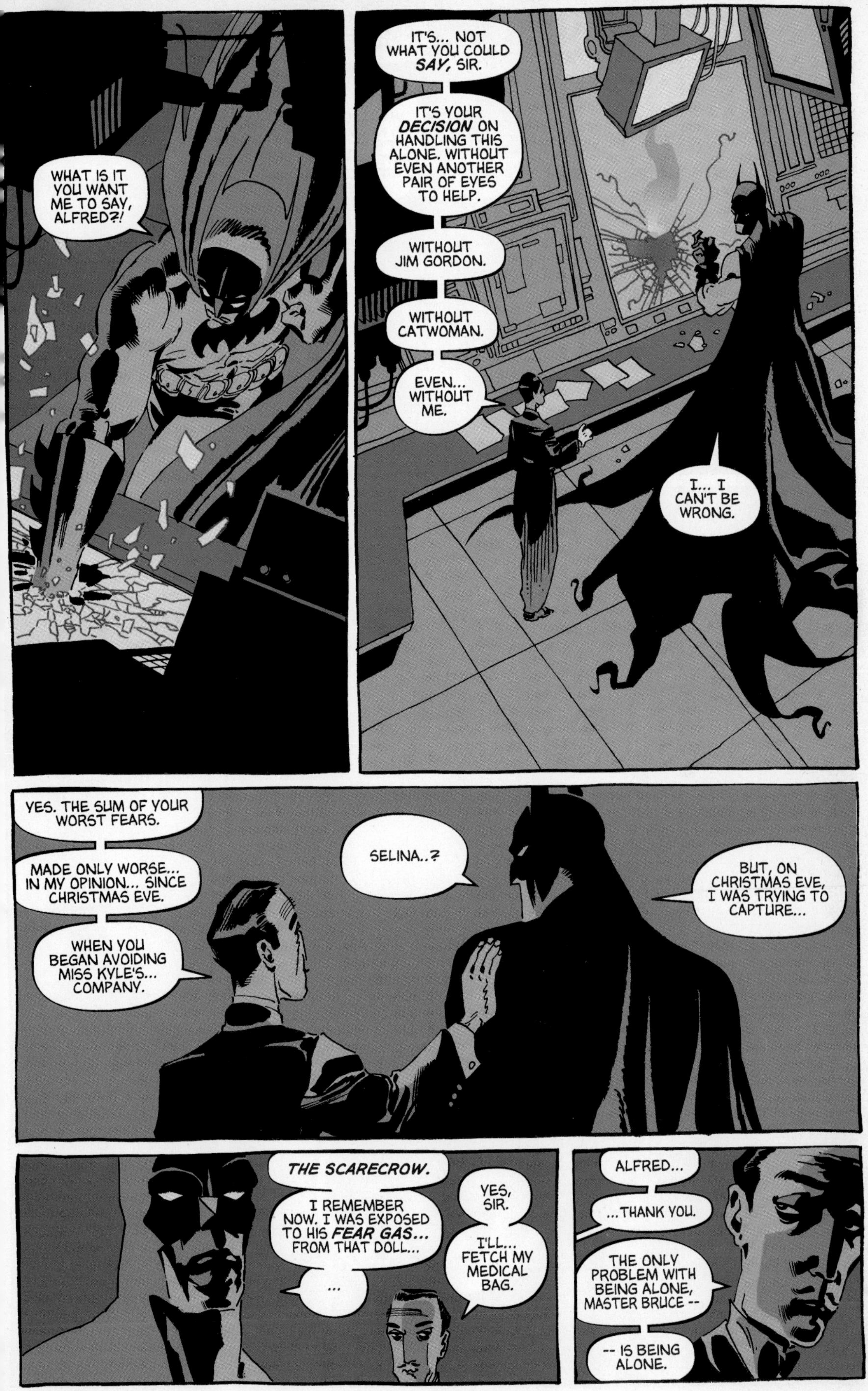
WHAT IS IT YOU WANT ME TO SAY, ALFRED?!
IT'S... NOT WHAT YOU COULD SAY, SIR.
IT'S YOUR DECISION ON HANDLING THIS ALONE. WITHOUT EVEN ANOTHER PAIR OF EYES TO HELP.
WITHOUT JIM GORDON.
WITHOUT CATWOMAN.
EVEN... WITHOUT ME.
I... I CAN'T BE WRONG.
YES. THE SUM OF YOUR WORST FEARS.
MADE ONLY WORSE... IN MY OPINION... SINCE CHRISTMAS EVE.
WHEN YOU BEGAN AVOIDING MISS KYLE'S... COMPANY.
SELINA..?
BUT, ON CHRISTMAS EVE, I WAS TRYING TO CAPTURE...
THE SCARECROW.
I REMEMBER NOW. I WAS EXPOSED TO HIS FEAR GAS... FROM THAT DOLL...
...
YES, SIR.
I'LL... FETCH MY MEDICAL BAG.
ALFRED...
...THANK YOU.
THE ONLY PROBLEM WITH BEING ALONE, MASTER BRUCE --
-- IS BEING ALONE.

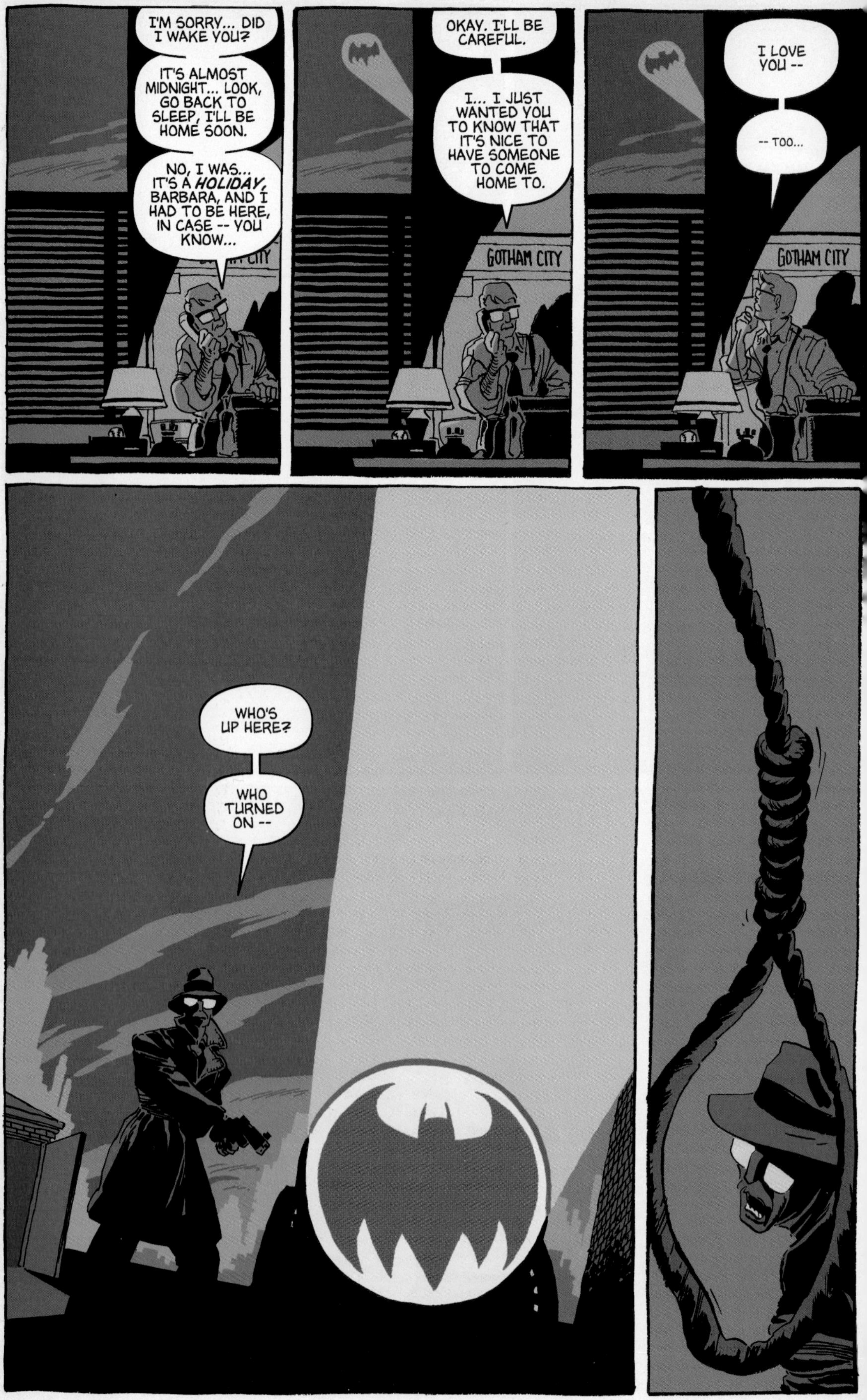
I'M SORRY... DID I WAKE YOU?
IT'S ALMOST MIDNIGHT... LOOK, GO BACK TO SLEEP, I'LL BE HOME SOON.
NO, I WAS... IT'S A *HOLIDAY*, BARBARA, AND I HAD TO BE HERE, IN CASE -- YOU KNOW...
OKAY. I'LL BE CAREFUL.
I... I JUST WANTED YOU TO KNOW THAT IT'S NICE TO HAVE SOMEONE TO COME HOME TO.
GOTHAM CITY
I LOVE YOU --
-- TOO...
GOTHAM CITY
WHO'S UP HERE?
WHO TURNED ON --

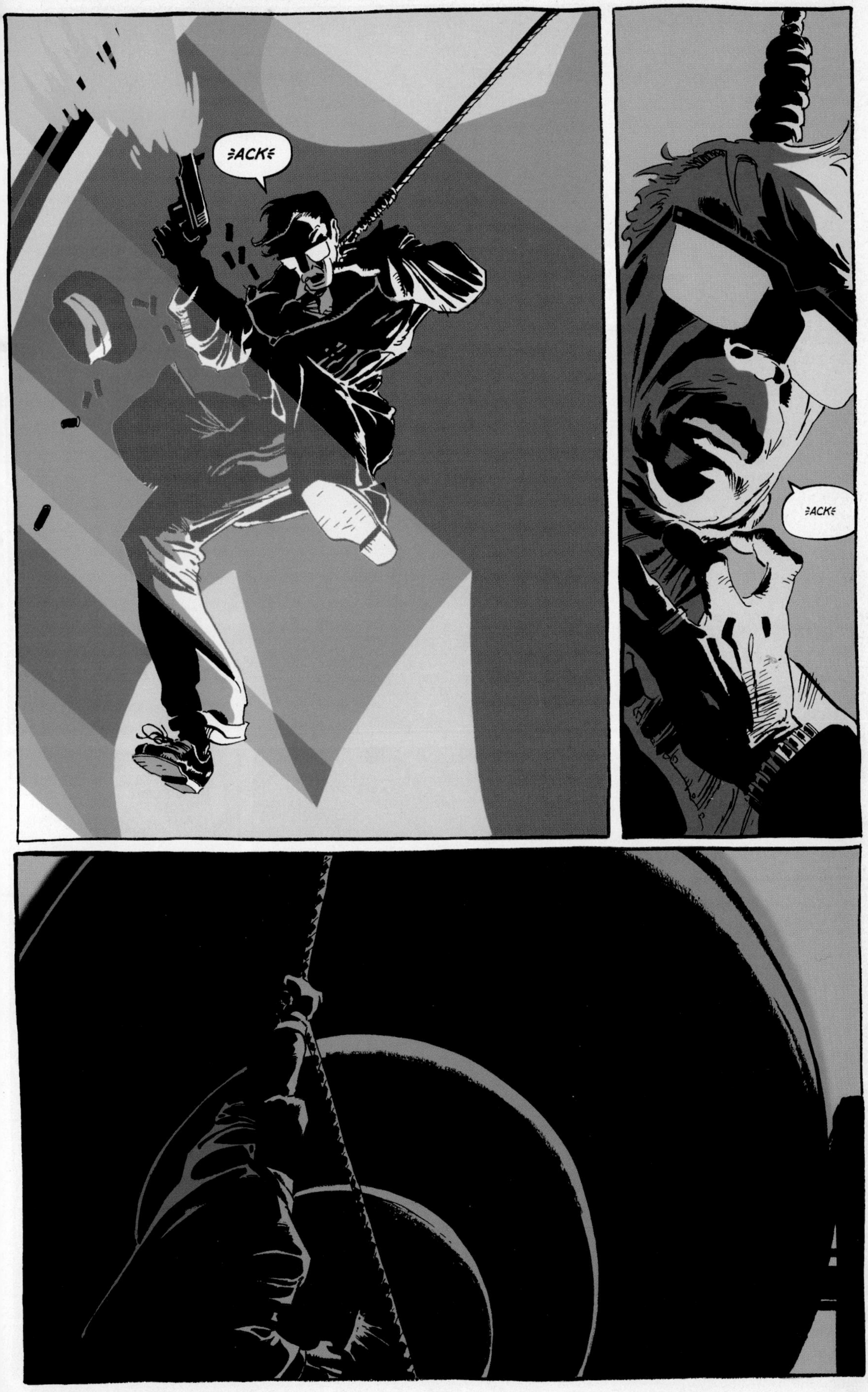

ACK
ACK

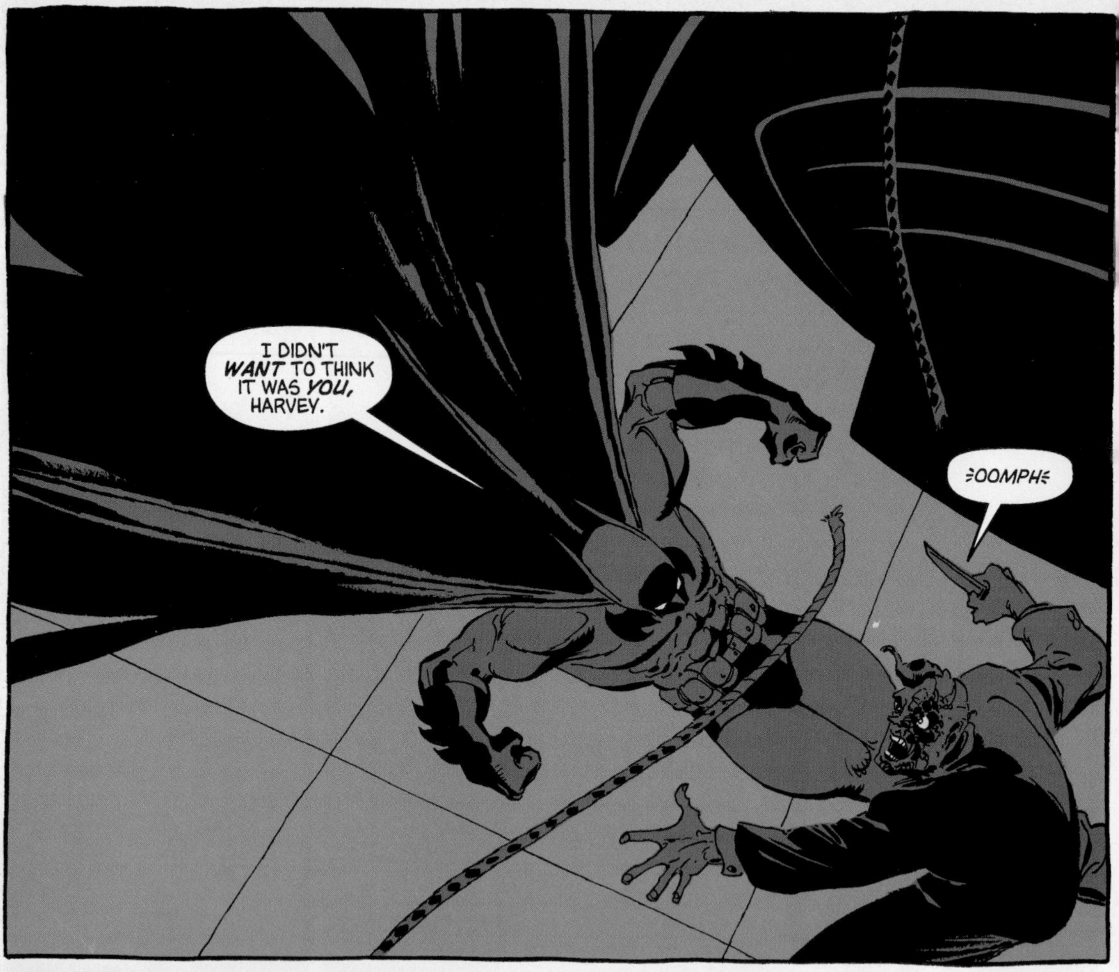
I DIDN'T WANT TO THINK IT WAS YOU, HARVEY.
OOMPH

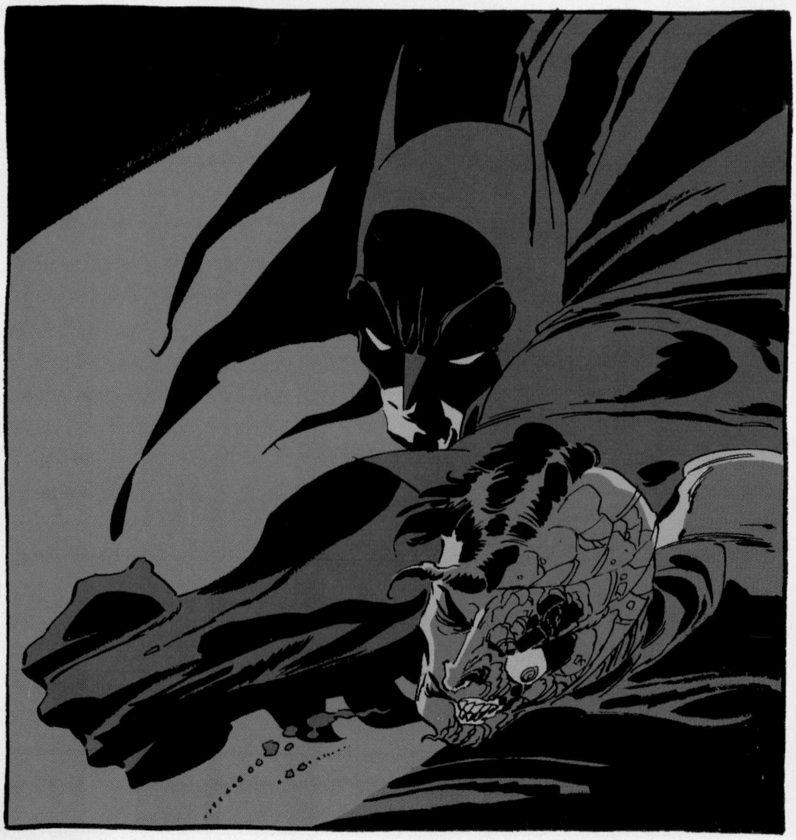

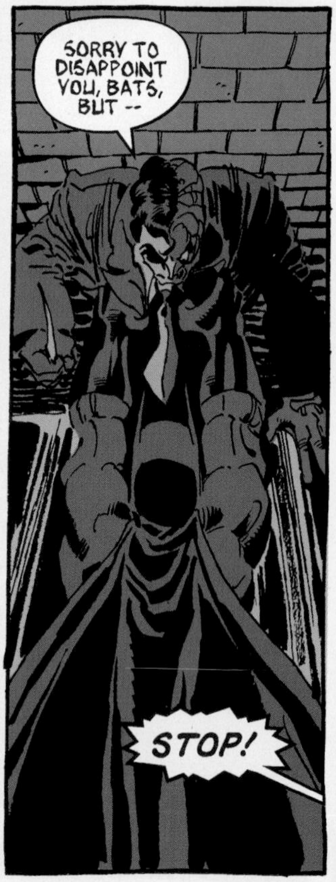
SORRY TO DISAPPOINT YOU, BATS, BUT --
STOP!

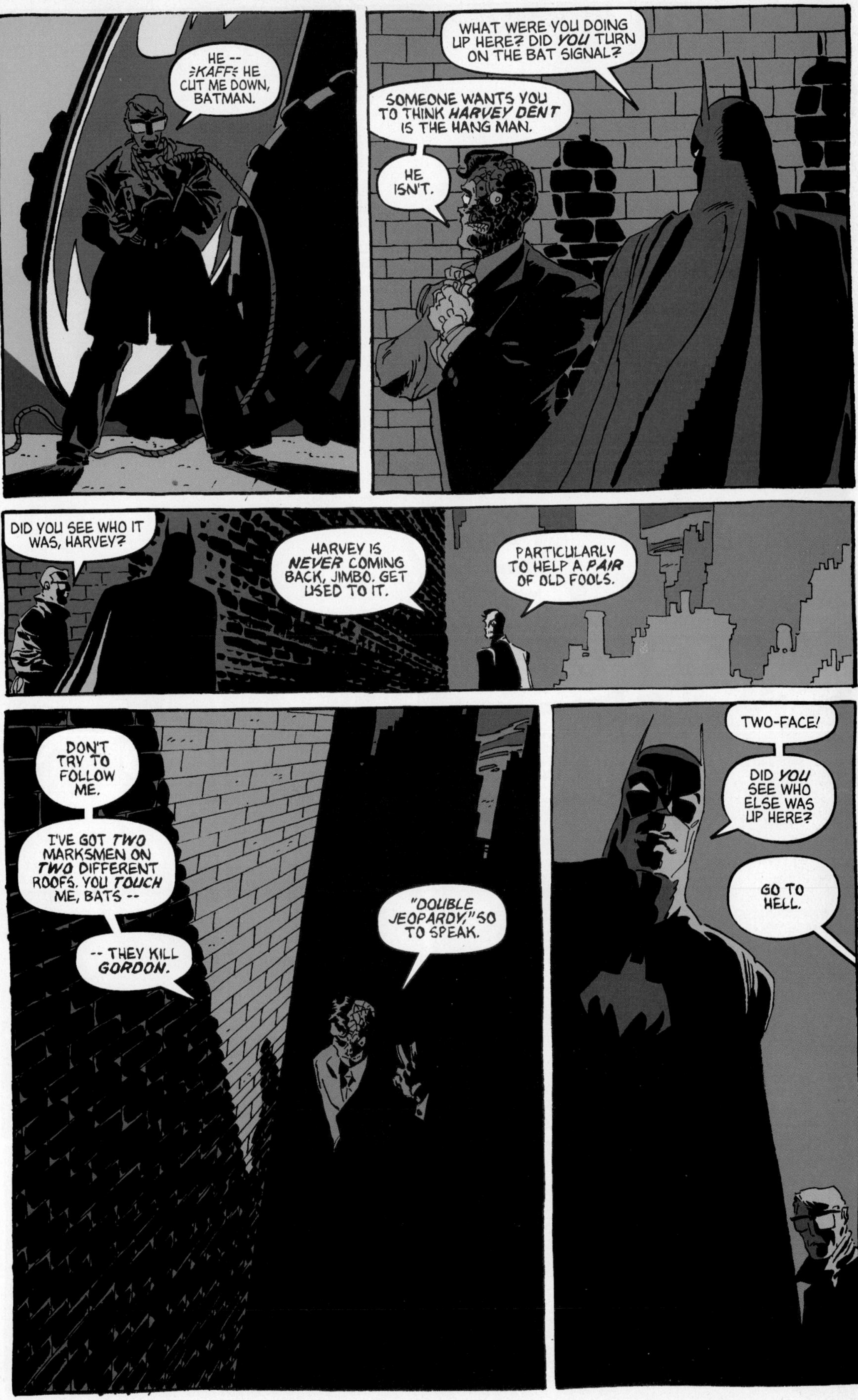
HE -- =KAFF= HE CUT ME DOWN, BATMAN.
WHAT WERE YOU DOING UP HERE? DID YOU TURN ON THE BAT SIGNAL?
SOMEONE WANTS YOU TO THINK HARVEY DENT IS THE HANG MAN.
HE ISN'T.
DID YOU SEE WHO IT WAS, HARVEY?
HARVEY IS NEVER COMING BACK, JIMBO. GET USED TO IT.
PARTICULARLY TO HELP A PAIR OF OLD FOOLS.
DON'T TRY TO FOLLOW ME.
I'VE GOT TWO MARKSMEN ON TWO DIFFERENT ROOFS. YOU TOUCH ME, BATS --
-- THEY KILL GORDON.
"DOUBLE JEOPARDY," SO TO SPEAK.
TWO-FACE!
DID YOU SEE WHO ELSE WAS UP HERE?
GO TO HELL.

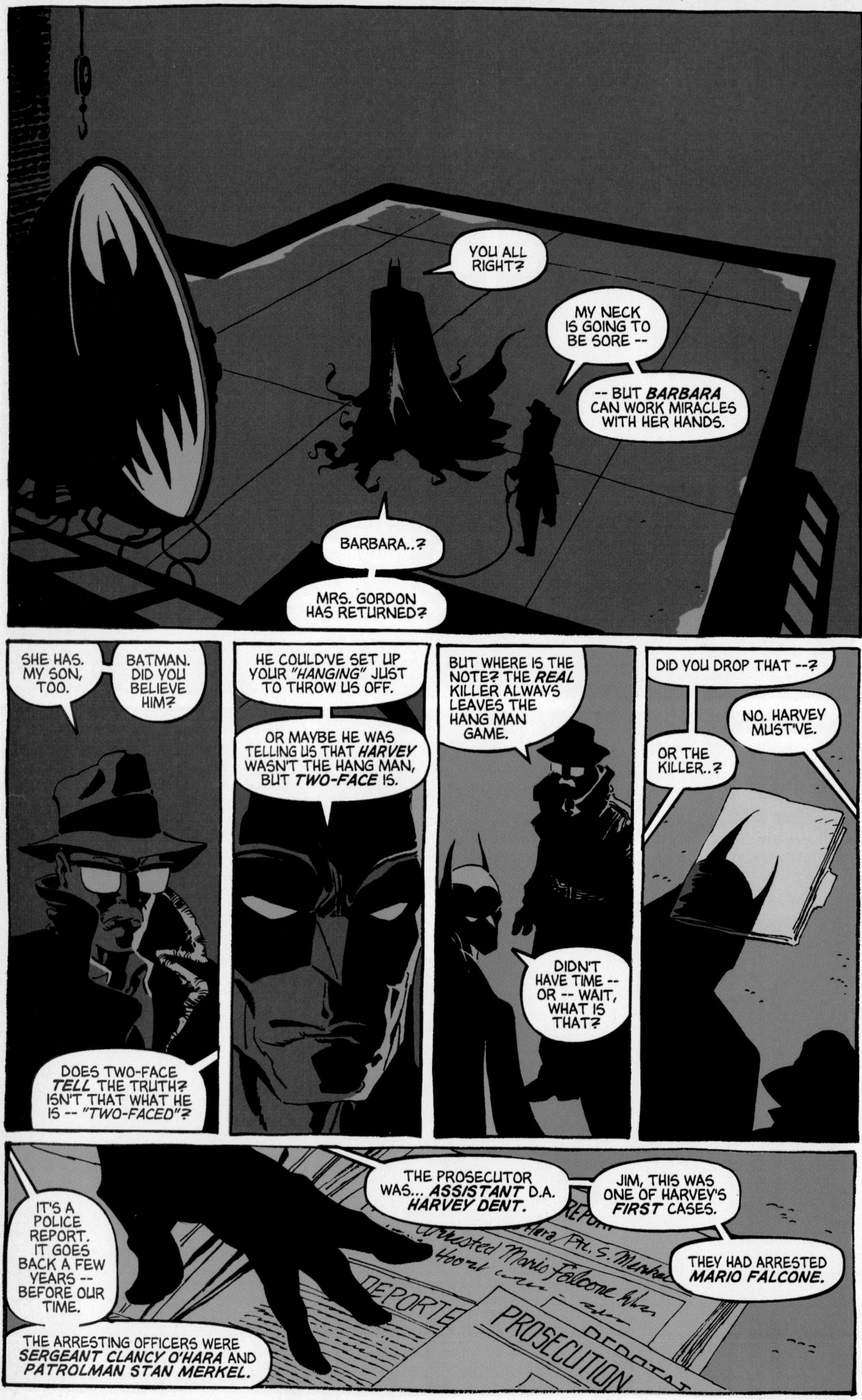

YOU ALL RIGHT?
MY NECK IS GOING TO BE SORE --
-- BUT BARBARA CAN WORK MIRACLES WITH HER HANDS.
BARBARA..?
MRS. GORDON HAS RETURNED?
SHE HAS. MY SON, TOO.
BATMAN. DID YOU BELIEVE HIM?
DOES TWO-FACE TELL THE TRUTH? ISN'T THAT WHAT HE IS -- "TWO-FACED"?
HE COULD'VE SET UP YOUR "HANGING" JUST TO THROW US OFF.
OR MAYBE HE WAS TELLING US THAT HARVEY WASN'T THE HANG MAN, BUT TWO-FACE IS.
BUT WHERE IS THE NOTE? THE REAL KILLER ALWAYS LEAVES THE HANG MAN GAME.
DIDN'T HAVE TIME -- OR -- WAIT, WHAT IS THAT?
DID YOU DROP THAT --?
OR THE KILLER..?
NO. HARVEY MUST'VE.
IT'S A POLICE REPORT. IT GOES BACK A FEW YEARS -- BEFORE OUR TIME.
THE PROSECUTOR WAS... ASSISTANT D.A. HARVEY DENT.
JIM, THIS WAS ONE OF HARVEY'S FIRST CASES.
THEY HAD ARRESTED MARIO FALCONE.
THE ARRESTING OFFICERS WERE SERGEANT CLANCY O'HARA AND PATROLMAN STAN MERKEL.
PROSECUTION

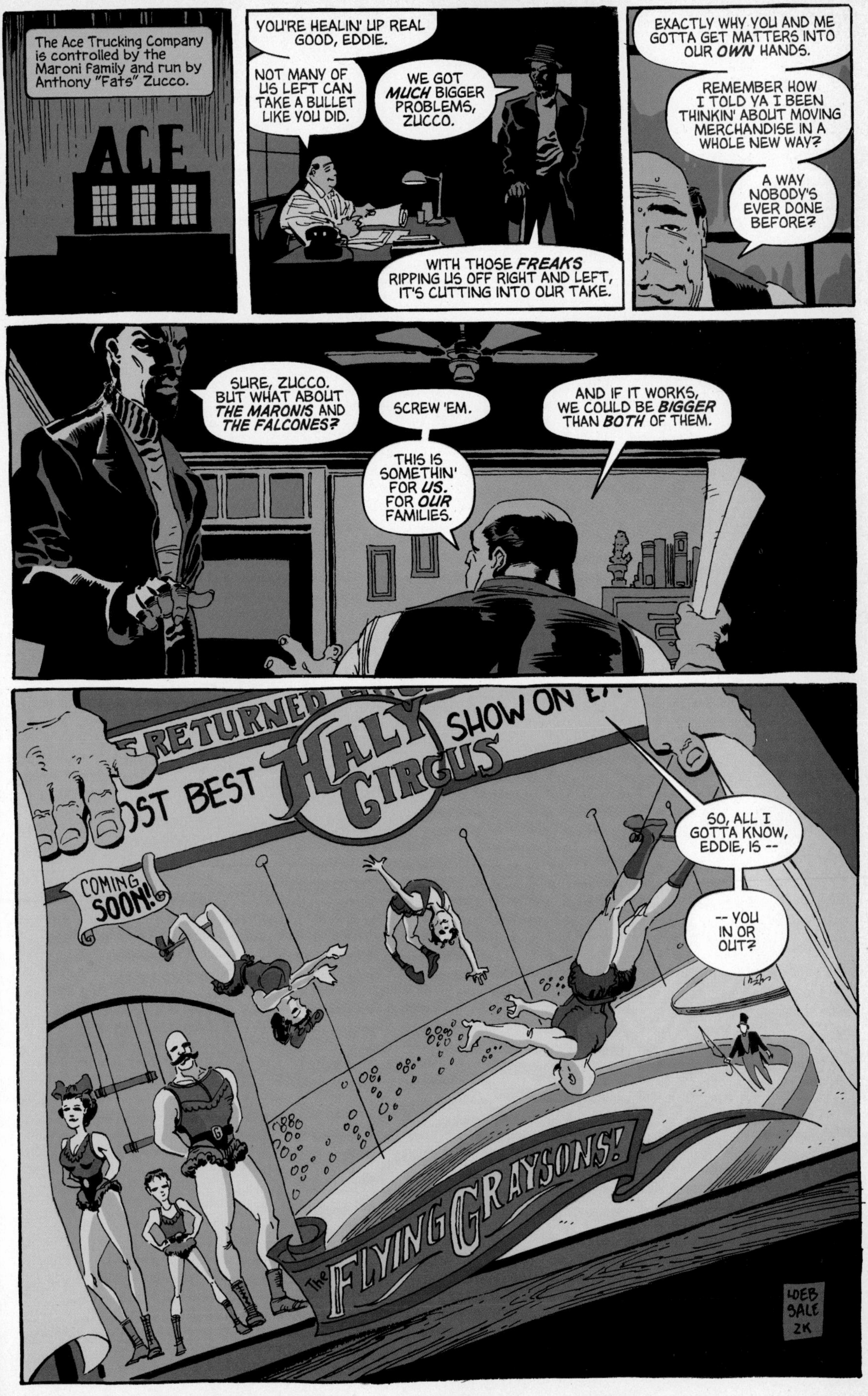

The Ace Trucking Company is controlled by the Maroni family and run by Anthony "Fats" Zucco.
ACE
YOU'RE HEALIN' UP REAL GOOD, EDDIE.
NOT MANY OF US LEFT CAN TAKE A BULLET LIKE YOU DID.
WE GOT MUCH BIGGER PROBLEMS, ZUCCO.
WITH THOSE FREAKS RIPPING US OFF RIGHT AND LEFT, IT'S CUTTING INTO OUR TAKE.
EXACTLY WHY YOU AND ME GOTTA GET MATTERS INTO OUR OWN HANDS.
REMEMBER HOW I TOLD YA I BEEN THINKIN' ABOUT MOVING MERCHANDISE IN A WHOLE NEW WAY?
A WAY NOBODY'S EVER DONE BEFORE?
SURE, ZUCCO. BUT WHAT ABOUT THE MARONIS AND THE FALCONES?
SCREW 'EM.
THIS IS SOMETHIN' FOR US. FOR OUR FAMILIES.
AND IF IT WORKS, WE COULD BE BIGGER THAN BOTH OF THEM.
RETURNED
SHOW ON
OST BEST
HALY CIRCUS
COMING SOON!
SO, ALL I GOTTA KNOW, EDDIE, IS --
-- YOU IN OR OUT?
The FLYING GRAYSONS!
LOEB SALE 2K

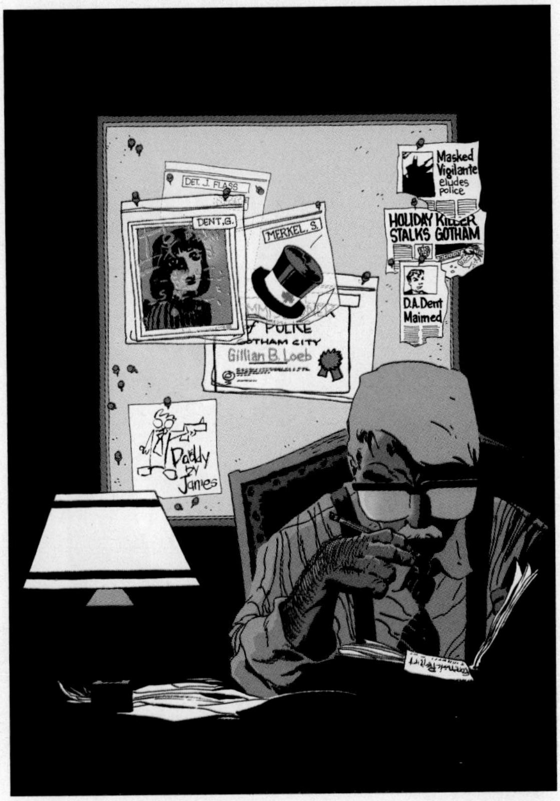
DET. J. FLASS
DENT, G.
MERKEL, S.
POLICE
Gillian B. Loeb
Masked Vigilante eludes police
HOLIDAY KILLER STALKS GOTHAM
D.A. Dent Maimed
Daddy by James

8

B A T T L E

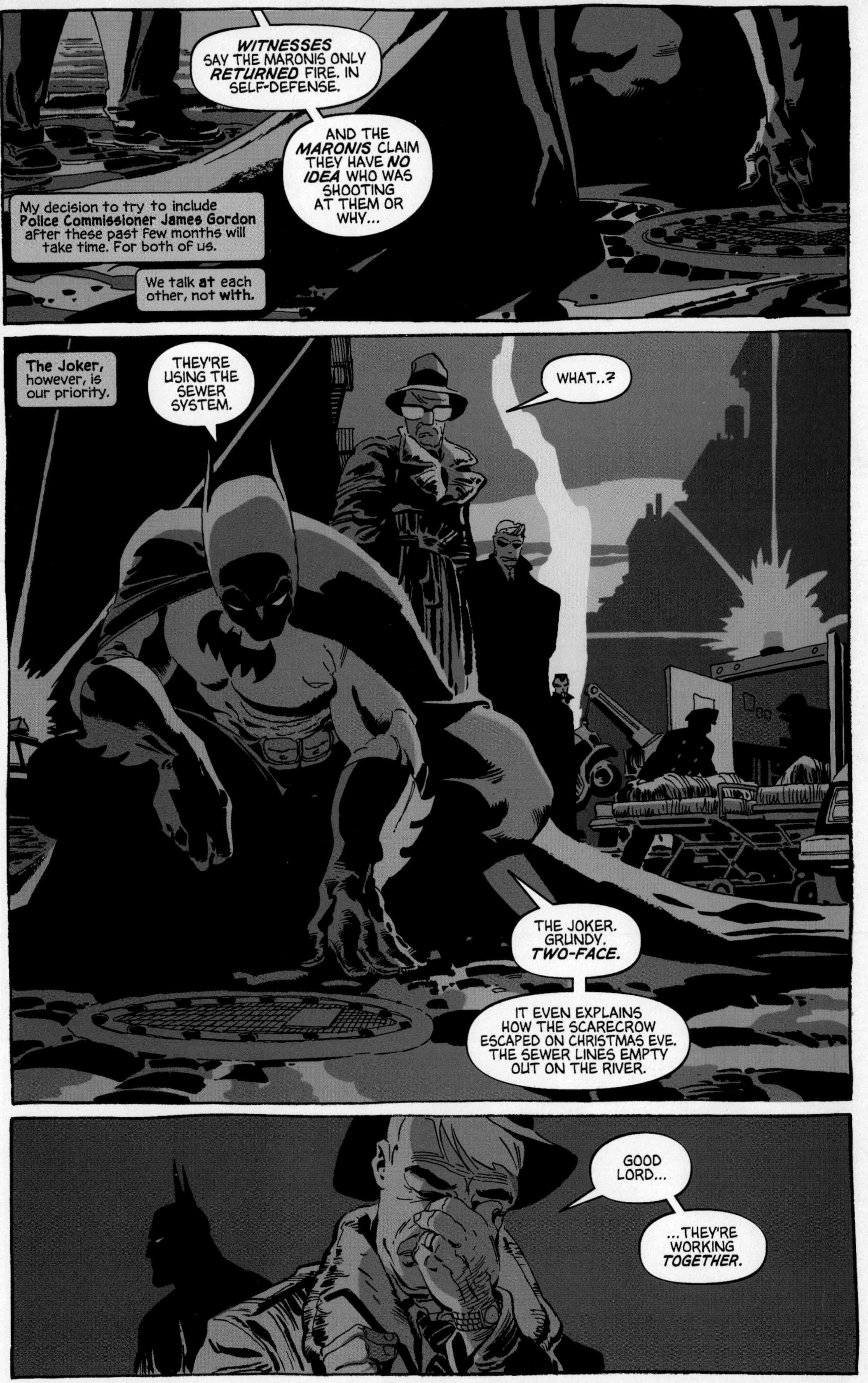
WITNESSES SAY THE MARONIS ONLY RETURNED FIRE. IN SELF-DEFENSE.
AND THE MARONIS CLAIM THEY HAVE NO IDEA WHO WAS SHOOTING AT THEM OR WHY...
My decision to try to include Police Commissioner James Gordon after these past few months will take time. For both of us.
We talk at each other, not with.
The Joker, however, is our priority.
THEY'RE USING THE SEWER SYSTEM.
WHAT..?
THE JOKER. GRUNDY. TWO-FACE.
IT EVEN EXPLAINS HOW THE SCARECROW ESCAPED ON CHRISTMAS EVE. THE SEWER LINES EMPTY OUT ON THE RIVER.
GOOD LORD...
...THEY'RE WORKING TOGETHER.

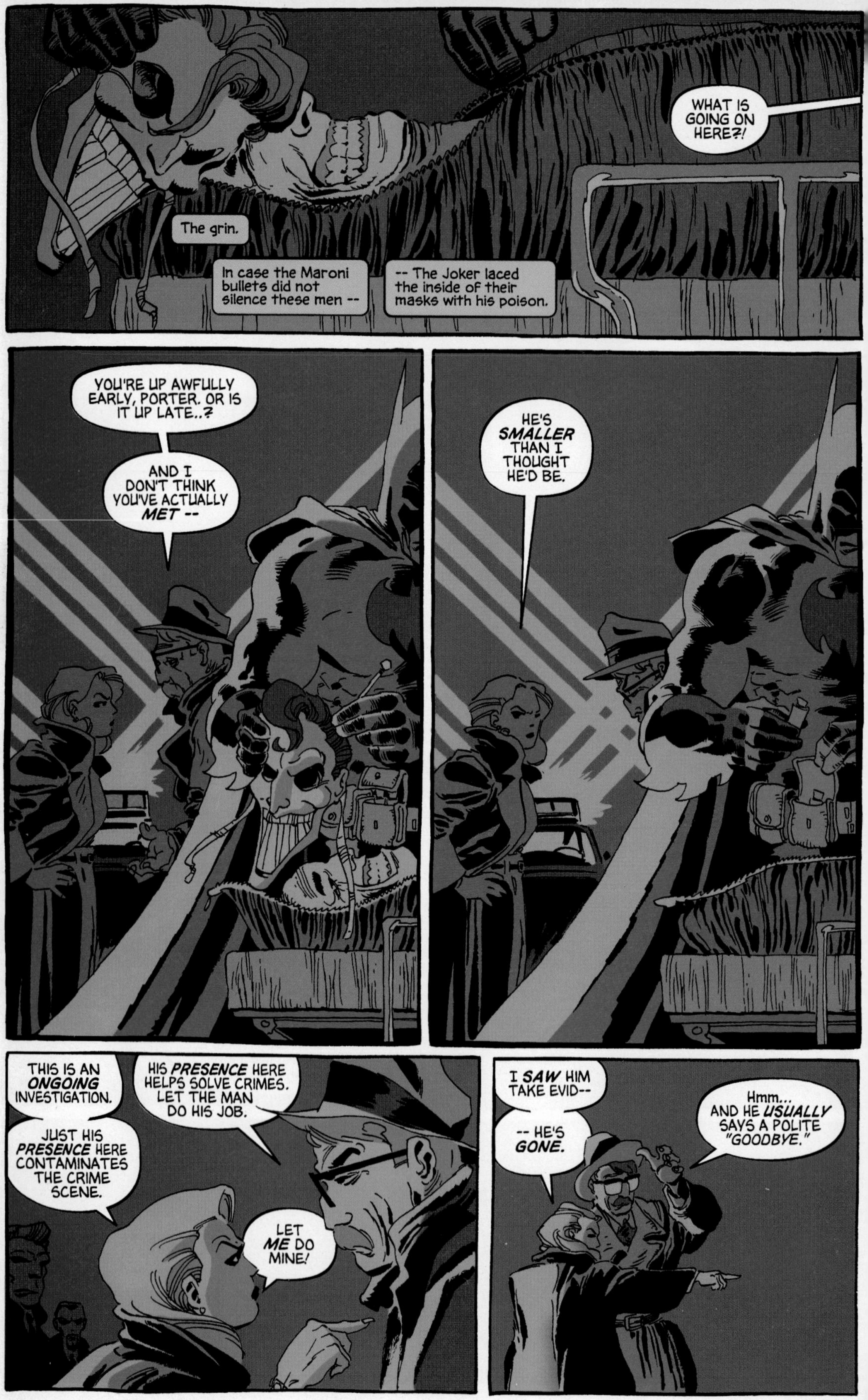
WHAT IS GOING ON HERE?!
The grin.
In case the Maroni bullets did not silence these men --
-- The Joker laced the inside of their masks with his poison.
YOU'RE UP AWFULLY EARLY, PORTER. OR IS IT UP LATE..?
AND I DON'T THINK YOU'VE ACTUALLY MET --
HE'S SMALLER THAN I THOUGHT HE'D BE.
THIS IS AN ONGOING INVESTIGATION.
JUST HIS PRESENCE HERE CONTAMINATES THE CRIME SCENE.
HIS PRESENCE HERE HELPS SOLVE CRIMES. LET THE MAN DO HIS JOB.
LET ME DO MINE!
I SAW HIM TAKE EVID--
-- HE'S GONE.
Hmm... AND HE USUALLY SAYS A POLITE "GOODBYE."

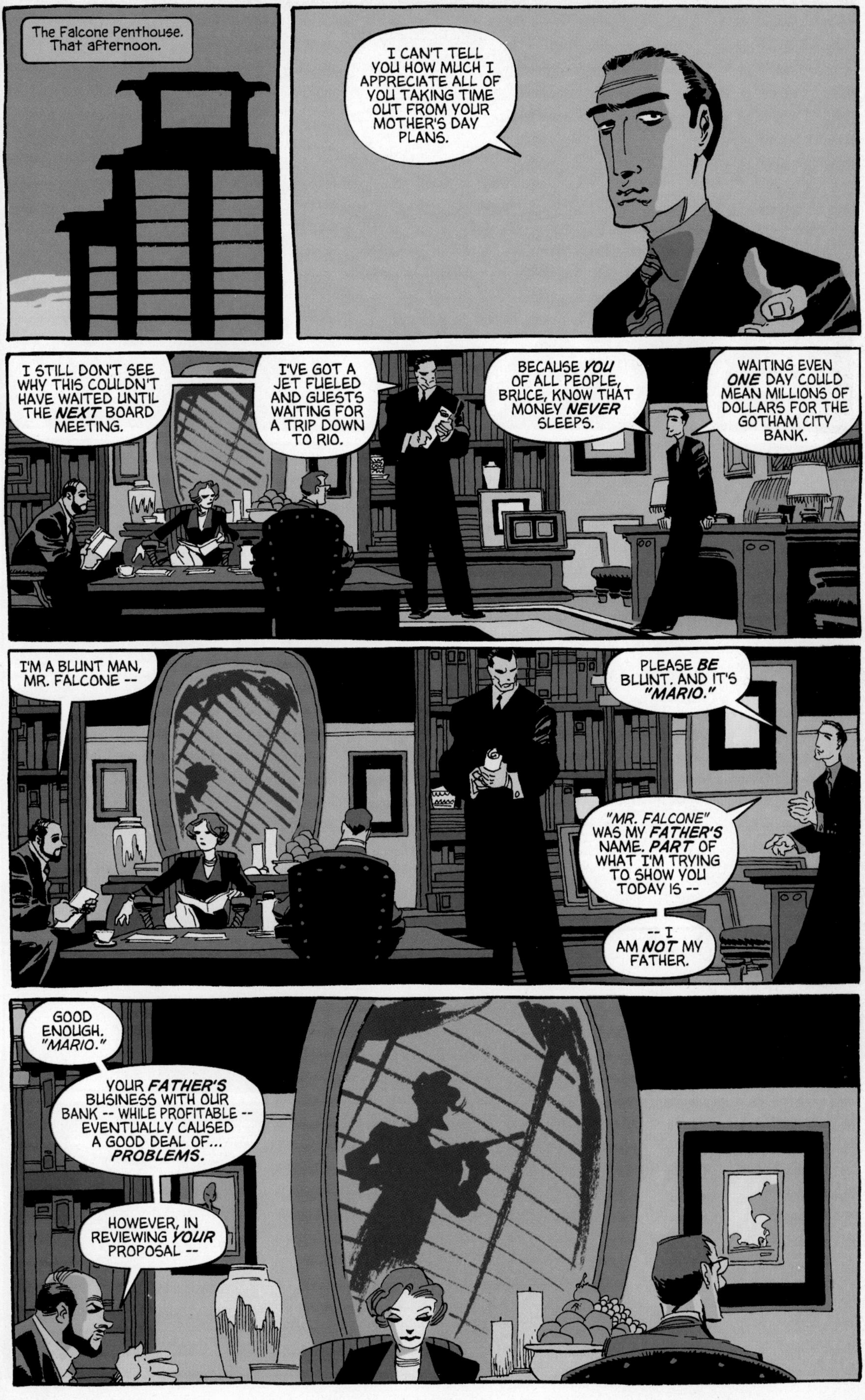

The Falcone Penthouse. That afternoon.
I CAN'T TELL YOU HOW MUCH I APPRECIATE ALL OF YOU TAKING TIME OUT FROM YOUR MOTHER'S DAY PLANS.
I STILL DON'T SEE WHY THIS COULDN'T HAVE WAITED UNTIL THE *NEXT* BOARD MEETING.
I'VE GOT A JET FUELED AND GUESTS WAITING FOR A TRIP DOWN TO RIO.
BECAUSE *YOU* OF ALL PEOPLE, BRUCE, KNOW THAT MONEY *NEVER* SLEEPS.
WAITING EVEN *ONE* DAY COULD MEAN MILLIONS OF DOLLARS FOR THE GOTHAM CITY BANK.
I'M A BLUNT MAN, MR. FALCONE --
PLEASE *BE* BLUNT. AND IT'S *"MARIO."*
"MR. FALCONE" WAS MY *FATHER'S* NAME. *PART* OF WHAT I'M TRYING TO SHOW YOU TODAY IS --
-- I AM *NOT* MY FATHER.
GOOD ENOUGH. *"MARIO."*
YOUR *FATHER'S* BUSINESS WITH OUR BANK -- WHILE PROFITABLE -- EVENTUALLY CAUSED A GOOD DEAL OF... *PROBLEMS.*
HOWEVER, IN REVIEWING *YOUR* PROPOSAL --

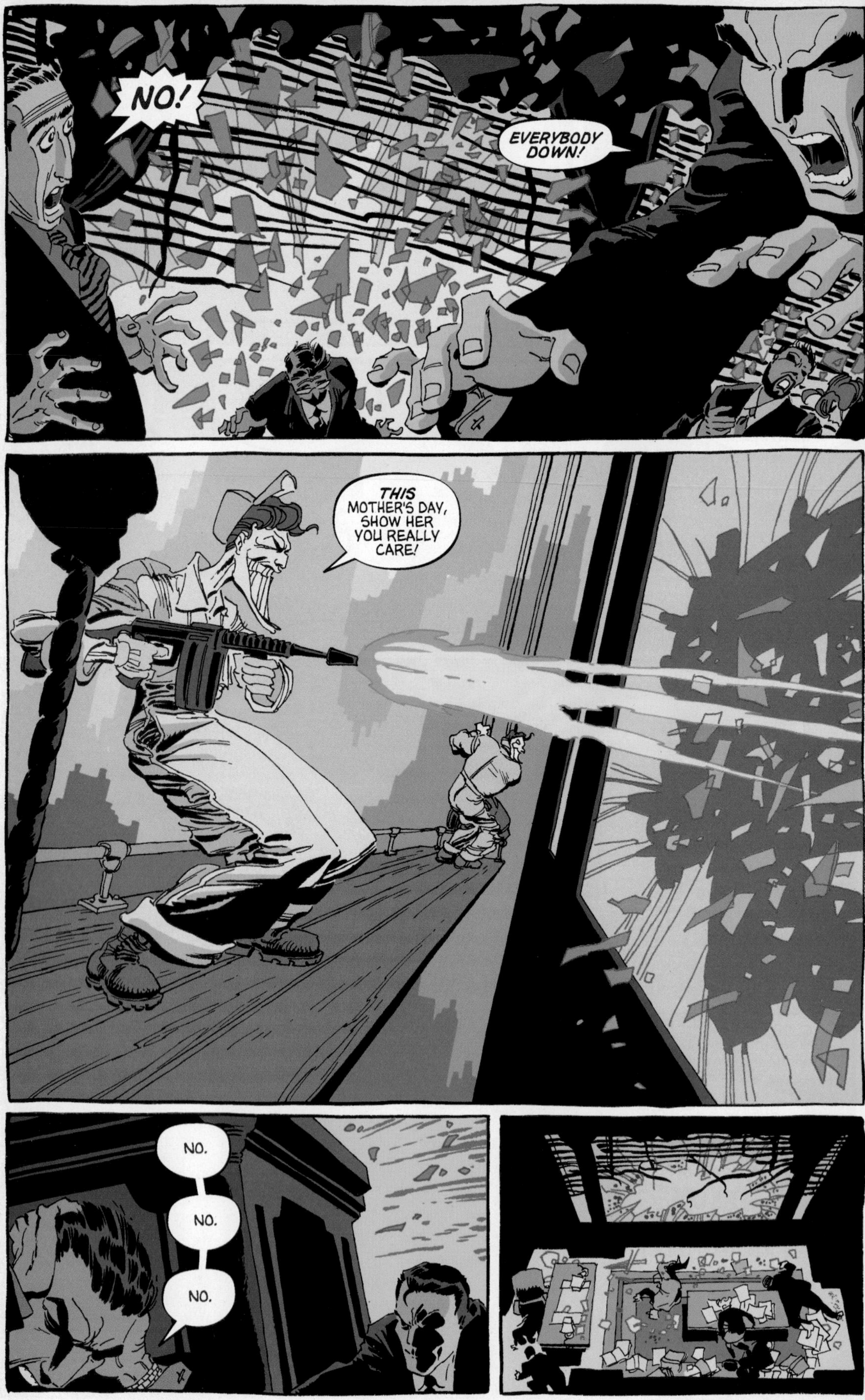
NO!
EVERYBODY DOWN!
THIS MOTHER'S DAY, SHOW HER YOU REALLY CARE!
NO.
NO.
NO.

ARE YOU HURT?

NO.

CALL THE POLICE.

The Joker. Again.

First, the Maronis. Now, here.

He has never killed in a logical **progression** before.

Why now?

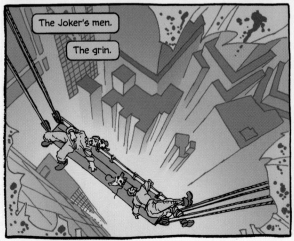

The Joker's men.

The grin.

I HAD BETTER NOT FIND OUT YOU HAD *ANYTHING* TO DO WITH THIS, FALCONE.

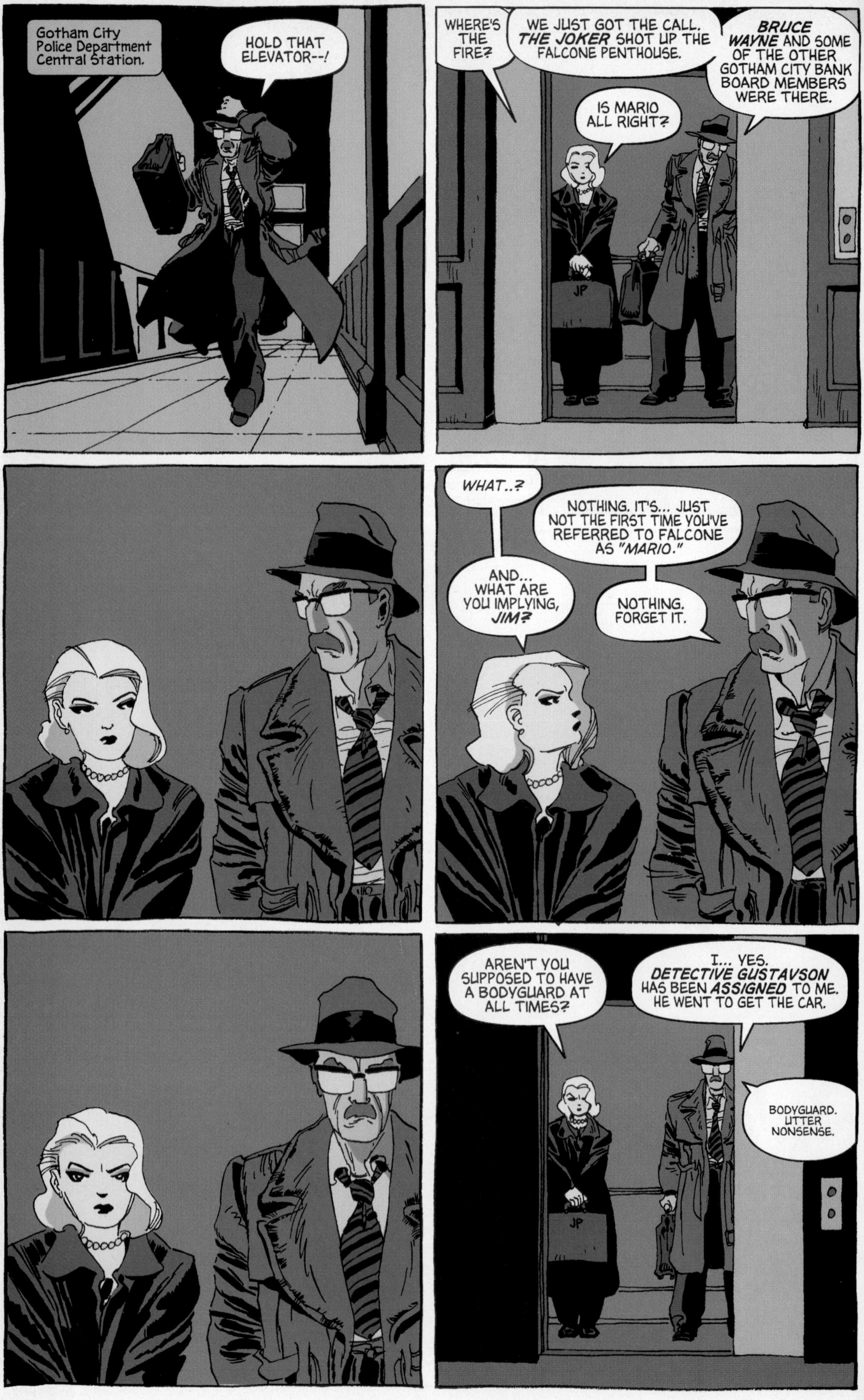
Gotham City Police Department Central Station.
HOLD THAT ELEVATOR--!
WHERE'S THE FIRE?
WE JUST GOT THE CALL. THE JOKER SHOT UP THE FALCONE PENTHOUSE.
BRUCE WAYNE AND SOME OF THE OTHER GOTHAM CITY BANK BOARD MEMBERS WERE THERE.
IS MARIO ALL RIGHT?
JP
WHAT..?
NOTHING. IT'S... JUST NOT THE FIRST TIME YOU'VE REFERRED TO FALCONE AS "MARIO."
AND... WHAT ARE YOU IMPLYING, JIM?
NOTHING. FORGET IT.
AREN'T YOU SUPPOSED TO HAVE A BODYGUARD AT ALL TIMES?
I... YES. DETECTIVE GUSTAVSON HAS BEEN ASSIGNED TO ME. HE WENT TO GET THE CAR.
BODYGUARD. UTTER NONSENSE.
JP

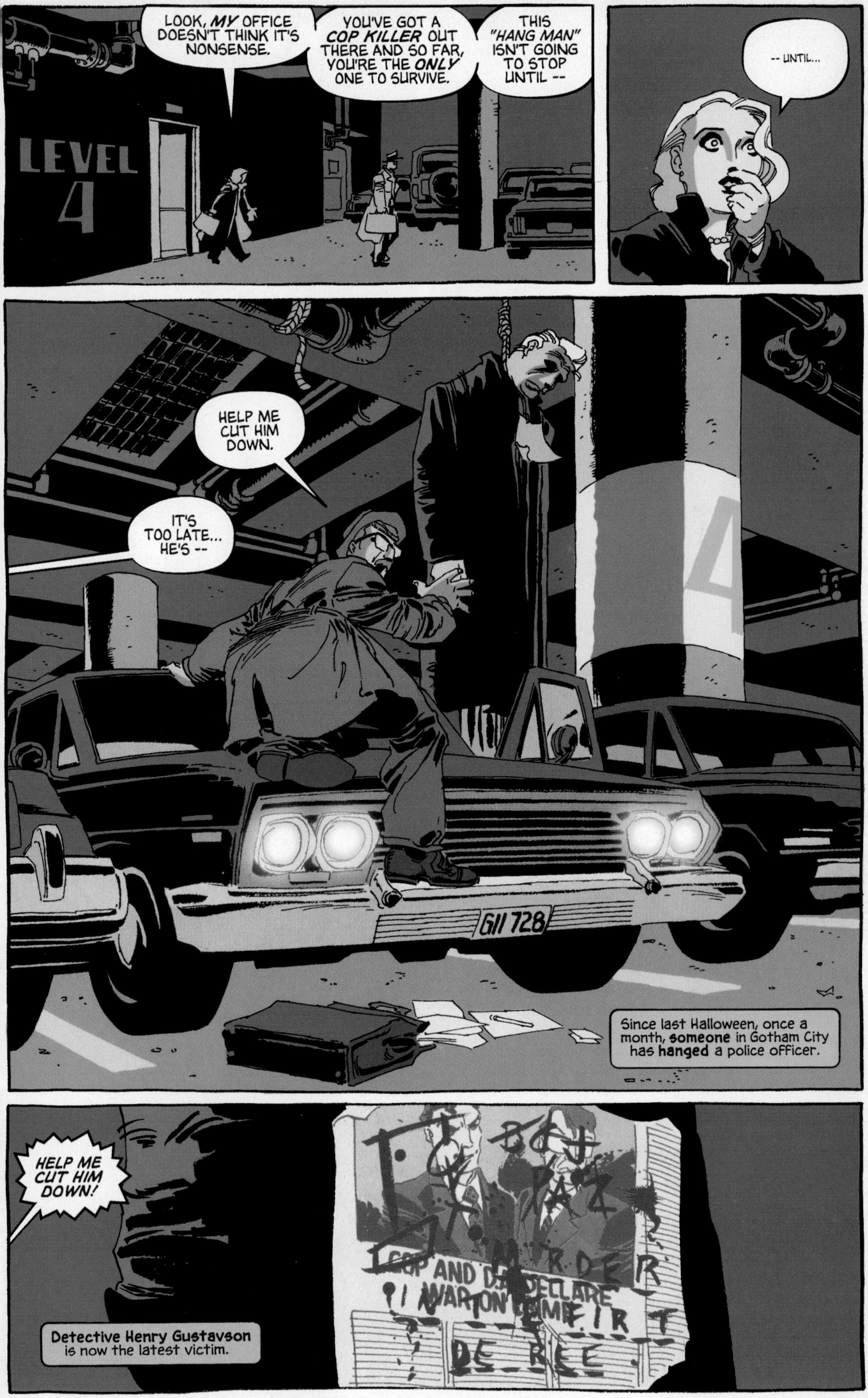
LOOK, MY OFFICE DOESN'T THINK IT'S NONSENSE.
YOU'VE GOT A COP KILLER OUT THERE AND SO FAR, YOU'RE THE ONLY ONE TO SURVIVE.
THIS "HANG MAN" ISN'T GOING TO STOP UNTIL --
LEVEL 4
-- UNTIL...
HELP ME CUT HIM DOWN.
IT'S TOO LATE... HE'S --
GII 728
Since last Halloween, once a month, someone in Gotham City has hanged a police officer.
HELP ME CUT HIM DOWN!
Detective Henry Gustavson is now the latest victim.

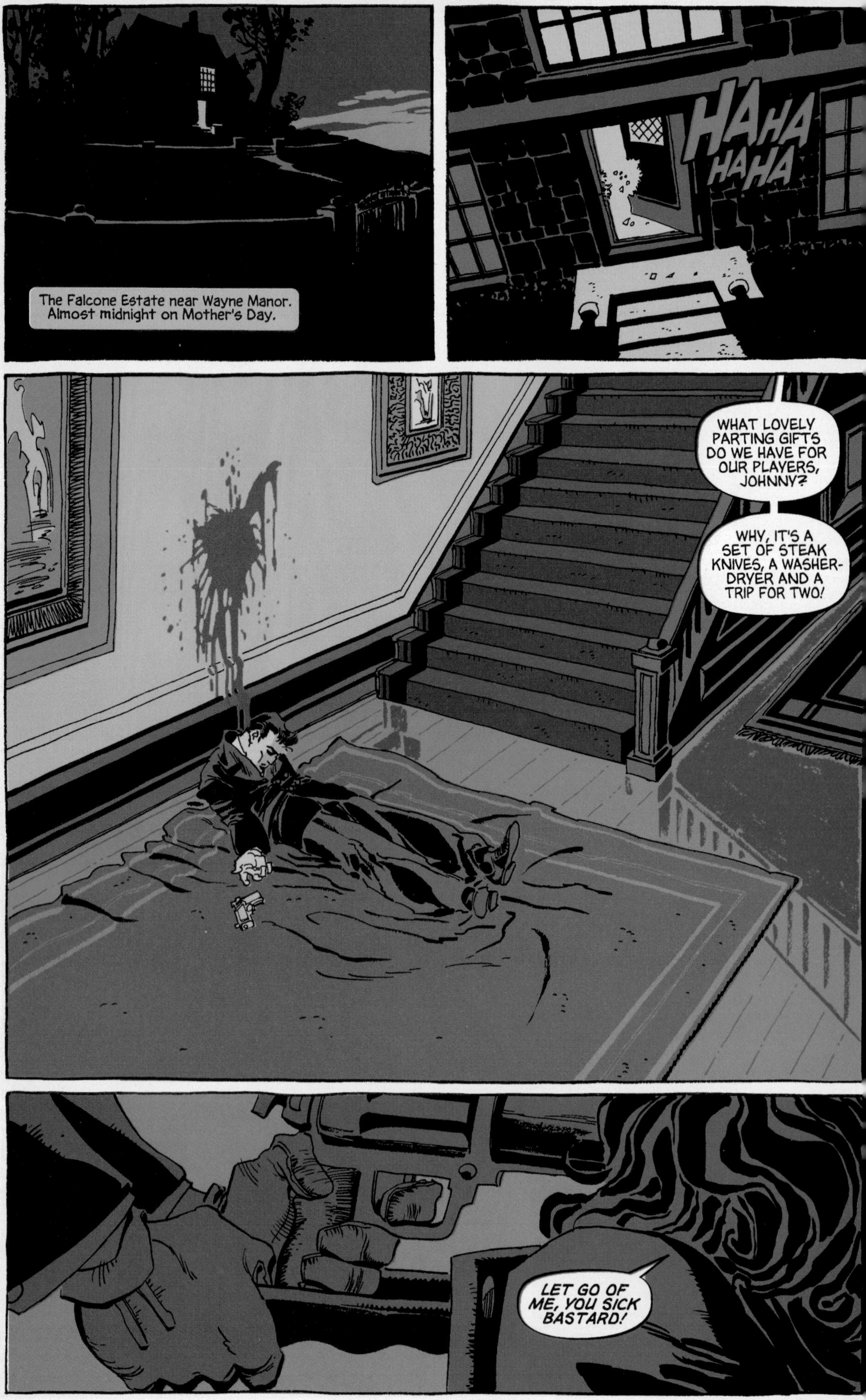

The Falcone Estate near Wayne Manor. Almost midnight on Mother's Day.
HAHA HAHA
WHAT LOVELY PARTING GIFTS DO WE HAVE FOR OUR PLAYERS, JOHNNY?
WHY, IT'S A SET OF STEAK KNIVES, A WASHER-DRYER AND A TRIP FOR TWO!
LET GO OF ME, YOU SICK BASTARD!

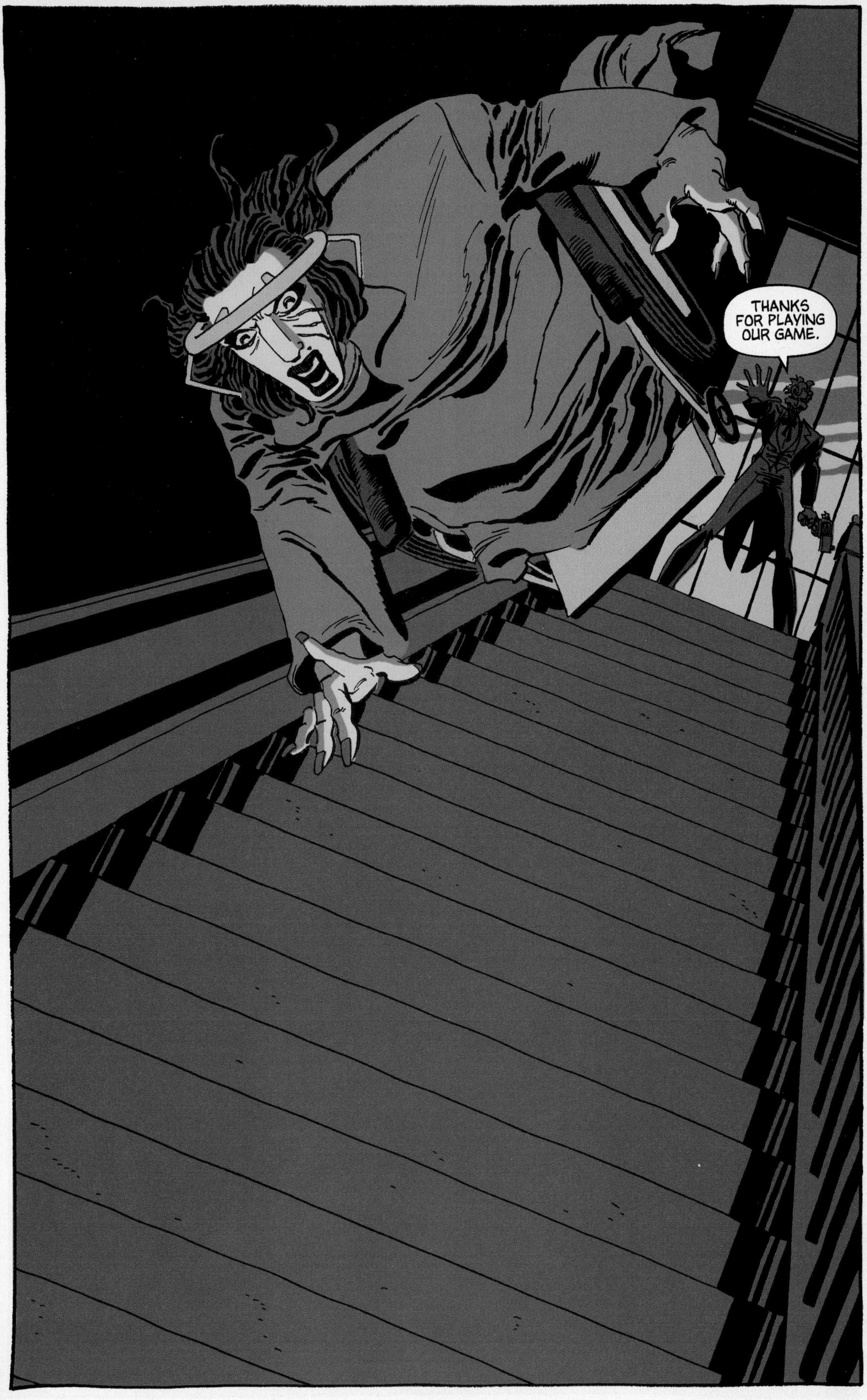
THANKS FOR PLAYING OUR GAME.

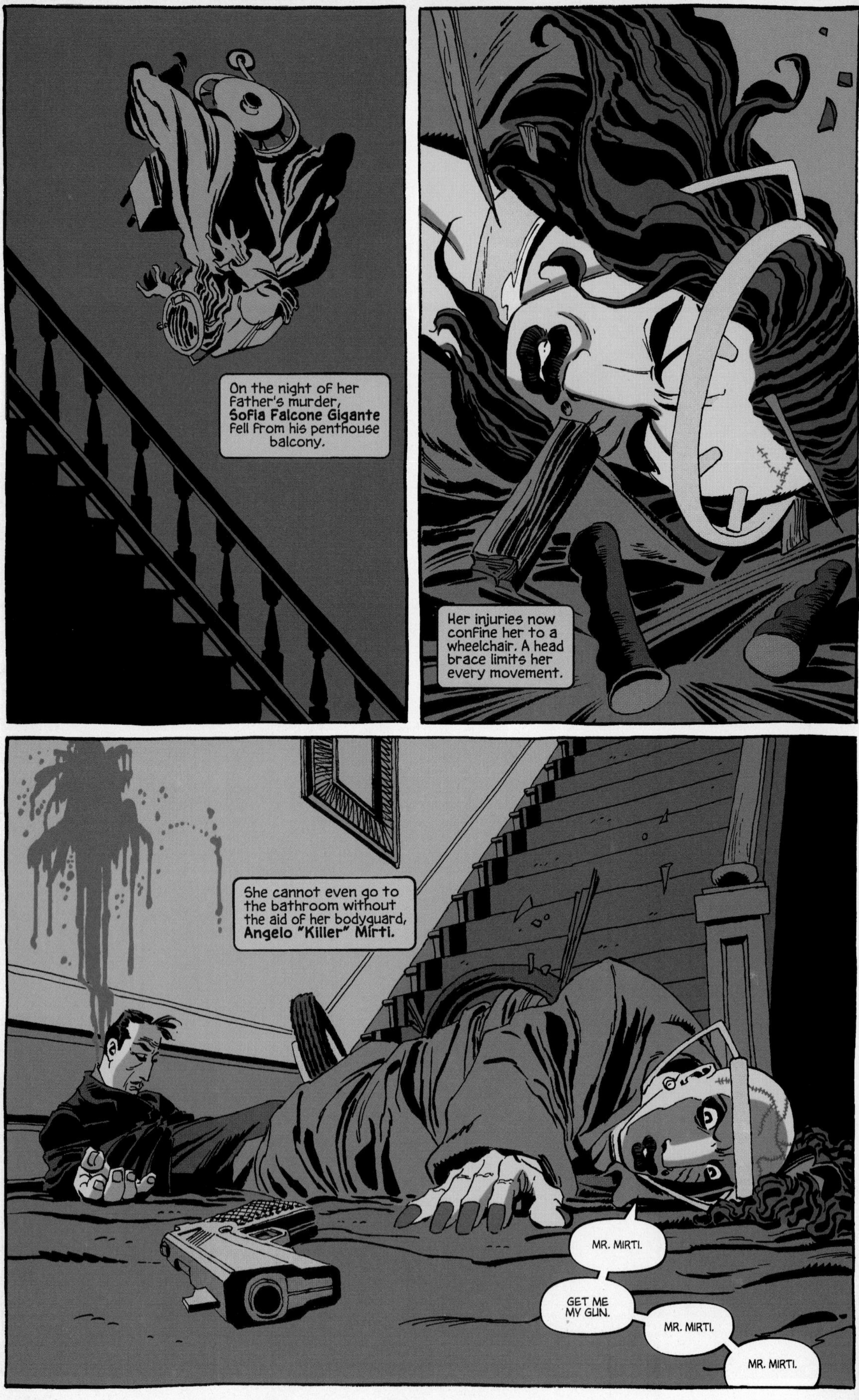

On the night of her father's murder, **Sofia Falcone Gigante** fell from his penthouse balcony.
Her injuries now confine her to a wheelchair. A head brace limits her every movement.
She cannot even go to the bathroom without the aid of her bodyguard, **Angelo "Killer" Mirti.**
MR. MIRTI.
GET ME MY GUN.
MR. MIRTI.
MR. MIRTI.

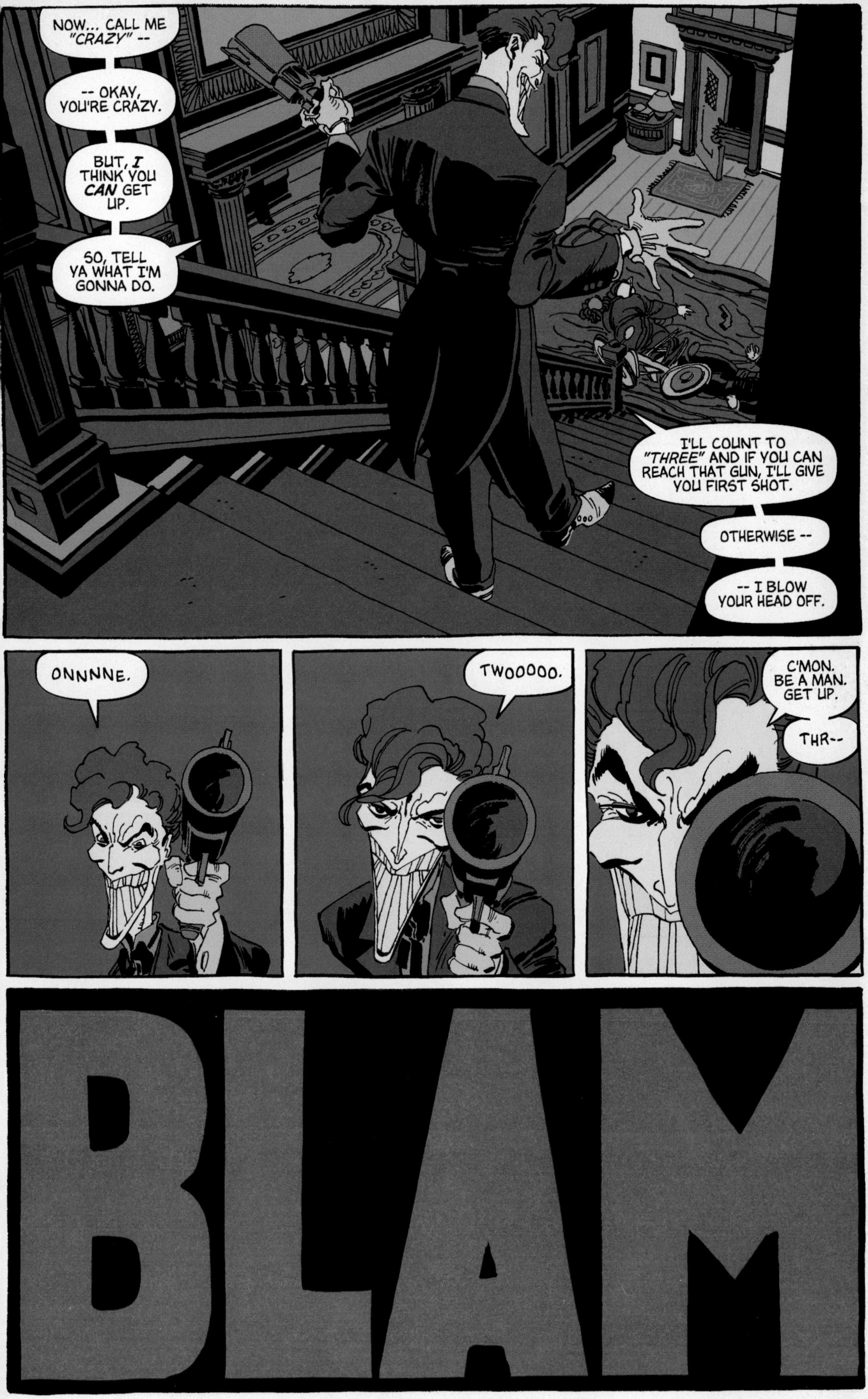
NOW... CALL ME "CRAZY" --
-- OKAY, YOU'RE CRAZY.
BUT, I THINK YOU CAN GET UP.
SO, TELL YA WHAT I'M GONNA DO.
I'LL COUNT TO "THREE" AND IF YOU CAN REACH THAT GUN, I'LL GIVE YOU FIRST SHOT.
OTHERWISE --
-- I BLOW YOUR HEAD OFF.
ONNNNE.
TWOOOOO.
C'MON. BE A MAN. GET UP.
THR--
BLAM

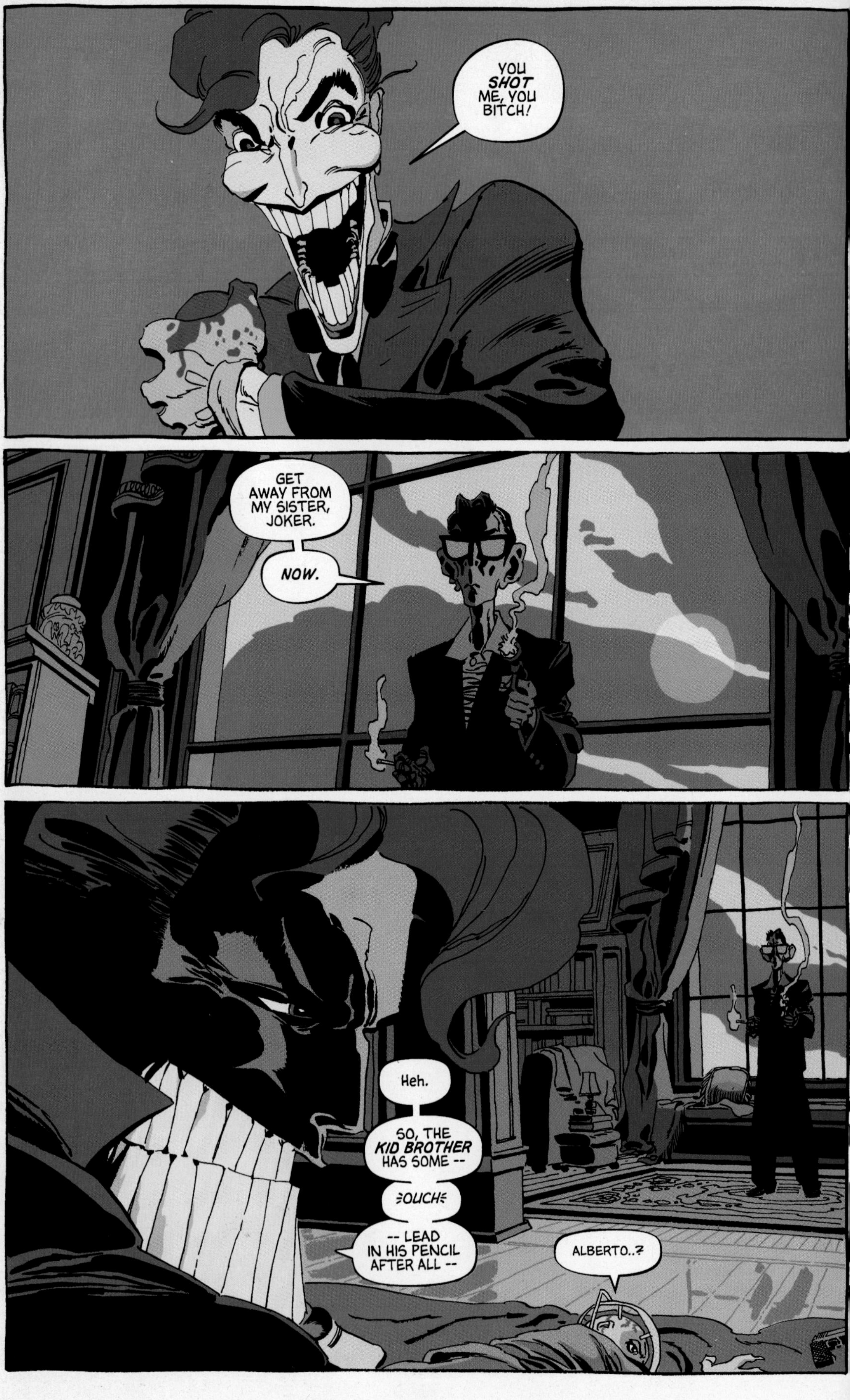
YOU SHOT ME, YOU BITCH!
GET AWAY FROM MY SISTER, JOKER.
NOW.
Heh.
SO, THE KID BROTHER HAS SOME --
OUCH
-- LEAD IN HIS PENCIL AFTER ALL --
ALBERTO..?

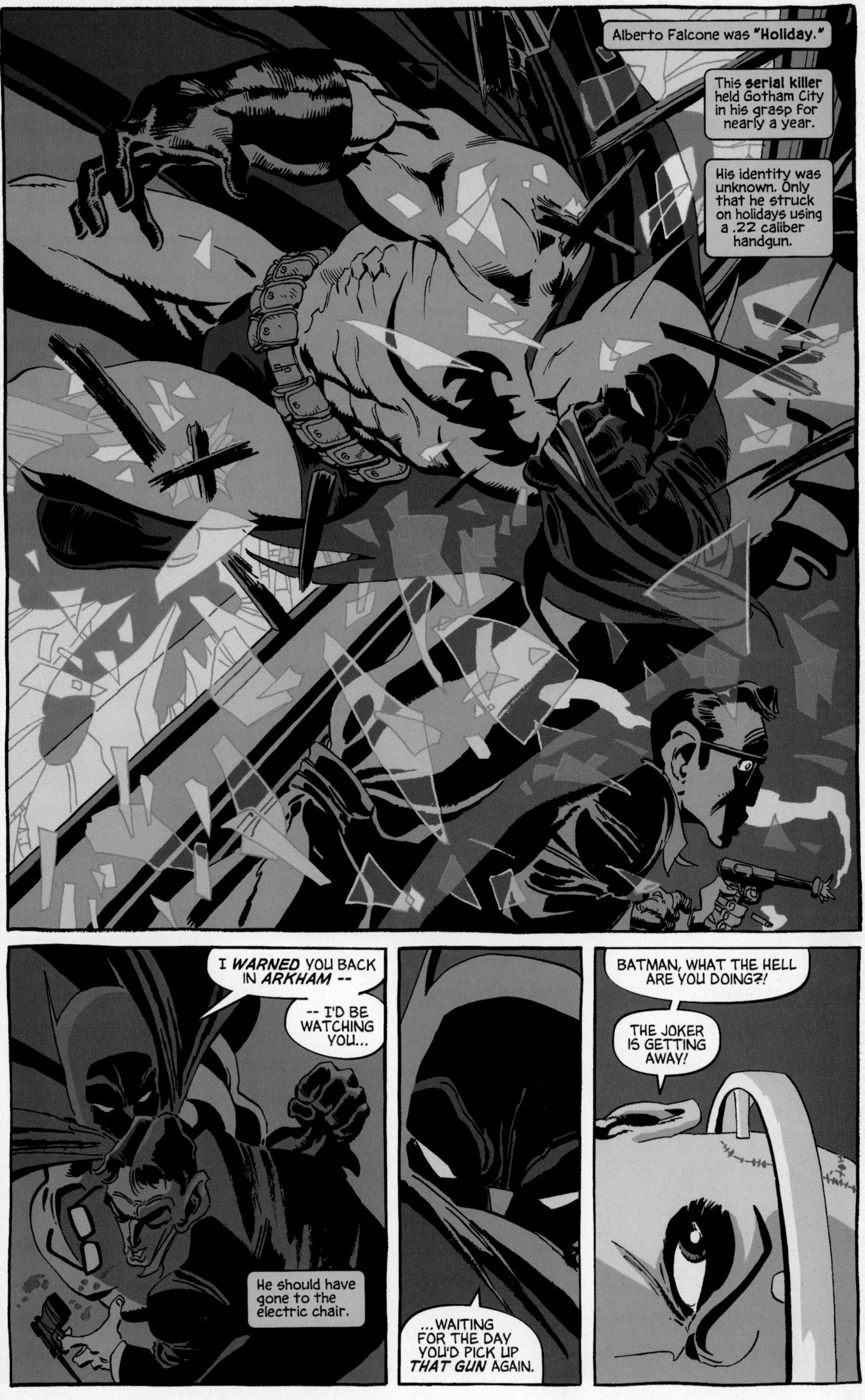

Alberto Falcone was "Holiday."
This serial killer held Gotham City in his grasp for nearly a year.
His identity was unknown. Only that he struck on holidays using a .22 caliber handgun.
I WARNED YOU BACK IN ARKHAM --
-- I'D BE WATCHING YOU...
He should have gone to the electric chair.
...WAITING FOR THE DAY YOU'D PICK UP THAT GUN AGAIN.
BATMAN, WHAT THE HELL ARE YOU DOING?!
THE JOKER IS GETTING AWAY!

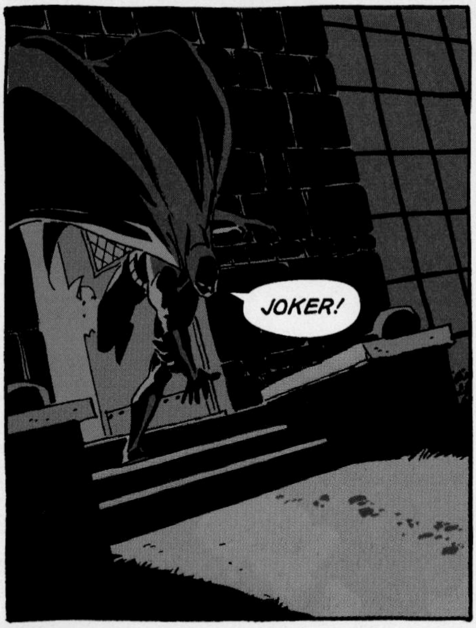
JOKER!

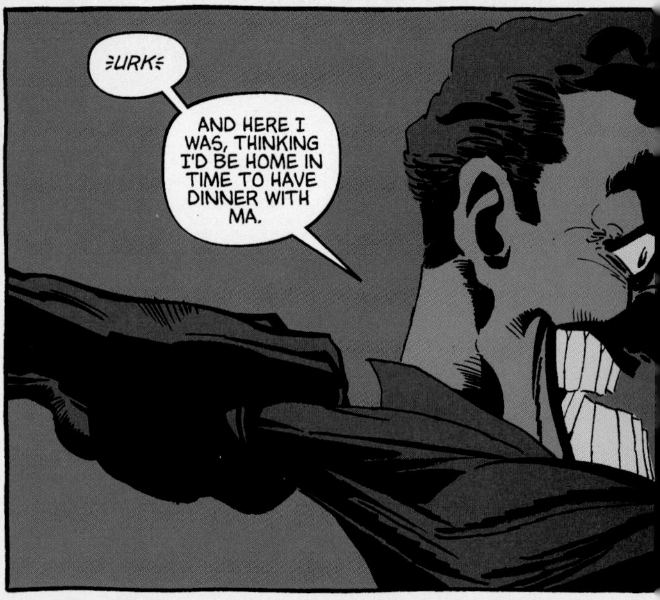
≡URK≡
AND HERE I WAS, THINKING I'D BE HOME IN TIME TO HAVE DINNER WITH MA.

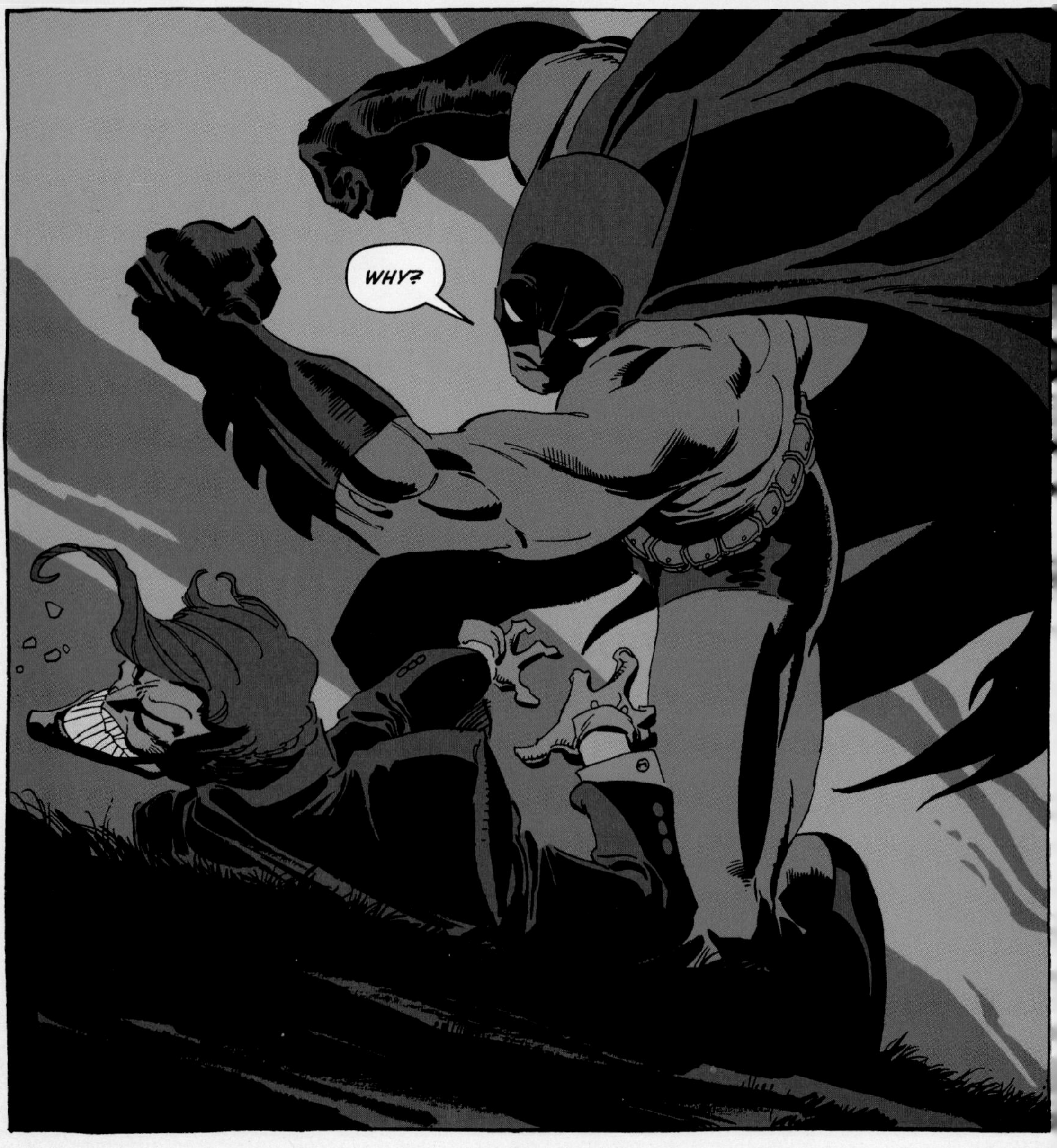
WHY?

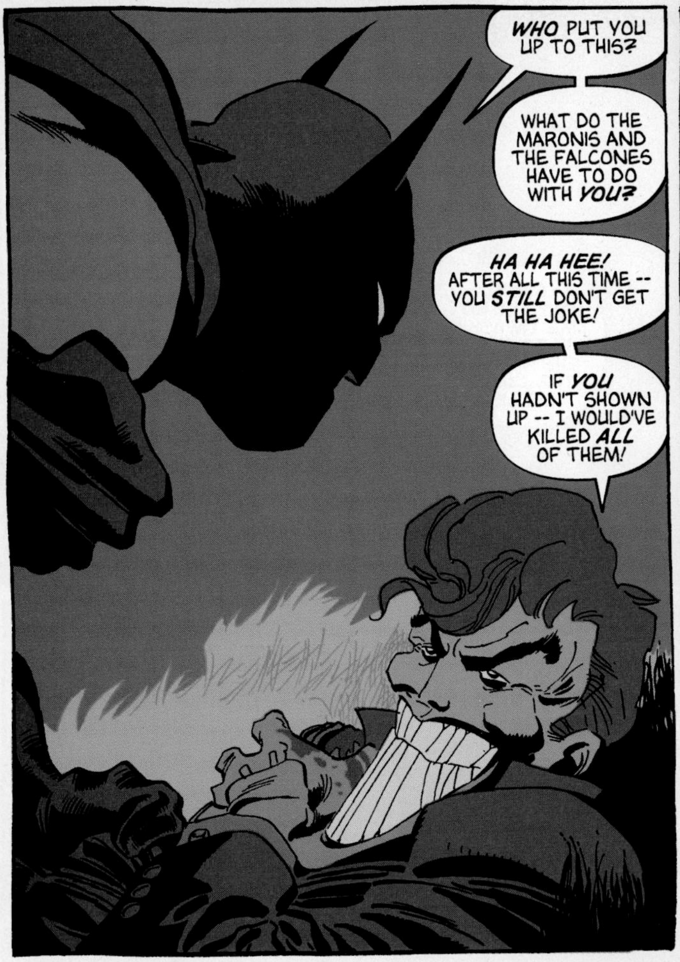
WHO PUT YOU UP TO THIS?
WHAT DO THE MARONIS AND THE FALCONES HAVE TO DO WITH YOU?
HA HA HEE! AFTER ALL THIS TIME -- YOU STILL DON'T GET THE JOKE!
IF YOU HADN'T SHOWN UP -- I WOULD'VE KILLED ALL OF THEM!

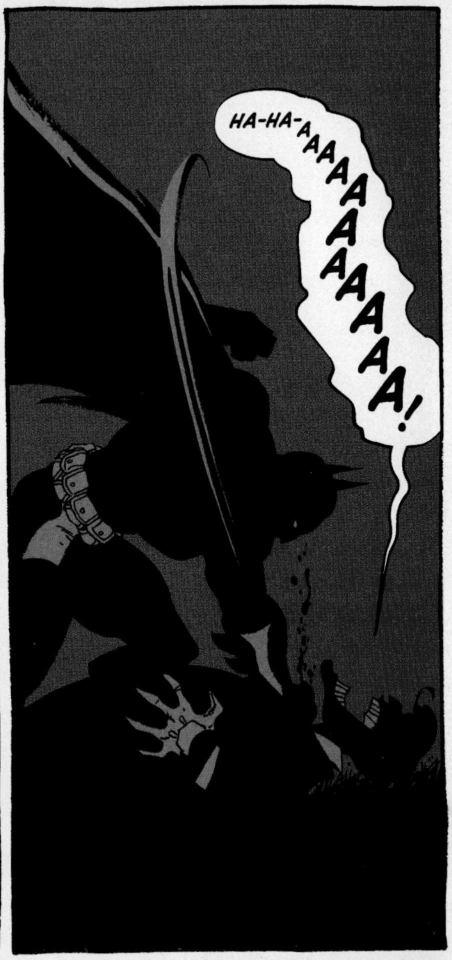
HA-HA-AAAAAAAAAAAA!

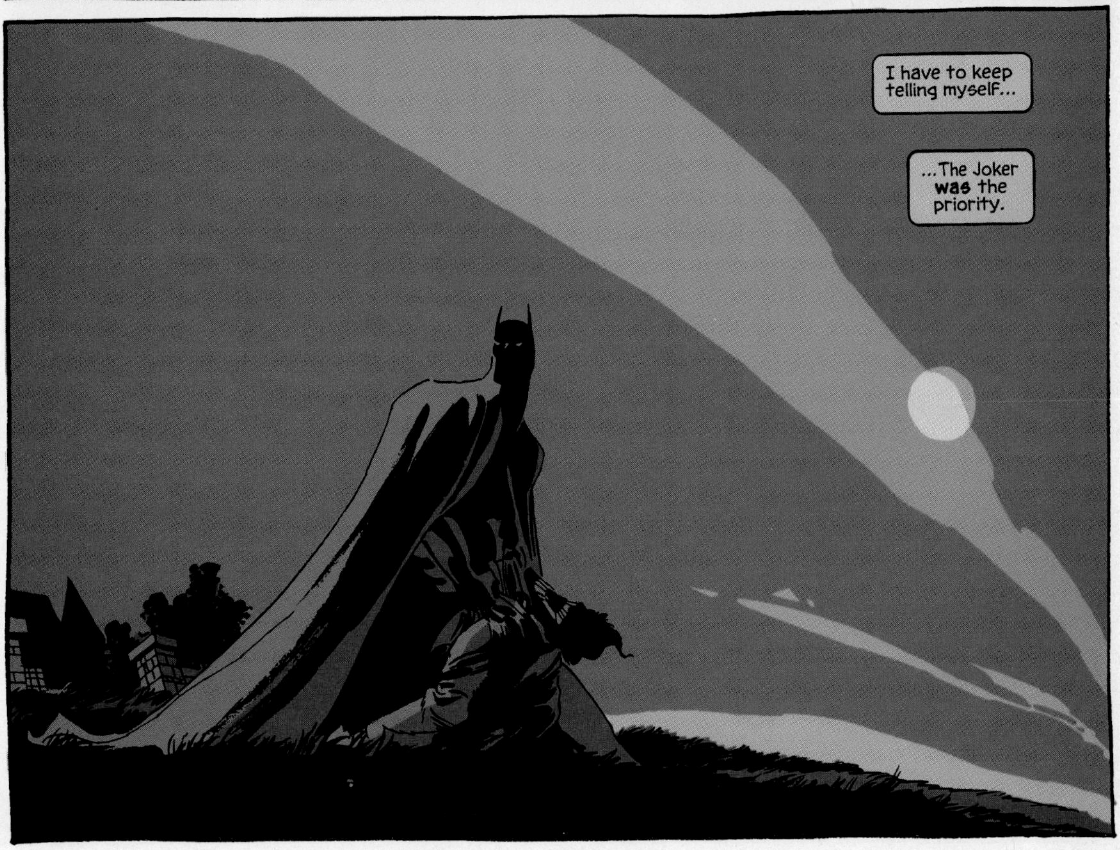
I have to keep telling myself...
...The Joker was the priority.

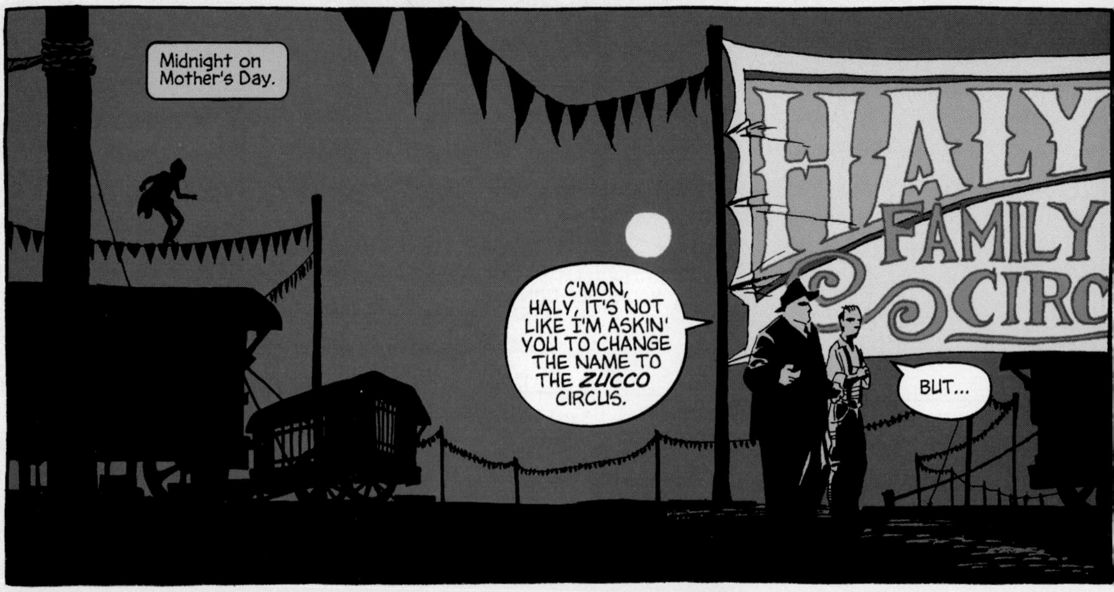
Midnight on Mother's Day.
HALY
FAMILY
CIRC
C'MON, HALY, IT'S NOT LIKE I'M ASKIN' YOU TO CHANGE THE NAME TO THE *ZUCCO* CIRCUS.
BUT...

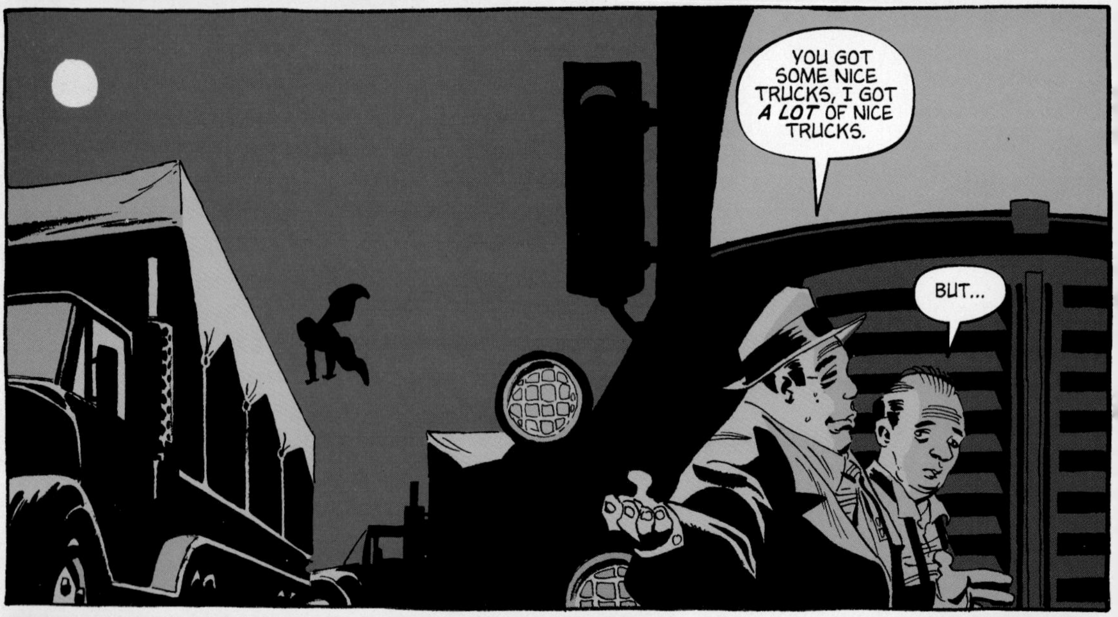
YOU GOT SOME NICE TRUCKS, I GOT *A LOT* OF NICE TRUCKS.
BUT...

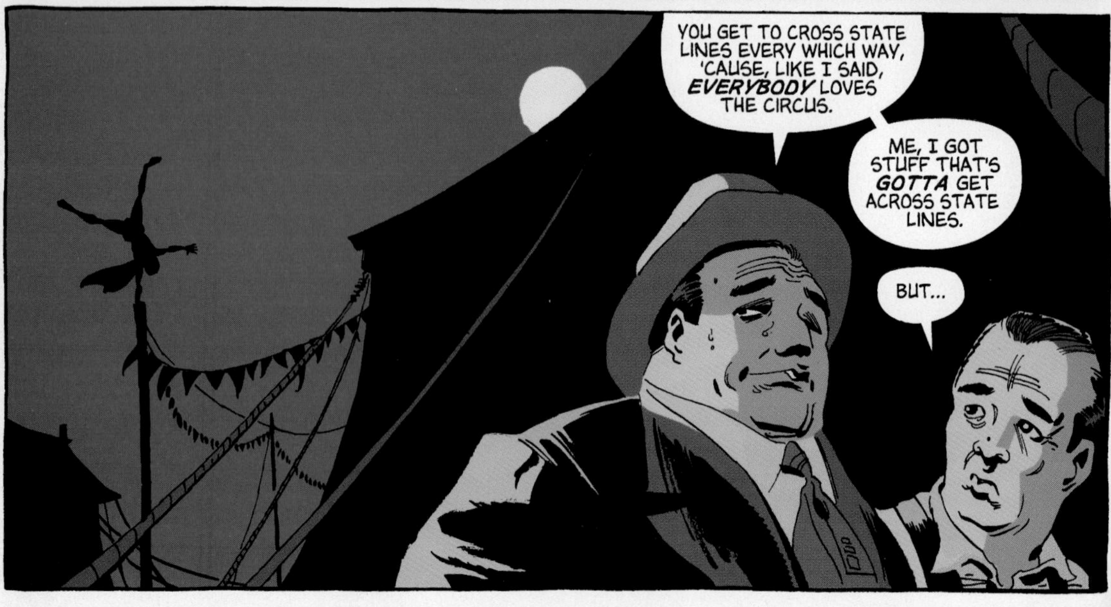
YOU GET TO CROSS STATE LINES EVERY WHICH WAY, 'CAUSE, LIKE I SAID, *EVERYBODY* LOVES THE CIRCUS.
ME, I GOT STUFF THAT'S *GOTTA* GET ACROSS STATE LINES.
BUT...

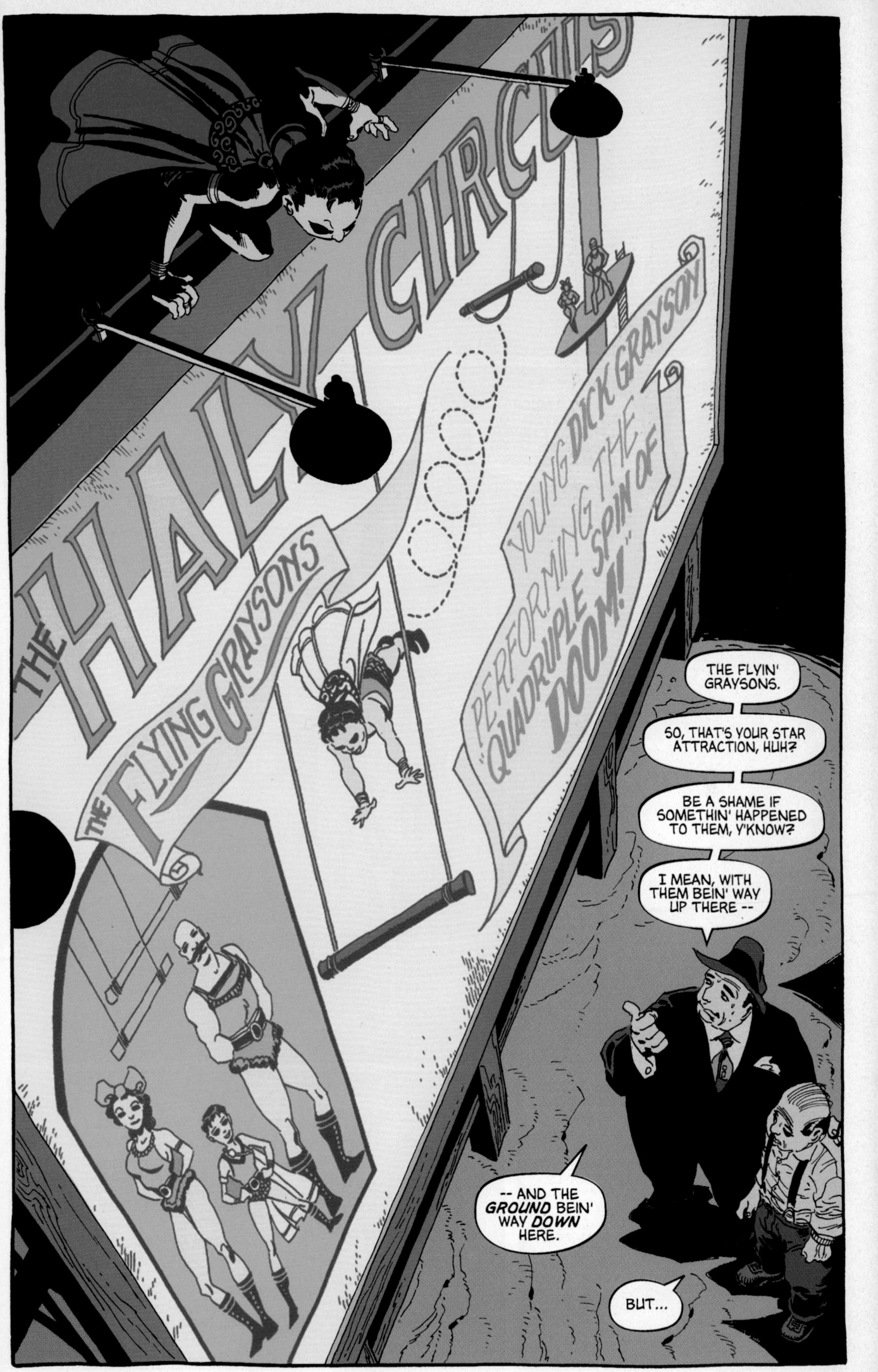
THE HALY CIRCUS
THE FLYING GRAYSONS
YOUNG DICK GRAYSON PERFORMING THE "QUADRUPLE SPIN OF DOOM!"
THE FLYIN' GRAYSONS.
SO, THAT'S YOUR STAR ATTRACTION, HUH?
BE A SHAME IF SOMETHIN' HAPPENED TO THEM, Y'KNOW?
I MEAN, WITH THEM BEIN' WAY UP THERE --
-- AND THE *GROUND* BEIN' WAY *DOWN* HERE.
BUT...

Wayne Manor. My father's house, except --

-- on nights such as this, I think of my mother.

LONG DAY, SIR?

AH, FORGIVE ME. THEY'RE *ALL* LONG DAYS, AREN'T THEY?

I... AS MUCH AS I WANTED TO, ALFRED... I NEVER FOUND TIME TO GO UP AND VISIT HER.

NOW, MOTHER'S DAY IS OVER...

WHAT ARE THESE..?

THEY ARE *CIRCUS* TICKETS, SIR. YOU MADE A CHARITABLE DONATION, I BELIEVE.

AT THE TIME, YOU HAD PLANNED ON TAKING MISS KYLE.

OH.

SEE THAT THEY'RE GIVEN TO SOMEONE WHO NEEDS THEM, THEN.

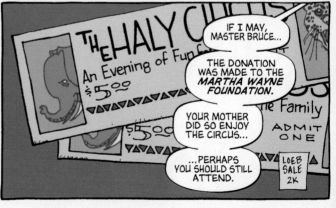

THE HALY CIRCUS
An Evening of Fun f...
$5.00

the Family
$5.00
ADMIT ONE

IF I MAY, MASTER BRUCE...

THE DONATION WAS MADE TO THE *MARTHA WAYNE FOUNDATION.*

YOUR MOTHER DID SO ENJOY THE CIRCUS...

...PERHAPS YOU SHOULD STILL ATTEND.

LOEB SALE 2K

236

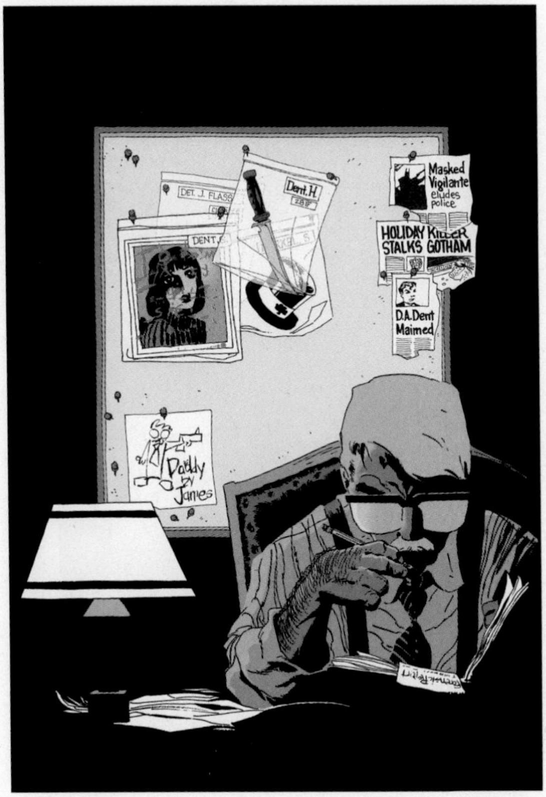

DET. J. FLASS
Dent.H.
Masked Vigilante eludes police
HOLIDAY KILLER STALKS GOTHAM
D.A. Dent Maimed
Daddy by James

9

ORPHANS

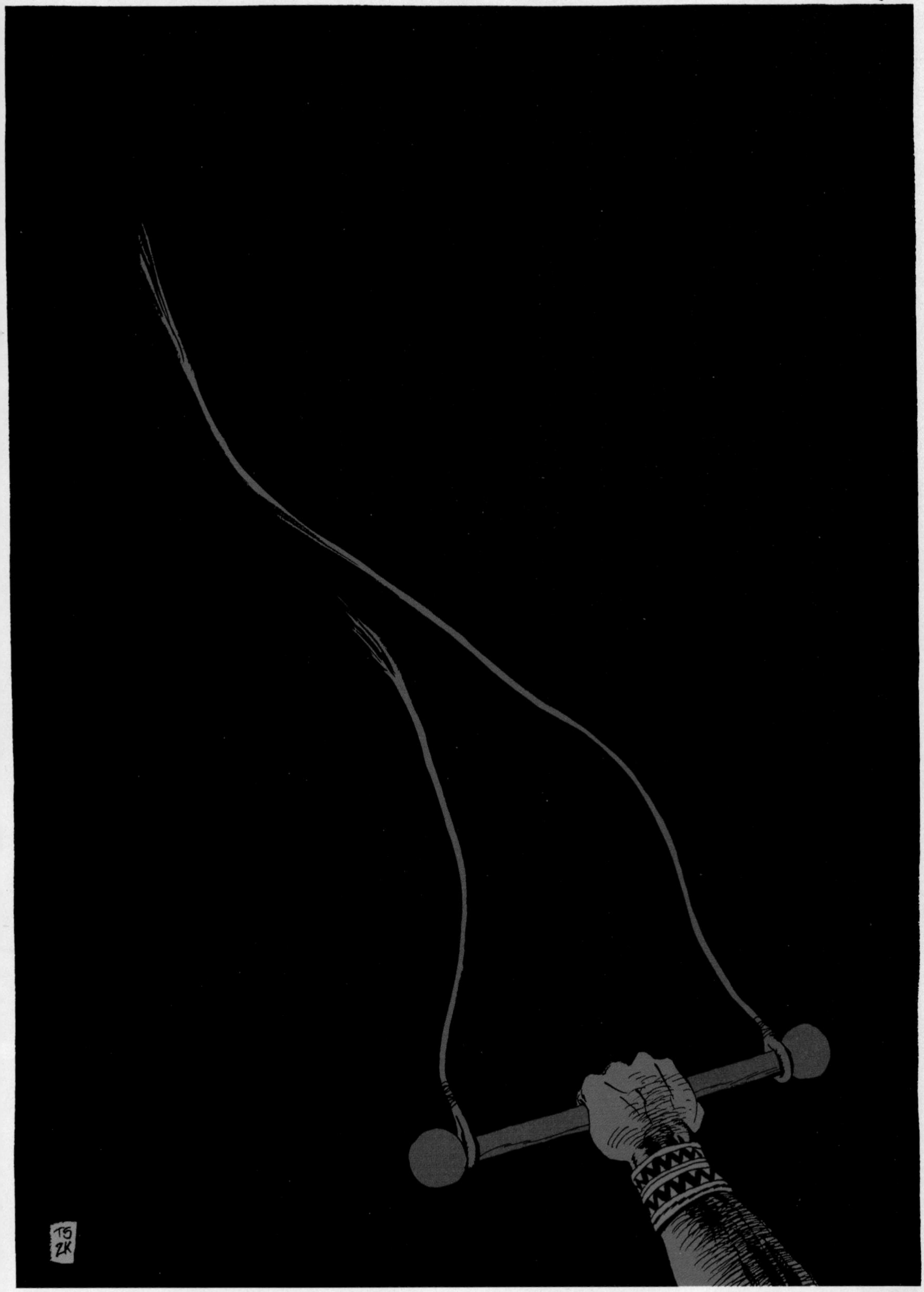
TS
2K

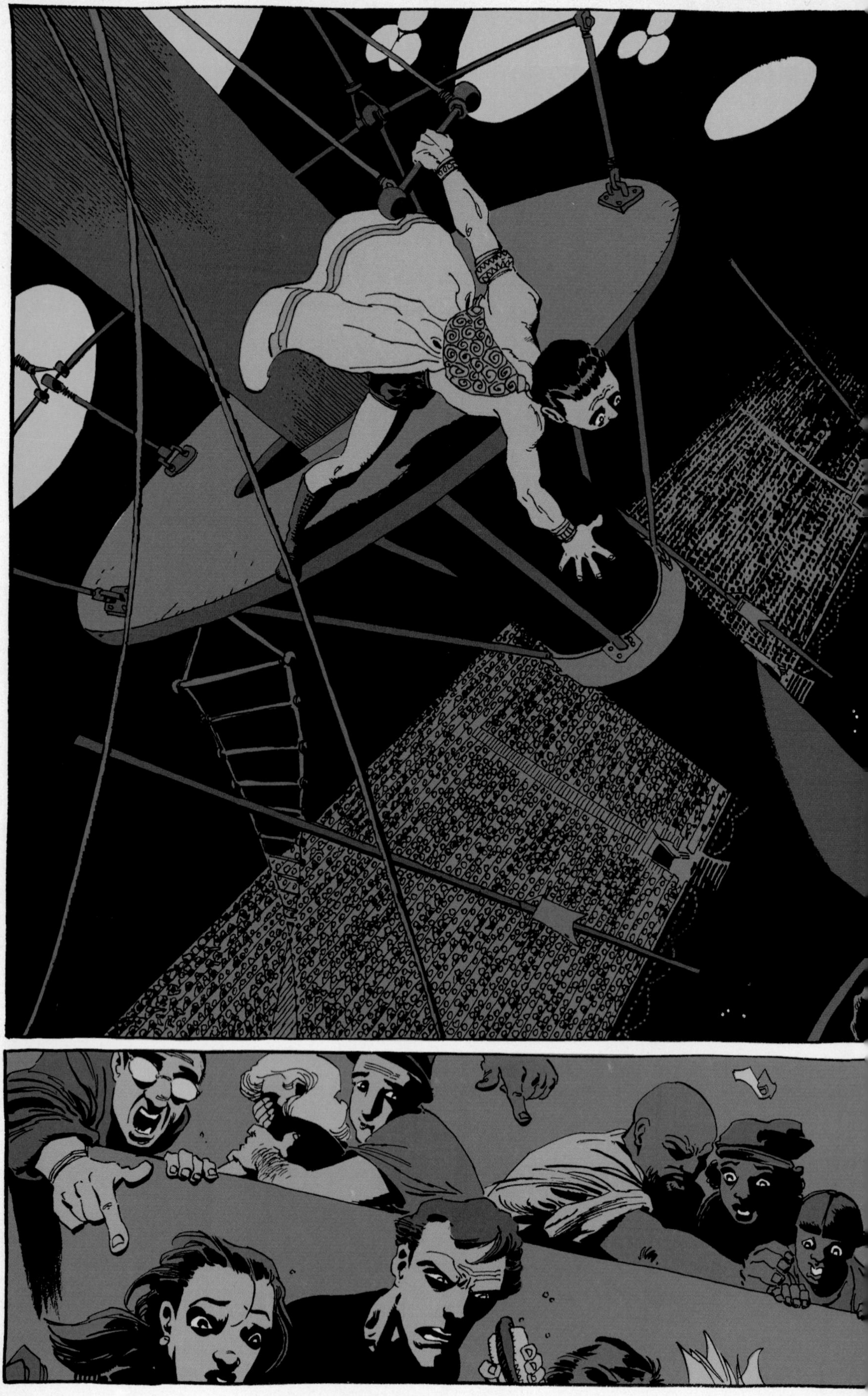

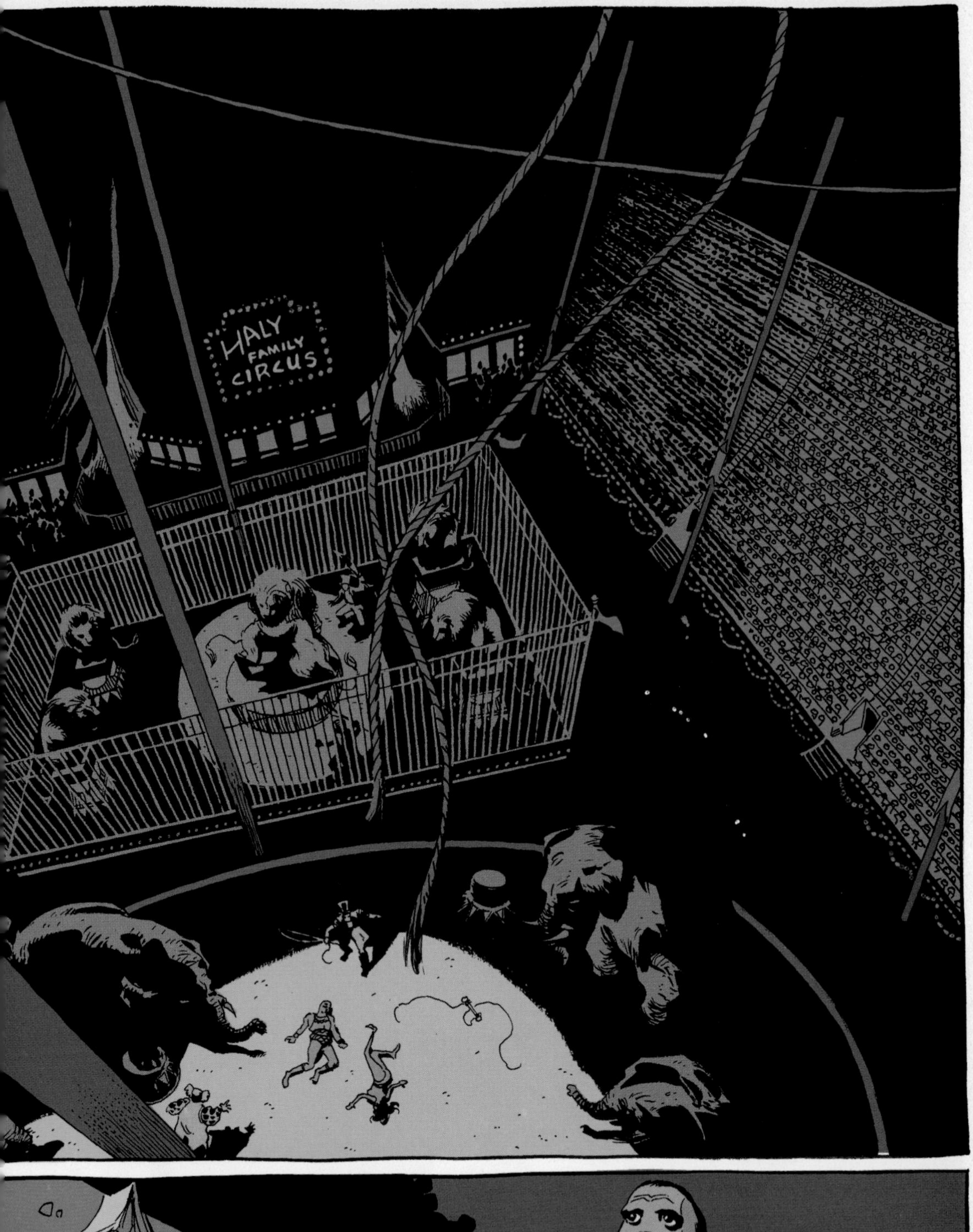

HALY
FAMILY
CIRCUS

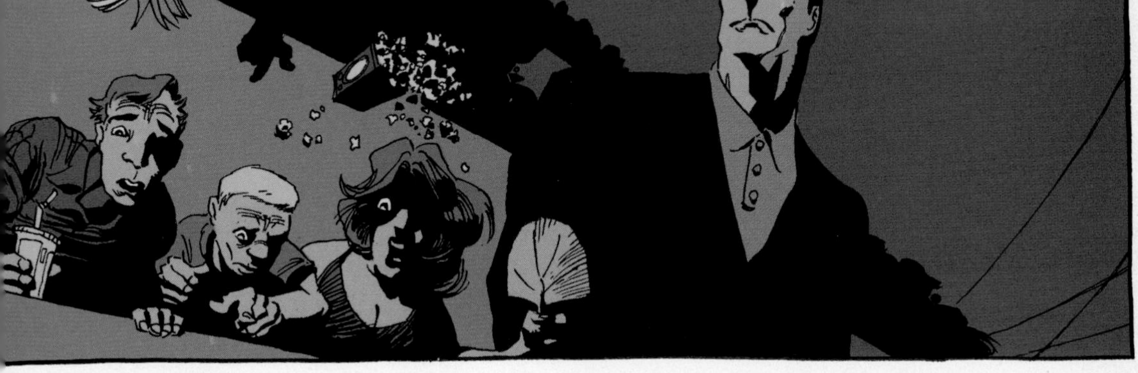

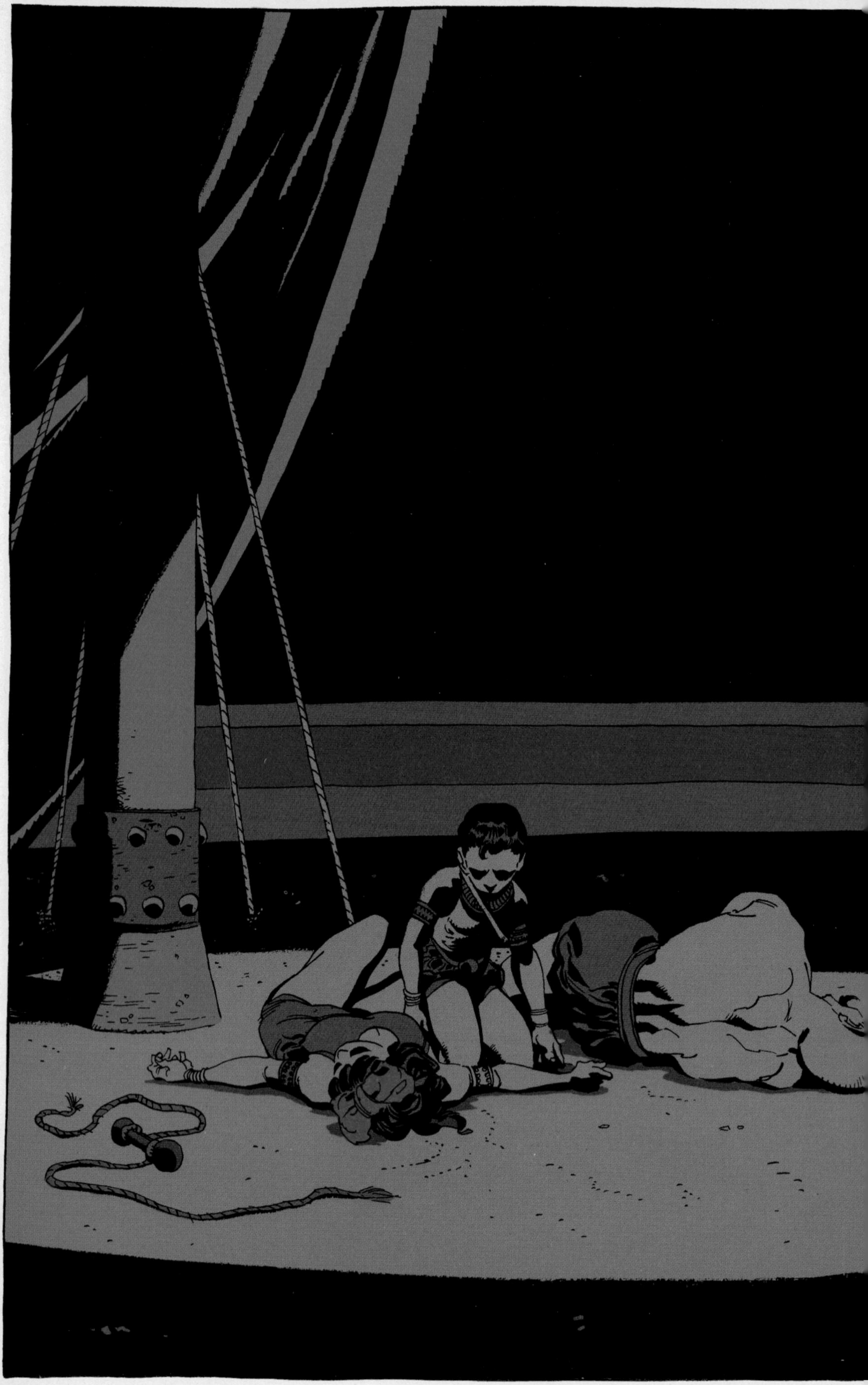

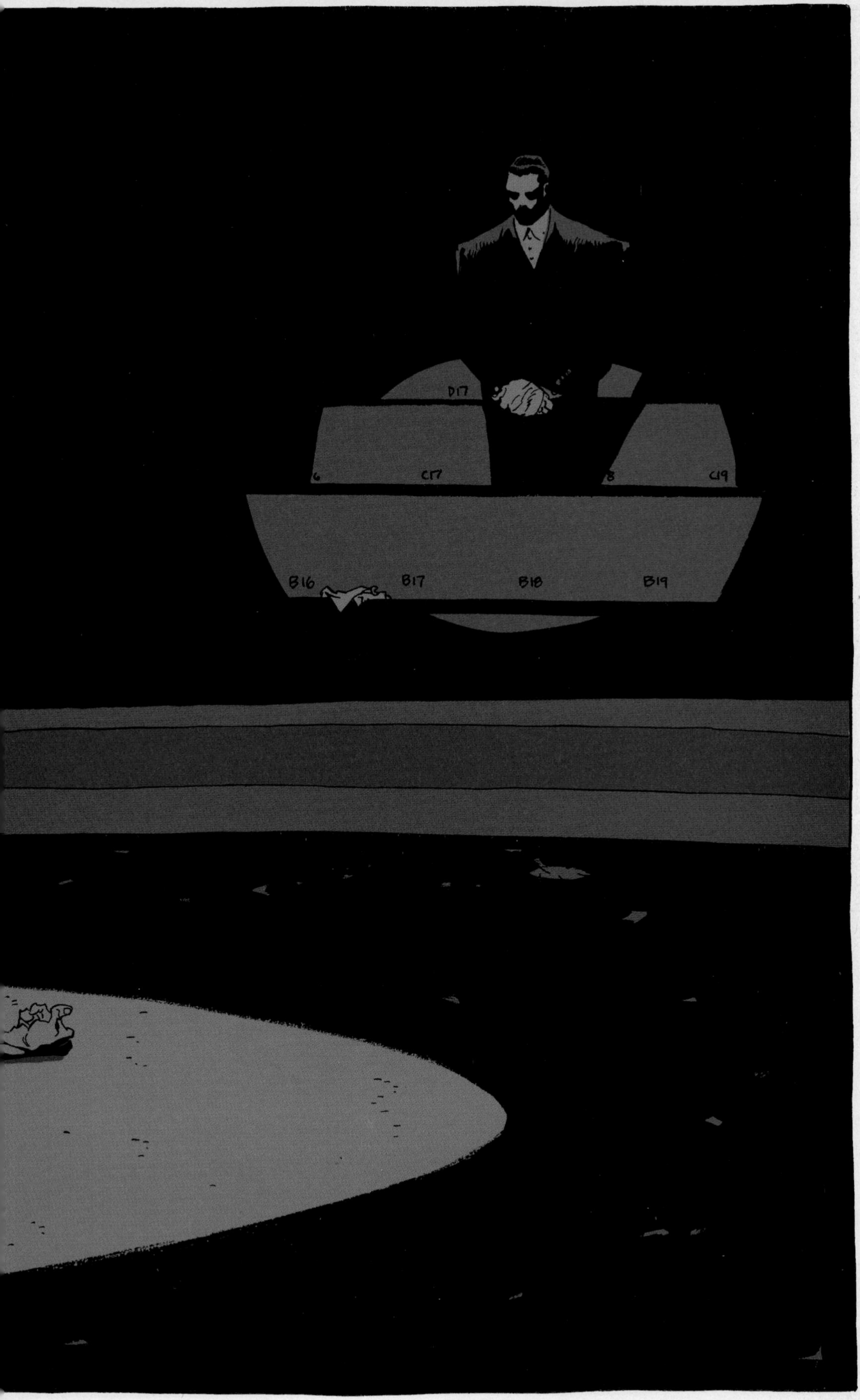
D17
C17
C19
B16
B17
B18
B19

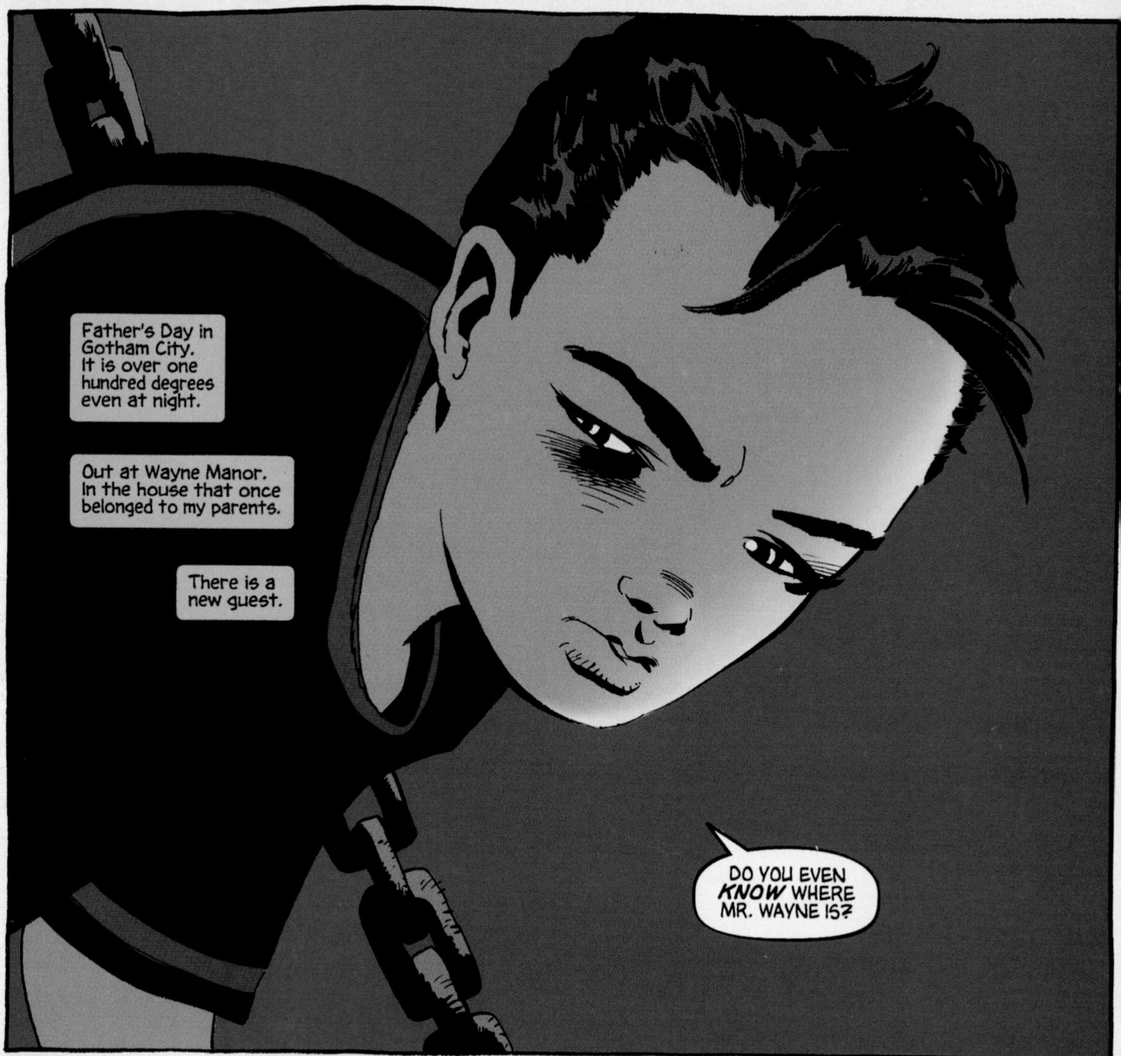
Father's Day in Gotham City. It is over one hundred degrees even at night.
Out at Wayne Manor. In the house that once belonged to my parents.
There is a new guest.
DO YOU EVEN KNOW WHERE MR. WAYNE IS?

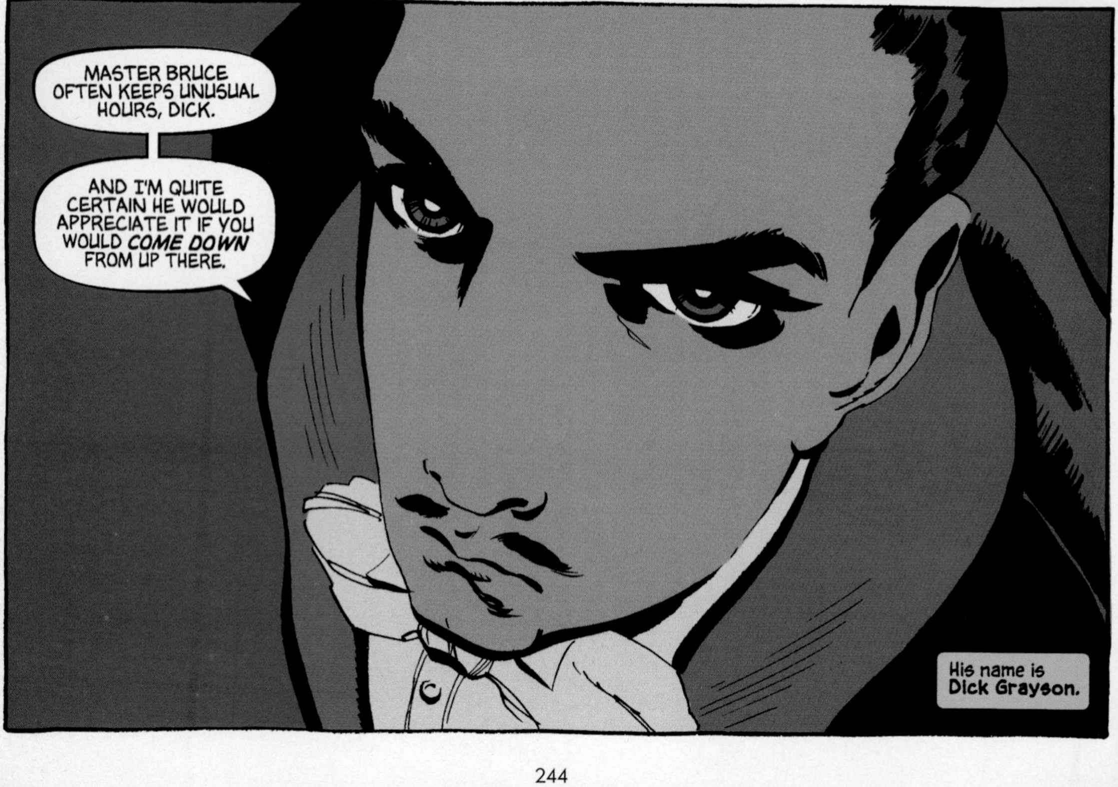
MASTER BRUCE OFTEN KEEPS UNUSUAL HOURS, DICK.
AND I'M QUITE CERTAIN HE WOULD APPRECIATE IT IF YOU WOULD COME DOWN FROM UP THERE.
His name is Dick Grayson.

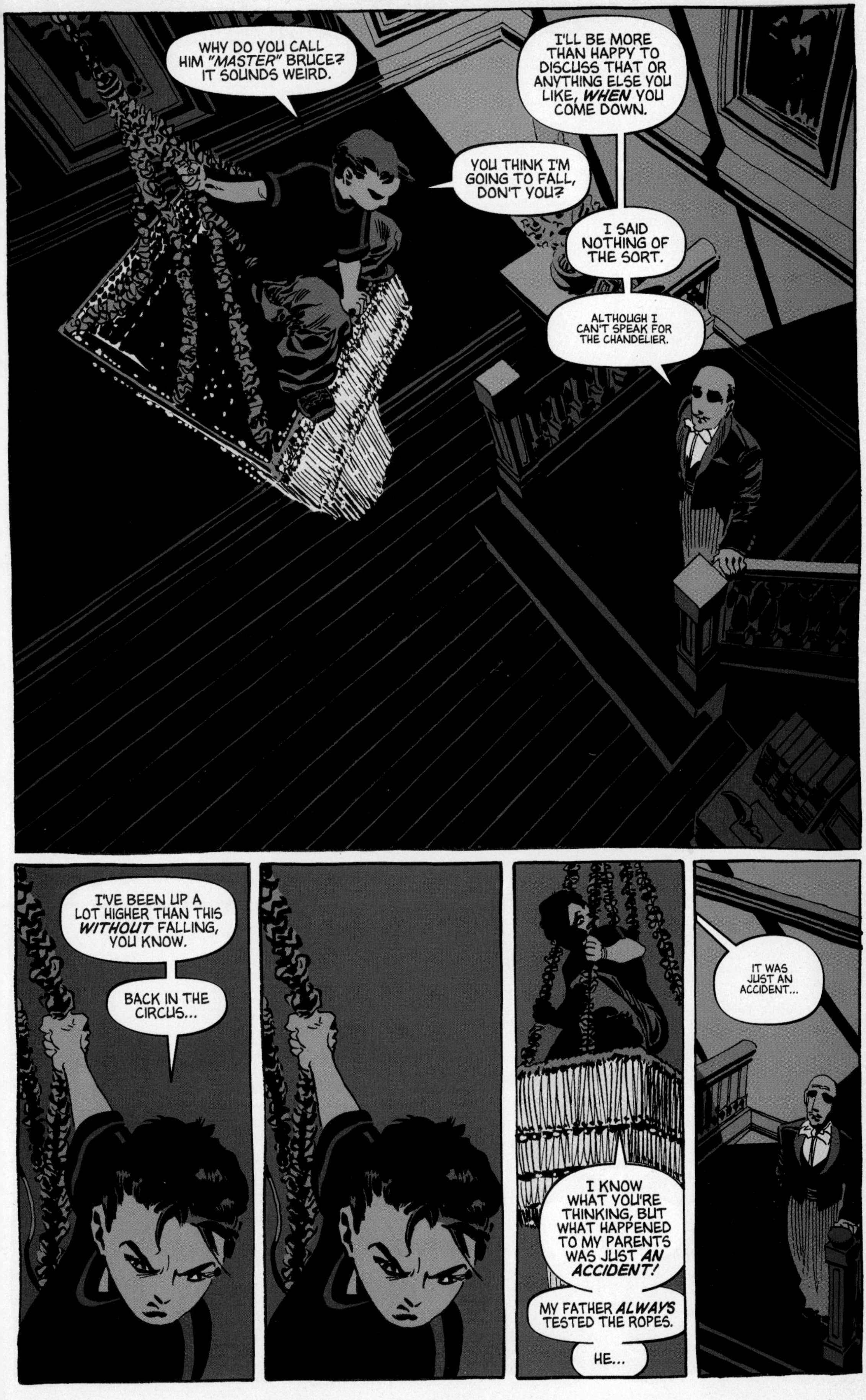
WHY DO YOU CALL HIM "MASTER" BRUCE? IT SOUNDS WEIRD.
I'LL BE MORE THAN HAPPY TO DISCUSS THAT OR ANYTHING ELSE YOU LIKE, WHEN YOU COME DOWN.
YOU THINK I'M GOING TO FALL, DON'T YOU?
I SAID NOTHING OF THE SORT.
ALTHOUGH I CAN'T SPEAK FOR THE CHANDELIER.
I'VE BEEN UP A LOT HIGHER THAN THIS WITHOUT FALLING, YOU KNOW.
BACK IN THE CIRCUS...
I KNOW WHAT YOU'RE THINKING, BUT WHAT HAPPENED TO MY PARENTS WAS JUST AN ACCIDENT!
MY FATHER ALWAYS TESTED THE ROPES.
HE...
IT WAS JUST AN ACCIDENT...

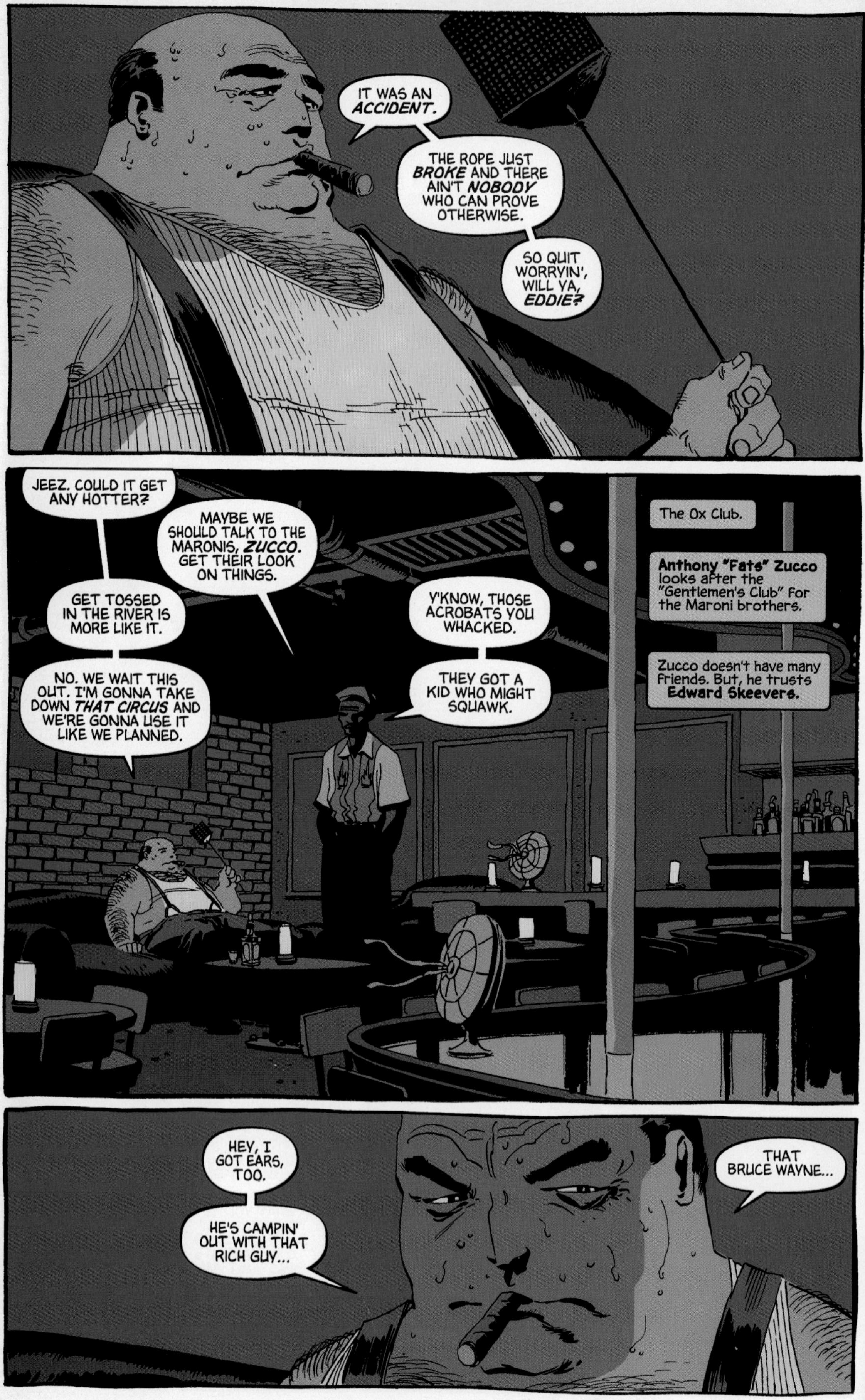
IT WAS AN ACCIDENT.
THE ROPE JUST BROKE AND THERE AIN'T NOBODY WHO CAN PROVE OTHERWISE.
SO QUIT WORRYIN', WILL YA, EDDIE?
The Ox Club.
Anthony "Fats" Zucco looks after the "Gentlemen's Club" for the Maroni brothers.
Zucco doesn't have many friends. But, he trusts Edward Skeevers.
JEEZ. COULD IT GET ANY HOTTER?
MAYBE WE SHOULD TALK TO THE MARONIS, ZUCCO. GET THEIR LOOK ON THINGS.
GET TOSSED IN THE RIVER IS MORE LIKE IT.
NO. WE WAIT THIS OUT. I'M GONNA TAKE DOWN THAT CIRCUS AND WE'RE GONNA USE IT LIKE WE PLANNED.
Y'KNOW, THOSE ACROBATS YOU WHACKED.
THEY GOT A KID WHO MIGHT SQUAWK.
HEY, I GOT EARS, TOO.
HE'S CAMPIN' OUT WITH THAT RICH GUY...
THAT BRUCE WAYNE...

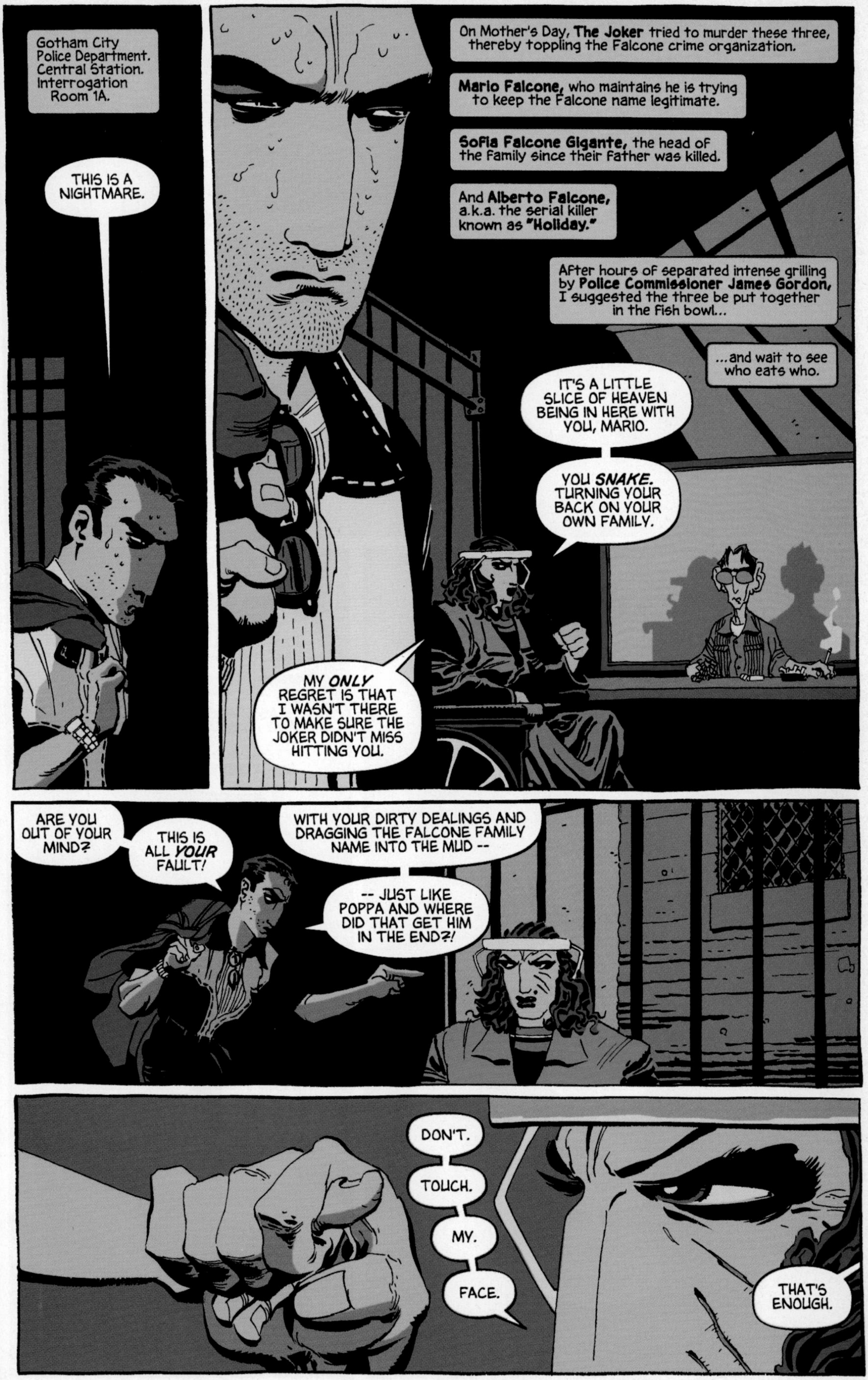
Gotham City Police Department. Central Station. Interrogation Room 1A.
THIS IS A NIGHTMARE.
On Mother's Day, The Joker tried to murder these three, thereby toppling the Falcone crime organization.
Mario Falcone, who maintains he is trying to keep the Falcone name legitimate.
Sofia Falcone Gigante, the head of the family since their father was killed.
And Alberto Falcone, a.k.a. the serial killer known as "Holiday."
After hours of separated intense grilling by Police Commissioner James Gordon, I suggested the three be put together in the fish bowl...
...and wait to see who eats who.
IT'S A LITTLE SLICE OF HEAVEN BEING IN HERE WITH YOU, MARIO.
YOU SNAKE. TURNING YOUR BACK ON YOUR OWN FAMILY.
MY ONLY REGRET IS THAT I WASN'T THERE TO MAKE SURE THE JOKER DIDN'T MISS HITTING YOU.
ARE YOU OUT OF YOUR MIND?
THIS IS ALL YOUR FAULT!
WITH YOUR DIRTY DEALINGS AND DRAGGING THE FALCONE FAMILY NAME INTO THE MUD --
-- JUST LIKE POPPA AND WHERE DID THAT GET HIM IN THE END?!
DON'T.
TOUCH.
MY.
FACE.
THAT'S ENOUGH.

EVERY WORD WE SAY IN THIS ROOM CAN BE HEARD ON THE OTHER SIDE OF THE MIRROR BEHIND ME.

SO, I SUGGEST YOU BOTH REMAIN SILENT UNTIL OUR *LAWYERS* GET US RELEASED.

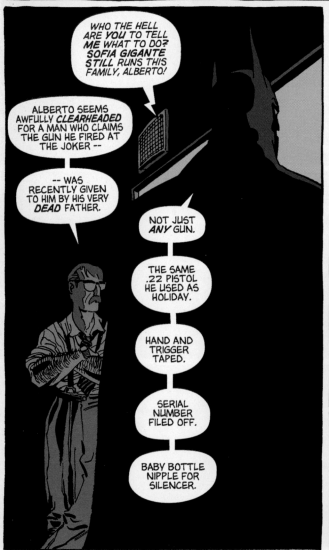

WHO THE HELL ARE *YOU* TO TELL *ME* WHAT TO DO? *SOFIA GIGANTE STILL* RUNS THIS FAMILY, ALBERTO!

ALBERTO SEEMS AWFULLY *CLEARHEADED* FOR A MAN WHO CLAIMS THE GUN HE FIRED AT THE JOKER --

-- WAS RECENTLY GIVEN TO HIM BY HIS VERY *DEAD* FATHER.

NOT JUST *ANY* GUN.

THE SAME .22 PISTOL HE USED AS HOLIDAY.

HAND AND TRIGGER TAPED.

SERIAL NUMBER FILED OFF.

BABY BOTTLE NIPPLE FOR SILENCER.

ONCE A SERIAL KILLER..?

THEN, WE'LL HOLD THEM UNTIL PAST MIDNIGHT --

-- ASSUMING THIS *HANG MAN* MADMAN WILL FOLLOW THE PATTERN AND STRIKE ON FATHER'S DAY.

WE *CAN'T* HOLD THEM ANY LONGER.

WHAT..?

THEIR LAWYERS ARGUED THAT THEY WERE EACH *VICTIMS* IN THE JOKER KILLINGS AND --

-- JUDGE HARKNESS HAS ORDERED THEIR *IMMEDIATE* RELEASE.

WHAT'S *BATMAN* DOING IN HERE?

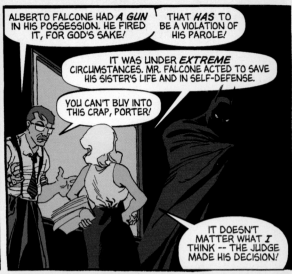

ALBERTO FALCONE HAD *A GUN* IN HIS POSSESSION. HE FIRED IT, FOR GOD'S SAKE!

THAT *HAS* TO BE A VIOLATION OF HIS PAROLE!

IT WAS UNDER *EXTREME* CIRCUMSTANCES. MR. FALCONE ACTED TO SAVE HIS SISTER'S LIFE AND IN SELF-DEFENSE.

YOU CAN'T BUY INTO THIS CRAP, PORTER!

IT DOESN'T MATTER WHAT *I* THINK -- THE JUDGE MADE HIS DECISION!

DISTRICT ATTORNEY PORTER.

HOW WELL DID YOU KNOW ALBERTO FALCONE WHILE YOU ATTENDED HARVARD TOGETHER?

YOU SHOULD DO YOUR HOMEWORK BETTER.

BY THE TIME I TRANSFERRED INTO HARVARD, MR. FALCONE HAD LEFT FOR OXFORD.

AND STAY THE HELL OUT OF MY PRIVATE LIFE...

...UNLESS YOU'D LIKE ME TO LOOK INTO *YOURS*.

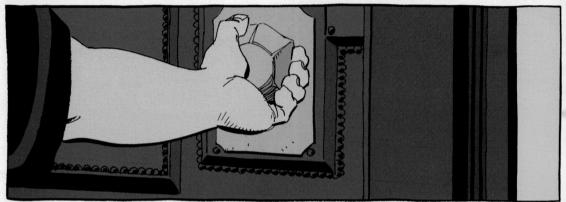

WHAT ARE YOU DOING IN HERE?

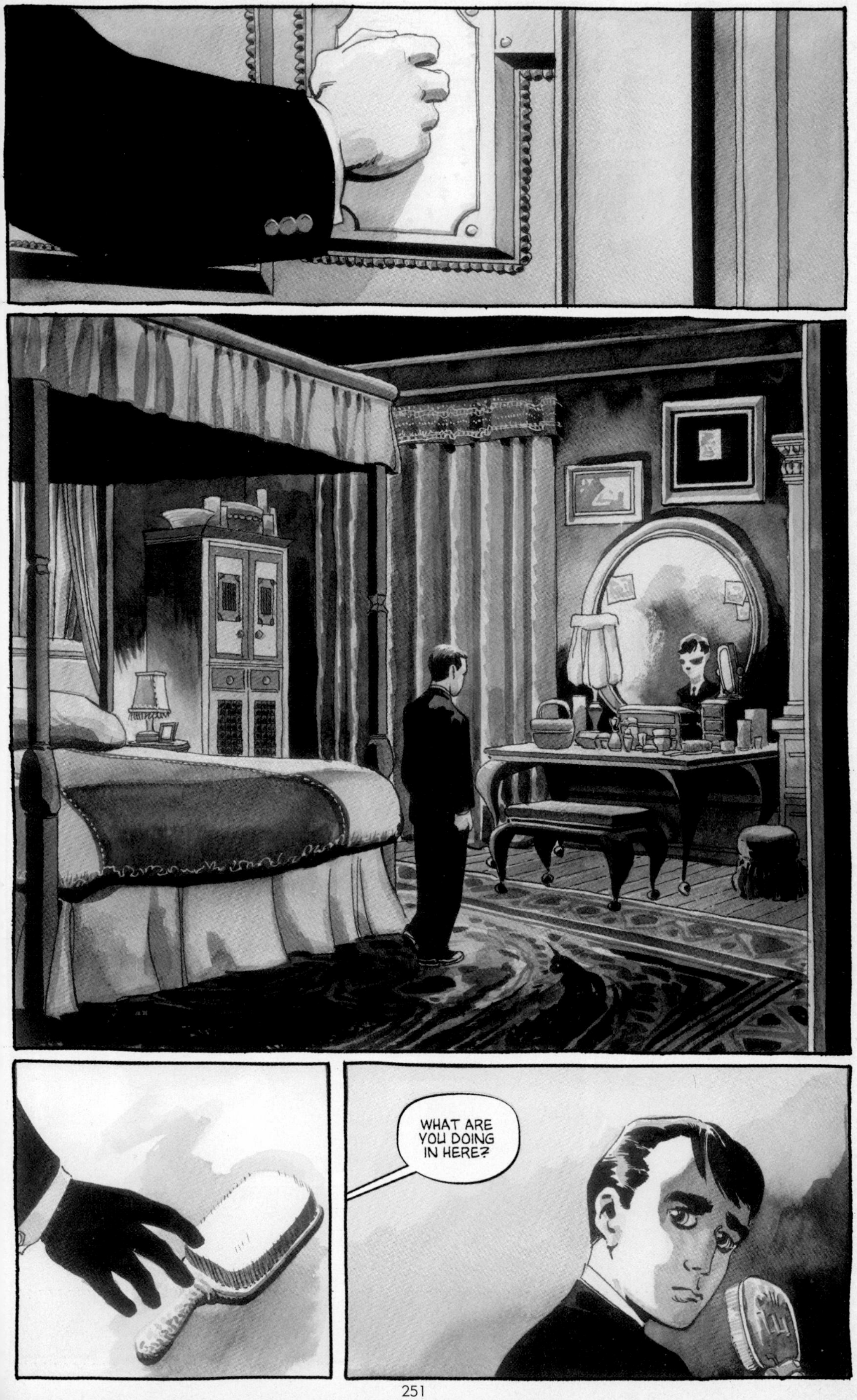
WHAT ARE YOU DOING IN HERE?

MY MOM HAD A BRUSH LIKE THIS.

SHE WOULD BRUSH HER HAIR BEFORE *EVERY* PERFORMANCE.

MY DAD WOULD GET SO MAD. HE NEVER WANTED US TO BE LATE FOR A SHOW.

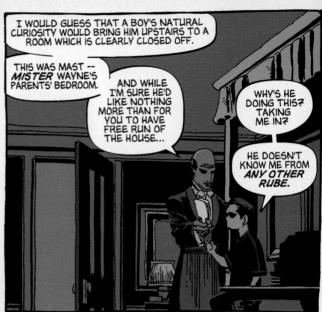

I WOULD GUESS THAT A BOY'S NATURAL CURIOSITY WOULD BRING HIM UPSTAIRS TO A ROOM WHICH IS CLEARLY CLOSED OFF.

THIS WAS MAST -- *MISTER* WAYNE'S PARENTS' BEDROOM.

AND WHILE I'M SURE HE'D LIKE NOTHING MORE THAN FOR YOU TO HAVE FREE RUN OF THE HOUSE...

WHY'S HE DOING THIS? TAKING ME IN?

HE DOESN'T KNOW ME FROM *ANY OTHER RUBE.*

I... IT'S NOT REALLY MY PLACE TO SAY FOR CERTAIN.

BUT, AS A BOY HE HAD THE MISFORTUNE OF WITNESSING HIS PARENTS' DEATHS AS WELL.

SO... WE'RE BOTH ORPHANS...

I NEVER SPENT FATHER'S DAY BY MYSELF.

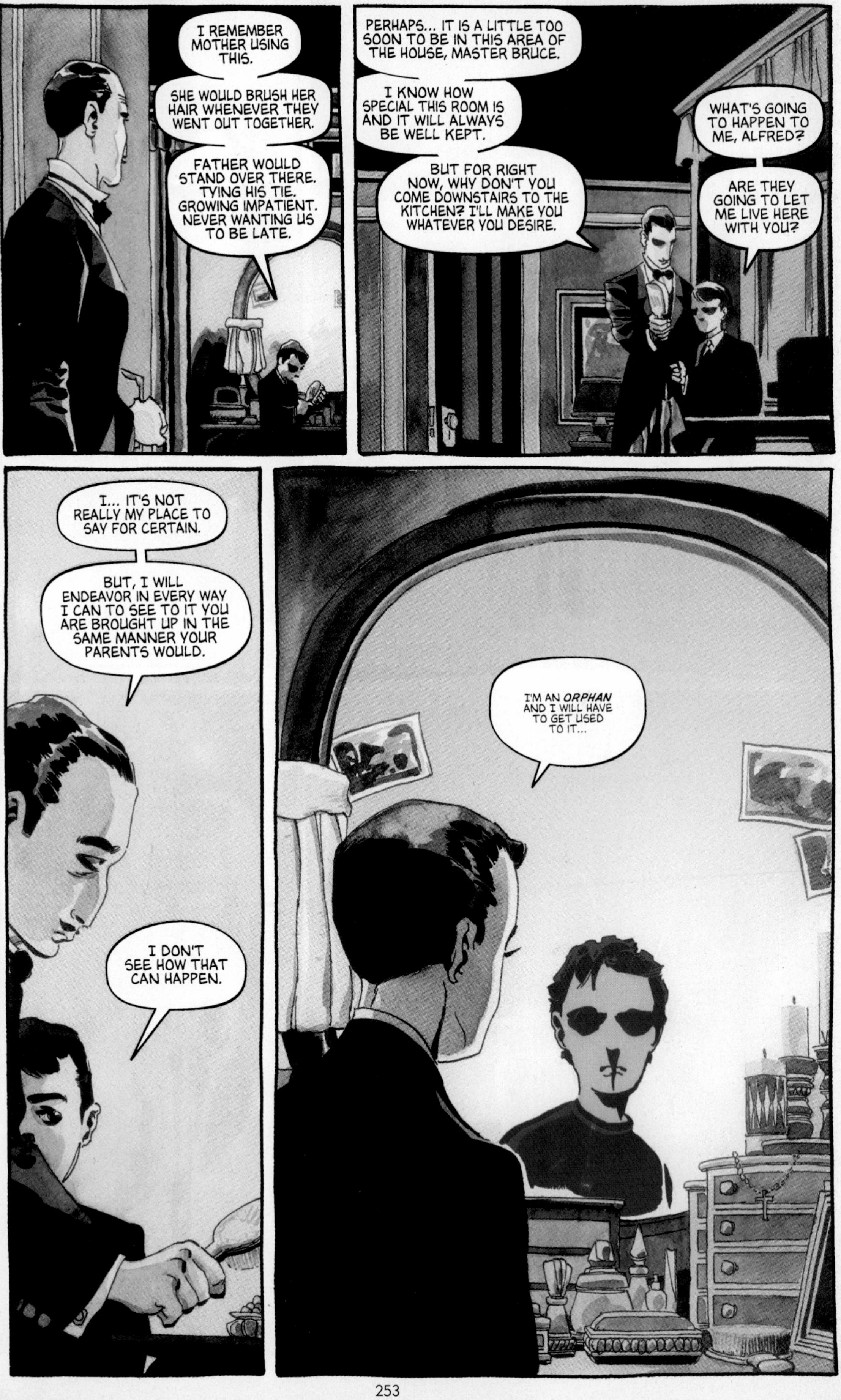

I REMEMBER MOTHER USING THIS.
SHE WOULD BRUSH HER HAIR WHENEVER THEY WENT OUT TOGETHER.
FATHER WOULD STAND OVER THERE. TYING HIS TIE. GROWING IMPATIENT. NEVER WANTING US TO BE LATE.
PERHAPS... IT IS A LITTLE TOO SOON TO BE IN THIS AREA OF THE HOUSE, MASTER BRUCE.
I KNOW HOW SPECIAL THIS ROOM IS AND IT WILL ALWAYS BE WELL KEPT.
BUT FOR RIGHT NOW, WHY DON'T YOU COME DOWNSTAIRS TO THE KITCHEN? I'LL MAKE YOU WHATEVER YOU DESIRE.
WHAT'S GOING TO HAPPEN TO ME, ALFRED?
ARE THEY GOING TO LET ME LIVE HERE WITH YOU?
I... IT'S NOT REALLY MY PLACE TO SAY FOR CERTAIN.
BUT, I WILL ENDEAVOR IN EVERY WAY I CAN TO SEE TO IT YOU ARE BROUGHT UP IN THE SAME MANNER YOUR PARENTS WOULD.
I DON'T SEE HOW THAT CAN HAPPEN.
I'M AN ORPHAN AND I WILL HAVE TO GET USED TO IT...

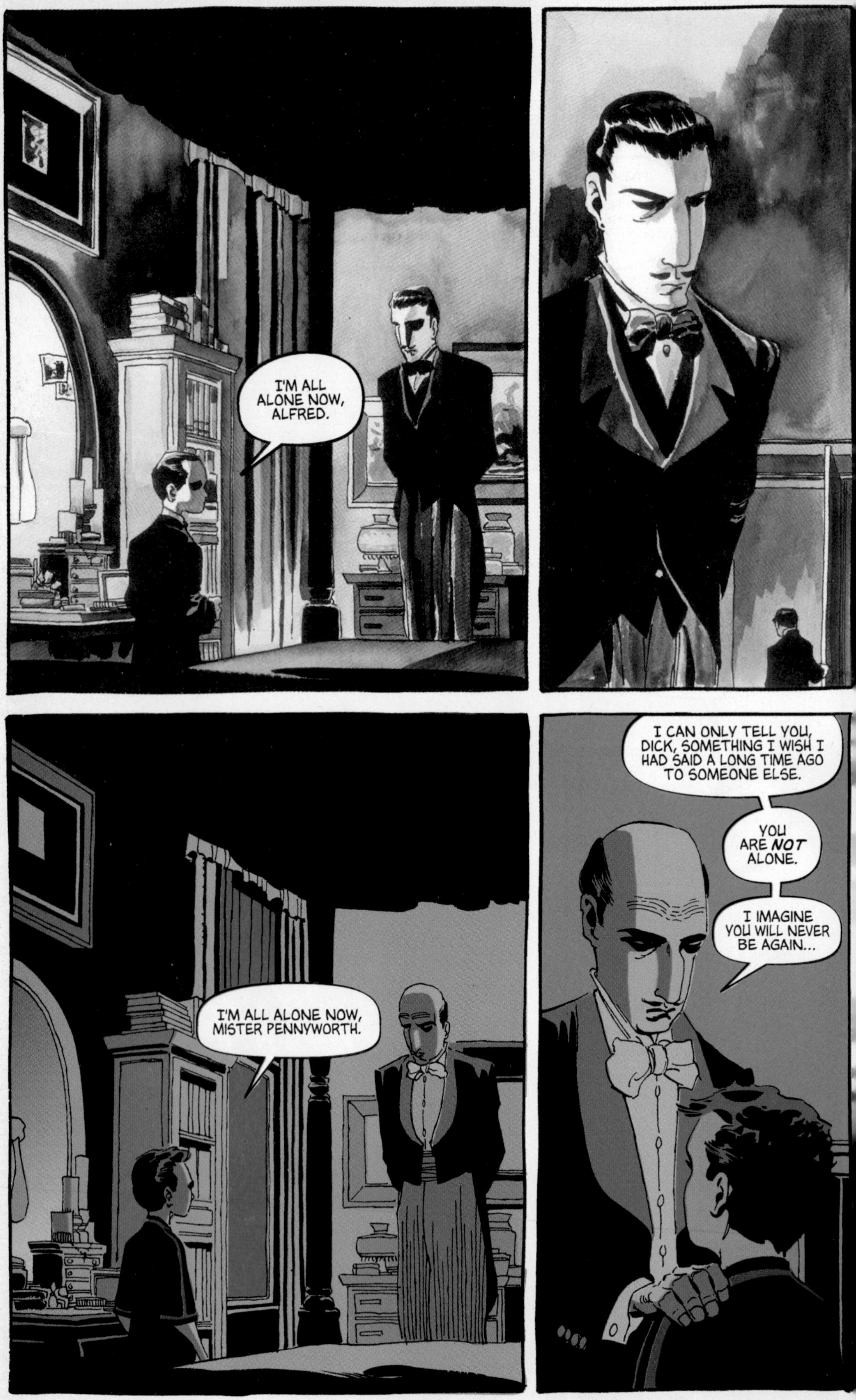
I'M ALL ALONE NOW, ALFRED.
I'M ALL ALONE NOW, MISTER PENNYWORTH.
I CAN ONLY TELL YOU, DICK, SOMETHING I WISH I HAD SAID A LONG TIME AGO TO SOMEONE ELSE.
YOU ARE *NOT* ALONE.
I IMAGINE YOU WILL NEVER BE AGAIN...

THE HANG MAN KILLINGS.

I THOUGHT... I DON'T KNOW WHY...

I WANTED TO BELIEVE THAT *THE FIVE* OF YOU WERE... UNTOUCHABLE.

BUT, WITH *GUSTAVSON'S* DEATH...

COMMISSIONER.

I APOLOGIZE FOR INTERRUPTING, BUT I THINK WE ALL KNOW WHERE THIS IS GOING.

DON'T GIVE UP ON US. WE KNEW THE RISKS GOING IN.

WE'RE *STILL* THE BEST CHANCE THIS DEPARTMENT HAS TO CATCH THIS KILLER --

-- OR YOU WOULDN'T HAVE PICKED US IN THE FIRST PLACE.

KING IS RIGHT, SIR.

IF ALL THE VICTIMS HAD PAST RELATIONSHIPS WITH *HARVEY DENT* -- THEN HE OR SHE OR *THEY* HAVE NOW BROKEN THE PATTERN WITH *GUSTAVSON.*

WE WANT TO KNOW WHY.

AND I KNOW IT SEEMS OBVIOUS, BUT HAS ANYONE NOTICED THAT ALL THE VICTIMS ARE *MEN?*

THOSE... SEEM LIKE PROMISING LEADS, *LOPEZ.*

IT'S LATE...

...I SHOULD GET HOME AND SPEND A FEW MINUTES WITH MY SON...

...FATHER'S DAY AND ALL...

ANY OF YOU KNOW WHERE *O'CONNOR* IS? HE GOT ASSIGNED AS MY DRIVER.

WILCOX..?

I SPOKE TO HIM ABOUT AN HOUR AGO.

HE SAID HE WAS GOING TO GRAB A QUICK SHOWER AND MEET US HERE...

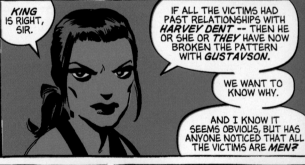

Detective Mark O'Connor spent most of his career teaching Firearms at the Police Academy.

An expert marksman, he thought his gift was best shared with the young police officers, training them.

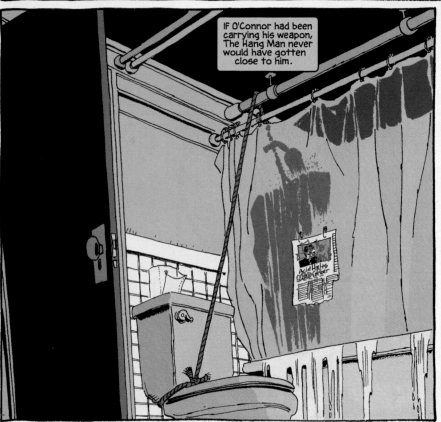

IF O'Connor had been carrying his weapon, The Hang Man never would have gotten close to him.

Acid Halts D.A's Career

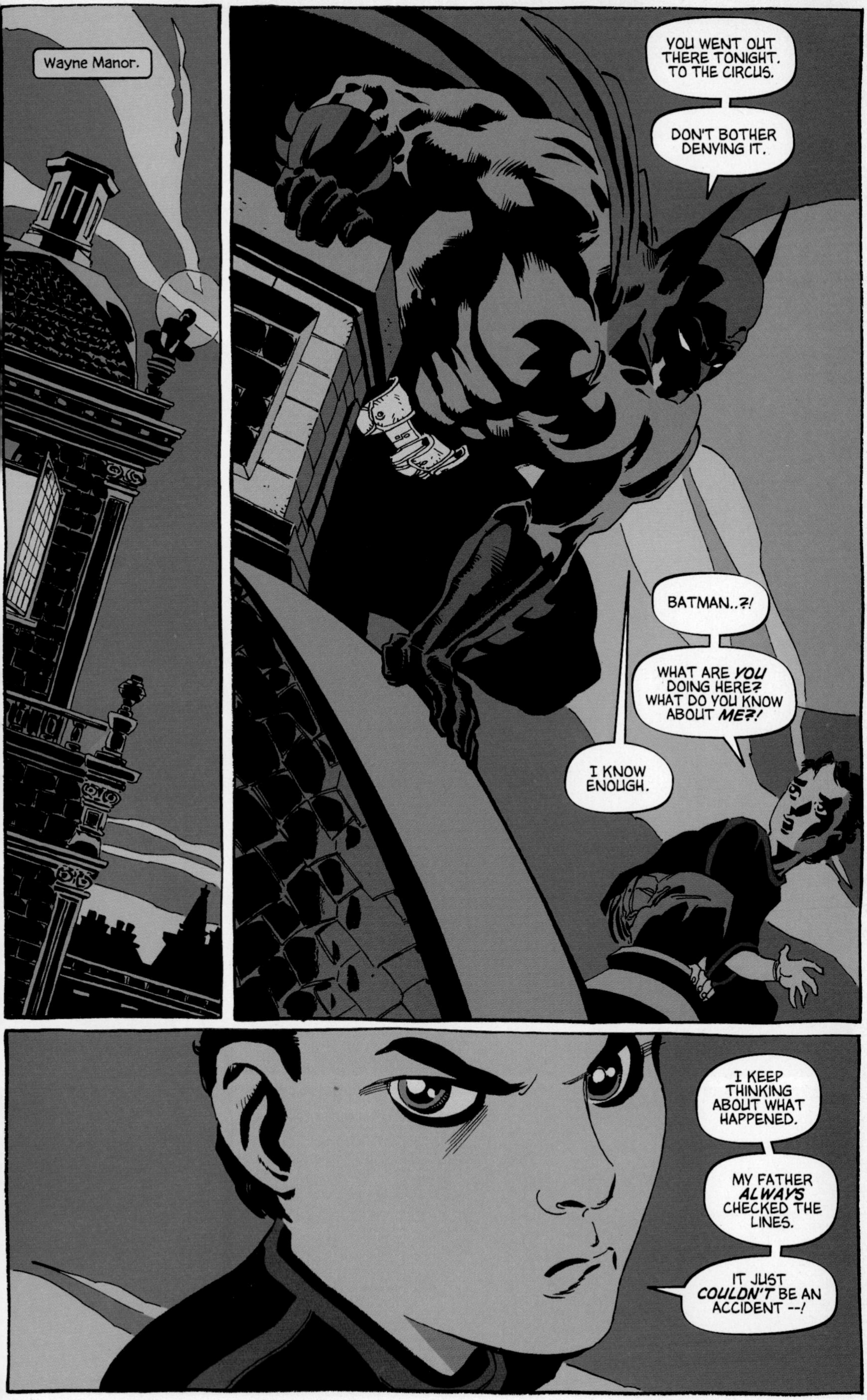
Wayne Manor.
YOU WENT OUT THERE TONIGHT. TO THE CIRCUS.
DON'T BOTHER DENYING IT.
BATMAN..?!
WHAT ARE YOU DOING HERE? WHAT DO YOU KNOW ABOUT ME?!
I KNOW ENOUGH.
I KEEP THINKING ABOUT WHAT HAPPENED.
MY FATHER ALWAYS CHECKED THE LINES.
IT JUST COULDN'T BE AN ACCIDENT --!

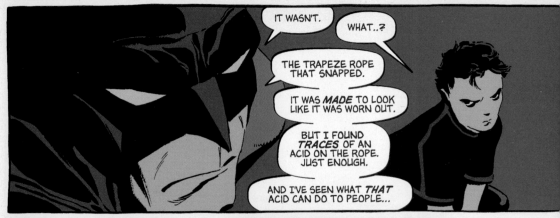

IT WASN'T.

WHAT..?

THE TRAPEZE ROPE THAT SNAPPED.

IT WAS *MADE* TO LOOK LIKE IT WAS WORN OUT.

BUT I FOUND *TRACES* OF AN ACID ON THE ROPE. JUST ENOUGH.

AND I'VE SEEN WHAT *THAT* ACID CAN DO TO PEOPLE...

I WANT TO HELP.

YOU WILL. WHEN THE TIME IS RIGHT.

I PROMISE.

I REMEMBER SEEIN' A *GUY* TALKING TO *MISTER HALY* AT THE CIRCUS.

HE SAID SOMETHING ABOUT HOW IT'D BE A SHAME IF ANYTHING HAPPENED TO MY...

HE WAS A BIG FAT GUY.

YOU SHOULD GO BACK INSIDE NOW.

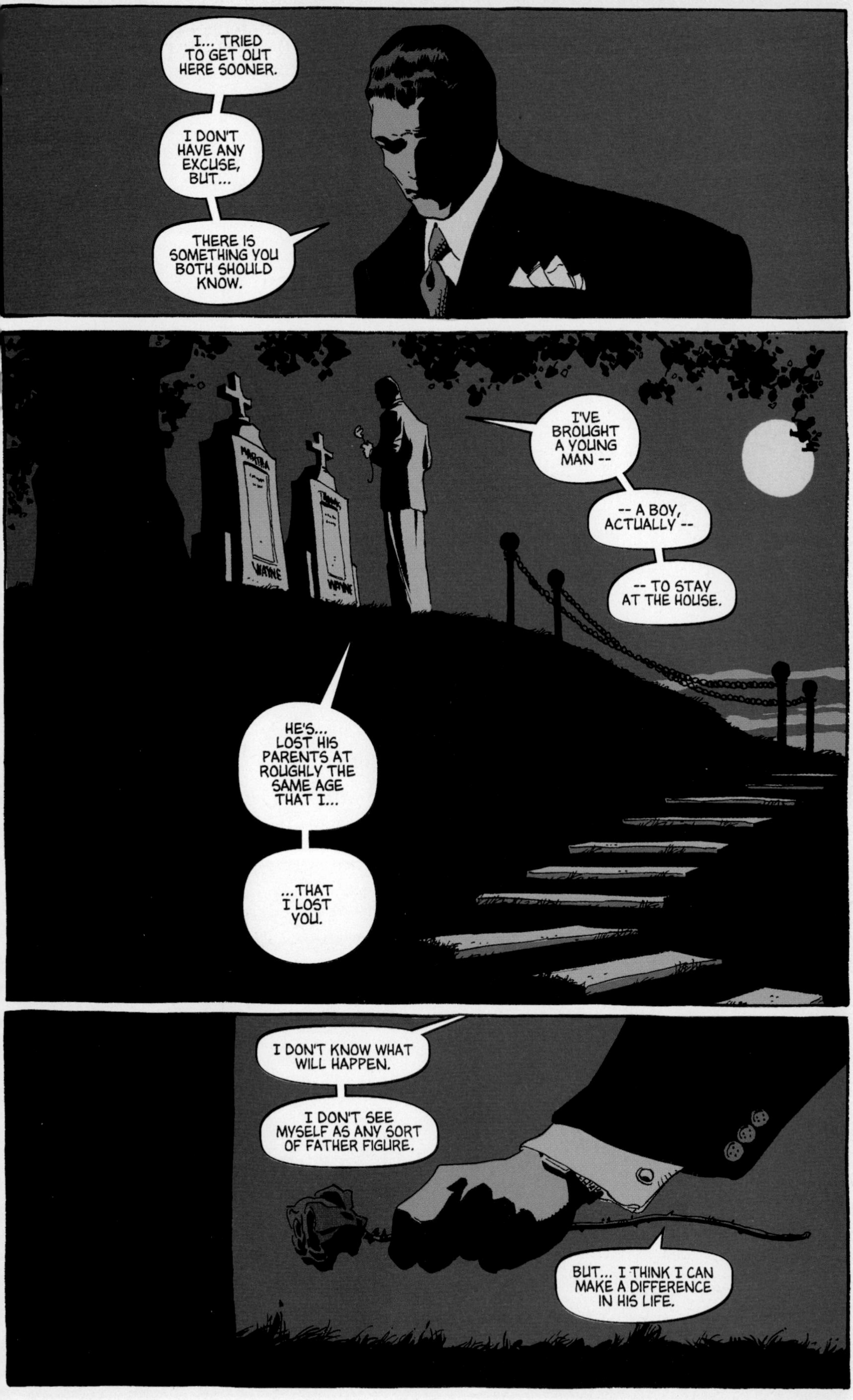

I... TRIED TO GET OUT HERE SOONER.
I DON'T HAVE ANY EXCUSE, BUT...
THERE IS SOMETHING YOU BOTH SHOULD KNOW.
I'VE BROUGHT A YOUNG MAN --
-- A BOY, ACTUALLY --
-- TO STAY AT THE HOUSE.
HE'S... LOST HIS PARENTS AT ROUGHLY THE SAME AGE THAT I...
...THAT I LOST YOU.
I DON'T KNOW WHAT WILL HAPPEN.
I DON'T SEE MYSELF AS ANY SORT OF FATHER FIGURE.
BUT... I THINK I CAN MAKE A DIFFERENCE IN HIS LIFE.

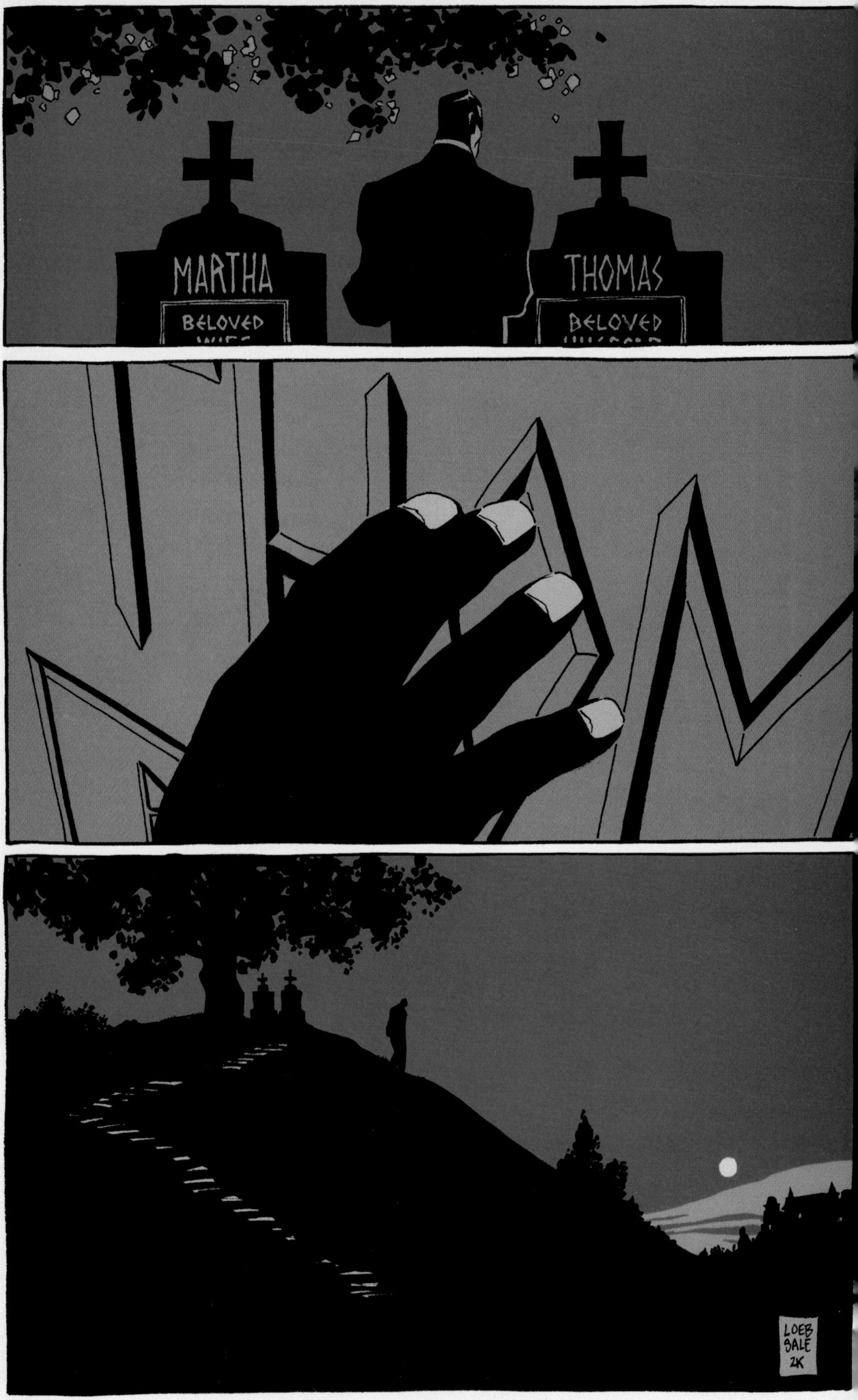
MARTHA
BELOVED
THOMAS
BELOVED
LOEB
SALE
2K

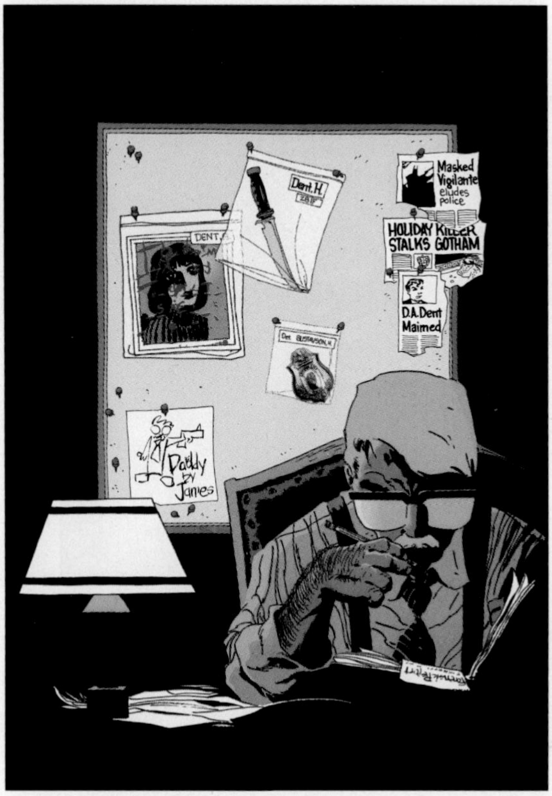
Dent. H.
Masked Vigilante eludes police
HOLIDAY KILLER STALKS GOTHAM
D.A. Dent Maimed
Daddy by James

JUSTICE

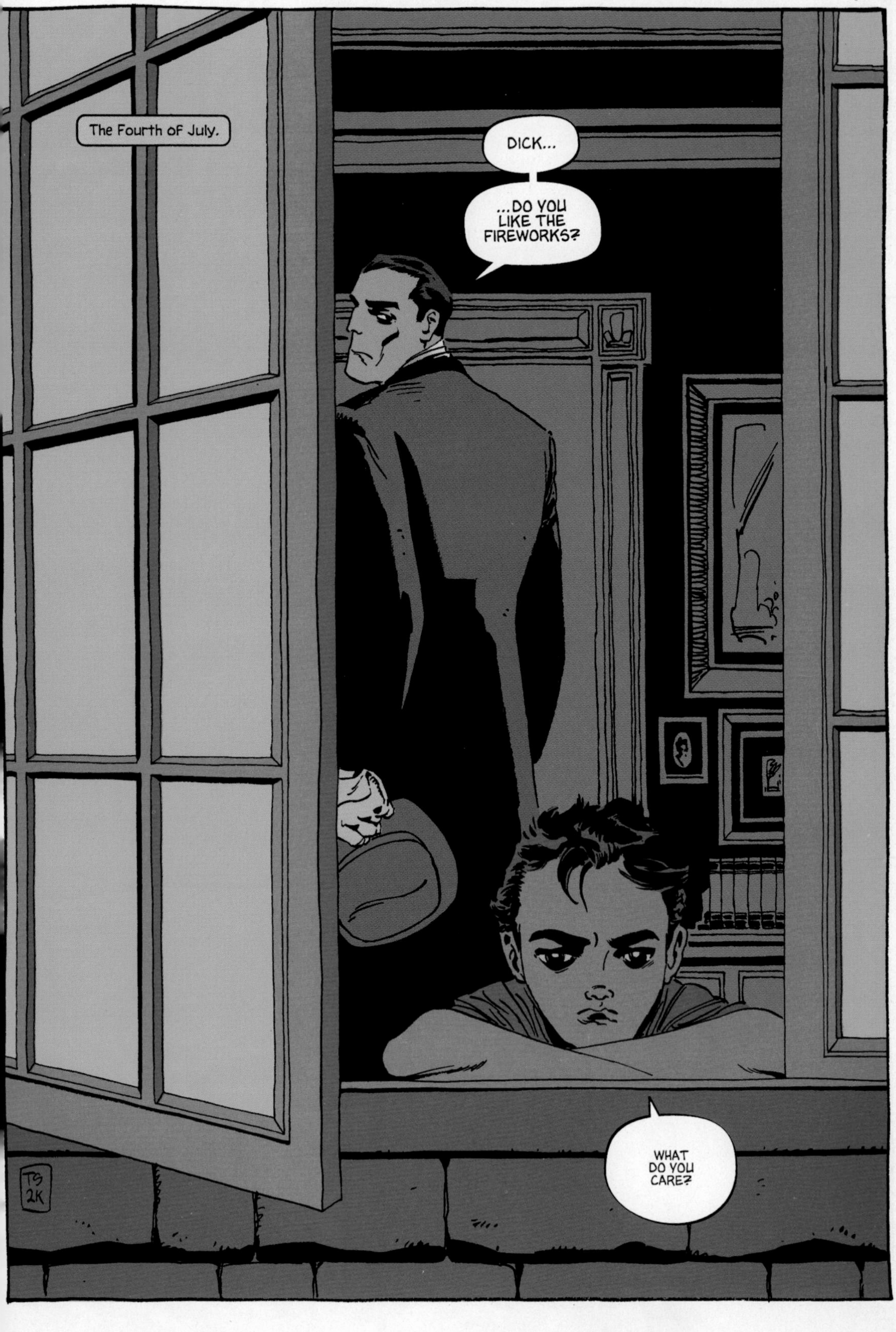
The Fourth of July.
DICK...
...DO YOU LIKE THE FIREWORKS?
WHAT DO YOU CARE?
TS 2K

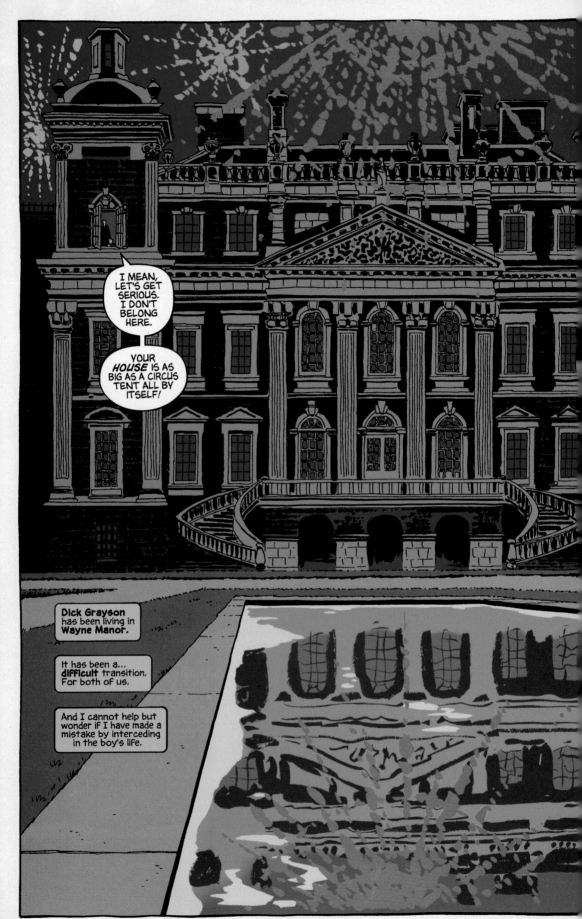

I MEAN, LET'S GET SERIOUS. I DON'T BELONG HERE.

YOUR *HOUSE* IS AS BIG AS A CIRCUS TENT ALL BY ITSELF!

Dick Grayson has been living in **Wayne Manor.**

It has been a... **difficult** transition. For both of us.

And I cannot help but wonder if I have made a mistake by interceding in the boy's life.

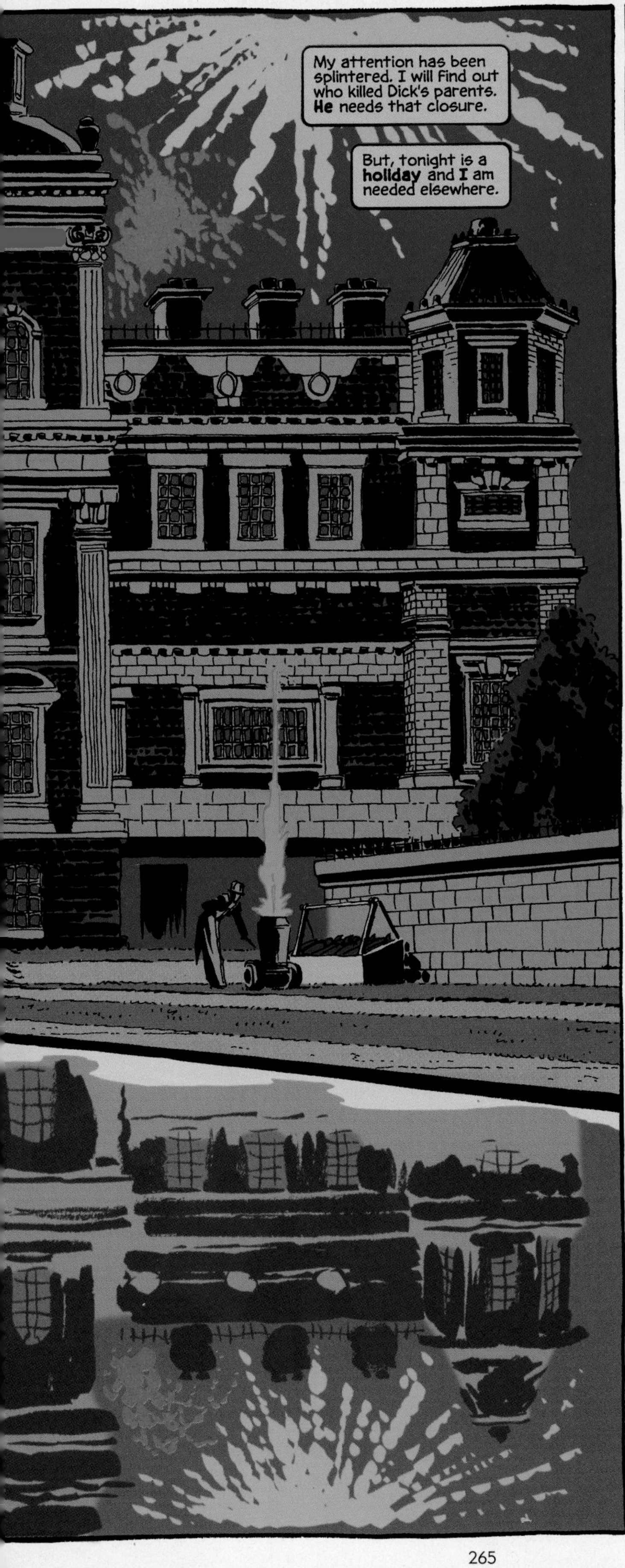
My attention has been splintered. I will find out who killed Dick's parents. **He** needs that closure.
But, tonight is a **holiday** and **I** am needed elsewhere.

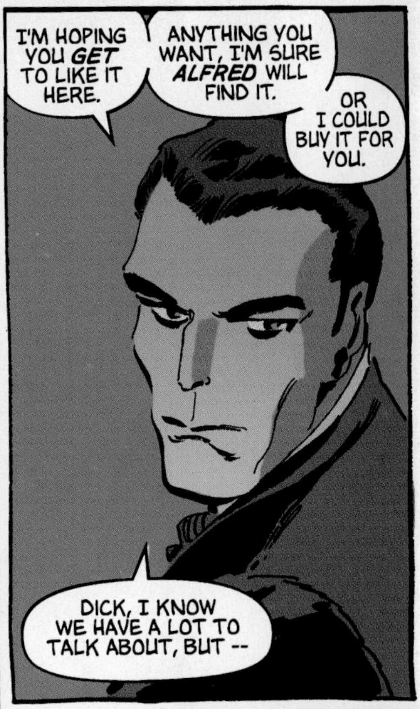
I'M HOPING YOU ***GET*** TO LIKE IT HERE.
ANYTHING YOU WANT, I'M SURE ***ALFRED*** WILL FIND IT.
OR I COULD BUY IT FOR YOU.
DICK, I KNOW WE HAVE A LOT TO TALK ABOUT, BUT --

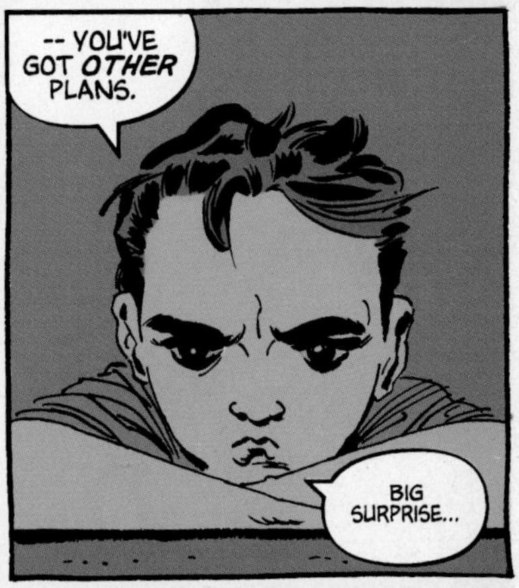
-- YOU'VE GOT ***OTHER*** PLANS.
BIG SURPRISE...

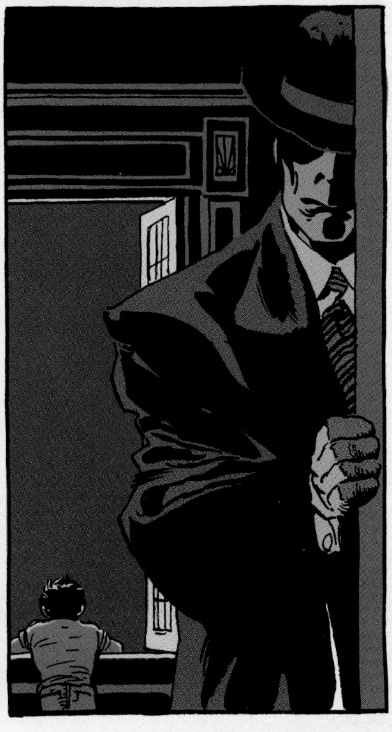

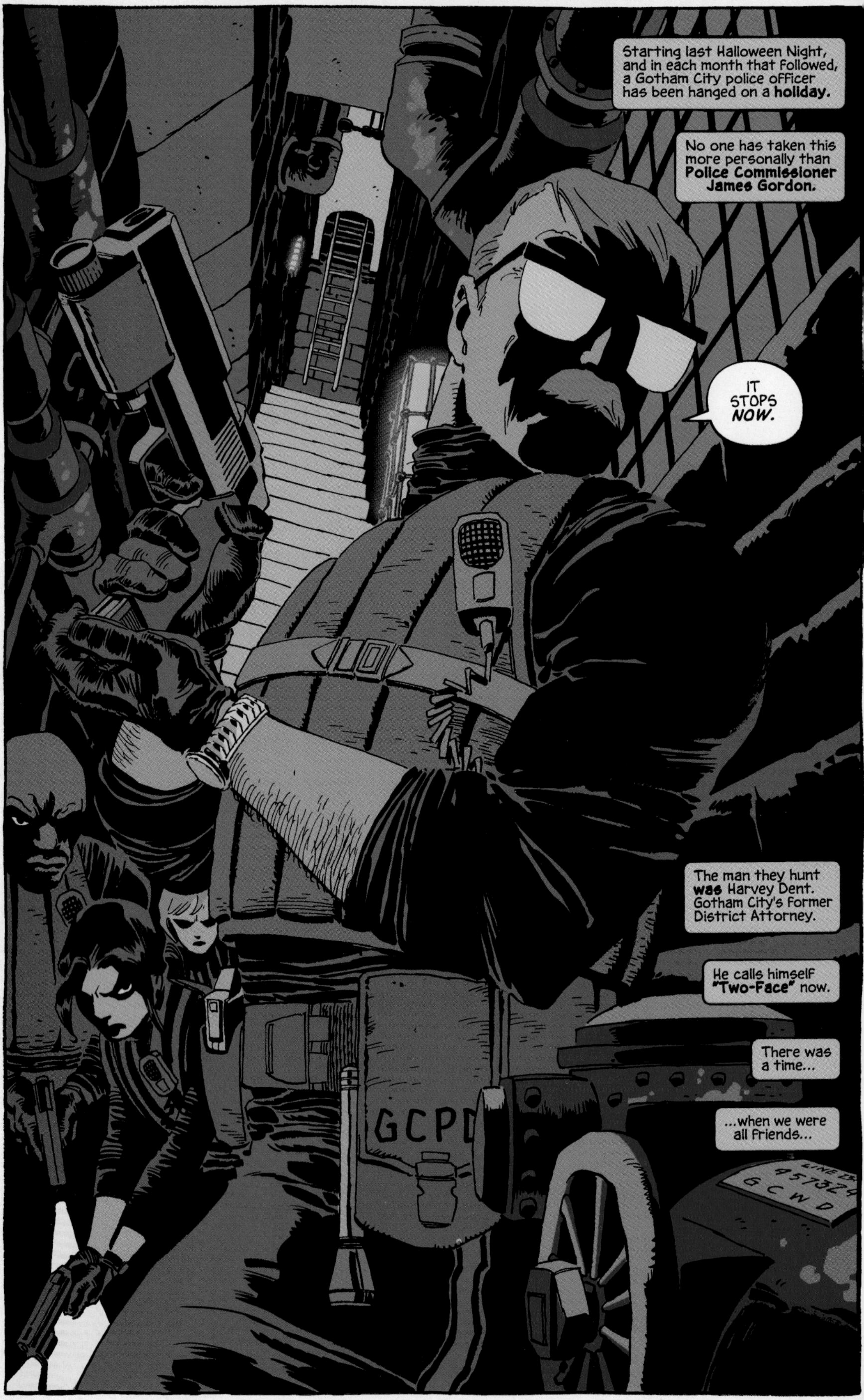
Starting last Halloween Night, and in each month that followed, a Gotham City police officer has been hanged on a **holiday.**
No one has taken this more personally than **Police Commissioner James Gordon.**
IT STOPS *NOW.*
The man they hunt **was** Harvey Dent. Gotham City's former District Attorney.
He calls himself **"Two-Face"** now.
There was a time...
...when we were all friends...
GCPD
GCWD

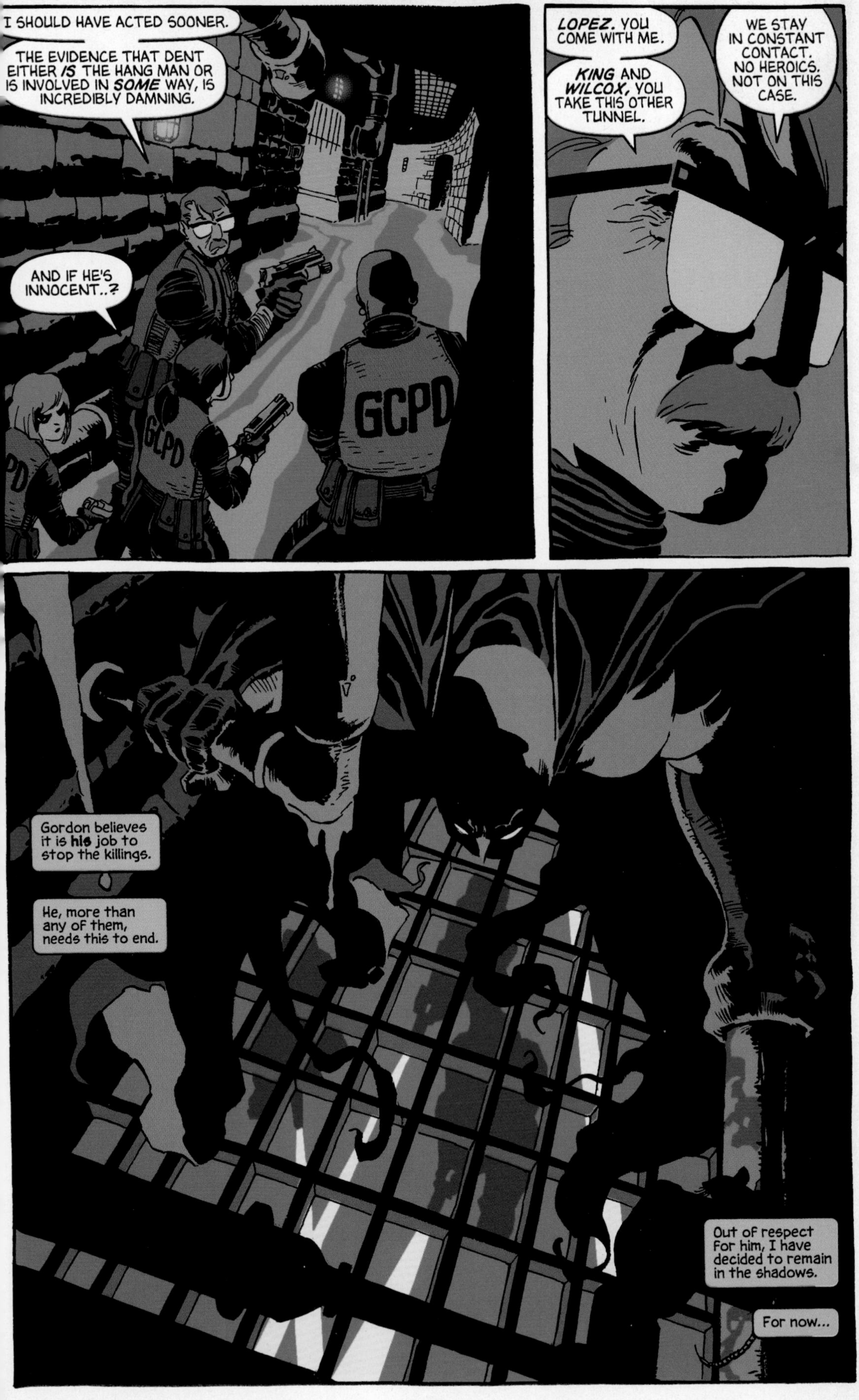

I SHOULD HAVE ACTED SOONER.
THE EVIDENCE THAT DENT EITHER *IS* THE HANG MAN OR IS INVOLVED IN *SOME* WAY, IS INCREDIBLY DAMNING.
AND IF HE'S INNOCENT..?
GCPD
GCPD
PD
LOPEZ. YOU COME WITH ME.
KING AND WILCOX, YOU TAKE THIS OTHER TUNNEL.
WE STAY IN CONSTANT CONTACT. NO HEROICS. NOT ON THIS CASE.
Gordon believes it is **his** job to stop the killings.
He, more than any of them, needs this to end.
Out of respect for him, I have decided to remain in the shadows.
For now...

HAVE YOU EVER BEEN IN LOVE?

WHAT THE HELL HAS THAT GOT TO DO WITH ANYTHING?

WHEN YOU ARE DEALING WITH ME, IT HAS TO DO WITH *EVERYTHING*.

I DO NOT CARE WHAT YOUR *LARGER* PLANS ARE.

IT IS ONLY ABOUT THE *MONEY* YOU HAVE PROMISED ME.

SO YOU'VE *SAID,* VICTOR.

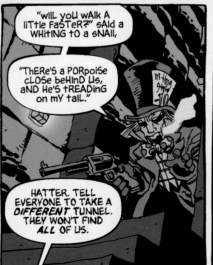

"WILL YOU WALK A LITTLE FASTER?" SAID A WHITING TO A SNAIL,

"THERE'S A PORPOISE CLOSE BEHIND US, AND HE'S TREADING ON MY TAIL."

HATTER. TELL EVERYONE TO TAKE A *DIFFERENT* TUNNEL. THEY WON'T FIND *ALL* OF US.

AND FREEZE. REMEMBER.

IF I DON'T GET OUT --

-- YOU'LL GET *NOTHING*.

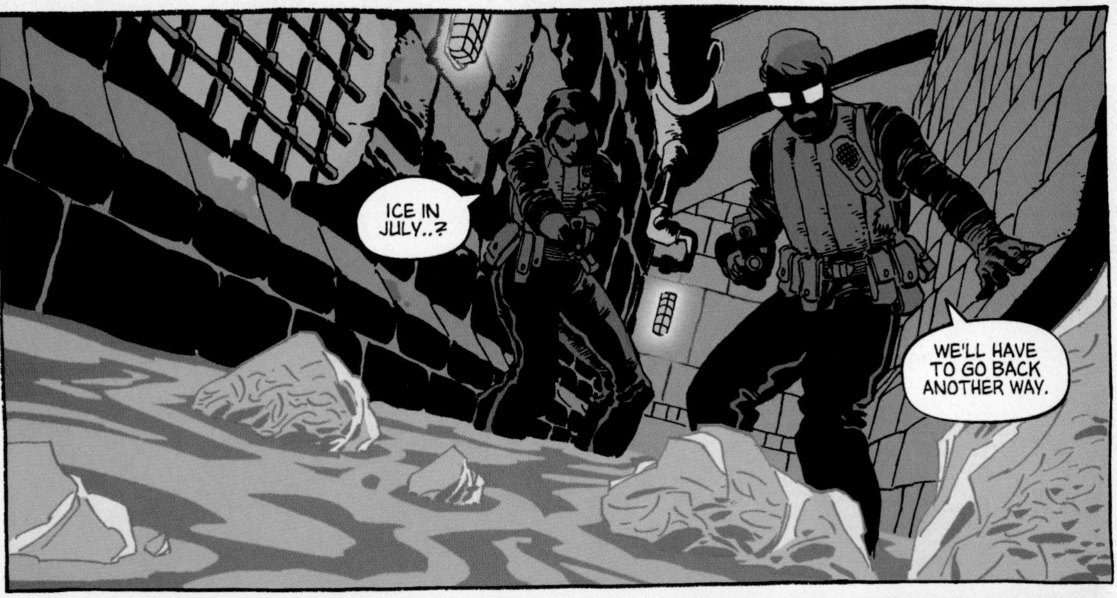
ICE IN JULY..?
WE'LL HAVE TO GO BACK ANOTHER WAY.

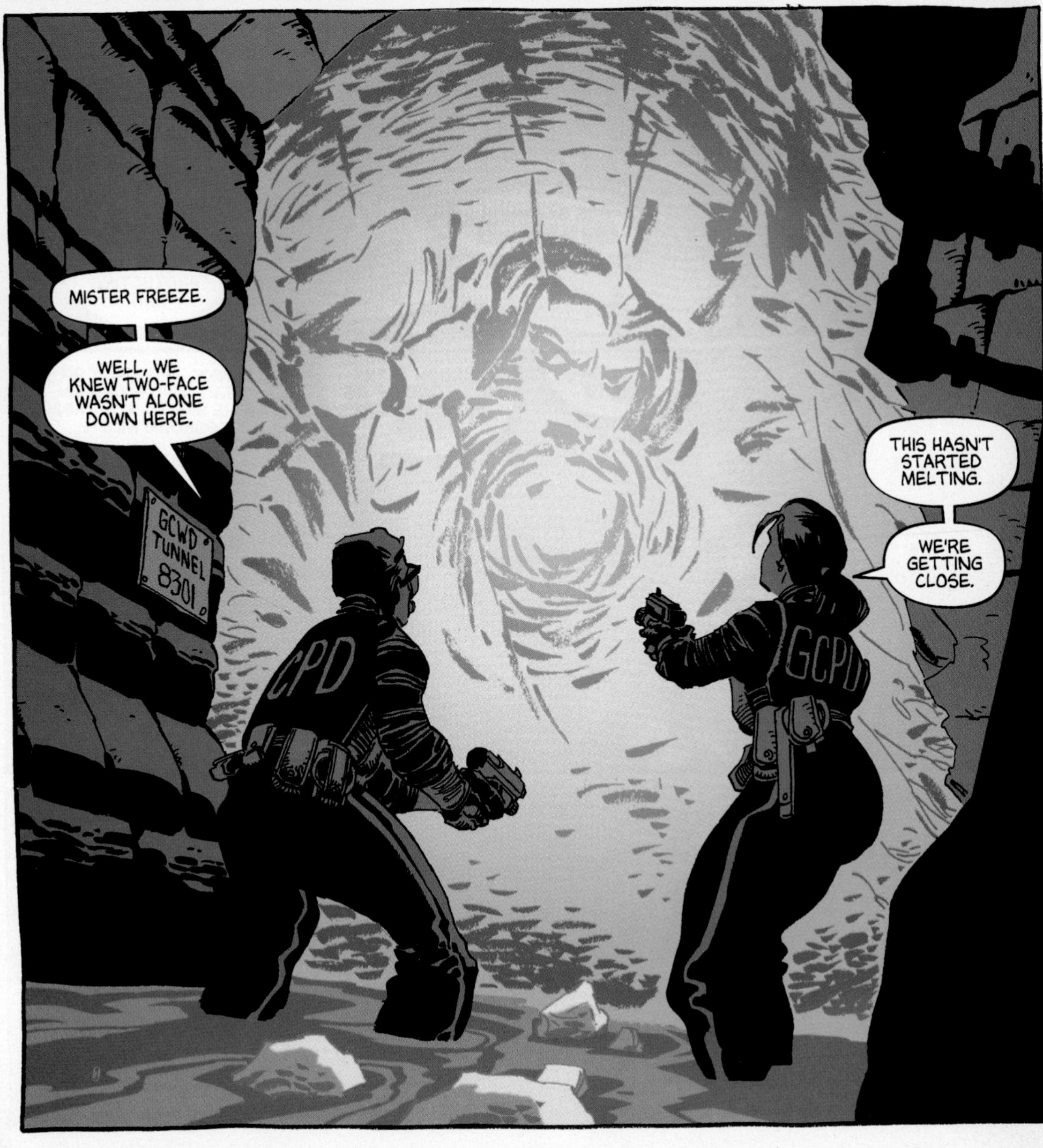
MISTER FREEZE.
WELL, WE KNEW TWO-FACE WASN'T ALONE DOWN HERE.
GCWD TUNNEL 8301
THIS HASN'T STARTED MELTING.
WE'RE GETTING CLOSE.
GCPD
GCPD

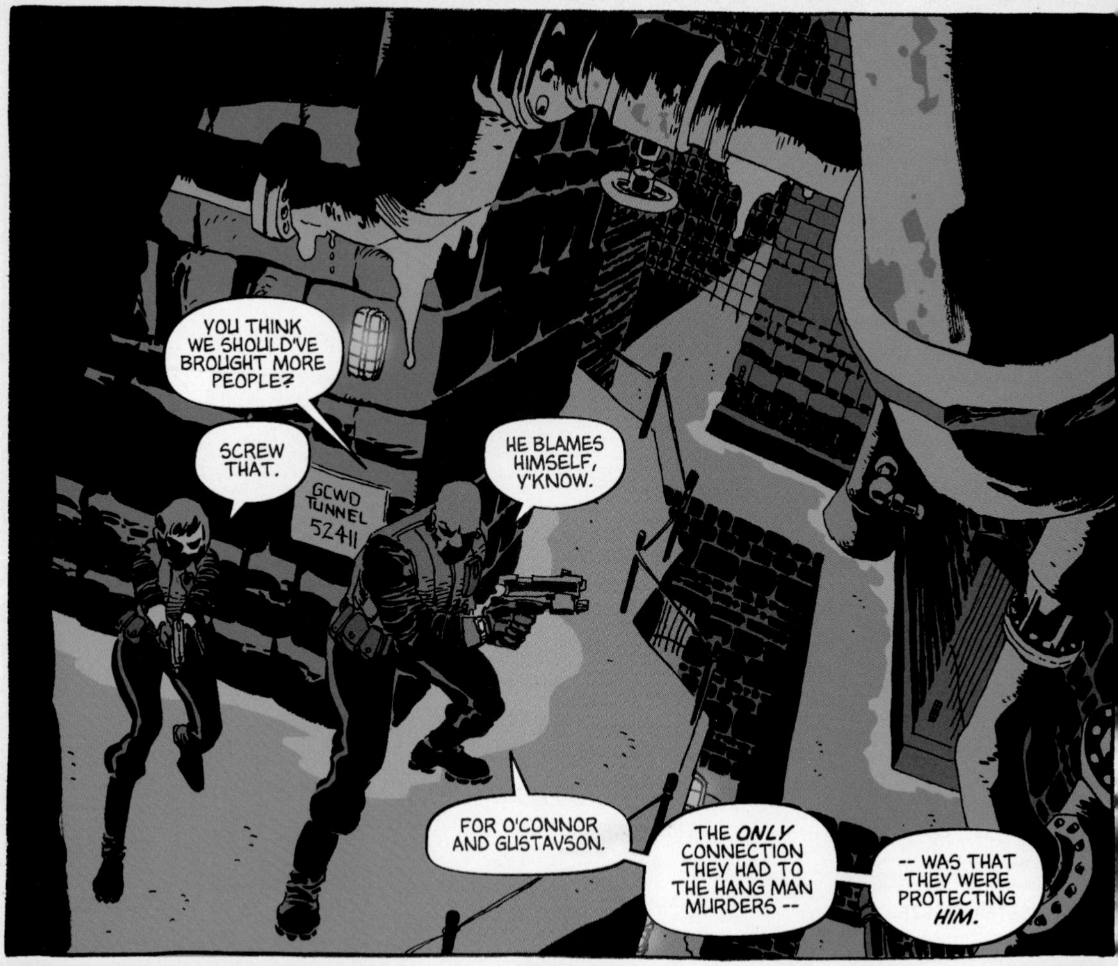
YOU THINK WE SHOULD'VE BROUGHT MORE PEOPLE?
SCREW THAT.
GCWD TUNNEL 52411
HE BLAMES HIMSELF, Y'KNOW.
FOR O'CONNOR AND GUSTAVSON.
THE *ONLY* CONNECTION THEY HAD TO THE HANG MAN MURDERS --
-- WAS THAT THEY WERE PROTECTING *HIM.*

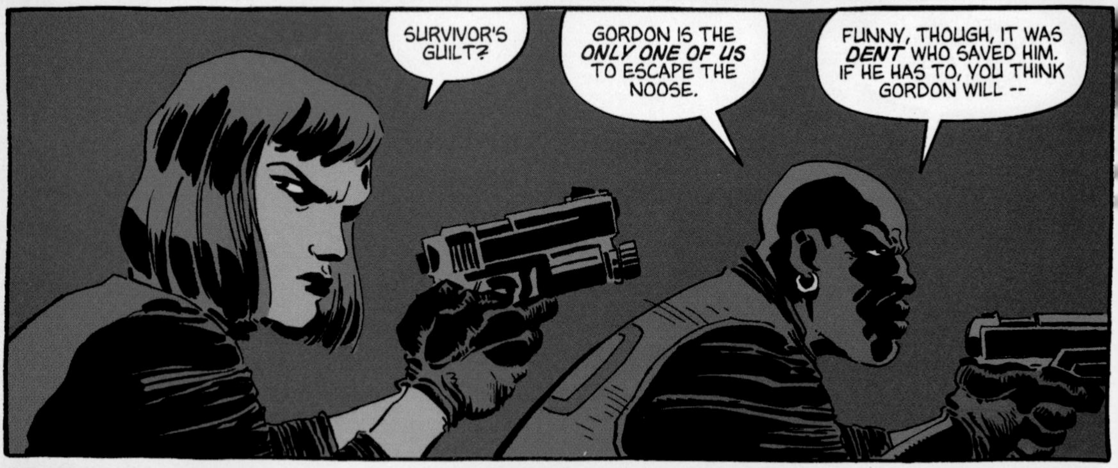
SURVIVOR'S GUILT?
GORDON IS THE *ONLY ONE OF US* TO ESCAPE THE NOOSE.
FUNNY, THOUGH, IT WAS *DENT* WHO SAVED HIM. IF HE HAS TO, YOU THINK GORDON WILL --

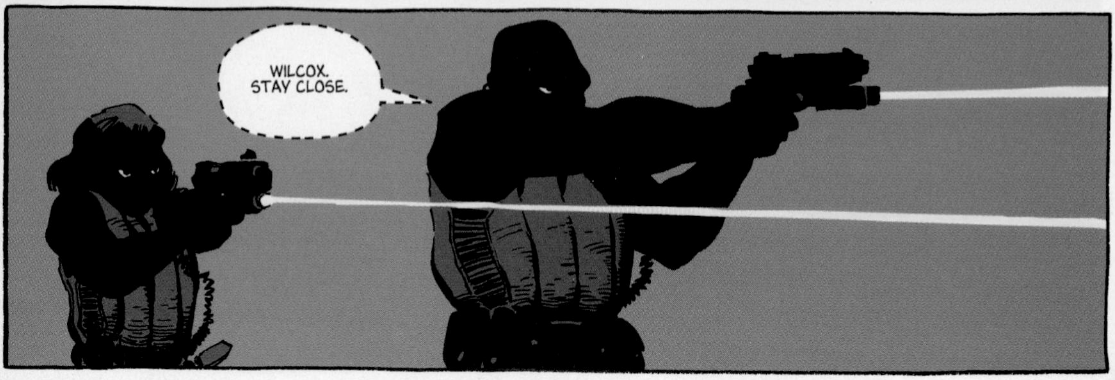
WILCOX. STAY CLOSE.

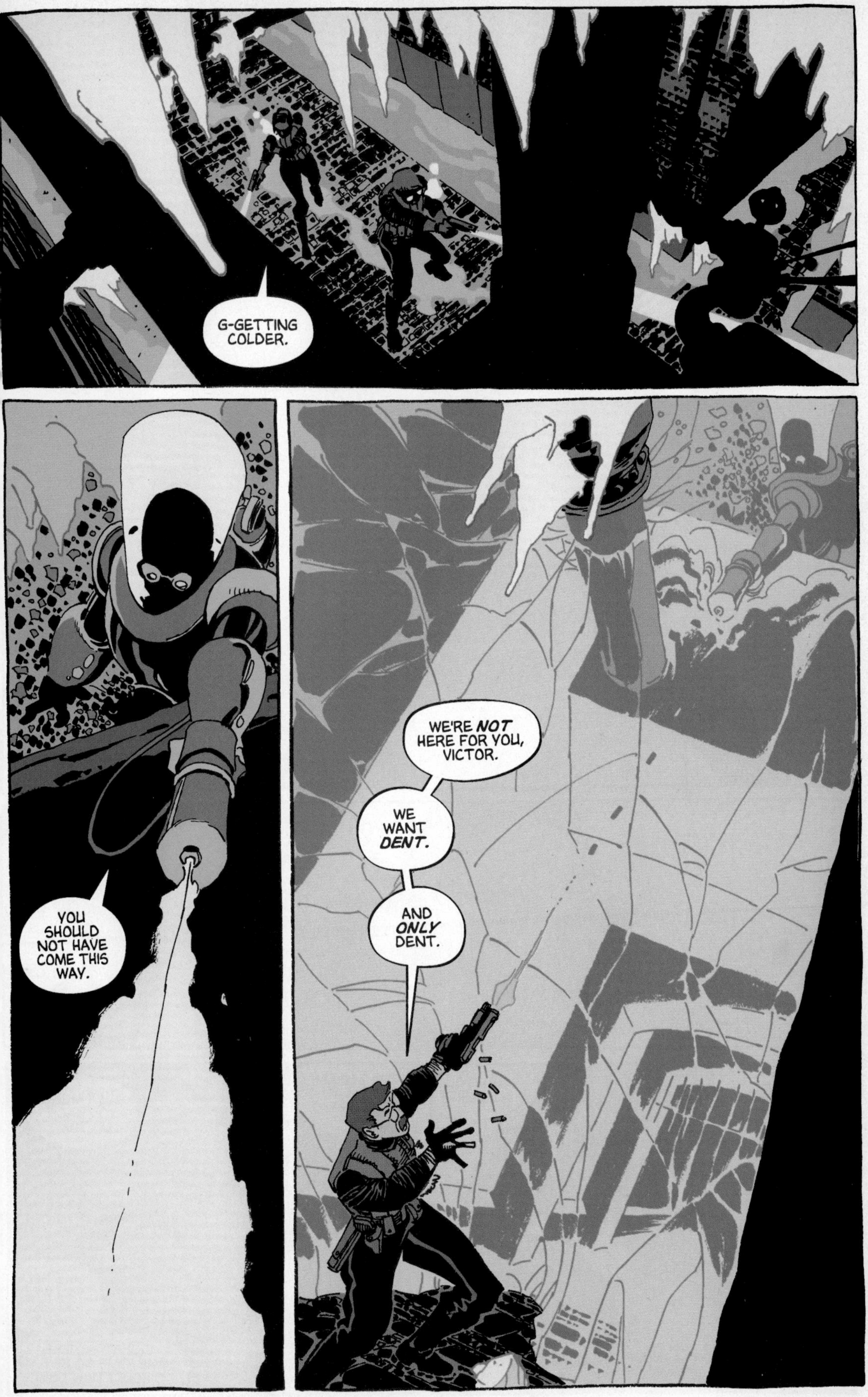
G-GETTING COLDER.
YOU SHOULD NOT HAVE COME THIS WAY.
WE'RE *NOT* HERE FOR YOU, VICTOR.
WE WANT *DENT.*
AND *ONLY* DENT.

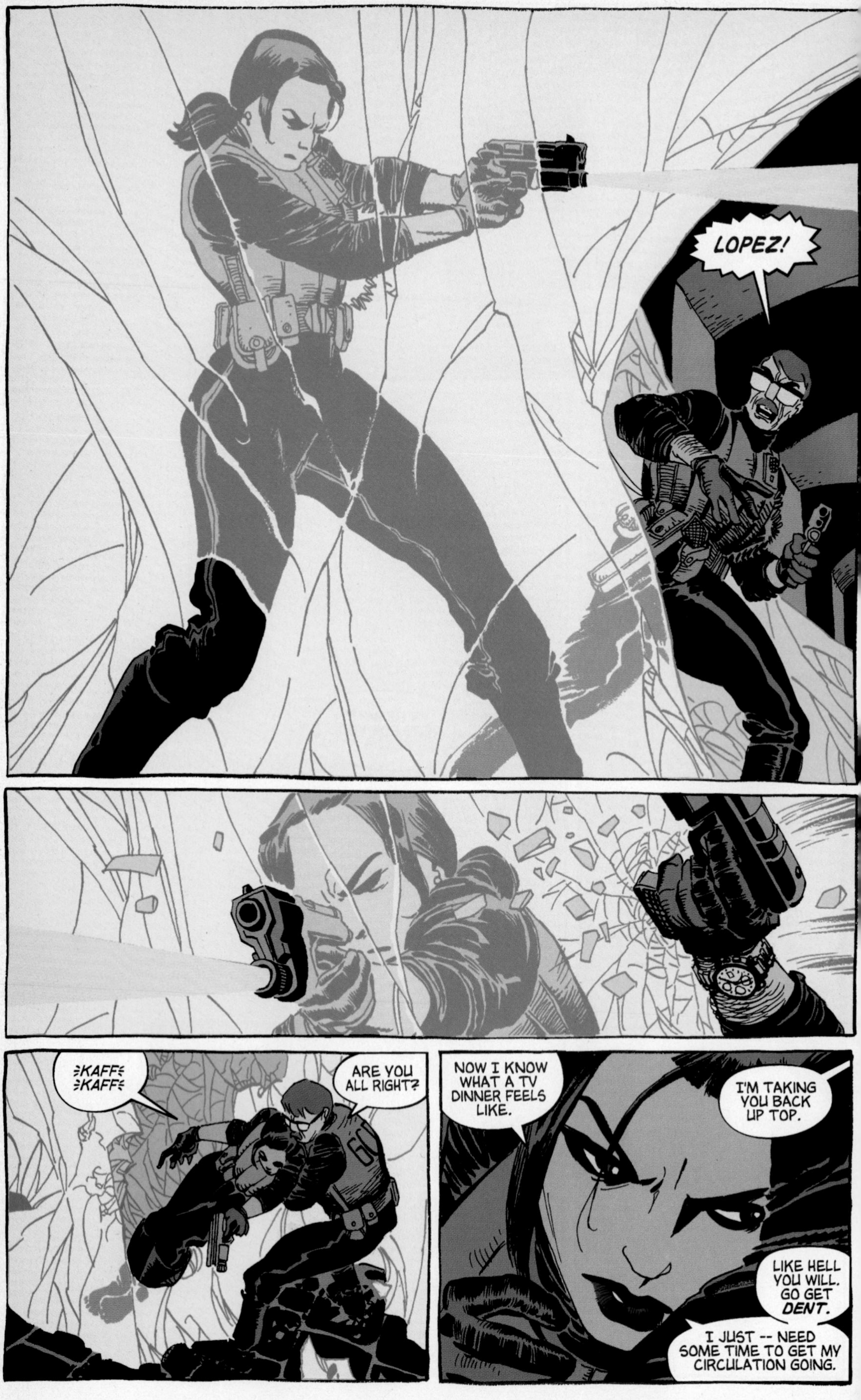
LOPEZ!
ƎKAFFƎ ƎKAFFƎ
ARE YOU ALL RIGHT?
NOW I KNOW WHAT A TV DINNER FEELS LIKE.
I'M TAKING YOU BACK UP TOP.
LIKE HELL YOU WILL. GO GET DENT.
I JUST -- NEED SOME TIME TO GET MY CIRCULATION GOING.

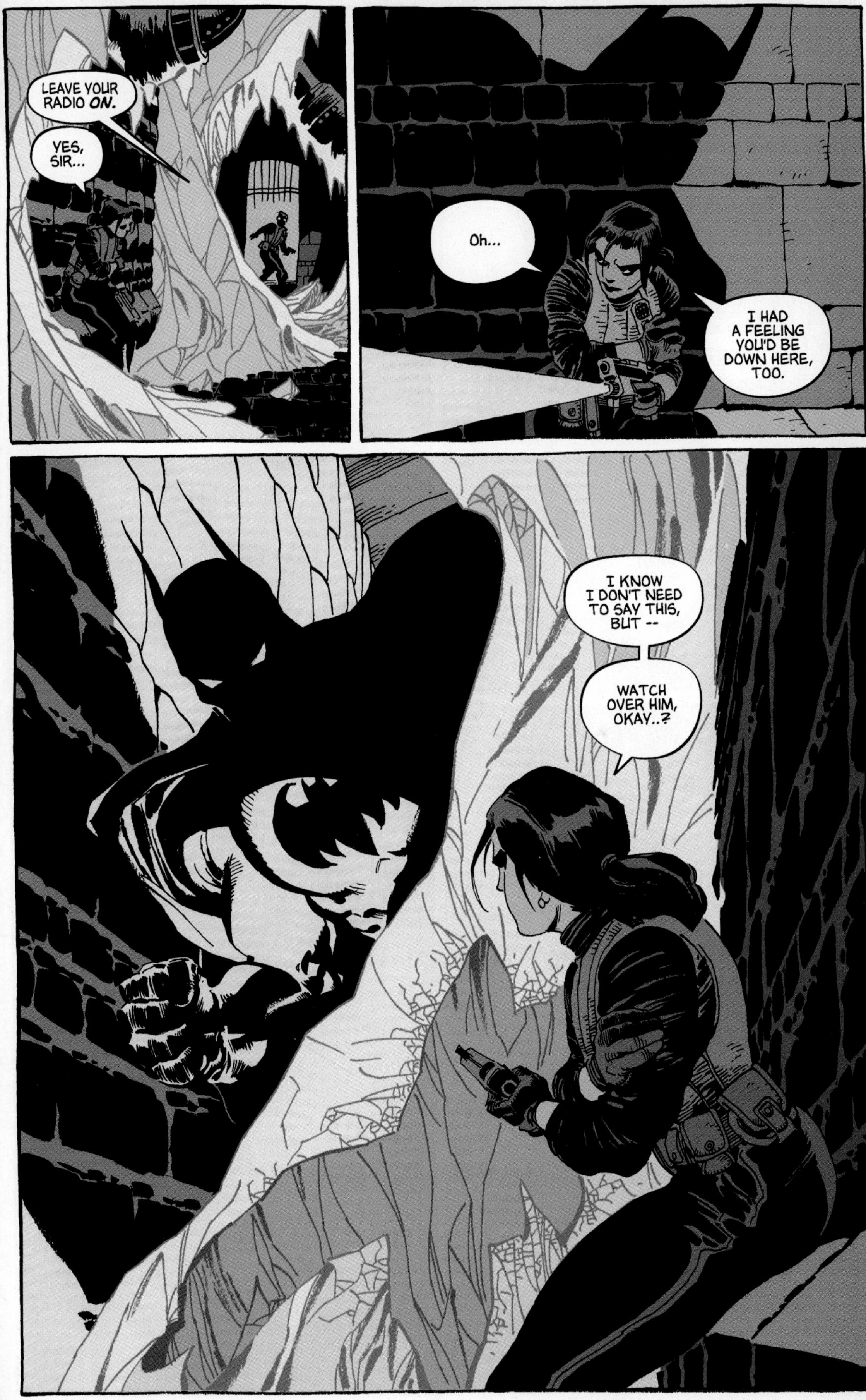
LEAVE YOUR RADIO ON.
YES, SIR...
Oh...
I HAD A FEELING YOU'D BE DOWN HERE, TOO.
I KNOW I DON'T NEED TO SAY THIS, BUT --
WATCH OVER HIM, OKAY..?

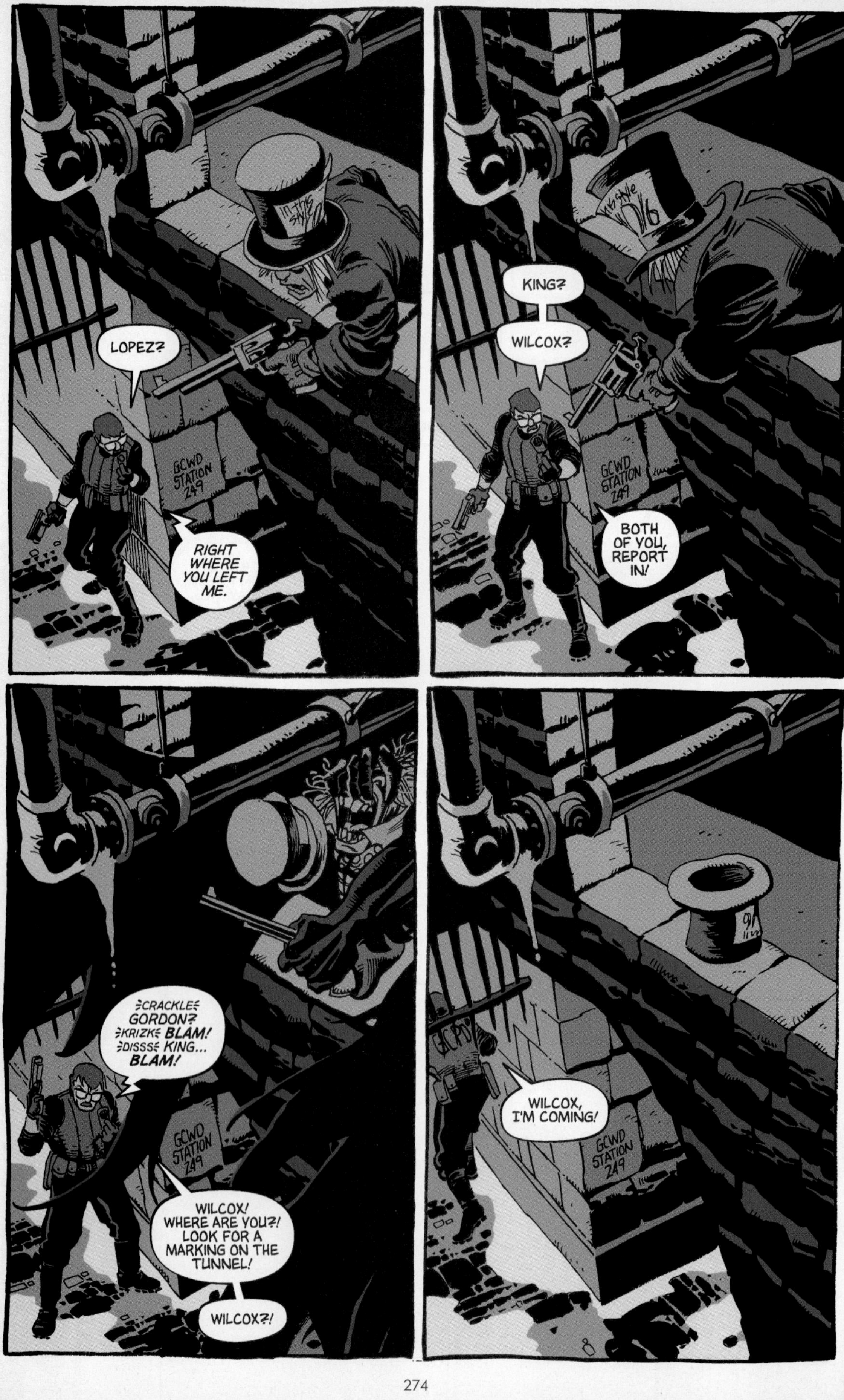

LOPEZ?
RIGHT WHERE YOU LEFT ME.
KING?
WILCOX?
BOTH OF YOU, REPORT IN!
CRACKLE GORDON? KRIZK BLAM! DISSS KING... BLAM!
WILCOX! WHERE ARE YOU?! LOOK FOR A MARKING ON THE TUNNEL!
WILCOX?!
WILCOX, I'M COMING!

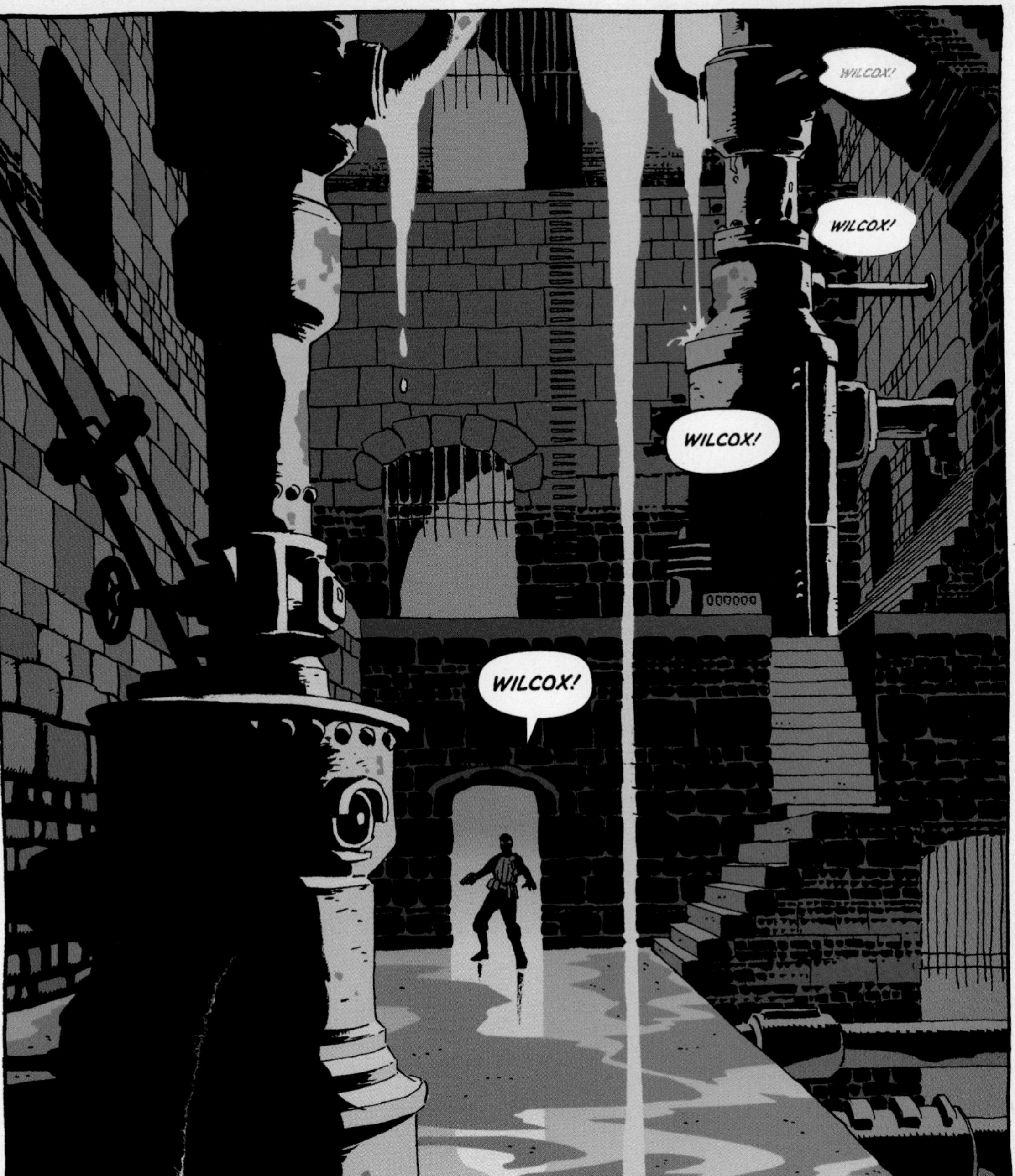
WILCOX!
WILCOX!
WILCOX!
WILCOX!

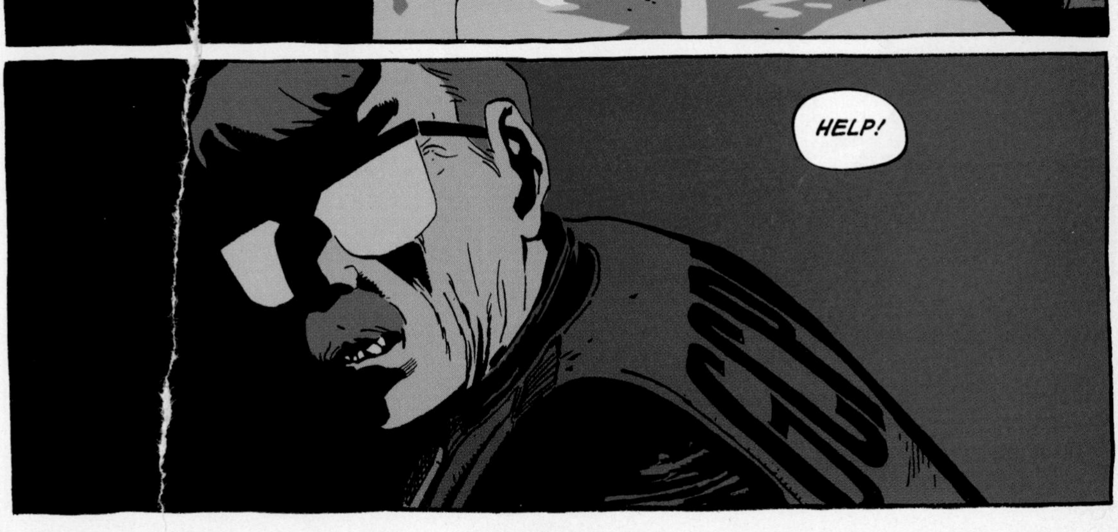
HELP!

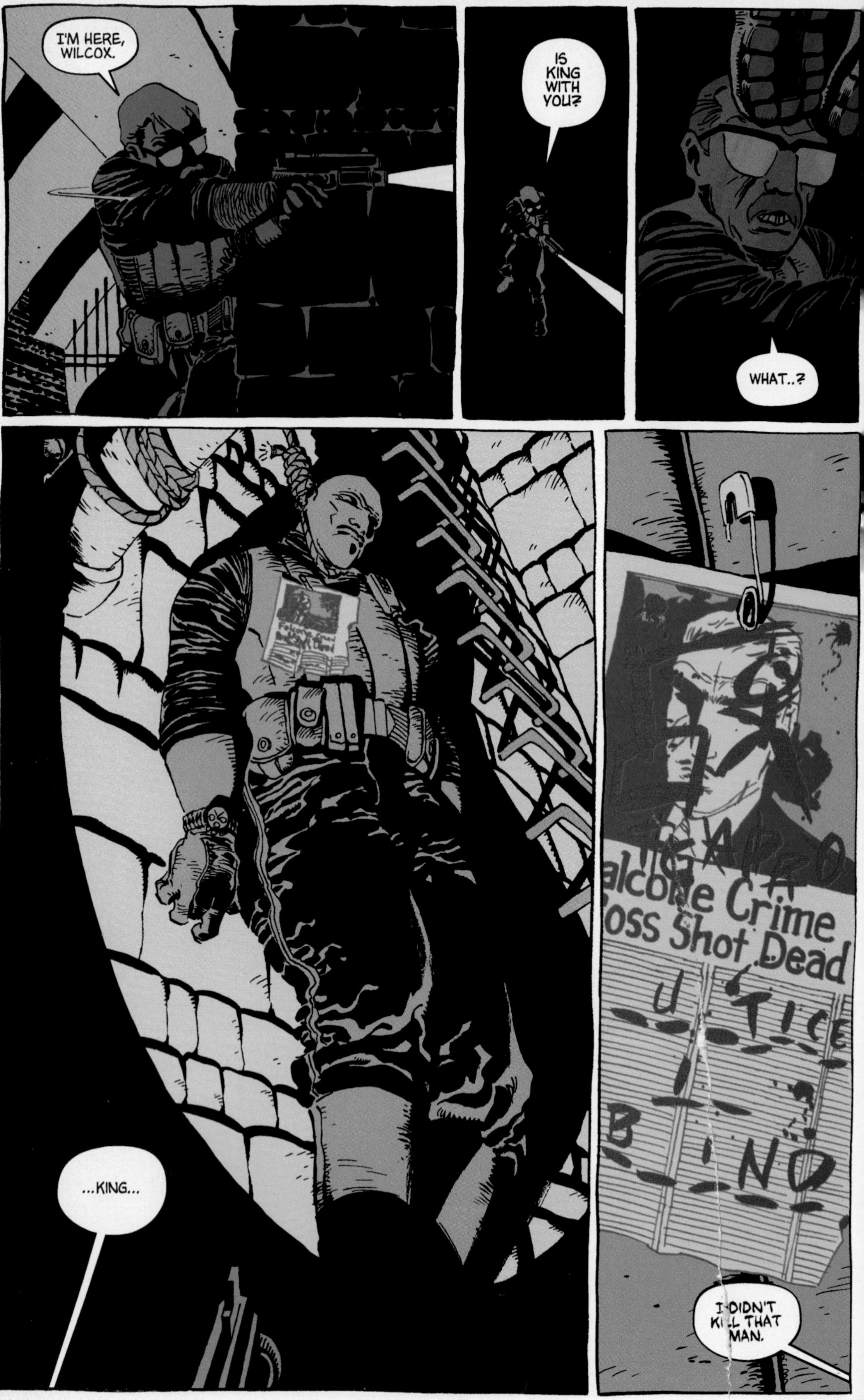
I'M HERE, WILCOX.
IS KING WITH YOU?
WHAT..?
...KING...
alcone Crime
oss Shot Dead
I DIDN'T KILL THAT MAN.

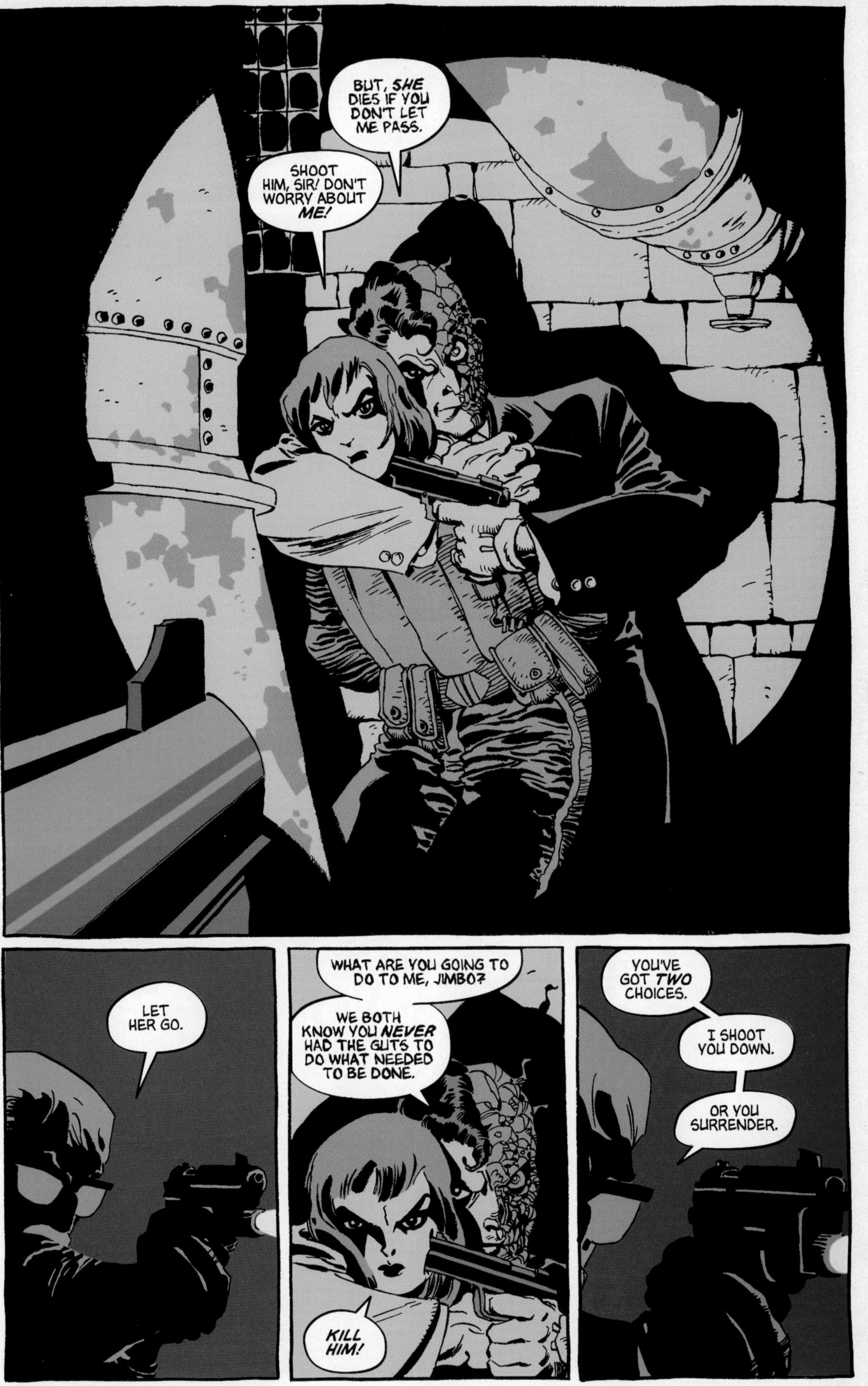
BUT, *SHE* DIES IF YOU DON'T LET ME PASS.
SHOOT HIM, SIR! DON'T WORRY ABOUT *ME!*
LET HER GO.
WHAT ARE YOU GOING TO DO TO ME, JIMBO?
WE BOTH KNOW YOU *NEVER* HAD THE GUTS TO DO WHAT NEEDED TO BE DONE.
KILL HIM!
YOU'VE GOT *TWO* CHOICES.
I SHOOT YOU DOWN.
OR YOU SURRENDER.

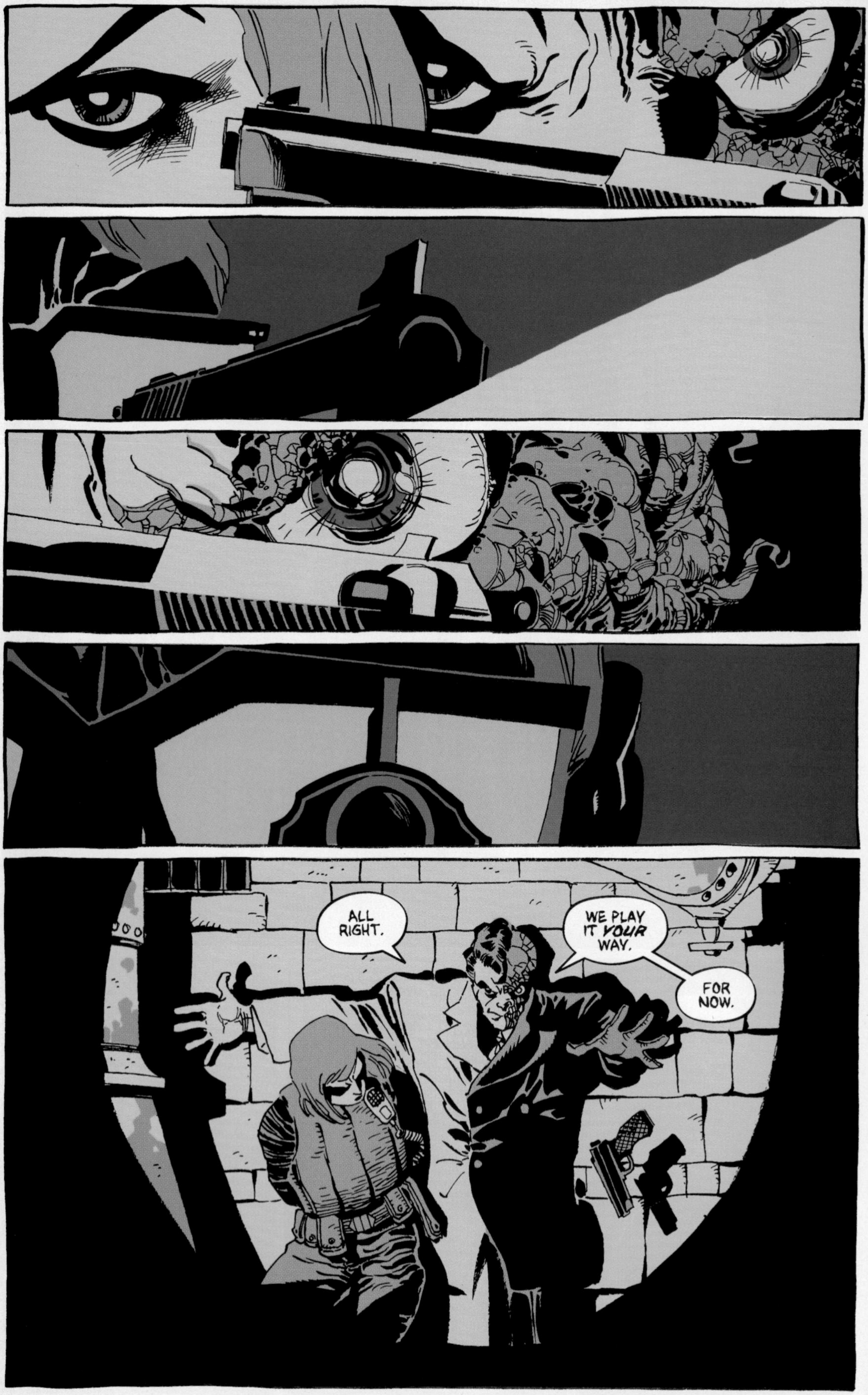
ALL RIGHT.
WE PLAY IT YOUR WAY.
FOR NOW.

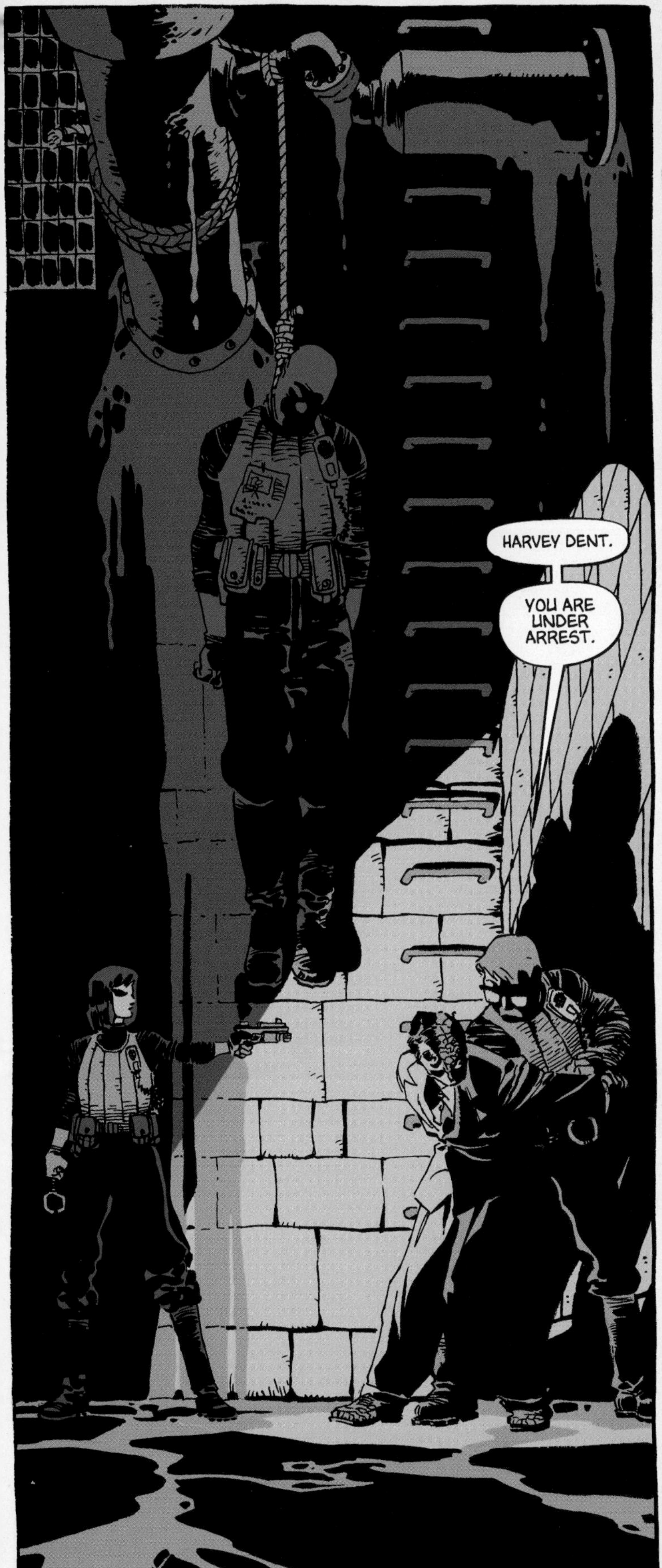
HARVEY DENT.
YOU ARE UNDER ARREST.

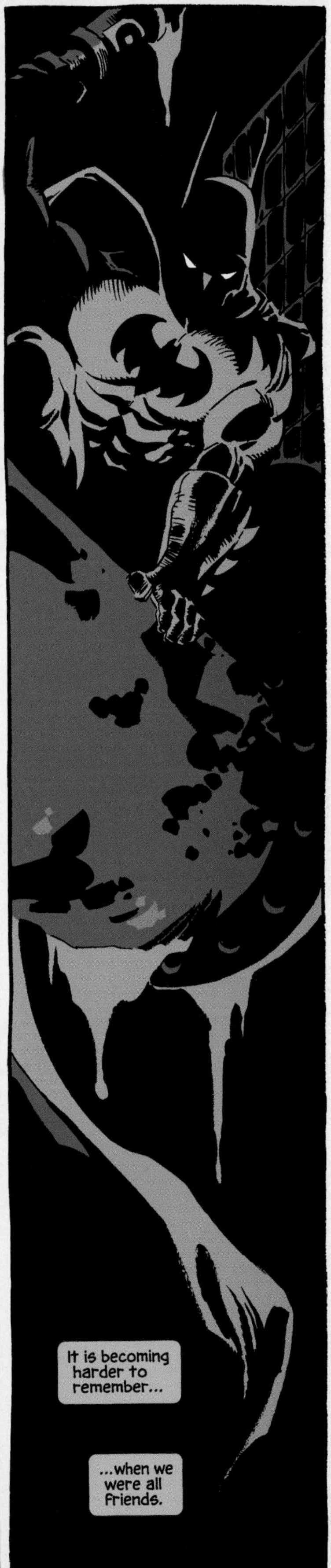
It is becoming harder to remember...
...when we were all friends.

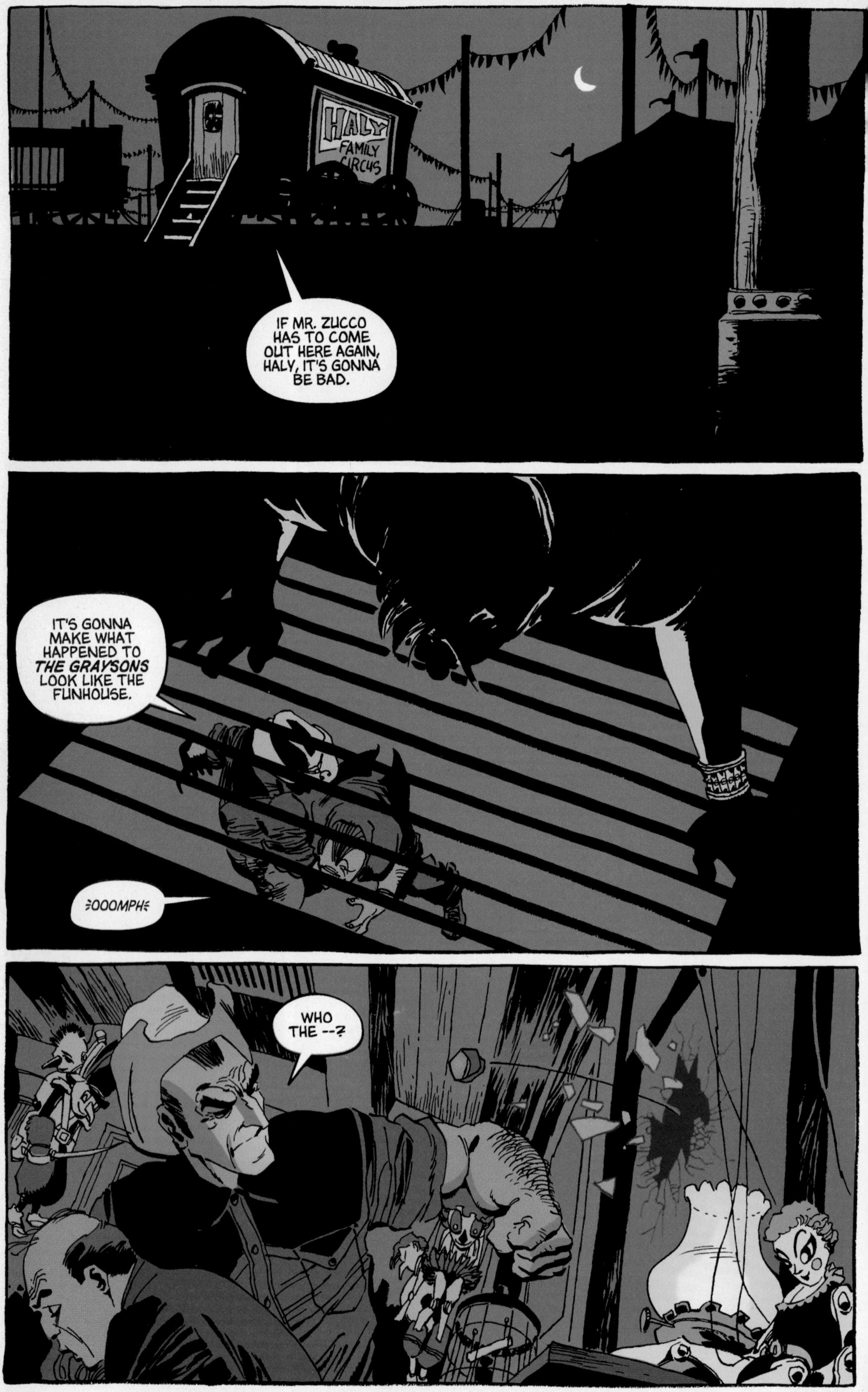
HALY FAMILY CIRCUS
IF MR. ZUCCO HAS TO COME OUT HERE AGAIN, HALY, IT'S GONNA BE BAD.
IT'S GONNA MAKE WHAT HAPPENED TO THE GRAYSONS LOOK LIKE THE FUNHOUSE.
OOOMPH
WHO THE --?

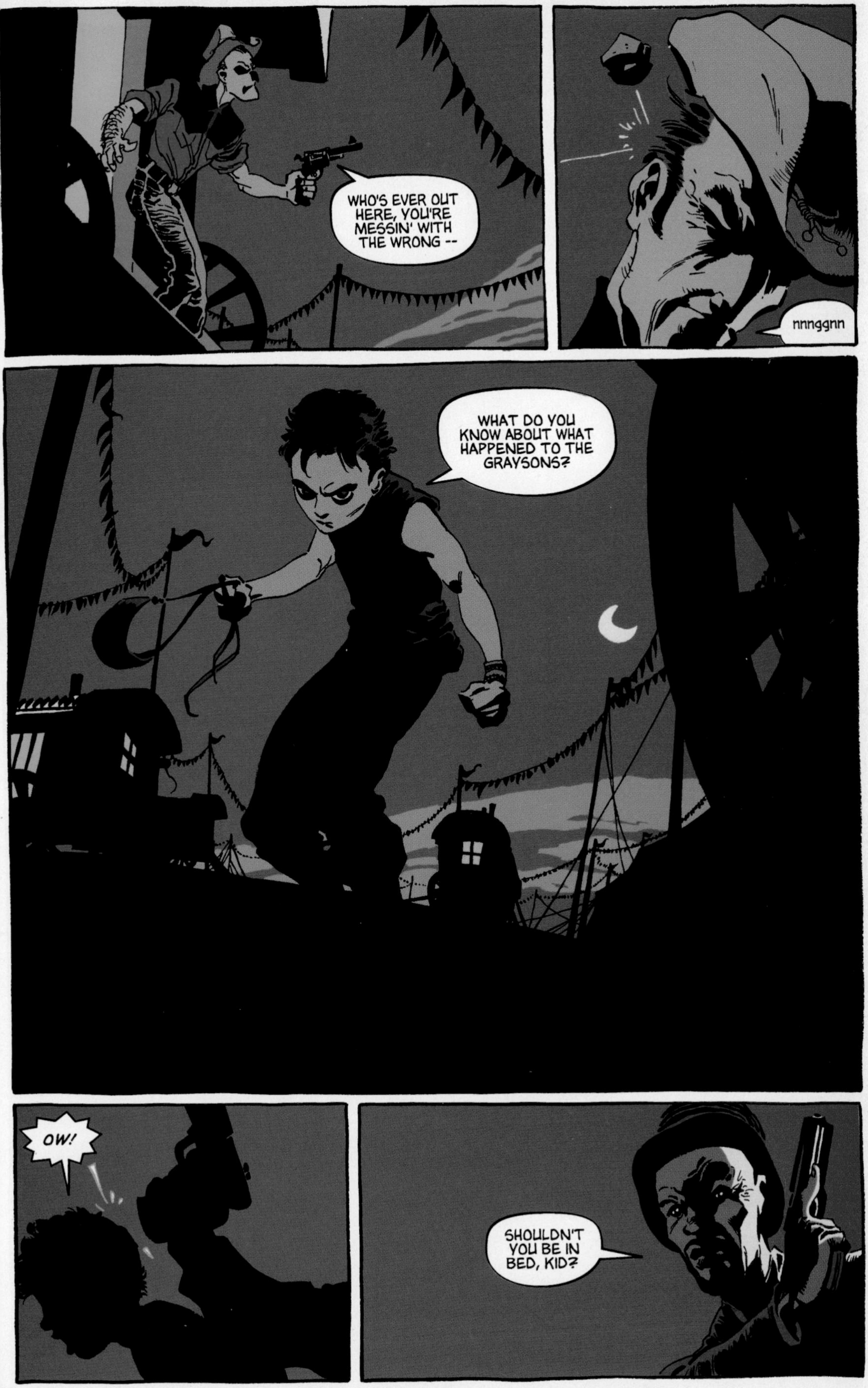
WHO'S EVER OUT HERE, YOU'RE MESSIN' WITH THE WRONG --
nnnggnn
WHAT DO YOU KNOW ABOUT WHAT HAPPENED TO THE GRAYSONS?
OW!
SHOULDN'T YOU BE IN BED, KID?

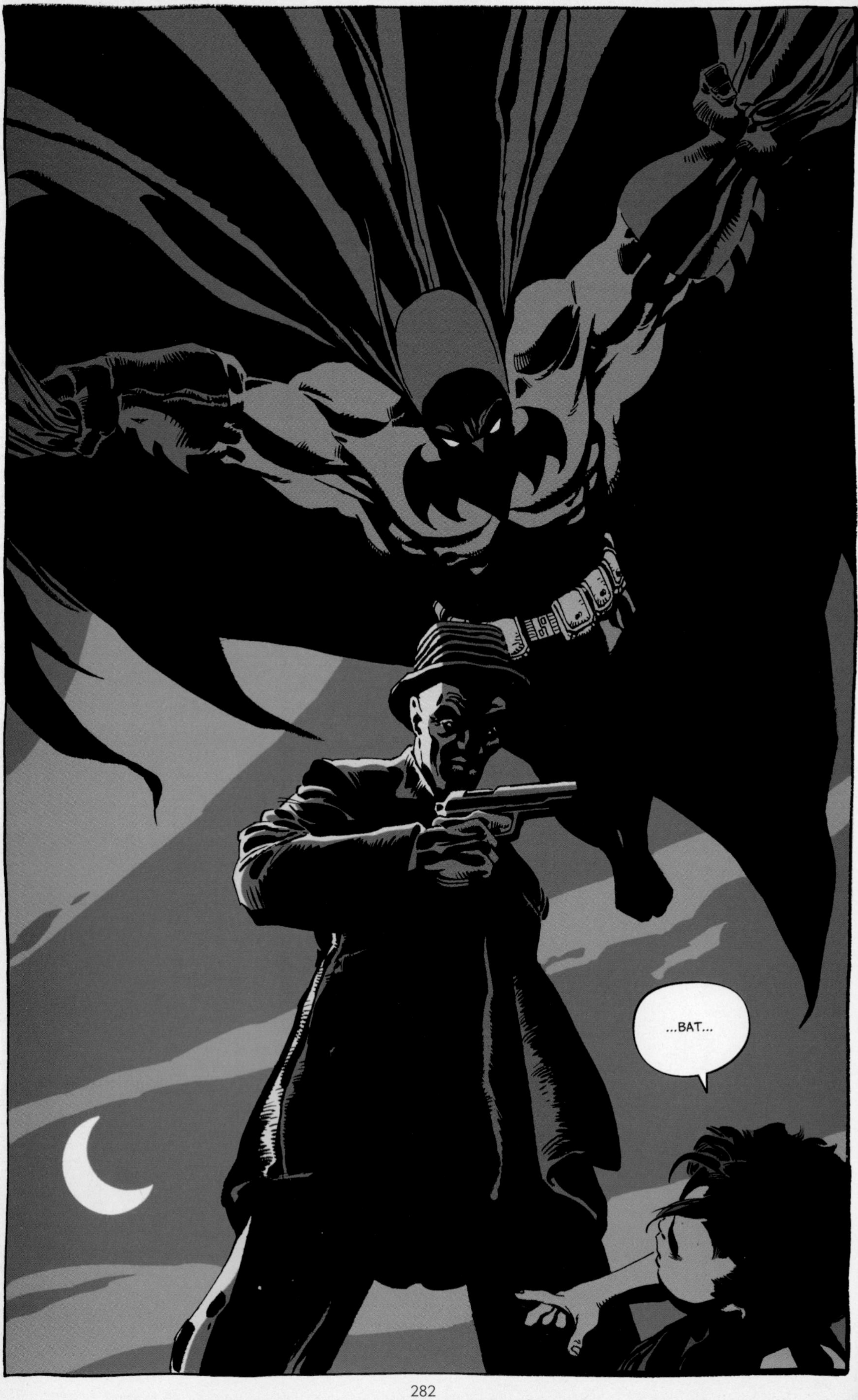
...BAT...

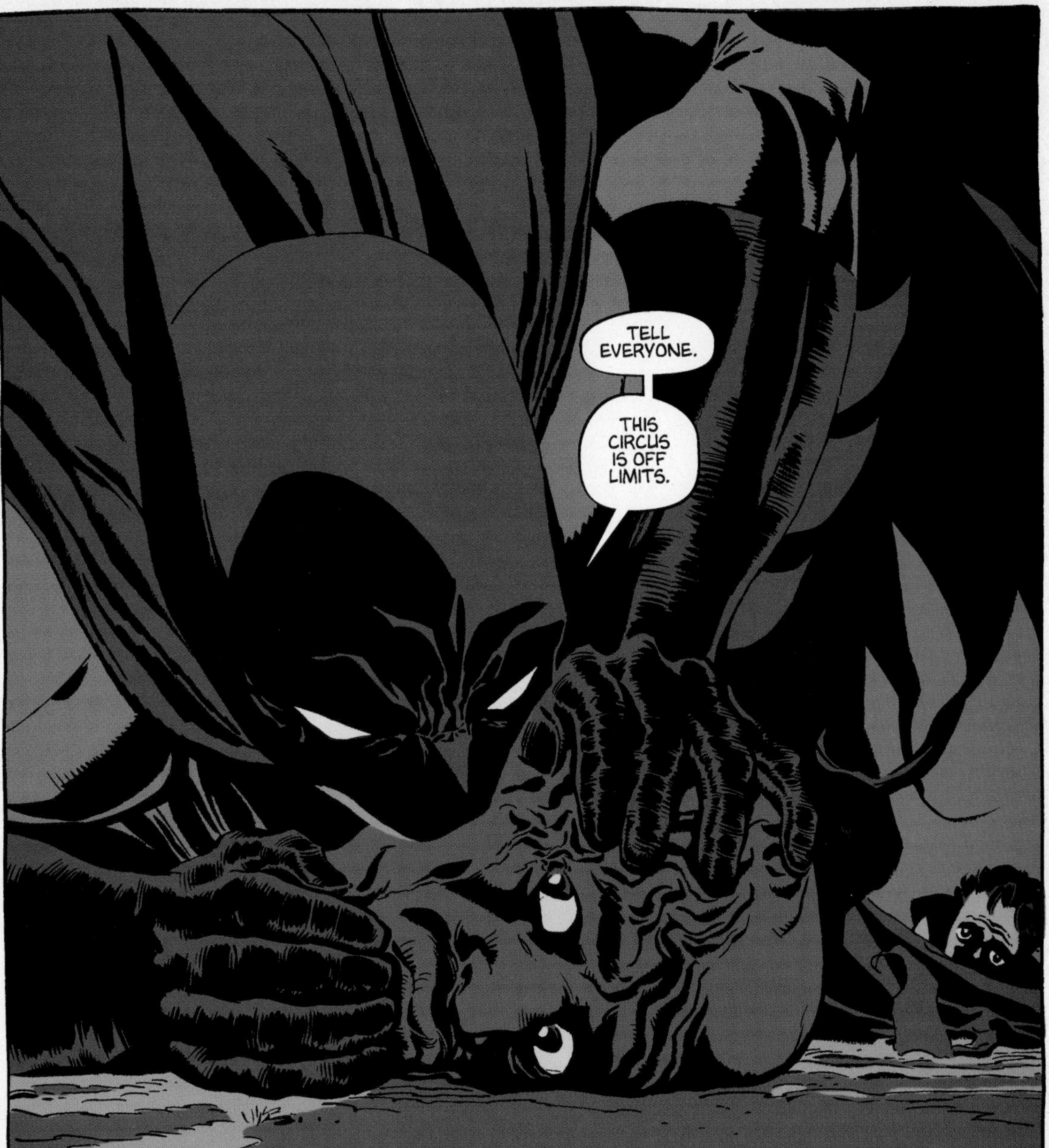
TELL EVERYONE.
THIS CIRCUS IS OFF LIMITS.

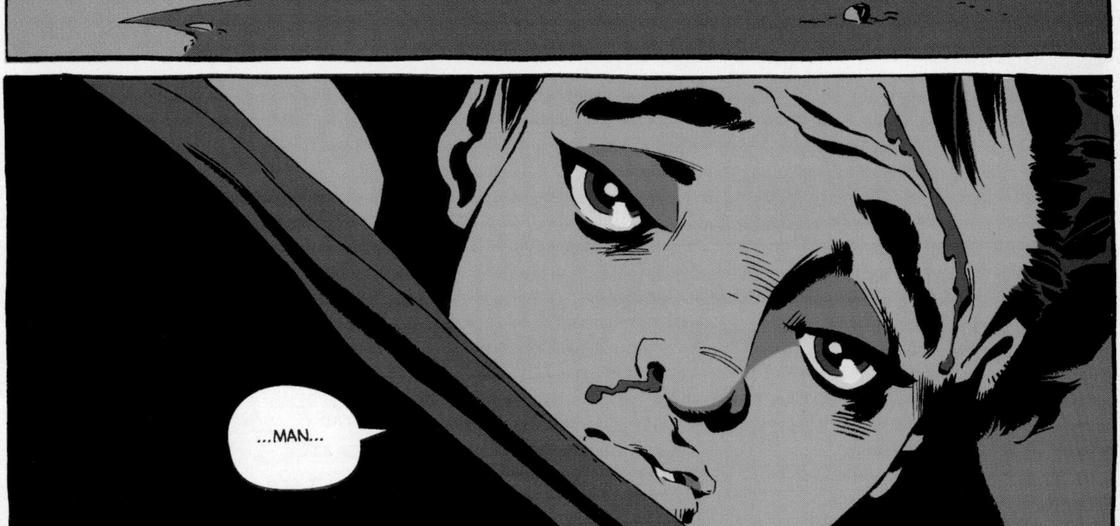
...MAN...

Just before the **acid** was thrown in his face...

...I was nearly ready to tell Harvey Dent **the truth**.

WHAT... WHAT IS THIS PLACE?

About who I was. About my parents. All of it.

I NEVER THOUGHT TO GIVE IT A NAME.

YOU WANT TO FIND OUT WHO KILLED YOUR MOTHER AND FATHER.

YES.

I CAN'T LET YOU GO OUT THERE. **UNTRAINED.**

ALL YOU'LL DO IS GET **HURT** OR **WORSE.**

Had Harvey **known** he had someone who trusted him and believed in him...

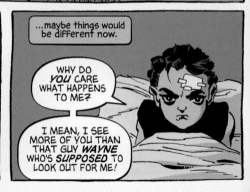

...maybe things would be different now.

WHY DO **YOU** CARE WHAT HAPPENS TO ME?

I MEAN, I SEE MORE OF YOU THAN THAT GUY **WAYNE** WHO'S **SUPPOSED** TO LOOK OUT FOR ME!

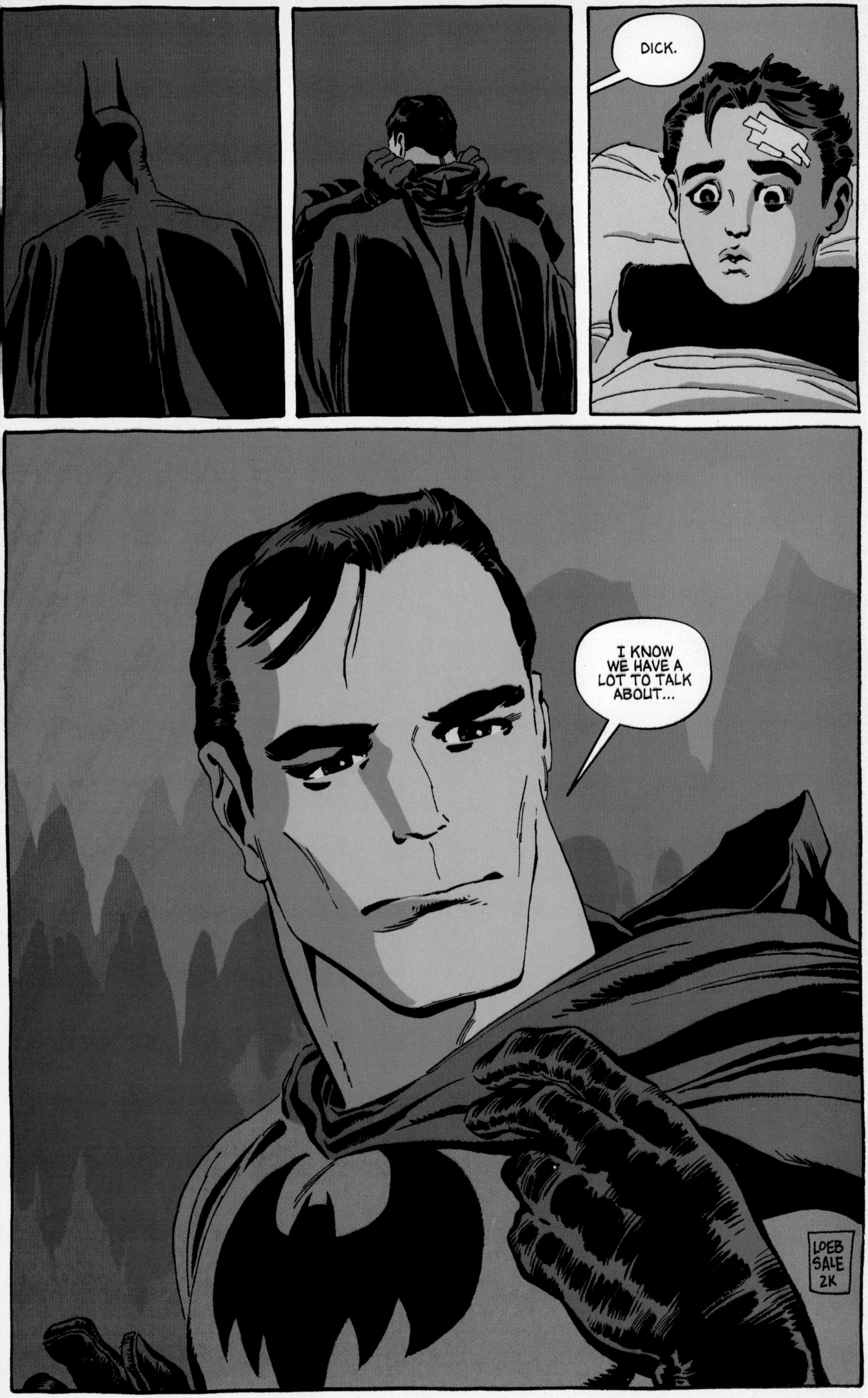
DICK.
I KNOW WE HAVE A LOT TO TALK ABOUT...
LOEB SALE 2K

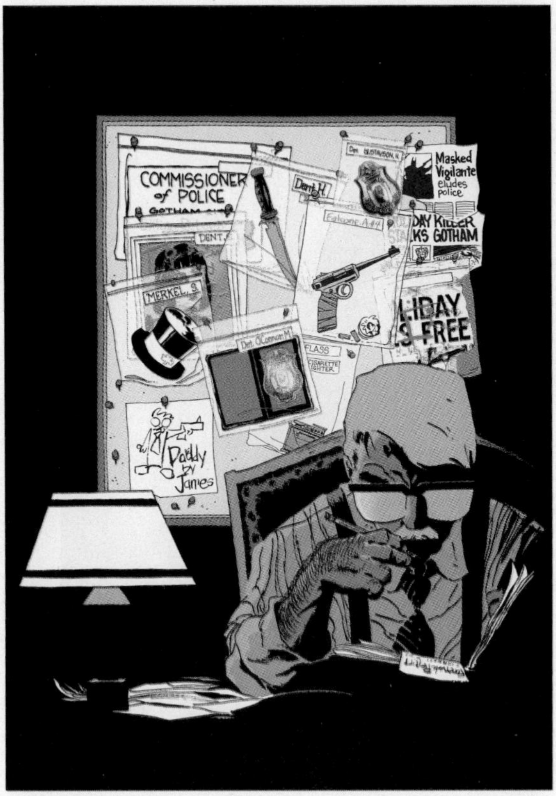
COMMISSIONER
of POLICE
Masked Vigilante
eludes police
MERKEL, S.
FLASS
Daddy
by
James

11

PASSION

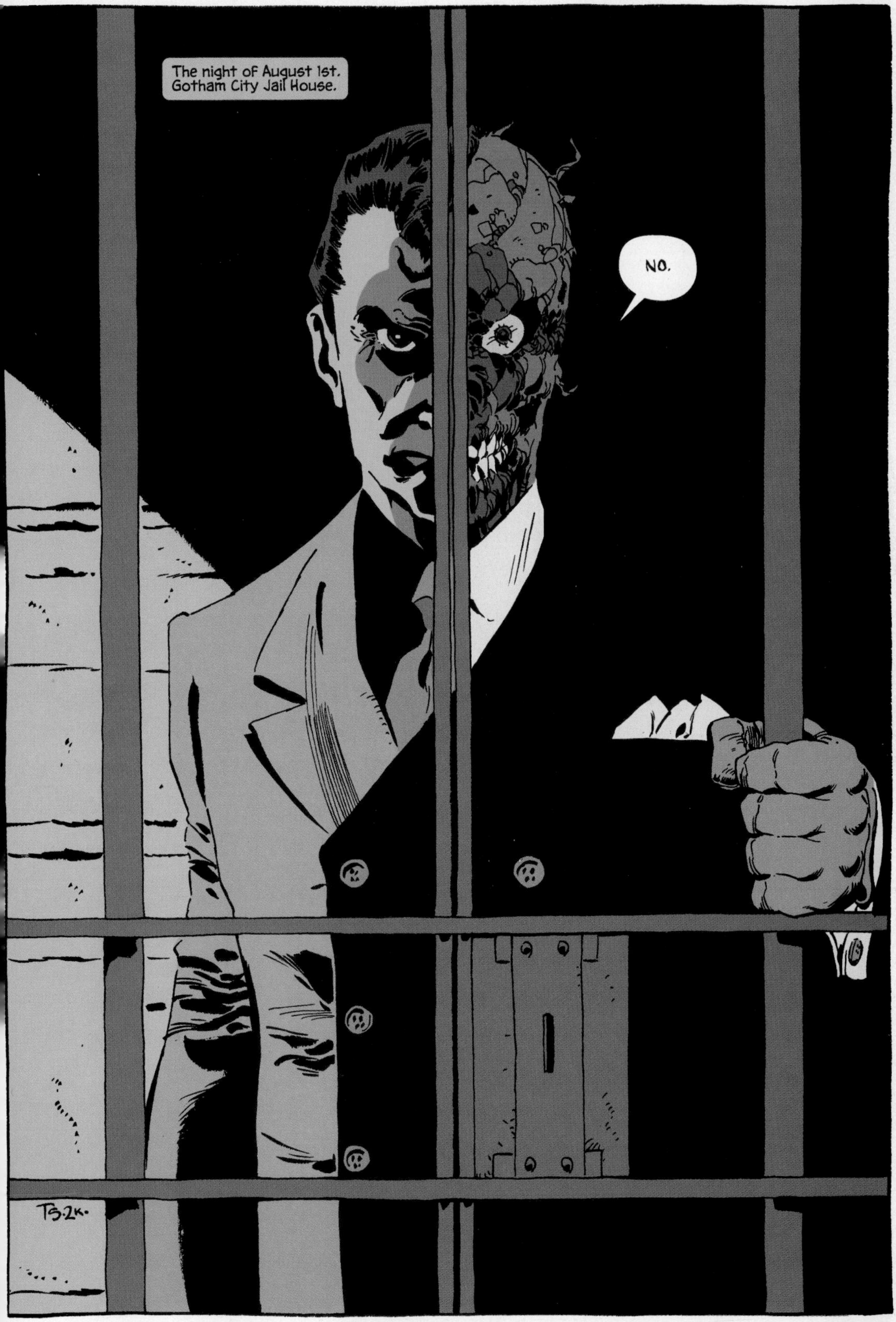
The night of August 1st.
Gotham City Jail House.
NO.
TS.2K.

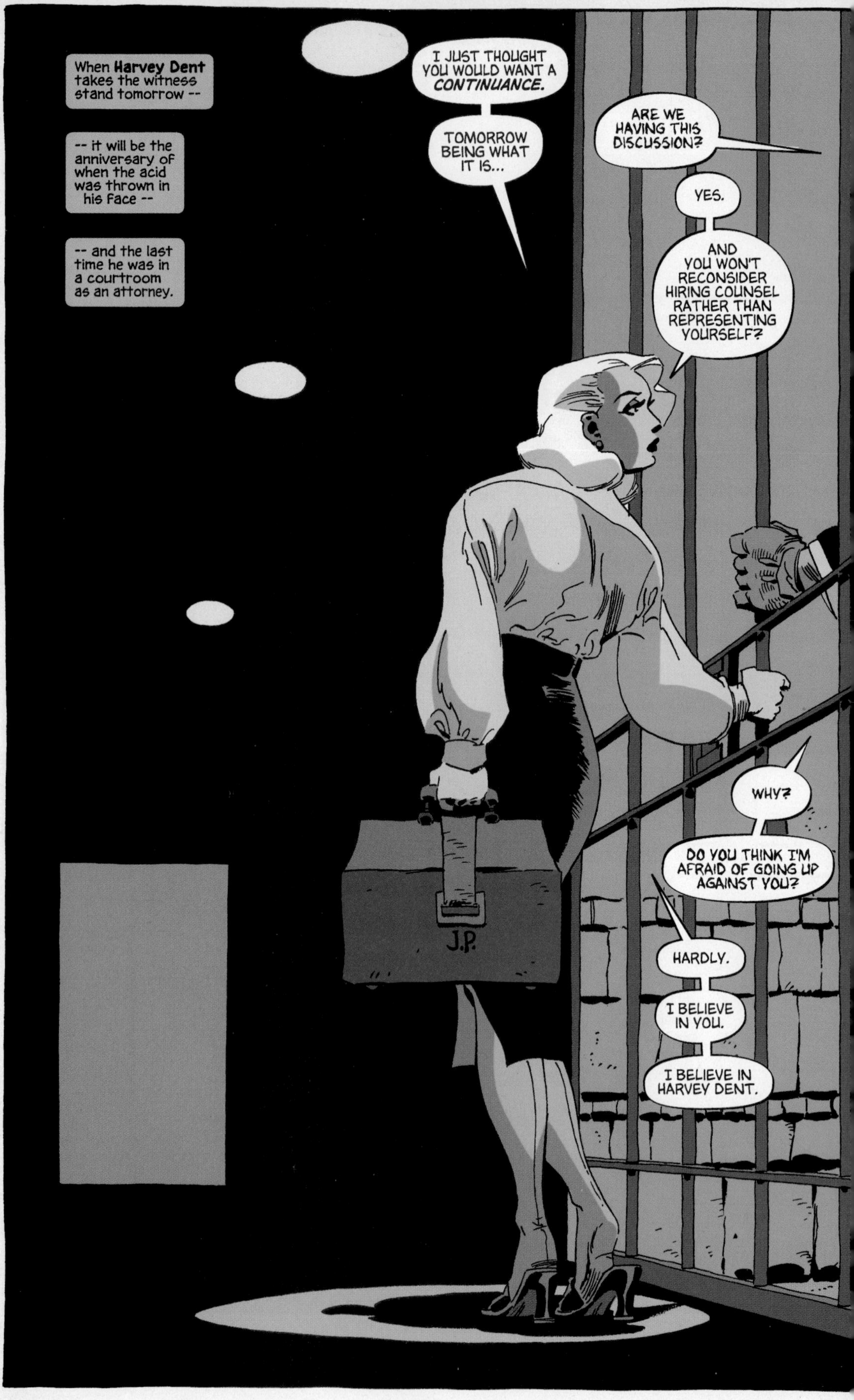

When Harvey Dent takes the witness stand tomorrow --
-- it will be the anniversary of when the acid was thrown in his face --
-- and the last time he was in a courtroom as an attorney.
I JUST THOUGHT YOU WOULD WANT A CONTINUANCE.
TOMORROW BEING WHAT IT IS...
ARE WE HAVING THIS DISCUSSION?
YES.
AND YOU WON'T RECONSIDER HIRING COUNSEL RATHER THAN REPRESENTING YOURSELF?
WHY?
DO YOU THINK I'M AFRAID OF GOING UP AGAINST YOU?
HARDLY.
I BELIEVE IN YOU.
I BELIEVE IN HARVEY DENT.
J.P.

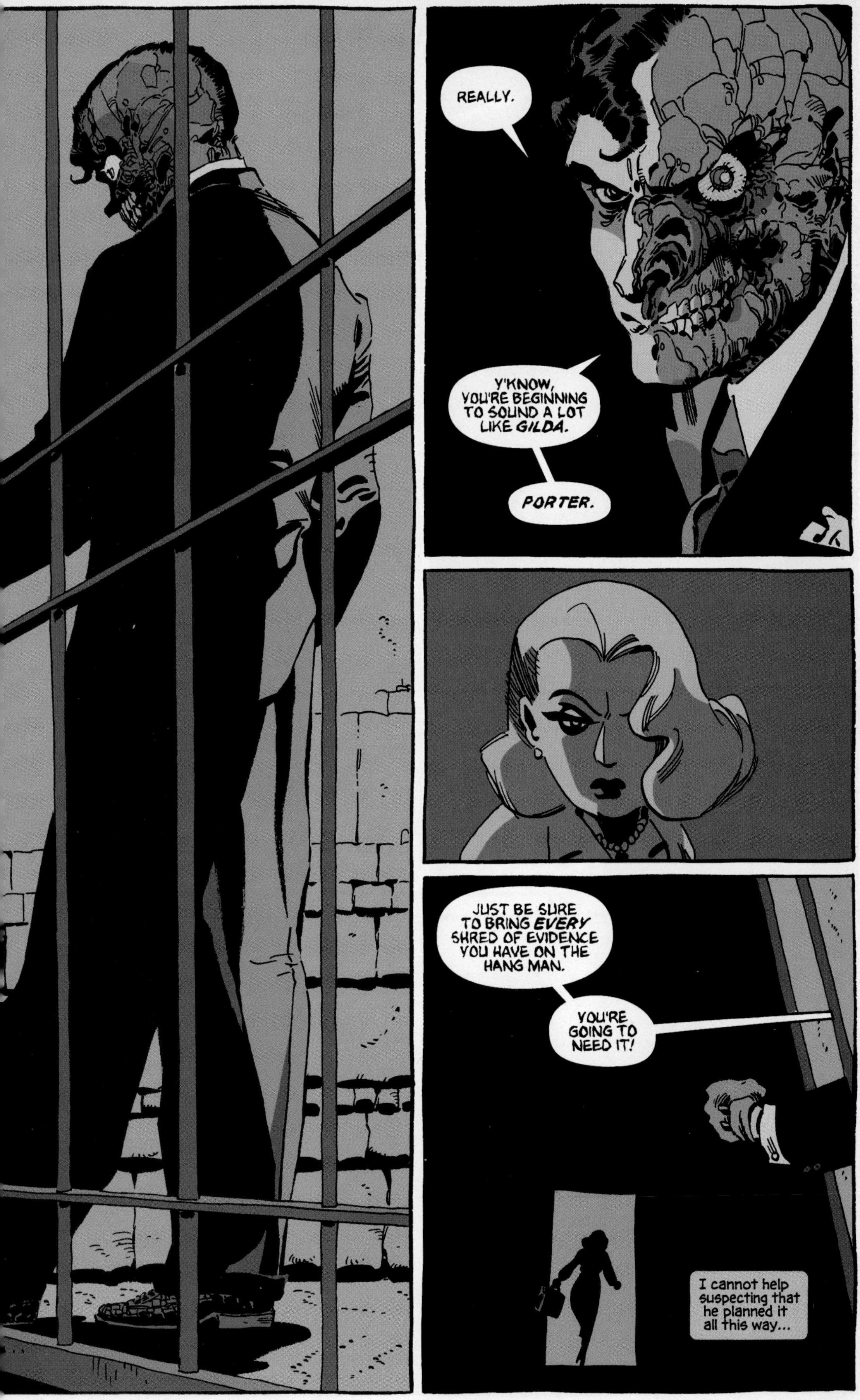

REALLY.
Y'KNOW, YOU'RE BEGINNING TO SOUND A LOT LIKE *GILDA*.
PORTER.
JUST BE SURE TO BRING *EVERY* SHRED OF EVIDENCE YOU HAVE ON THE HANG MAN.
YOU'RE GOING TO NEED IT!
I cannot help suspecting that he planned it all this way...

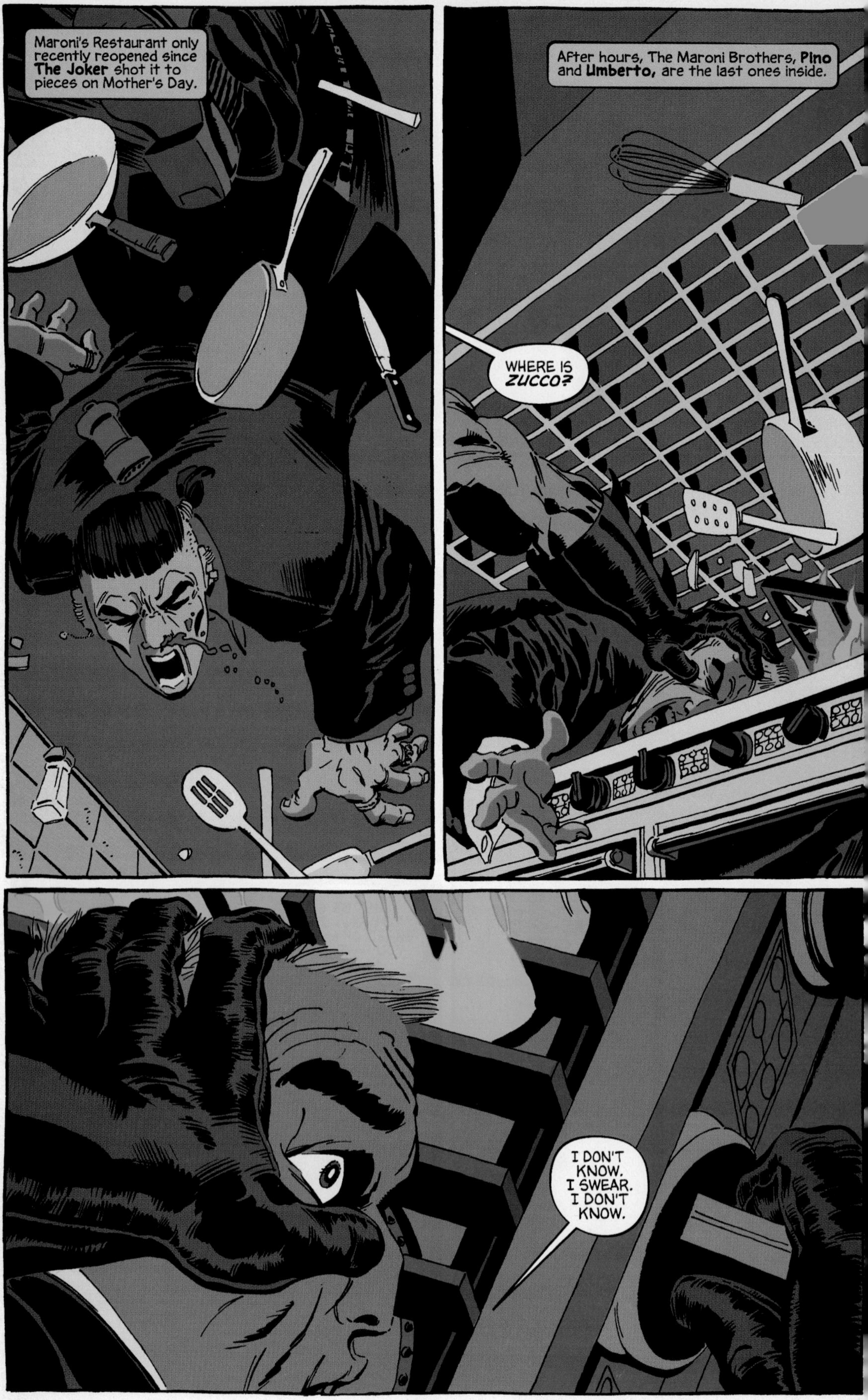
Maroni's Restaurant only recently reopened since The Joker shot it to pieces on Mother's Day.
After hours, The Maroni Brothers, Pino and Umberto, are the last ones inside.
WHERE IS ZUCCO?
I DON'T KNOW. I SWEAR. I DON'T KNOW.

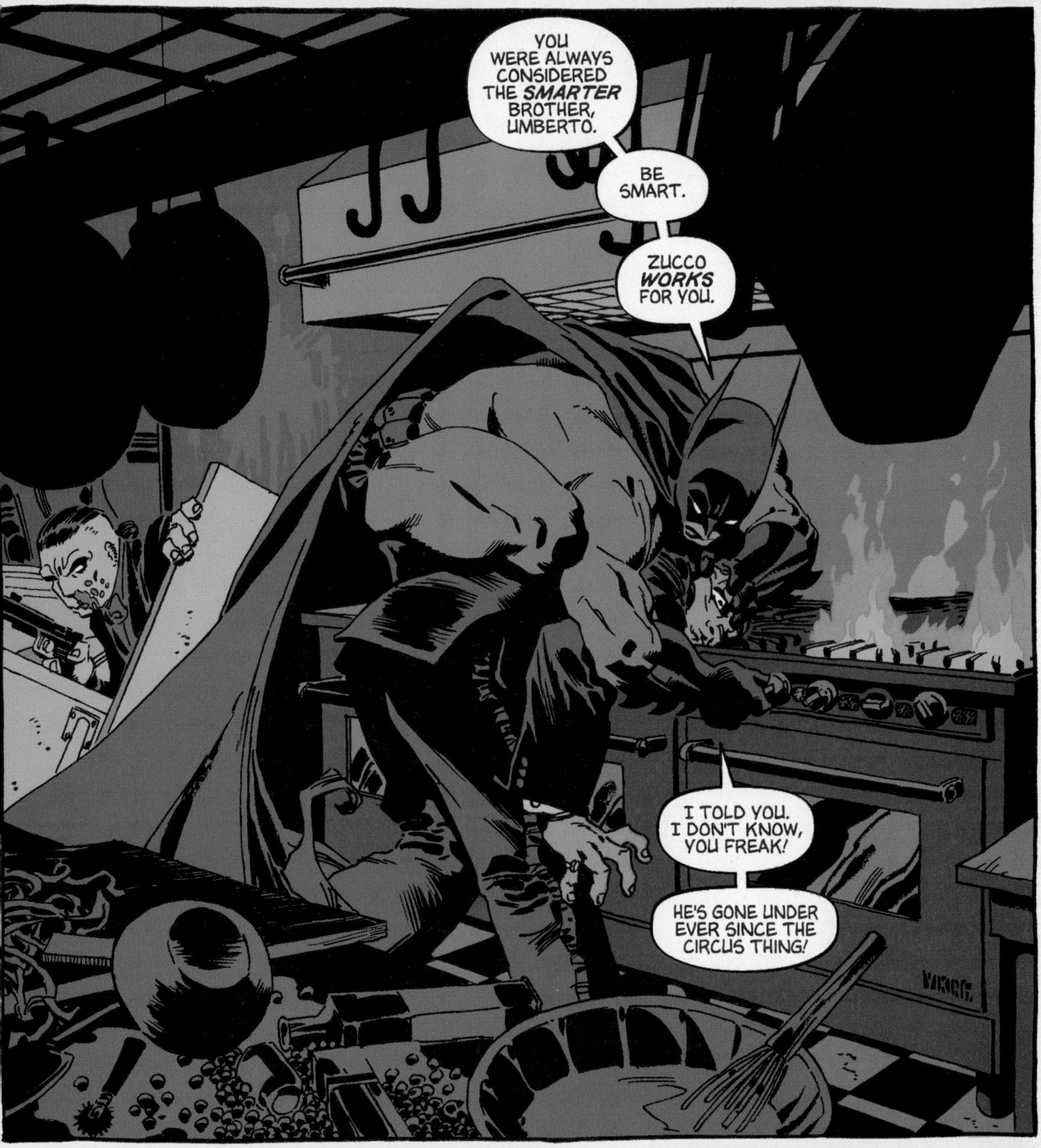
YOU WERE ALWAYS CONSIDERED THE SMARTER BROTHER, UMBERTO.
BE SMART.
ZUCCO WORKS FOR YOU.
I TOLD YOU. I DON'T KNOW, YOU FREAK!
HE'S GONE UNDER EVER SINCE THE CIRCUS THING!
VIKING

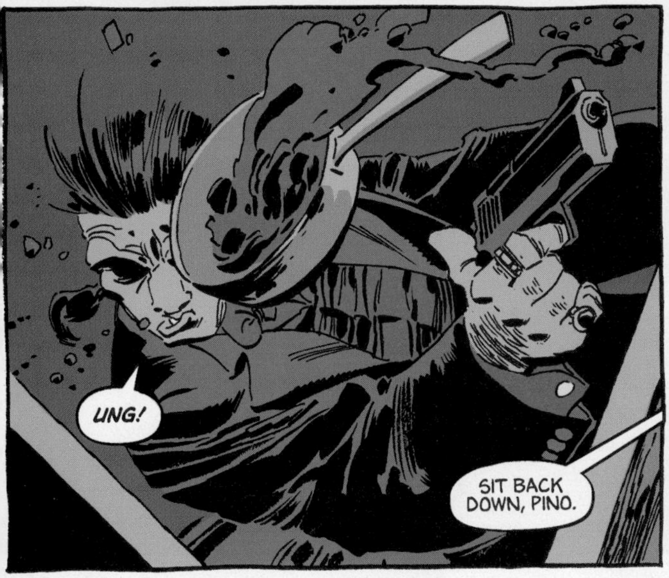
UNG!
SIT BACK DOWN, PINO.

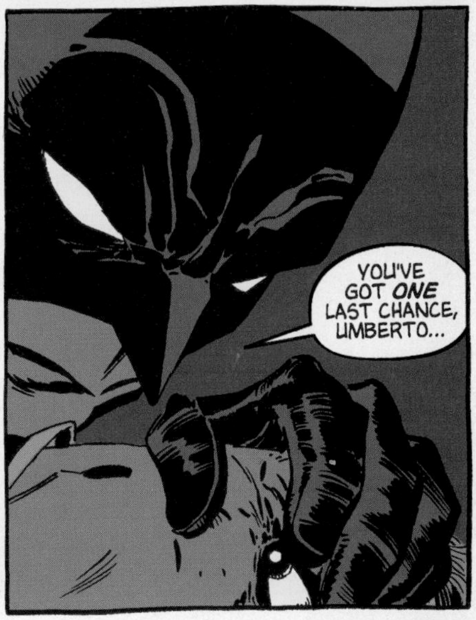
YOU'VE GOT ONE LAST CHANCE, UMBERTO...

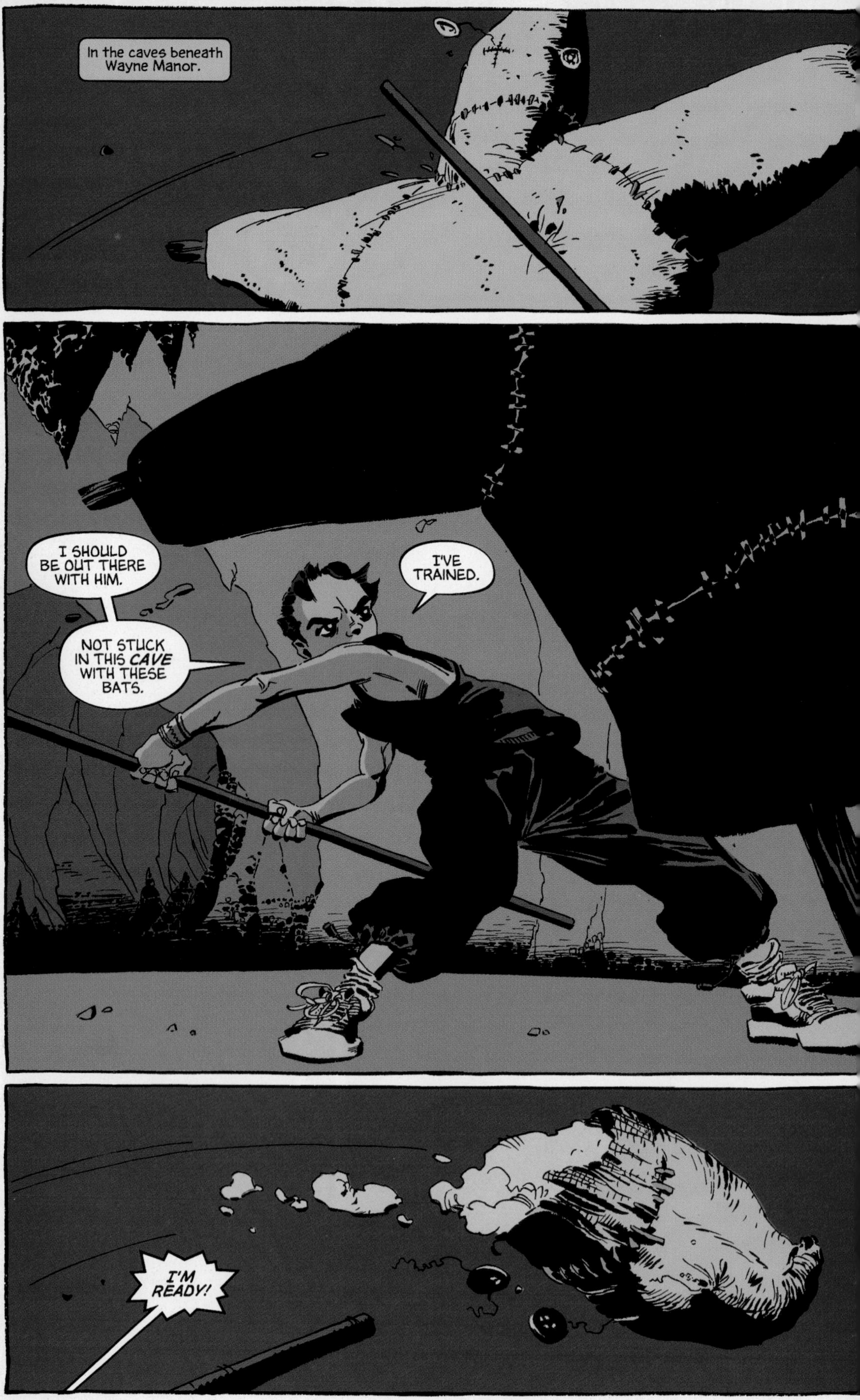
In the caves beneath Wayne Manor.
I SHOULD BE OUT THERE WITH HIM.
NOT STUCK IN THIS *CAVE* WITH THESE BATS.
I'VE TRAINED.
I'M READY!

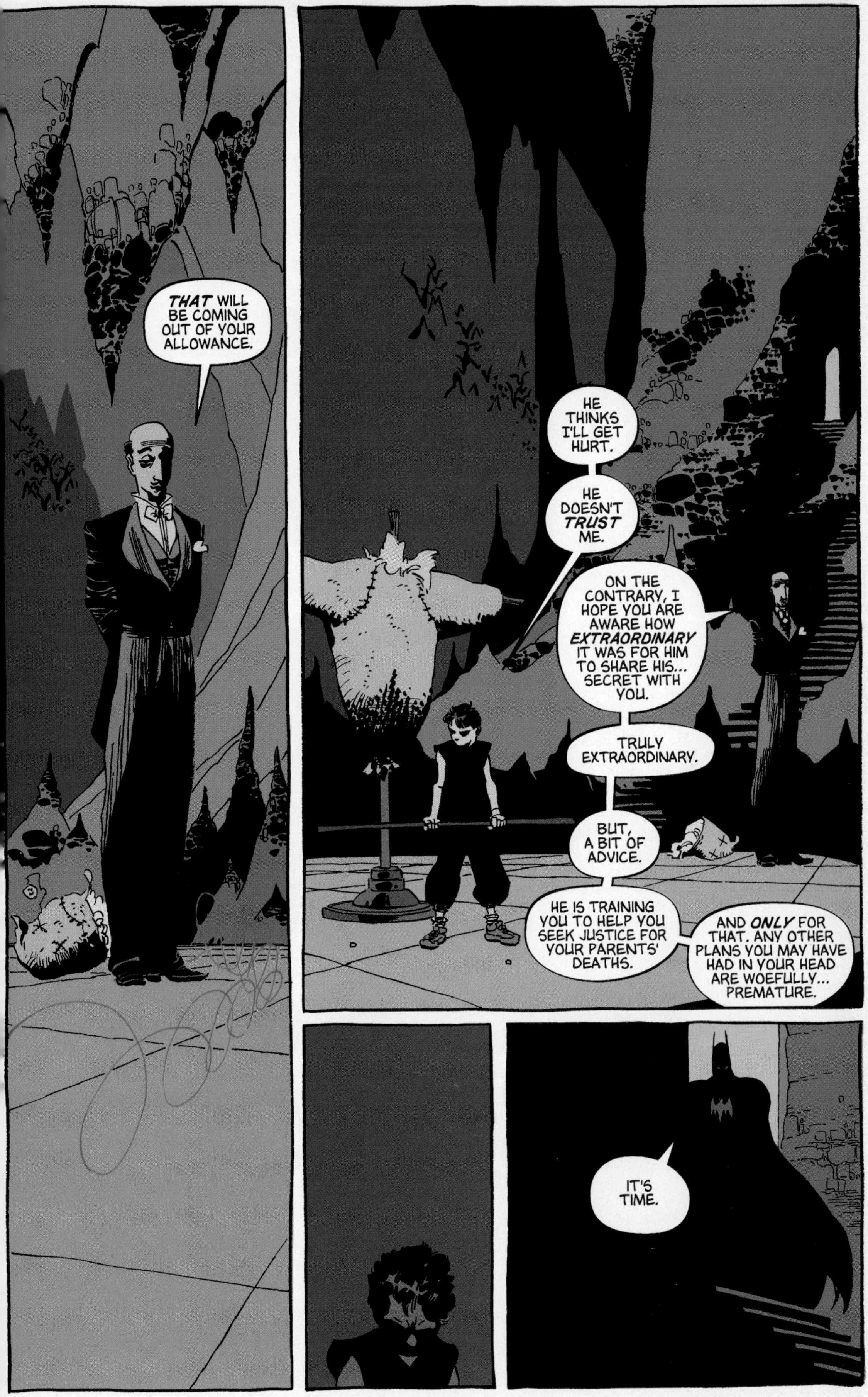
THAT WILL BE COMING OUT OF YOUR ALLOWANCE.
HE THINKS I'LL GET HURT.
HE DOESN'T TRUST ME.
ON THE CONTRARY, I HOPE YOU ARE AWARE HOW EXTRAORDINARY IT WAS FOR HIM TO SHARE HIS... SECRET WITH YOU.
TRULY EXTRAORDINARY.
BUT, A BIT OF ADVICE.
HE IS TRAINING YOU TO HELP YOU SEEK JUSTICE FOR YOUR PARENTS' DEATHS.
AND ONLY FOR THAT. ANY OTHER PLANS YOU MAY HAVE HAD IN YOUR HEAD ARE WOEFULLY... PREMATURE.
IT'S TIME.

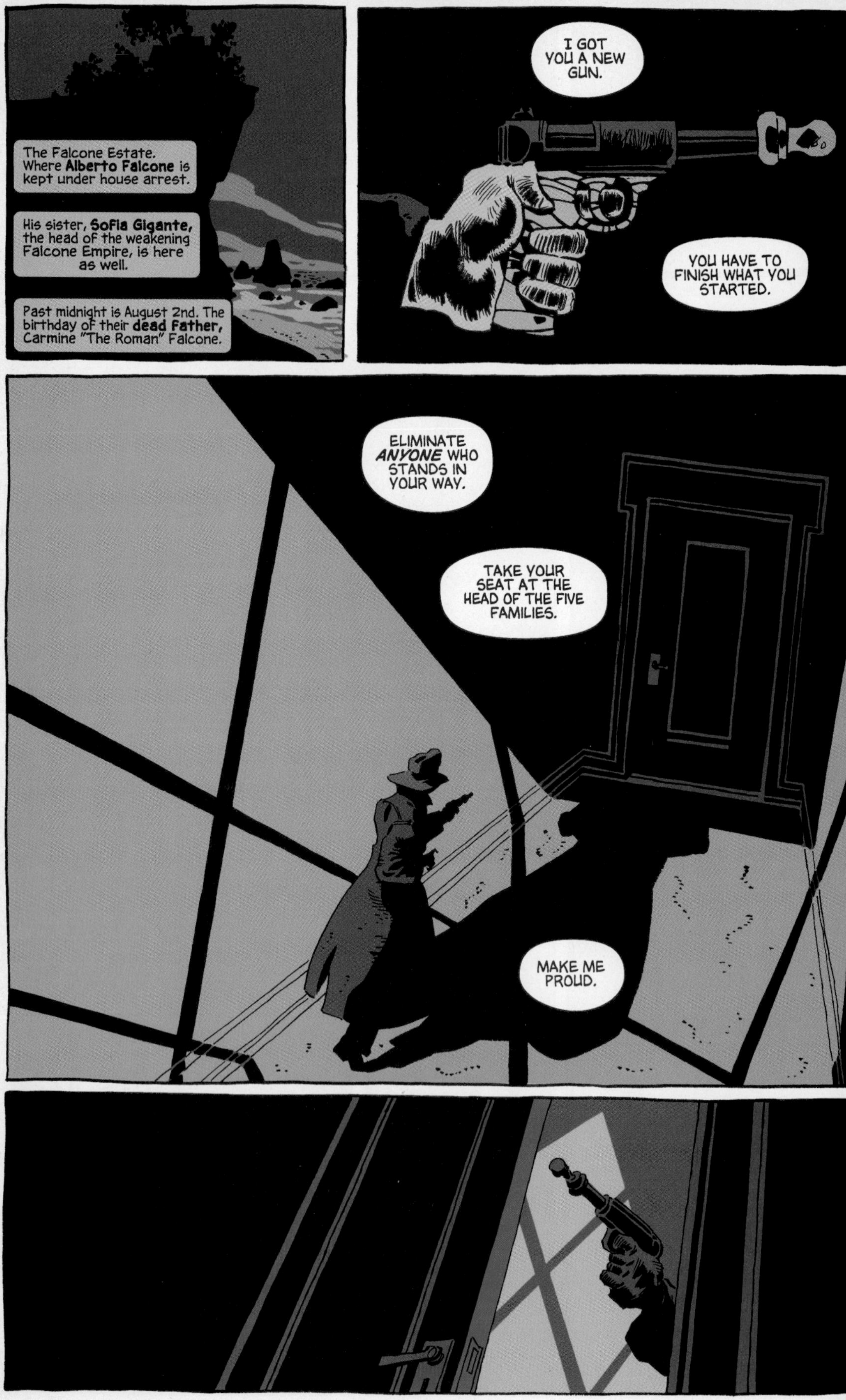

The Falcone Estate. Where Alberto Falcone is kept under house arrest.
His sister, Sofia Gigante, the head of the weakening Falcone Empire, is here as well.
Past midnight is August 2nd. The birthday of their dead Father, Carmine "The Roman" Falcone.
I GOT YOU A NEW GUN.
YOU HAVE TO FINISH WHAT YOU STARTED.
ELIMINATE ANYONE WHO STANDS IN YOUR WAY.
TAKE YOUR SEAT AT THE HEAD OF THE FIVE FAMILIES.
MAKE ME PROUD.

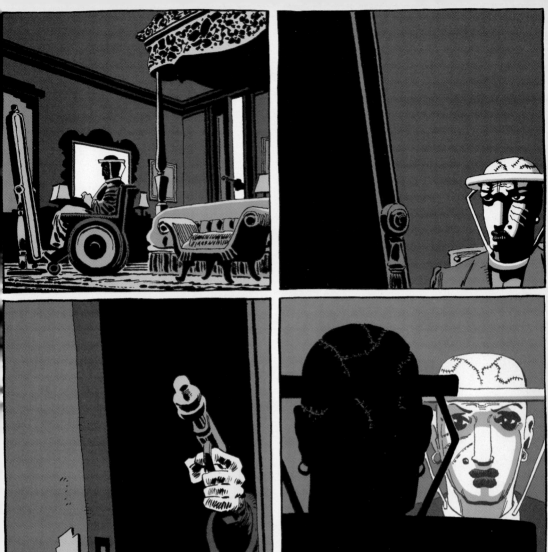

POPPA.

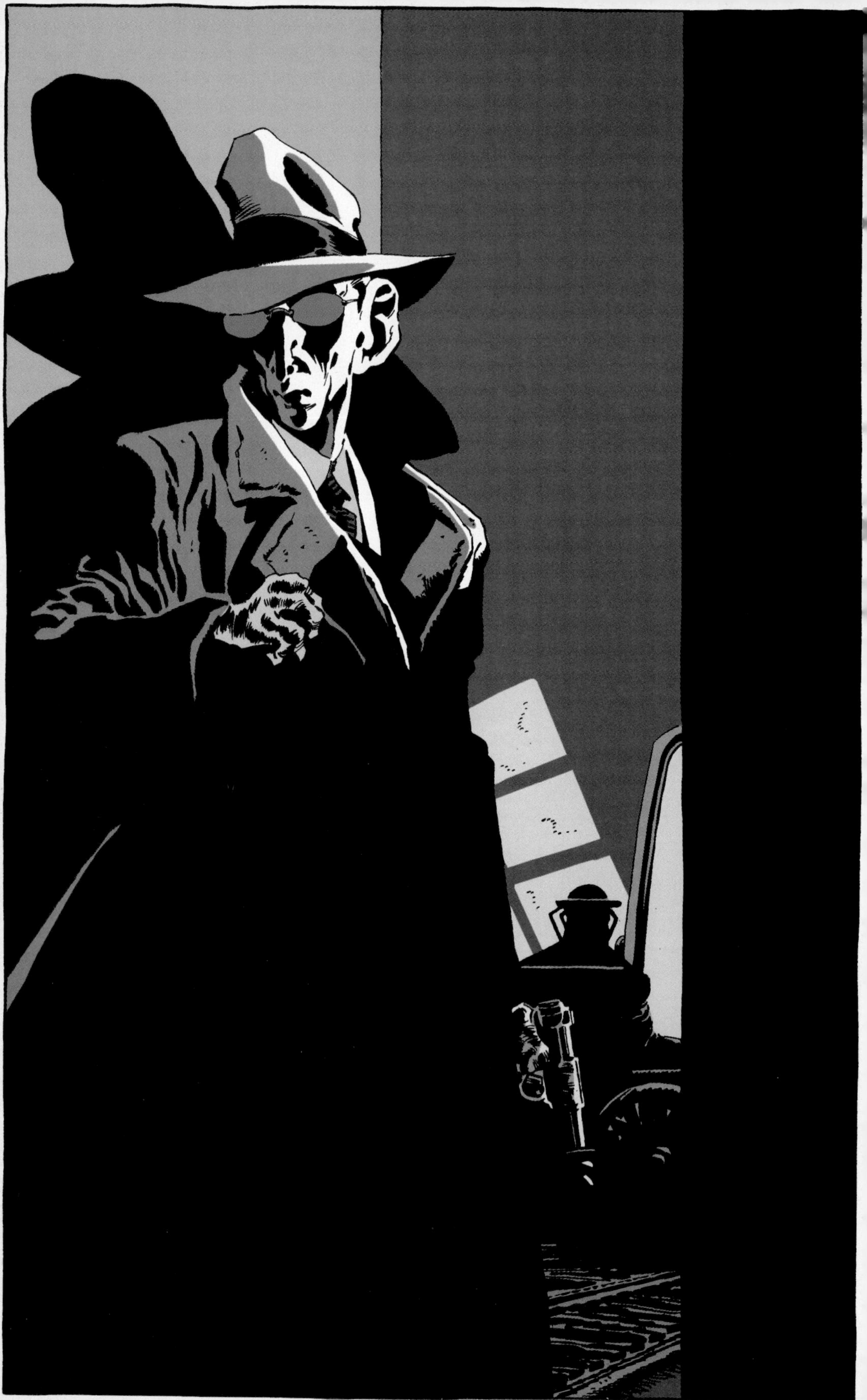

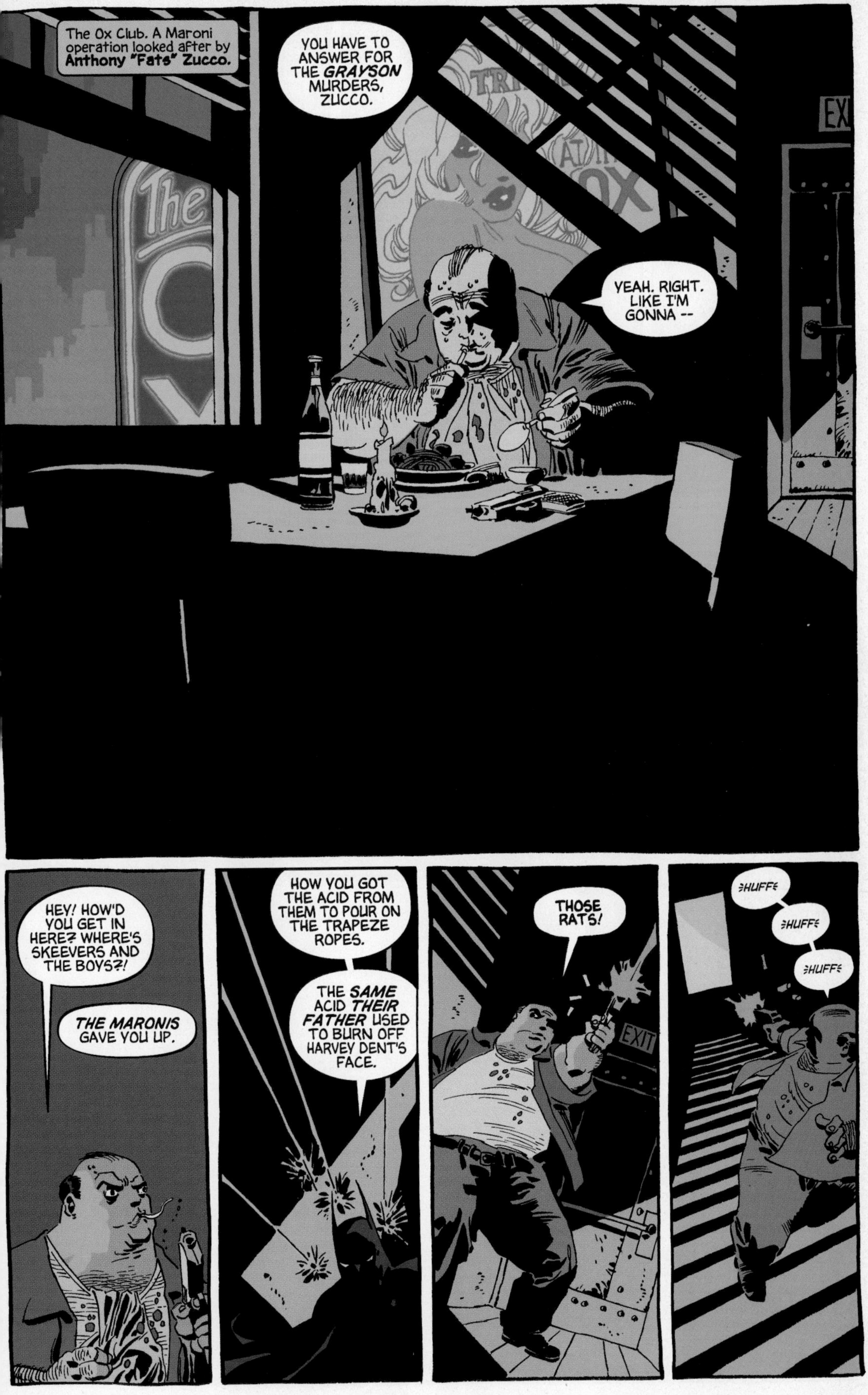
The Ox Club. A Maroni operation looked after by Anthony "Fats" Zucco.
YOU HAVE TO ANSWER FOR THE GRAYSON MURDERS, ZUCCO.
YEAH. RIGHT. LIKE I'M GONNA --
HEY! HOW'D YOU GET IN HERE? WHERE'S SKEEVERS AND THE BOYS?!
THE MARONIS GAVE YOU UP.
HOW YOU GOT THE ACID FROM THEM TO POUR ON THE TRAPEZE ROPES.
THE SAME ACID THEIR FATHER USED TO BURN OFF HARVEY DENT'S FACE.
THOSE RATS!
EXIT
HUFF
HUFF
HUFF

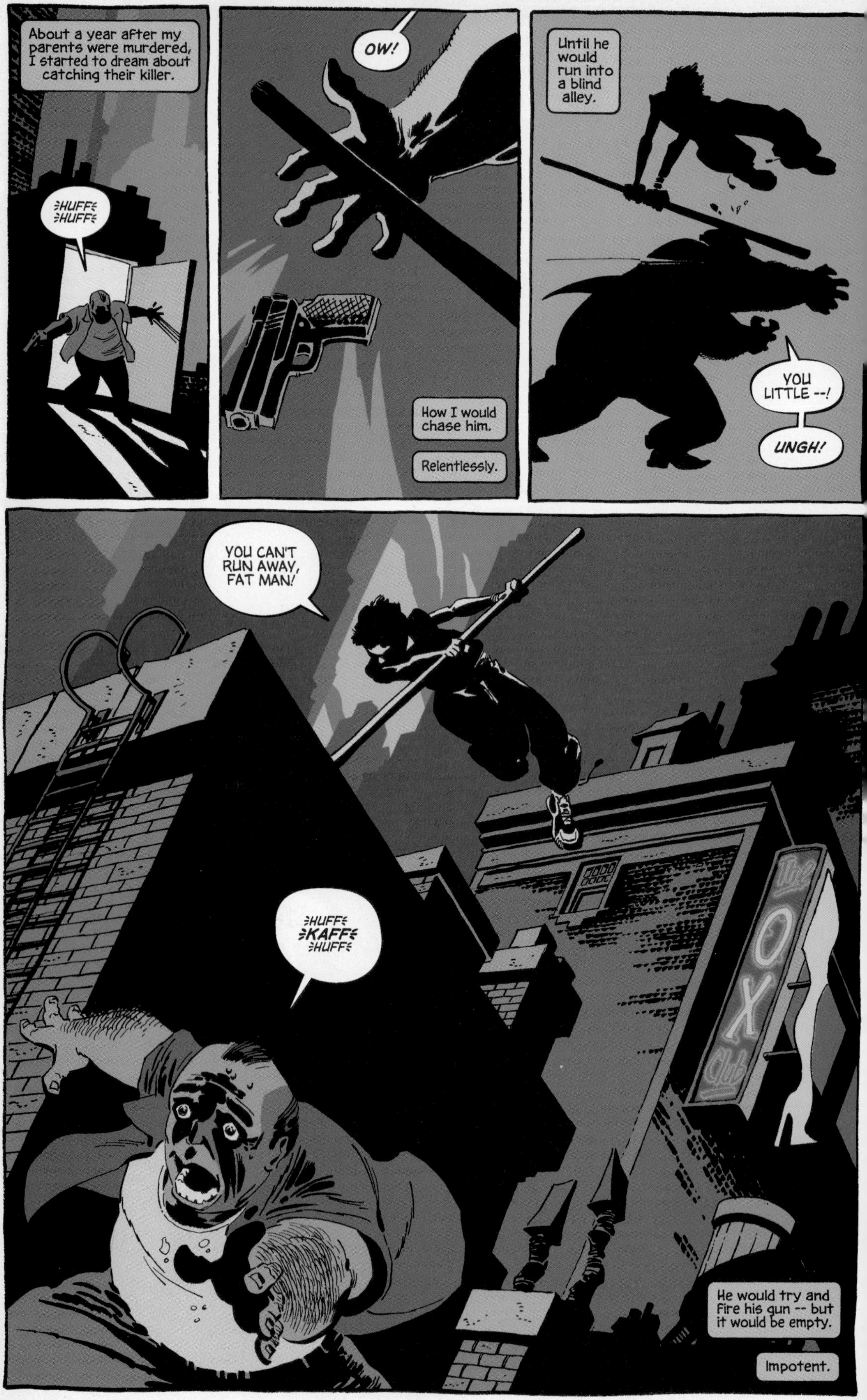

About a year after my parents were murdered, I started to dream about catching their killer.
HUFF HUFF
OW!
How I would chase him.
Relentlessly.
Until he would run into a blind alley.
YOU LITTLE --!
UNGH!
YOU CAN'T RUN AWAY, FAT MAN!
HUFF KAFF HUFF
The OX Club
He would try and fire his gun -- but it would be empty.
Impotent.

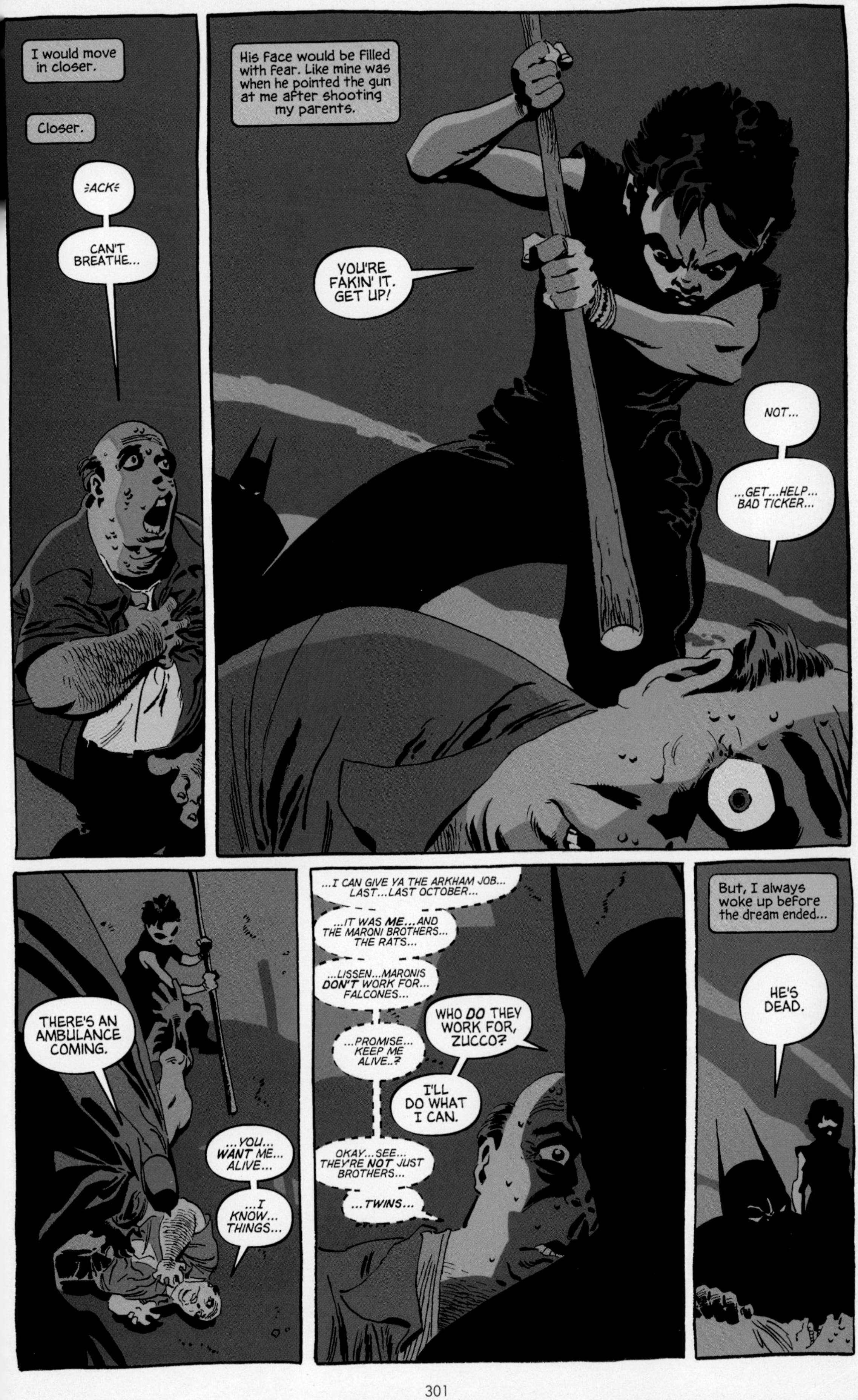
I would move in closer.
Closer.
ACK
CAN'T BREATHE...
His face would be filled with fear. Like mine was when he pointed the gun at me after shooting my parents.
YOU'RE FAKIN' IT. GET UP!
NOT...
...GET...HELP... BAD TICKER...
THERE'S AN AMBULANCE COMING.
...YOU... WANT ME... ALIVE...
...I KNOW... THINGS...
...I CAN GIVE YA THE ARKHAM JOB... LAST...LAST OCTOBER...
...IT WAS ME...AND THE MARONI BROTHERS... THE RATS...
...LISSEN...MARONIS DON'T WORK FOR... FALCONES...
WHO DO THEY WORK FOR, ZUCCO?
...PROMISE... KEEP ME ALIVE..?
I'LL DO WHAT I CAN.
OKAY...SEE... THEY'RE NOT JUST BROTHERS...
...TWINS...
But, I always woke up before the dream ended...
HE'S DEAD.

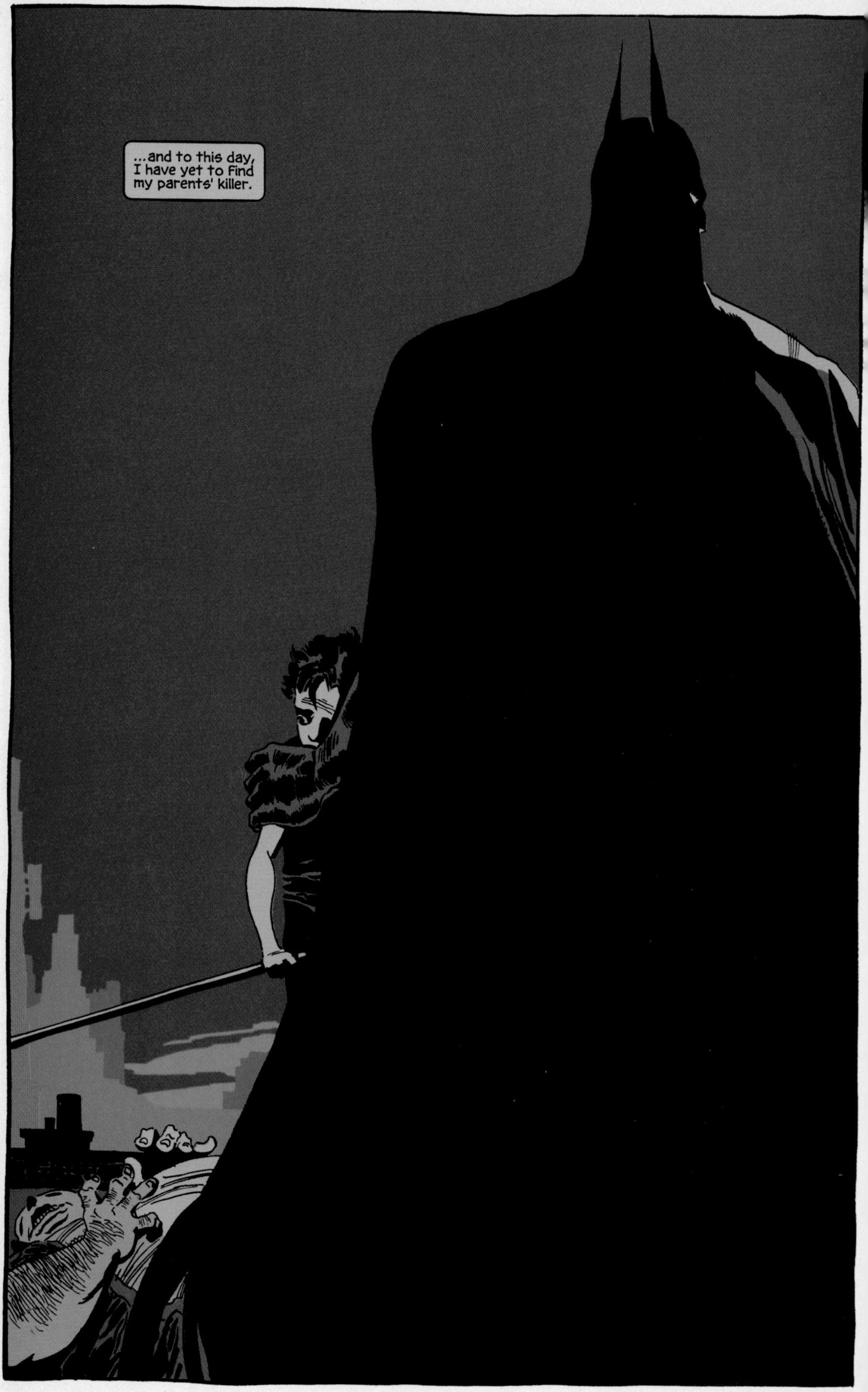
...and to this day, I have yet to find my parents' killer.

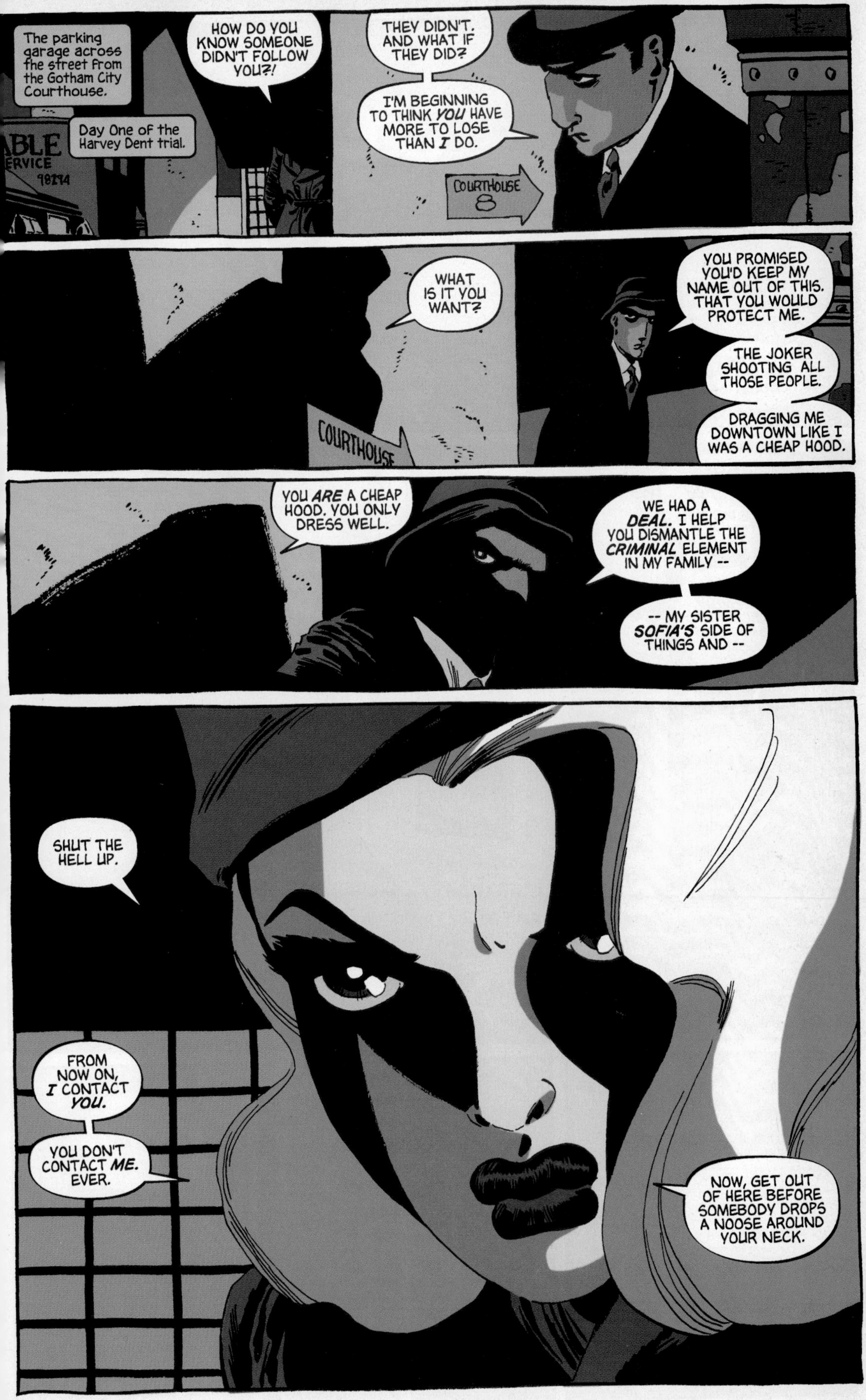
The parking garage across the street from the Gotham City Courthouse.
Day One of the Harvey Dent trial.
HOW DO YOU KNOW SOMEONE DIDN'T FOLLOW YOU?!
THEY DIDN'T. AND WHAT IF THEY DID?
I'M BEGINNING TO THINK YOU HAVE MORE TO LOSE THAN I DO.
COURTHOUSE
WHAT IS IT YOU WANT?
YOU PROMISED YOU'D KEEP MY NAME OUT OF THIS. THAT YOU WOULD PROTECT ME.
THE JOKER SHOOTING ALL THOSE PEOPLE.
DRAGGING ME DOWNTOWN LIKE I WAS A CHEAP HOOD.
COURTHOUSE
YOU ARE A CHEAP HOOD. YOU ONLY DRESS WELL.
WE HAD A DEAL. I HELP YOU DISMANTLE THE CRIMINAL ELEMENT IN MY FAMILY --
-- MY SISTER SOFIA'S SIDE OF THINGS AND --
SHUT THE HELL UP.
FROM NOW ON, I CONTACT YOU.
YOU DON'T CONTACT ME. EVER.
NOW, GET OUT OF HERE BEFORE SOMEBODY DROPS A NOOSE AROUND YOUR NECK.

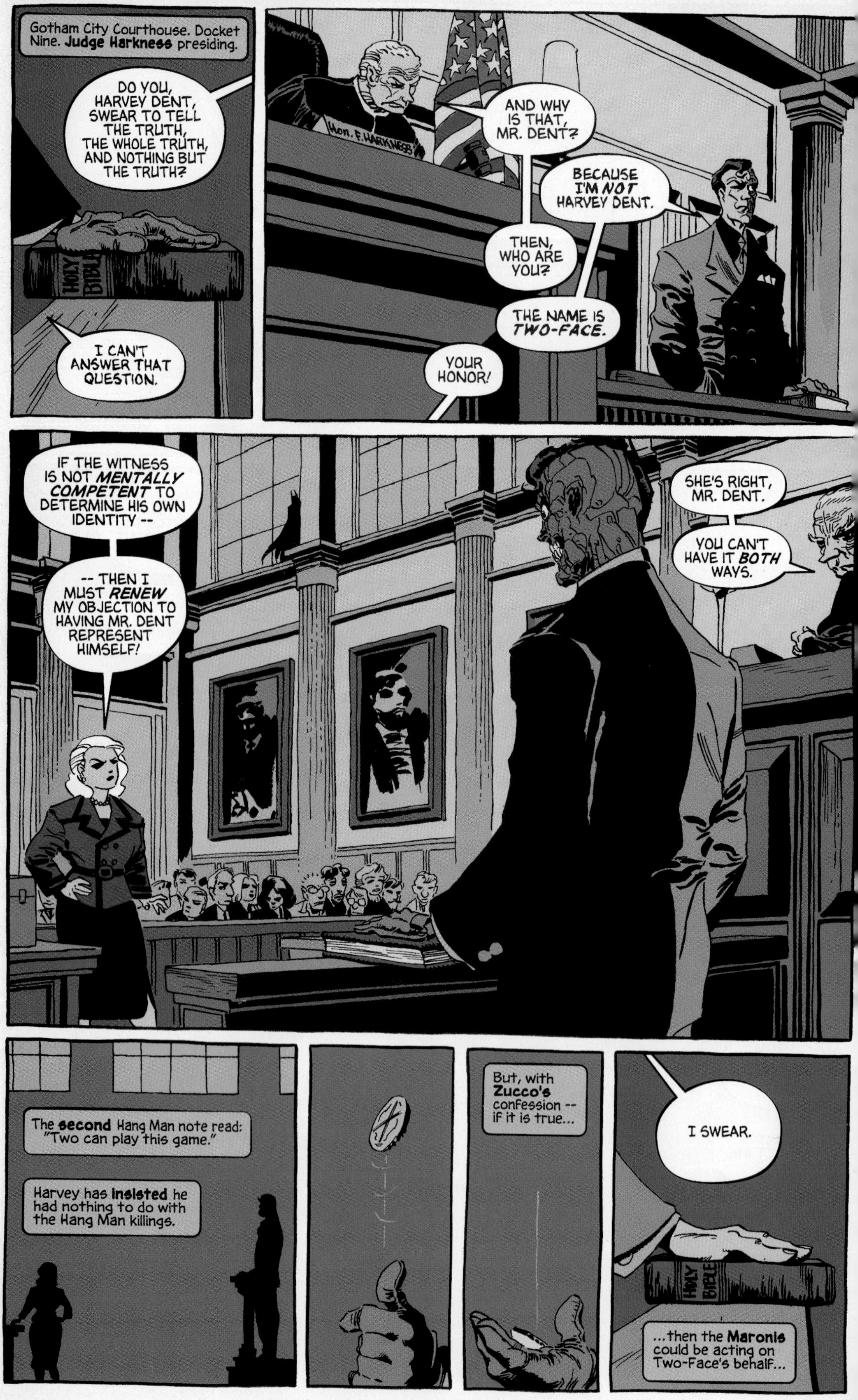
Gotham City Courthouse. Docket Nine. Judge Harkness presiding.
DO YOU, HARVEY DENT, SWEAR TO TELL THE TRUTH, THE WHOLE TRUTH, AND NOTHING BUT THE TRUTH?
HOLY BIBLE
I CAN'T ANSWER THAT QUESTION.
HON. F. HARKNESS
AND WHY IS THAT, MR. DENT?
BECAUSE I'M NOT HARVEY DENT.
THEN, WHO ARE YOU?
THE NAME IS TWO-FACE.
YOUR HONOR!
IF THE WITNESS IS NOT MENTALLY COMPETENT TO DETERMINE HIS OWN IDENTITY --
-- THEN I MUST RENEW MY OBJECTION TO HAVING MR. DENT REPRESENT HIMSELF!
SHE'S RIGHT, MR. DENT.
YOU CAN'T HAVE IT BOTH WAYS.
The second Hang Man note read: "Two can play this game."
Harvey has insisted he had nothing to do with the Hang Man killings.
But, with Zucco's confession -- if it is true...
I SWEAR.
HOLY BIBLE
...then the Maronis could be acting on Two-Face's behalf...

The courtroom is filled with families of the Hanged Police Officers.

If Dent **is** convicted, **Gordon** will have a tough time getting him out of here alive.

MR. DENT. THESE STRONG BOXES ARE FILLED WITH EVIDENCE RELATING TO THE *HANG MAN KILLINGS*.

NINE MEN FROM THE GOTHAM CITY POLICE FORCE, PAST AND PRESENT, HAVE BEEN HANGED.

ALL WERE PINNED WITH NOTES THAT HAD TO DO WITH *YOU*, BOTH PERSONALLY AND PROFESSIONALLY.

HOW DO YOU EXPLAIN THAT?

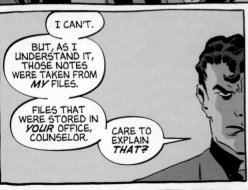

I CAN'T.

BUT, AS I UNDERSTAND IT, THOSE NOTES WERE TAKEN FROM *MY* FILES.

FILES THAT WERE STORED IN *YOUR* OFFICE, COUNSELOR.

CARE TO EXPLAIN *THAT?*

I... IT IS A MATTER OF RECORD THAT THOSE FILES WERE *STOLEN* FROM MY OFFICE *BEFORE* THE FIRST MURDER.

HOW CONVENIENT.

OH.

I AM NOT THE ONE ON TRIAL HERE, MR. DENT!

WHAT TIME IS IT?

Something is wrong. Two-Face is wearing a watch.

IT'S JUST ABOUT TWO O'CLOCK.

WHY?

Two...

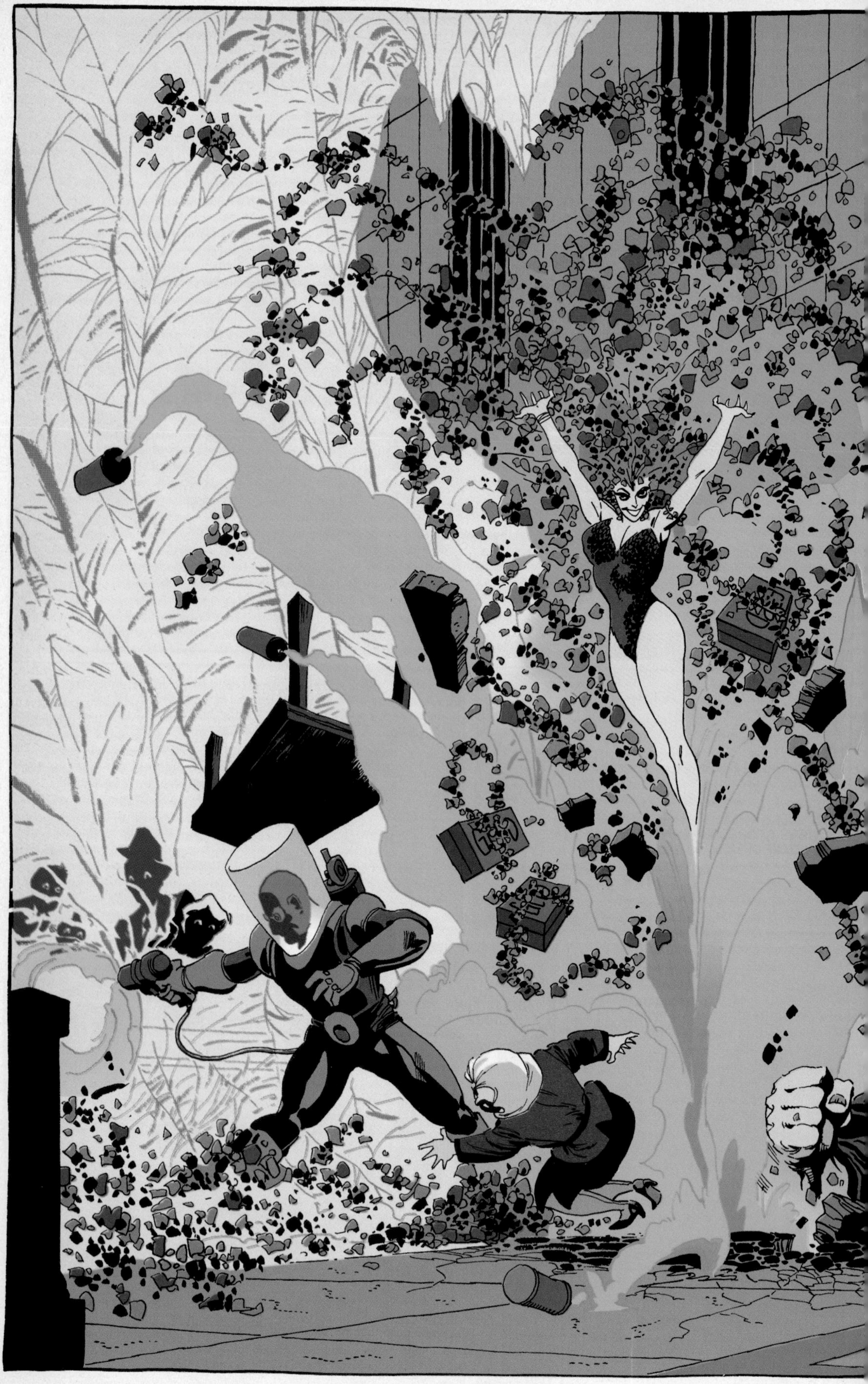

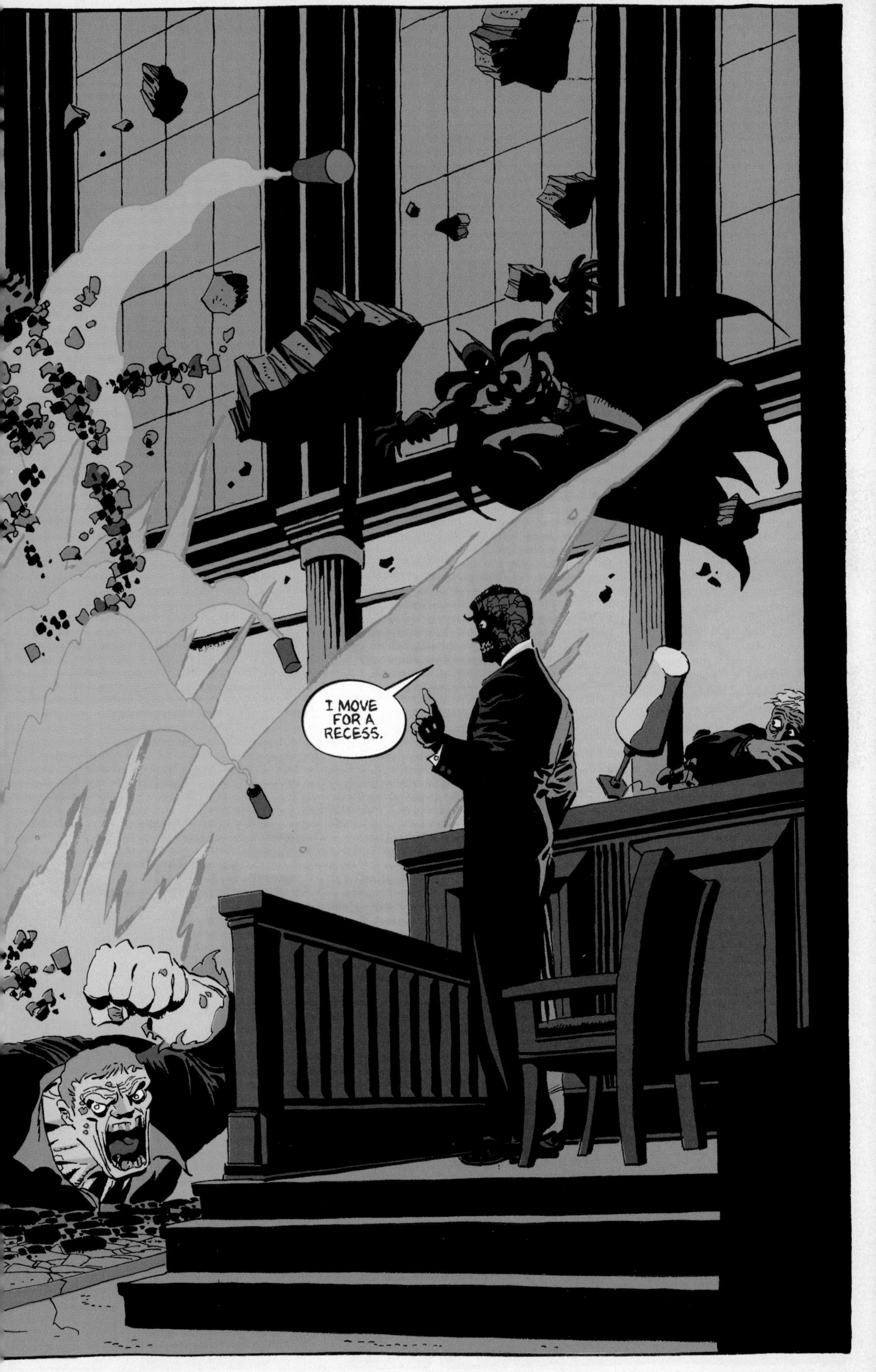
I MOVE FOR A RECESS.

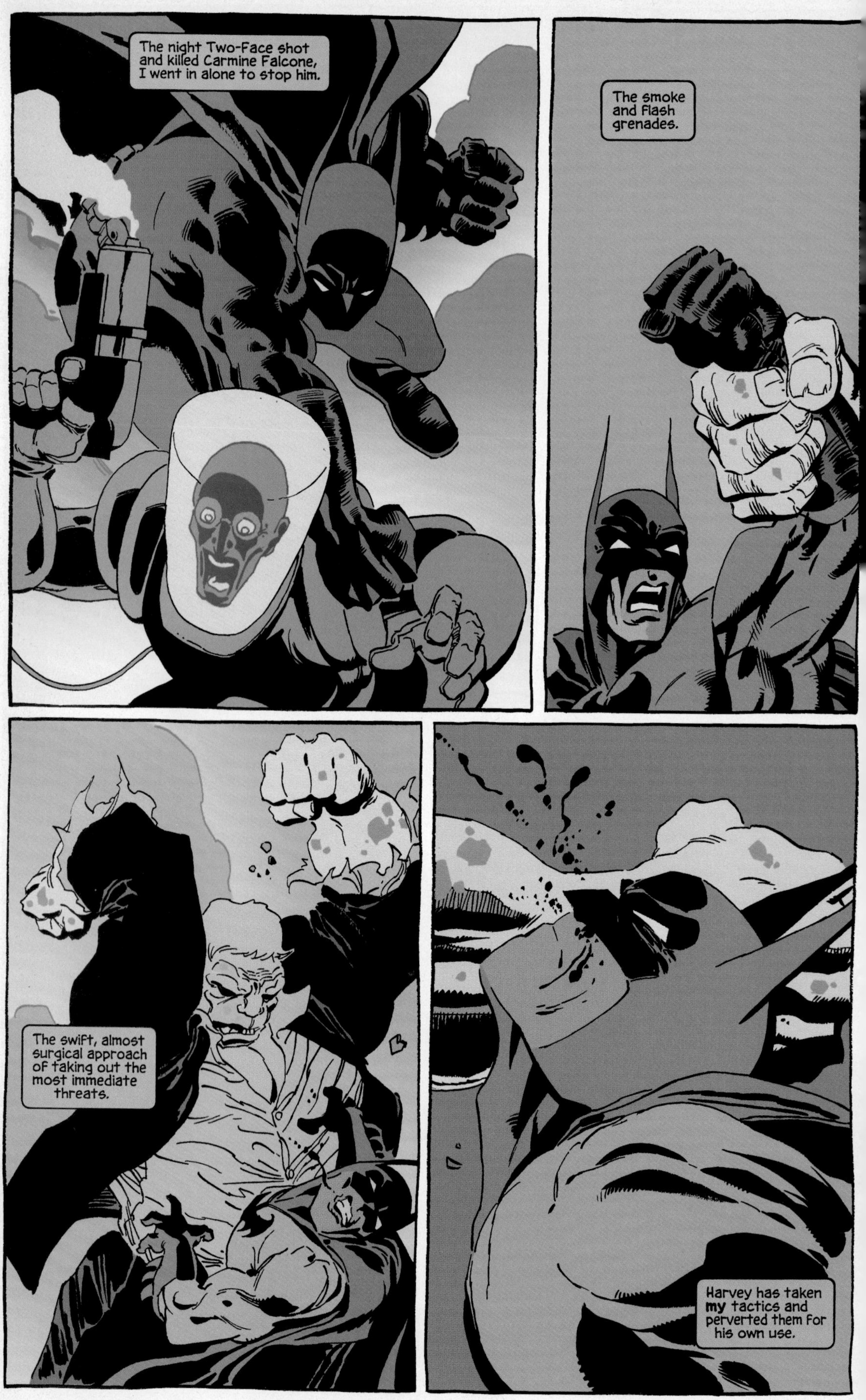
The night Two-Face shot and killed Carmine Falcone, I went in alone to stop him.
The smoke and flash grenades.
The swift, almost surgical approach of taking out the most immediate threats.
Harvey has taken **my** tactics and perverted them for his own use.

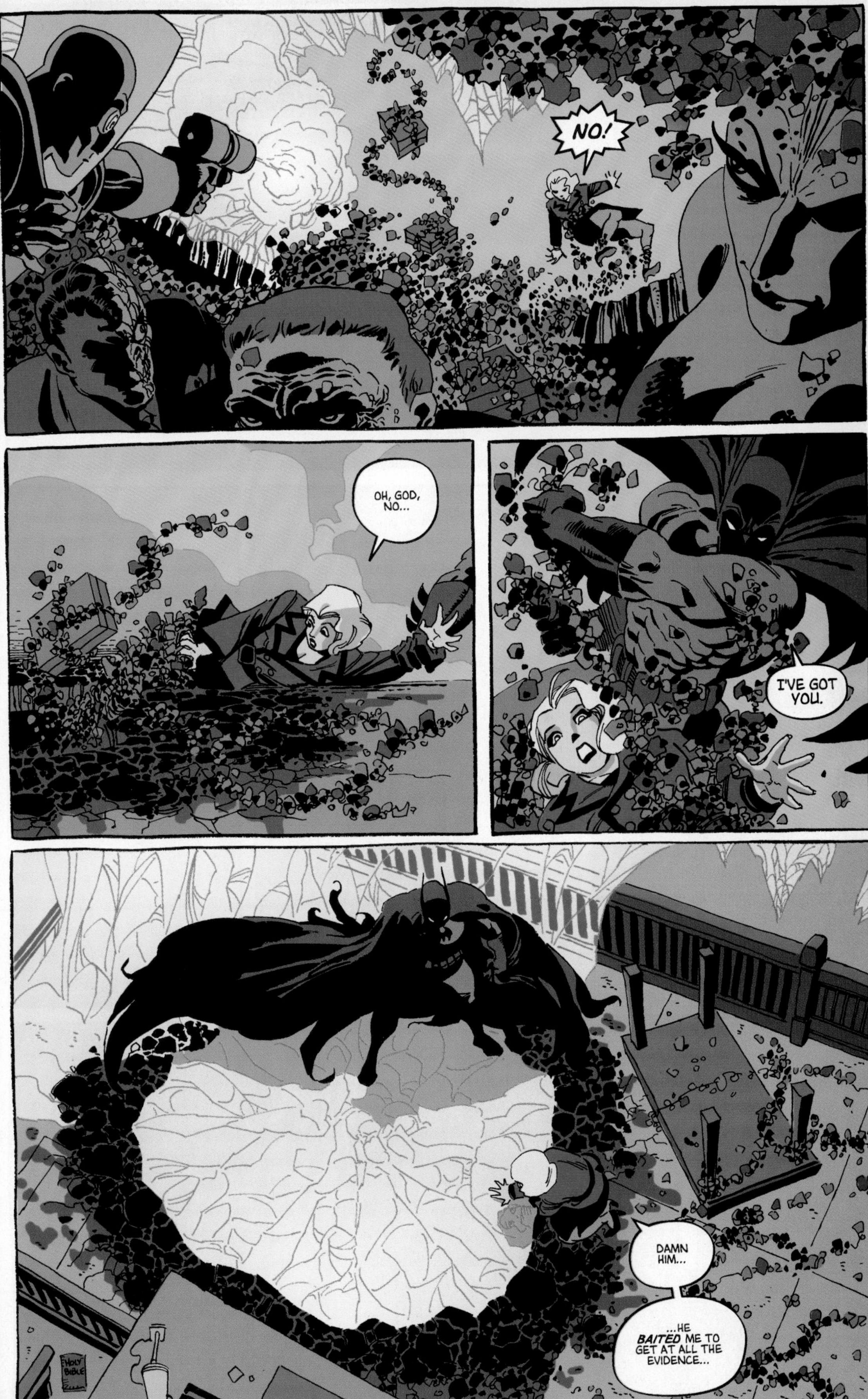
NO!
OH, GOD, NO...
I'VE GOT YOU.
HOLY BIBLE
DAMN HIM...
...HE BAITED ME TO GET AT ALL THE EVIDENCE...

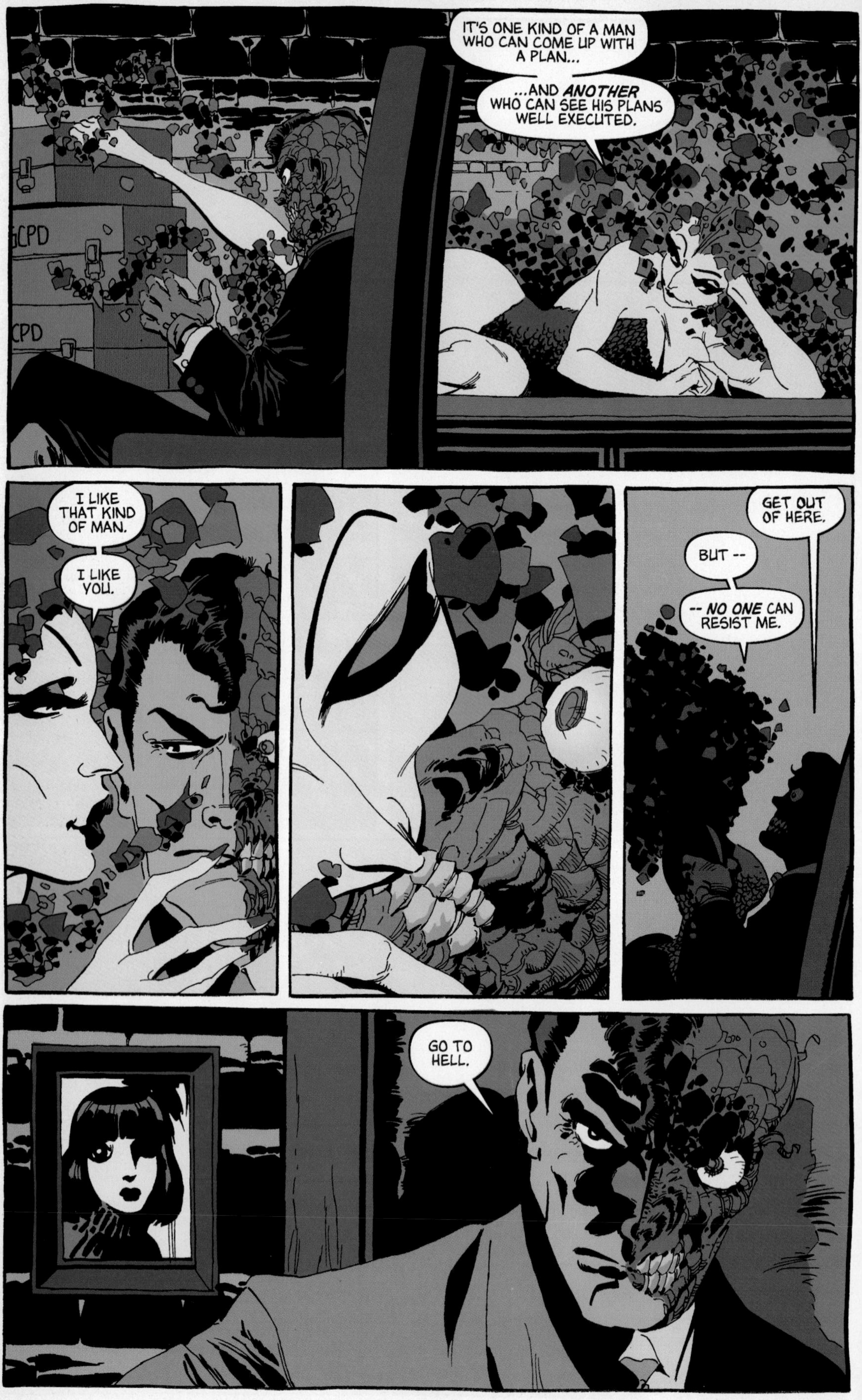
IT'S ONE KIND OF A MAN WHO CAN COME UP WITH A PLAN...
...AND ANOTHER WHO CAN SEE HIS PLANS WELL EXECUTED.
GCPD
GCPD
I LIKE THAT KIND OF MAN.
I LIKE YOU.
GET OUT OF HERE.
BUT --
-- NO ONE CAN RESIST ME.
GO TO HELL.

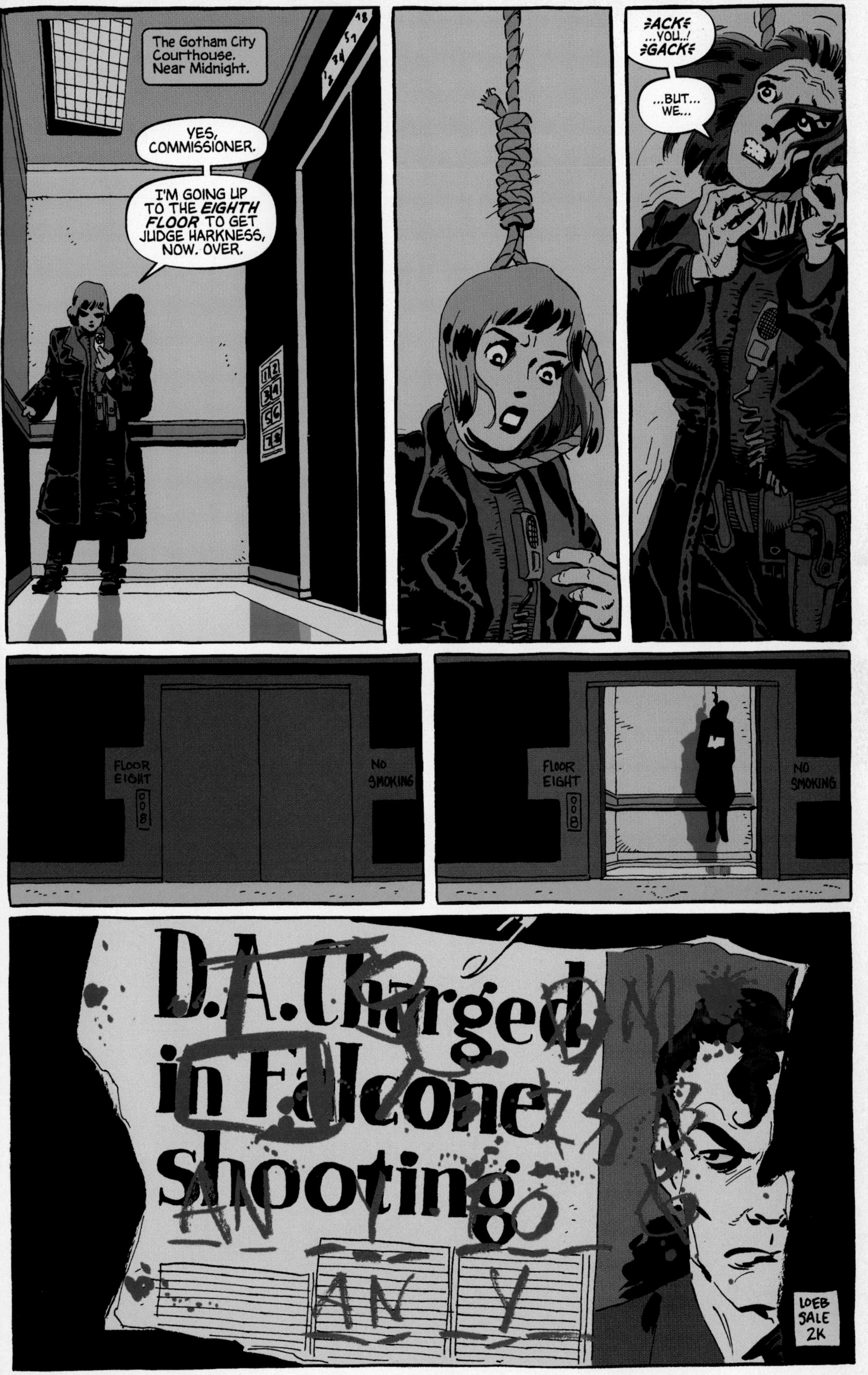

The Gotham City Courthouse. Near Midnight.
YES, COMMISSIONER.
I'M GOING UP TO THE *EIGHTH FLOOR* TO GET JUDGE HARKNESS, NOW. OVER.
ACK ...YOU..! GACK
...BUT... WE...
FLOOR EIGHT
NO SMOKING
FLOOR EIGHT
NO SMOKING
D.A. Charged in Falcone Shooting
LOEB SALE 2K

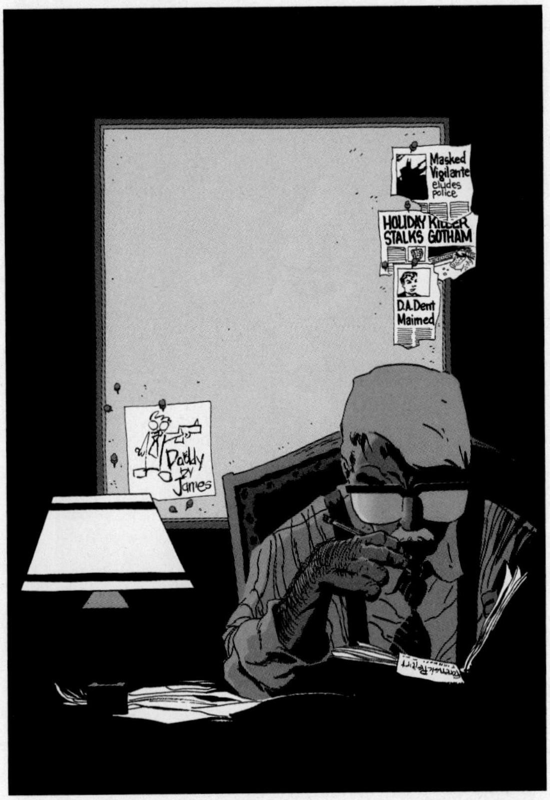

Masked Vigilante eludes police
HOLIDAY KILLER STALKS GOTHAM
D.A. Dent Maimed
Daddy by James

12

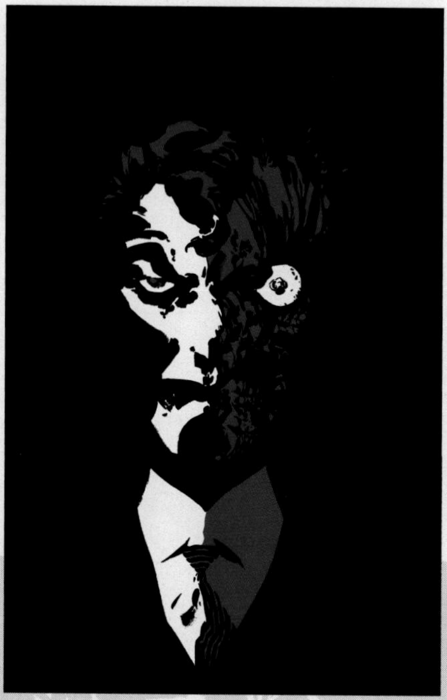

R E V E N G E

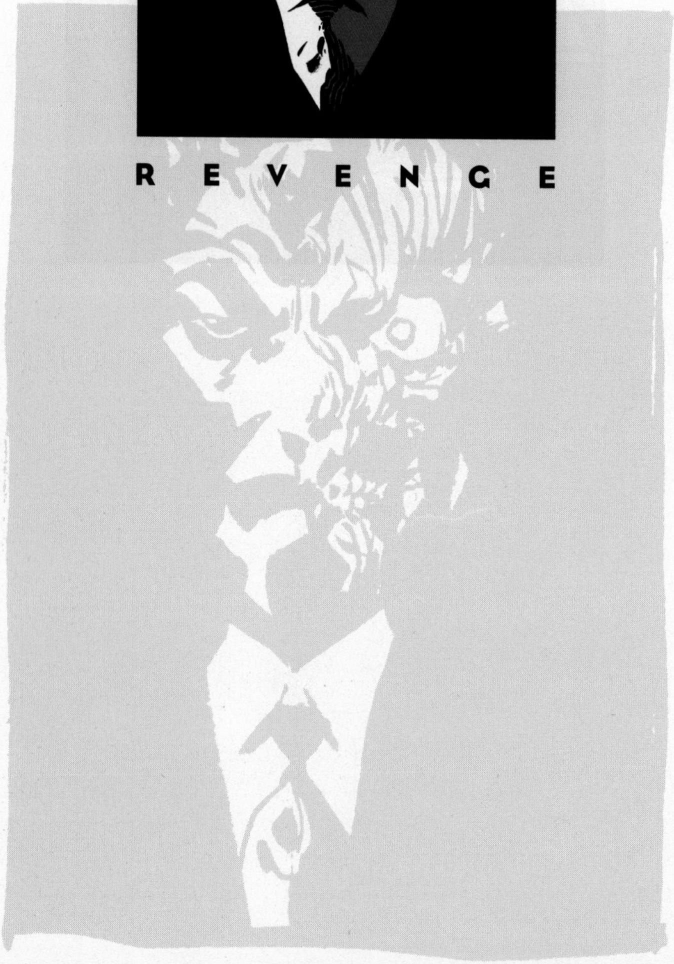

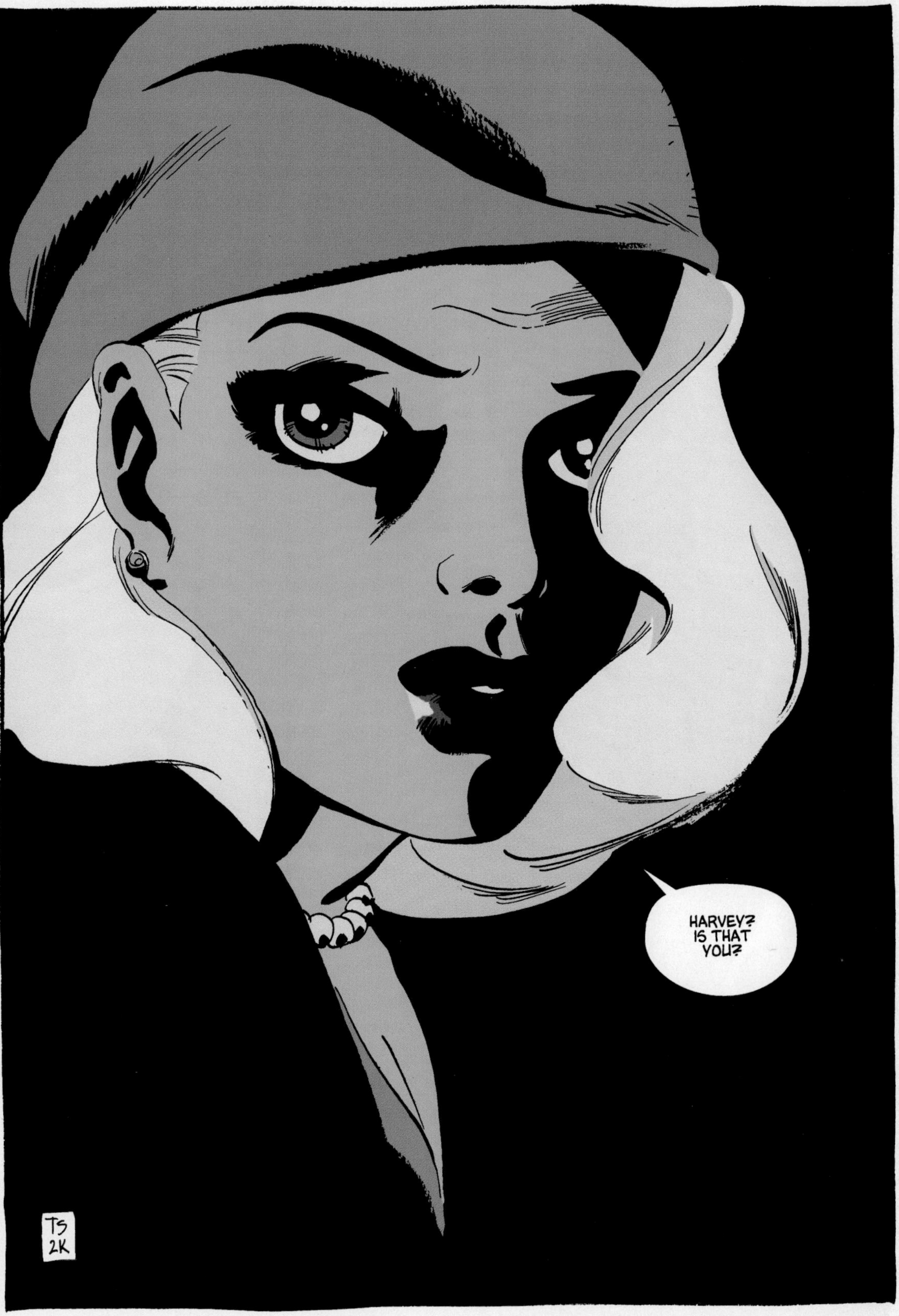
HARVEY? IS THAT YOU?
TS 2K

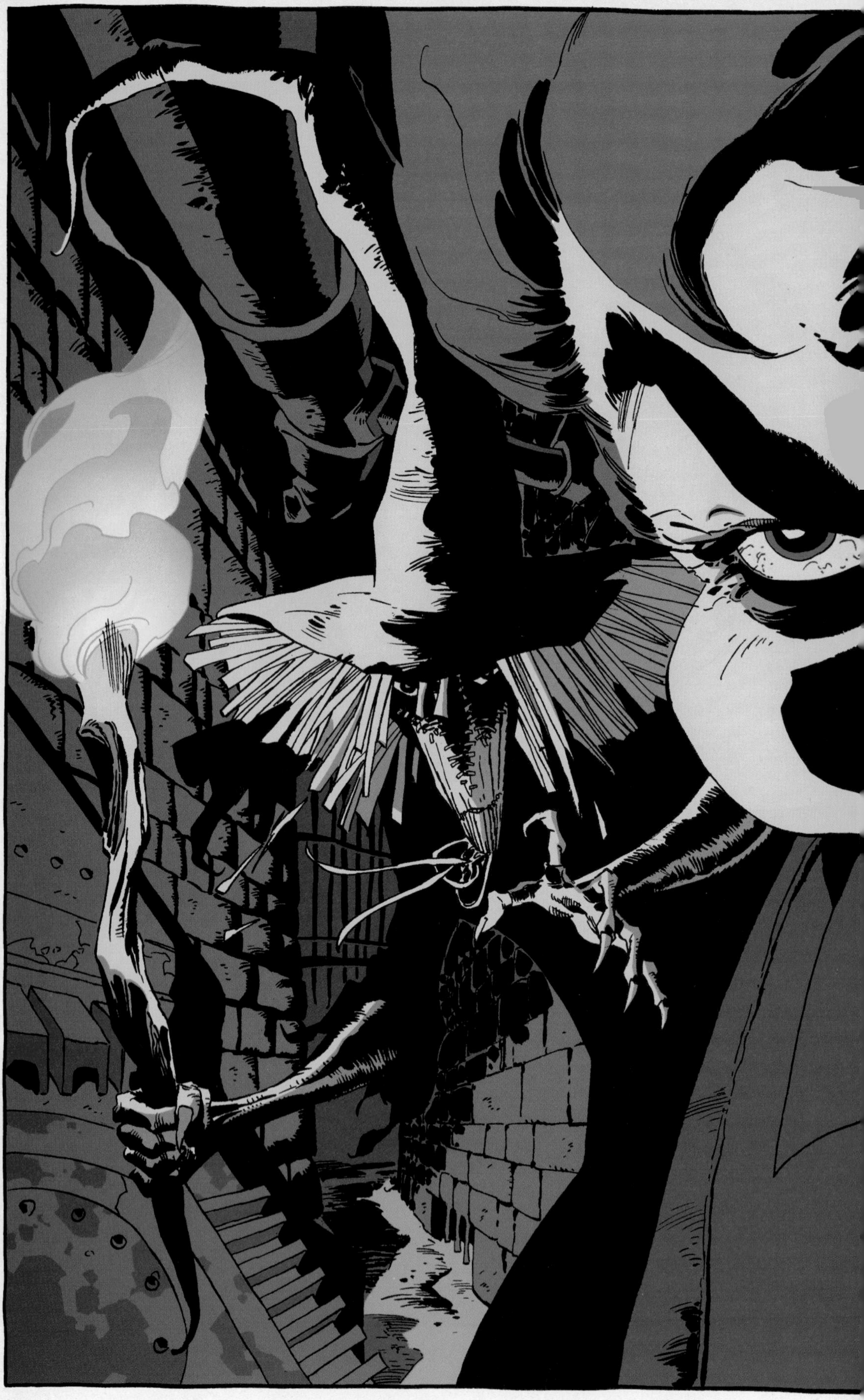

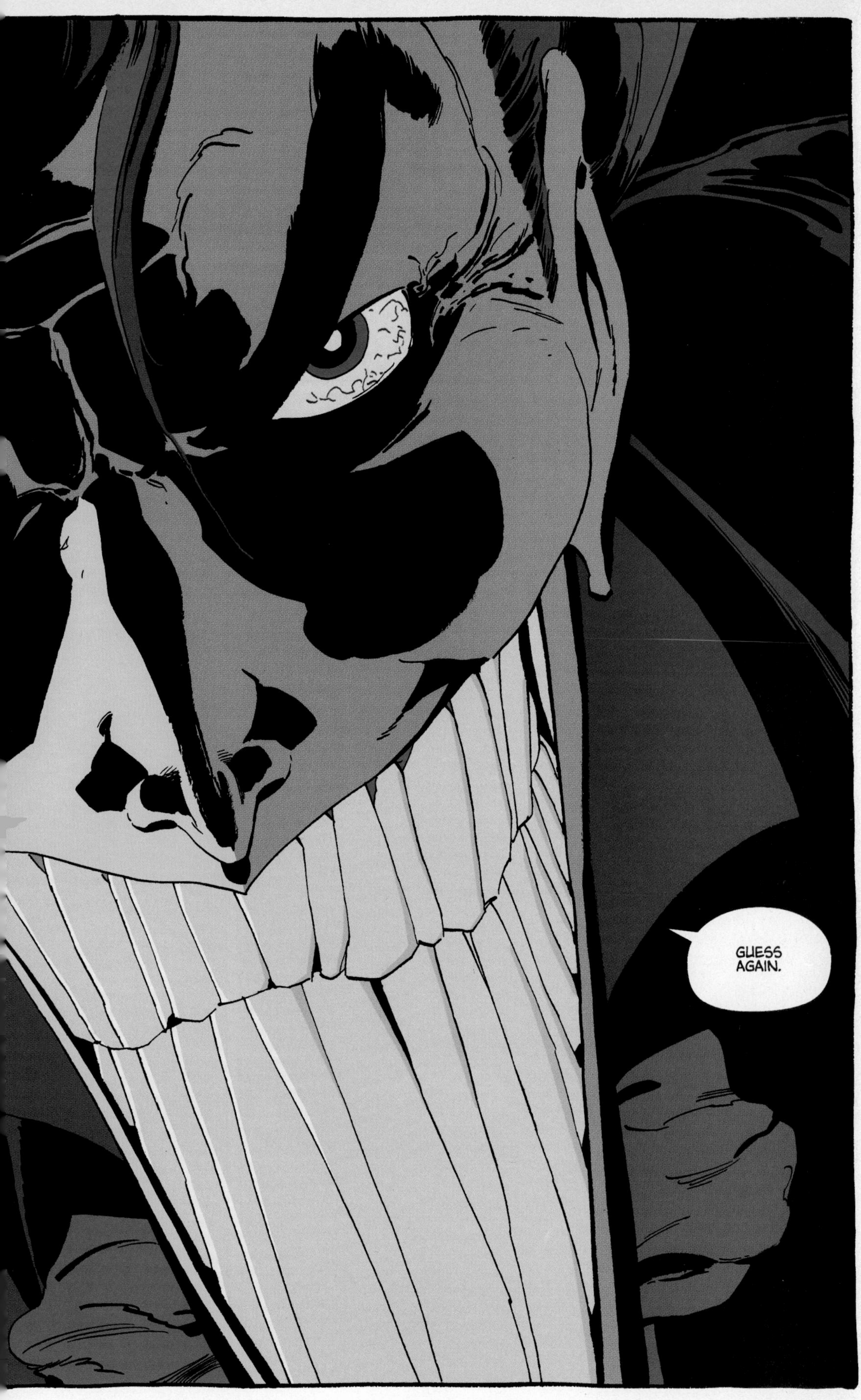
GUESS AGAIN.

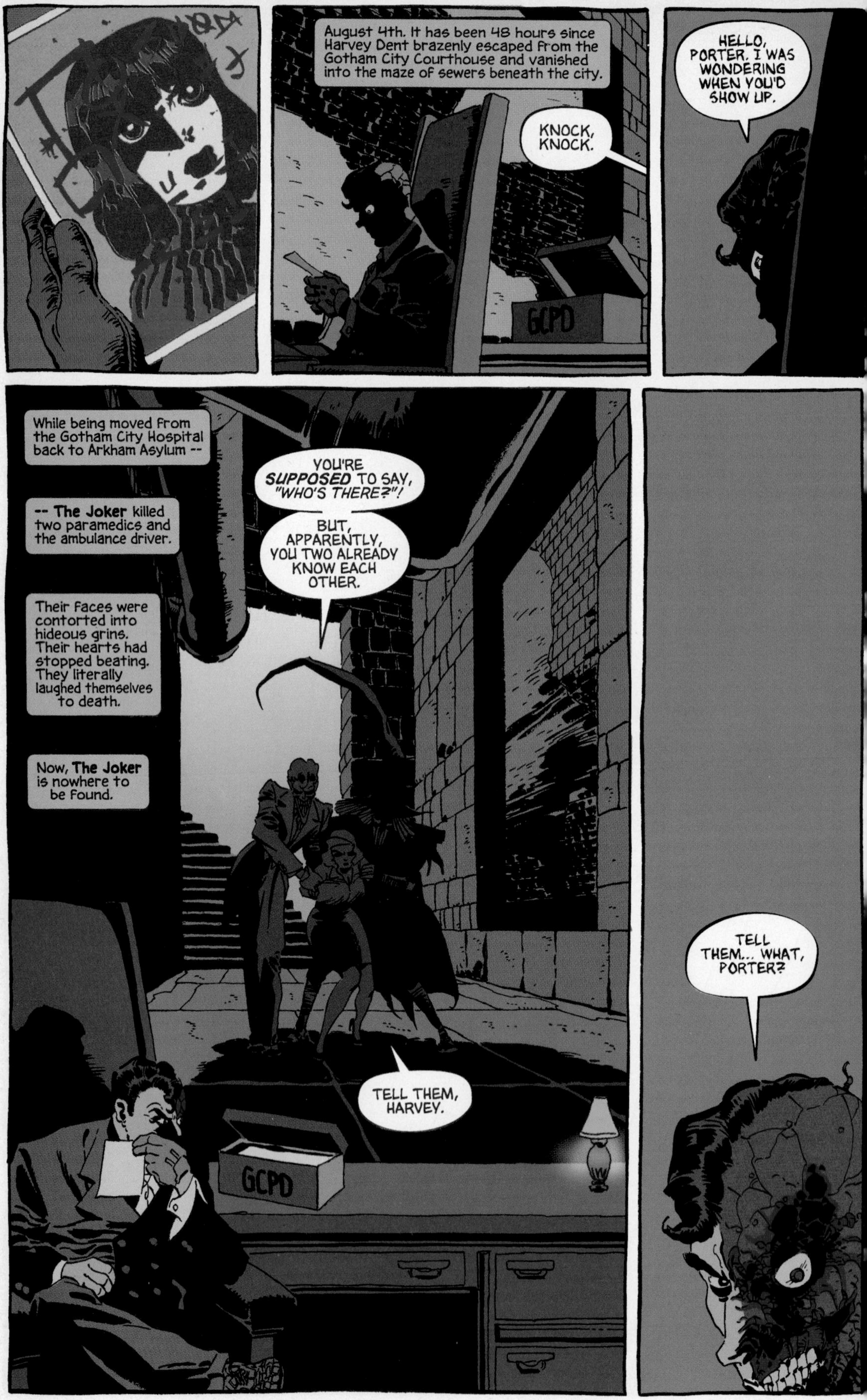

August 4th. It has been 48 hours since Harvey Dent brazenly escaped from the Gotham City Courthouse and vanished into the maze of sewers beneath the city.
KNOCK, KNOCK.
HELLO, PORTER. I WAS WONDERING WHEN YOU'D SHOW UP.
While being moved from the Gotham City Hospital back to Arkham Asylum --
-- The Joker killed two paramedics and the ambulance driver.
Their faces were contorted into hideous grins. Their hearts had stopped beating. They literally laughed themselves to death.
Now, The Joker is nowhere to be found.
YOU'RE SUPPOSED TO SAY, "WHO'S THERE?"!
BUT, APPARENTLY, YOU TWO ALREADY KNOW EACH OTHER.
TELL THEM, HARVEY.
TELL THEM... WHAT, PORTER?
GCPD

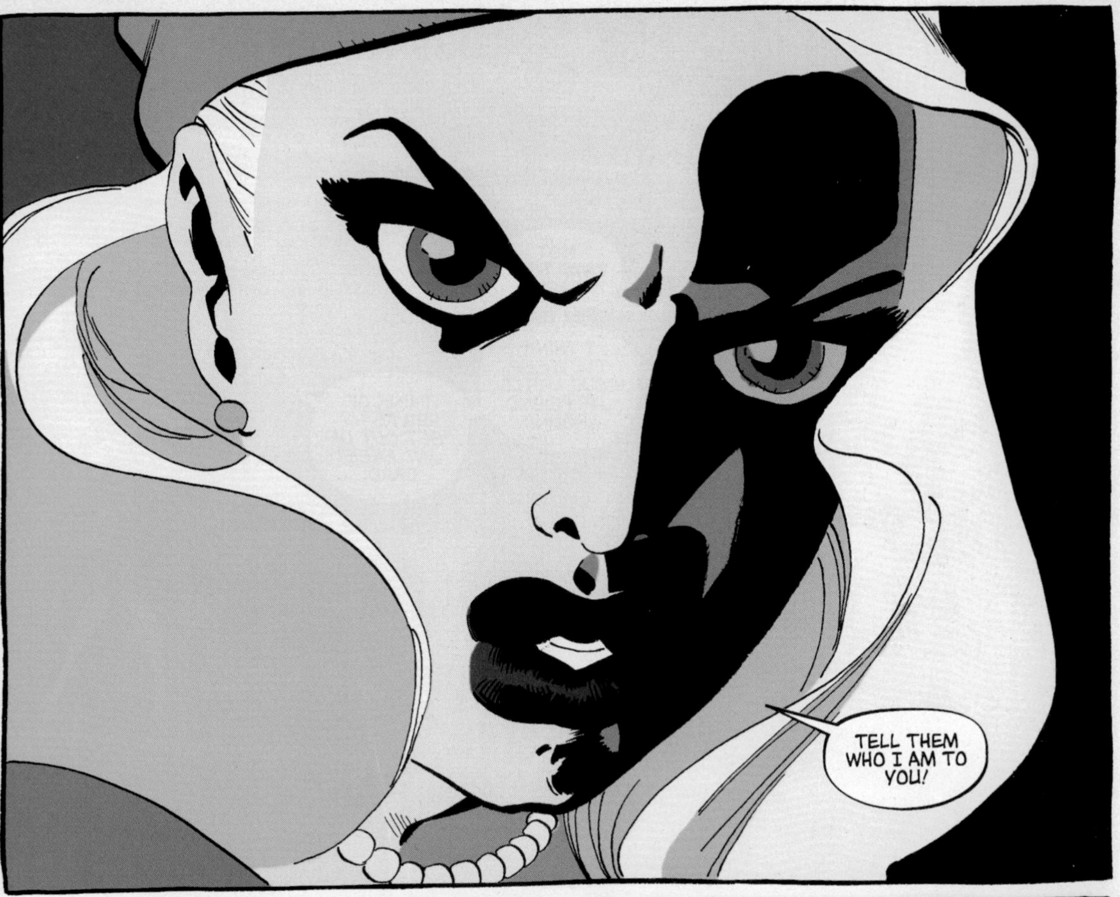
TELL THEM WHO I AM TO YOU!

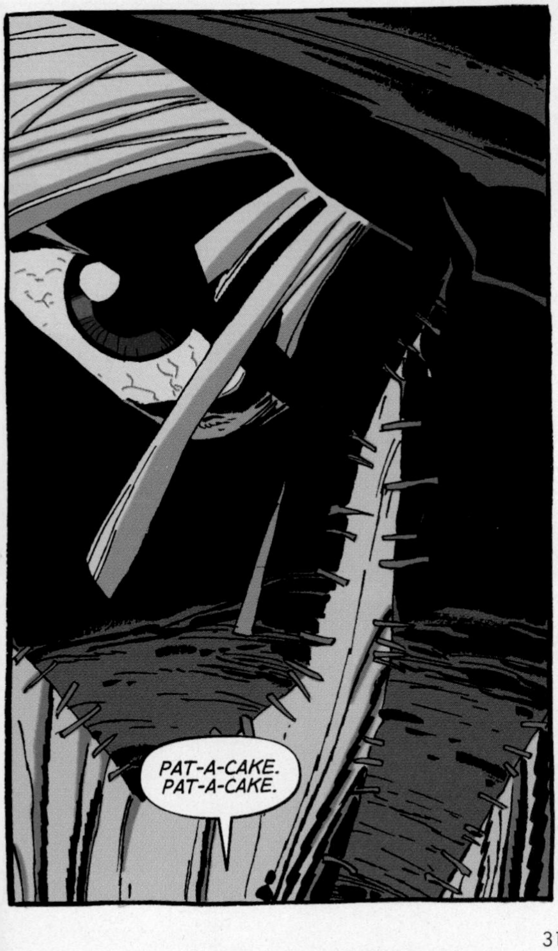
PAT-A-CAKE. PAT-A-CAKE.

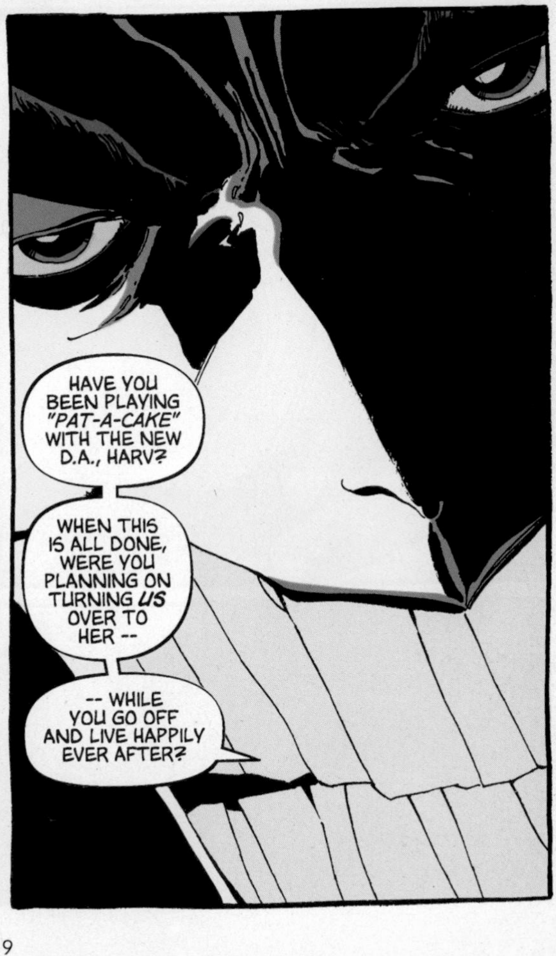
HAVE YOU BEEN PLAYING "PAT-A-CAKE" WITH THE NEW D.A., HARV?
WHEN THIS IS ALL DONE, WERE YOU PLANNING ON TURNING US OVER TO HER --
-- WHILE YOU GO OFF AND LIVE HAPPILY EVER AFTER?

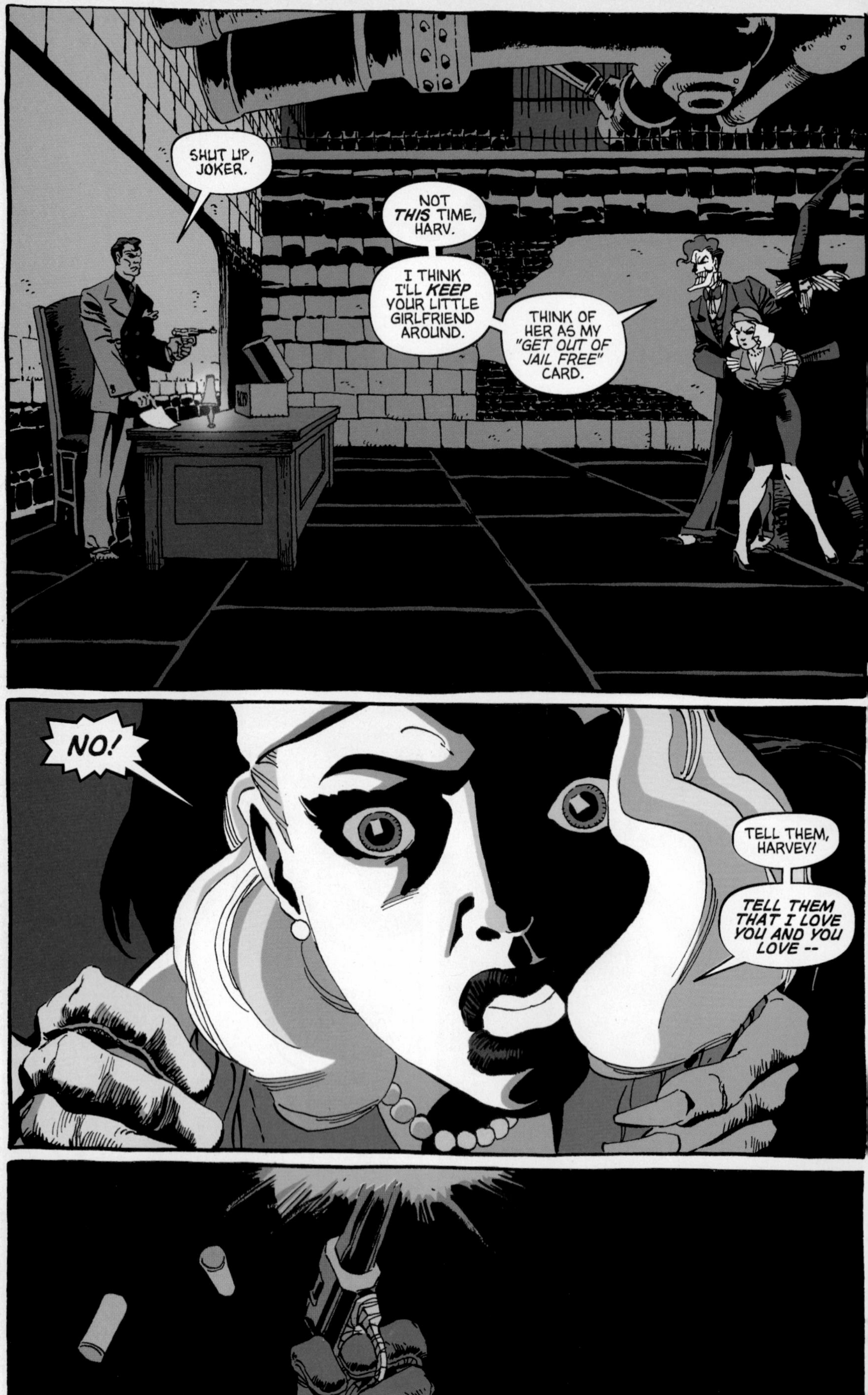
SHUT UP, JOKER.
NOT THIS TIME, HARV.
I THINK I'LL KEEP YOUR LITTLE GIRLFRIEND AROUND.
THINK OF HER AS MY "GET OUT OF JAIL FREE" CARD.
NO!
TELL THEM, HARVEY!
TELL THEM THAT I LOVE YOU AND YOU LOVE --

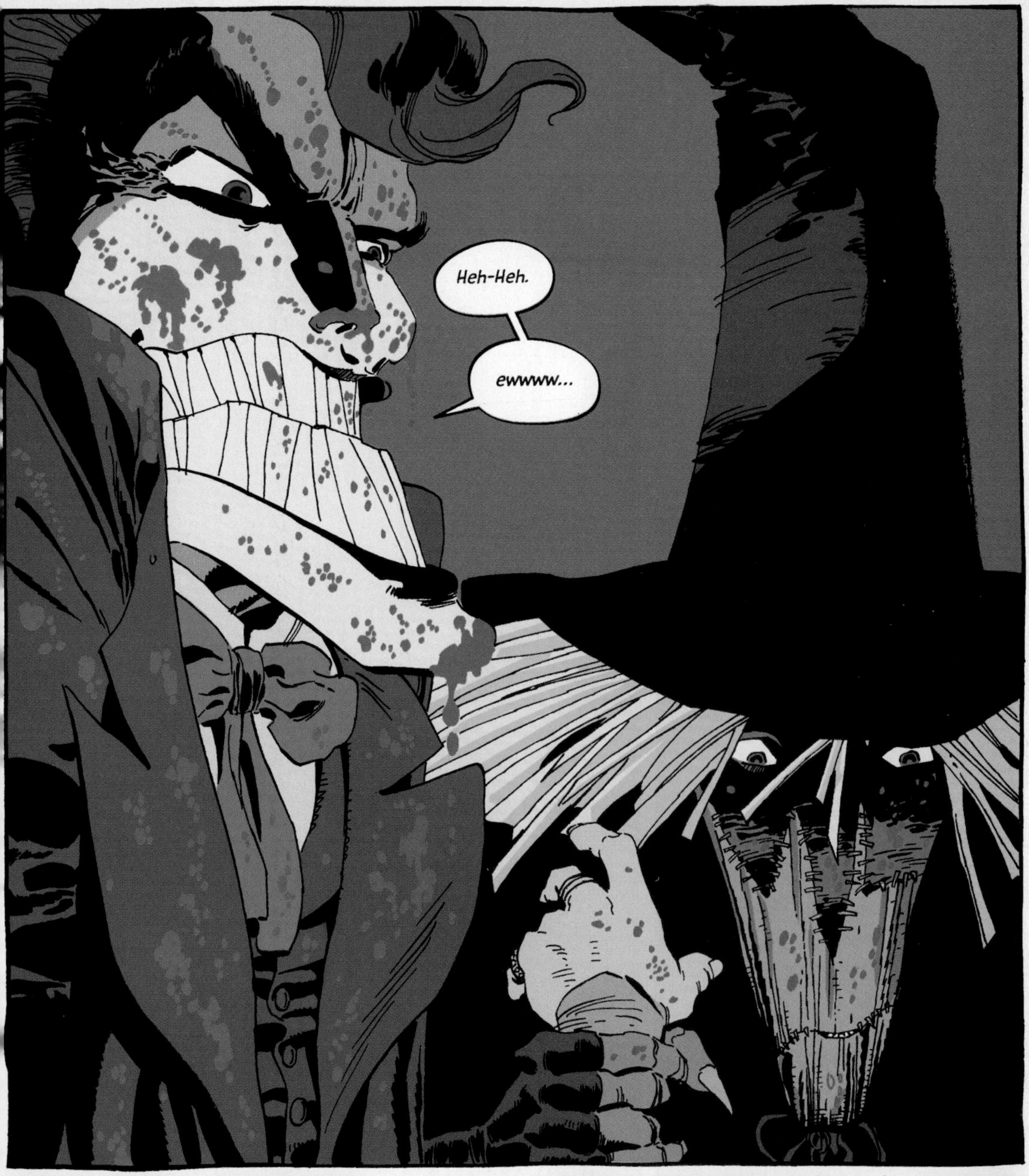
Heh-Heh.
ewwww...

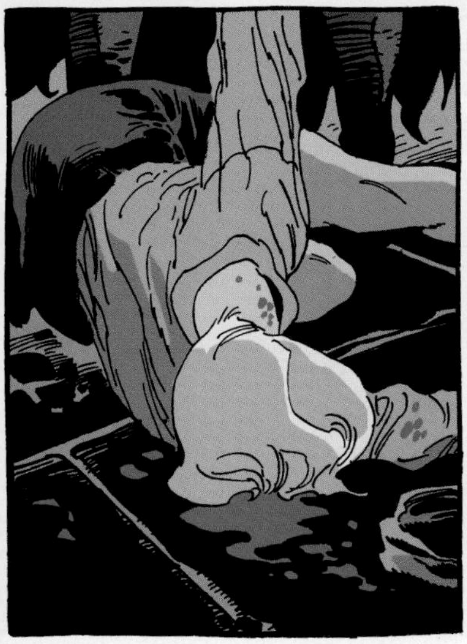

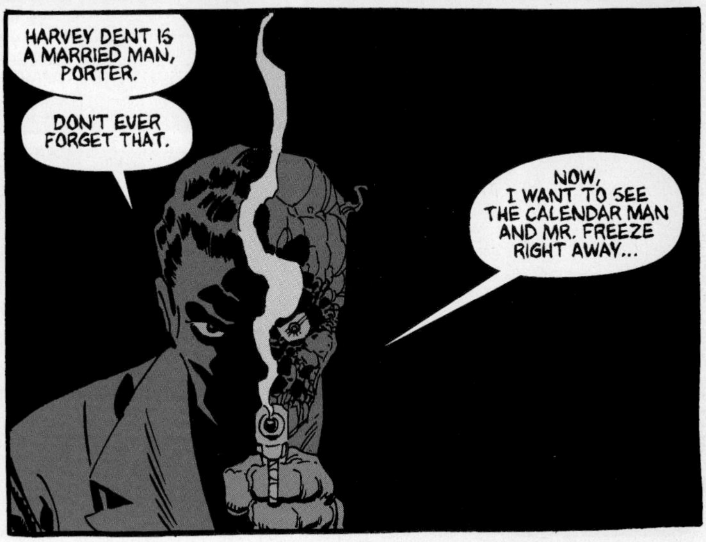
HARVEY DENT IS A MARRIED MAN, PORTER.
DON'T EVER FORGET THAT.
NOW, I WANT TO SEE THE CALENDAR MAN AND MR. FREEZE RIGHT AWAY...

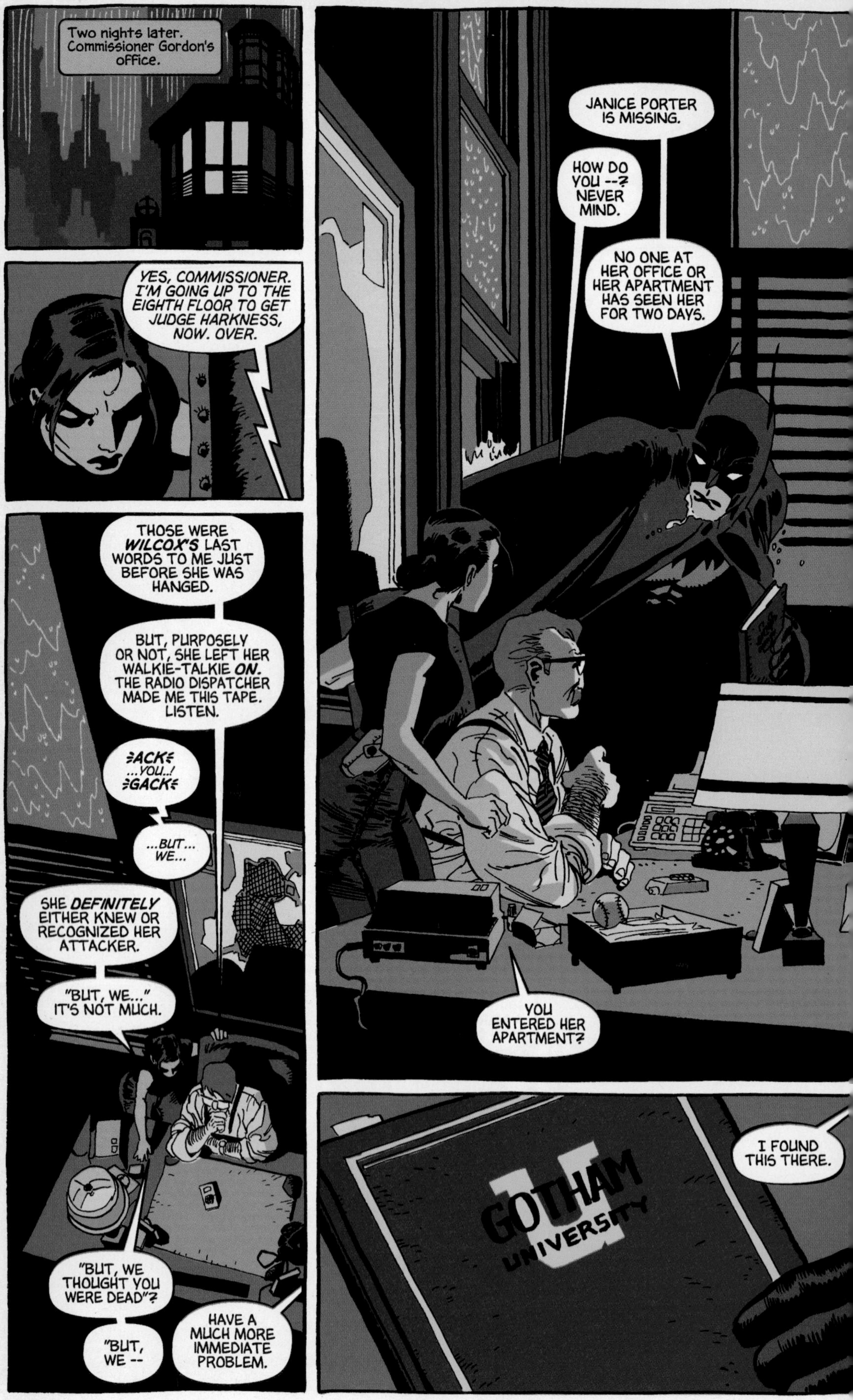
Two nights later. Commissioner Gordon's office.
YES, COMMISSIONER. I'M GOING UP TO THE EIGHTH FLOOR TO GET JUDGE HARKNESS, NOW. OVER.
THOSE WERE WILCOX'S LAST WORDS TO ME JUST BEFORE SHE WAS HANGED.
BUT, PURPOSELY OR NOT, SHE LEFT HER WALKIE-TALKIE ON. THE RADIO DISPATCHER MADE ME THIS TAPE. LISTEN.
ACK ...YOU..! GACK
...BUT... WE...
SHE DEFINITELY EITHER KNEW OR RECOGNIZED HER ATTACKER.
"BUT, WE..." IT'S NOT MUCH.
"BUT, WE THOUGHT YOU WERE DEAD"?
"BUT, WE --
HAVE A MUCH MORE IMMEDIATE PROBLEM.
JANICE PORTER IS MISSING.
HOW DO YOU --? NEVER MIND.
NO ONE AT HER OFFICE OR HER APARTMENT HAS SEEN HER FOR TWO DAYS.
YOU ENTERED HER APARTMENT?
I FOUND THIS THERE.
GOTHAM UNIVERSITY

DO YOU REMEMBER WHEN I ASKED PORTER IF SHE HAD KNOWN *ALBERTO FALCONE* AT HARVARD?

SHE SAID SOMETHING ABOUT FALCONE HAVING LEFT FOR OXFORD BY THE TIME SHE GOT THERE, BATMAN.

SPECIFICALLY, SHE SAID, "BY THE TIME SHE *TRANSFERRED* TO HARVARD, FALCONE HAD LEFT FOR OXFORD."

FROM GOTHAM UNIVERSITY?

WHERE SHE KNEW A YOUNG PROFESSOR NAMED *"HARVEY DENT"*...

...AND TRANSFERRED OUT THE YEAR HE MARRIED *GILDA DENT*.

Favorite Subject: Iᴇᴏɴᴇ

JANICE PORTER

LAW SCHOOL (1)

Voted Most Likely to be D.A.
Favorite Subject: Criminal Law

JIM.

IT'S POSSIBLE *EVERYTHING* YOU'VE SHARED WITH PORTER --

-- *TWO-FACE* KNOWS...

CITY

323

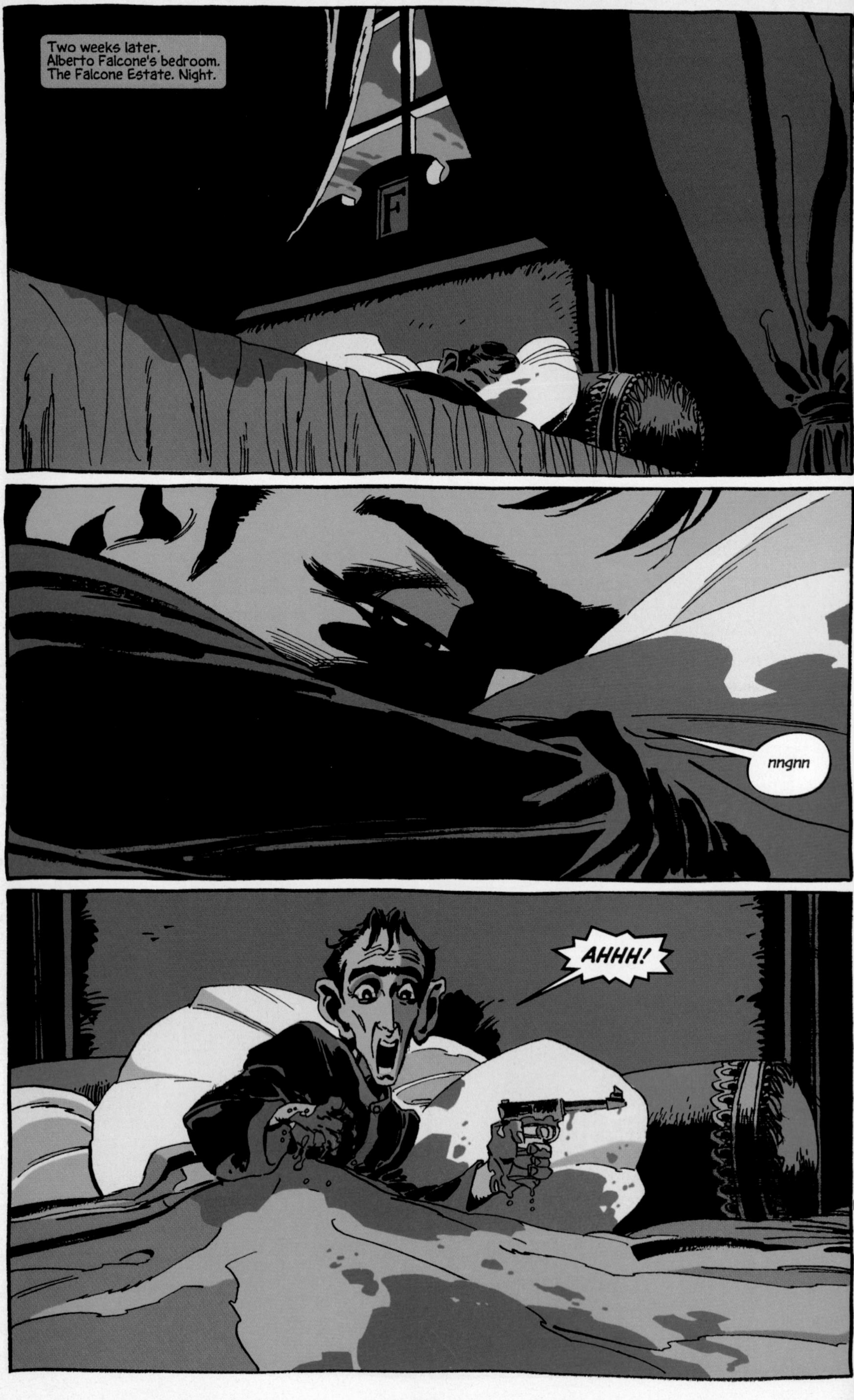
Two weeks later.
Alberto Falcone's bedroom.
The Falcone Estate. Night.
nngnn
AHHH!

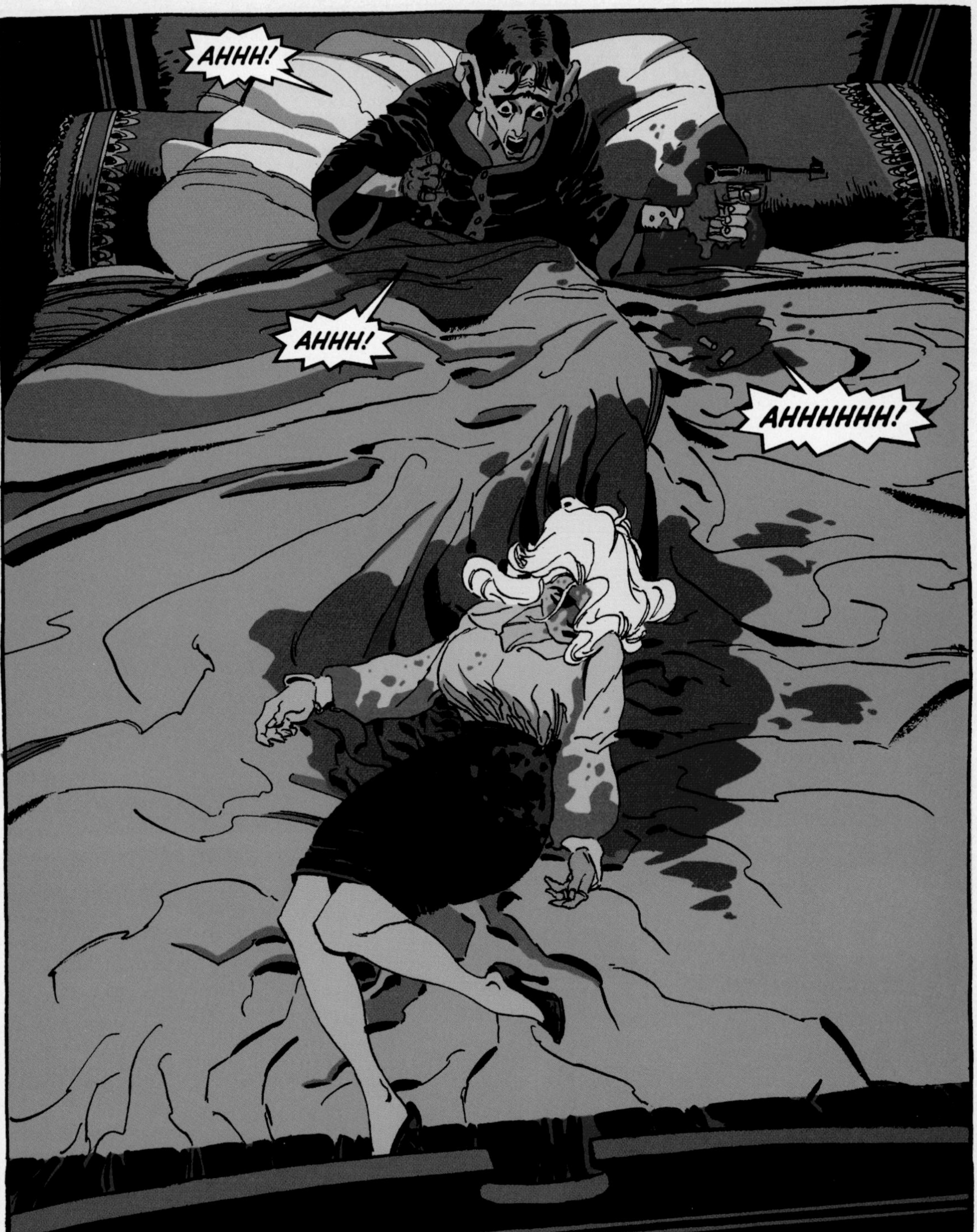
AHHH!
AHHH!
AHHHHHH!

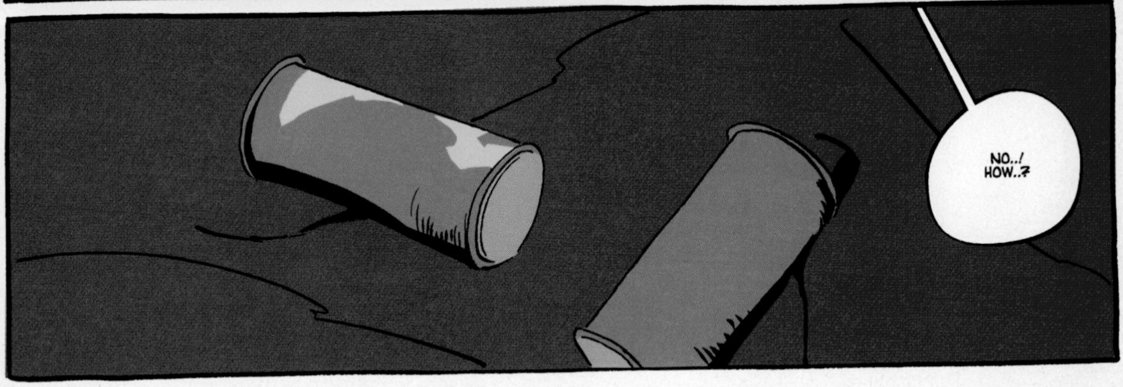
NO..! HOW..?

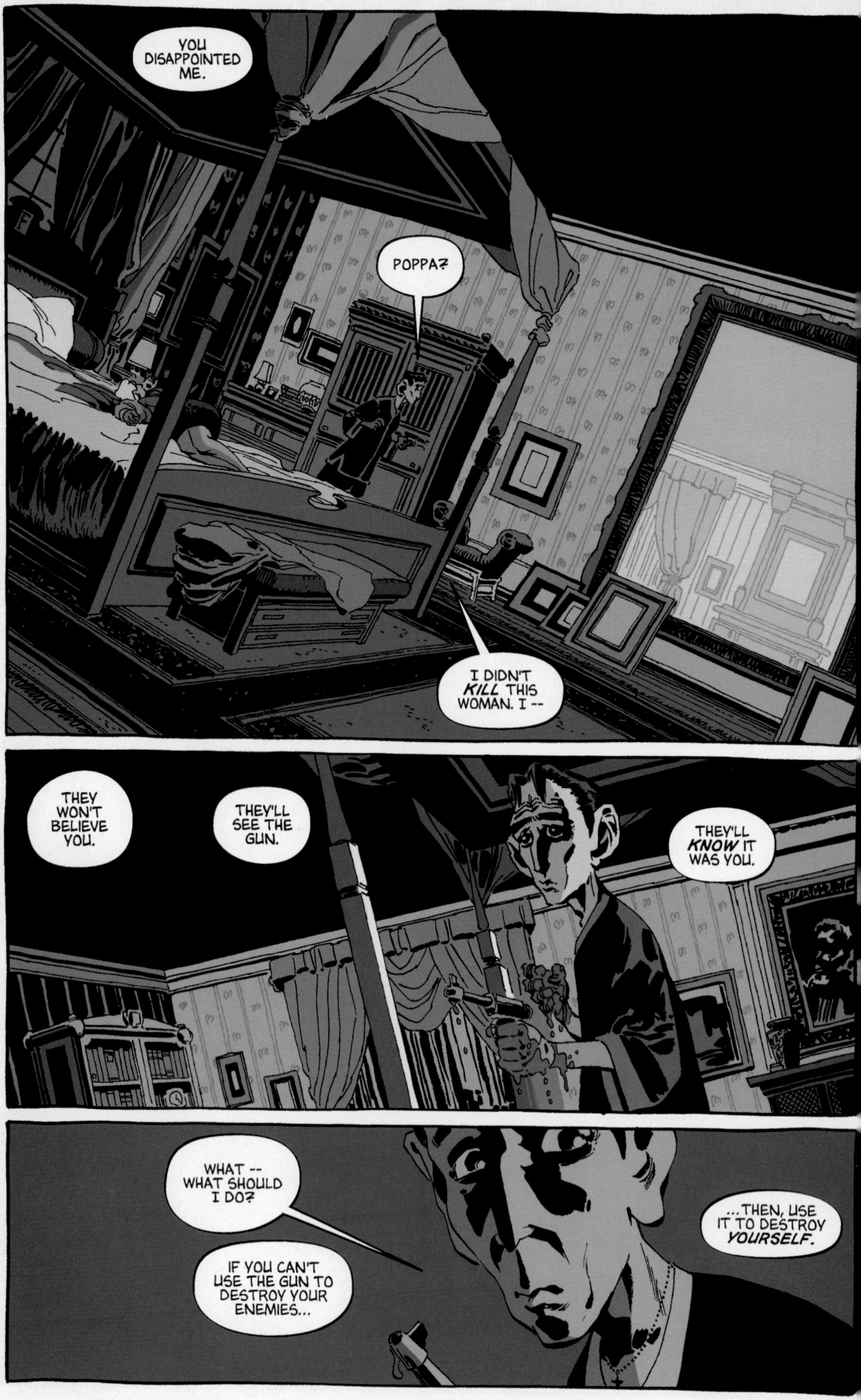
YOU DISAPPOINTED ME.
POPPA?
I DIDN'T KILL THIS WOMAN. I --
THEY WON'T BELIEVE YOU.
THEY'LL SEE THE GUN.
THEY'LL KNOW IT WAS YOU.
WHAT -- WHAT SHOULD I DO?
IF YOU CAN'T USE THE GUN TO DESTROY YOUR ENEMIES...
...THEN, USE IT TO DESTROY YOURSELF.

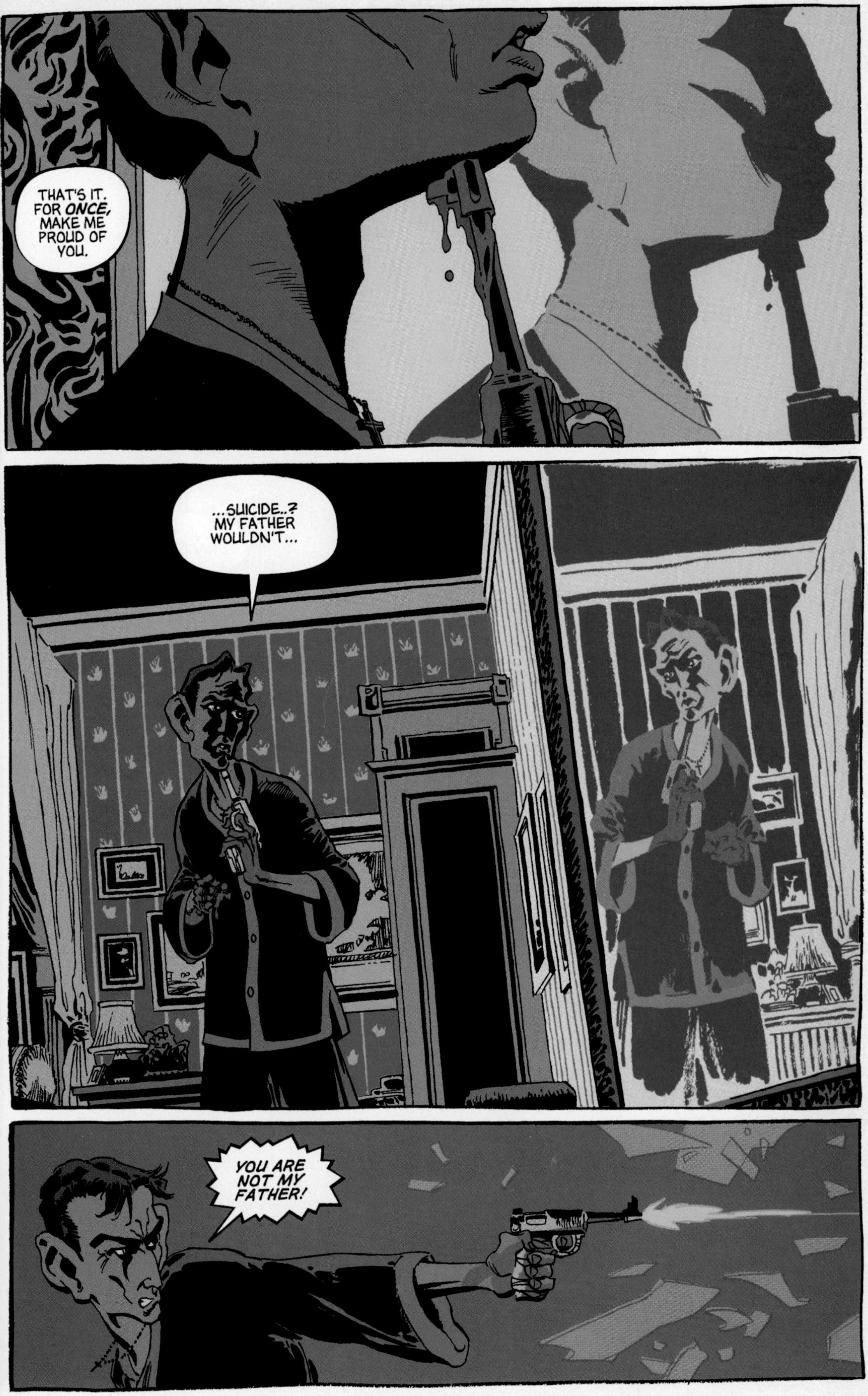
THAT'S IT. FOR *ONCE,* MAKE ME PROUD OF YOU.
...SUICIDE..? MY FATHER WOULDN'T...
YOU ARE NOT MY FATHER!

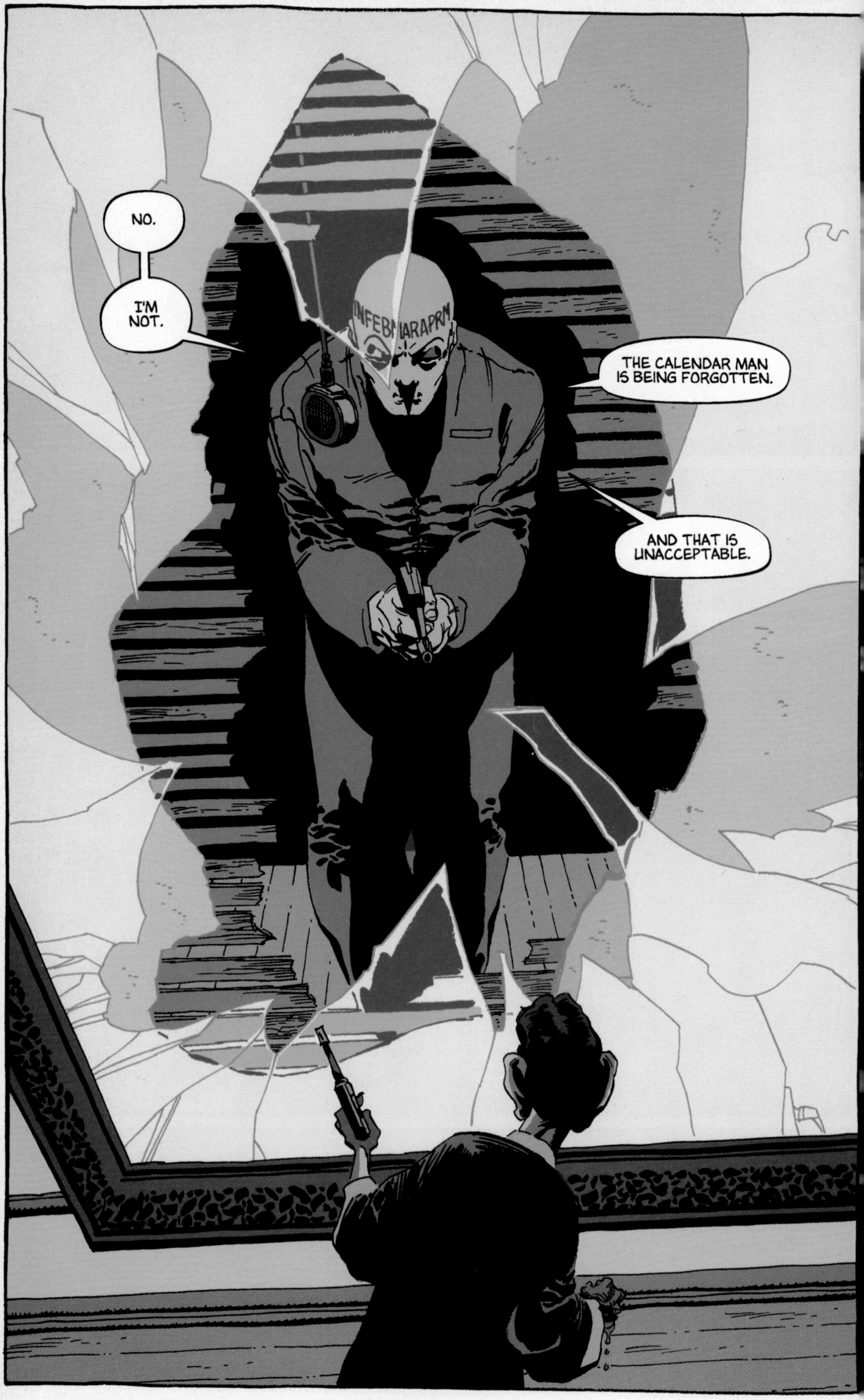
NO.
I'M NOT.
THE CALENDAR MAN IS BEING FORGOTTEN.
AND THAT IS UNACCEPTABLE.

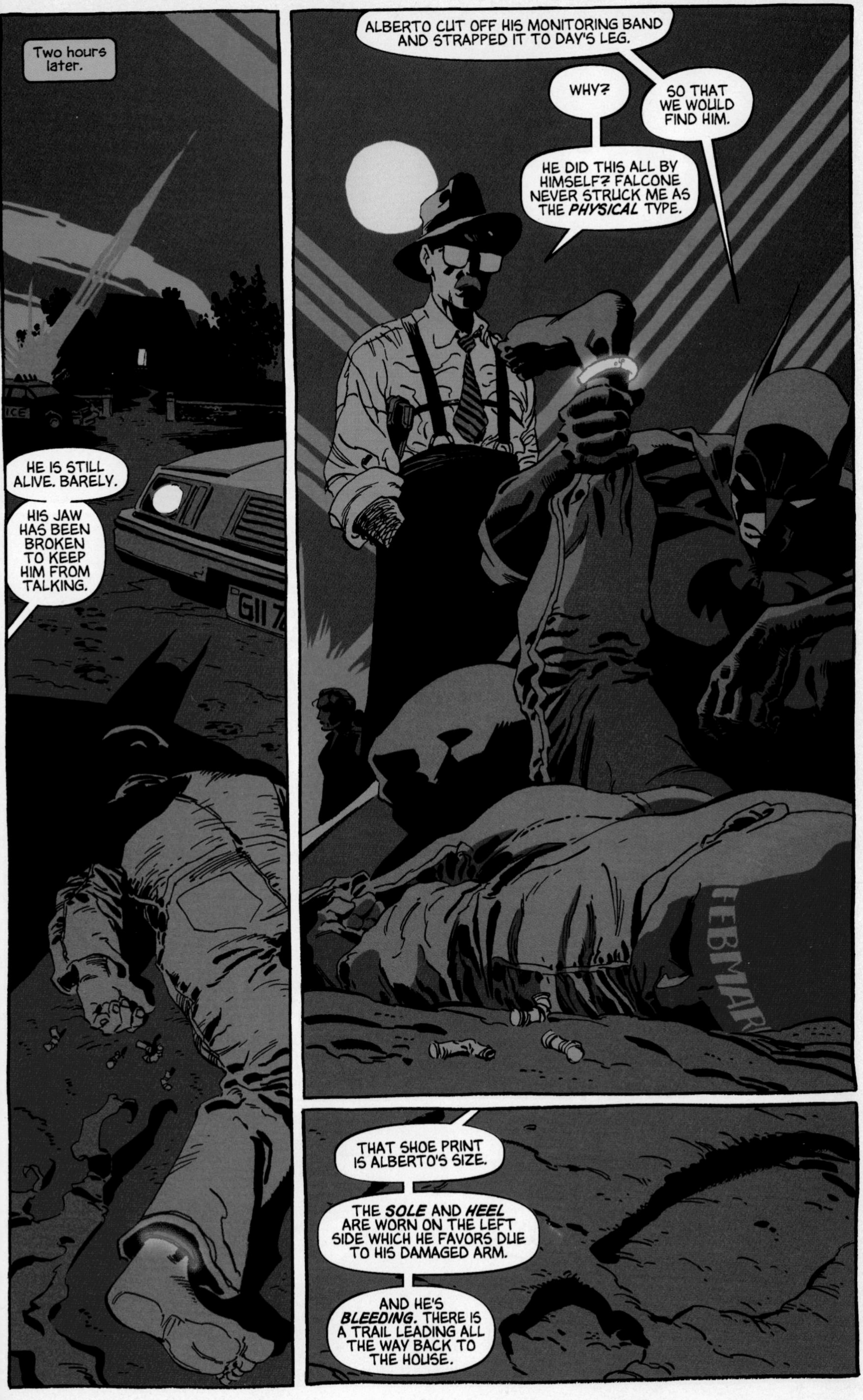
Two hours later.
HE IS STILL ALIVE. BARELY.
HIS JAW HAS BEEN BROKEN TO KEEP HIM FROM TALKING.
ALBERTO CUT OFF HIS MONITORING BAND AND STRAPPED IT TO DAY'S LEG.
WHY?
SO THAT WE WOULD FIND HIM.
HE DID THIS ALL BY HIMSELF? FALCONE NEVER STRUCK ME AS THE PHYSICAL TYPE.
THAT SHOE PRINT IS ALBERTO'S SIZE.
THE SOLE AND HEEL ARE WORN ON THE LEFT SIDE WHICH HE FAVORS DUE TO HIS DAMAGED ARM.
AND HE'S BLEEDING. THERE IS A TRAIL LEADING ALL THE WAY BACK TO THE HOUSE.

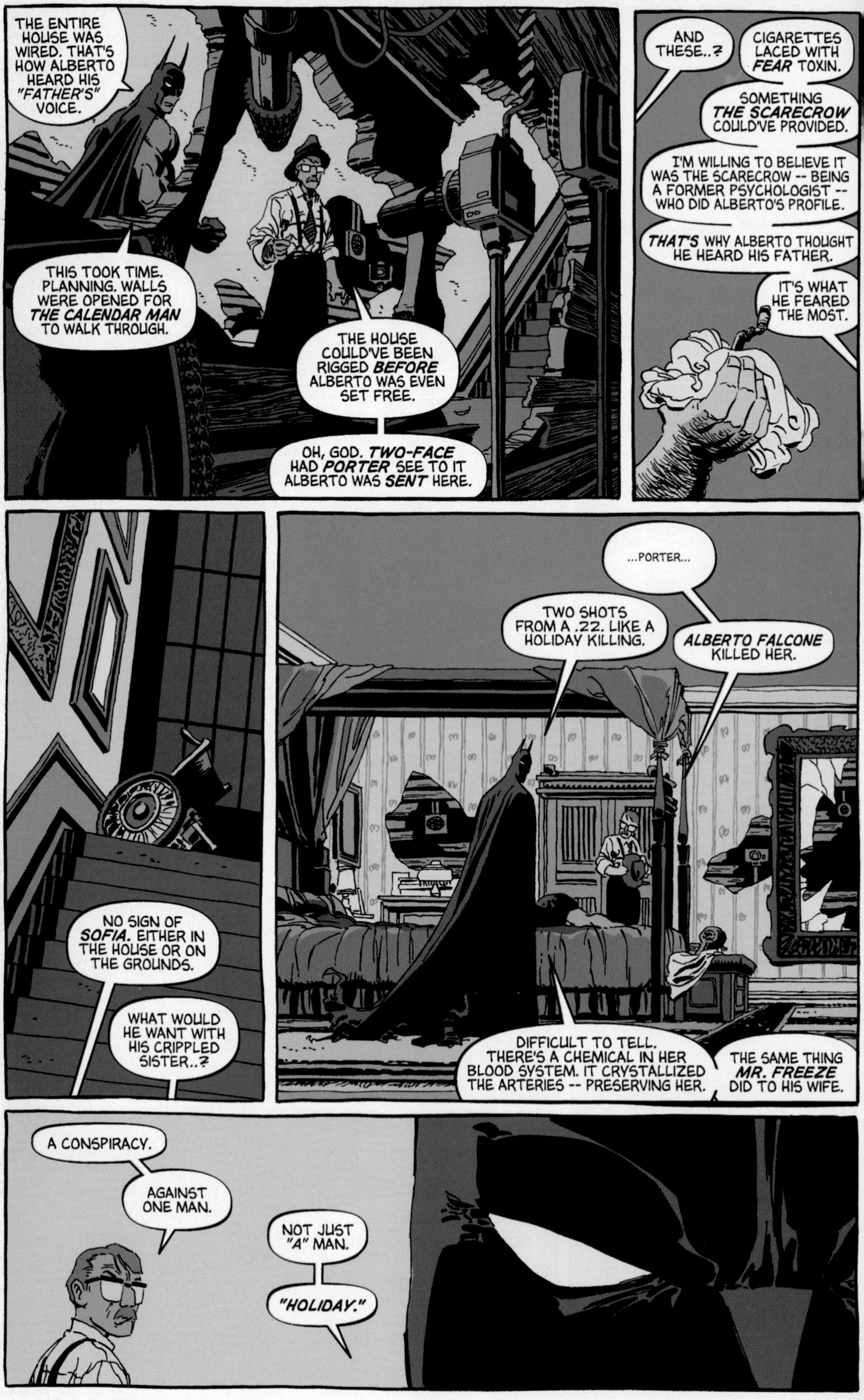
THE ENTIRE HOUSE WAS WIRED. THAT'S HOW ALBERTO HEARD HIS "FATHER'S" VOICE.
THIS TOOK TIME. PLANNING. WALLS WERE OPENED FOR THE CALENDAR MAN TO WALK THROUGH.
THE HOUSE COULD'VE BEEN RIGGED BEFORE ALBERTO WAS EVEN SET FREE.
OH, GOD. TWO-FACE HAD PORTER SEE TO IT ALBERTO WAS SENT HERE.
AND THESE..?
CIGARETTES LACED WITH FEAR TOXIN.
SOMETHING THE SCARECROW COULD'VE PROVIDED.
I'M WILLING TO BELIEVE IT WAS THE SCARECROW -- BEING A FORMER PSYCHOLOGIST -- WHO DID ALBERTO'S PROFILE.
THAT'S WHY ALBERTO THOUGHT HE HEARD HIS FATHER.
IT'S WHAT HE FEARED THE MOST.
NO SIGN OF SOFIA. EITHER IN THE HOUSE OR ON THE GROUNDS.
WHAT WOULD HE WANT WITH HIS CRIPPLED SISTER..?
...PORTER...
TWO SHOTS FROM A .22. LIKE A HOLIDAY KILLING.
ALBERTO FALCONE KILLED HER.
DIFFICULT TO TELL. THERE'S A CHEMICAL IN HER BLOOD SYSTEM. IT CRYSTALLIZED THE ARTERIES -- PRESERVING HER.
THE SAME THING MR. FREEZE DID TO HIS WIFE.
A CONSPIRACY.
AGAINST ONE MAN.
NOT JUST "A" MAN.
"HOLIDAY."

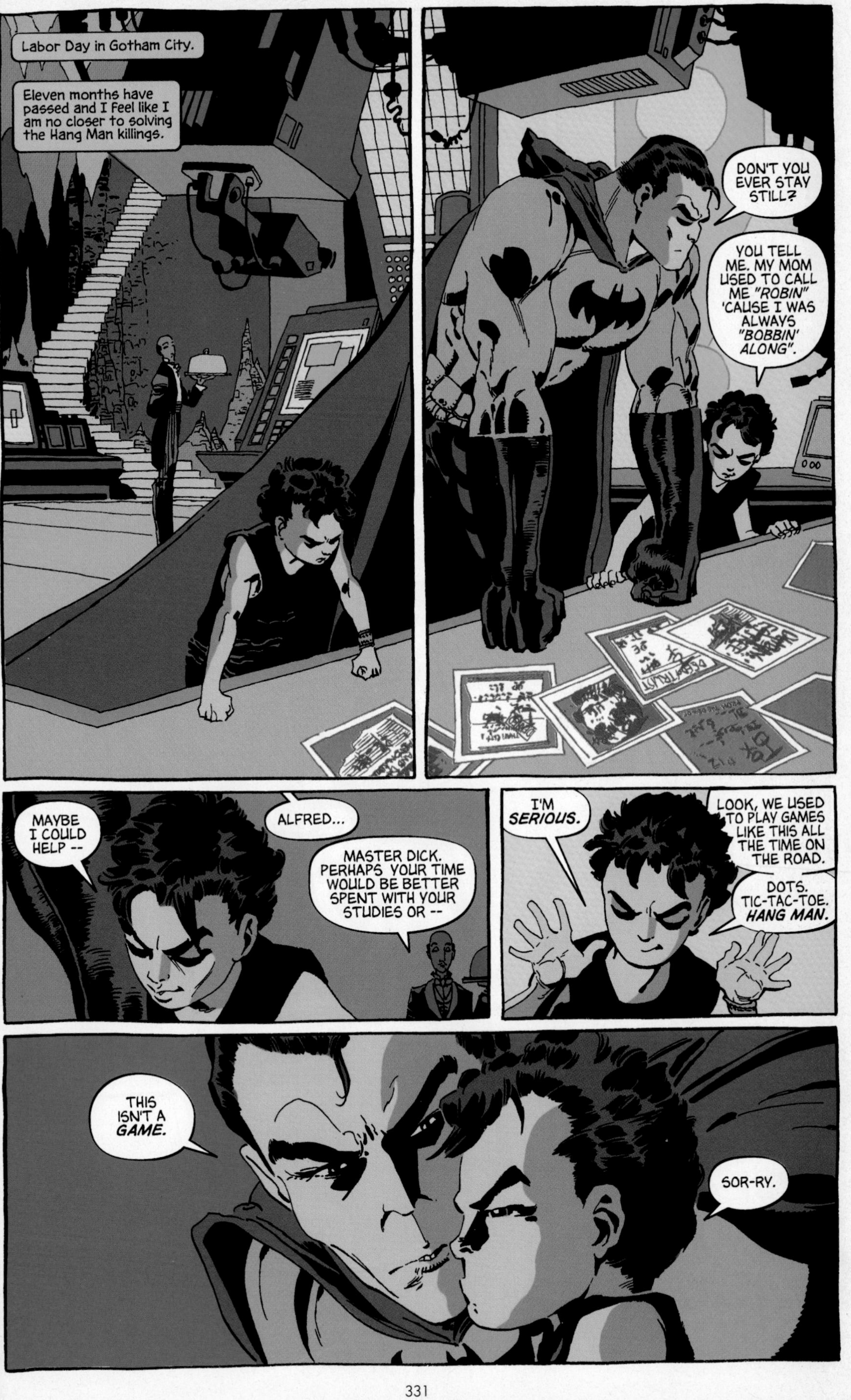

Labor Day in Gotham City.
Eleven months have passed and I feel like I am no closer to solving the Hang Man killings.
DON'T YOU EVER STAY STILL?
YOU TELL ME. MY MOM USED TO CALL ME "ROBIN" 'CAUSE I WAS ALWAYS "BOBBIN' ALONG".
MAYBE I COULD HELP --
ALFRED...
MASTER DICK. PERHAPS YOUR TIME WOULD BE BETTER SPENT WITH YOUR STUDIES OR --
I'M SERIOUS.
LOOK, WE USED TO PLAY GAMES LIKE THIS ALL THE TIME ON THE ROAD.
DOTS. TIC-TAC-TOE. HANG MAN.
THIS ISN'T A GAME.
SOR-RY.

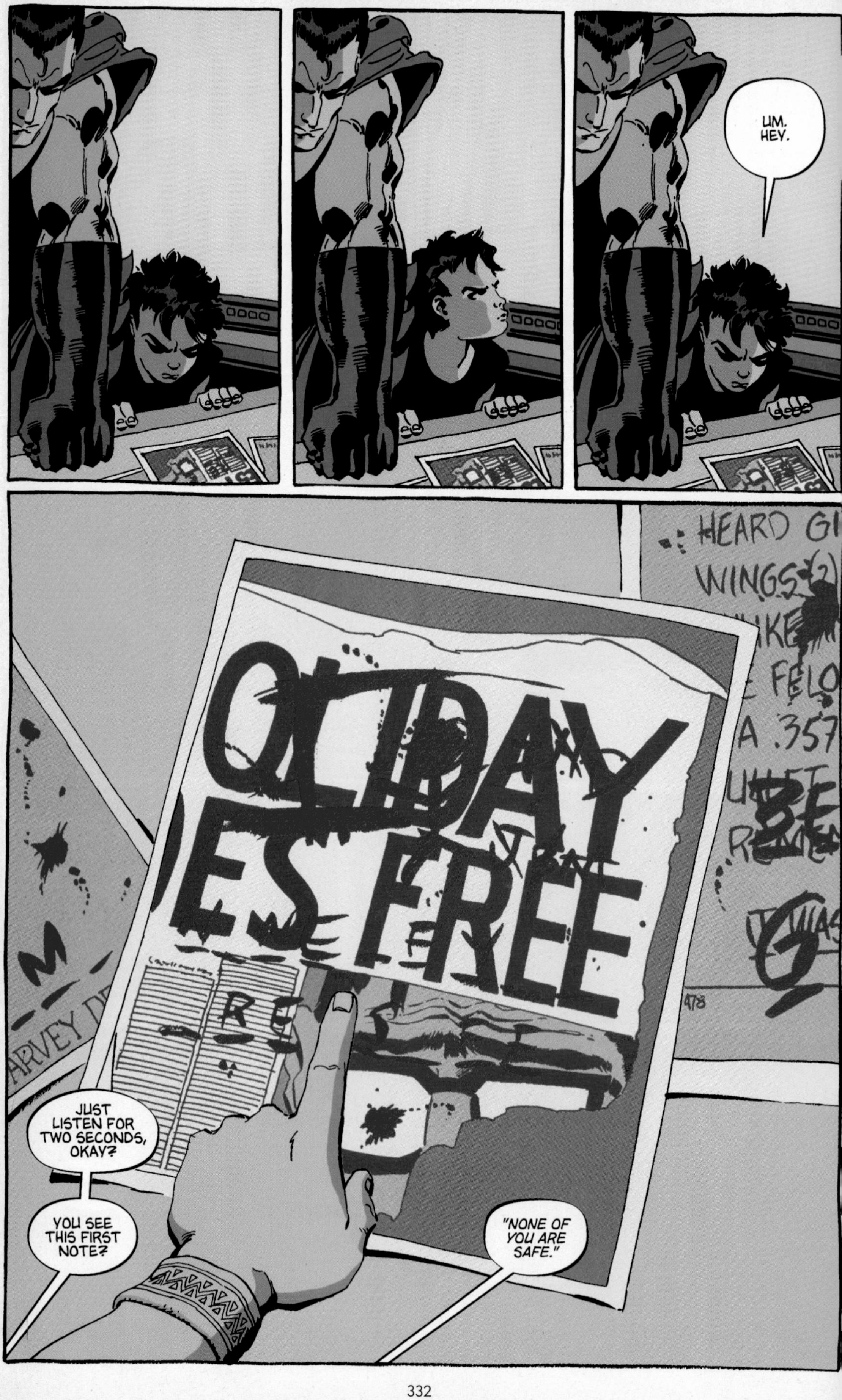

UM. HEY.
JUST LISTEN FOR TWO SECONDS, OKAY?
YOU SEE THIS FIRST NOTE?
"NONE OF YOU ARE SAFE."

FALCONE CRIME EMPIRE
COMPILED BY JANICE PORTER DISTRICT ATTORNEY GOTHAM CITY

FALCONE FAMILY
GOTHAM CITY

SOFIA FALCONE GIGANTE

MARIO FALCONE   ALBERTO FALCONE

THE MARONI FAMILY
GOTHAM CITY

UMBERTO MARONI   PINO MARONI

THE VITI FAMILY
CHICAGO

LUCIA VITI

ANTHONY "FATS" ZUCCO

THE GAZZO FAMILY
METROPOLIS

BOBBY "THE DON" GAZZO

WHAT IF IT'S SUPPOSED TO READ --

"*NINE* OF YOU ARE SAFE."

Y'KNOW. LIKE A MESSAGE -- NOT A CLUE.

HUH? HUH? WHAT DO YOU THINK?

The boy... shows promise.

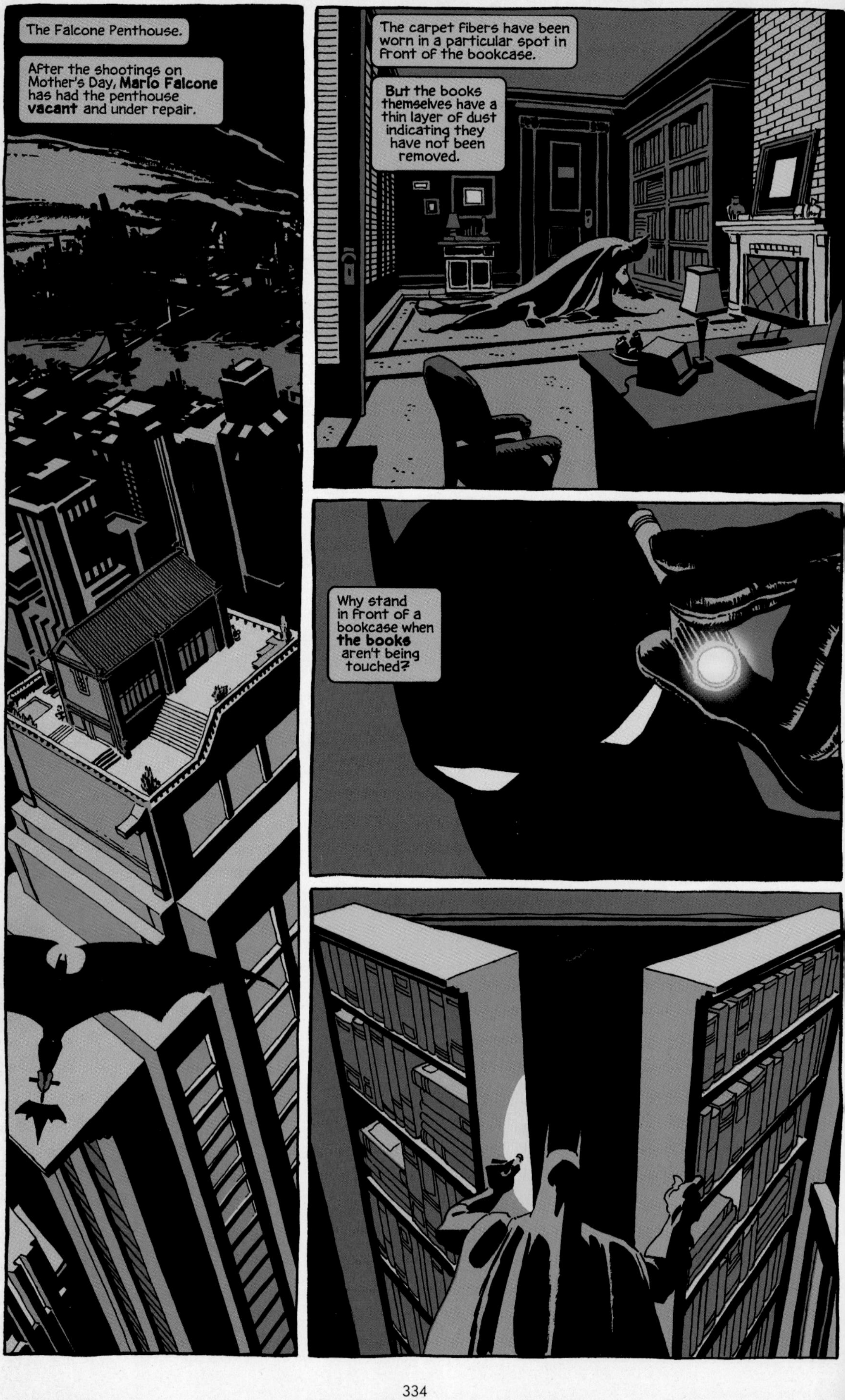

The Falcone Penthouse.
After the shootings on Mother's Day, **Mario Falcone** has had the penthouse **vacant** and under repair.
The carpet fibers have been worn in a particular spot in front of the bookcase.
But the books themselves have a thin layer of dust indicating they have not been removed.
Why stand in front of a bookcase when **the books** aren't being touched?

ACK

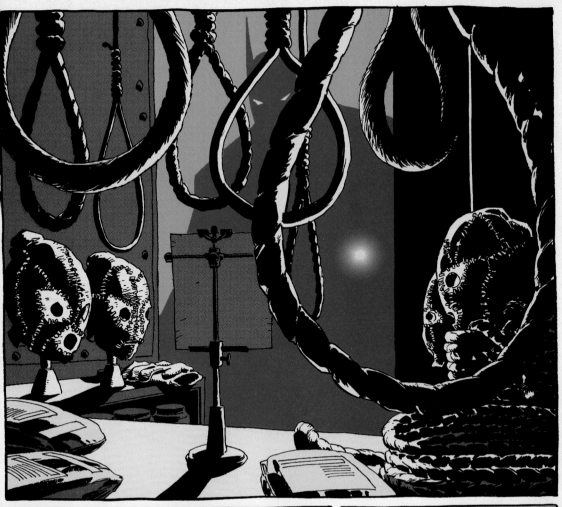

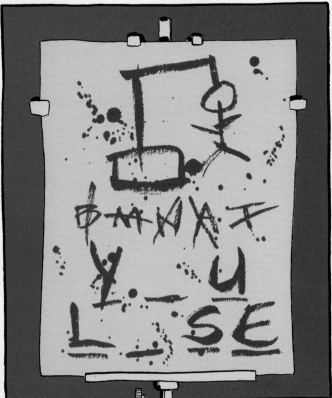

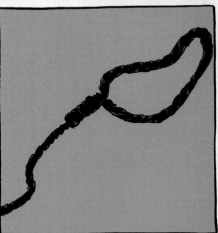

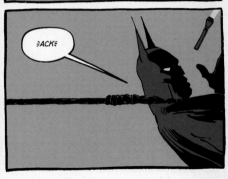

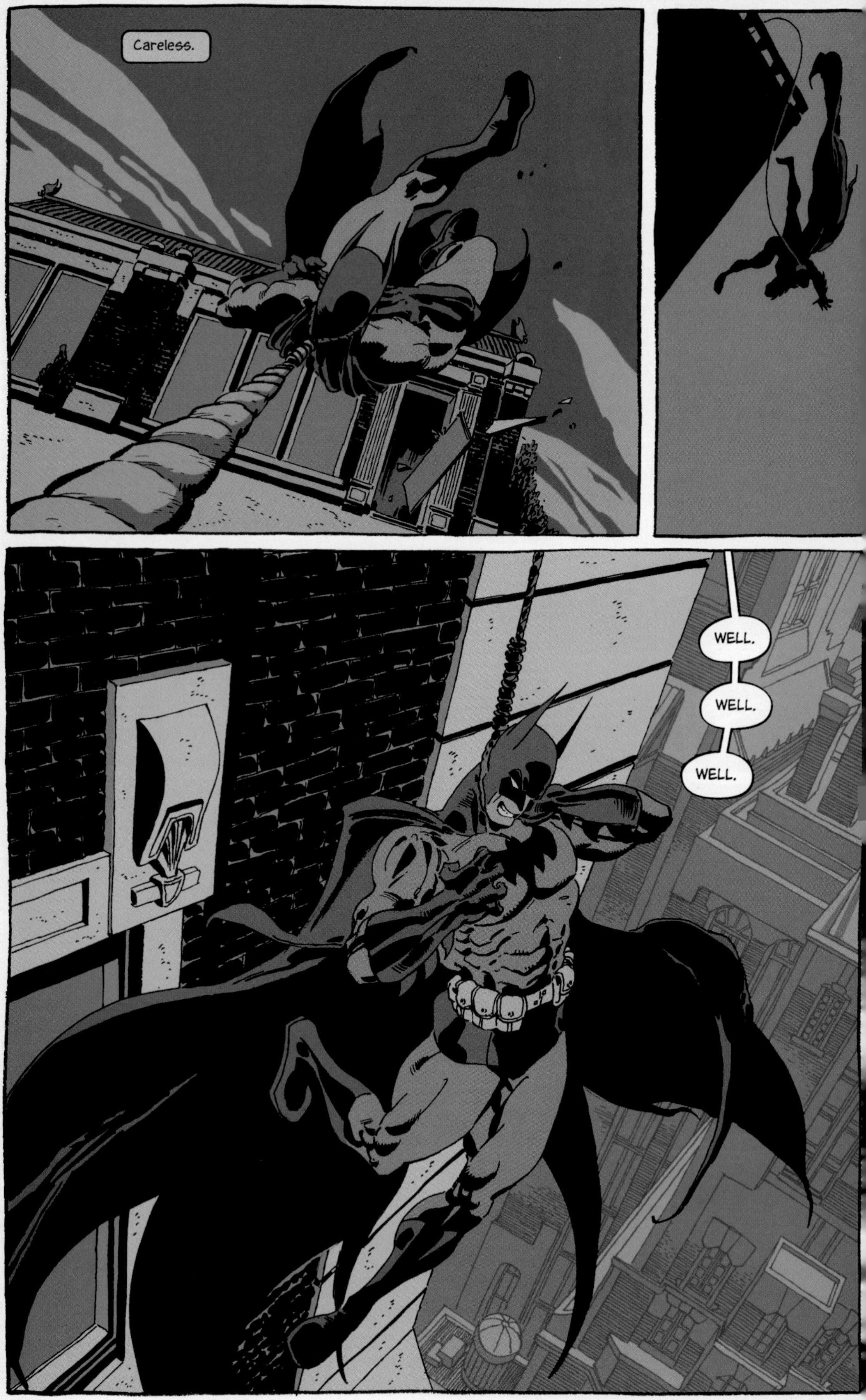
Careless.
WELL.
WELL.
WELL.

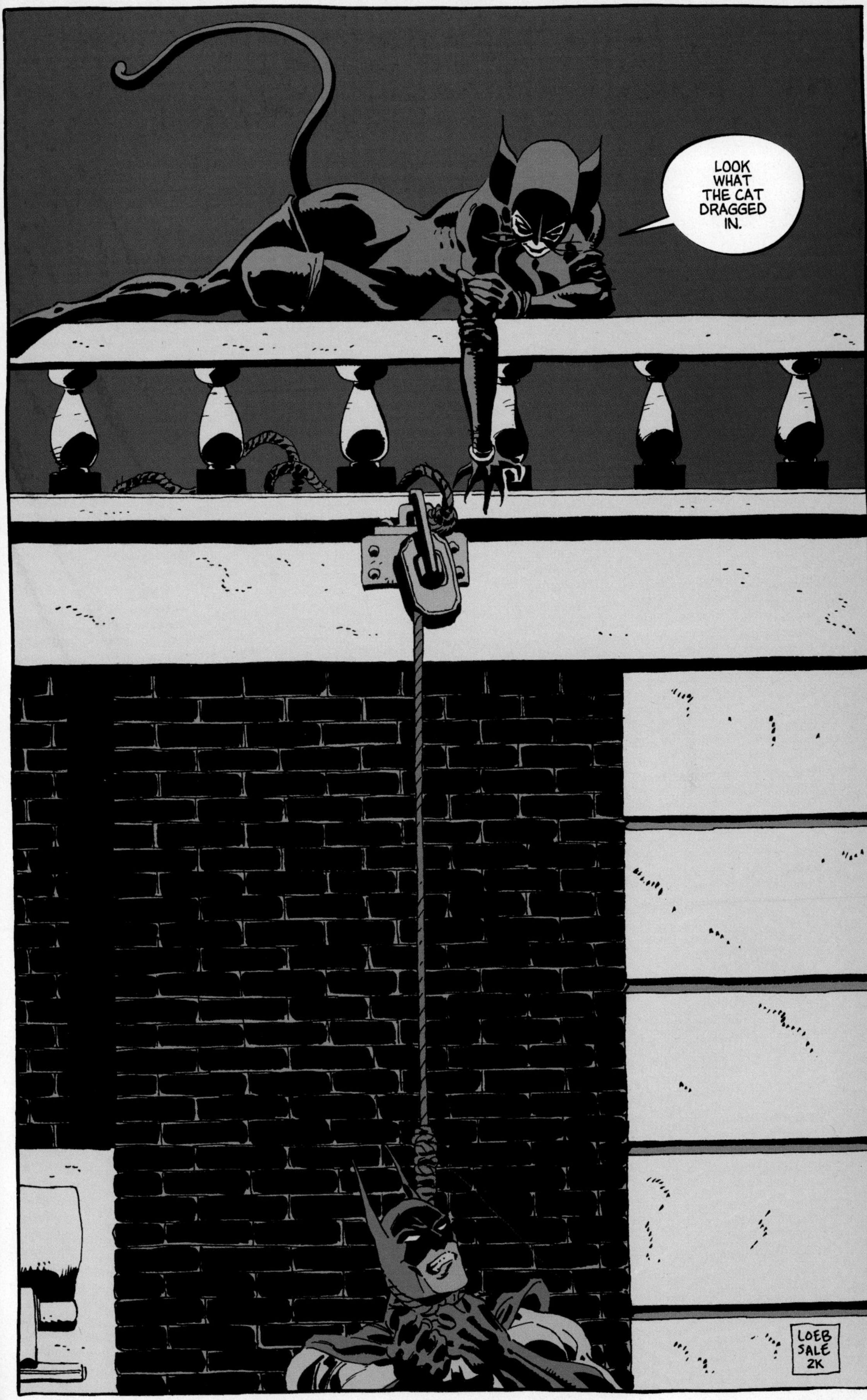
LOOK WHAT THE CAT DRAGGED IN.
LOEB SALE 2K

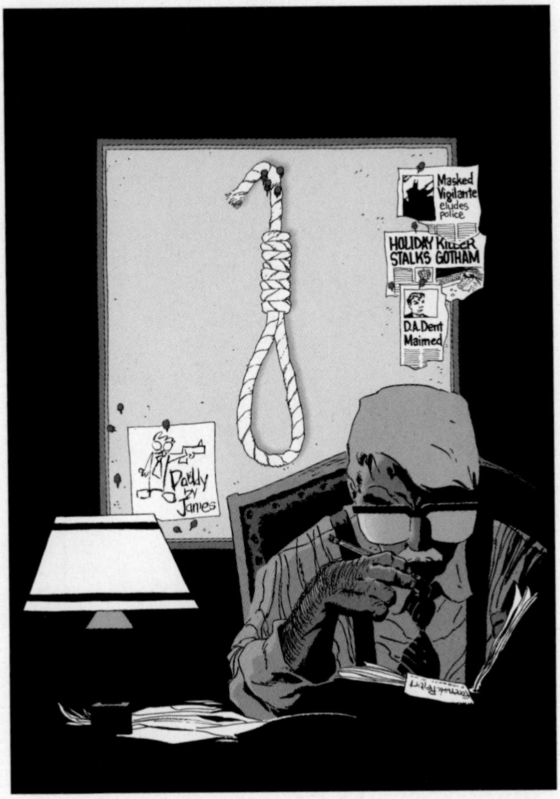
Masked Vigilante eludes police
HOLIDAY KILLER STALKS GOTHAM
D.A. Dent Maimed
Daddy by James

13

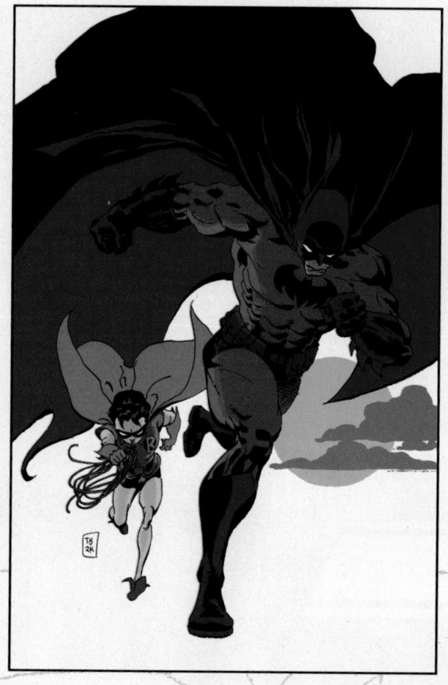

P E A C E

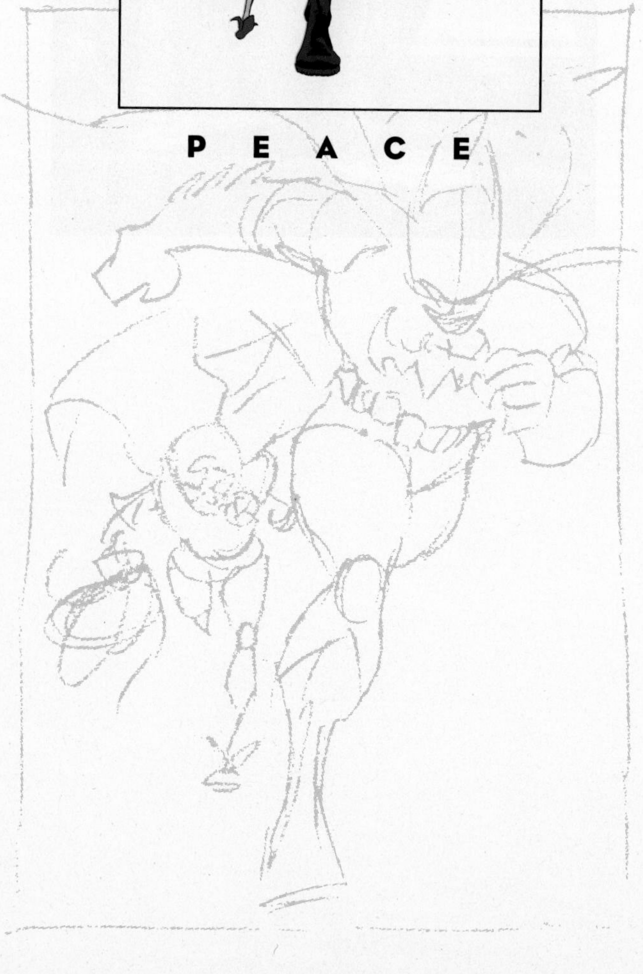

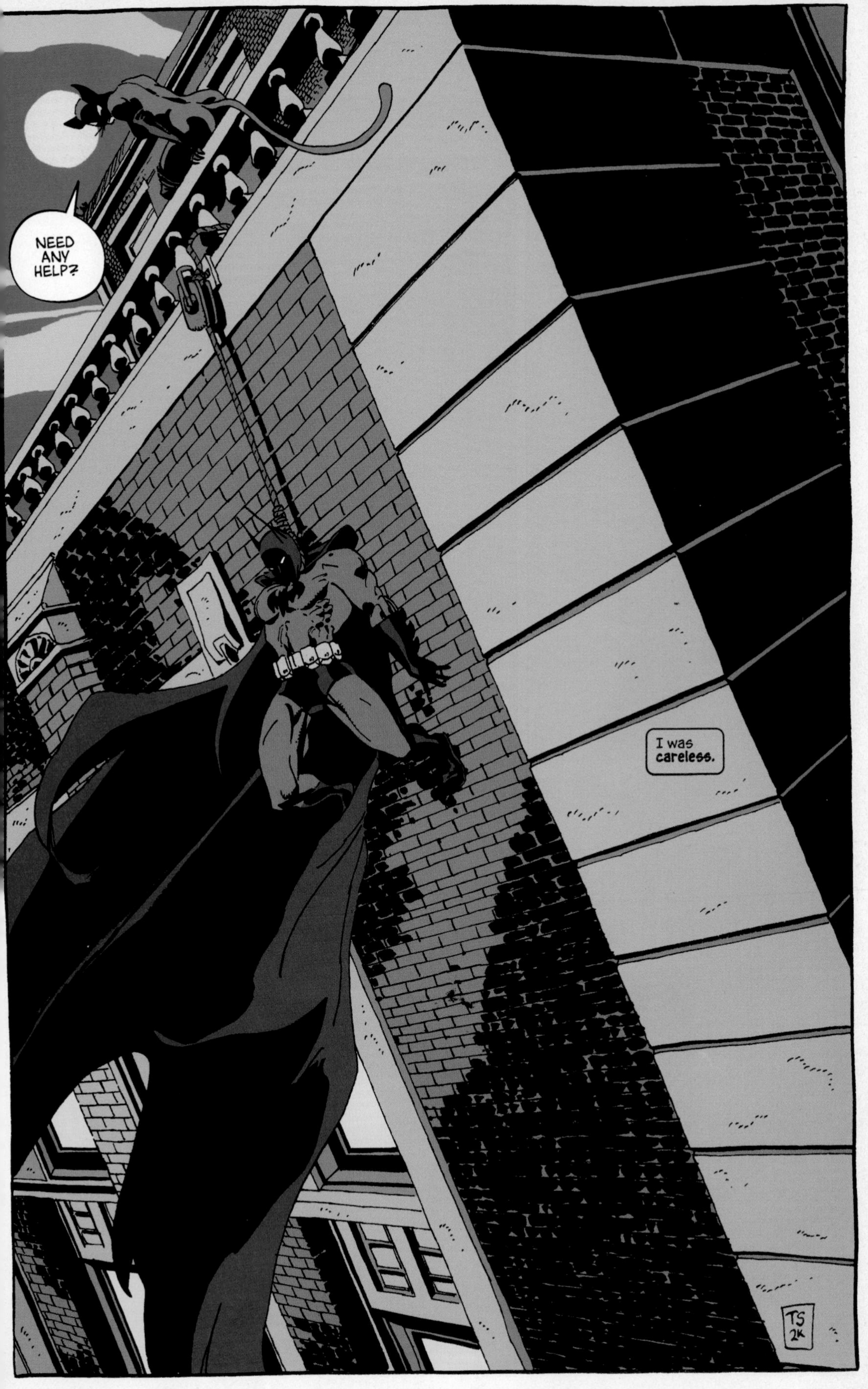
NEED ANY HELP?
I was careless.
TS 2K

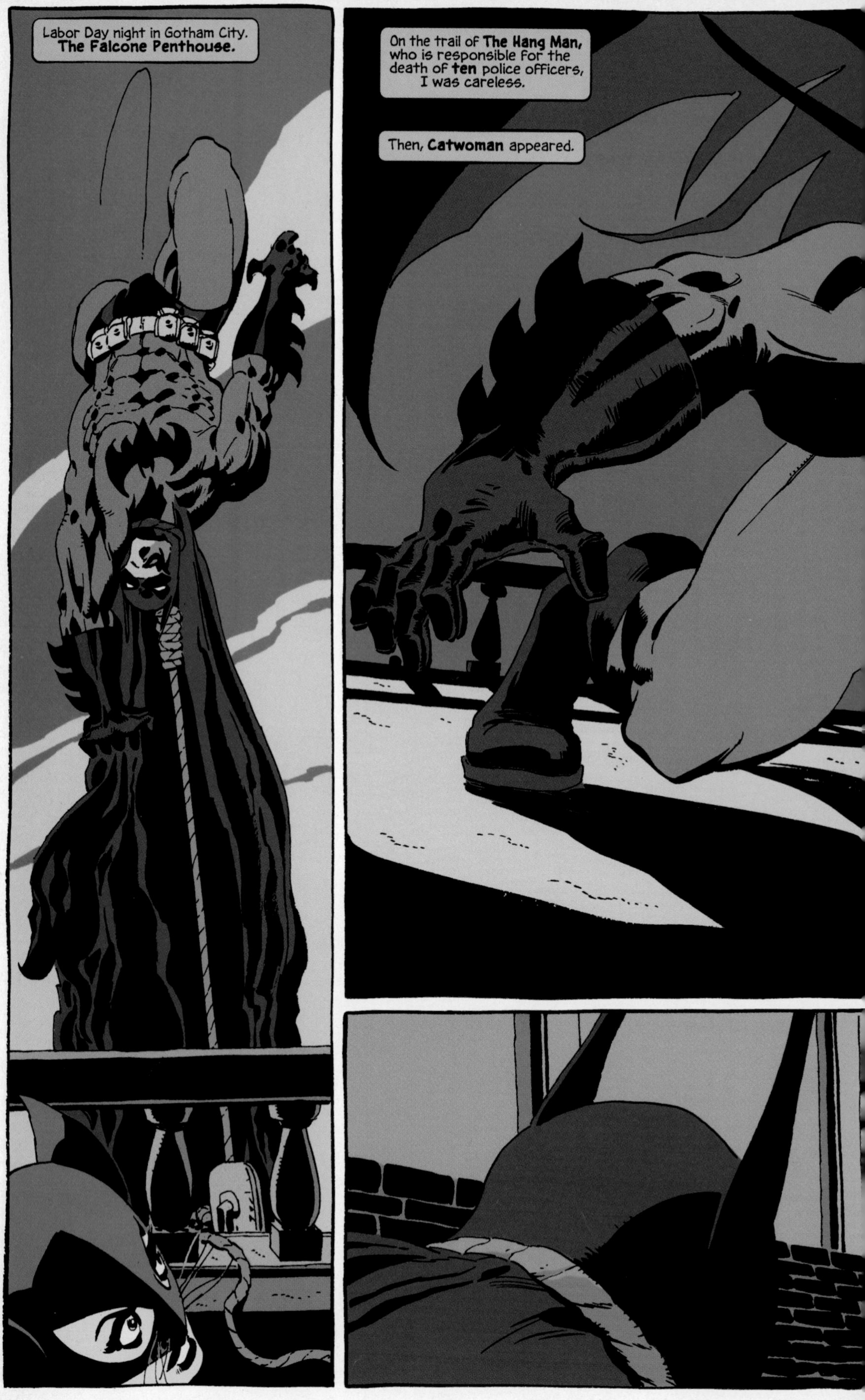

Labor Day night in Gotham City.
The Falcone Penthouse.
On the trail of **The Hang Man,** who is responsible for the death of **ten** police officers, I was careless.
Then, **Catwoman** appeared.

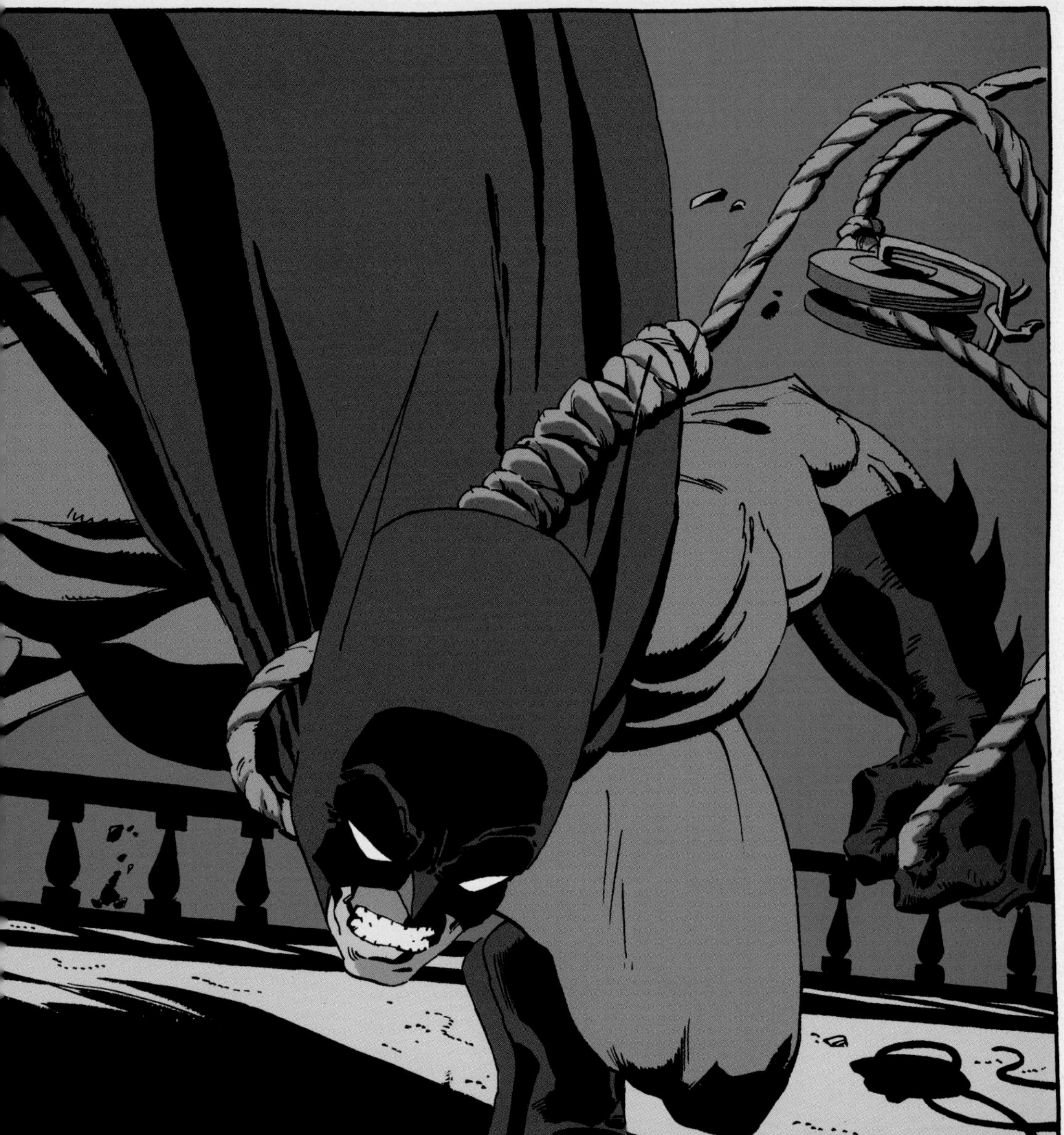

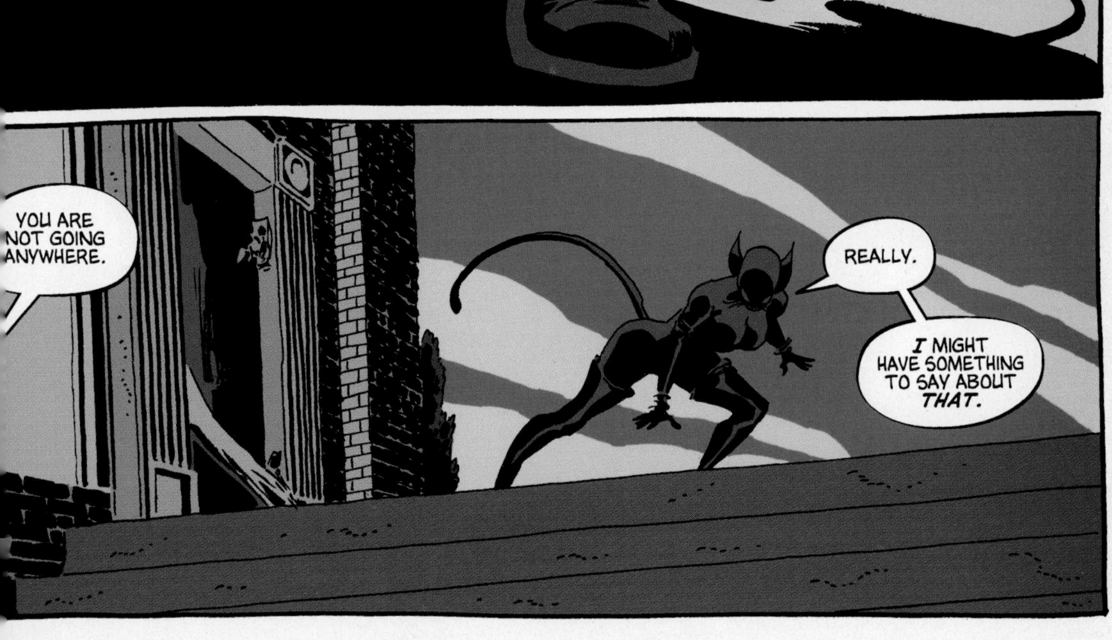

YOU ARE NOT GOING ANYWHERE.
REALLY.
I MIGHT HAVE SOMETHING TO SAY ABOUT THAT.

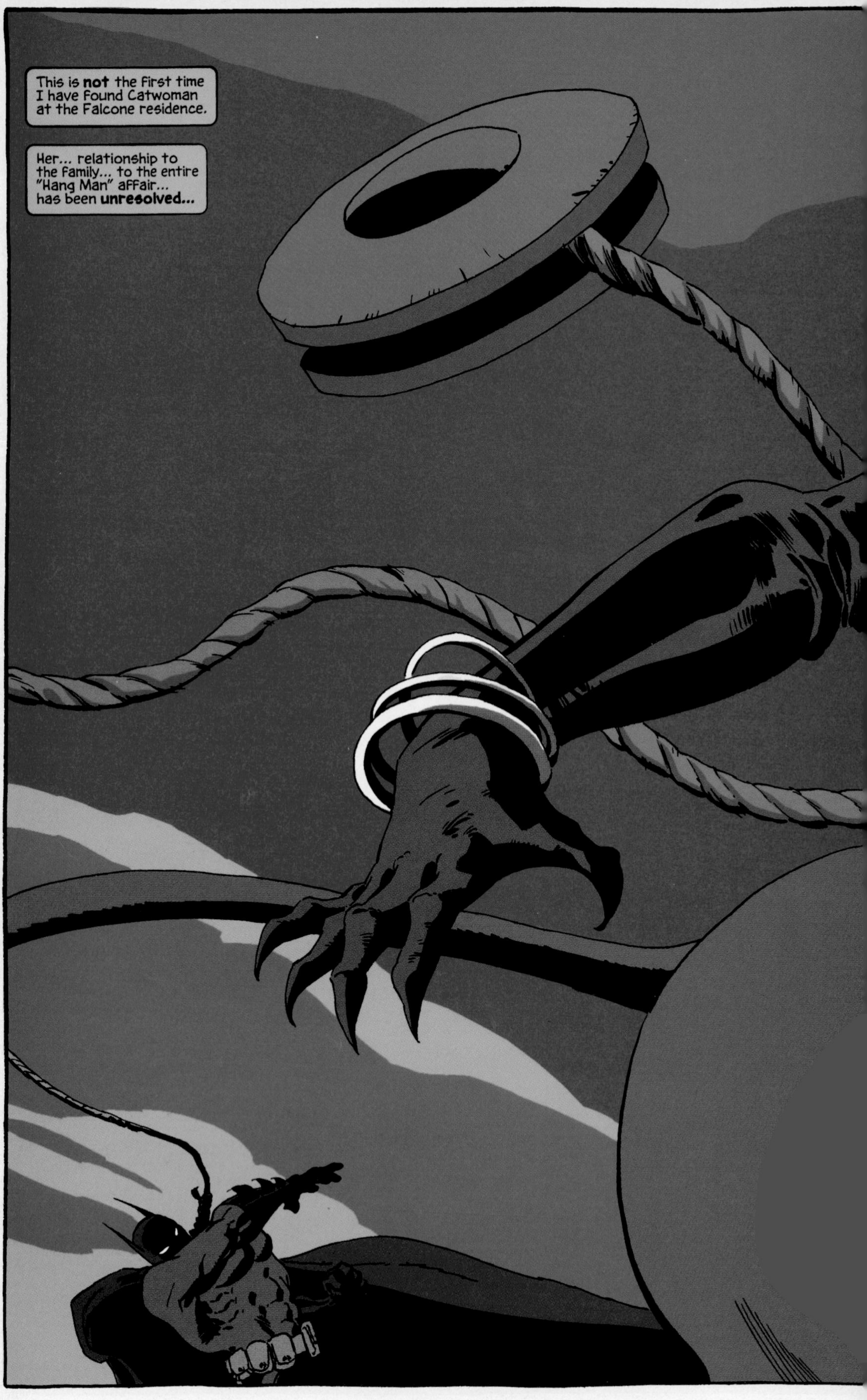
This is **not** the first time I have found Catwoman at the Falcone residence.
Her... relationship to the family... to the entire "Hang Man" affair... has been **unresolved...**

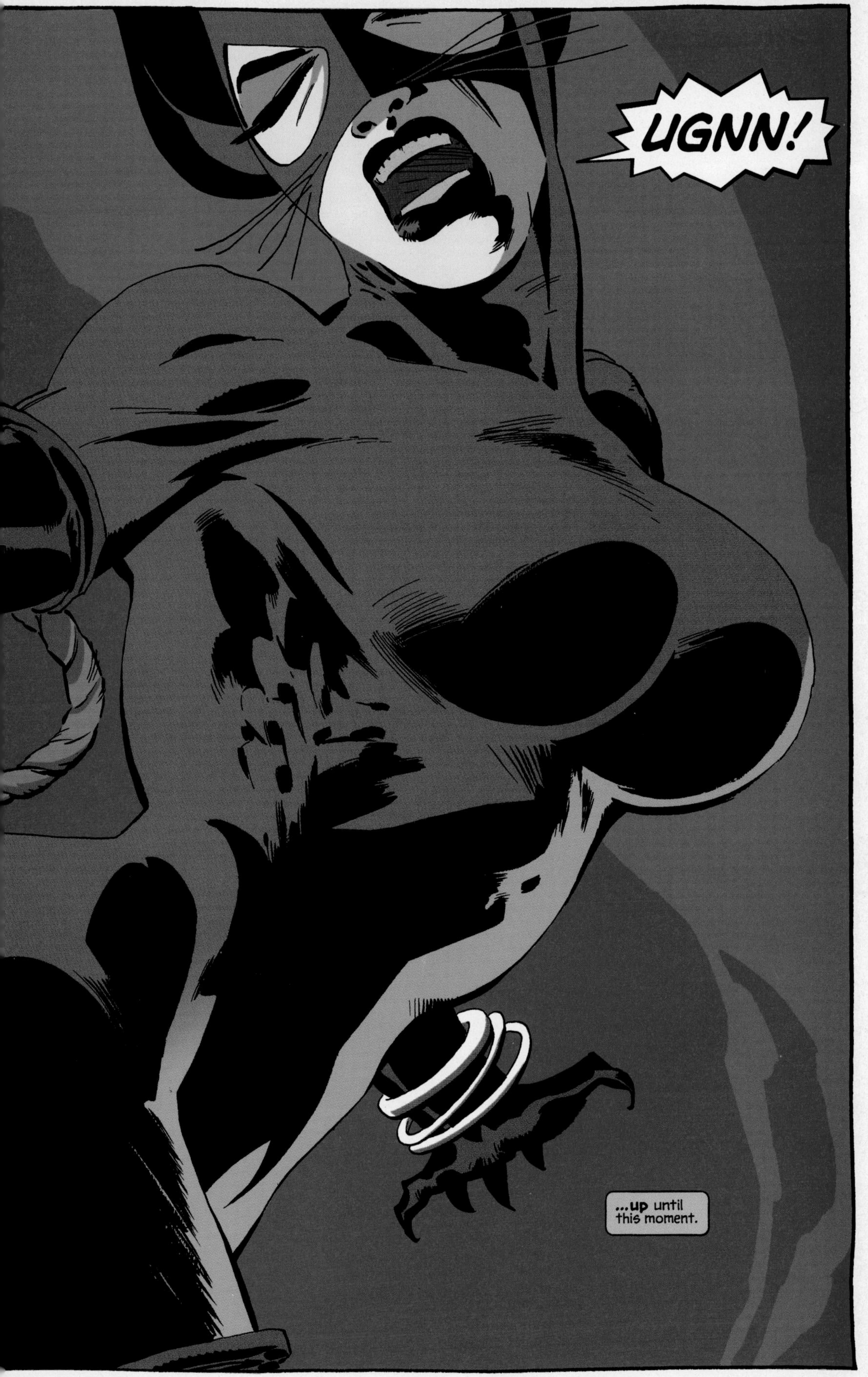
UGNN!
...up until this moment.

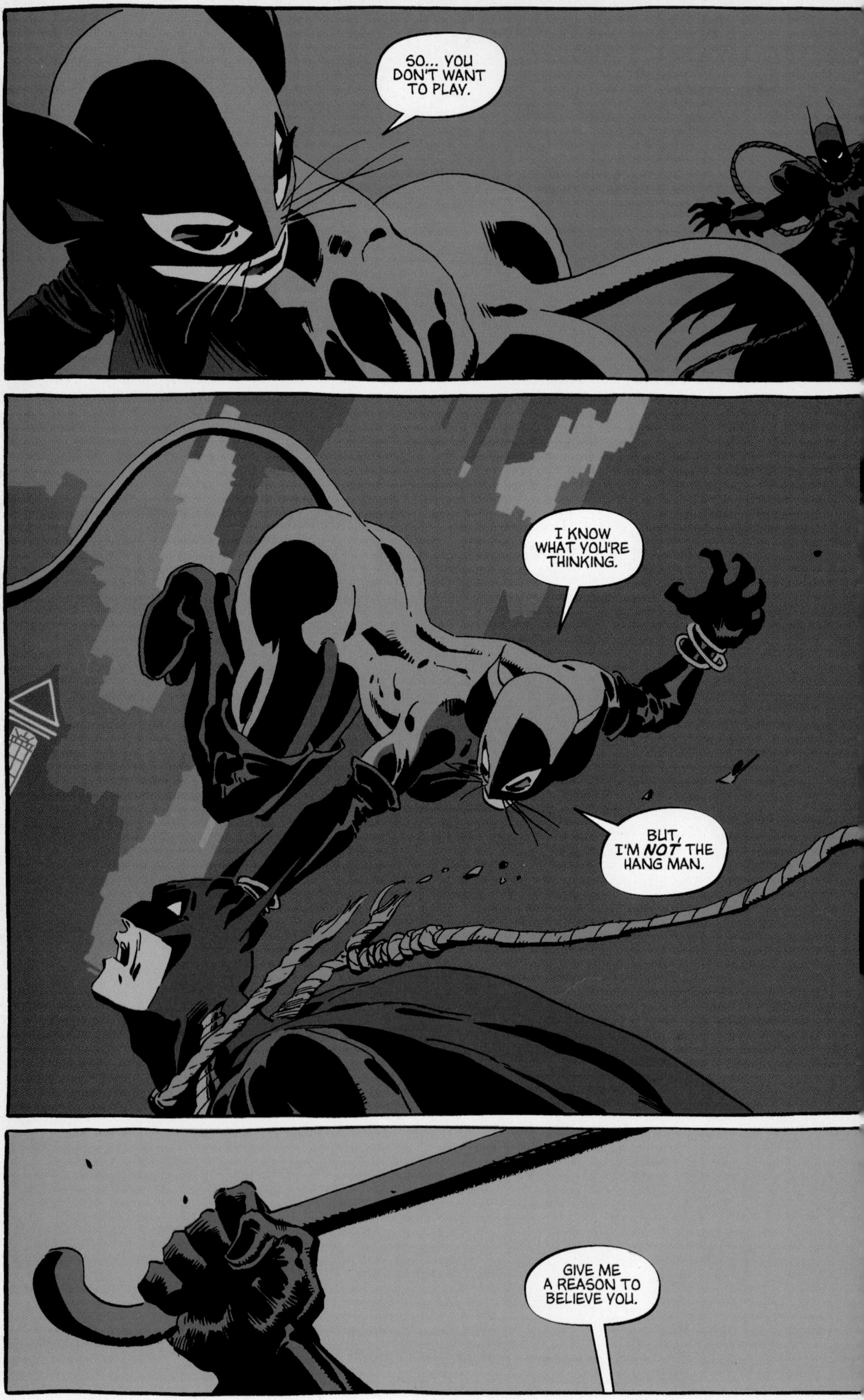
SO... YOU DON'T WANT TO PLAY.
I KNOW WHAT YOU'RE THINKING.
BUT, I'M *NOT* THE HANG MAN.
GIVE ME A REASON TO BELIEVE YOU.

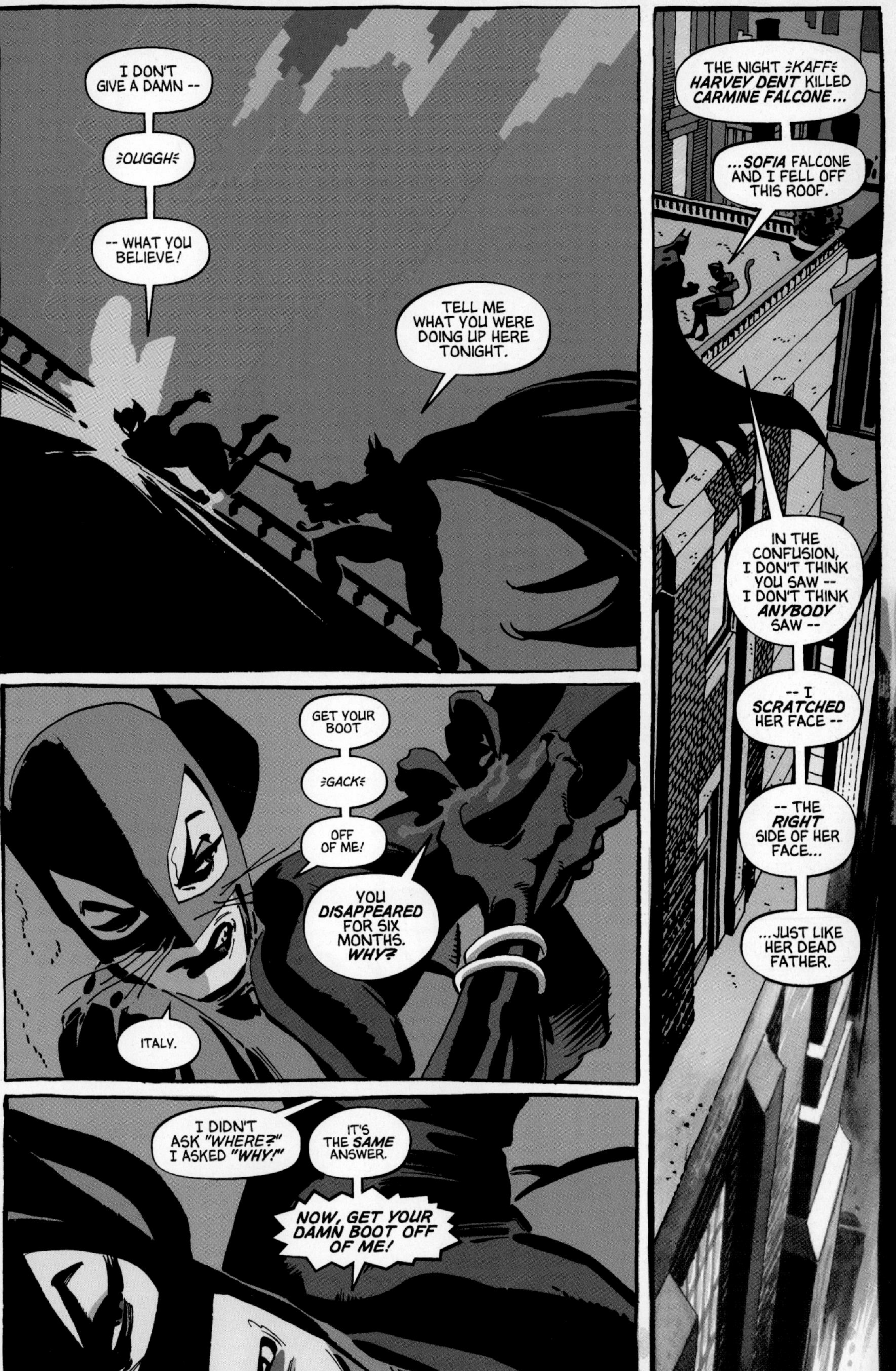
I DON'T GIVE A DAMN --
≷OUGGH≶
-- WHAT YOU BELIEVE!
TELL ME WHAT YOU WERE DOING UP HERE TONIGHT.
GET YOUR BOOT
≷GACK≶
OFF OF ME!
YOU DISAPPEARED FOR SIX MONTHS. WHY?
ITALY.
I DIDN'T ASK "WHERE?" I ASKED "WHY!"
IT'S THE SAME ANSWER.
NOW, GET YOUR DAMN BOOT OFF OF ME!
THE NIGHT ≷KAFF≶ HARVEY DENT KILLED CARMINE FALCONE...
...SOFIA FALCONE AND I FELL OFF THIS ROOF.
IN THE CONFUSION, I DON'T THINK YOU SAW -- I DON'T THINK ANYBODY SAW --
-- I SCRATCHED HER FACE --
-- THE RIGHT SIDE OF HER FACE...
...JUST LIKE HER DEAD FATHER.

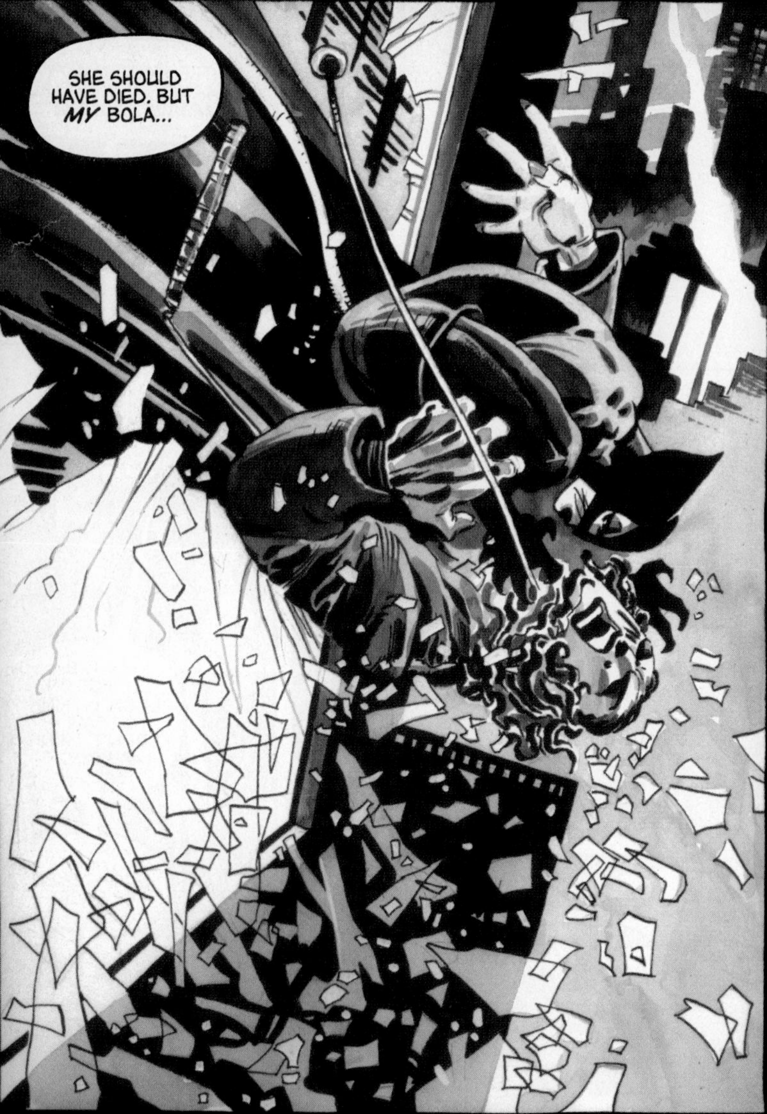
SHE SHOULD
HAVE DIED. BUT
MY BOLA...

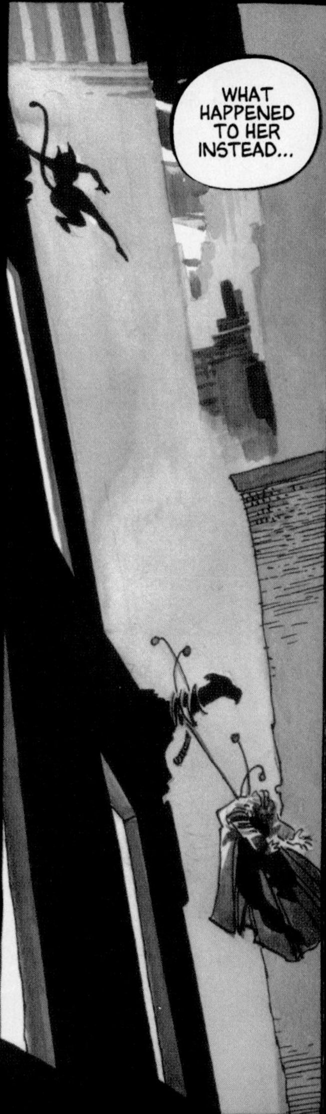
WHAT
HAPPENED
TO HER
INSTEAD...

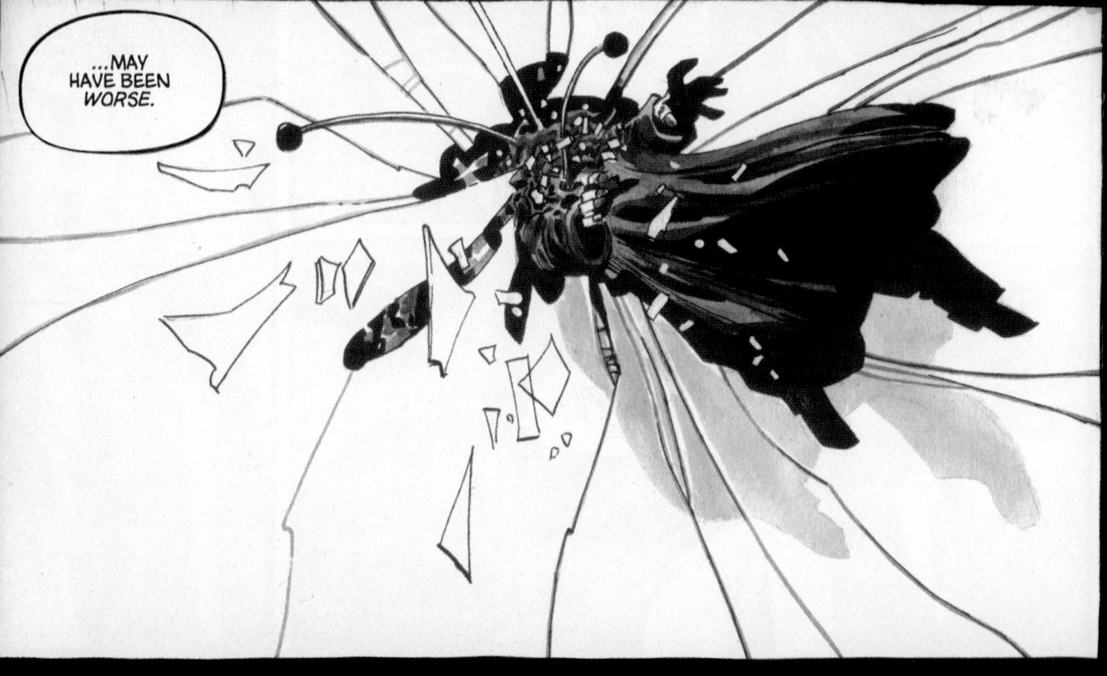
...MAY
HAVE BEEN
WORSE.

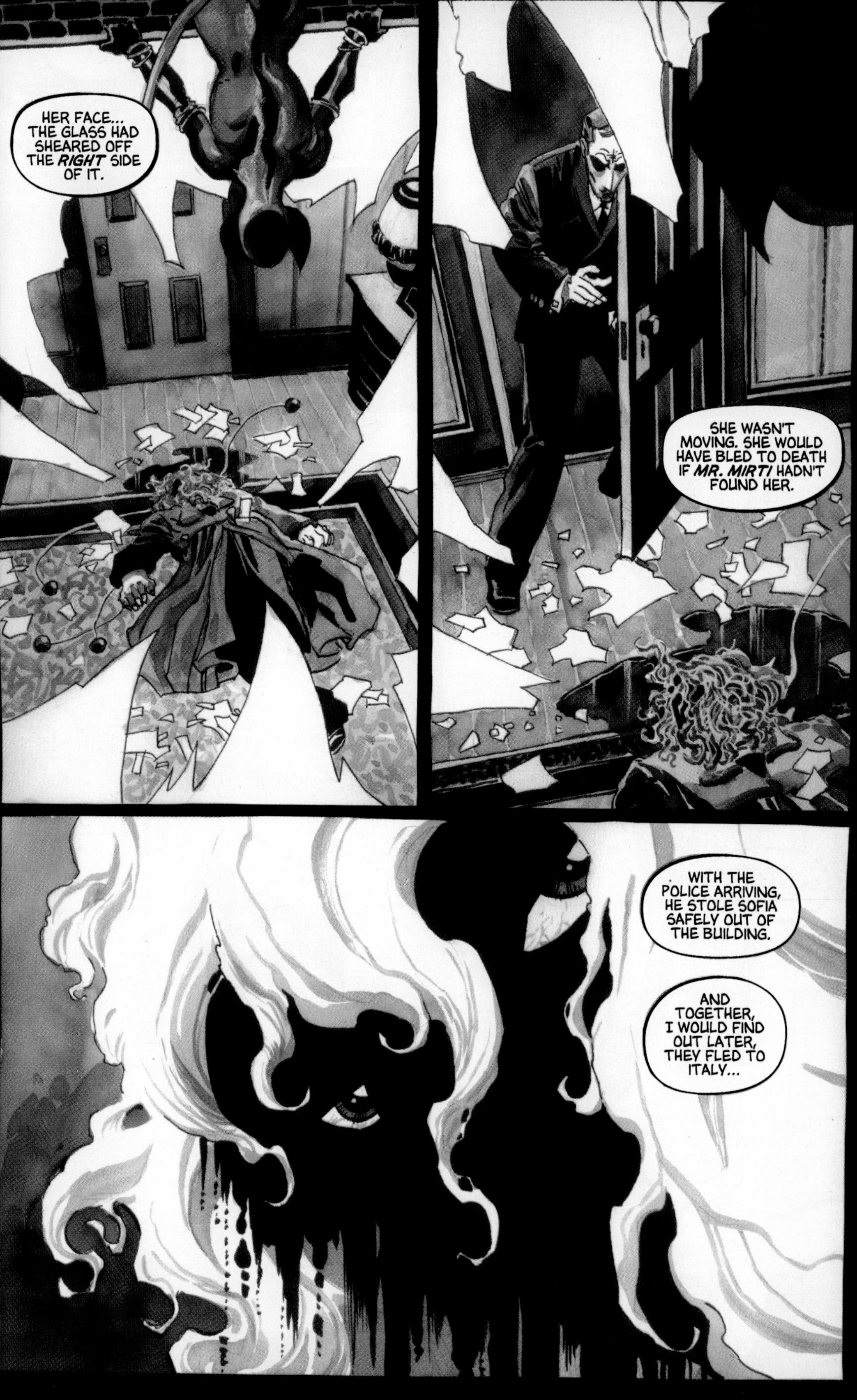
HER FACE... THE GLASS HAD SHEARED OFF THE *RIGHT* SIDE OF IT.
SHE WASN'T MOVING. SHE WOULD HAVE BLED TO DEATH IF *MR. MIRTI* HADN'T FOUND HER.
WITH THE POLICE ARRIVING, HE STOLE SOFIA SAFELY OUT OF THE BUILDING.
AND TOGETHER, I WOULD FIND OUT LATER, THEY FLED TO ITALY...

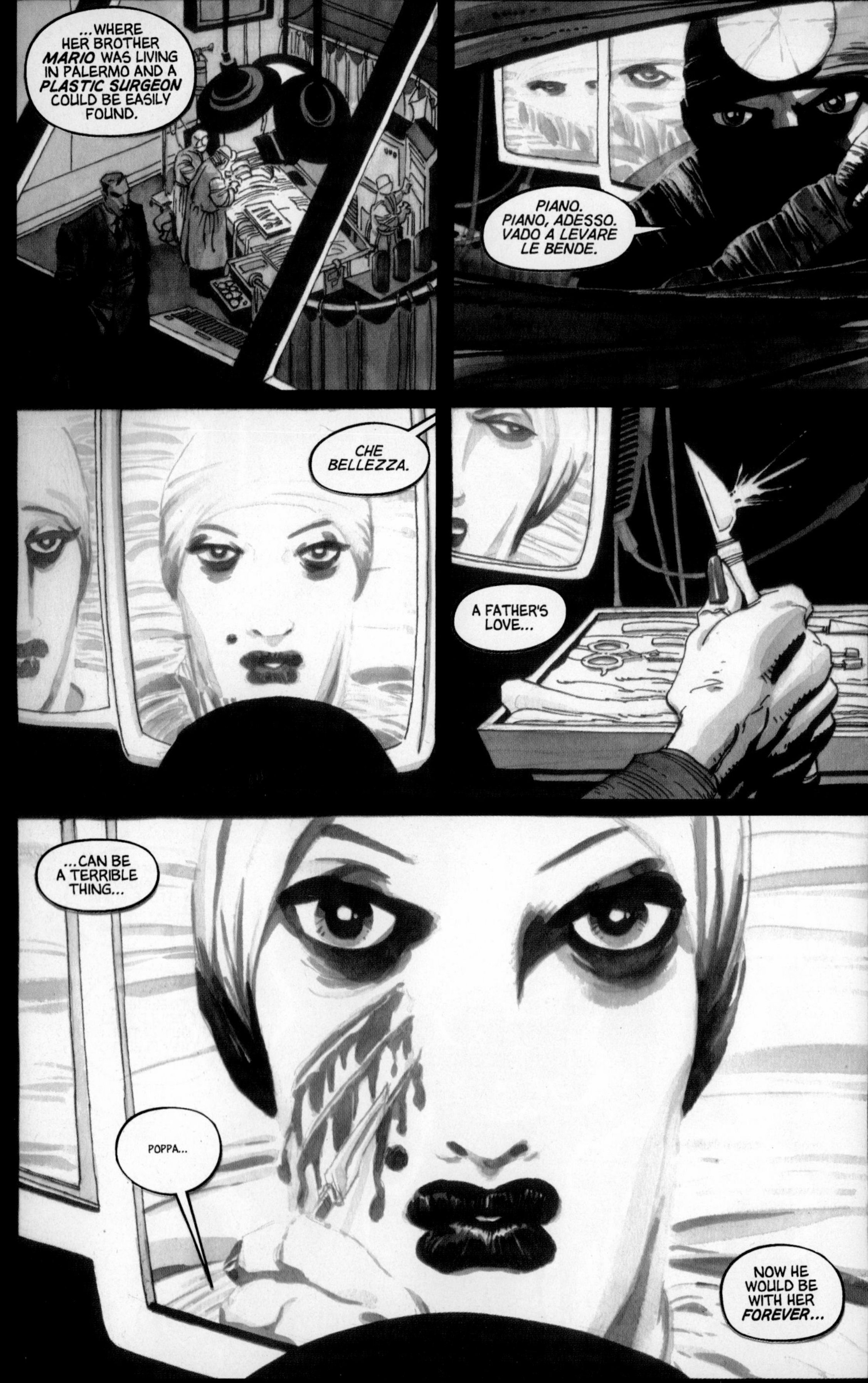
...WHERE HER BROTHER *MARIO* WAS LIVING IN PALERMO AND A *PLASTIC SURGEON* COULD BE EASILY FOUND.
PIANO. PIANO, ADESSO. VADO A LEVARE LE BENDE.
CHE BELLEZZA.
A FATHER'S LOVE...
...CAN BE A TERRIBLE THING...
POPPA...
NOW HE WOULD BE WITH HER *FOREVER*...

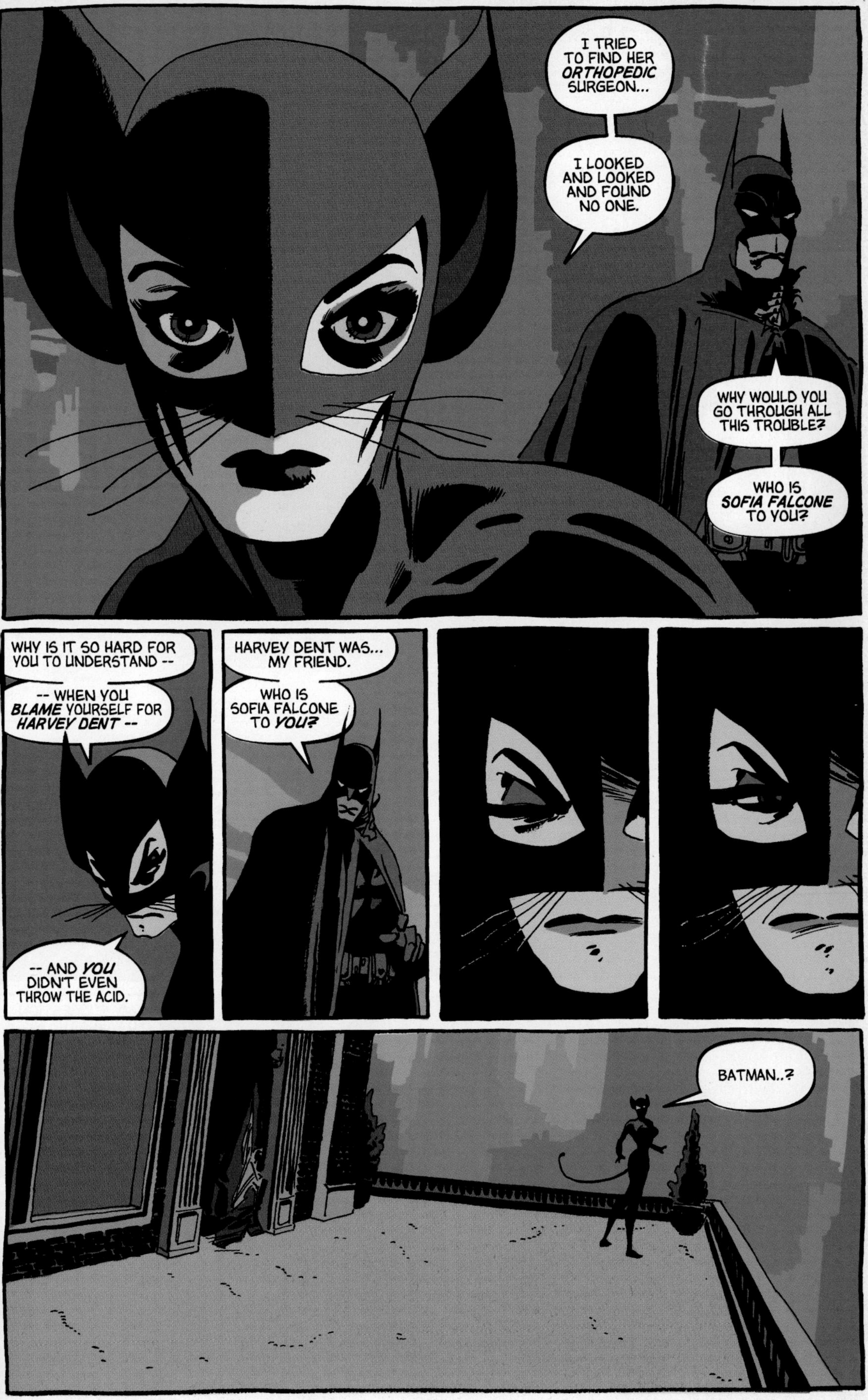
I TRIED TO FIND HER ORTHOPEDIC SURGEON...
I LOOKED AND LOOKED AND FOUND NO ONE.
WHY WOULD YOU GO THROUGH ALL THIS TROUBLE?
WHO IS SOFIA FALCONE TO YOU?
WHY IS IT SO HARD FOR YOU TO UNDERSTAND --
-- WHEN YOU BLAME YOURSELF FOR HARVEY DENT --
-- AND YOU DIDN'T EVEN THROW THE ACID.
HARVEY DENT WAS... MY FRIEND.
WHO IS SOFIA FALCONE TO YOU?
BATMAN..?

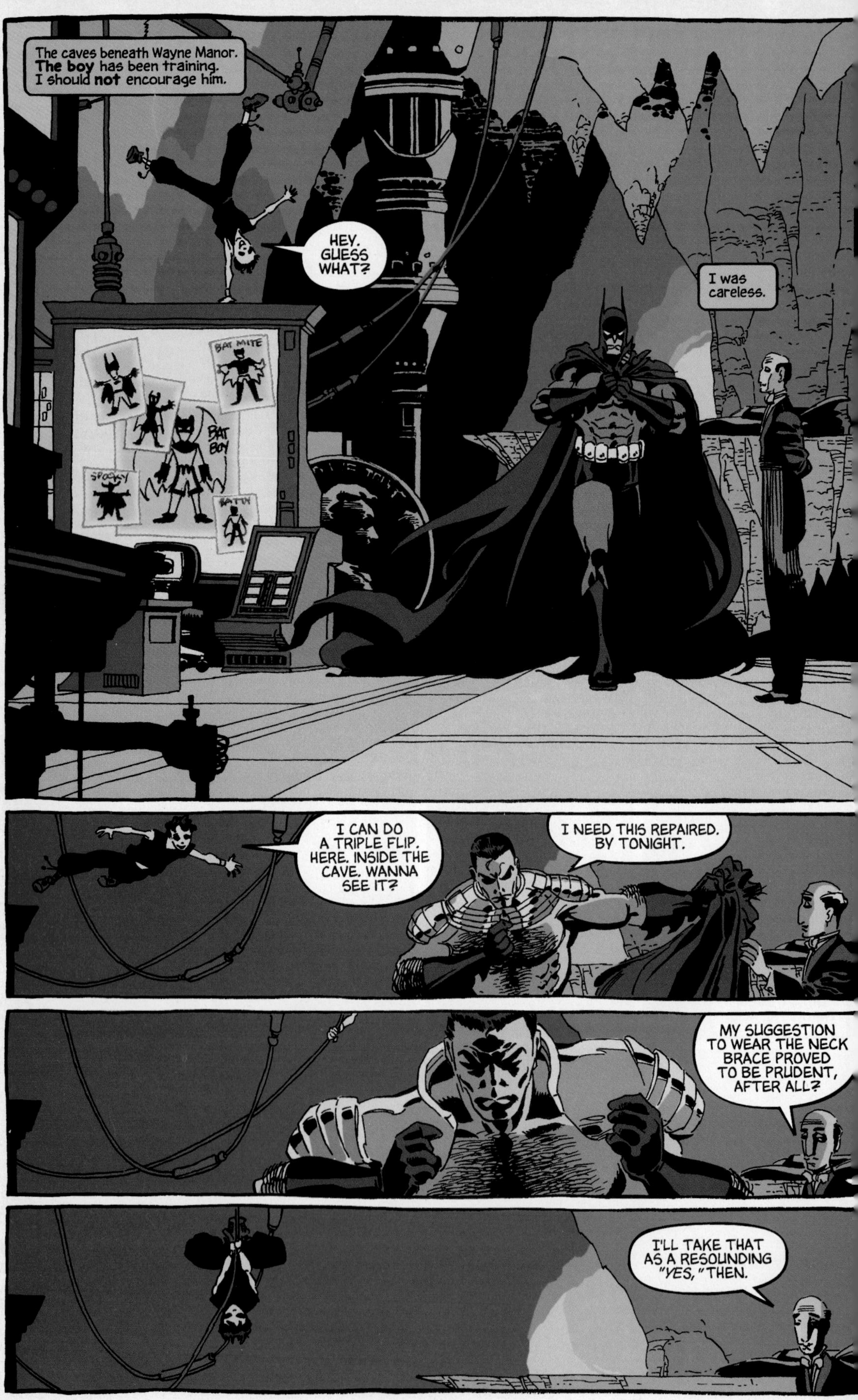

The caves beneath Wayne Manor. **The boy** has been training. I should **not** encourage him.
HEY. GUESS WHAT?
I was careless.
BAT MITE
BAT BOY
SPOOKY
BATTY
I CAN DO A TRIPLE FLIP. HERE. INSIDE THE CAVE. WANNA SEE IT?
I NEED THIS REPAIRED. BY TONIGHT.
MY SUGGESTION TO WEAR THE NECK BRACE PROVED TO BE PRUDENT, AFTER ALL?
I'LL TAKE THAT AS A RESOUNDING *"YES,"* THEN.

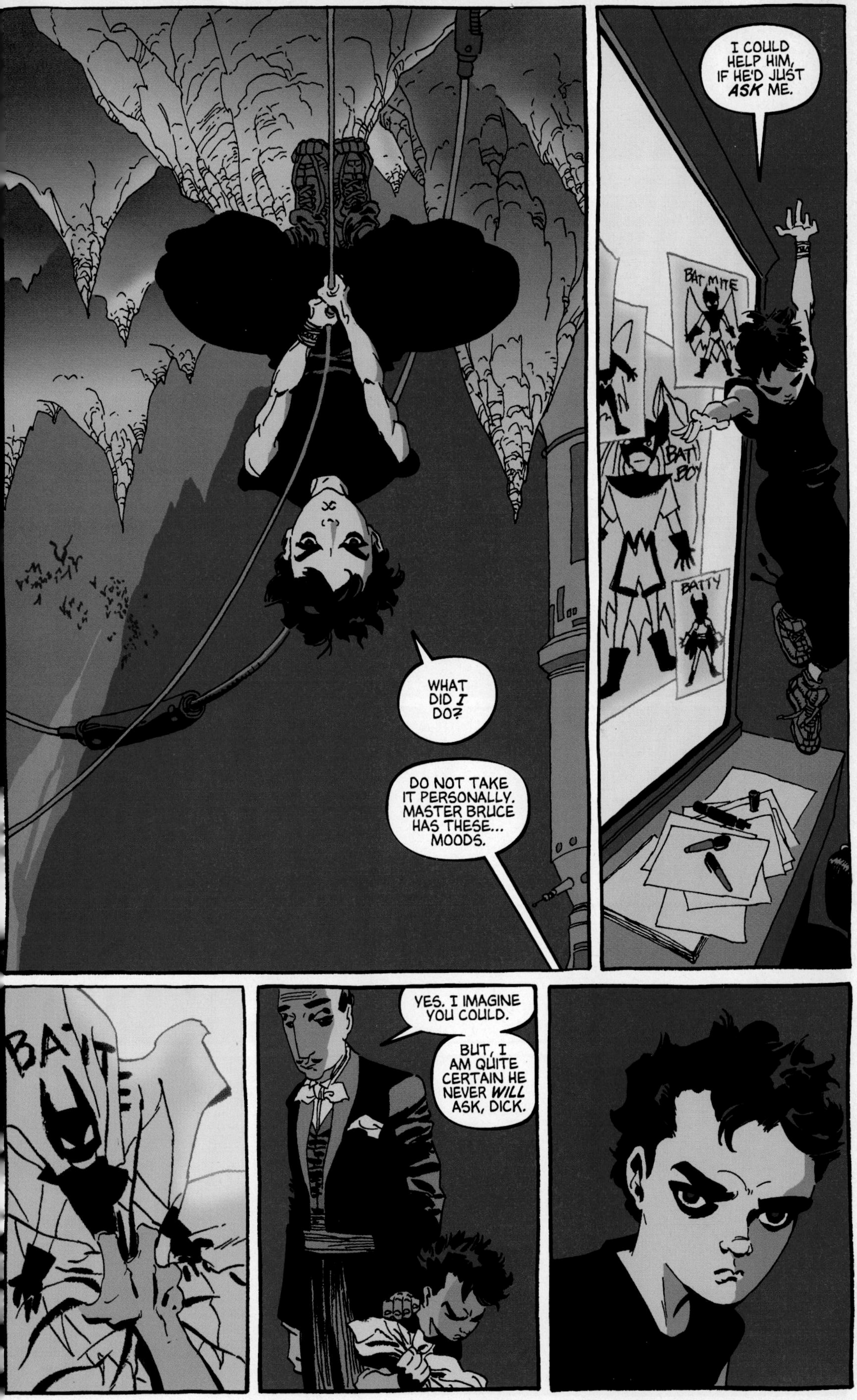

I COULD HELP HIM, IF HE'D JUST ASK ME.
WHAT DID I DO?
DO NOT TAKE IT PERSONALLY. MASTER BRUCE HAS THESE... MOODS.
BAT MITE
BAT BOY
BATTY
YES. I IMAGINE YOU COULD.
BUT, I AM QUITE CERTAIN HE NEVER WILL ASK, DICK.

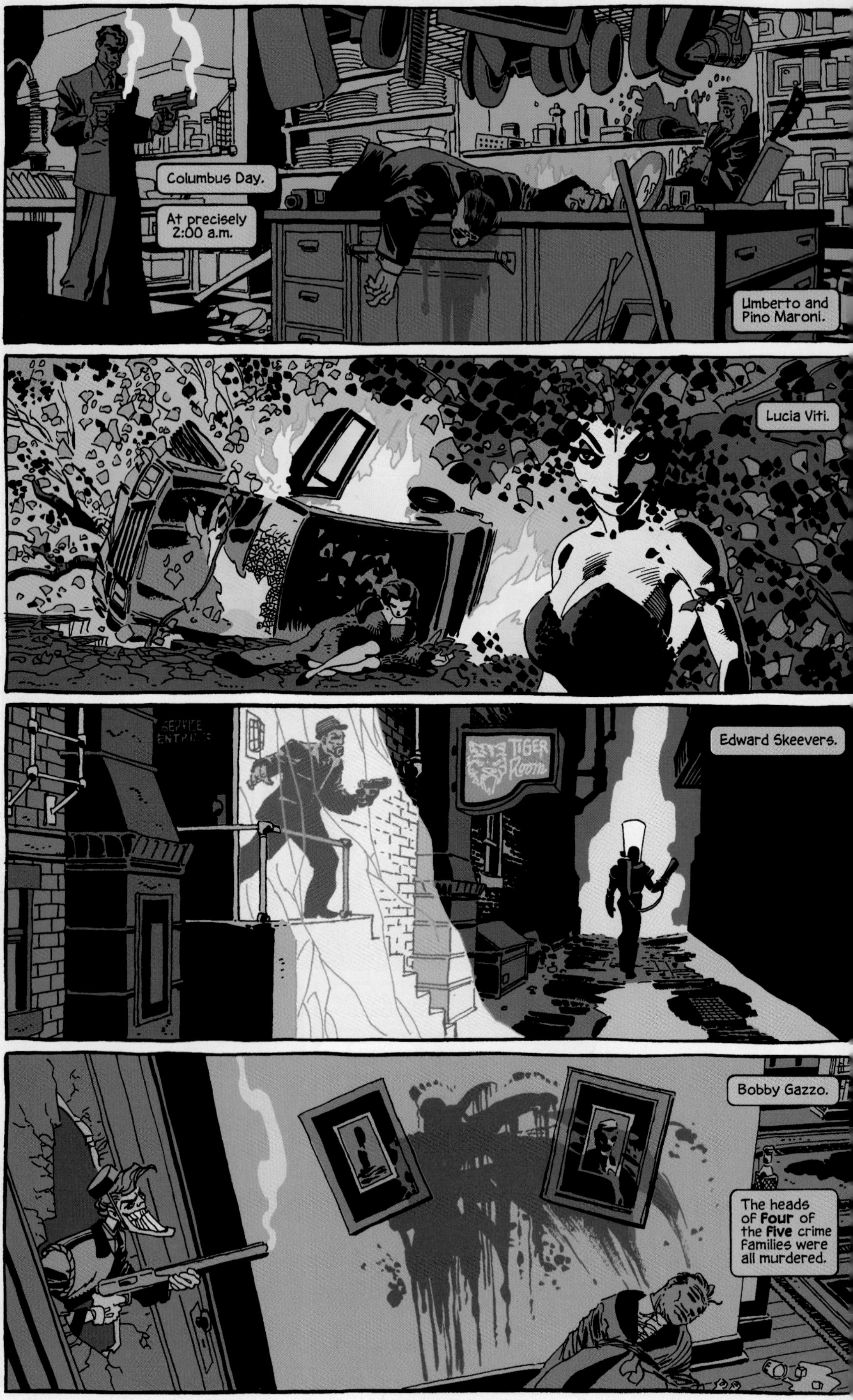

Columbus Day.
At precisely 2:00 a.m.
Umberto and Pino Maroni.
Lucia Viti.
Edward Skeevers.
TIGER Room
Bobby Gazzo.
The heads of **Four** of the **Five** crime Families were all murdered.

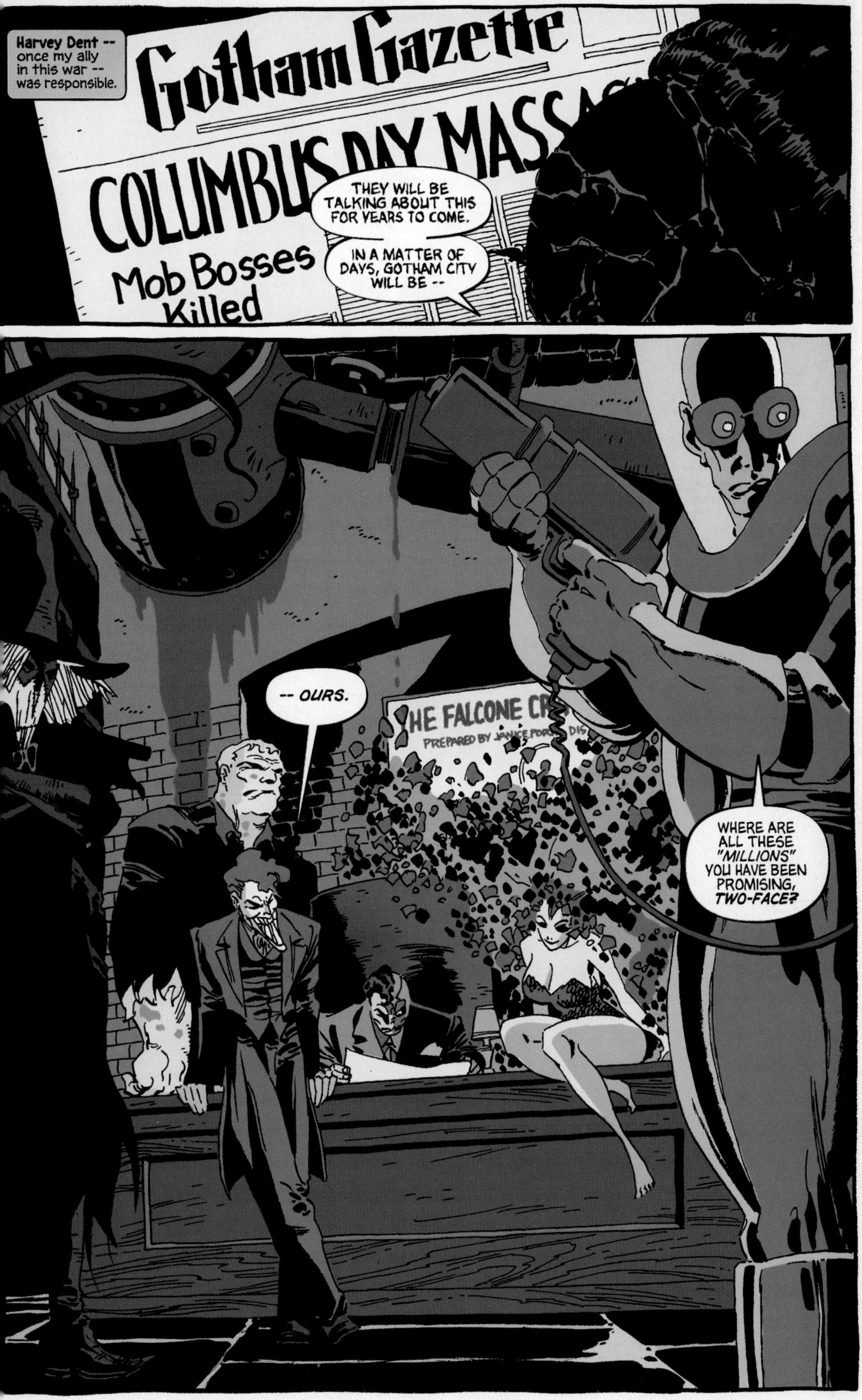
Harvey Dent -- once my ally in this war -- was responsible.
Gotham Gazette
COLUMBUS DAY MASSA
Mob Bosses Killed
THEY WILL BE TALKING ABOUT THIS FOR YEARS TO COME.
IN A MATTER OF DAYS, GOTHAM CITY WILL BE --
-- OURS.
HE FALCONE CR
WHERE ARE ALL THESE "MILLIONS" YOU HAVE BEEN PROMISING, TWO-FACE?

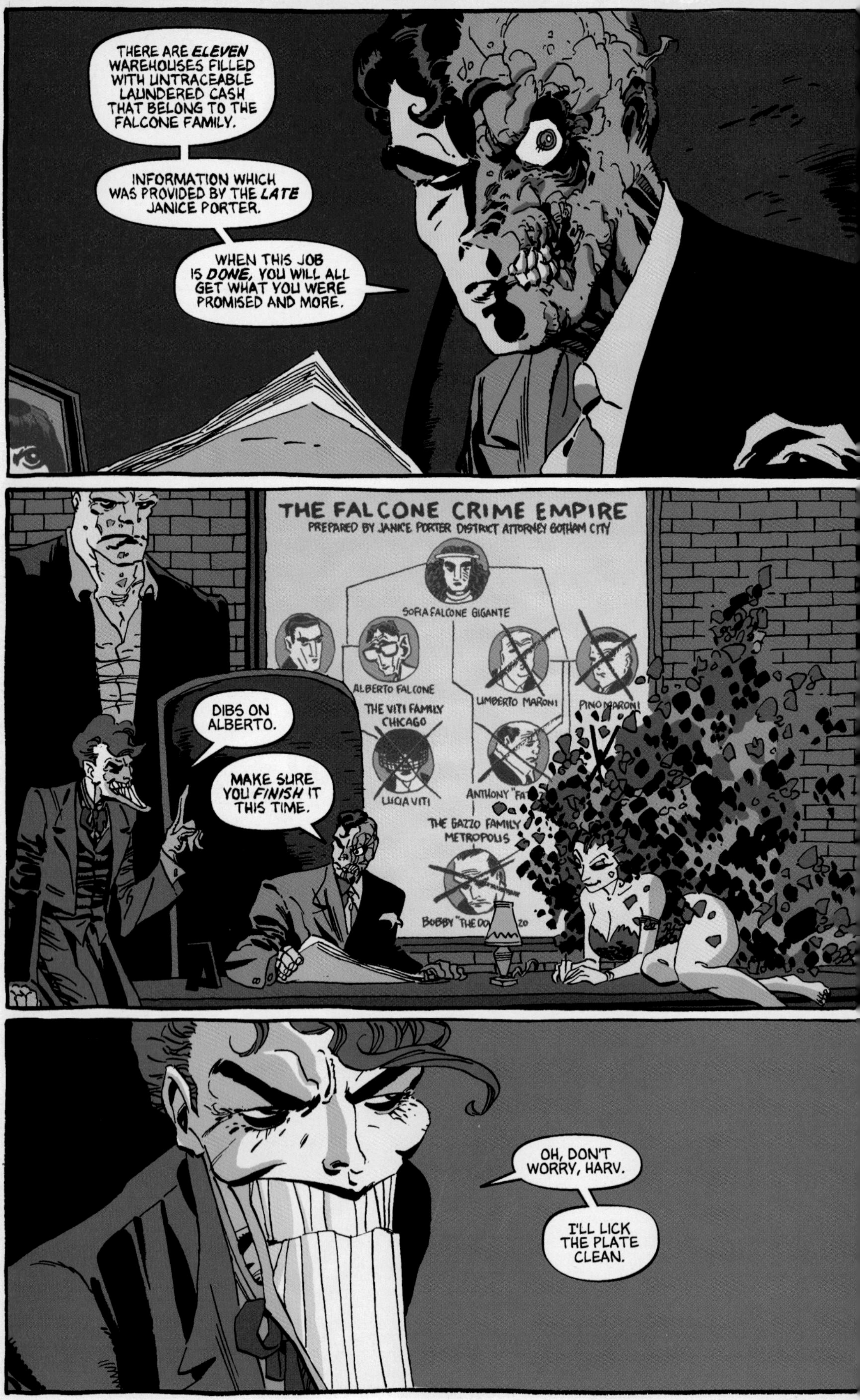

THERE ARE *ELEVEN* WAREHOUSES FILLED WITH UNTRACEABLE LAUNDERED CASH THAT BELONG TO THE FALCONE FAMILY.
INFORMATION WHICH WAS PROVIDED BY THE *LATE* JANICE PORTER.
WHEN THIS JOB IS *DONE*, YOU WILL ALL GET WHAT YOU WERE PROMISED AND MORE.
THE FALCONE CRIME EMPIRE
PREPARED BY JANICE PORTER DISTRICT ATTORNEY GOTHAM CITY
SOFIA FALCONE GIGANTE
ALBERTO FALCONE
UMBERTO MARONI
THE VITI FAMILY CHICAGO
LUCIA VITI
THE GAZZO FAMILY METROPOLIS
DIBS ON ALBERTO.
MAKE SURE YOU *FINISH* IT THIS TIME.
OH, DON'T WORRY, HARV.
I'LL LICK THE PLATE CLEAN.

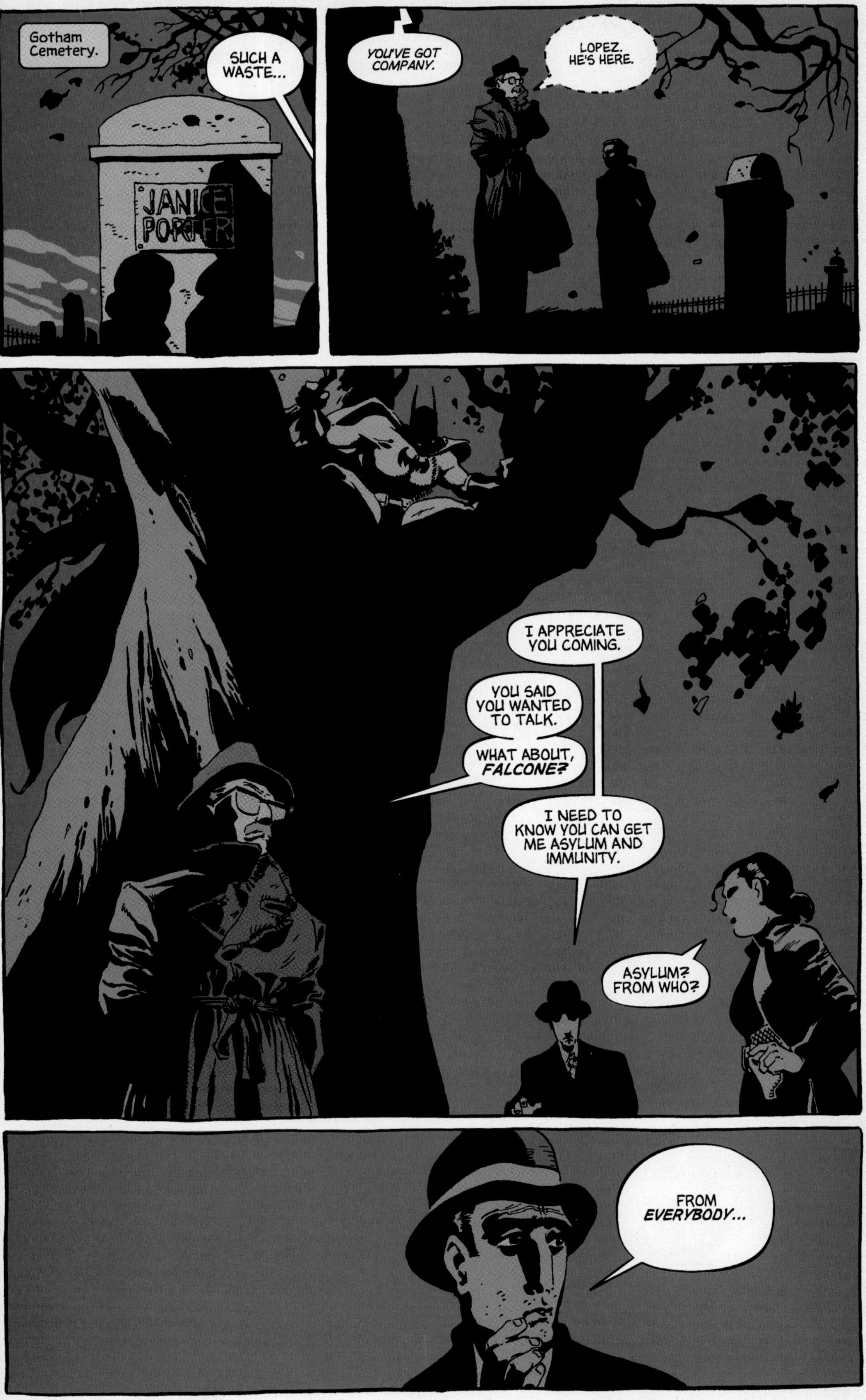
Gotham Cemetery.
SUCH A WASTE...
JANICE PORTER
YOU'VE GOT COMPANY.
LOPEZ. HE'S HERE.
I APPRECIATE YOU COMING.
YOU SAID YOU WANTED TO TALK.
WHAT ABOUT, *FALCONE?*
I NEED TO KNOW YOU CAN GET ME ASYLUM AND IMMUNITY.
ASYLUM? FROM WHO?
FROM *EVERYBODY...*

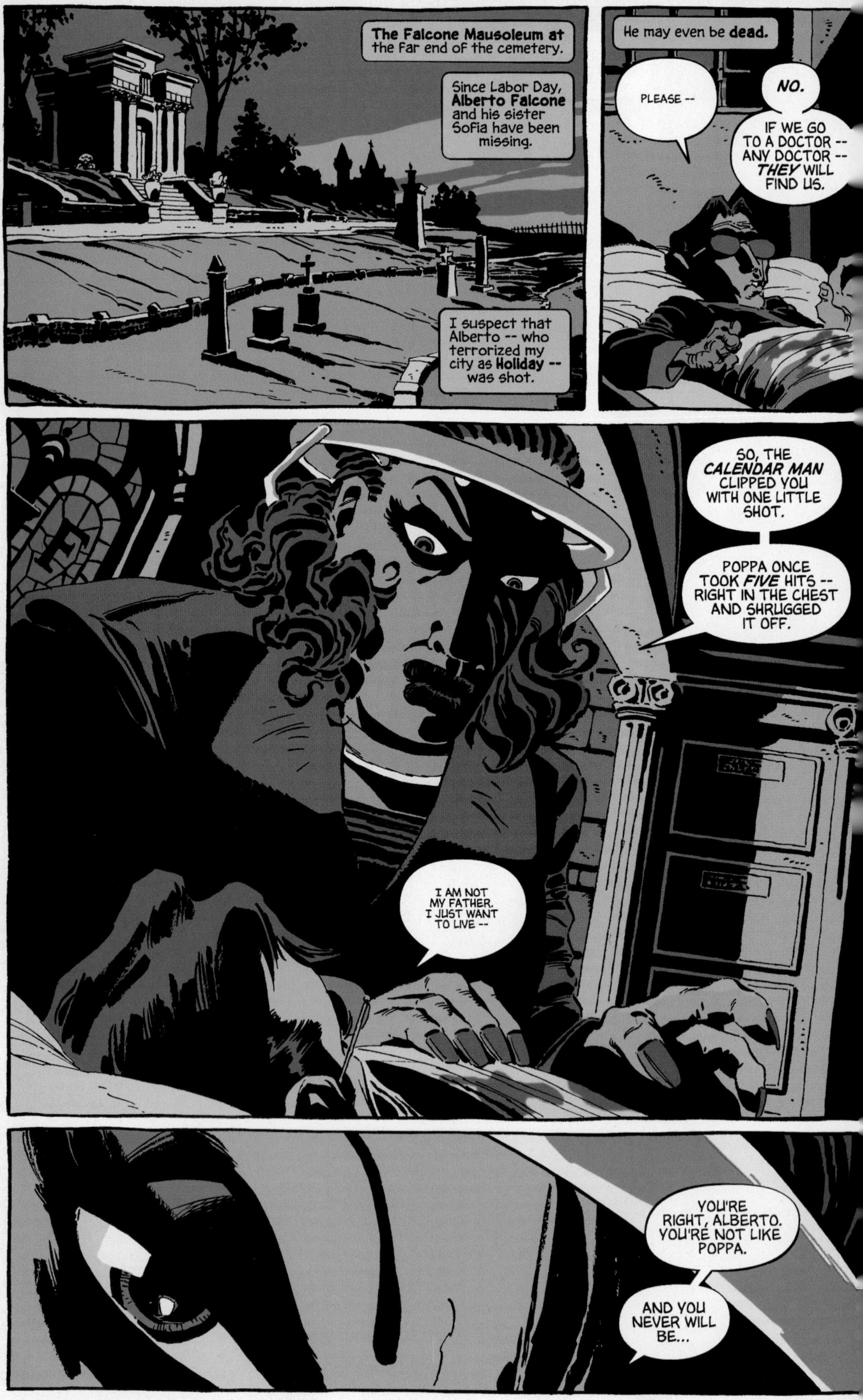
The Falcone Mausoleum at the far end of the cemetery.
Since Labor Day, Alberto Falcone and his sister Sofia have been missing.
I suspect that Alberto -- who terrorized my city as Holiday -- was shot.
He may even be dead.
PLEASE --
NO.
IF WE GO TO A DOCTOR -- ANY DOCTOR -- THEY WILL FIND US.
SO, THE CALENDAR MAN CLIPPED YOU WITH ONE LITTLE SHOT.
POPPA ONCE TOOK FIVE HITS -- RIGHT IN THE CHEST AND SHRUGGED IT OFF.
I AM NOT MY FATHER. I JUST WANT TO LIVE --
YOU'RE RIGHT, ALBERTO. YOU'RE NOT LIKE POPPA.
AND YOU NEVER WILL BE...

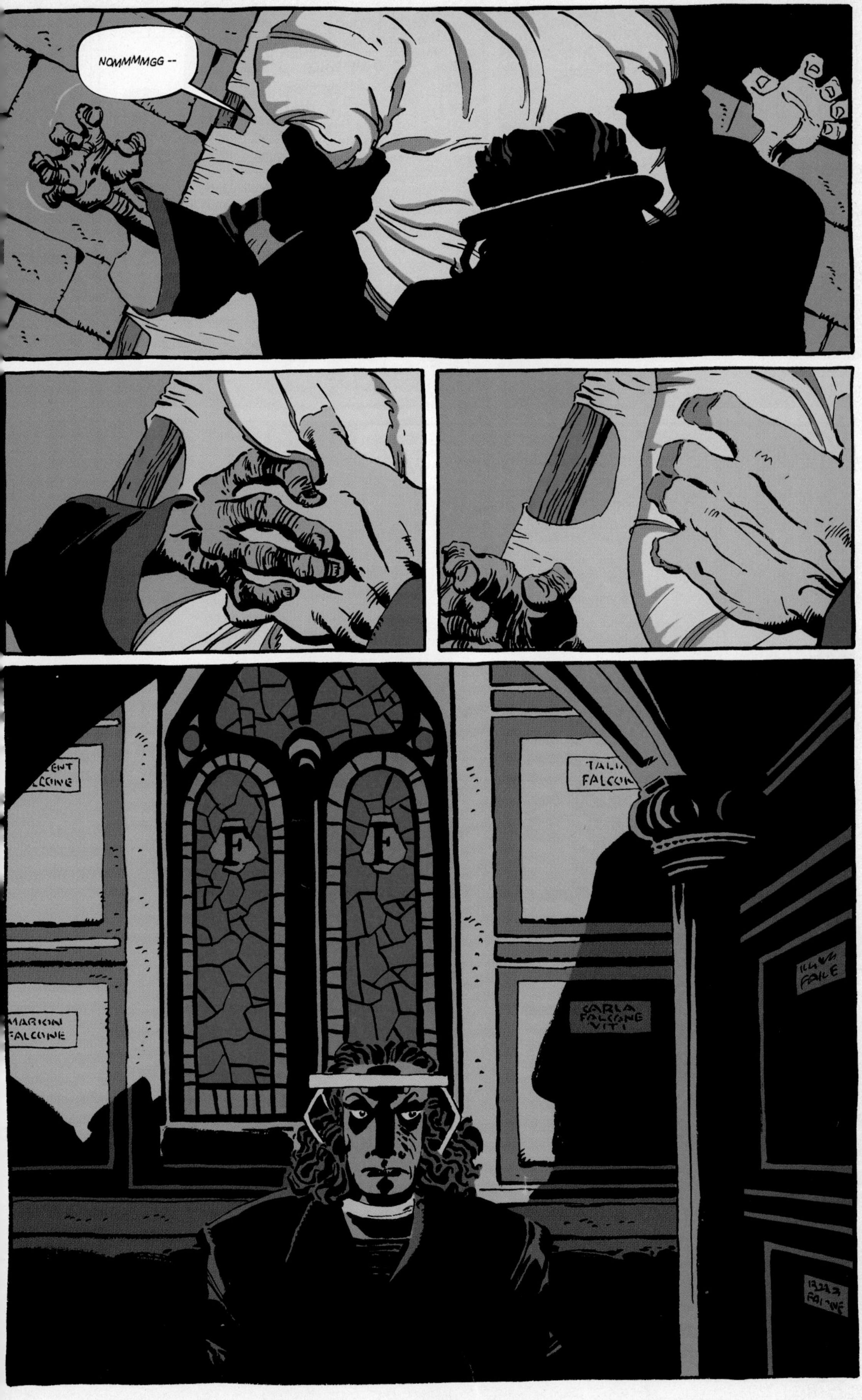
NOMMMMGG --
MARION FALCONE
CARLA FALCONE VITI

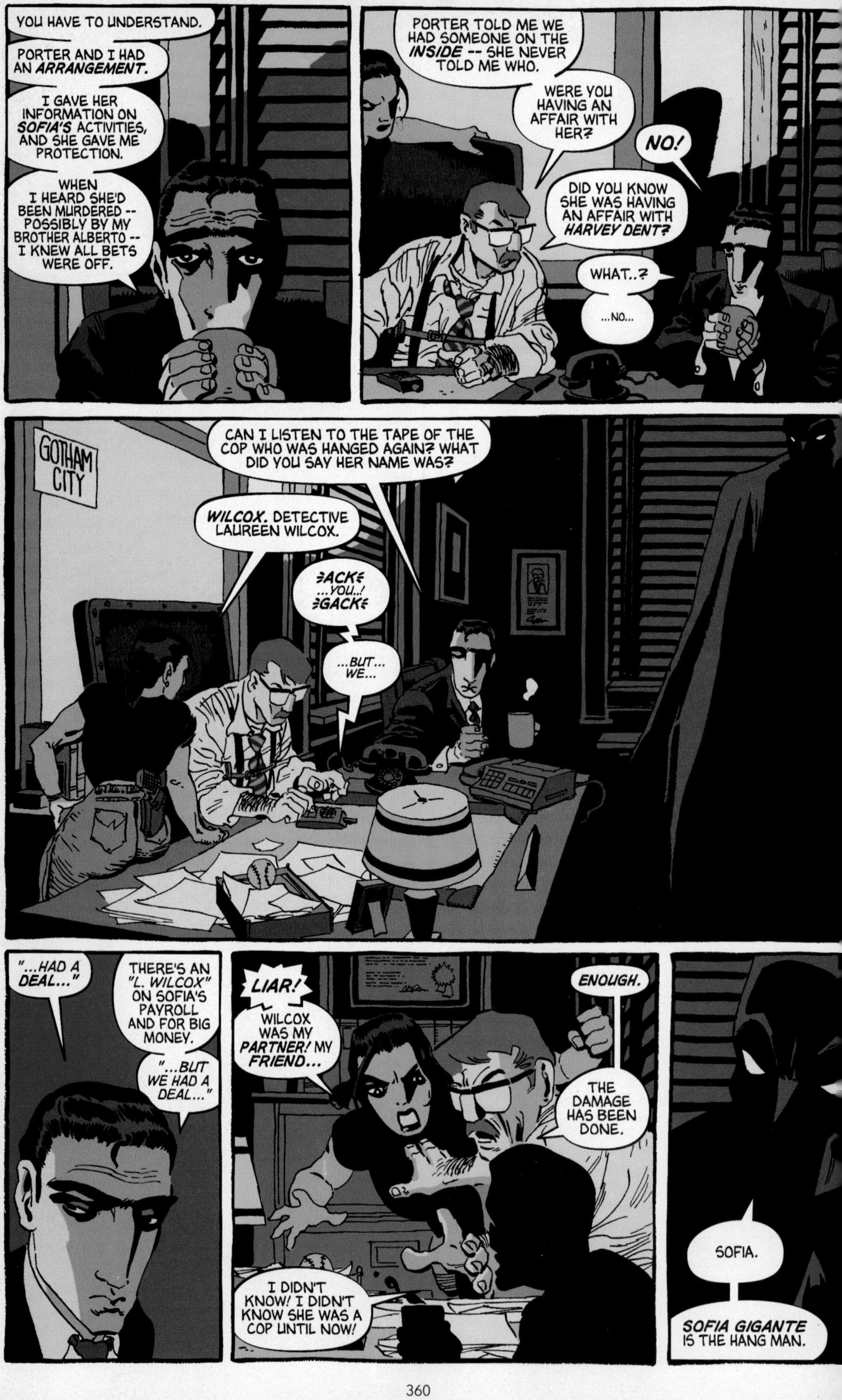
YOU HAVE TO UNDERSTAND.
PORTER AND I HAD AN *ARRANGEMENT.*
I GAVE HER INFORMATION ON *SOFIA'S* ACTIVITIES, AND SHE GAVE ME PROTECTION.
WHEN I HEARD SHE'D BEEN MURDERED -- POSSIBLY BY MY BROTHER ALBERTO -- I KNEW ALL BETS WERE OFF.
PORTER TOLD ME WE HAD SOMEONE ON THE *INSIDE* -- SHE NEVER TOLD ME WHO.
WERE YOU HAVING AN AFFAIR WITH HER?
NO!
DID YOU KNOW SHE WAS HAVING AN AFFAIR WITH *HARVEY DENT?*
WHAT..?
...NO...
GOTHAM CITY
CAN I LISTEN TO THE TAPE OF THE COP WHO WAS HANGED AGAIN? WHAT DID YOU SAY HER NAME WAS?
WILCOX. DETECTIVE LAUREEN WILCOX.
ACK ...YOU..! *GACK*
...BUT... WE...
"...HAD A *DEAL*..."
THERE'S AN "L. WILCOX" ON SOFIA'S PAYROLL AND FOR BIG MONEY.
"...BUT WE HAD A DEAL..."
LIAR!
WILCOX WAS MY *PARTNER!* MY *FRIEND...*
I DIDN'T KNOW! I DIDN'T KNOW SHE WAS A COP UNTIL NOW!
ENOUGH.
THE DAMAGE HAS BEEN DONE.
SOFIA.
SOFIA GIGANTE IS THE HANG MAN.

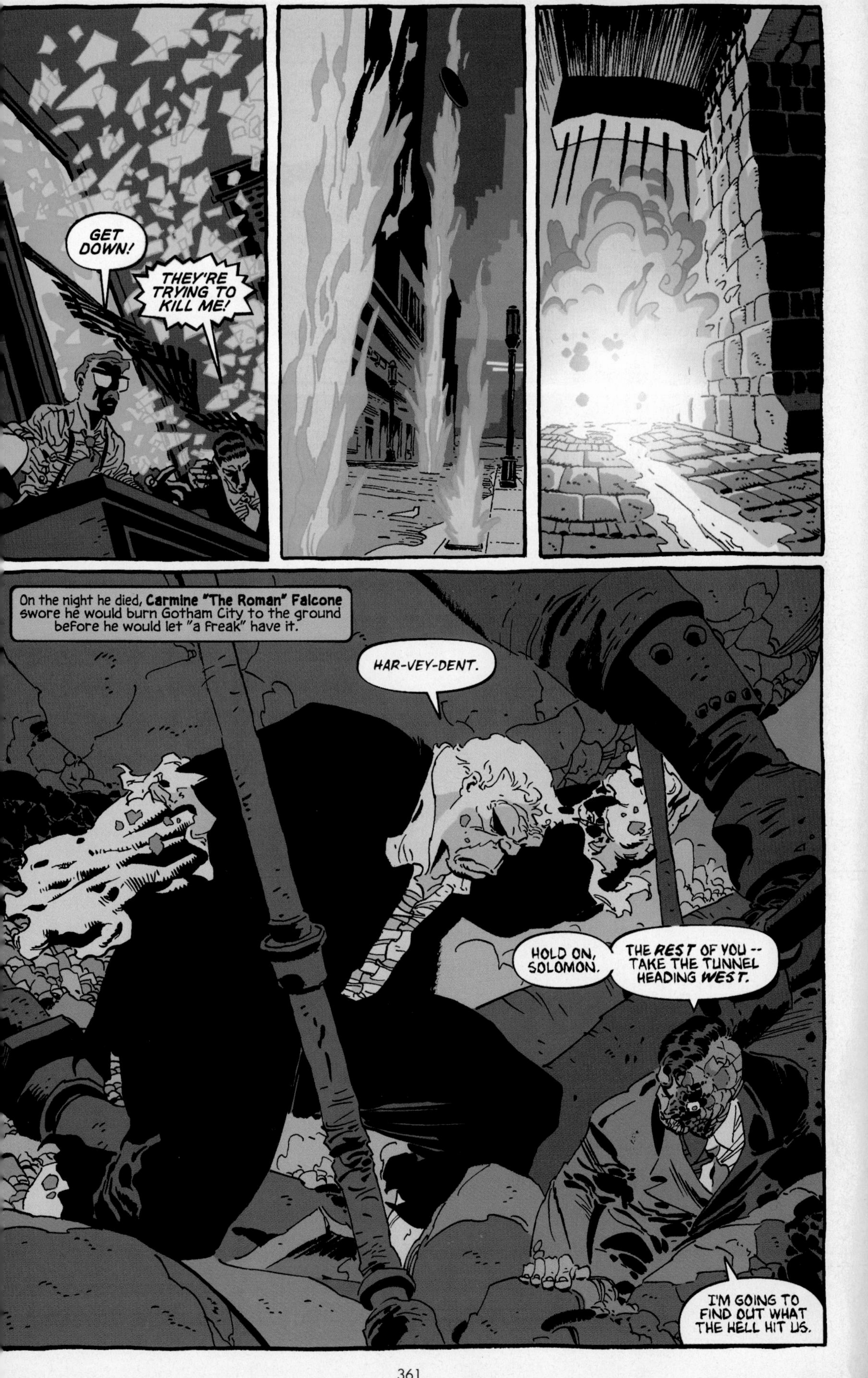
GET DOWN!
THEY'RE TRYING TO KILL ME!
On the night he died, Carmine "The Roman" Falcone swore he would burn Gotham City to the ground before he would let "a freak" have it.
HAR-VEY-DENT.
HOLD ON, SOLOMON.
THE REST OF YOU -- TAKE THE TUNNEL HEADING WEST.
I'M GOING TO FIND OUT WHAT THE HELL HIT US.

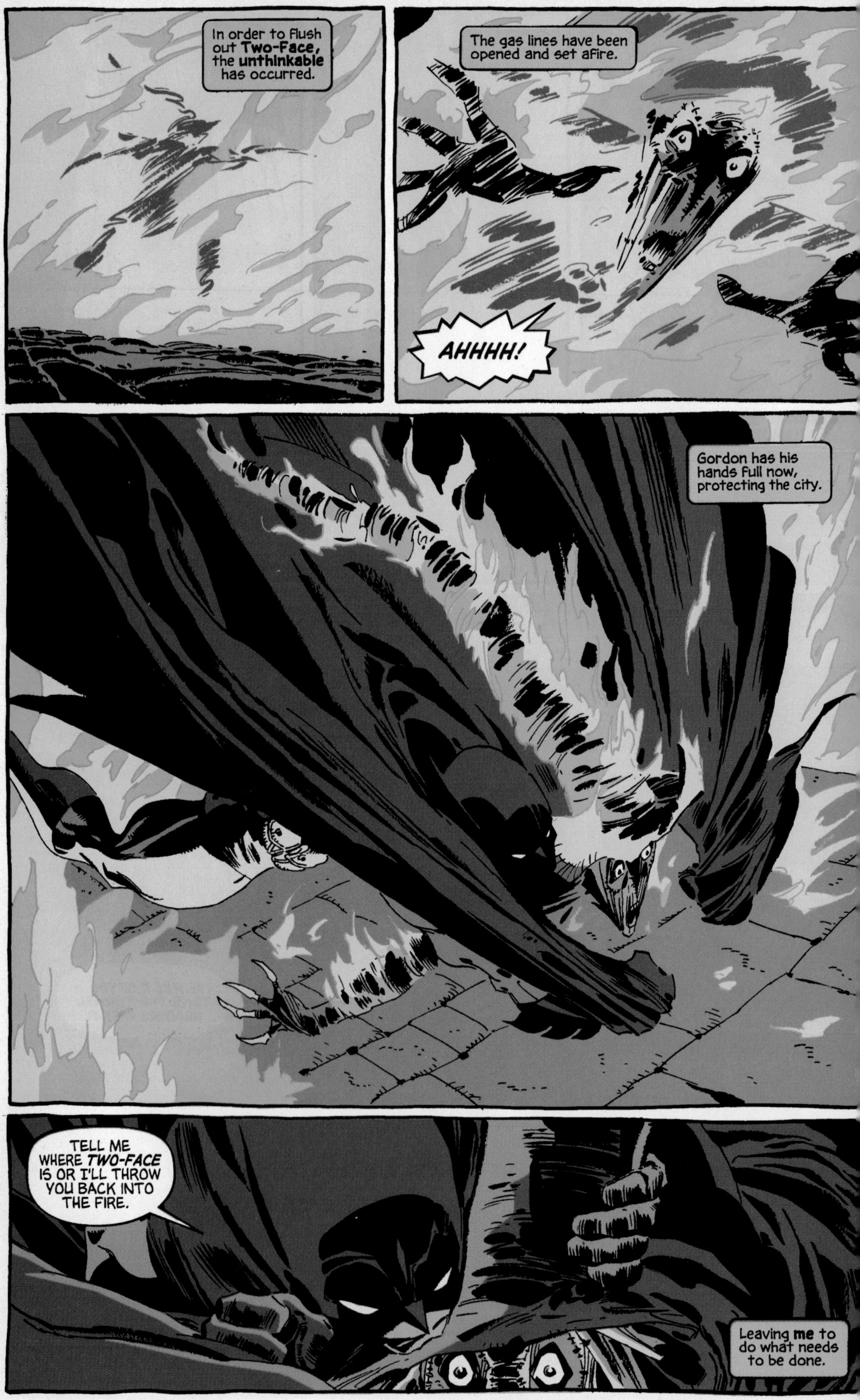

In order to flush out **Two-Face,** the **unthinkable** has occurred.
The gas lines have been opened and set afire.
AHHHH!
Gordon has his hands full now, protecting the city.
TELL ME WHERE *TWO-FACE* IS OR I'LL THROW YOU BACK INTO THE FIRE.
Leaving **me** to do what needs to be done.

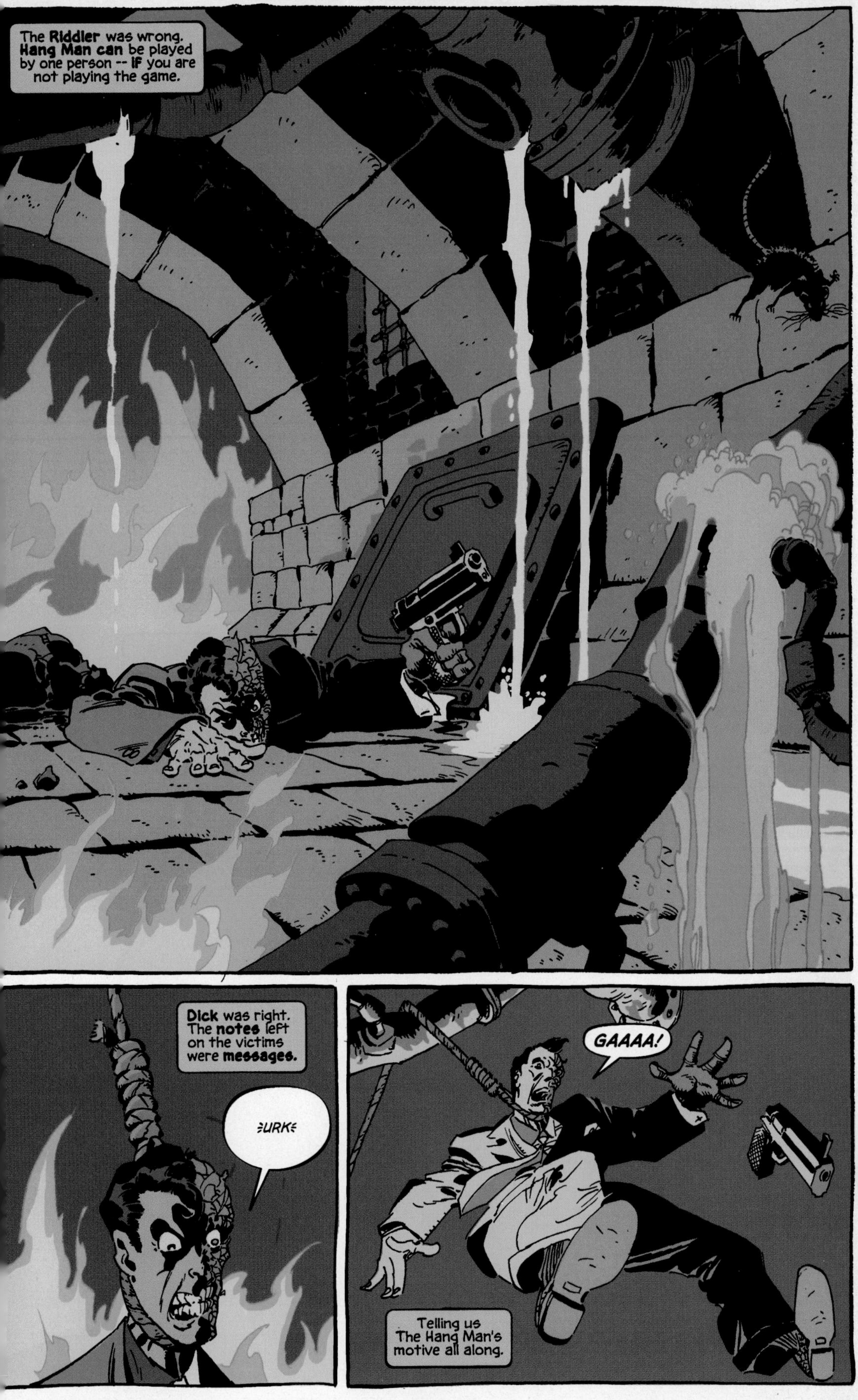

The Riddler was wrong. Hang Man can be played by one person -- if you are not playing the game.
Dick was right. The notes left on the victims were messages.
URK
GAAAA!
Telling us The Hang Man's motive all along.

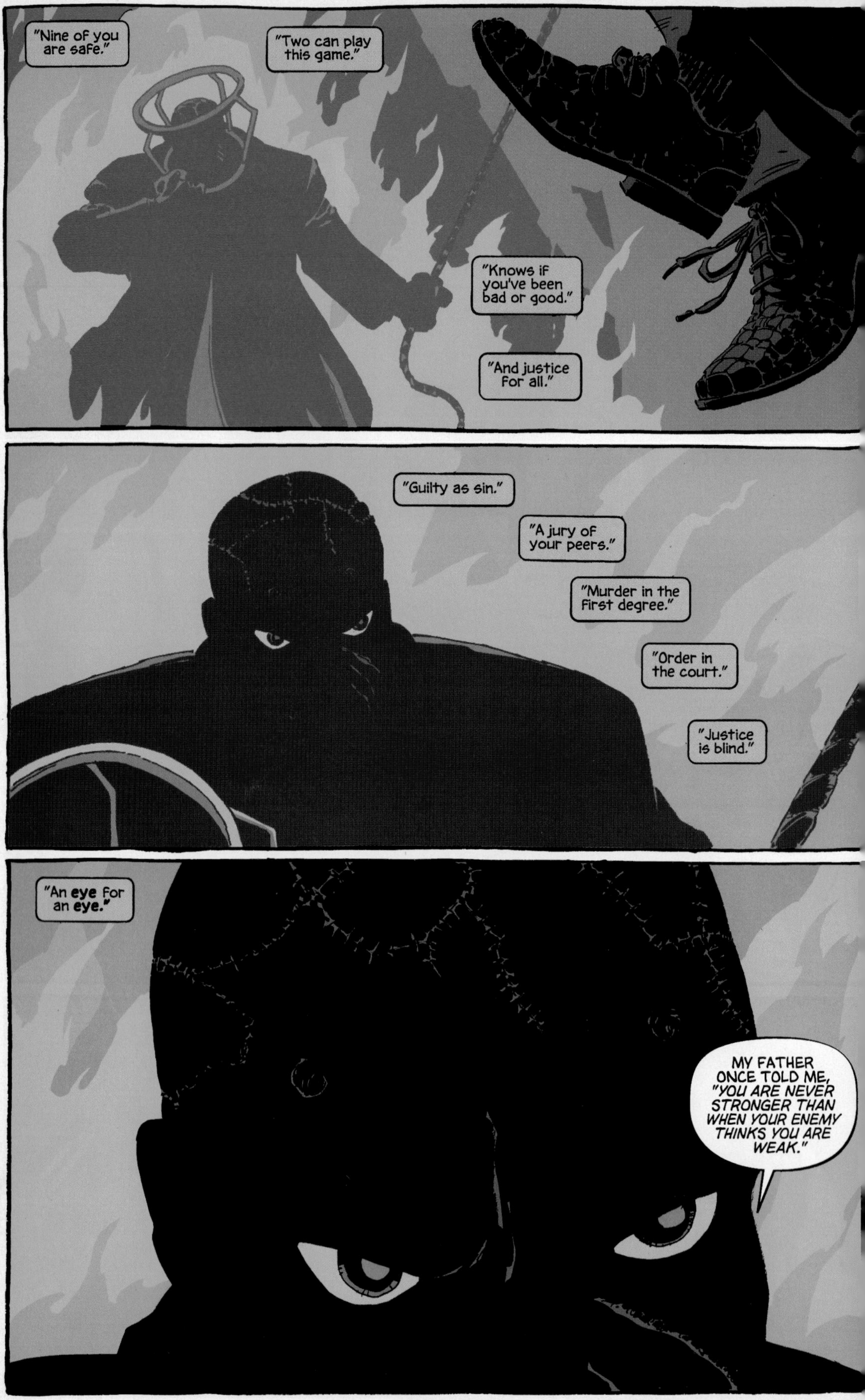
"Nine of you are safe."
"Two can play this game."
"Knows if you've been bad or good."
"And justice for all."
"Guilty as sin."
"A jury of your peers."
"Murder in the first degree."
"Order in the court."
"Justice is blind."
"An **eye** for an **eye**."
MY FATHER ONCE TOLD ME, *"YOU ARE NEVER STRONGER THAN WHEN YOUR ENEMY THINKS YOU ARE WEAK."*

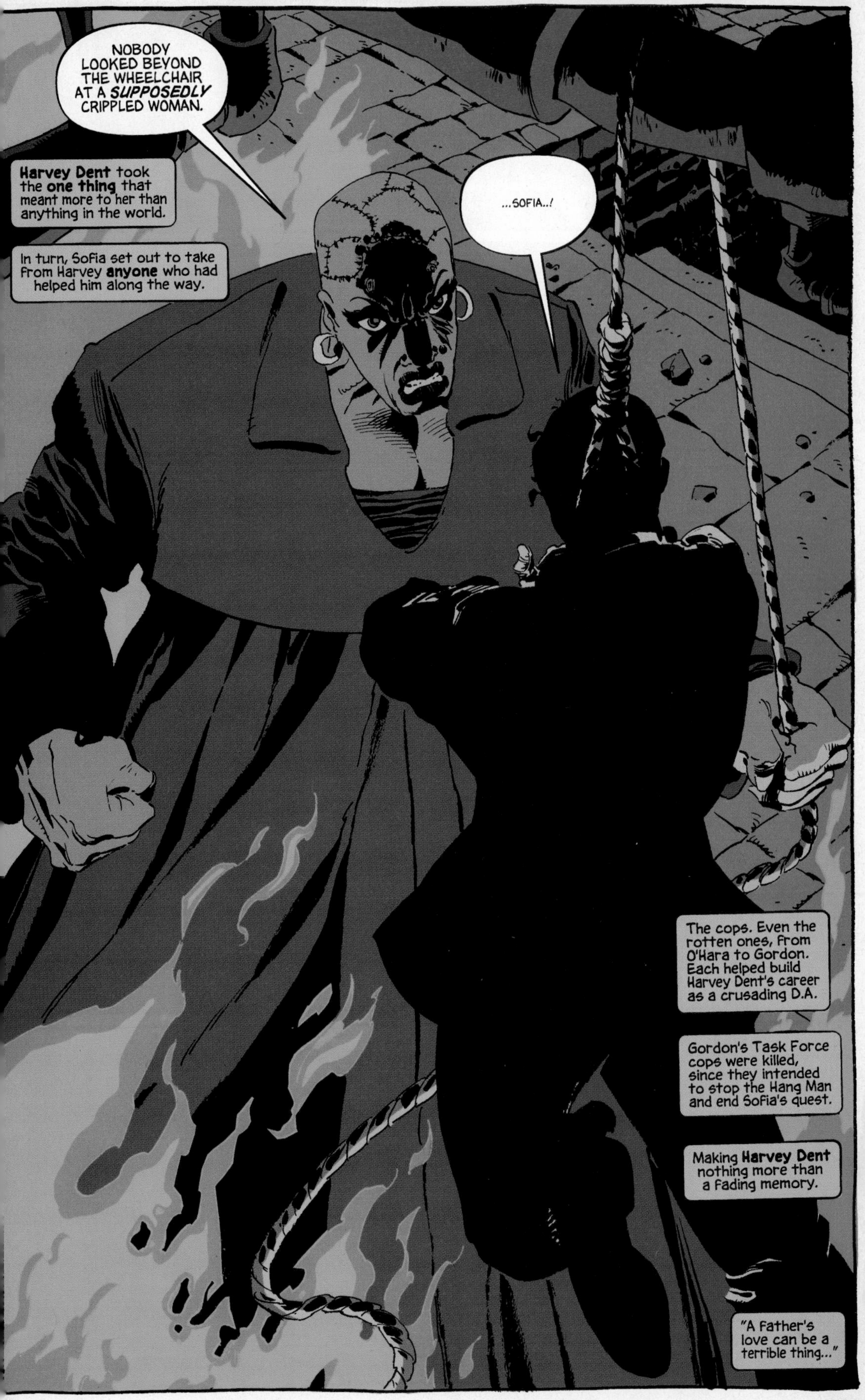
NOBODY LOOKED BEYOND THE WHEELCHAIR AT A SUPPOSEDLY CRIPPLED WOMAN.
Harvey Dent took the one thing that meant more to her than anything in the world.
In turn, Sofia set out to take from Harvey anyone who had helped him along the way.
...SOFIA..!
The cops. Even the rotten ones, from O'Hara to Gordon. Each helped build Harvey Dent's career as a crusading D.A.
Gordon's Task Force cops were killed, since they intended to stop the Hang Man and end Sofia's quest.
Making Harvey Dent nothing more than a fading memory.
"A Father's love can be a terrible thing..."

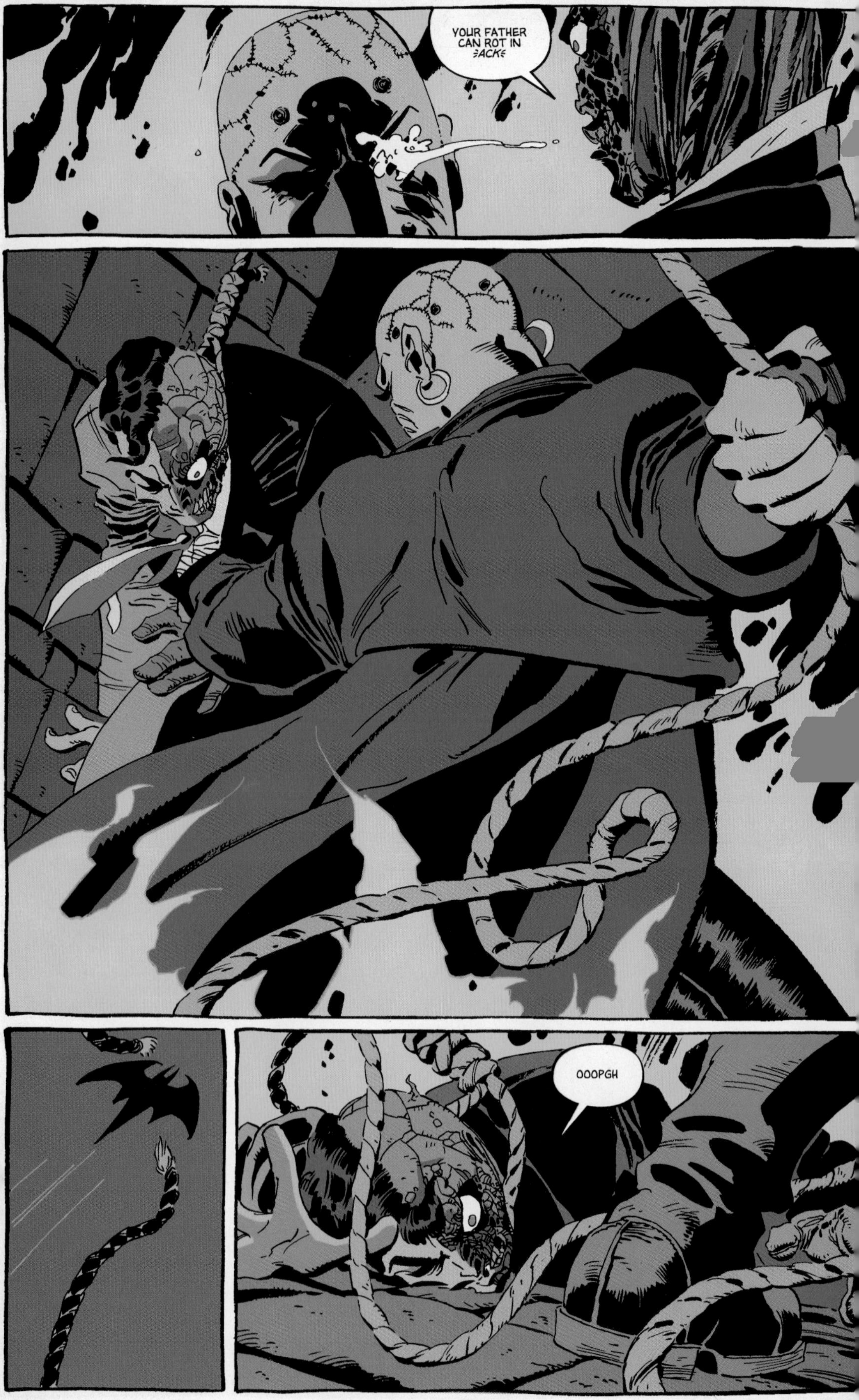
YOUR FATHER
CAN ROT IN
ACK
OOOPGH

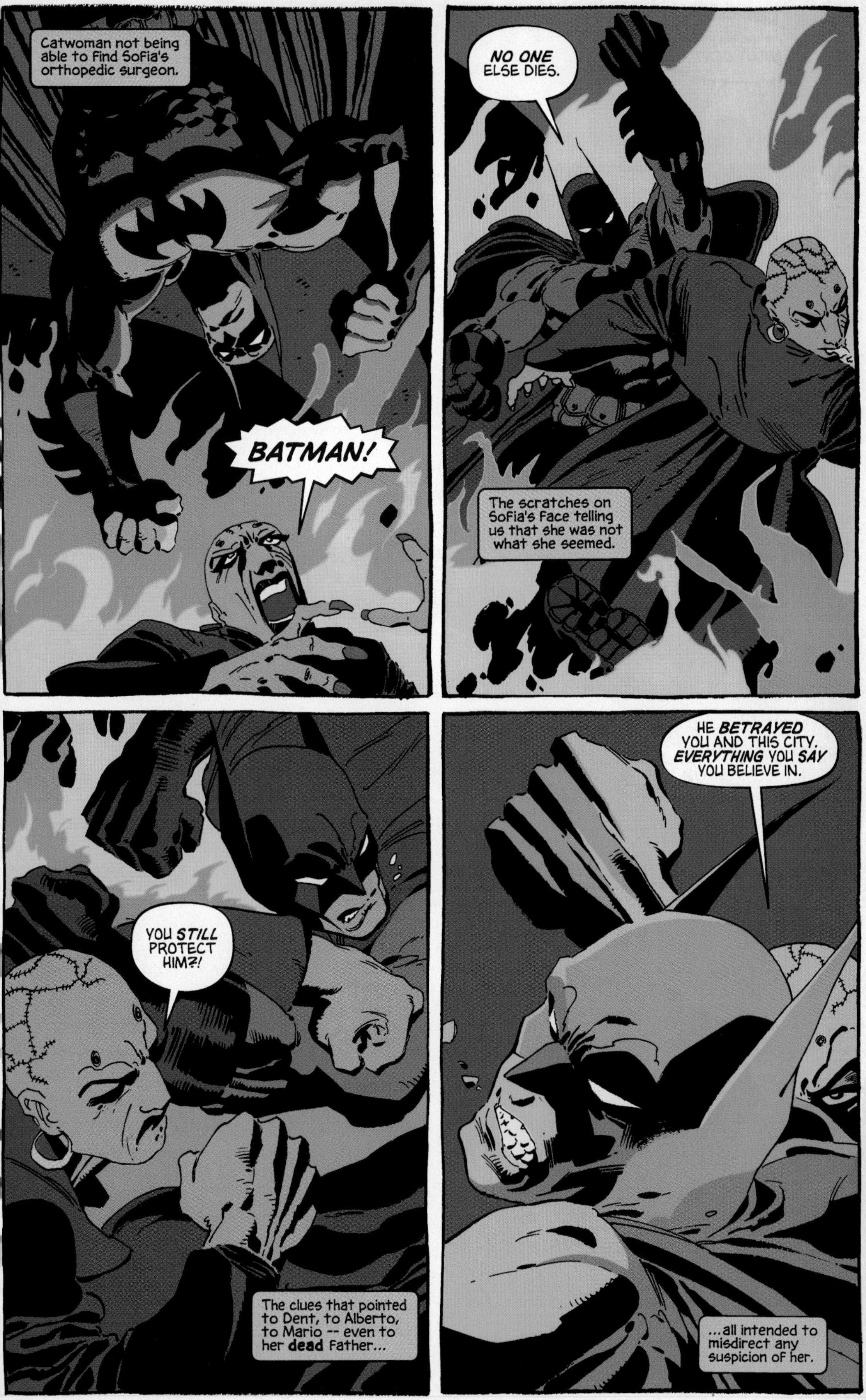

Catwoman not being able to find Sofia's orthopedic surgeon.
BATMAN!
NO ONE ELSE DIES.
The scratches on Sofia's face telling us that she was not what she seemed.
YOU STILL PROTECT HIM?!
The clues that pointed to Dent, to Alberto, to Mario -- even to her dead father...
HE BETRAYED YOU AND THIS CITY. EVERYTHING YOU SAY YOU BELIEVE IN.
...all intended to misdirect any suspicion of her.

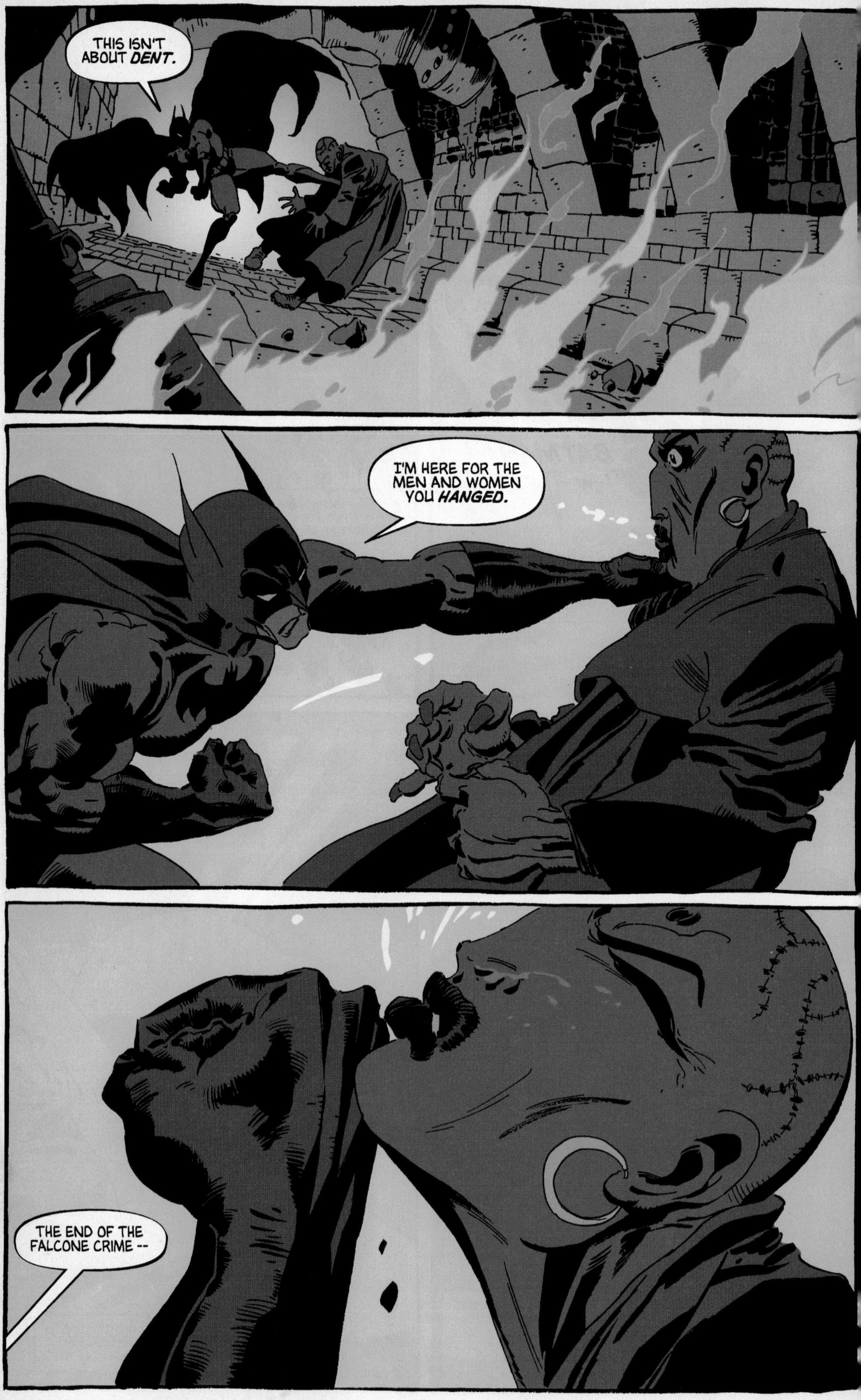
THIS ISN'T ABOUT *DENT*.
I'M HERE FOR THE MEN AND WOMEN YOU *HANGED*.
THE END OF THE FALCONE CRIME --

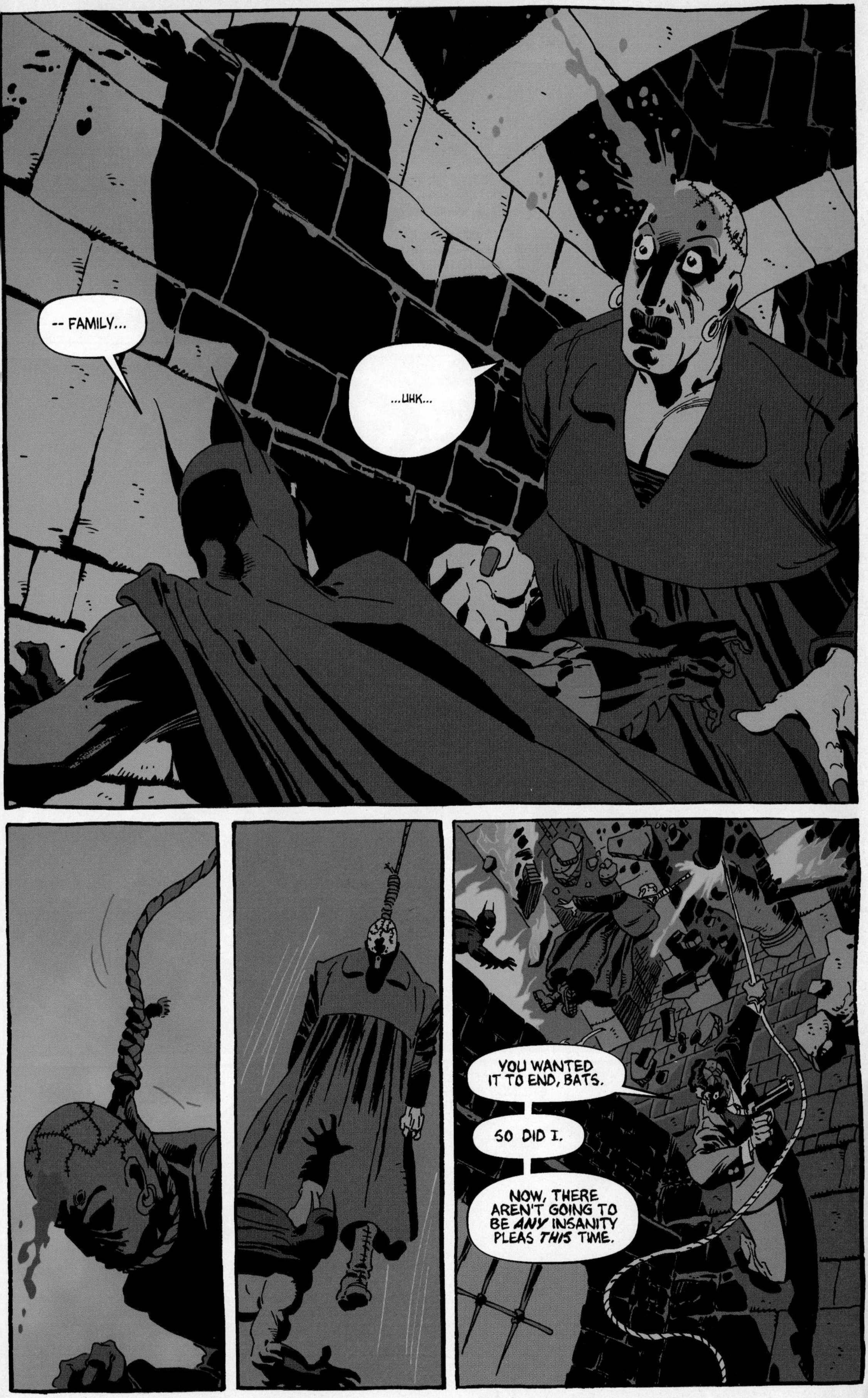
-- FAMILY...
...UHK...
YOU WANTED IT TO END, BATS.
SO DID I.
NOW, THERE AREN'T GOING TO BE ANY INSANITY PLEAS THIS TIME.

GUNSHOTS...

...AND A *DEAD* END.

DANGER HIGH VOLTAGE

WE'LL HAVE TO SHOW OUR PAL HARVEY OUR *APPRECIATION* FOR THIS ESCAPE ROUTE.

SOLOMON. OPEN THE GATE AND SEE WHERE IT TAKES US.

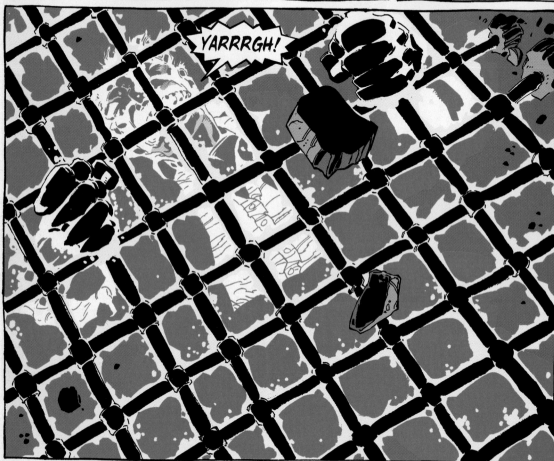

YARRRGH!

TWO-FACE! ALL GRUNDY WAS -- WAS *LOYAL* TO YOU.

HE'S *DEAD!*

HE'S DIED *BEFORE.*

HE'LL LIVE AGAIN. LET'S GO!

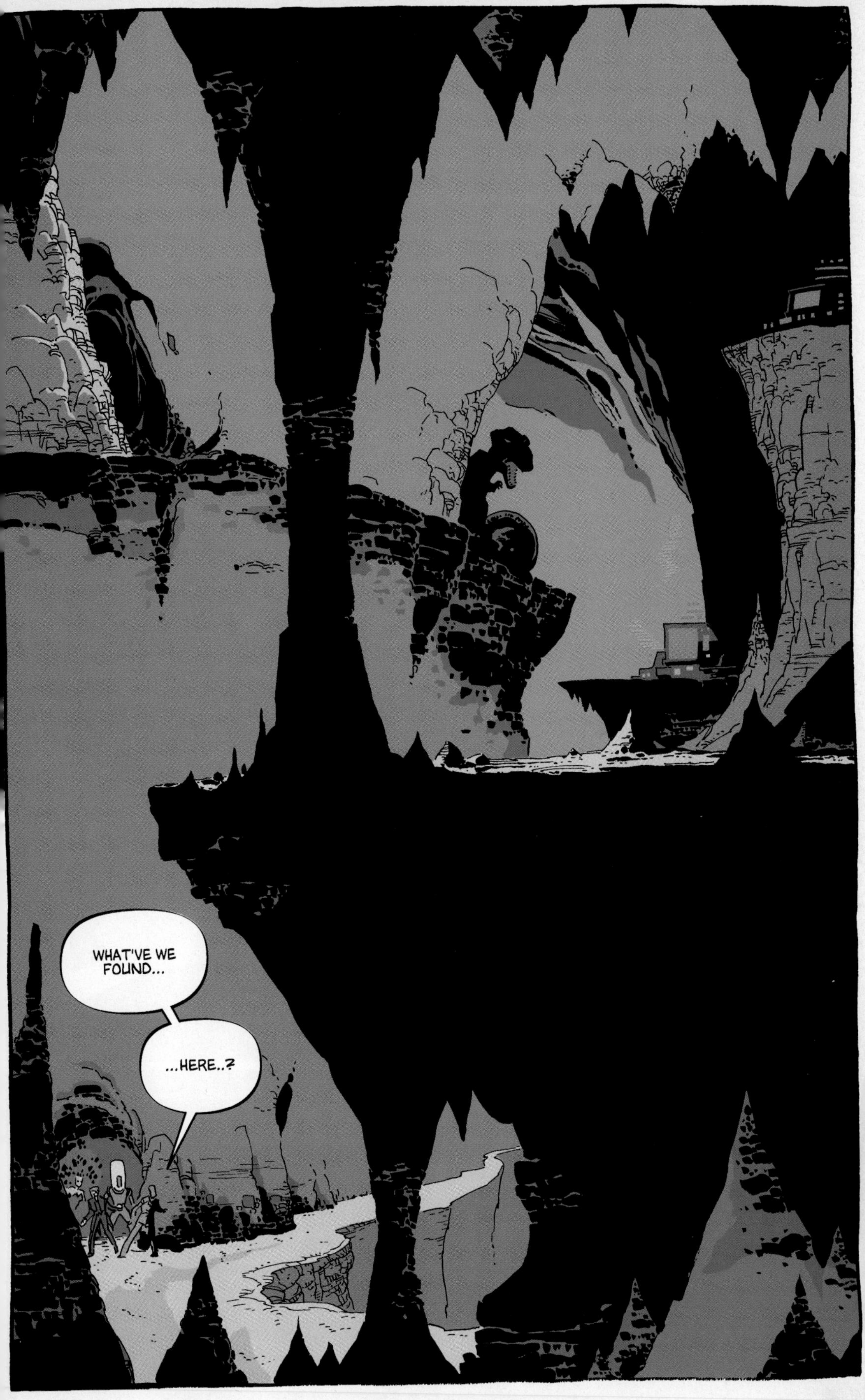
WHAT'VE WE FOUND...
...HERE..?

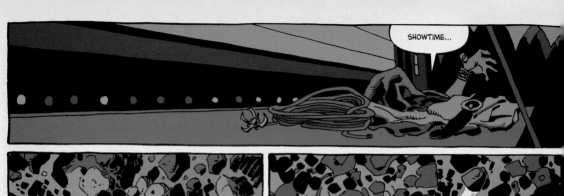

SHOWTIME...

WATCH OUT!

OWWHHHHH

Heh.

THERE'S *SOMEONE* ELSE DOWN -- NGGGNNN

Dick..?

...UH-OH...

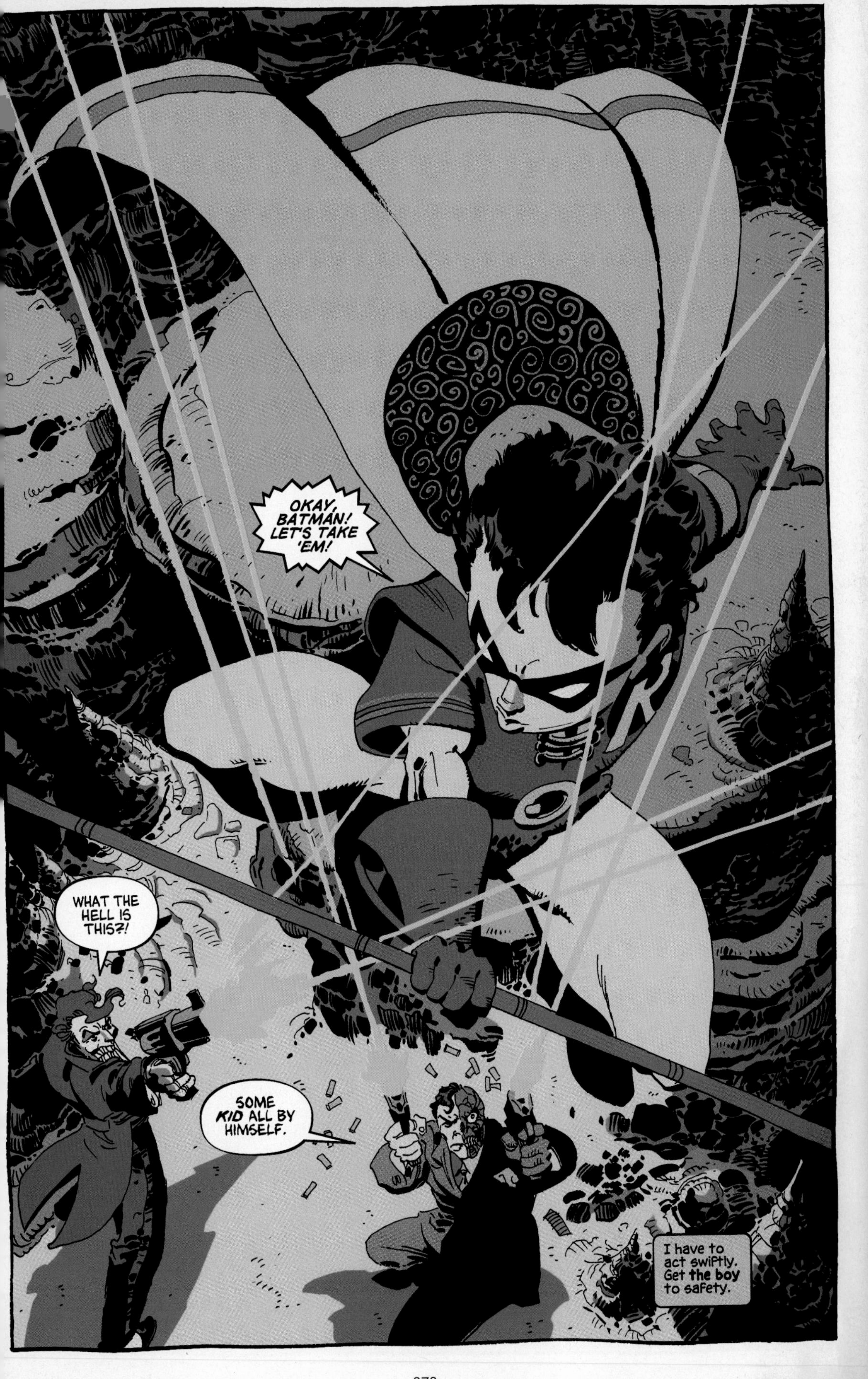
OKAY, BATMAN! LET'S TAKE 'EM!
WHAT THE HELL IS THIS?!
SOME KID ALL BY HIMSELF.
I have to act swiftly. Get the boy to safety.

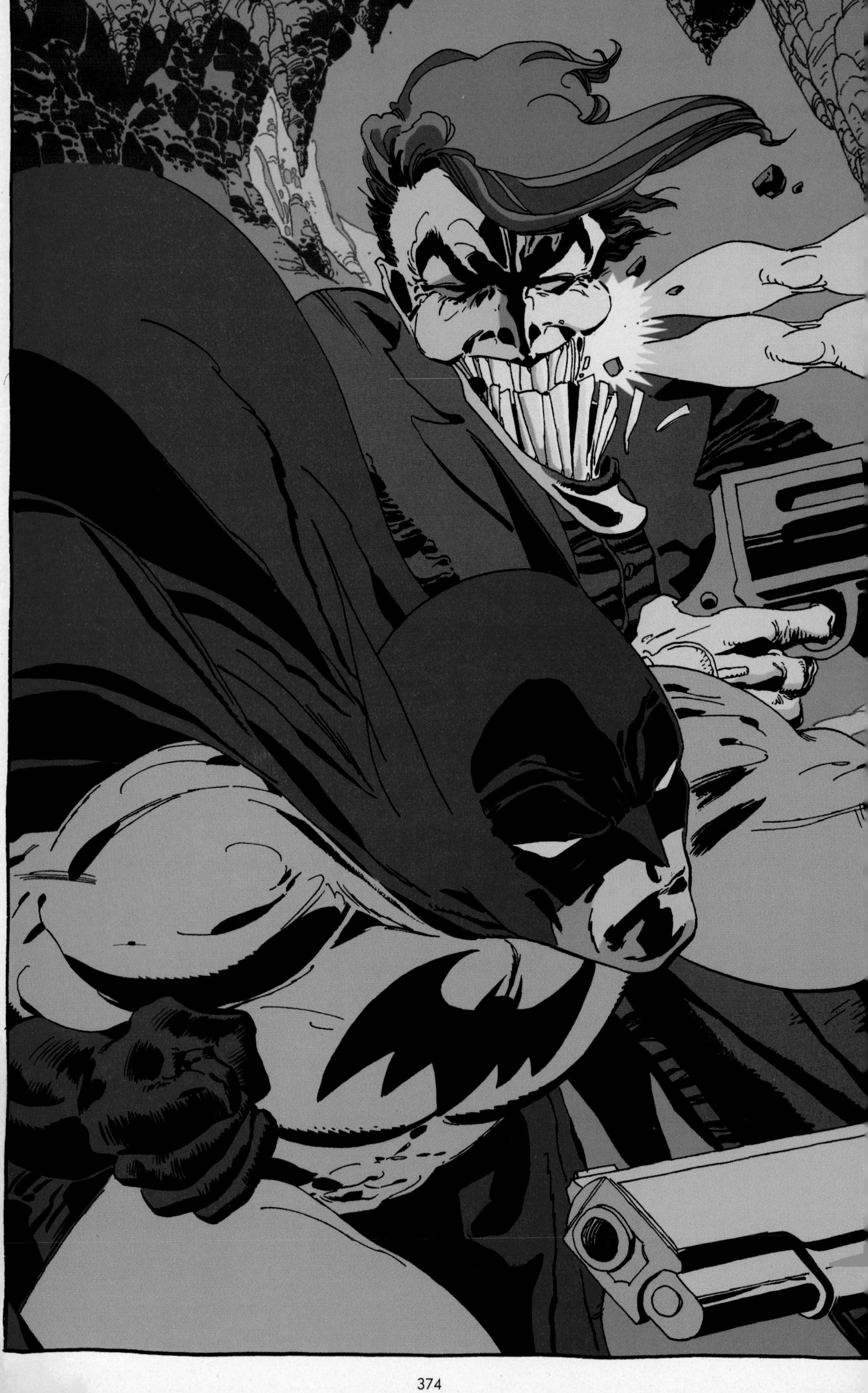

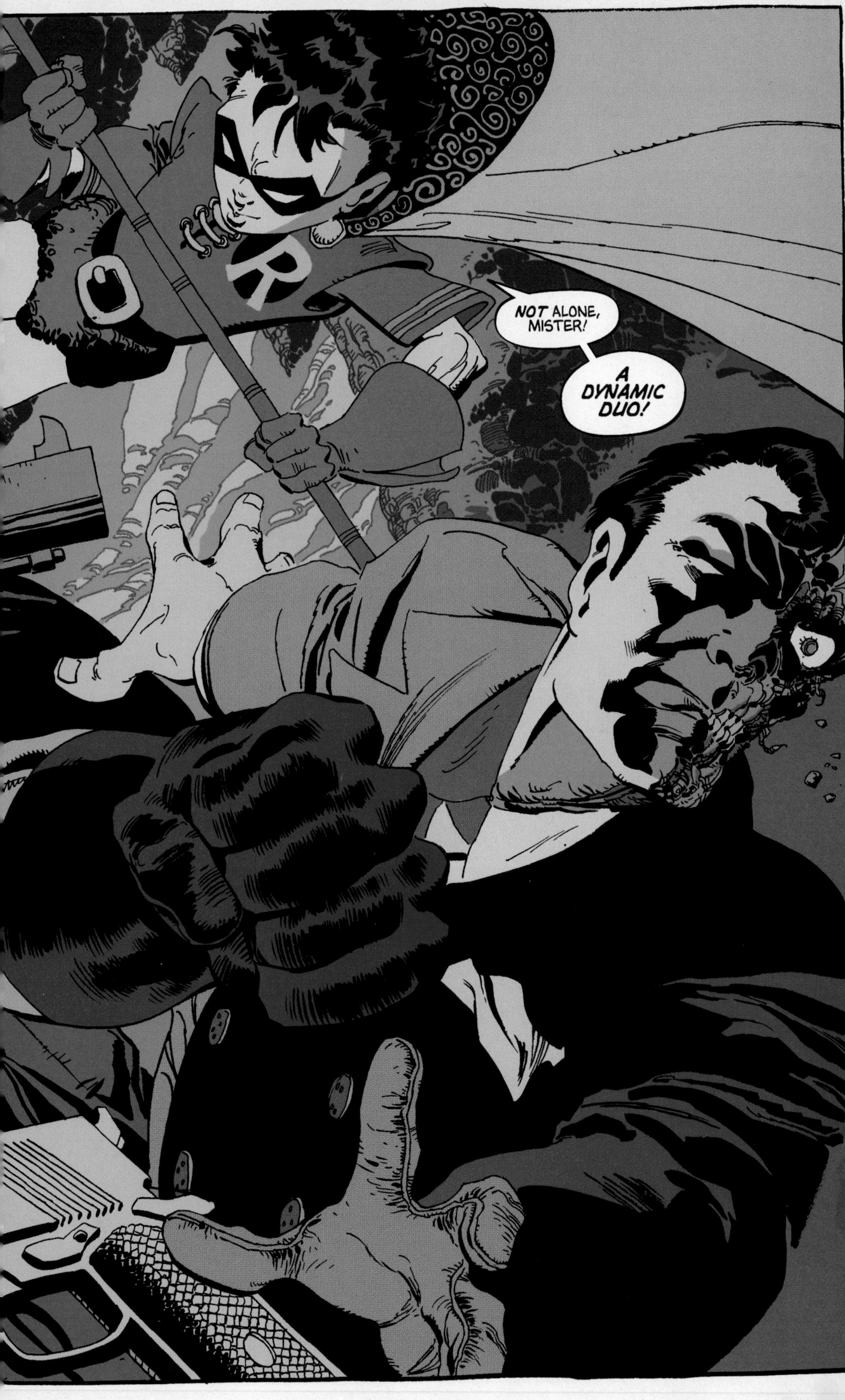
NOT ALONE, MISTER!
A DYNAMIC DUO!

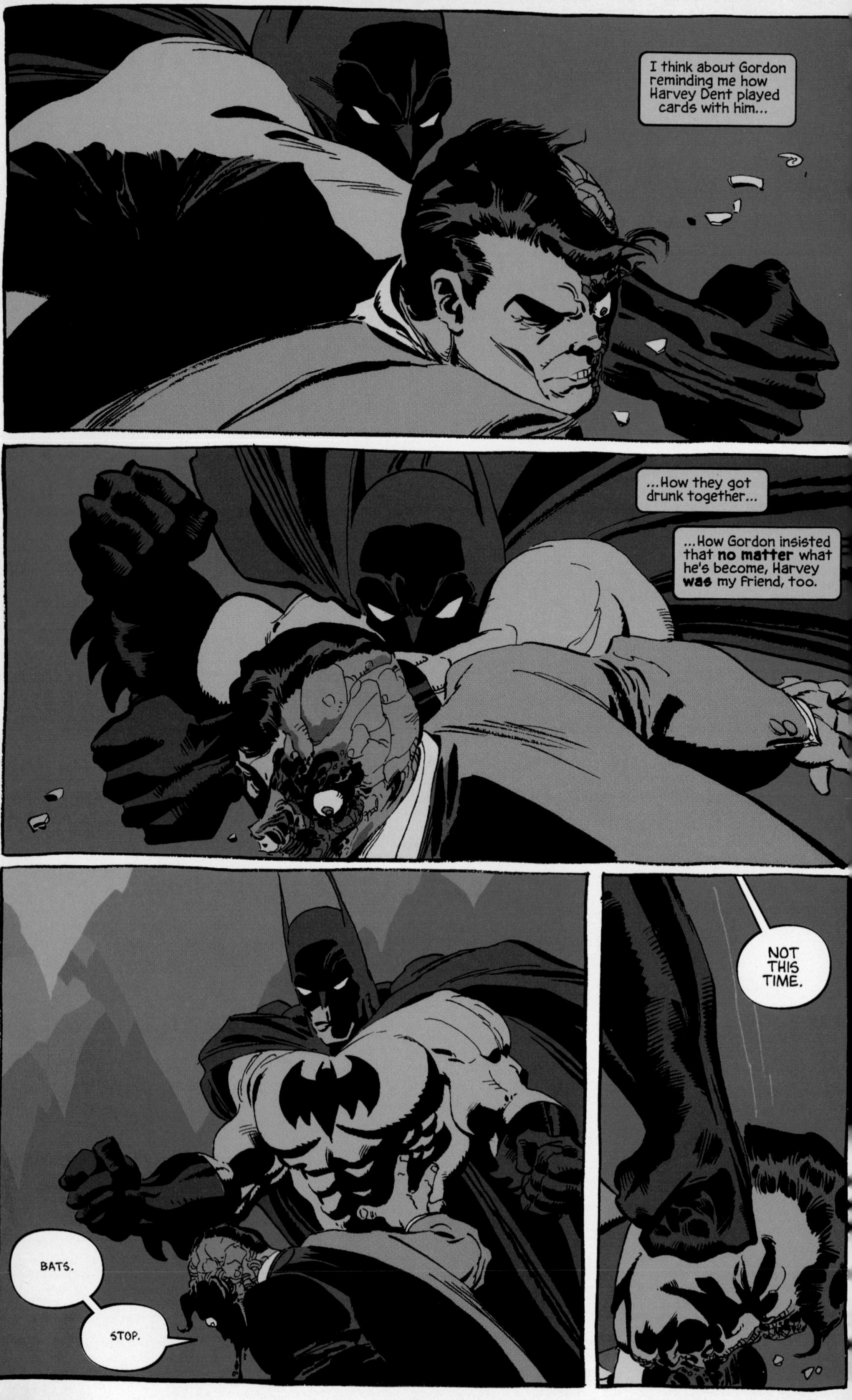
I think about Gordon reminding me how Harvey Dent played cards with him...
...How they got drunk together...
...How Gordon insisted that **no matter** what he's become, Harvey **was** my friend, too.
BATS.
STOP.
NOT THIS TIME.

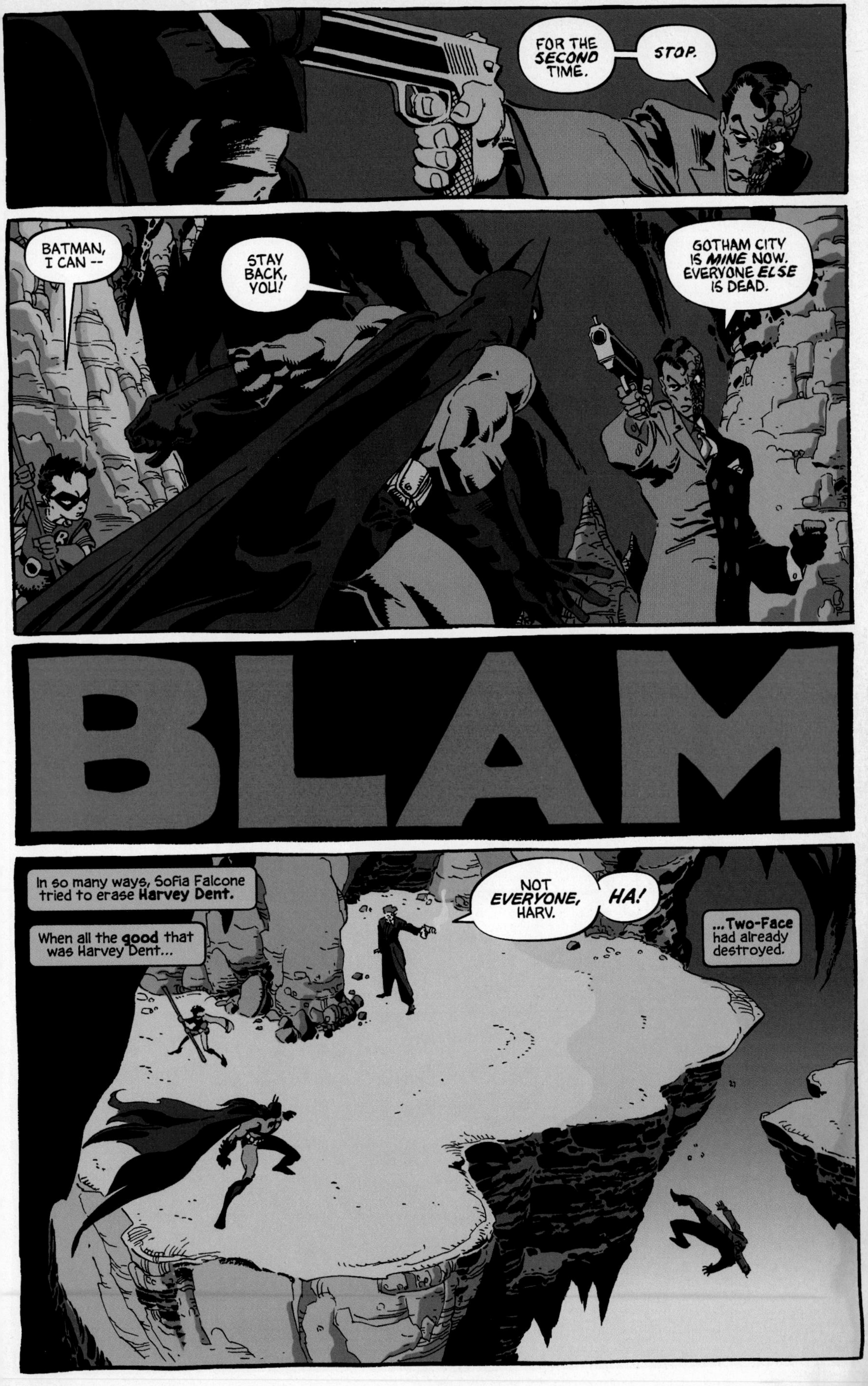

STOP.
FOR THE SECOND TIME.
BATMAN, I CAN --
STAY BACK, YOU!
GOTHAM CITY IS MINE NOW. EVERYONE ELSE IS DEAD.
BLAM
In so many ways, Sofia Falcone tried to erase Harvey Dent.
When all the good that was Harvey Dent...
NOT EVERYONE, HARV.
HA!
...Two-Face had already destroyed.

WELL. I WASN'T GOING TO LET HIM HAVE IT *ALL.*

FOR ALL HIS TALK, WHAT DID *TWO-FACE* REALLY WANT?

GETTING RID OF A BUNCH OF *GANGSTERS.*

SAME AS OL' HARV.

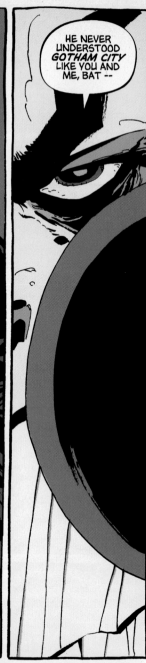

HE NEVER UNDERSTOOD *GOTHAM CITY* LIKE YOU AND ME, BAT --

SCREWBALL IN THE CORNER POCKET.

AGGG!

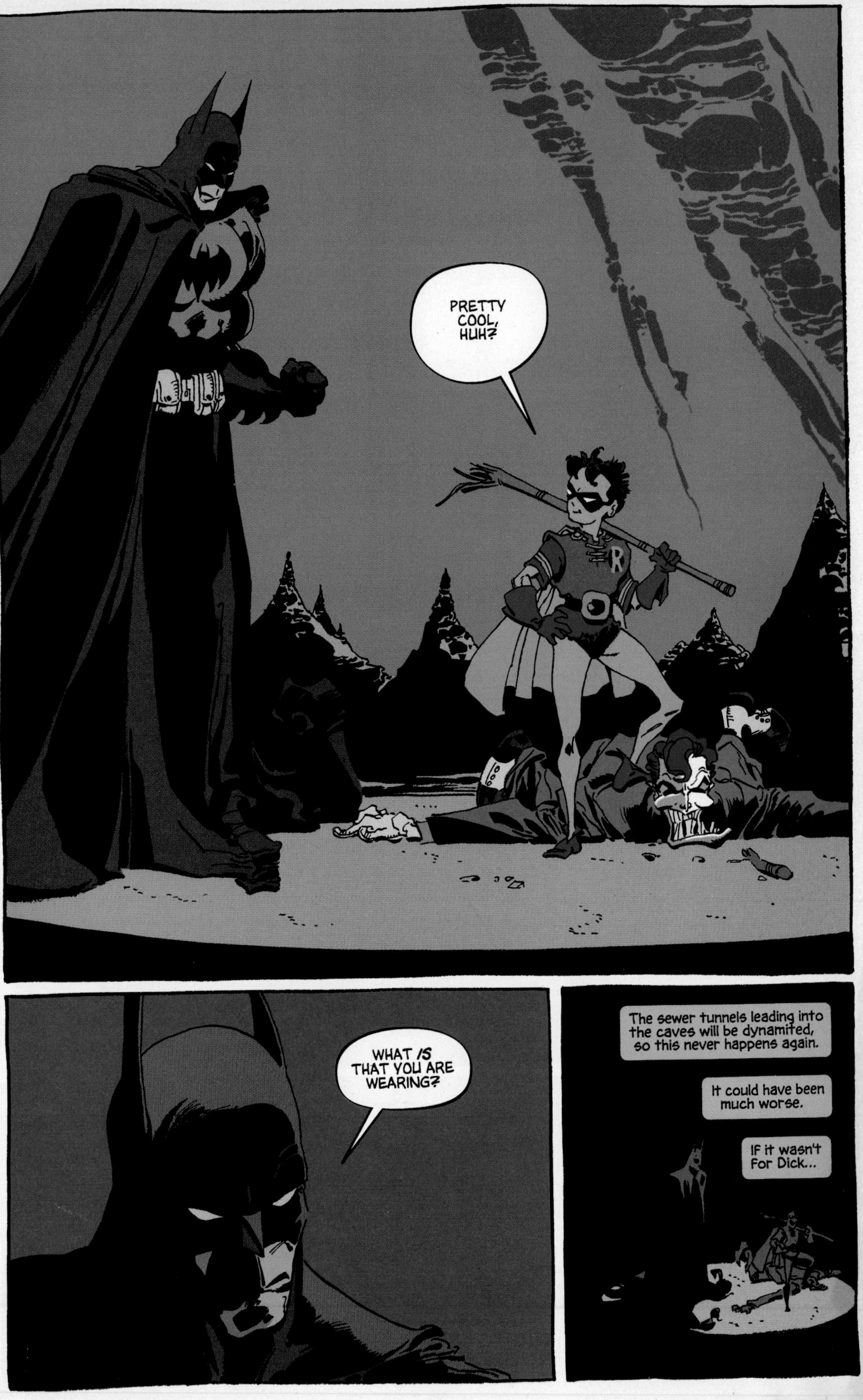
PRETTY COOL, HUH?
WHAT IS THAT YOU ARE WEARING?
The sewer tunnels leading into the caves will be dynamited, so this never happens again.
It could have been much worse.
If it wasn't For Dick...

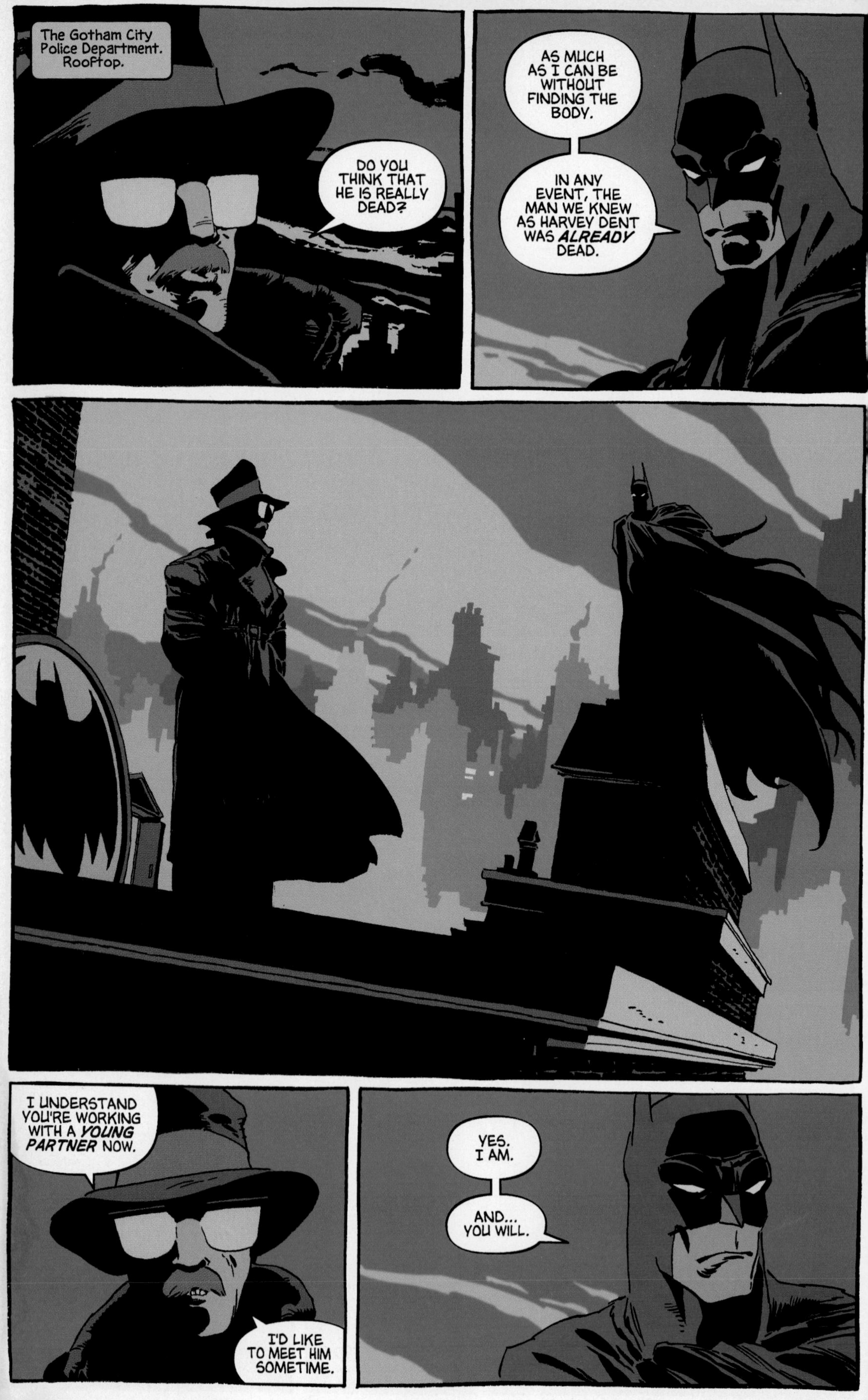
The Gotham City Police Department. Rooftop.
DO YOU THINK THAT HE IS REALLY DEAD?
AS MUCH AS I CAN BE WITHOUT FINDING THE BODY.
IN ANY EVENT, THE MAN WE KNEW AS HARVEY DENT WAS *ALREADY* DEAD.
I UNDERSTAND YOU'RE WORKING WITH A *YOUNG PARTNER* NOW.
I'D LIKE TO MEET HIM SOMETIME.
YES. I AM.
AND... YOU WILL.

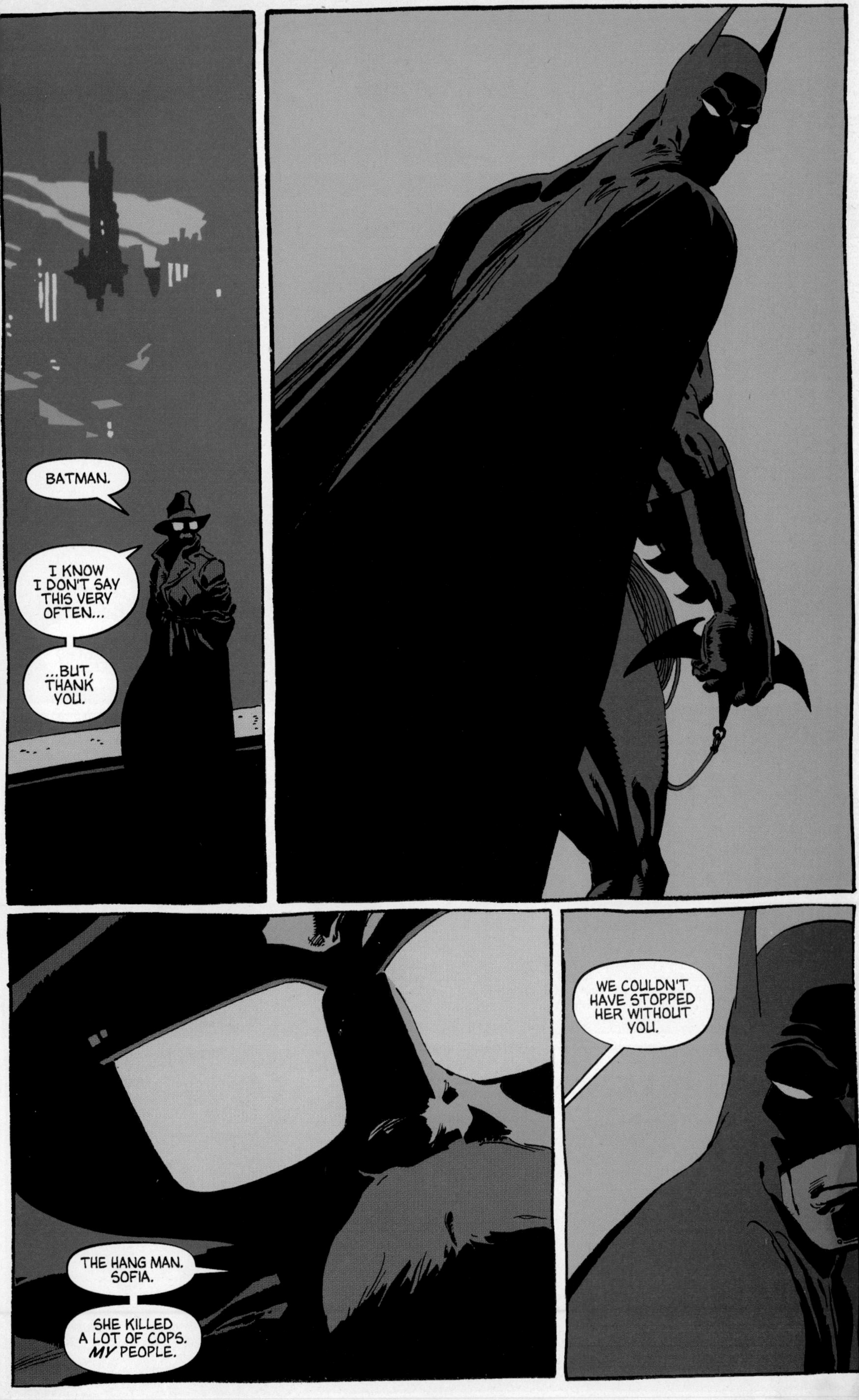
BATMAN.
I KNOW I DON'T SAY THIS VERY OFTEN...
...BUT, THANK YOU.
THE HANG MAN. SOFIA.
SHE KILLED A LOT OF COPS. *MY* PEOPLE.
WE COULDN'T HAVE STOPPED HER WITHOUT YOU.

Halloween night in Gotham City.

HONESTLY? I DON'T KNOW WHAT I'M GOING TO DO.

THIS CASE -- I SAW SOME THINGS...

Former DA Presumed Dead...

WILCOX! I TRUSTED HER...

I CAN ONLY IMAGINE HOW YOU FEEL, JULIA.

IT'S BEEN A HARD YEAR FOR *ALL* OF US.

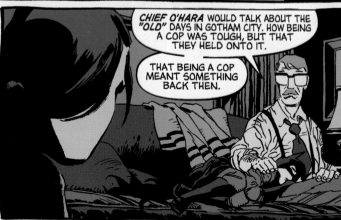

CHIEF O'HARA WOULD TALK ABOUT THE *"OLD"* DAYS IN GOTHAM CITY. HOW BEING A COP WAS TOUGH, BUT THAT THEY HELD ONTO IT.

THAT BEING A COP MEANT SOMETHING BACK THEN.

I THINK IT CAN AGAIN, *LOPEZ.* THE G.C.P.D. NEEDS GOOD PEOPLE.

AND I'M GOING TO BE LOOKING FOR A *NEW* CHIEF SOON.

I...

...I ALWAYS LIKED O'HARA....

382

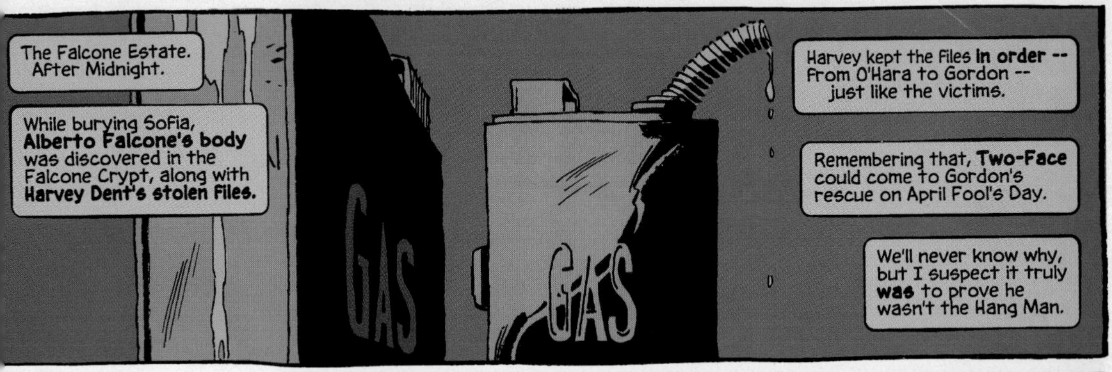
The Falcone Estate.
After Midnight.
While burying Sofia, Alberto Falcone's body was discovered in the Falcone Crypt, along with Harvey Dent's stolen files.
Harvey kept the files in order -- from O'Hara to Gordon -- just like the victims.
Remembering that, Two-Face could come to Gordon's rescue on April Fool's Day.
We'll never know why, but I suspect it truly was to prove he wasn't the Hang Man.
GAS
GAS

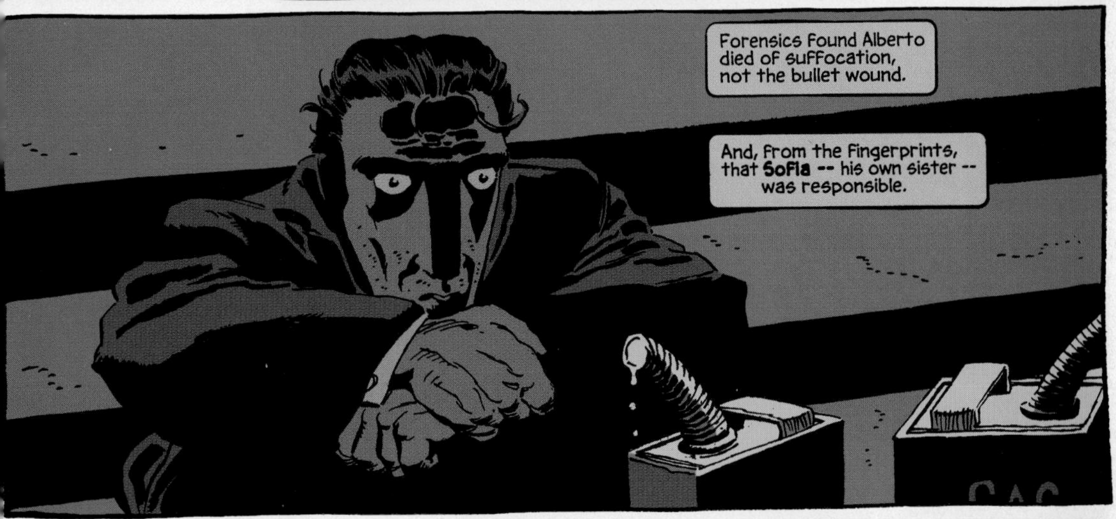
Forensics found Alberto died of suffocation, not the bullet wound.
And, from the fingerprints, that Sofia -- his own sister -- was responsible.

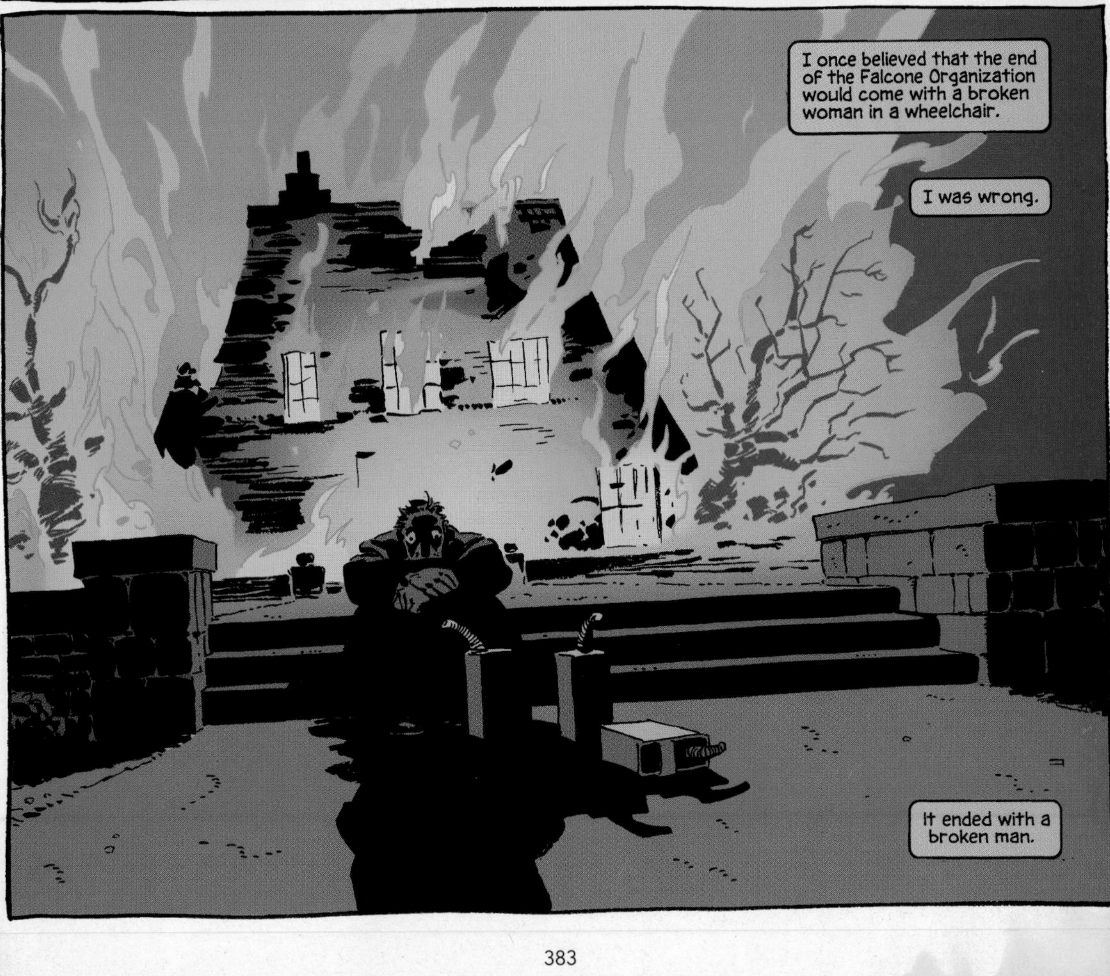
I once believed that the end of the Falcone Organization would come with a broken woman in a wheelchair.
I was wrong.
It ended with a broken man.

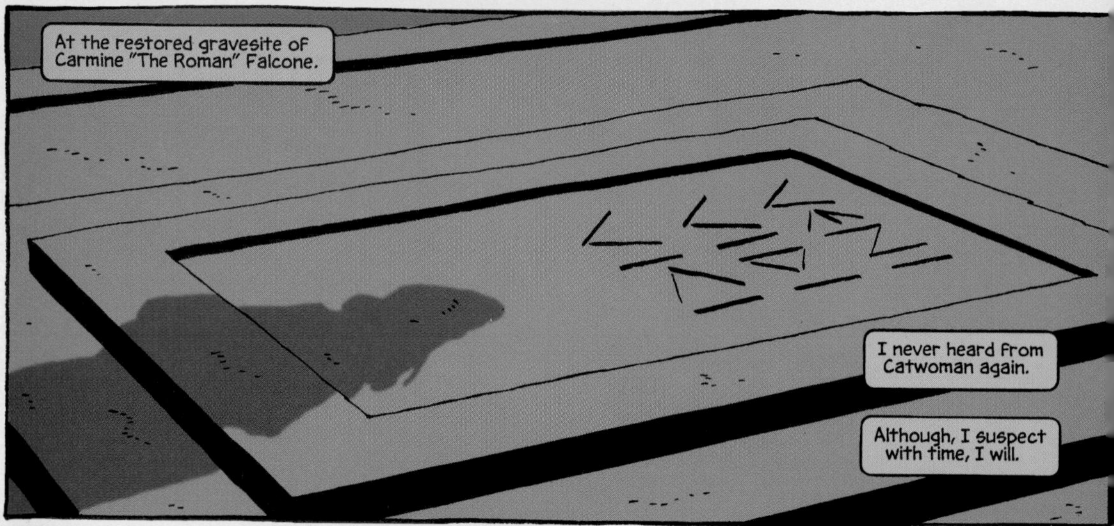
At the restored gravesite of Carmine "The Roman" Falcone.
I never heard from Catwoman again.
Although, I suspect with time, I will.

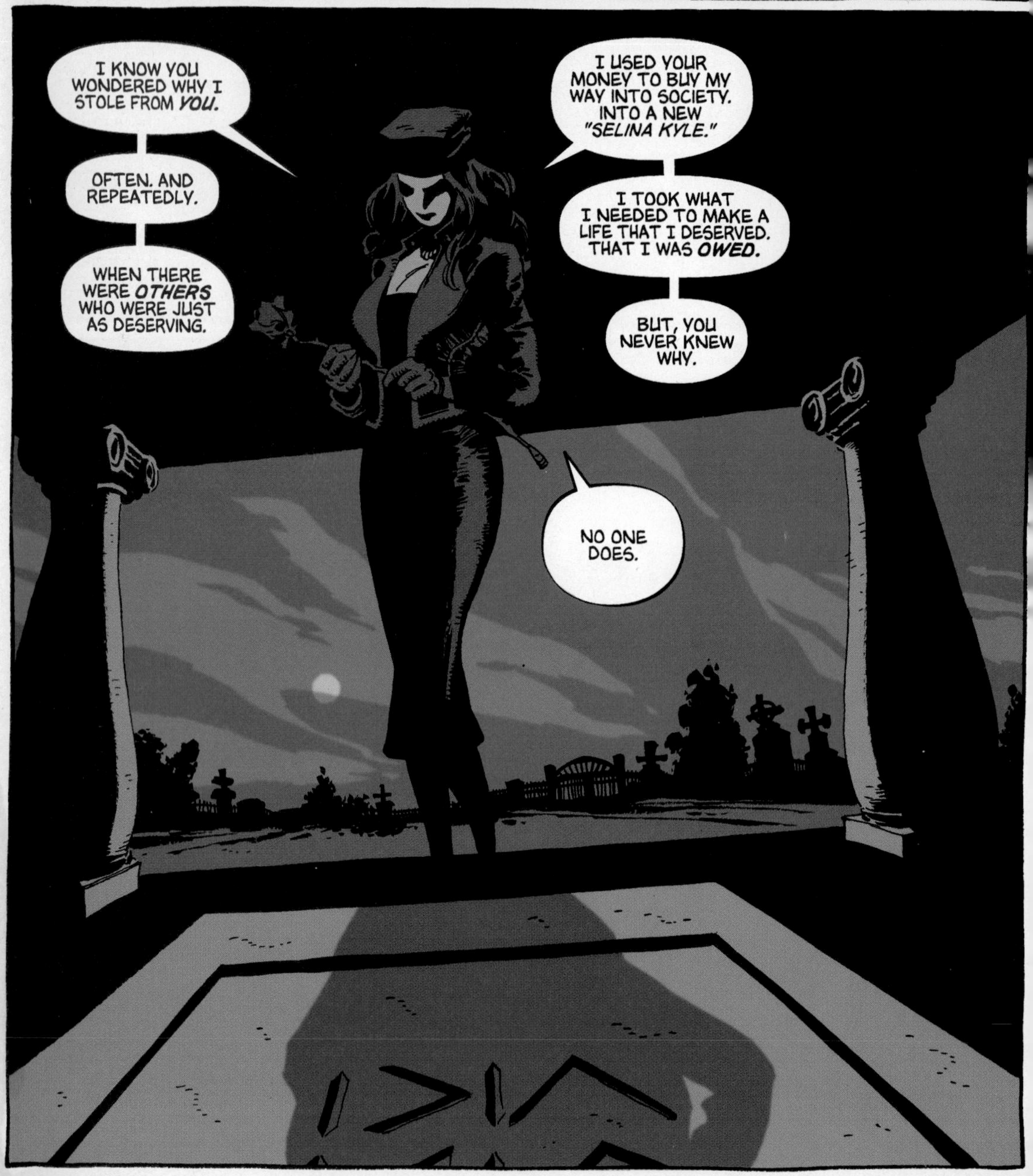
I KNOW YOU WONDERED WHY I STOLE FROM *YOU.*
OFTEN. AND REPEATEDLY.
WHEN THERE WERE *OTHERS* WHO WERE JUST AS DESERVING.
I USED YOUR MONEY TO BUY MY WAY INTO SOCIETY. INTO A NEW *"SELINA KYLE."*
I TOOK WHAT I NEEDED TO MAKE A LIFE THAT I DESERVED. THAT I WAS *OWED.*
BUT, YOU NEVER KNEW WHY.
NO ONE DOES.

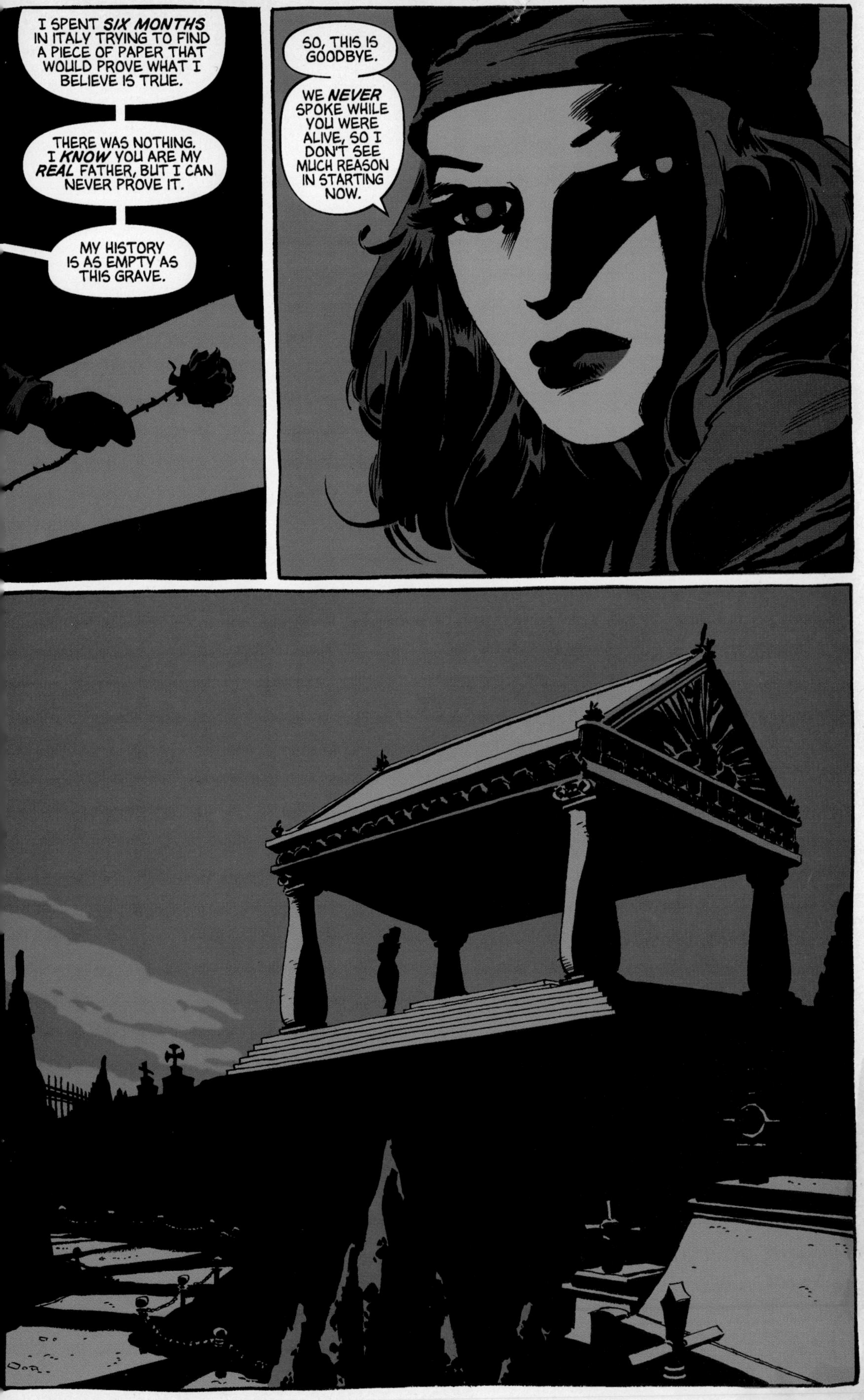
I SPENT SIX MONTHS IN ITALY TRYING TO FIND A PIECE OF PAPER THAT WOULD PROVE WHAT I BELIEVE IS TRUE.
THERE WAS NOTHING. I KNOW YOU ARE MY REAL FATHER, BUT I CAN NEVER PROVE IT.
MY HISTORY IS AS EMPTY AS THIS GRAVE.
SO, THIS IS GOODBYE.
WE NEVER SPOKE WHILE YOU WERE ALIVE, SO I DON'T SEE MUCH REASON IN STARTING NOW.

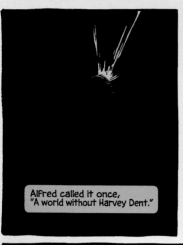

Alfred called it once,
"A world without Harvey Dent."

It is a better
world for that.

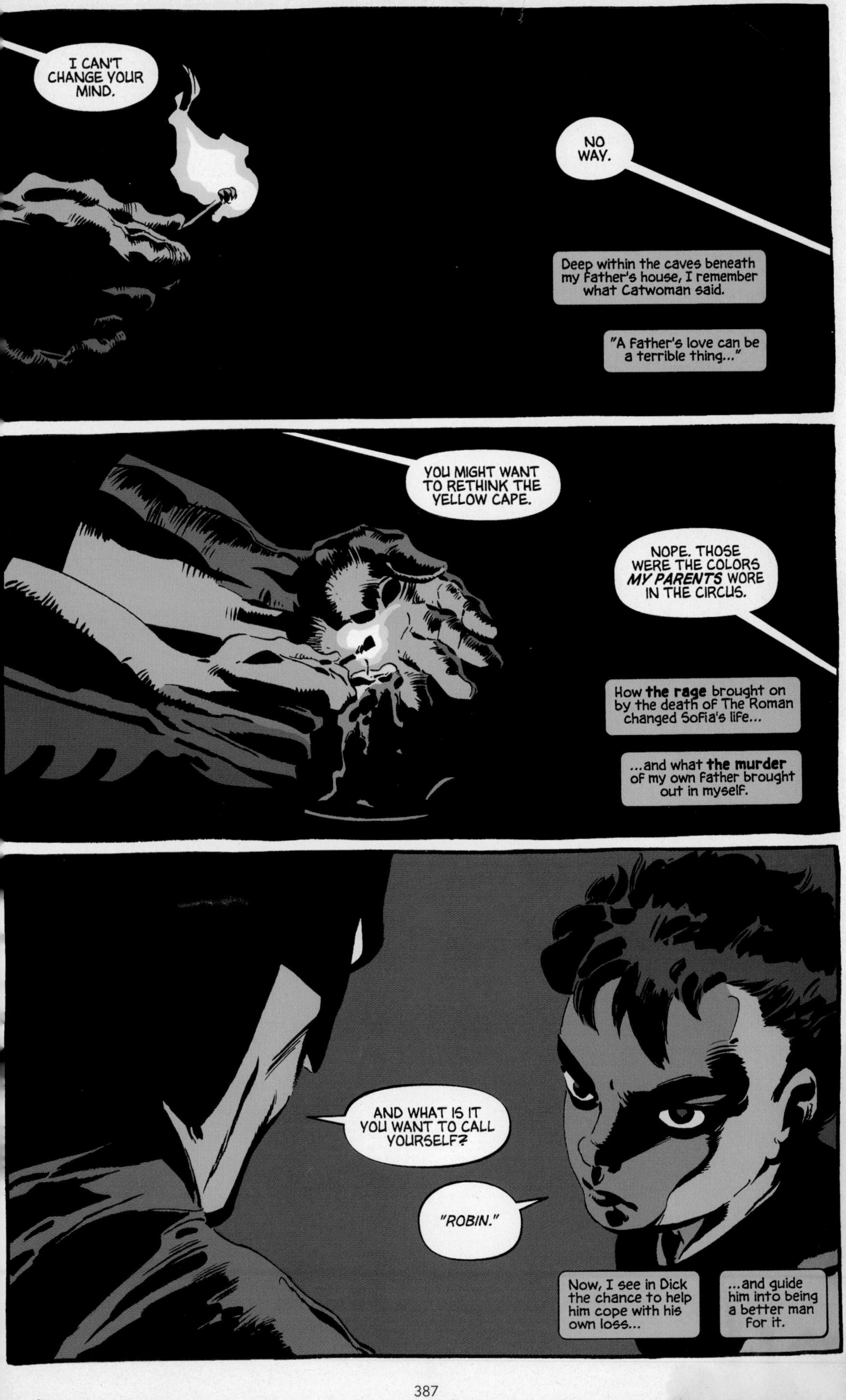
I CAN'T CHANGE YOUR MIND.
NO WAY.
Deep within the caves beneath my father's house, I remember what Catwoman said.
"A father's love can be a terrible thing..."
YOU MIGHT WANT TO RETHINK THE YELLOW CAPE.
NOPE. THOSE WERE THE COLORS *MY PARENTS* WORE IN THE CIRCUS.
How **the rage** brought on by the death of The Roman changed Sofia's life...
...and what **the murder** of my own father brought out in myself.
AND WHAT IS IT YOU WANT TO CALL YOURSELF?
"ROBIN."
Now, I see in Dick the chance to help him cope with his own loss...
...and guide him into being a better man for it.

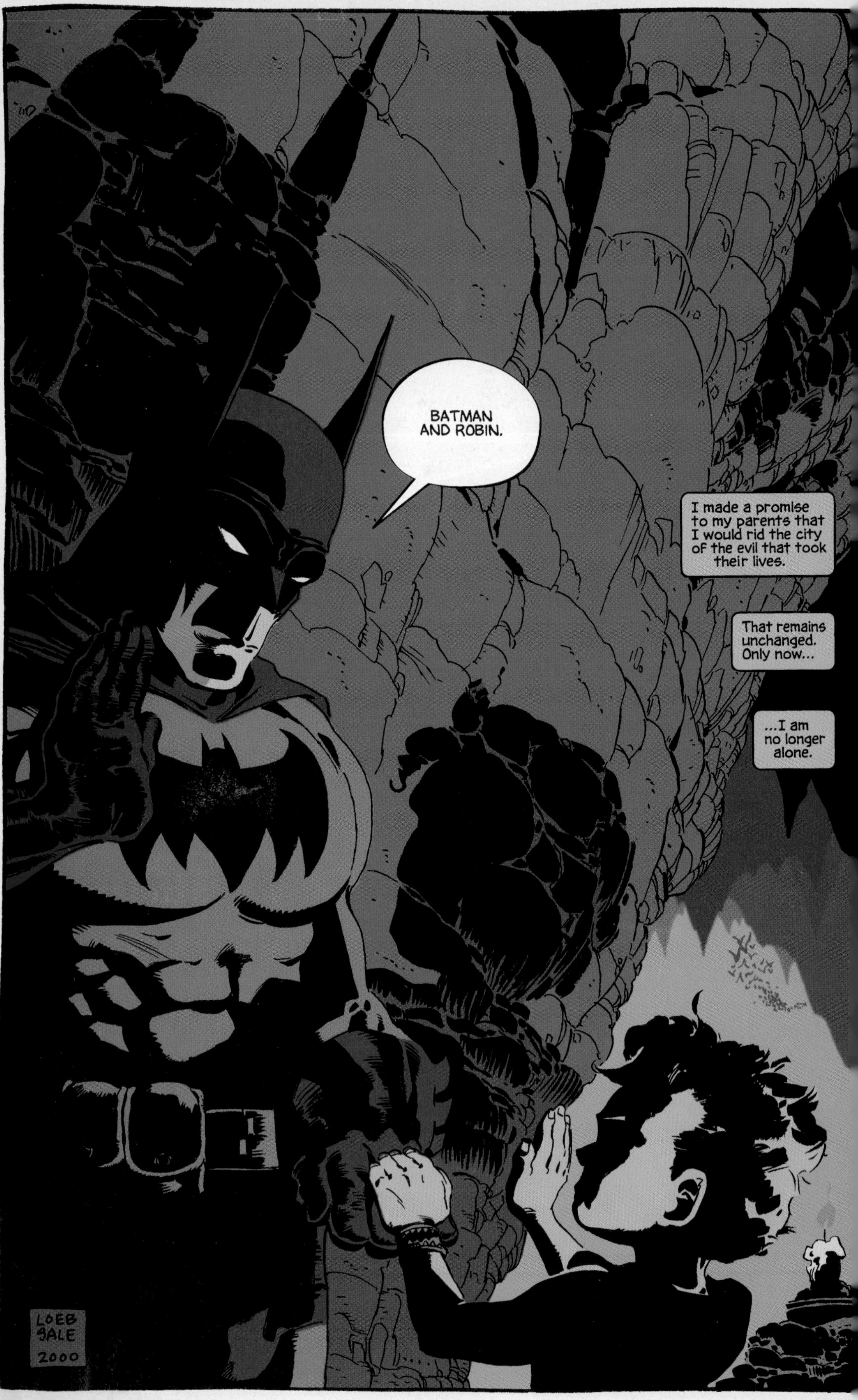
BATMAN AND ROBIN.
I made a promise to my parents that I would rid the city of the evil that took their lives.
That remains unchanged. Only now...
...I am no longer alone.
LOEB GALE 2000

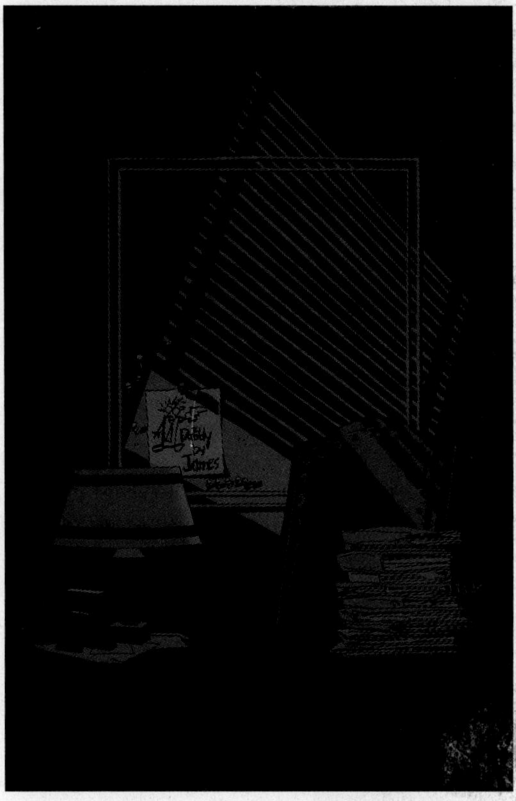
by
James

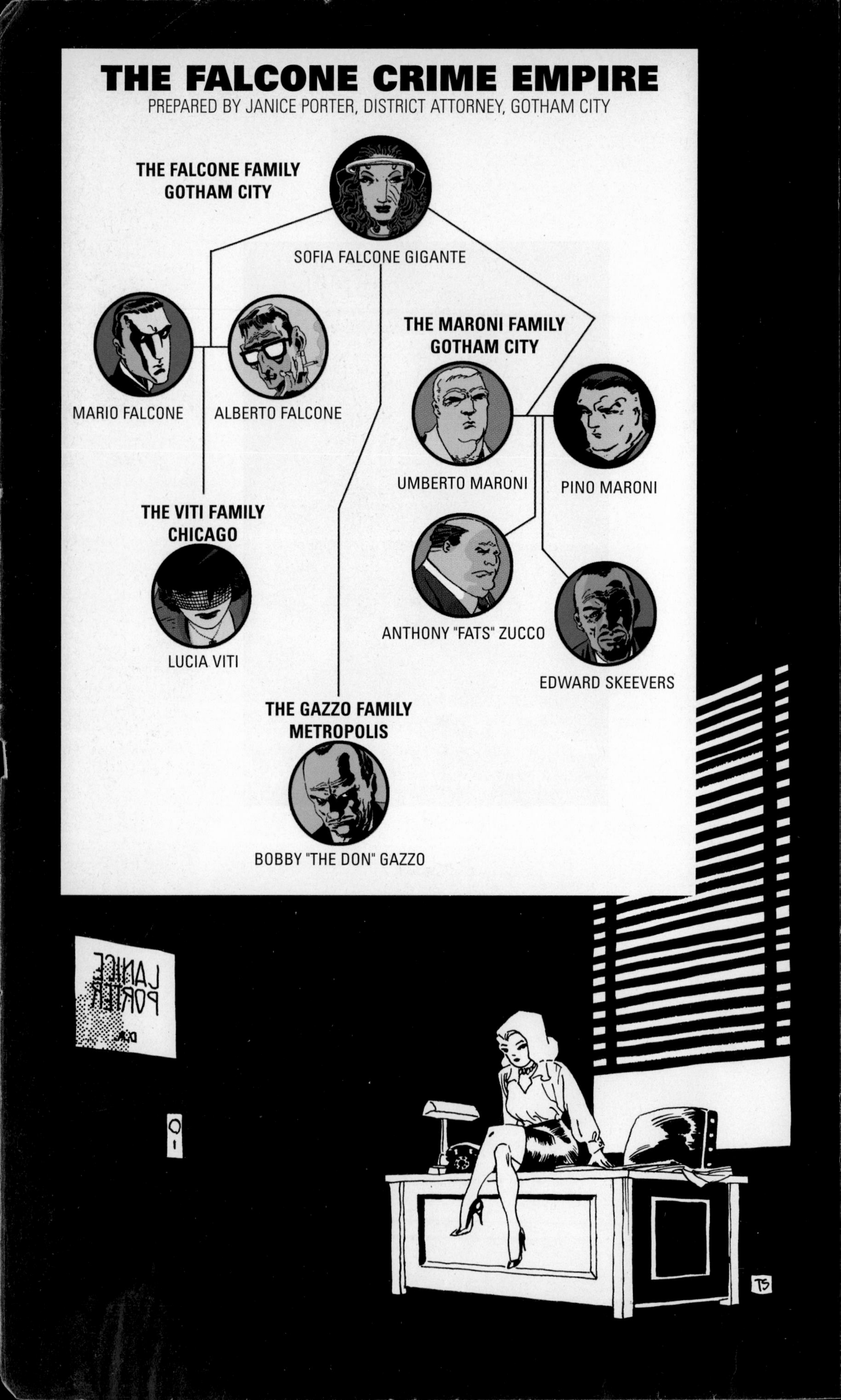
THE FALCONE CRIME EMPIRE
PREPARED BY JANICE PORTER, DISTRICT ATTORNEY, GOTHAM CITY
THE FALCONE FAMILY
GOTHAM CITY
SOFIA FALCONE GIGANTE
MARIO FALCONE
ALBERTO FALCONE
THE MARONI FAMILY
GOTHAM CITY
UMBERTO MARONI
PINO MARONI
THE VITI FAMILY
CHICAGO
LUCIA VITI
ANTHONY "FATS" ZUCCO
EDWARD SKEEVERS
THE GAZZO FAMILY
METROPOLIS
BOBBY "THE DON" GAZZO
JANICE
PORTER
TS

S K E T C H E S

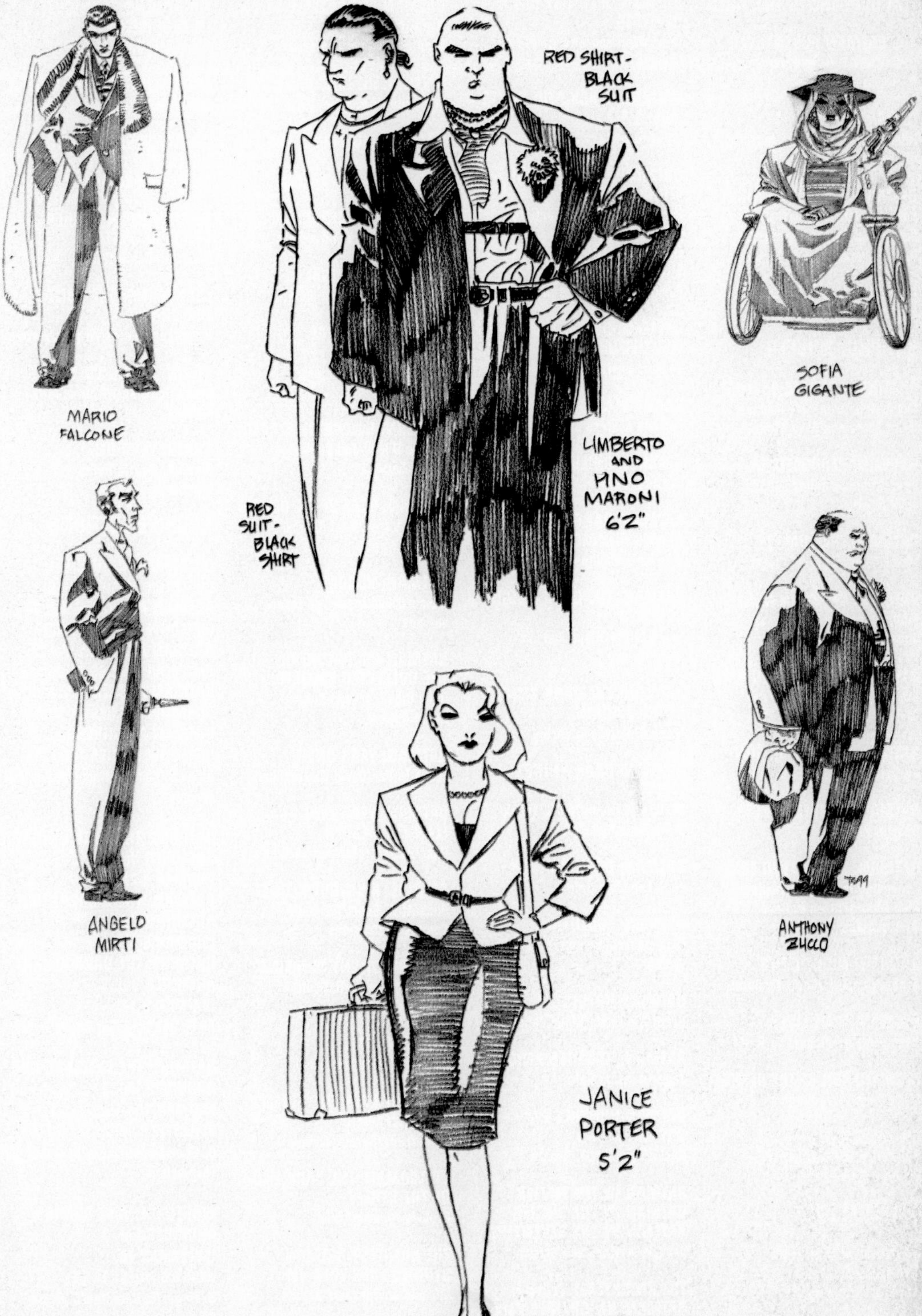
MARIO
FALCONE
RED SHIRT-
BLACK
SUIT
SOFIA
GIGANTE
UMBERTO
AND
PINO
MARONI
6'2"
RED
SUIT-
BLACK
SHIRT
ANGELO
MIRTI
ANTHONY
ZUCCO
JANICE
PORTER
5'2"
TB99

THE DARK VICTORY ROGUES GALLERY: MOBSTER CHARACTER SKETCHES AND JANICE PORTER, GOTHAM'S NEWEST DISTRICT ATTORNEY WHOSE DESIGN WAS INFLUENCED BY LANA TURNER.

B A T M A N

THE QUEST FOR JUSTICE CONTINUES IN THESE BOOKS FROM DC:

FOR READERS OF ALL AGES

THE BATMAN ADVENTURES
K. Puckett/T. Templeton/
R. Burchett/various

BATMAN BEYOND
Hilary Bader/Rick Burchett/
various

BATMAN: THE DARK KNIGHT ADVENTURES
Kelley Puckett/Mike Parobeck/
Rick Burchett

BATMAN: WAR ON CRIME
Paul Dini/Alex Ross

GRAPHIC NOVELS

BATMAN: ARKHAM ASYLUM
Suggested for mature readers
Grant Morrison/Dave McKean

BATMAN: BLOODSTORM
Doug Moench/Kelley Jones/
John Beatty

BATMAN: THE CHALICE
Chuck Dixon/John Van Fleet

BATMAN: CRIMSON MIST
Doug Moench/Kelley Jones/
John Beatty

BATMAN/DRACULA: RED RAIN
Doug Moench/Kelley Jones/
Malcolm Jones III

BATMAN: FORTUNATE SON
Gerard Jones/Gene Ha

BATMAN: HARVEST BREED
George Pratt

BATMAN: THE KILLING JOKE
Suggested for mature readers
Alan Moore/Brian Bolland/
John Higgins

BATMAN: NIGHT CRIES
Archie Goodwin/Scott Hampton

BATMAN: NINE LIVES
Dean Motter/Michael Lark

BATMAN: SON OF THE DEMON
Mike Barr/Jerry Bingham

CATWOMAN: SELINA'S BIG SCORE
Darwyn Cooke

COLLECTIONS

BATMAN: A DEATH IN THE FAMILY
Jim Starlin/Jim Aparo/
Mike DeCarlo

BATMAN: A LONELY PLACE OF DYING
Marv Wolfman/George Pérez/
various

BATMAN BLACK AND WHITE Vols. 1 & 2
Various writers and artists

BATMAN: BRUCE WAYNE — MURDERER?
Various writers and artists

BATMAN: BRUCE WAYNE — FUGITIVE Vol. 1
Various writers and artists

BATMAN: BRUCE WAYNE — FUGITIVE Vol. 2
Various writers and artists

BATMAN: CATACLYSM
Various writers and artists

BATMAN: CHILD OF DREAMS
Kia Asamiya

BATMAN: DANGEROUS DAMES & DEMONS
Dini/Timm/various

BATMAN: THE DARK KNIGHT RETURNS
Frank Miller/Klaus Janson/
Lynn Varley

BATMAN: THE DARK KNIGHT STRIKES AGAIN
Frank Miller/Lynn Varley

BATMAN: DARK KNIGHT DYNASTY
M. Barr/S. Hampton/G. Frank/
S. McDaniels/various

BATMAN: DARK VICTORY
Jeph Loeb/Tim Sale

BATMAN: EVOLUTION
Rucka/Martinbrough/Mitchell/
various

BATMAN: GOTHIC
Grant Morrison/Klaus Janson

BATMAN: HAUNTED KNIGHT
Jeph Loeb/Tim Sale

BATMAN/HUNTRESS: CRY FOR BLOOD
Rucka/Burchett/T. Beatty

BATMAN IN THE FIFTIES
BATMAN IN THE SIXTIES
BATMAN IN THE SEVENTIES
Various writers and artists

THE KNIGHTFALL Trilogy
BATMAN: KNIGHTFALL Part 1: Broken Bat
BATMAN: KNIGHTFALL Part 2: Who Rules the Night
BATMAN: KNIGHTFALL Part 3: KnightsEnd
Various writers and artists

BATMAN: THE LONG HALLOWEEN
Jeph Loeb/Tim Sale

BATMAN: NO MAN'S LAND Vols. 1 - 5
Various writers and artists

BATMAN: OFFICER DOWN
Various writers and artists

BATMAN: PRODIGAL
Various writers and artists

BATMAN: STRANGE APPARITIONS
S. Englehart/M. Rogers/
T. Austin/various

BATMAN: SWORD OF AZRAEL
Dennis O'Neil/Joe Quesada/
Kevin Nowlan

BATMAN: TALES OF THE DEMON
Dennis O'Neil/Neal Adams/
various

BATMAN: VENOM
Dennis O'Neil/Trevor Von Eeden/
various

BATMAN VS. PREDATOR: THE COLLECTED EDITION
Dave Gibbons/Andy Kubert/
Adam Kubert

BATMAN: YEAR ONE
Frank Miller/David Mazzucchelli

BATMAN: YEAR TWO — FEAR THE REAPER
Barr/Davis/McFarlane/various

BATGIRL: A KNIGHT ALONE
Puckett/D. Scott/Turnbull/
Campanella/various

BATGIRL: SILENT RUNNING
Puckett/Peterson/D. Scott/
Campanella

BIRDS OF PREY
Various writers and artists

BIRDS OF PREY: OLD FRIENDS, NEW ENEMIES
Dixon/Land/Geraci/various

CATWOMAN: THE DARK END OF THE STREET
Brubaker/Cooke/Allred

THE GREATEST BATMAN STORIES EVER TOLD Vol. 1
Various writers and artists

THE GREATEST JOKER STORIES EVER TOLD
Various writers and artists

NIGHTWING: A KNIGHT IN BLÜDHAVEN
Dixon/McDaniel/Story

NIGHTWING: ROUGH JUSTICE
Dixon/McDaniel/Story

NIGHTWING: LOVE AND BULLETS
Dixon/McDaniel/Story

NIGHTWING: A DARKER SHADE OF JUSTICE
Dixon/McDaniel/Story

NIGHTWING: THE HUNT FOR ORACLE
Dixon/Land/Guice/Zircher/various

ROBIN: FLYING SOLO
Dixon/Grummett/P. Jimenez/
various

ROBIN: YEAR ONE
Dixon/S. Beatty/Pulido/
Martin/Campanella

ARCHIVE EDITIONS

BATMAN ARCHIVES Vol. 1
(DETECTIVE COMICS 27-50)
BATMAN ARCHIVES Vol. 2
(DETECTIVE COMICS 51-70)
BATMAN ARCHIVES Vol. 3
(DETECTIVE COMICS 71-86)
BATMAN ARCHIVES Vol. 4
(DETECTIVE COMICS 87-102)
BATMAN ARCHIVES Vol. 5
(DETECTIVE COMICS 103-119)
All by B. Kane/B. Finger/D. Sprang/
various

BATMAN: THE DARK KNIGHT ARCHIVES Vol. 1
(BATMAN 1-4)
BATMAN: THE DARK KNIGHT ARCHIVES Vol. 2
(BATMAN 5-8)
BATMAN: THE DARK KNIGHT ARCHIVES Vol. 3
(BATMAN 9-12)
All by Bob Kane/Bill Finger/various

BATMAN: THE DYNAMIC DUO ARCHIVES Vol. 1
(BATMAN 164-167,
DETECTIVE COMICS 327-333)
B. Kane/Giella/Finger/Broome/
Fox/various

WORLD'S FINEST COMICS ARCHIVES Vol. 1
(SUPERMAN 76,
WORLD'S FINEST 71-85)
B. Finger/E. Hamilton/C. Swan/
Sprang/various

TO FIND MORE COLLECTED EDITIONS AND MONTHLY COMIC BOOKS FROM DC COMICS,
CALL 1-888-COMIC BOOK FOR THE NEAREST COMICS SHOP OR GO TO YOUR LOCAL BOOK STORE.

Visit us at www.dccomics.com

BM0012